Sources of American Indian Oral Literature

EDITORS

Douglas R. Parks
Raymond J. DeMallie

This series offers new editions of works previously published,
as well as works never before published,
on Native American oral tradition

THE PAWNEE MYTHOLOGY

George A. Dorsey

Introduction to the Bison Books Edition
by Douglas R. Parks

University of Nebraska Press
Lincoln and London

First Bison Books printing: 1997

Library of Congress Cataloging-in-Publication Data
Dorsey, George Amos, 1868–1931.
[Pawnee mythology (part I)]
The Pawnee mythology / George A. Dorsey; introduction to the Bison Books
edition by Douglas R. Parks.
p. cm.
Originally published: The Pawnee mythology (part I). Washington, D.C.:
Carnegie Institution of Washington, 1906. (Carnegie Institution of Wash-
ington publication; no. 59)
Part II was never published.
ISBN 0-8032-6603-0 (pa)
1. Pawnee mythology. 2. Pawnee Indians—Folklore. 3. Legends—Great
Plains. I. Parks, Douglas R.
E99.P3D6 1997
398'.089'979—dc21
97-12832 CIP

Reprinted from the original 1906 edition by the Carnegie Institution of
Washington, Washington DC, publication no. 59, titled *The Pawnee: Mythology (Part I)*.

INTRODUCTION TO THE BISON BOOKS EDITION

Douglas R. Parks

During the waning decades of the nineteenth century, when Plains Indian tribes were still adapting to new lives on reservations and to the strong acculturative pressures of a dominant American society, anthropology as a science of humankind—as a profession committed to documenting and studying human diversity—was developing in two complementary contexts, museums and universities. The earlier of those contexts was museums, and dominant among them was the Smithsonian Institution in the nation's capital, founded in 1849. Joseph Henry, its first secretary, as part of his plan for the development of American science, committed the new institution to the study of the linguistics, archaeology, and ethnology of America's native peoples; and later, in 1879, the great naturalist John Wesley Powell established within the Smithsonian the Bureau of Ethnology (later the Bureau of American Ethnology), which served as the sponsor of massive field studies and publication projects documenting American Indian life, producing records that today are among the richest sources on the native peoples of the Americas.

Nearly simultaneous with the founding of the Smithsonian Institution's Bureau of Ethnology was the development of the Peabody Museum at Harvard University, the first university museum in the United States. Beginning in 1874 under the direction of Frederick Ward Putnam, an archaeologist, the museum not only sponsored field studies, developed collections, and mounted exhibits, but equally importantly established a close association with an anthropology program at Harvard that Putnam himself established in 1890. His commitment to a close association between a museum, with its research and curatorial activities, and an academic program that provided professional anthropological training became a model that would later be followed by other American universities in which museums were established as adjuncts to anthropology programs or departments.

Putnam's influence in the development of American anthropology was not limited to the creation of museums in academic contexts; in the closing decade of the nineteenth century he was equally responsible for implementing vigorous, far-sighted anthropological programs in the two greatest public natural history museums in the United

States, the Field Columbia Museum (later the Field Museum of Natural History) in Chicago and the American Museum of Natural History in New York City. In both of those cities he envisioned the formation of great ethnological museums built upon field expeditions to tribes throughout North America to collect prehistoric artifacts and contemporary cultural objects as well as to make ethnographic records, all designed to provide a grand panorama of human life in America from prehistoric times to the period of European contact. Those collections, reasoned Putnam and his contemporaries, would illustrate the stages of the development of humankind on the American continent, "spread out as an open book from which all could read" (Dexter 1966:315–32).

Putnam's first opportunity to implement his plan occurred in Chicago. In 1893 the city hosted the World Columbian Exposition, a grand effort to bring science and culture to the public in exhibit form. Putnam was appointed chief of its Department of Ethnology and Archaeology, and during the two years preceding the exhibit he sent field workers throughout the Western Hemisphere to assemble a vast collection of material objects representing the prehistoric and contemporary native peoples of the Americas. Together with his assistant Franz Boas, he succeeded in producing the grand-scale exhibit he envisaged—later heralded as "one of the marvels of the Fair"—and, at the same time, provided that the collections he amassed would, after the Exposition, serve as the core of a permanent collection for a great anthropological museum. In 1894, the year following the Exposition, a natural history museum was in fact founded, endowed by the philanthropist Marshall Field and named in his honor. It included a Department of Anthropology, initially headed by Franz Boas, Putnam's assistant throughout the Exposition. Although Putnam's association with the new museum, as well as that of Boas, ended within a year of its founding, the scientific course that he had charted for its anthropology program was subsequently carried out by his student George A. Dorsey, who became Curator of Anthropology in 1897.

Meanwhile, in 1894 Putnam was appointed part-time head of the Department of Anthropology in the American Museum of Natural History, where in 1896 he again employed Franz Boas to develop research and collections in the museum. Here, as in Chicago, Putnam envisioned a grand plan for anthropological research combined with education, and Boas was instrumental in implementing it. The plan bore fruit since the anthropology department of the American Museum went on to become one of the major research programs in the United States. Boas, who was initially given a part-time appointment at Columbia

University, left the museum in 1905 to establish the foremost anthropology program in an American university in the early twentieth century and become, during his lifetime, the most influential figure in academic anthropology.

At the same time that anthropology was developing as a scholarly discipline focused on the description of native cultures, American Indian life throughout most of North America was undergoing rapid, radical change. Acculturation meant that knowledge of the past was rapidly disappearing, and consequently for American anthropology a major—in fact, *the* major—goal was to preserve as full a record as possible of the former lifeways of America's native peoples while it was still possible. It was an urgent documentary task.

This volume, *Pawnee Mythology*, is a product of that turn-of-the-century period, when museum research was efflorescing and academic anthropology was starting to form around Franz Boas and his students. It is one important part of Dorsey's research agenda while he was curator at the Field Museum during the first decade of the twentieth century. It is, moreover, a product of the collaborative efforts of two men, Dorsey the museum researcher and James R. Murie, an educated native Pawnee. Dorsey conceptualized and secured support for the project of which this book is a part—an ambitious, comprehensive plan for documenting Pawnee culture and language—and then employed Murie to work with him, as a collector in the field and as a compiler in Chicago. Together the two men produced this book and others, as well as an archive of Pawnee culture that in their aggregate represent a major achievement in the documentation of one tribe's culture.

THE PAWNEES

Throughout the late eighteenth and early nineteenth centuries the Pawnees lived along major tributaries of the Missouri River in central Nebraska and northern Kansas. Historically they were one of the largest and most prominent peoples on the Great Plains, numbering some ten thousand or more individuals during the period of early contact with Europeans. From the end of the eighteenth century to the present, four divisions, generally designated as bands, have been recognized. Northernmost were the Skiris, who spoke a distinct dialect of Pawnee and virtually formed a separate tribe. Until the early nineteenth century they lived along the north bank of the Loup River, at one time in perhaps as many as thirteen villages, but during the early historical period in a single village. To the south of them, generally on the south

bank of the Platte River, but ranging as far south as the Republican
River in Kansas, lived the Chawis, the Kitkahahkis, and the
Pitahawiratas, each of whom usually comprised one village each. The
latter three groups, today generally designated the South Band Pawnees, spoke a single dialect of the language. (See fig. 1 for variant
names and spellings of Pawnee subdivision designations.)

Pawnee Name and Translation	Contemporary English Designation	Variant English Spellings	Historical Designations
Ckíri 'Wolf'	Skiri	Skidi	Panimahas, Loups, Loup Pawnees, Wolf Pawnees
Cawi'i (no translation)	Chawi	Chaui, Tsawi	Grand Pawnees
Kítkahahki 'Little Earth Lodge Village'	Kitkahahki	Kitkehahki, Kitkahaki	Republican Pawnees
Piitahaawíraata 'Man Going East'	Pitahawirata	Pitahauirat, Pitahauerat	Tappage Pawnees, Noisy Pawnees

Fig. 1. Variant Names of Pawnee Subdivisions.

Closely related to these Pawnee groups are the Arikaras, who during the early historical period were living along the Missouri River in
central and later northern South Dakota.[1] They, too, were an aggregate of villages or bands. Arikara speech, frequently said to be a dialect of Pawnee, is no longer mutually intelligible with Pawnee and for
at least the past two centuries has constituted a separate language.[2]
More remotely related to the Pawnees are the Kitsais, who formerly
inhabited northeastern Texas, and the Wichitas, who lived in a wide
area of northern Texas and Oklahoma. The languages of all these
groups, together with that of the Caddos, another aggregate of related
peoples living in eastern Texas and western Louisiana, form the
Caddoan language family.

The Pawnees were a semi-sedentary people who represented the
horticultural tradition on the Plains. Their life was characterized by
alternating patterns of cultivation and high-plains buffalo hunting.
For them, the annual round of life began in the spring, when they
were living in their permanent villages of dome-shaped earth lodges,
domiciles that frequently housed two or more families and as many as
twenty or more people. During this season economic and ritual activity focused on horticulture: women prepared and planted gardens of
corn, beans, and squash, while men engaged in religious rituals associated with gardening. In June, after the crops were growing, mem-

bers of each village traveled west onto the high plains, where for nearly three months they lived in temporary bowl-shaped shelters and hunted buffalo. In late August they returned to their earth lodge villages to harvest the now-mature crops and to take up again a rich, variegated ritual life. In late October or November the people once again left their earth lodge villages, now for the winter hunt, during which they lived in buffalo-hide tipis. This hunt lasted until February or March, when the groups returned to their earth lodges to begin the annual cycle anew.

The basic unit of Pawnee social organization was the village. In the first half of the nineteenth century the village and band frequently coincided, although at different times the number of villages in a band varied from two to five or six, each comprising 40 to 200 lodges and ranging in population from 800 to 3,500. At an earlier period the number of villages was apparently greater and the population of each much smaller.

Governing each band or village were four chiefs, a head chief and three subordinate chiefs, who wielded considerable authority. The head chief's position, and undoubtedly that of the others as well, was hereditary, although an individual could achieve chiefly status through success in war, as many narratives attest. An important symbol of the chief's office, as well as a symbol of the village itself, was the sacred bundle, a religious shrine that represented the history of the band or village. Although the chief owned the bundle, and his wife cared for it, a priest—and not the chief—knew its rituals and performed the religious ceremonies associated with it. In secular Pawnee society there were other notable offices that also figure in traditional narratives. Each chief, for example, was assisted by four warriors who carried out his orders, and he had living in his lodge a crier or herald who made announcements to the village. Chiefs and successful warriors also lodged one or more young men, and sometimes an older man who had never achieved status. Known as "boys," they were aides or squires who ran errands, performed chores, and in other ways assisted the man of status.

Fundamental to Pawnee ceremonial life, and to an understanding of Pawnee traditional narratives, is a cultural dichotomy between religion and shamanism that was manifested respectively in the rituals of priests and those of doctors—rituals that to a large extent dominated Pawnee life and distinguished the Pawnees from other Plains tribes. Although both priests and doctors shared a general concern with the supernatural and attempted to control natural phenomena, what distinguished them were the differences in their objectives, the deities they invoked, and the means by which they sought to achieve their ends.[3]

Priests (*kúrahus*) sought to promote village welfare as mediators between the people and the deities of the heavens, where everything in the world had its origin. Through long, repetitive liturgies and sacrificial offerings, priests sought good fortune and an orderly world. They themselves had no power; they only knew the complex rituals and knowledge associated with each village's sacred bundle, which was a collection of symbolic and ritual objects wrapped up in a buffalo hide casing. The bundle traced back to a supernatural encounter, to a vision in which a heavenly being had come to an ancestor to bestow on him knowledge and power, which were symbolized by the bundle's rituals. The objects in the bundle represented that encounter and the instructions given to the visionary, and thus the bundle represented the origin of the village as well. Its rituals, then, typically recounted the origin of the world and the village. Every village had a sacred bundle, which served as its palladium—as a sacred object that would save the village—and which also served as an altar for its rituals.

Bundle rituals invoked heavenly deities—stars and other celestial phenomena—who were arranged hierarchically. At the top was Tirawahat (South Band *tiraawaahat*, Skiri *tiráwaahat*), an amorphous being who created the universe.[4] Below him were Evening Star and Morning Star, Sun and Moon, and a host of other star beings who had had roles in the creation of the world as the Pawnees knew it and who continued to control the universe. Thus they were responsible for the weather, plant growth, fertility, and other generalized human concerns—concerns that for Pawnees translated primarily as bountiful crops, plentiful buffalo, and success in war.

The deities of doctors (*kuraa'u'*), in contrast, were animals, birds, and other beings on earth. The powers of these terrestrial beings were curative, although they also included the ability to mesmerize people or to bring some malady or misfortune on an individual. Among the animals and birds there was no hierarchy. Although some, like the bear, were thought to be especially powerful, all animals—and, in fact, even insects—had their distinctive powers that they could impart to humans. They came to individuals in dreams, usually when a person was in a pitiful state, and taught them their knowledge, "blessing them" as Pawnees say today. Often, as among most Plains tribes, a single animal would bestow such power, but among the Pawnees an additional, distinctive theme is the bestowal of various powers by a group

of animals in an animal lodge. Such lodges were usually located un-
derwater or on the bank of a body of water, and in them animals of
various species were said to meet, arranging themselves in the same
manner as Pawnee doctors in the doctors' lodge and performing like
Pawnee doctors. Typically, a young man would fall asleep beside a body
of water, and an animal would approach him, mesmerize him, and
take him below into the animal lodge. There the animals would debate
whether they should kill him or let him live, and in the end they would
invariably pity the young man and bestow their powers on him. Afterward, he would be taken back to the bank where he had been sleeping.[5]

Although Pawnee doctors had short ceremonies in the spring, they
concentrated most of their ritual activity in one massive performance,
the Doctors' Dance, sometimes designated the Medicine Lodge, which
took place in September, near the end of the ritual season. The important doctors, together with their apprentices, met for a month in the
lodge of a leading doctor. This meeting, during which the doctors lived
in the lodge, was a staged event in which drama predominated. Doctors took turns impersonating their animal guardians and performing
sleight-of-hand, the purpose of which was to demonstrate their powers publicly—to convince people of their mysterious abilities and inspire awe. In such performances a man might be shot dead and then
brought back to life; a body part would be severed, taken around the
lodge, and then reattached to the person's body; or a corn plant might
be grown from seed before the eyes of spectators. So adept were the
doctors at magic that they convinced not only their own people but
gained a reputation among surrounding tribes for their mysterious
powers. Even early European and American visitors to the Pawnees
remarked on the doctors' exceptional skills as magicians.

A NINETEENTH CENTURY HISTORICAL OVERVIEW

During the nineteenth century, Pawnees were subjected to an inces-
sant, ever-increasing interplay of outside forces, mostly destructive,
that radically changed their lives. All of those forces were in large part
the result of the rapidly increasing influences of an expansionist United
States. One was white emigration and transcontinental travel that
went directly through traditional Pawnee territory. As the century
progressed, emigration swelled, putting increased demands on the limited natural resources of the region—on the buffalo herds and other
game upon which the Pawnees depended for food, on the pastures and

other forage that they needed for their horses, on the wood they needed for their houses and for fuel, and, ultimately, upon the very land that they considered their own. Simultaneous with that early emigration was another encroachment, the forced removal of tribes from east of the Mississippi River to land west of it, adding approximately a thirty percent increase to the native population of the eastern Plains and creating even more subsistence demands on an already economically uncertain environment. With the increase in population came pressure on the Pawnees to relinquish large portions of their territory. In 1833, the four Pawnee bands, now treated by the government as a single tribal entity, ceded their lands south of the Platte River. Finally, in 1857, in a treaty signed at Table Creek, Nebraska Territory, they yielded their independence by accepting a small reservation on the Loup Fork of the Platte River, together with monetary and other economic provisions.

White emigration and Indian removal from the East brought two other devastating effects to Pawnee and, more widely, Indian life on the eastern Plains: disease and warfare. Throughout the century a relentless series of epidemics took a deep, steady toll on the Pawnee population. In 1849, for example, cholera took the lives of over a thousand individuals and in 1852 a smallpox epidemic, only one of many, decimated the tribe. But even more demoralizing than the loss of life from disease was the loss from the unremitting attacks of their enemies, particularly the Sioux. The Pawnees had always been at war with most Plains tribes. Their only friends had been the Arikaras, Mandans, and Wichitas. They had also enjoyed intermittent peace with the Omahas, Poncas, and Otos but only because they had inspired fear in the latter tribes. With all others—particularly the large nomadic ones—there was a perpetual state of conflict. After the treaty of 1833, however, the Pawnees gave up their weapons and renounced warfare, agreeing to take up new lives as agrarians and ostensibly to be protected by the U.S. government in that endeavor. The effect of this new life of dependency, combined with the severe population loss from disease, left the Pawnees vulnerable—or, more precisely, at the mercy of their enemies. The Sioux, in particular, vowed a war of extermination, and for a period of forty years after that treaty, the Pawnees, essentially weaponless and unprotected, endured constant attacks by Sioux war parties of varying size that inflicted a major loss of life. So demoralizing was the unceasing harassment that, finally, in 1874 the tribe began a two-year removal to Indian Territory, where the Pawnees would begin new lives.

From the treaty of 1833 until their move to Indian Territory, Pawnees were also under progressively increasing pressure to change from
their traditional lifestyle to the new agrarian one represented by white
farmers of the period. Missionary efforts began in 1831, with the arrival of the Presbyterians John Dunbar and Samuel Allis. Government farmers soon settled among the Pawnees as well, and Allis opened
a school for Pawnee children. Until 1860, most of these efforts at changing Pawnee life were desultory and had little effect on it. After the
tribe settled on a reservation, however, government efforts at acculturation intensified. Many Pawnees, conscious of the gradual disappearance of the buffalo, were becoming more amenable to an agricultural way of life by individual families and to education. Nevertheless,
right up to their removal from Nebraska, Pawnees still clung to their
village life in which most people lived in earth lodges, cultivated corn,
beans, and squash in the traditional manner, and depended on buffalo
hunting for a portion of their subsistence.

After arriving in Oklahoma between 1874 and 1876, the Pawnees
settled into a pattern of life much like the one they had known in
Nebraska. Each band settled on a large, separate tract of land assigned to it and, initially, began to farm the band tract cooperatively.
For a short time an attenuated form of their old village life was maintained in which the chiefs, priests, and doctors continued to organize
Pawnee social, economic, and religious life. Nevertheless, many
younger, progressive Pawnees soon began to move onto individual farms
during their first decade in Indian Territory, and by 1890 most of the
Skiris and a large proportion of the Chawis were living in houses on
their own farms, dressing like contemporary whites, and speaking
English in daily life. Some children were attending the local Pawnee
Industrial Boarding School, at which they received a minimal education, while others were going off to such boarding schools as Carlisle
Indian School (in Pennsylvania) and Hampton Institute (in Virginia),
where significant numbers of Pawnee youth received good educations.

By the close of the century, then, Pawnee culture had changed fundamentally. The symbols of the old were now by and large vestiges.
Village life had been replaced by life on individual farms; a mixed
horticultural-hunting subsistence pattern had given way to agriculture and government rations; the authority of chiefs had been replaced
by that of the agent; and religious ceremonies and the knowledge of
sacred bundles were rapidly disappearing as the priests who possessed
that knowledge died and no successors came forward. Doctors' dances
were to continue in attenuated form for several decades, but after 1878

the protracted late-summer Doctors' Dance, in which the doctors demonstrated their powers, ceased.[6]

DORSEY'S AND MURIE'S STUDIES OF THE PAWNEE

When George A. Dorsey went to Oklahoma in 1901, he was five years beyond completion of his doctorate in anthropology at Harvard University and was still at the beginning of an ambitious anthropological career in which American Indians, and particularly Plains Indians, would figure as only a small part. Dorsey was known as a man of boundless enthusiasm and energy, and those qualities helped him to secure funding for expeditions to all parts of the world to acquire ethnological collections for the Field Columbian Museum and in the process to carry out the program charted by Putnam, his teacher. His trip to Oklahoma in the summer of 1901 was only one of many field expeditions that would provide materials for Plains Indian exhibits and ethnographic monographs. On this one he collected among the Osages, Pawnees, and Wichitas, but also visited the Arapahos and Cheyennes. Later that year he planned a return trip to visit the Pawnees, Otos, and Kickapoos that undoubtedly included other stops as well.

In a letter that Dorsey wrote in 1905 to F. J. V. Skiff, director of the museum, he told his superior that until 1902 his investigations had been desultory but in that year he had finally become profoundly interested in the social organization of the Pawnees, Arapahos, and Cheyennes and since then was devoting his time to studying those tribes. His study of the Arapahos had actually begun in 1901, however, when he employed as his field assistant an educated Arapaho named Cleaver Warden, who for a period of six years recorded ethnographic information and traditional stories for him. During the same six-year period Dorsey followed a similar procedure in his study of the Cheyennes, working with Richard Davis.

Dorsey's studies of the Pawnees, which ultimately became the most extensive and elaborate of his career, extended over the same period. When visiting the Pawnees on his summer trip in 1901, Dorsey laid the foundation for a protracted study among the tribe that was similar to the one he developed for the Arapahos and Cheyennes. On that trip he met James R. Murie, an educated Skiri Pawnee who was already employed by Alice C. Fletcher, an ethnologist affiliated with both the Harvard Peabody Museum and the Bureau of American Ethnology. For five years Fletcher had been studying Pawnee ritualism, and Murie was assisting her by introducing her to knowledgeable elders, translating for her, recording songs and chants, and transcribing and translating their lyrics. On that visit Murie proposed that Dorsey hire him, and the next year, in April 1902 when Dorsey returned to Pawnee, Oklahoma, again, he employed Murie as an assistant for his Pawnee studies.

In early January 1903, Dorsey submitted a proposal to the Carnegie Institution of Washington for support of a four-year project "to carry on ethnological researches among Indian tribes of the Caddoan stock," tribes that he considered particularly interesting because of their intermediate position between those of the High Plains and those of the Southeast. All the Caddoan groups had a comparatively rich material culture, distinctive domiciles—the earth lodges of the Arikaras and Pawnees and the grass lodges of the Wichitas—and rich, complex ritual lives. His was a broad, ambitious plan that had two parts. The first was to document the mythology and languages of all four Caddoan tribes—Arikaras, Caddos, Pawnees, and Wichitas. The second part was specific to the Pawnees: to document their religious rituals, including the hundreds of songs intrinsic to them. The task of documenting Pawnee religion, he argued, was an onerous one that had never been accomplished before because the rituals were regarded as personal property and securing information on them was expensive, requiring payment of goods and money. Moreover, such a project required an interpreter who was influential in the community and "of the priesthood," a person who had entree to religious leaders and their knowledge and who could as well record the ritual songs on a phonograph and then write out and translate them. Dorsey had chosen Murie as his collaborator, and in his proposal to the Carnegie Institution he asked for funds in two equal amounts, one to cover project expenses and the other to pay the salary of Murie, who would work both in the field and in Chicago. The project was approved later that month.

The chronology of Dorsey's and Murie's work, as well as an appreciation of their methodicalness, can be seen in Dorsey's annual reports on their accomplishments.[7] During 1903, the first year of the project, they compiled large, representative collections of traditional narratives (or mythology) for the Skiri Pawnees, Arikaras, and Wichitas. Although they completed the first two collections in 1903, the collection of Wichita narratives extended into 1904. For many Skiri stories, Murie also recorded on wax cylinders the songs that accompanied them. In 1904 three volumes were printed (Dorsey 1904b, c, d), one for each tribe, representing most of the narratives they had collected, with the exception of the Skiri stories that had songs—they were being reserved for a later publication—and some stories that were published separately in journals (for Wichita, see Dorsey 1902a, 1903a, 1904a; for Pawnee, see Dorsey 1902b, 1903b).

During the second year of their project, Murie and Dorsey also began to collect narratives for two additional volumes, one representing the other three Pawnee subdivisions (the South Bands), the other the Caddos. They completed both collections the following year, in 1905, and submitted them for publication. The Caddo volume was published that same year (Dorsey 1905) and the Pawnee volume, the largest of the five collections, was printed in 1906. Again, for these tribes Dorsey published some additional material in journals (for Caddo, see Dorsey 1905c; for Pawnee, see Dorsey 1905b, 1906b, the latter a collection of war tales). Thus, within a four-year period Dorsey and Murie had achieved one of their major goals, publication of representative collections of mythology for each of the five surviving Caddoan tribes.

During that same period, Dorsey and Murie were also observing surviving Pawnee and Arikara rituals and recording the songs that were part of them. When Murie visited the Arikaras in North Dakota in summer 1903, for example, he witnessed several ceremonies of the doctors' societies as well as other rituals, took notes on them, and recorded eighteen cylinders of songs. In that same year he, and perhaps Dorsey as well, observed many more Pawnee rituals: eight doctors' society ceremonies, four Bear society ceremonies, one lance or warriors' society ritual, and twenty sacred bundle rituals. In addition, they recorded songs that filled an additional sixty cylinders.

In 1904 both Murie and Dorsey gave more attention to Pawnee religion and ritualism. They continued their field study of Skiri rituals and expanded their efforts to include Chawi ceremonies as well. Moreover, they brought to Chicago an elderly monolingual Skiri priest, Roaming Scout, who had previously furnished ritual information to Alice Fletcher and on one occasion had visited her in Washington, D.C. On this trip to Chicago, one of at least two, Roaming Scout remained for several weeks, during which he provided information on the rituals of sacred bundles and doctors and recorded songs. Dorsey also reported that "an important member" of the Wichita tribe visited Chicago that year as well, and that the man's visit allowed him to begin a study of Wichita ceremonies. There are, however, no extant notes or other material from that visit.

Dorsey, with Murie's assistance both in Pawnee, Oklahoma, and in Chicago, took the project even further in 1905. He reported that they now had over five hundred cylinders of recorded songs, the largest number for any tribe in North America, and that through their field investigations they had "extended our knowledge of Pawnee social and ceremonial organization." At the end of the year he was ready to begin writing a monograph on the latter topic.

The following year, 1906, was one in which Dorsey brought more work to culmination. Besides submitting *The Pawnee: Mythology* to the printer, he spent most of the year writing a book-length manuscript entitled "Society and Religion of the Skidi Pawnee," completing most, but not all, of it.[8] He also stated that he had begun a study comparing Caddoan mythology with that of neighboring tribes, a project that he intended to complete the following year.[9] In addition to these endeavors, Dorsey enlisted the collaboration of the noted German musicologist Erich von Hornbostel, who came from Berlin to Chicago and then visited the Pawnees in Oklahoma. The result was that for several years after he returned home von Hornbostel transcribed the music to many of the songs Murie and Dorsey had recorded and prepared an analysis of Pawnee music; but this material, too, was never published.

In 1906, Murie again brought Roaming Scout to Chicago, this time to record narratives in the Pawnee language on wax cylinders, an endeavor that would produce descriptions of Pawnee thought and culture in the words of a Skiri intellectual and at the same time provide a large body of linguistic material for a study of Pawnee grammar. While there, the elderly priest recorded over seven hours of narration that covered a range of ethnographic topics—discussions of life, death, the nature of mysterious power, healing, constellations and individual stars, and religious rituals—as well as Roaming Scout's autobiography, reminiscences, and several myths.[10] Later, Murie wrote out the Skiri text of the narratives and then prepared a literal word-for-word translation of them. The next year, once Murie had completed the transcriptional work, he and Dorsey went to New York for several weeks of linguistic training under Franz Boas, by then the leading figure in the study of American Indian languages. Subsequently, over a two-year period Dorsey continued to refine Murie's transcriptions and to analyze Pawnee grammatical structure based on the texts themselves.

In his 1907 report to the Carnegie Institution Dorsey asked for an additional year of support that would enable him to prepare for publication three more volumes: part two of *The Pawnee: Mythology*,[11] the monograph "Society and Religion of the Skiri Pawnee," and a volume comprising the Roaming Scout narratives together with English translations and grammatical notes. For reasons that are not entirely clear, but apparently reflecting a tighter Carnegie budget, Dorsey's request was denied. Two years earlier, in 1905, Dorsey had written Skiff that once his Pawnee and Arapaho work was finished, he planned no further ethnological studies in North America; he hoped, instead, to devote himself to the physical anthropology collections in the museum. The rejection by the Carnegie Institution essentially ended his Pawnee work. Although Dorsey continued to study the Roaming Scout texts off and on through 1909, he never published again on the Pawnee.

For its time, Dorsey's plan for documenting Caddoan mythology comparatively and Pawnee culture specifically was one of the most comprehensive projects ever attempted in American anthropology and, had it been completed in its entirety, would have resulted in one of the most thorough and insightful descriptions of an American Indian tribe. Not only did he and Murie compile splendid collections of oral traditions for each of the Caddoan tribes, but for the Pawnees they conceptualized a grand descriptive scheme that encompassed social organization, religion, oral tradition, music, and material culture, all seen as inextricably related and expressed through language and song. Dorsey, with Murie's indispensable collaboration, recognized the importance of recording ethnography verbatim from members of the culture and from as many individuals as possible. He recognized, moreover, the importance of recording that information, whenever possible, in the native language, or at least in close English translation. Moreover, because of the sheer number of wax cylinder recordings of Pawnee songs and spoken texts, Dorsey and Murie were unique among anthropologists of the time in their use of technology to preserve a documentary record. This commitment to documenting native accounts and letting members of a culture speak for themselves was, then, a hallmark of Dorsey's anthropology and gives a timeless value to the material that he and Murie recorded.

THIS VOLUME

Of the five volumes of Caddoan oral traditions, this one, comprising 148 narratives, is the largest and most comprehensive. It covers nearly the entire gamut of Pawnee oral genres: myths, with casts of heavenly and other supernatural characters, that tell of world origins and mythic dramas; legends, or vision stories, that relate how individuals were pitied by supernatural beings and given power, often in the form of rituals that they subsequently performed for their own or for tribal benefit; and tales, or fables, that were fictional and were told for amusement. In the Pawnee world view these categories represent two major genres: the first two, true stories, or history; the latter, fiction.

No matter the type, all these narratives are set in a time and world that preceded Europeans—in a world inhabited by Pawnees and the animals and other supernatural beings that from time to time interacted with them; by other tribes known to the Pawnees or by supernatural characters or beings who comprised the Pawnee conception of the world before it assumed its historical form, when Pawnee life had not been disrupted by the entry of Europeans. This timeless period preceded the historical past and constitutes a large part of true history as Pawnees conceived it. Interestingly, history as Euro-Americans conceive it—of events and encounters between ethnic groups set within a chronological framework—is not represented here. As a result, even though they first encountered European fur traders at least two centuries ago, there are no accounts here of Pawnee interaction with Europeans throughout the period of time after those early encounters. In fact, there are *no* references to Europeans or Americans in any of these traditions. It is, then, an exclusively Pawnee world that is portrayed throughout.

Included in this collection are forty-five Skiri narratives that Dorsey had purposefully omitted from his earlier Skiri monograph (Dorsey 1904b). They are tales containing one or more songs, as well as some miscellaneous stories. Dorsey had intended to publish them as a separate volume, as a sequel to the earlier Skiri monograph, but then decided to include them in this collection instead. What he did not include in this volume, however, are war tales, a popular narrative genre, especially among men. They are accounts of intertribal warfare, usually of individual exploits, that occurred during the nineteenth century when Pawnee men still set out in war parties to capture horses, take enemy scalps, and count coups on foes. The war stories that Dorsey and Murie recorded are presented in two separate, article-length publications (Dorsey 1903b, 1906b).

This collection is especially distinctive for its representativeness. Unlike most collections of mythology of an American Indian tribe, which comprise stories told by either a single individual or a relatively small number of storytellers, Murie and Dorsey recorded stories from thirty-nine individuals from the four Pawnee subdivisions. At the turn of the century, when the Pawnee population had sunk to an all-time low of five hundred individuals, those thirty-nine represented essentially the entire story-telling population of the Pawnees. Although Dorsey states in his introduction that the Chawi and Pitahawirata stories do not

adequately represent the traditions of those divisions (7), it is nevertheless fair to assume that the traditions presented here, in their aggregate, provide a rich portrayal of the Pawnees as a whole.

Classification and presentation. Dorsey, as he states in the introduction to this volume, chose to present the narratives here as a single
collection representing the Pawnees as a unitary tribe. That arrangement was inevitable since, during the period when the stories were
recorded, the reduction of the Pawnee population to a mere remnant
of its former size had forced members of the four subdivisions to intermarry, and intermarriage necessarily leveled most cultural differences
that formerly existed among them. In the early twentieth century, for
example, when elderly Pawnees tried to revive many rituals, it was
necessary for the few men from each of the subdivisions who had some
knowledge of nearly forgotten ceremonies to pool their knowledge in
order to perform the rituals. The result was that late-nineteenth and
early-twentieth century ritualism was an amalgam of what individuals from each subdivision remembered.

Pawnees, like their kindred the Arikaras (Parks 1991, 3:44–49), clas-
sified their oral traditions into two large groups, true stories and fables.
The former category includes what folklorists now designate as myths
and legends, as well as historical accounts from the past century. For
Pawnees, however, they constitute history: what occurred in times past,
from the beginning of the world until recently. Fables, in contrast,
generally called Coyote stories by Pawnees, are tales recognized as
fictional and told to amuse or to impart some moral.

Dorsey, like others who have published large collections of oral narratives, chose to develop a more elaborate classificatory scheme. He
utilized four categories, each one based on common thematic elements
as well as on the characters of the stories:

- *myths* generally associated with sacred bundles and rituals; the characters are usually heavenly beings
- *myths* or *legends* that are hero, or poor boy, stories in which the
  protagonist performs some feat, usually a miraculous one, benefit-
  ing the tribe. The Pawnees refer to such stories as Ready-to-Give
  tales, based on the deity Kawaharu (*káwahaaru'*), a name that literally means 'good fortune' and refers to the ultimate source of the
  hero's power. These stories are generally recognized as fictional.
- *legends* that recount the acquisition of power, usually referred to as
  vision stories

- *Coyote tales* that recount the antics or foibles of the trickster Coyote (*ckírihki*)

Arranging stories by characters was, in fact, the way in which Pawnees themselves grouped stories, according to Dorsey. He recognized the problems of such a classification, in part because most stories have a unique character rather than a stock, or distinctively Pawnee, one. Moreover, the protagonist of the same story often will have a different name in a version told by a different individual.

Another basic problem with the classification here is that many stories of the same type or theme are placed in different sections. There are, for example, many buffalo-calling stories, in which an individual has or acquires the power to bring the buffalo during a period of starvation and save the people. In part I there are at least nine such stories (nos. 3, 21–28), and in part II there are sixteen (nos. 51–66), with no apparent reason for separating them. Similarly, in part I there are nine vision stories (nos. 11, 12, 14, 19–21, 23, 25, 31), in which an individual acquires power; they, like many of the buffalo-calling stories, would seem to be more appropriately placed in part III, even though Dorsey states that the basis for classifying stories in parts I–III is largely determined by source of power, that is, from heavenly beings, from Kawaharu, or from earthly beings. Sometimes, too, the same story, told by different narrators, is occasionally placed in different sections. Thus, four versions of the story of the buffalo wife (nos. 16, 18, 26, 28), a widespread Plains story, appear in part I, while another variant (no. 57) occurs in part II.[12]

These classificatory problems suggest an alternative arrangement based on a combination of narrative features: of time period in which the story is set, its function, and its perceived veracity. Thus, rather than utilizing source of power (heavenly or earthly) as the criterion for arrangement, one could employ a simple temporal scheme that is cross-cut by a true-ficticious distinction. Thus, the first section would comprise myths that tell of events preceding the world as the Pawnee knew it, or during the period when it was taking its present form, all of which are perceived to be true. The second section would comprise dream, or vision, stories (now part III but including stories in part I), also recognized as true. A third section would encompass fables—all stories deemed as fictional—which fall into two major groups: Coyote stories and most of the stories in Dorsey's part II. Alternatively, since most of the stories in Dorsey's part II hover between myth and fable, one could arrange them in a subsection of myths in the first section.

Presentation. Although Dorsey does not describe Murie's methods of recording the stories in this collection, it appears that he took them down in dictation, apparently translating them from Pawnee into English as they were told, since most if not all the narrators spoke no English. Some may have been retellings by Murie, written out later after he had heard them, but, given the length and detail of most of the narratives, as well as their style, they do not appear to be retellings.

The narratives do, however, lack many, if not most of, the characteristic features of Pawnee oral narrative style. Such common sentence and paragraph introducers as *náwah* 'now,' *na* and *a* 'and,' and *tsu* 'but,' as well as the often used emotive particle *aáka'a* 'oh, oh my,' do not occur in these English versions. Repetition, a feature that serves to emphasize a statement, or to indicate spatial or temporal extension, has also been eliminated from the translations. Similarly, common Pawnee framing statements such as 'This is what he said' or 'This is what he did' are lacking altogether.[13]

Despite the lack of such features of Pawnee oral style, these stories do appear to hew closely to the narrators' renditions in Pawnee and to lack the explanatory embellishments often provided in English versions. Precisely how closely they follow the original Pawnee, however, will remain a question since the recordings of the original narrations no longer exist.

Relationship to other collections of Pawnee narratives. Although sources of Pawnee oral narratives are relatively plentiful, they were collected by a small number of individuals. Preceding Murie and Dorsey was the great nineteenth-century naturalist George Bird Grinnell. Beginning in 1870 and continuing over two decades, Grinnell visited the Pawnees, first in Nebraska and later in their new home in Indian Territory. His avowed task among the Pawnees, as it was among the Cheyennes and Blackfeet, whom he also visited, was to be a cultural recorder, and on his visits he documented traditional stories, historical reminiscences, and ethnography, often assisted by Murie as his translator. For the Pawnees, Grinnell's major work is *Pawnee Hero Stories and Folk-Tales*, the first half of which is a collection of oral narratives and the second half a combination of Pawnee history and ethnography. The narratives in the book divide into two groups, historical accounts of heroic feats (what Grinnell calls hero stories) and legends of events that reach further back into a dimmer past of Pawnee history (Grinnell's folk tales). In addition to this collection, Grinnell published many stories in journals, either singly or as smaller collections (Grinnell 1891, 1892, 1893, 1894), and included several Pawnee examples in a collection of stories from various tribes (Grinnell 1901).

Following Grinnell's documentary efforts were those of Dorsey and Murie, which spanned the period 1903 to 1906. After Dorsey forsook his Pawnee studies, Murie was engaged by the Bureau of American Ethnology beginning in 1910 to record descriptions of surviving Pawnee rituals, which at that time were primarily the doctors' dances. In the course of that work, extending over several years, Clark Wissler, Curator of Anthropology at the American Museum of Natural History, arranged in 1912 for Murie to collect information on the former men's societies among the Pawnee. Murie's work for Wissler resulted in a short monograph that contains descriptions as well as the origin stories of those societies (Murie 1914). Subsequently, Murie collaborated with Wissler on an elaborate documentary study of Skiri ceremonialism. That work, begun in 1914, extended through 1921, when Wissler combined into a single monograph their Skiri study and Murie's descriptions of three South Band doctors' dances, written for the Bureau, to produce a documentary record of Pawnee religious and medical ritualism (Murie 1981). That work is a rich source of religious narratives as well as an unparalleled collection of vision stories that underlay Pawnee doctors' rites.

In 1919 and 1920, when Murie was finishing his work with Wissler, Frances Densmore visited Pawnee, Oklahoma, to record songs as part of her larger comparative documentary project to record American Indian music. Murie assisted Densmore, as he had all previous anthropologists, by transcribing and translating the lyrics of the songs she recorded. The monograph that resulted from her study (Densmore 1929) contains eighty-six songs, and for a majority of them she includes in English translation the story explaining the song. Thus the volume is as much a source of oral tradition as it is music.

Nearly a decade after Murie's collaborative work with Dorsey and Wissler, the anthropologist Gene Weltfish, a student of Franz Boas at Columbia University, visited the Pawnees in Oklahoma from 1929 to 1931, and during the course of her work she recorded a collection of stories from various South Band Pawnees. Weltfish's method was to take the stories down in dictation in the Pawnee language and afterward write out for each one a word-by-word literal translation followed by a free translation. The published collection is a combination of vision stories, fables, personal reminiscences, and cultural descriptions—a collection designed to record the Pawnee oral tradition in the native language and thereby preserve its stylistic and other characteristic features (Weltfish 1937). It is, consequently, an essential source on Pawnee oral traditions.

More recently Parks (1977, 1994) has published several stories that were recorded in the course of his linguistic study of Pawnee extending from 1965 to the present.

CONCLUSION

The Pawnee Mythology, together with its companion volume *Traditions of the Skidi Pawnee*, comprises a unique, priceless contribution to the documentation of nineteenth-century Pawnee oral traditions, recorded at nearly the last possible moment, when Pawnee life was being radically transformed by acculturation and the people were suffering the loss of the last generation that had grown up with the worldview expressed in the stories. As a large, representative collection of the tribe's literary heritage, the volume affords a rich, intimate portrayal of that earlier Pawnee conception of the world and their history—of how tribal social and ritual life took its shape, and of what and who were important in the Pawnee past—as told by individual Pawnees themselves in the narrative form they had always used for the transmission of tradition. The stories thus contextualize the Pawnees' existence in their world, giving it meaning as well as temporal and social orientation. Consequently, they convey to contemporary and future readers a depth of understanding of historical Pawnee culture that can only be derived from a people's own perspectives, embodied in their historical and literary texts.

That we are still able to share in that Pawnee world, a century after the narrators represented in this volume have passed on and the Pawnee narrative tradition no longer survives, is a tribute to the foresight and perseverance of George A. Dorsey and James R. Murie, who dedicated themselves to the documentary goals of anthropology during its formative period. Today, when anthropology and such related fields as folklore and comparative literature are returning to collections of late-nineteenth- and early-twentieth-century texts as unique, essential sources of worldview and of native literary style, collections such as this one assume a new importance and demonstrate their enduring value. At the same time, Pawnees today, who have not had the privilege of growing up hearing these oral traditions, as well as other people who seek to enter into the Pawnee world illustrated in these stories, still have that opportunity.

NOTES

1. During most of the nineteenth century the Arikaras lived along the Missouri River in North Dakota. Today they live on the Fort Berthold Indian Reservation in west central North Dakota.

2. The Arikaras are often said to be an "offshoot" of, or historically derived from, the Skiris. There is, however, no linguistic or historical evidence to support that interpretation, which seems to be based on a misinterpretation of historical visiting patterns between Arikaras and Skiris.

3. For a more comprehensive overview of Pawnee religion and shamanism, see Murie (1981, 1:7–18).

4. In this volume and in other writings at the turn of the century, Murie and other writers attempted to make a distinction between a discrete supreme being, putatively designated Tirawa, and the vast expanse of the heavens, termed Tirawahat. In fact, there is no such distinction in the Pawnee language, only the form *tiraawaahat*, which literally means 'this expanse' and is the term used to designate both the heavens or sky and the pervading force of that expanse that is the deity (Murie 1981, 1:179 n.16). As such it is usually translated as 'the Heavens.' In prayer, Pawnees address Tirawahat as *atí'as títaku ahrakítaku,* 'our Father who is above.'

5. For a discussion of Pawnee animal lodges and historical locations of them, see Parks and Wedel (1985).

6. A more comprehensive overview of Pawnee history is presented in Lesser (1933:1–52).

7. Most of the information in this section is taken from the Dorsey file of correspondence and reports in the archives of the Carnegie Institution of Washington.

8. This manuscript, which Dorsey intended to publish in 1906, was never finished entirely. It is, however, being edited for publication by this writer.

9. Today there is no known archival manuscript, partial or complete, on this topic.

10. These narratives were also never published, but are currently being prepared for publication.

11. In his introduction to this volume, Dorsey states that in "Part II of this memoir will be found the results of a comparative study" of narratives for each of the Pawnee subdivisions as well as with American Indian narratives in general (9). Not only was this study never submitted for publication, but no copy of the manuscript seems to survive today.

12. Several stories are misplaced. One (no. 20) is set in historical times but is placed in part I, which comprises myths; it should go to part III. Placed in part II is a Coyote story (no. 64) that belongs in part III. Placed in part III is a Burnt Belly story (no. 107) that actually belongs in part II with the other stories of Burnt Belly.

13. For a detailed discussion of the stylistic features of Arikara oral traditions, which are nearly identical to those of Pawnee, see Parks (1991, 3:64–82).

BIBLIOGRAPHY

Cole, Fay-Cooper
1931   George A. Dorsey. *American Anthropologist* 33:413–14.
Darnell, Regna Diebold
1969   The Development of American anthropology 1879–1920: From the Bureau of American Ethnology to Franz Boas. Ph.D. diss., University of Pennsylvania.
Densmore, Frances
1929   *Pawnee Music*. Bureau of American Ethnology Bulletin 93. Washington DC: GPO.
Dexter, Ralph W.
1966   Putnam's Problems Popularizing Anthropology. *American Scientist* 54 (3):315–32.
Dorsey, George A.
1902a Wichita Tales. *Journal of American Folk-Lore* 15:215–39.
1902b One of the Sacred Altars of the Pawnee. In *Proceedings of the Thirteenth International Congress of Americanists*. New York.
1903a Wichita Tales. *Journal of American Folk-Lore* 16:160–79.
1903b How the Pawnee Captured the Cheyenne Medicine Arrows. *American Anthropologist* 5:644–58.
1904a Wichita Tales. *Journal of American Folk-Lore* 17:153–60.
1904b *Traditions of the Skidi Pawnee*. American Folk-Lore Society, memoir 8. Boston: Houghton, Mifflin.
1904c *Traditions of the Arikara*. Carnegie Institution of Washington, pub. 17. Washington DC.
1904d *The Mythology of the Wichita*. Carnegie Institution of Washington, pub. 21. Washington DC.
1904e An Arikara Story-Telling Contest. *American Anthropologist* 6:240–43.
1905a *Traditions of the Caddo*. Carnegie Institution of Washington, pub. 41. Washington DC.
1905b A Pawnee Personal Medicine Shrine. *American Anthropologist* 7:496–98.
1905c Caddo Customs of Childhood. *Journal of American Folk-Lore* 18:226–28.
1906a *The Pawnee: Mythology (Part I)*. Carnegie Institution of Washington, pub. 59. Washington DC. Reprinted as *The Pawnee Mythology*, with an introduction by Douglas R. Parks, Lincoln: University of Nebraska Press, 1997.
1906b Pawnee War Tales. *American Anthropologist* 8:337–45.
Fletcher, Alice Cunningham
1903   Pawnee Star Lore. *Journal of American Folk-Lore* 16:10–15.
Grinnell, George Bird
1889   *Pawnee Hero Stories and Folk-Tales*. New York: Forest and Stream.

1891 The Young Dog's Dance. *Journal of American Folk-Lore* 4:307–13.

1892 Development of a Pawnee Myth. *Journal of American Folk-Lore* 5:127–34.

1893 Pawnee Mythology. *Journal of American Folk-Lore* 6:113–30.

1894 A Pawnee Star Myth. *Journal of American Folk-Lore* 7:197–200.

1901 *The Punishment of the Stingy and Other Indian Stories.* New York: Harper and Brothers.

Lesser, Alexander

1933 *The Pawnee Ghost Dance Hand Game: Ghost Dance Revival and Ethnic Identity.* Columbia Contributions to Anthropology, vol. 16. New York: Columbia University Press. Reprint, Madison: University of Wisconsin Press, 1978, and, with an introduction by Alice Beck Kehoe, Lincoln: University of Nebraska Press, 1996.

Murie, James R.

1914 *Pawnee Indian Societies.* Anthropological Papers of the American Museum of Natural History, vol. 11, pt. 7. New York.

1981 *Ceremonies of the Pawnee.* Ed. Douglas R. Parks. Smithsonian Contributions to Anthropology, no. 27. Washington DC: Smithsonian Institution Press. Reprint, Lincoln: University of Nebraska Press, 1989.

Parks, Douglas R.

1977 Pawnee Texts: Skiri and South Band. In: Caddoan Texts, ed. Douglas R. Parks, Native American Text Series, *International Journal of American Linguistics* 2(1):65–90.

1991 *Traditional Narratives of the Arikara Indians.* 4 vols. Lincoln: University of Nebraska Press.

1994 Three Skiri Pawnee Stories. *In Coming to Light: Contemporary Translations of the Native Literatures of North America,* ed. Brian Swann, 377–402. New York: Random House.

Parks, Douglas R. and Raymond J. DeMallie

1992 Plains Indian Native Literatures. *Boundary 2* special issue, 1492–1992: American Indian Persistence and Resurgence, ed. Karl Kroeber, 105–47.

Parks, Douglas R. and Waldo R. Wedel

1985 Pawnee Geography: Historical and Sacred. *Great Plains Quarterly* 5:143–76.

Weltfish, Gene

1936 The Vision Story of Fox-Boy, a South Band Pawnee Text. *International Journal of American Linguistics* 9:44–76.

1937 *Caddoan Texts: Pawnee, South Band Dialect.* Publications of the American Ethnological Society, vol. 17. New York: G. E. Stechert.

1965 *The Lost Universe.* New York: Basic Books.

CONTENTS

CONTENTS

* The letters C, K, S, and P indicate, respectively, the Chaui Kitkehahki, Skidi, and Pitahauirat.

II. Tales of Ready-to-Give.

III. The Origin of Medicine Ceremonies or Power.

IV. Coyote Tales.

PREFACE.

This present memoir forms part of a series of investigations begun by the author among the tribes of the Caddoan stock on behalf of the Field Museum of Natural History, and continued since the beginning of 1903 under the auspices of the Carnegie Institution of Washington. The results of this investigation, which have appeared up to the present time, are as follows:

1. Wichita Tales. 1. Origin. *J. Am. Folk-Lore*, vol. xv, pp. 215-239.
2. One of the sacred altars of the Pawnee. *Trans. Int. Cong. of Americanists*, pp. 67-74, 1902.
3. How the Pawnee captured the Cheyenne medicine arrows. *Am. Anth.* (n. s.), vol. v, pp. 644-658.
4. Wichita Tales. 2. The story of Weksalahos or the Shooting Stars. *J. Am. Folk-Lore*, vol. xvi, pp. 160-179.
5. An Arikara story-telling contest. *Am. Anth.* (n. s.), vol. vi, pp. 240-243, 1904.
6. Wichita Tales. 3. The two boys who slew the monsters and became stars. *J. Am. Folk-Lore*, vol. xvii, pp. 153-160, 1904.
7. Traditions of the Skidi Pawnee. *Mem. Am. Folk-Lore*, vol. viii, 1904.
8. Traditions of the Arikara. Pub. 17, *Carnegie Institution of Washington*, 1904.
9. The mythology of the Wichita. Pub. 21, *Carnegie Institution of Washington*, 1904.
10. A Pawnee personal medicine shrine. *Am. Anth.* (n. s.), pp. 496-498, 1905.
11. Caddo customs of childhood. *J. Am. Folk-Lore*, vol. xviii, pp. 226-228, 1905.
12. Traditions of the Caddo. Pub. 41, *Carnegie Institution of Washington*, 1905.

Part I of the mythology here presented contains the tales of the Kitkehahki, Pitahauirat, and Chaui bands of Pawnee, as well as a few miscellaneous Skidi tales, and completes the work of recording the traditions of the Caddoan tribes; it will be followed by Part II, in which will be presented the music which belongs to certain tales of this memoir, and which will give the results of a comparative study of the tales of the various tribes of this stock, both among themselves and with the tales of other tribes of North America.

The share of the work performed by Mr. James R. Murie has been as great in this present volume as in previous volumes, and without his keen interest and untiring patience the production of the memoir would not have been possible.

GEORGE A. DORSEY.

May 1, 1906.

INTRODUCTION.

The present memoir comprises one hundred and forty-eight tales, of which forty-five were obtained from nineteen Skidi informants, seventeen from five Pitahauirat informants, seventy-three from ten Kitkehahki informants, and thirteen from five Chaui informants. Concerning this representation it seems advisable to say a word. First, it should be noted that the Skidi tales here presented are to be regarded as supplementary to those already printed in my "Traditions of the Skidi Pawnee." In the introduction to that volume a statement was made that tales which contained songs would be reserved for publication in a later volume. The forty-five Skidi tales here presented contain all those which were omitted in the memoir just referred to, and include also several others which have been obtained during the last two years. Next, it should be remembered that the Skidi to-day exceed in population the other three bands combined. In the Chaui band there are but two men living who may be regarded as full-blooded Chaui. Others, however, have married Chaui women, have become possessors of Chaui traditions and their bundles brought to them by their wives, and are generally considered as Chaui to-day. The Pitahauirat band is also small in numbers. The Kitkehahki is relatively more numerous than the two bands just mentioned, but the great number of tales from this band is rather due to the fact that thirty-four of the tales were obtained from a single informant.

It appears that from the four bands thirty-nine informants are represented. These collectively represent practically the entire story-telling population of the Pawnee, for the tribe to-day numbers about five hundred, whereas at the time of the removal of the Pawnee from Nebraska to Oklahoma, in 1874, they numbered over two thousand. This great decimation of their ranks, together with the almost total abandonment of their religious observances, has undoubtedly greatly influenced the volume of mythology in the tribe; especially is this known to be the case among the Skidi, where certain villages are no longer represented and nothing is known of the ritual accompanying the sacred bundle which belonged to that village and consequently nothing of the tales of its origin. Again, it may be pointed out that in the representations of the Pitahauirat and Chaui of to-day it is not at all likely that anything approaching a fair representation of their mythology may be obtained. It seems, however, that the inequality in the number of tales representing the bands is not as serious as might seem at first consideration; for, although the four bands have long been recognized as distinct, the Pawnee themselves are firm in the belief that the Chaui, Pitahauirat, and Kitkehahki originally formed a single band or division known as the Kawarahkis. The time of this union is believed to have been long before the advent of the whites; the belief is based on historic tradition and hence must be accepted as at least provisionally true. According to this tradition the Kawarahkis at this time made their home near the present site of Nemaha, in the southeastern corner of Nebraska, near the Missouri River. From this point the Chaui and Kitkehahki, after their separation, went north, the Kitkehahki locating on the Republican River, where they were found by Pike, and the Chaui going to the northwest, where they settled south of the Platte River. After the departure of these two bands, the Kawarahkis remained in the neighborhood of Nemaha for a long period and the remnant finally became known as the Pitahauirat. Early in this century they also migrated to the northwest and occupied the area between the Chaui and the Kitkehahki. According to this tradition, therefore, the Chaui, Pitahauirat, and Kitkehahki form to-day remnants of what was once a single tribe, just as we have reason to believe that the Arikara and Skidi once formed a single tribe. The mythology of the three bands also leads to this belief, for their origin myths are practically the same, the variation which exists being due probably to the fact that since the bands became distinct each has acquired, generally from the Skidi, certain ceremonies or rites along with a story of origin. Thus it appears that the Pitahauirat, Kitkehahki, and Chaui would be likely to have a mythology which would show many points of difference from that of the Skidi. Were it possible to obtain a full account of their mythology, this difference, which undoubtedly exists, would probably be found to be much greater than now appears; at any rate it is known that their social organization and even many elements of their religion had much in common, but differed considerably from the Skidi. It may be further noted, however, that in general the tales of the four bands as they exist to-day form a unit and have many characteristic features in common. This is due to the fact that for the last forty years the four bands have been closely associated, and that since their removal to Oklahoma they have been treated by the government as a single tribe and have been forced to intermingle in a manner which formerly would not have been possible. The rapidly diminishing size of the tribe has also tended to bind the four tribes closer and closer together, and for several years past they have freely visited back and forth during ceremonies, at which gatherings story-telling has been a regular feature.

In Part II of this memoir will be found the results of a comparative study of the tales and incidents of the bands of the Pawnee, which in turn will be contrasted with the tales of other tribes of the so-called Caddoan stock and with the tales of American Indians in general. It might be pointed out at this time that in cosmogonic beliefs and in tales explanatory of rituals the Skidi more nearly approach the Arikara[1] than they do the other three bands of Pawnee. In the character of their so-called Coyote tales, however, the Skidi bears a closer resemblance to the other three bands than to the Arikara. This is as might be expected, for the Coyote tales would be much more likely to pass from one tribe to another through borrowing than would tales which relate to religious observances. It is interesting in this connection to note that the Skidi have had very little intercourse with the Arikara since their separation, about 1832.

In the introduction to the "Traditions of the Skidi Pawnee" will be found a general characterization of the religious life of the Skidi and the circumstances under which the tales were told. These remarks, in general, apply with equal force to the corresponding cultural elements of the other three bands. It should be noted, however, that the religion of the Chaui, Kitkehahki, and Pitahauirat collectively is not nearly so rich in ceremonies and accompanying rituals based upon the sacred bundles or altars as is that of the Skidi. Indeed, as stated before, there is some reason for believing that these three bands represent offshoots of the original Skidi through the single band of the Kawarahkis.

For obvious reasons the basis of the arrangement of the tales in the present volume is not the band; thus, Skidi tales are not found in one group, Chaui in another, etc. Such grouping would imply and might lead to the belief that the tales presented, for example, in the Chaui group belong to the Chaui rather than to the other three bands, whereas the fact that a tale is ascribed to a Chaui informant means that and nothing more. It is quite possible, and generally more than likely, that the other three bands have a similar tale; indeed, in many cases variants have been obtained from other bands, some of which are here presented, but where they present no new incident they have not been recorded. The basis of the present grouping has been determined by considering the tales as forming the available mythology of a single tribe, and the basis of the grouping is that which is recognized by the Pawnee themselves, namely, the character of the tale. The arrangement has been made only after long and extended inquiry among the leading informants, and especially after carefully considering the subject with Mr. Murie, who is at the present time probably the best informed man in his tribe. One of the dif-

See "Traditions of the Arikara," p. 5.

ficulties early discovered in the grouping of the tales is the fact that one version of a tale may be considered as having a certain character, while a slightly different version is related by another informant in another band, or even in the same band, and is considered as having an entirely different character. Hence it is that in one or two instances one version of a tale is found in one group, while another version is found in another group. Further difficulty of arrangement was encountered in the fact that a few tales lie close to the borderland of one or another group, and it often becomes a matter of considerable difficulty in deciding upon the proper position of a tale. In nearly every case, however, the estimate of the character of the tale as held by the informant has been observed.

The Pawnee clearly recognizes two great categories of tales—those which are true and which are supposed to relate to things or events which actually happened, and those which are false and which are considered to have been invented by the Pawnee, especially by the old men, for the purpose of impressing some moral precept, illustrating some phase of ethical life, or of conveying a warning, etc. A division slightly more extended, however, than the one just noted has been followed, and the tales are divided into four groups, each group being preceded by a statement which presents with sufficient fullness the common ground and common facts which connect together the tales of that group. Thus there are distinguished: (1) Tales which are true and which especially concern the supernatural beings of the heavens. Many of these tales are cosmogonic in nature, and nearly all possess some religious element. (2) Tales of Ready-to-Give, the major part of which are cultural hero tales which may be or may not be true, but which are associated with one of the supernatural beings of the north who is the supreme guardian deity of the people in matters pertaining to food quests. (3) Stories which are supposed to be true and which treat of the wonderful doings of the supernatural beings of the earth. The majority of these are concerned with the acquisition of an individual medicine or manitou, which may be transferred by sale or gift, but which is not necessarily hereditary. (4) Coyote tales, none of which are supposed to be true, but nearly all of which point a moral. It is interesting to note, concerning the Coyote tales as a group, that throughout the Coyote appears as a mean trickster and that his position as transformer is secondary to that of certain heroes found in the second group. There is reason to believe that, while the Pawnee were in Nebraska, the word Coyote was rarely or possibly never used in connection with these tales, and that they were called instead Wolf tales, the Wolf being the mean trickster and not the Coyote. These Coyote or Wolf tales, in general, suggest to the Pawnee the mischievous performances of the Wolf sent by the Wolf-Star, who, in attempting to steal people from Lightning, introduces mortality on earth, and through Lightning's failure to sacrifice Wolf the earth becomes subject to warfare and death. Thus the original wolf is a transformer of far-reaching consequences and at the same time a veritable trickster. This latter element appears throughout all the Coyote tales. The transformer element, as already noted, is as a rule much less prominent.

It has not been possible to obtain, up to the present time, any lengthy connected story of creation such as has been recorded from the Navaho. It seems probable, however, that such tales as the one just referred to represent a studied effort on the part of the narrator or observer to combine many elements in a continuous story. The Pawnee know of no such tale. It now seems quite certain to me, however, that a complete knowledge of the rituals associated with the sacred bundles of the Skidi would furnish us with a fairly well-connected tale of origin of unusual interest. This, however, it will never be possible to obtain, as many chapters or sections of such a tale disappeared with the village and its bundle. Many sections of the story are still available, a few of which have already been given in popular form in the "Traditions of the Skidi Pawnee." The comment there made may be here repeated, namely, that as a rule myths which seem to be explanatory of rituals do not represent the official version. This is embodied in the ritual itself, which is chanted or sung during the ceremony. The meaning of the words of the ritual is generally obscure, often unintelligible even to the priest himself. In this connection it may be interesting to note that not for thirty years have the bundle ceremonies been held or their rituals chanted. It is all the more surprising that the priests remember as much about them as they do.

Nearly one-half of the stories are accompanied by music and song, but only a free translation of the songs is given in the body of the stories. The music and text of the songs will be found in Part II. It is known that formerly songs existed with many of the other tales, but their words or music or both have been lost. The music and words of many songs have also been obtained from the narrators of many of the medicine stories. These songs, however, form an intrinsic part of the medicine-man's ceremonies, and consideration of them is reserved for a more appropriate place.

Accompanying the title of each tale is a note which bears the name of the informant and band. With a large number of tales there is also a brief explanatory note, in which is set forth the reason, as given by the informant, why the tale is told, and which supplements the general statement given at the beginning of each group of tales. This information, with the grouping of the stories from the view point of the Indian, will, it is believed, assist materially in a proper understanding of the tales. With the note to many of the tales I have added a few words of explanation where such seemed advisable.

In a few instances the titles of tales are given in their proper places, but the tales themselves are found only in the abstracts, where they are presented in an abbreviated form. This has been done in order the more clearly to bring out the rank given the tale by the narrator. It would have been possible to have brought about a further shortening of the tales by omitting in a few other instances the full tale and presenting it only in abstract form. In such cases, however, where apparently this might have been done but has not, the tales from the point of view of the Pawnee are different not only in character but in their origin, and either relate to different ceremonies or customs or point an entirely different moral.

I. TRUE STORIES OF THE HEAVENLY BEINGS.

The stories in the first group, as the division headline indicates, are all supposed to be true and to describe events which actually took place. Furthermore, these tales are nearly all connected with the sacred bundle or altar ceremonies, and in general may be considered as explanatory of the ceremony, or of some episode of the ceremony, or even as accounting for the very origin of the ceremony. These tales, as a rule, are told only during ceremonies, especially during the intermissions or pauses in the ceremony which occur from time to time between rites, or during resting periods in the chanting of a long ritual. During such intermissions anyone of those present may ask of the priests for such a tale. Especially is it the privilege of the one who has made the ceremony possible, by providing the food for the sacrifice and feast, to ask that such a tale be related. These tales may also, under certain circumstances, be told outside the ceremonial lodge, as, for example, a group of young men, by presenting on an appropriate occasion a ceremonial pipe to one who knows the story, could ask him to relate what he had heard during his presence in a ceremony. These stories are told, as a rule, in the fall and winter rather than in the spring and summer, and the chief object in relating them is to furnish instruction. Collectively they form a popular account of the Pawnee belief in the doings and performances of the supernatural beings.

---

1. ORIGIN OF THE CHAUI.[1]

After Tirawa had created the sun, moon, stars, the heavens, the earth, and all things upon the earth, he spoke, and at the sound of his voice a woman appeared upon the earth. Tirawa spoke to the gods in the heavens and asked them what he should do to make the woman happy and

[1] Told by Roaming-Chief, hereditary chief of the Chaui. The grandfather of Roaming-Chief was a Kitkehahki who married a Chaui woman and finally became chief of the Chaui. The result of this union was two children, one of whom was the famous Pitalesaru who was appointed by the United States Government as chief of the confederated bands of the Pawnee. His sister was the mother of Roaming-Chief. The tale possibly contains Kitkehahki elements, although it is claimed to be representative of the Chaui. It has its origin from a bundle on one of the sacred altars, and is handed down from one generation to another. Anyone making an offering of buffalo meat for the opening of the altar is privileged to hear the story. It is supposed especially to instill the belief of the great power of Tirawa and to inspire confidence in his ability to send the buffalo.

13

that she might give increase. The Moon spoke and said, "All things that you have made, you have made in pairs, as the Heavens and the Earth, the Sun and the Moon. Give a mate to the woman so that the pair may live together and help one another in life." Tirawa made a man and sent him to the woman; then he said: "Now I will speak to both of you. I give you the earth. You shall call the earth 'mother.' The heavens you shall call 'father.' You shall also call the moon 'mother,' for she rises in the east; and you shall call the sun 'father,' for he rises in the east. In time you, woman, shall be known as 'mother,' and the man shall be known as 'father.' I give you the sun to give you light. The moon will also give you light. The earth I give you, and you are to call her 'mother,' for she gives birth to all things. The timber that shall grow upon the earth you shall make use of in many ways. Some of the trees will have fruit upon them. Shrubs will grow from the ground and they will have berries upon them. All these things I give you and you shall eat of them. Never forget to call the earth 'mother,' for you are to live upon her. You must love her, for you must walk upon her. I will now show you how to build a lodge, so that you will not be cold or get wet from the rain. Go and get timber. Cut ten forked sticks and set them in a circle. Cut some poles to lay across the forks. Four of the upright forks must form a parallelogram, with the longest sides extending east and west. The posts that are set in the ground to uphold the lodge represent the four gods who hold up the heavens in the northeast, northwest, southwest, and southeast. There are minor gods between these, with powers that connect the power of one god to another. There is also an outer circle of many gods, and you shall cut poles to represent them; their power also extends from one god to another. The south side of the lodge will be for the men, for the men will be strong, and so they must be on the right. The north side shall be for the women, for they are not as strong as the men and so must be on the left. The entrance of the lodge shall always face the east, for the lodge that you are to build shall breathe as if human. Five posts are on the south side, representing the five branches of the man, two legs, two arms and head. The five forks at the north also stand for the five branches of the woman. You shall net willows together. These shall be thrown upon the east side of the four posts that stand for the gods in the heavens. These netted willows represent the ribs of the gods that the posts represent. When the lodge is complete, dig in the center for the fireplace and I will give you fire-sticks so that you can make your fire. These fire-sticks belong to the sun. When you make the fireplace, dig up the dirt in the center of the lodge and take it out and place it in front of the lodge in the form of a mound, so that when the sun shall rise in the east he will see that mound. Fire will do many things for you. After you have completed the fireplace, make the ground even inside of the lodge, leaving only one small mound in the west for an altar. Kill a buffalo and place the skull on the altar. Though the skull has no life in it, I, Tirawa, or the spirit of the buffalo will be present there when the rays of the sun shine upon it. For this reason always keep the skull on the altar, facing east, so that the first rays of the sun, as it enters the lodge, will shine upon it. Whenever you kill an animal, take fat and grease the parts so that you will remember that there are gods in the heavens, located as the posts of your lodge are. Whenever I, or the buffalo spirit, am away from the altar the minor gods will dwell there until we return. I will give you a sacred bundle to hang upon the wall over the altar. The woman will have charge of the bundle, and it is to be opened at certain times, so that you may see the things that are in it. I also give you a pipe and native tobacco and mother-corn, and painted sticks with scalps on them. Keep these painted sticks stuck around outside of the lodge, one in each of the four directions. All of the animals and all of the birds shall have power from the bundle and they shall go in pairs and have increase, as you shall have. Remember the skull, for I have placed it in your lodge to live with you and communicate with you. Listen to the thunder, for it is your father's voice. You must sacrifice things to him and to the other gods in the heavens. I now give you, man, a bow and arrows, which are to be known as the 'wonderful bow and arrows.' You, too, woman, I give a bow and arrows and also a hoe made from the shoulder blade of a buffalo; and seeds of four different colors, red, yellow, black, and white, and you shall have corn of these colors. Make a pot from the clay of the earth and cook the corn on the fire and eat it. I will tell you what herbs to eat and what ones to give to the sick. Eat these things and the flesh of animals."

When they had completed the lodge the woman was the first to enter it. She had with her some corn that she had raised from the seeds, and this she offered to the four gods, the southeast, southwest, northeast, and northwest. As she put the corn upon each post she pressed it upon the posts and rubbed upwards. The man killed an animal with his bow and arrows, from which he took the fat, and he greased the four posts and placed the skull upon the altar. After a time Tirawa spoke to them again and asked the man if he knew what the lodge represented. The man did not know. Tirawa then spoke and said: "I told you to call the earth 'mother.' The lodge represents the mother's breast. The smoke that escapes from the opening is like the milk that flows from the mother's breast. You also have a fireplace where your food is cooked. When you eat the things that are cooked, it is like sucking a mother's breast, because you eat and grow strong. I make you to live in the lodge, and you shall increase, but you are not to live forever. You are to die, and will be placed under the ground again. You and your children must always remember that I gave you life, but you are to return to the earth again. You, woman, take this speckled corn that I give you and put it in a clay pot with water and place it upon the fire to boil. After the water has boiled away and gone up into the air, eat of the dry mush that is left and feed it to your husband and you shall have increase." They ate of the mush and had increase. Then Tirawa spoke to them again and gave them many wonderful ceremonies. Two of the ceremonies have been handed down through all generations. One of the ceremonies is known as the Woman-dance, and it is to remind the people that it was Tirawa who gave them light. This was the first dance that Tirawa ever gave to the people. The other ceremony that has been handed down is known as the Starisu, Woman's dance, and it is formed as follows:

In the winter time, when the Pawnee are hunting buffalo, the chiefs will let the people know that they want meat for this particular ceremony. The young men of high birth will try to kill the fattest buffalo in the bunch, so that they can take this meat to the chief's lodge. Several buffalo will be killed for this purpose, and these buffalo will be taken to the chief's lodge, where the meat is jerked and dried. Early in the spring the people have planted their corn and it is now time for them to go buffalo hunting again. Then the four priests with one chief enter the lodge of a chief and they make known to him that they wish now to have the ceremony. The chief gives his consent. The women at once clear from the lodge their beds and other things, then the lodge is swept out with eagle-wing fans. The four priests take their seats at the west, the chief walks up, and the four priests make an opening in the center for him. The errand man is sent out by the chief to invite the young men and girls of high birth. These young people come in; the girls take their seats on the north side of the lodge, and the young men take theirs on the south side. The chief speaks and says: "My friends, this is a day that we have selected to have a dance, that Tirawa gave us. We were told in olden times that Tirawa promised to send buffalo to us if we should give this dance. We will now give the dance." He tells them to paint, dress, and prepare for the dance. The chief puts on his leggings, then takes the holy ointment from the bundle, arises and stands in front of them, and tells them that they must put upon themselves the grease of the buffalo, for they are about to imitate them. He tears the fat in two pieces and gives one piece to the first young man, the other to the first young woman. The boy greases his body, then hands the piece of fat to the next young man. After all of the young men have greased themselves, the fat is given to the two priests in the west, who also grease themselves. The fat that is given to the girl is also handed down to all the girls, who grease their faces, bodies, and hair. After they have used it they return it to the two priests in the west and they grease themselves. The two pieces of fat are then placed in front of the chief. The chief puts them together, then tells the people that Tirawa gave them this dance because the people were hungry. He tells them the following:

"The young man who had charge of the dance had given it and gone away, and left the people starving. He was guided by the Moon to a hilly country, and there on a hillside he was taken into a cave, and in the cave was a tipi and outside sat an old woman, who said: 'I am the Moon. I brought you here. I know the people are in need of food. Tirawa promised them that he would give them buffalo. Buffalo are scarce upon the earth, so we will have to send to them some buffalo that live under the ground. Take these pieces of fat and let the people eat or chew on it and get the grease out of it, and then they will feel better.' The young man returned and gave the people the fat, and everybody chewed a little of it. The young man went back into the cave and there found a young girl sitting outside of an earth-lodge. In front of her sat a basket with plum seeds in it. To her right were the gambling sticks. When the young woman saw him she took up the sticks and the ring and gave them to him, saying: 'Take this. Let the men of your people play with these sticks, so that they will not think about eating.' Then she picked up the basket with the plum seeds and said: 'Take this to the women. Let them play with the basket and seeds, so they will not think about eating. Take these two pieces of dried meat and gather the children and let them eat of it. The buffalo are far away. It will be some time before they can go out of the earth.' The young man returned to the people and gave the men the gambling sticks and the women the basket and seeds, and the children he gathered and gave them a piece of meat, so that they were filled. Several days afterward he went down to the pond and saw the same woman standing in the pond. She told him to go and stand outside of the entrance of the cave while she called the buffalo. She hallooed as follows:

> "Lihoo-oo-oo-oo!
> Lihoo-oo-oo-oo!
> Lihoo-oo-oo-oo!
> Lihoo-oo-oo-oo!

"At the last call the buffalo rushed out from the cave. The young man returned to the people and told them there were buffalo now on the prairie. The people went and killed many buffalo."

And so, as he concludes his story, he says: "We must perform the ceremony correctly; so that when we go out upon the hunt we may find many buffalo."

Then he is seated. He takes the four water drums and gives each of the priests one. He selects three of the older men to stay with the priests, to whom he gives the gourd rattles, keeping the largest rattle for himself, to show that he is the leader of the ceremony. He tells the two soldiers to prepare their costume. Each puts on a bustle made of crow feathers and a coyote tail, and each wears a red headdress. Then they take up their long sticks. When the chief sees that the soldiers are ready he puts his mysterious headdress upon his head, then covers it with black. He then leads and the priests follow, carrying their drums and rattles with them. A mat has been spread outside the lodge. There they seat themselves, the chief sitting at the west, facing the east, with the men on either side of him. They are now ready to sing. The chief then orders one of the chiefs to call the people out, as the young man called the buffalo, making the peculiar noise four times. When the chief has finished calling, the two men with the pipes, who are standing at the entrance, lead the procession out. First after the priests come four young men, then four young women, four young men, and so on, and finally the soldiers, who dance with the sticks as they come out. The song that is sung at this time is about a child growing from childhood to manhood. The procession comes out and goes around outside the singers four times, then stops dancing and sings another song. This song is about young men who can hunt buffalo and the enemy. When the song is completed they sing the song about calling the buffalo. Then they go around the singers four times, then stop and sing the last song, which is about the bulls and old cows dropping out from the main herd on account of old age. Then they enter the lodge. The chief, still wearing his mysterious headdress, takes one of the pipes, already filled with native tobacco, and smokes toward the east, then toward the south, then toward the west, then from the west to the fireplace, then from the fireplace to the west, then to the northeast. He then goes around by way of the north and lets one of the drummers smoke. He goes around the fireplace to the drummers by way of the south again and lets one of the drummers smoke. Then he goes to the singers and they all smoke. He takes the pipe, stands by the fireplace, facing the east, and empties the ashes from the pipe, then passes his hands over the pipe four times, above four times, upon the ground four times, then he gives the pipe to one of the priests, who says, "Nawa." Then all say, "Nawa." Two men are selected and they cut up the meat and boil it. The chief tells a certain young man to take some grease from the soup, to rub it upon the posts on the southeast, the southwest, the northwest, and the fireplace; then to the northeast. Then he is told to pour the grease into the center of the fireplace. He then gives the buffalo-horn spoon to the chief, who says, "Nawa," and sits down. The meat is divided among the people and the chief speaks and says: "I am satisfied. We are about to go hunting. We have gone through this ceremony given to us by our forefathers. I have tried to go through it as nearly as I could the way they were told to do by Tirawa. We have given the call of the buffalo. The buffalo under the earth have heard. They will help to send the buffalo to us on the buffalo hunt. Arise, and go out of the entrance that is known as the 'wonderful buffalo's entrance.' "

2. THE FOUR GODS IN THE WEST.[1]

A long time ago, when the people were first put upon the earth, they were placed near what is now Nemaha, Nebraska. There the people who were first created, two in number, made their earth-lodge. This earth-lodge faced west. As these two people increased they had many children and they married. The old people gave the children who were married separate lodges. Now, these three lodges of the people were living upon artichokes, ground beans, and other things which they could dig up. The two people in the first lodge had a sacred bundle, and they had many children, as well as the children who had married. These other two people who had married now also had many children. These people all moved west. One village was always made behind, while the two other villages were made in front of the other one. On their journey they stopped at one place. They began to play with the gambling sticks[2] on the south side of the village. Among the people was one who did not seem to care for anything. One day, as they were playing with the sticks, this man came and sat down close by where the people were playing. When it became too dark to play with the sticks the people took the

[1] Told by Thief, or Jackson-Crusoe, now one of the oldest members of the Kitkehahki tribe, and formerly of the recognized rank of warrior. This story is of special interest on account of its reference to Nemaha, Nebraska, as the original home of the ancestors of the Kitkehahki. The story of the four gods of the west is said to be the especial property of the altar originally in possession of the Kawarahkis, from which band, as noted in the introduction, the Kitkehahki, Pitahauirat, and Chaui are supposed to be descended.

[2] This refers to the ring and javelin game of the Pawnee, in which the ring is of small size and the javelin bears two cross bars and symbolizes the buffalo.

sticks home, but the man remained at the playground. Just as he was about to get up, he heard a grunting sound like that of a woman. He looked and he saw in the dusk a woman coming to the gambling grounds. She passed through the grounds and went around and back over the hill again. The man went home and told the people that he had seen a strange woman; that the woman had a covering over her which was all over her hair. Early the next morning this man went to the ground and he looked for the footprints of the woman. Instead of footprints of the woman he found tracks of an animal whose hoofs were split. He then cried toward the village for the people to come and see the tracks. The people came and saw them. The people did not like to play again upon the ground, but some said, "Play on, for we have seen the tracks." So the people began to play with the sticks again.

Late in the afternoon they saw a woman coming from a hill. When she reached the bottom of the hill she ran across the playground and passed the man who was seated nearby. She passed in front of him, and circling around, went over the hills and turned into a buffalo. The man who was seated jumped up and ran after the Buffalo. The man ran after the Buffalo for many, many days. After a while they came to a place where there was nothing but water. The man knew no more. Some time afterwards the Buffalo touched him and said, "Come with me." The man followed the Buffalo, and it led him into a lodge. In the lodge sat four men in the west. When the man entered the lodge these four old men greeted him with, "Nawa." Then the four men said: "We are the four gods in the west. The gods gave us power to create everything. We sent for you, for here in our lodge we have a buffalo. We want the people to live on buffalo, and before we turn these buffalo loose we wish to show you how to prepare your meat. You see this lodge is half filled with parfleches, and inside of the parfleches is dried meat. Each parfleche has a whole buffalo in it. We shall show you how your people must do." Then they opened a parfleche. They took therefrom the heart and tongue of a buffalo. They made a fire. They put the heart and tongue upon the fire. They said: "This you shall do for us when you have killed the buffalo. Take these seeds and give them to your people." The seeds were tied up in a little piece of buffalo skin. The seeds were corn, beans, squash, and native tobacco. They said: "We will now turn the buffalo loose. You must not go far from them, for we wish them to follow you to your village." A robe was placed upon the man and he was told to go. When he went out of the lodge he knew no more until a little blue bird touched him upon the back of his neck and he seemed to wake up. He had the robe on and so he knew that it was all true. He went to the people and told them of his journey, and that the gods in the west had sent him back with the buffalo. The people took their bows and arrows and in a day or so they saw the buffalo. The people were afraid of them, for this was the first time they had seen any buffalo. When they had killed some of them and tasted of the meat they thought it was very good. They offered the heart and tongue to the four gods in the west, as they had been told to do.

This is why the three bands, Pitahauirat, Chaui, and Kitkehahki, instead of making any offering to Tirawa, make their first offering to the four deities who stand in the west.

3. THE SMALL-ANTS BUNDLE AND THE BUFFALO.[1]

My grandfather told me that our people were put upon the earth a long time ago, when there were no seeds to plant or buffalo to hunt. They wandered from place to place and fed upon roots, berries, and pond lilies. After they had wandered for many years they reached the north country and there they found small game, which they killed and ate. While they were living in that distant and strange country, a young man told his father to speak to the chief of the people and tell them that they must go even farther north. The father listened to the words of the young man, for he knew that he was wise, and he knew that he spent many nights upon the top of a hill near the village in prayer. The father said, "My son, who told you that we must go farther north?" The boy answered his father and said: "Mother-Moon has told me to tell the people to continue their journey toward the north. She also told me that there were certain things that we must receive from Mother-Corn." The father then went and told the chief what the boy said. The chief was glad, and he told the people to continue their journey; that some young man had received word from above that the people should keep on their journey toward the north. The people were glad to hear this; but as they traveled on, roots and the things that they lived on became very scarce. The people began to complain. They called the chief names, and they wanted to know who the young man was who had told them to continue their journey.

One time the young man went ahead and there waited for the people. As they passed by him he said that he was the one who had told the chief

[1] Told by Red-Sun, a Chaui medicine-man who died in 1903 while on a visit to the Cheyenne. He was one of Captain Pratt's scouts. The tale has its origin from the altar known as the Small-Ant Altar, and was related during the intermission in the ceremony, if its telling was requested. The story teaches many things, and especially the origin of seeds and buffalo, which were obtained from Moon-Woman, who lived in a cave in the side of a hill, and it especially points out the folly of being careless in regard to food.

to continue the journey; that there was a certain place where they were
to go, and there they must make their village and stay. This place was
somewhere near what is now called Nemaha, Nebraska. They came to
a place where there were many ponds and the entire country was swampy,
so that the people did not have to go very far to find lilies, stems of reeds,
and other things to eat. Here they stopped and began to make grass-
lodges. Near these grass-lodges was a high hill. At the foot of the high
hill a spring gushed forth, and the water from the spring made the lands
swampy. The children played and swam in the ponds.

The people noticed that every night the young man went up on the
high hill that was near the village, and there he stood crying, sometimes
for several days and nights at a time. After a while he stopped going
out in the night, but every day he went up on the high hill and in the
evening he came down to the village. After a time the young man heard
the people complaining for want of food, for they had dug up nearly all
the roots and lilies there were in the ponds. The children cried for something to eat, and the young man felt sad. One day while he was upon
the hill crying another man came to him and asked him what he was crying about. The young man said that he was crying because the people
were poor and were hungry. The man said: "I have many children
and they cry for something to eat. We have eaten nearly all our pack
dogs." The two cried together and in the evening they went to the
village, and as the young man went into the pond to swim he heard some
one call him by name. He looked and he saw in the pond the Moon.
He swam to the place where he saw the Moon in the water, and when he
came close to the place he saw an old woman who looked at him. She
said: "I heard you crying. You are sorry for your people. It was I
who told you to command the people to come to this place. I promised
to give them certain things. Go to the high hill again to-night and cry.
Leave the other man alone." The old woman disappeared; then the
young man, instead of going to the village, went upon the high hill.
There he stood crying all night.

In the morning he came down, went to the spring to drink, and as he
knelt down to drink he looked up into the cave from which came the
stream of water, and he saw the old woman sitting there. She spoke
to the young man and said, "Go upon the hill again, and before sunset
come down and drink again of this spring." The young man went upon
the high hill and stood crying, and while he was there the other man came
and stood by him and cried. The young man stopped crying and went
to the man and said: "My brother, go down to the village to your people
and stay with them. Leave me alone upon this high hill. Encourage

the children and tell them that before very long they shall have something to eat." The man went down into the village and the young boy
was left upon the hill.

Before sunset he went down the hill, and as he knelt down to drink
from the spring he looked into the cave, and there sat a young girl. He
bowed his head to the water and drank. When he looked up there sat
an older woman. He drank again and when he looked up there sat a
middle-aged woman. He drank again and when he looked up there sat
the old woman. He drank again and when he looked up the old woman
had disappeared. Then he sat down at the mouth of the cave and waited.
After a while he heard a voice from the cave calling him. The young
man crawled up into the cave, and after he had crawled for some distance,
some one called to him and said, "Stand up and look." The young man
stood up and looked and he saw another country. The old woman took
him to her earth-lodge and said, "My son, stand at the entrance and look
west." The boy looked to the west and there he saw a young girl. She
told the young man to go farther into the lodge and look to the southwest. He did so, and there stood an older woman. She told him to go
farther into the lodge and look in the southwest. There in the southwest stood a middle-aged woman. She then told him to go farther into
the lodge and look toward the east. The boy looked and he saw the
old woman again. She disappeared. After a while some one spoke to
him where he stood at the west of the lodge. He looked around and there
the young girl stood and said, "Now do you know me?" The young
man said, "No." The young girl said, "I am the new Moon. The old
woman that you saw is a few days older than I am. The other woman
you saw is older by many days. Then you saw the old woman in the
east. She is the Moon become old. She disappears and I come again
as a girl. Let us now go out and I will speak to you outside." When
they were outside they sat down, and when the young man saw the girl
it was not the girl but the old woman who said: "The gods in the heavens are not yet ready to send the buffalo to your people, but the buffalo
are ready for the people, and the buffalo have given me these sticks
(buffalo game) with the ring. These you shall take into the village for
the young men to play with. This basket of plum seeds you shall also
take and give to the women to play with. I know that the people are
very hungry. Every morning the men must take these sticks and this
ring and play with them outside of the village. The men will play with
the sticks so that they will not think about being hungry. The women
will play the basket and seeds game so that they will not think about
eating. Now go back to your village, but return to us again." The

young man went into the village in the night and took with him the sticks and the ring, the basket and the seeds. In the morning the young man told his father to invite the chief and the leading men. The chief and the leading men came into their lodge. The boy said: "Chiefs and head men, take these sticks outside the village and call all the men and let them play with these sticks. Take also this basket and these plum seeds and give them to the women, so that they can play with them and not think about eating." The chief selected several men to take the sticks out and show the men how to play with them. The chief also selected two men to take the basket and plum seeds and to teach the women how to play with them. The men liked this game. There were so many men playing that other sticks were made for boys to play with. There were also so many women playing the basket game that some of the women made other baskets and seeds for their daughters, so that the girls could play the game. The young man was satisfied with the way the games were accepted.

He returned to the cave and the old woman was there to meet him. She said: "I want you to look through this land. There are many earth-lodges in this country." The young man looked, and he saw what appeared to him to be many ant-hills. He saw people coming out and going in again. The old woman said, "My son, you will have villages like these that you have seen; there will be many people." The old woman then took the boy into her own lodge and they stood on the west side, and the old woman said: "Now look. I want you to examine closely the way this lodge is built, for your people must build lodges like this. Where we stand the altar shall be. When you have killed the buffalo that I have promised you, you must place the skull at the altar." Then they went to the entrance on the north side, and she told the young man to sit down. She then went to the north of the lodge and picked up a wooden bowl filled with grains of corn. She told the young man to take the bowl full of corn with him and some night to give a few kernels to each individual in the village, so that all might eat of it. She went to the north side of the lodge and brought a small bowl of dried meat cut up. "This bowl of meat," she said, "you must put under your robe, and when the people come to get the corn you must give each a piece of this meat. Tell them to chew it, and not to swallow it for some time." The old woman then told the young man to go to the village and to feed the people. The young man went down, and went into his lodge. He set down the bowls of corn and meat and awoke his mother and told her to make a fire. When the fire was made the young man told his mother to tell all the people in the lodge to stay around by the fire. Then the young man took the bowls and went around, giving each a few grains of corn and a piece of meat. When the people in the lodge were satisfied the young man told his father to send for the chief. The chief came into the lodge and sat down by the young man. The young man reached and said, "I have brought this for you to eat." He gave him some corn. He then reached under his robe, took out a piece of meat and gave it to the chief, and told him to chew it for some time before swallowing it. The young man then told the chief to have the crier go through the village and tell the people to come to the young man's lodge. The people began to come in, and the boy gave them corn and meat. The men, women, and children all came and ate. There was still some corn and meat left. The young man sent for the man who had cried with him and told him to stay in his lodge, and for four nights to give corn and meat out to the people. Then he went back to the cave.

When he went into the cave the old woman was there and she said: "My son, the gods have given you the buffalo. The buffalo are to run out of this cave, and the first buffalo that shall go out shall be killed by your people. Its hide must be tanned, the head must be cut off, and the skull set up on this high hill. When the meat and everything has been cut off from the skull, it must be taken into the village and put in the lodge." The old woman gave the young man four bundles of corn of different colors, braided together. The old woman said, "These are the seeds for the people." She gave him a bunch of buffalo hair, and said, "This is the part of the buffalo that the gods have given your people." Among the buffalo hair was a downy feather with dark blue marks down the center. The old woman said: "When you want the buffalo to come out of the cave get out the feather and place it upon a pole, set it on the north side of the village. The first buffalo that shall go out shall be a wonderful buffalo and the people must kill it and place the skull upon the hill and take the hide and tan it. It shall be known as the holy buffalo." The old woman went into the lodge and when she came out she had a sacred bundle upon her back which she took off and placed upon the young man's back, and said: "This is your sacred bundle. You shall call it the Small-Ants bundle."

The young man took the things and went down to the village. He hung the sacred bundle inside of the lodge at the west side, while the corn he hung at the north side of the entrance. The buffalo hair he hung on top of the sacred bundle. In the meantime the people began to grumble and wanted the chief to tell the crier to move away from this place. The young man walked out through the village and saw that the women and girls were enjoying the game of basket and seeds (the dice game), and

that the men and boys were enjoying the game of ring and sticks.   The
young man went back to his lodge, sat down west of the fireplace, and told
his mother to get the bundle that was on top of the sacred bundle and
place it in front of him.   The young man then told his father in a whisper
to tell the people in this lodge to leave it.   The people all left the lodge.
Then the young man told his father to go and invite the chief.   The chief
came into the lodge and sat by the boy.   The boy said: "Chief, through
my advice our people came to this place.   Mother-Moon spoke to me in
my dreams, telling me that our people should come to this place.   She
promised me in my dreams that she would give certain things to the people.   Some of the things our people are enjoying, and yet some of them
are complaining.   Now it is time that we kill buffalo.   This is what Mother-
Moon has given us."   He opened the bunch of hair and said: "The gods
have given us many buffalo.   This day our people shall kill them.   The
skin of the first buffalo that they kill must be taken off.   The head must
be placed upon a high hill, and the meat brought to this lodge."   The
chief then stood up, passed his hands over the boy, and said: "My son,
you cried upon these hills for many days and nights.   The people and
myself made fun of you, but now I understand why you did this.   Let
the first buffalo come and I will select men to kill them.   All that you
have said shall be done."   The chief sat down, then sent for his crier.

The crier came and the chief told him to tell the people in the village
to put away their sticks and the basket game and to keep still.   When the
crier came, he said, "Chief, I have told the people what you told me to tell
them."   The chief then told the crier to go and tell four men to come to
the lodge where he was.   The young man then came into the lodge.   The
chief told the young man to instruct the men as to what they should do,
for they were ready to go with him to kill the buffalo.   The young man
sent one of the four men into the timber for a long willow.   The willow
was brought and peeled and at one end the young man tied the feather.
The bunch of buffalo hair was placed upon the bundle again, and the
young man led the four men out of the lodge and they went to their lodges
to get their bows and arrows.   The whole village was quiet, for everybody was now watching the young man.   The four men came with their
bows and arrows and the young man started toward the cave.   Half-way
between the cave and the village he stopped and stuck the stick, that had
the feather on, into the ground.   He told the men to look toward the hill.

After a while they saw a buffalo coming.   He told them to circle round
the buffalo and kill it.   The men circled around and crawled up to the
buffalo and shot it with their bows and arrows.   After a while the buffalo
fell and died.   Then the men skinned it and took the head off and placed

it on a high hill. The young man told the four men to put the meat upon their backs and follow him, one of them carrying the hide. They went into the boy's lodge and the meat was placed southeast of the entrance. The young man told his father to invite some of the older men. The father went and brought in some old men and when they came the young man said, "People, we must first make an offering to Mother-Corn, for she gave us the buffalo." Then the young man took the heart and tongue and said, "Boil these things." The men put the tongue and heart in a vessel and after it had boiled for some time he took it out. The young man then sent the crier through the village to tell all the men to be ready to try to get a piece of this heart and tongue and a little piece of fat to grease their families with. The young man went out of the lodge with the heart and tongue, the errand man following him with native tobacco in his hand. The young man went to the west of the village, and standing there he lifted the heart and tongue up toward the sky and gradually lowered them to the ground. He placed the heart and tongue on the ground, then the errand man handed him the tobacco. He lifted the tobacco toward the sky, lowered it and placed it upon the heart and tongue. Then as he turned to go back to the lodge he and the men ran to the place, and they piled one on top of another in their efforts to get a piece of the heart and tongue. Whenever a man got a piece of fat or heart or tongue he ran to his lodge, and after rubbing some of the grease upon himself he gave it to his people and told them to put the grease upon themselves, and when through with it to put it in the fire.

When the young man entered his lodge he sat down and spoke: "Chief, men, and old men, what I have done is not complete. Mother-Moon will tell us more of what to do. We must do as she says every time we kill the buffalo." Then the young man selected several men to take the meat and boil it. After they had taken the meat, the young man told the chief to tell the crier to go through the village and tell all the men to get their bows and arrows and follow the young man with the feather-stick. When the young man stuck the stick into the ground at the same place where he had it before, the buffalo rushed out of the cave and went toward the people. The men began to kill the buffalo. Some of the buffalo ran south, some west, some east, and some north. The men killed many buffalo and brought the meat to the village.

The people were satisfied. They began to cut timber to make their lodges, for the young man had instructed them to build earth-lodges. Every four days the young man went out, stuck his feathered stick into the ground, and again the buffalo rushed out of the cave. The fourth time the young man said: "This is all. The buffalo are out of the cave and there will be many upon the ground." The young man went back into the cave and the woman said: "I have given you all the things that I promised you. Now you must go and give the seeds to the people, and let them put them in the ground. I shall return to the place where I came from and shall stay there forever. When I want to speak to you I will come to your bedside, and talk to you in your dreams. Then you must tell the people what I tell you."

The young man returned to the village and told the people that it was now time that they should have seeds; that they must put them into the ground and take care of them until the corn-stalks were dry and the corn ready to be gathered. The people did as the boy told them and they had plenty of corn and plenty of meat. The young man went to the cave once more, and he found that the spring was dry and that the cave had closed in and there was no opening. When the people found this out they became dissatisfied and divided into bands, and they went in different directions.

4. THE FOUR GODS OF THE NORTH.[1]

After Tirawa created the world he created a man and put him upon the earth facing the north. Tirawa told this man to put his thumbs together and point towards the north. The man obeyed and his thumb-nails received the imprint of the faces of the two gods in the north. After the man's thumb-nails had grown out and the faces had disappeared, he was told by Tirawa again to point his two thumbs toward the north, and the imprint of the faces of the other two gods were placed upon them.[2] These four gods gave the man power to create a mate for himself. The gods in the north sent Kingfisher to the earth, who divided the earth so

[1] Told by High-Eagle, a Kitkehahki medicine-man, about sixty years old. This tale explains the origin of the ceremony of the four gods of the north. These are the gods who send buffalo to the people, and who send rain that the crops may grow. The chief object in relating the story is that the children who may be present, sitting about the entrance to the lodge, may always bear in mind that these four gods exist in the north and that there is especially one of them, known as Ready-to-Give, who is the special patron of the hunters. It is said that often the Pawnee when on the hunt, failing to find game, raise their hands to the north and say: "Nawa, Kawahar, you are the leader of all the gods of the north. Send me game that I may kill it for my people."

[2] In the ceremony referred to in this tale, four sticks are erected on the north side of the lodge, each one bearing a clam shell. Collectively they represent the four gods of the north referred to in this tale, which in turn represent the imprints of the faces placed on the thumb-nails as referred to in the text. In this connection it may be noted that the shell disk worn by the Kitkehahki on their heads is said to have had its origin from these four gods, as is the case among the Skidi. These sticks are covered with raven feathers, for the raven, like the coyote, is always successful in finding game. Ready-to-Give is supposed to be similarly endowed.

that part of it became water and part of it became land. When Kingfisher had done this it dropped by the man and he reached out his hand
and touched the bird and it turned into a woman.[1]

The man held a ceremony in honor of the four gods in the north and
he taught his offspring to conduct the ceremony. There were eight
priests. The bundle was opened and a bowl of water was placed in front
of the altar. This altar was in the west and the bundle rested there. In
the north of the lodge was another altar. This altar was for the gods.
The chief priest dressed himself to represent the god who carried out the
wishes of Tirawa. The priest first put on the top of his head a bunch of
downy feathers, about twenty-six in number, with turkey feathers around
it.[2] He had a string of blue beads in his right ear, with a clam shell at the
end of the string. From the shell hung a scalp. This priest also represented the first man. Now the priest took four sticks from the bundle
and clothed them with crow feathers. At the top were placed four shells.
The sticks were then set up in the north altar. Each of the north gods
had a face which was a shell. These faces were faces of Tirawa. This
is the reason why we once offered shells to the gods to remind them of
their power. The chief priest then put the holy ointment of red over his
body. Then he took from the bundle the holy moccasins. The moccasins were of buffalo hide with the hair outside. He also took from the
bundle a buffalo beard. This he tied about his waist to show people how
the first man was covered. The red ointment he passed to the other
seven priests. Then they invited the men to enter the lodge. The
women were not allowed to witness this ceremony.

When all the men had entered the lodge, the chief priest arose with a
kingfisher in his right hand. He stood in front of the wooden bowl. The
other priests arose with the gourd rattles in their right hands. Then all
the others arose and the seven priests began to sing. As the priests sang,
the high priest shook the ground, then he made a motion as if to turn the
bird loose, and lifted it toward the bowl of water several times and finally
he dipped it into the water. There was silence throughout the lodge. The
chief priest spoke and said, "This is the way Tirawa made the land to
appear out of the waters." They all sat down and the priest arose with
the pipe, lighted it, and gave a whiff of smoke to each of the four gods

[1] The conception of the kingfisher dividing the earth is quite different from the
Skidi belief in this regard. This idea, as well as that of the kingfisher becoming
a woman, is paralleled in the tales of the Arikara.

[2] The downy feathers in this connection are symbolic of eggs of the turkey, the
turkey feathers representing the turkey itself. The turkey is conceived of as
the most prolific of fowl, and the symbol has reference to the fact that during the
ceremony the priest receives the power which enables him to plan out the various
future activities of the camp, such as where and when they shall go on the hunt, etc.

in the north. Then he went west of the fireplace and gave one whiff towards the sky to Tirawa, then one whiff to Mother-Earth. He then went to the altar, gave one whiff to the bird, and several whiffs to the contents of the bundle. He then took his seat among the priests and gave his pipe to one of them. The pipe was passed from one priest to another, and after they had smoked, the ashes were dumped out in front of the altar and the pipe was returned to the high priest. After the offering of smoke, all the men who did not care to remain left the lodge. The dried meat was cut up and boiled. The first pile of meat taken from the kettle was placed upon a dried buffalo hide. Fat was taken from this piece of meat and offered to each god in the north, to Tirawa, to Mother-Earth, to the King-fisher, to the Bundle, and to Mother-Corn. The fat was then thrown into the fire so that the smoke would go to the heavens. The priest asked for the sticks or gods in the north and they were brought to him. He took the shells and the crow feathers off from them, and laid the sticks by the bundle. The priest called the errand man and asked him if he had the grass ready. The errand man said that he had. He brought the grass and laid it before the priest. The priest took up the sticks and gave them to the priests sitting nearest him, and he told them to prepare them. These sticks were plum sticks, and they represented the four gods who assisted Tirawa to create people. The priests took the plum sticks and covered them with grass. When they had finished, the priest selected four other priests to take sticks to the creek. The priests arose, received the sticks, and went to the creek and threw them into the water. The plum sticks were covered with grass, so that the gods would not see the sticks that represented them, and would not become angry. When the priests returned to the lodge there was a universal exclamation of satisfaction given throughout the lodge. The things used in the ceremony were waved through smoke of sweet grass, then placed in the bundle, and the bundle was tied up again and hung up at the west inside of the lodge. All of the meat was cooked and divided among the priests, and the high priest said: "The gods have received our offering. They will send good gifts to our people, so that they will not be poor. Now we rise and go to our homes."

5. LONG-TONGUE, THE ROLLING HEAD.[1]

Four girls went from a village in the winter time to gather firewood. After they had gathered the wood and tied it up with pack strings, they cut four long sticks and carried them down to the ice. They threw the sticks upon the ice to see which stick would slide farthest over the ice. While they were playing they smelt some root which had a very good odor. They kept playing with the sticks and the smell of the root seemed to come nearer to them. One of the girls said, "Let us go in the direction from which this odor comes, and try to find what makes it." The girls all agreed and they went toward the north, where the odor came from. After they had gone a little way one of the girls stopped and said, "I do not care to go any farther." The remaining three went on. After a while one of the girls stopped and said, "I am going back, I am not going." She went back, but the other two continued on their way. Soon one of the other girls stopped and said: "What is the use of going any farther? The sun is about to go down and we do not know where the smell comes from." The other girl wanted her to go on, but she would not, saying, "I am going home." The other girl said, "I am going on and find out where this odor comes from." One of the girls went home and so only one was left to find out where the smell came from.

She kept on her way until she saw at a distance a hillside covered with cedar trees. She went to the place and there she found a lodge which was built of rock. She stood near the rock-lodge and after a while a stone moved and a fine-looking young man came out from the lodge. He saw the girl and said: "You have been standing here some time. Come into my lodge." She said, "I am following a sweet odor, and if it is in your house I will come in." Then the boy said: "It is here that the odor comes from. Come right into the lodge."

The girl went in with the boy, and as soon as she stepped into the

[1] Told by Little-Chief, the present chief of the Chaui and great nephew of Pite-lesaru, the head chief of the Pawnee. He is the keeper of a sacred bundle and of the "buffalo pipe," which when exposed causes windstorms. This interesting version of the magic flight accounts for the origin among the Chaui of many objects, the possession of which was made possible through the theft from the stone house of the Rolling-Head of a sacred bundle, through the raven's assistance. This head was conceived of as an individual, round in shape, capable of traveling great distances with great rapidity, and as making while traveling a great noise. This being was finally overcome by the hawk, who was conceived of as striking it with a club, which is symbolic of the wing of the hawk by which it kills its prey, and severing the two parts by means of a flint axe, one part of the head becoming the sun and the other the moon. The daughter of the Evening-Star, who is instrumental in the accomplishment of the task just noted, later has connection with the red bird, which represents the winter storm, and she and her family become the Pleiades, which ultimately is to be increased to ten stars by the addition of herself, sister, and brother.

lodge the stone moved up and closed the opening. The girl looked around and she saw that there was no opening anywhere except at the top where the smoke escaped, and it was a very small hole. The young man went over to where there were some buffalo robes spread upon the ground and sat down. When the girl looked where the young man lay upon the buffalo robes, she saw there an ugly old man instead of the young man. The girl then began to cry. The old man said: "It will not do you any good to cry. You are here and I am going to kill you in a few days, but while you are living make yourself at home and try to be content, for you have but a short time to live." The girl looked around the lodge and she saw a sacred bundle, with five big gourd rattles upon it, hanging upon the side of the wall. The old man gave her a buffalo robe and she placed it upon the ground and then lay down.

The next morning he told her to cook some meat; that he was going out over the country that day. When the old man was ready to go out from the lodge he turned into a handsome young man again. He stood at the entrance and he spoke to the stone door and it moved. Then he stepped outside and was gone. The girl began to cry, and as she cried she heard some one speak to her, saying: "Woman, this being, whose name is Long-Tongue, is a round, rattling, rolling skull that kills people and other animals, but if you do as I tell you, you shall be saved. The odor which you smelt came from the roots in the sacred bundle which you see here. To-morrow when the being is in this lodge you ask him to let you go out for a few minutes. He will let the stone move. When you come out I will make the hackberry trees lower their limbs so that you can pick a handful of the berries. These you will place under your belt, and then you return to the lodge. I will come again and help you." When she looked up at the hole she saw a Raven sitting at the top of the opening. The Raven flew away and in the night Long-Tongue came back. As he stepped into the lodge he turned into the old man again. The next day when the sun was high she asked him to let her go out for a few moments. The old man spoke, the stone moved, and the girl was outside. She quickly picked a handful of the hackberries, then she returned to the lodge and sat down. About noon Long-Tongue said: "Make yourself at home. I am going away into the country, but will be back in the afternoon." At noon Long-Tongue went out of the lodge and disappeared.

After a while the Raven came and sat at the opening of the lodge. He said: "Woman, when Long-Tongue comes back he is going to ask you to take lice off of his head, and you must do as he tells you. When you have placed his head upon your lap you will find that his head is covered with ticks instead of lice.   He will say that when you take the lice from his head you must bite them with your teeth.   As you take the ticks off throw them away and at the same time bite a hackberry, so that it will make a noise.   When you have taken off all the ticks, Long-Tongue will lose his life just for a short time.   You must go to the entrance and say, 'Grandfather, move,' and the entrance stone will move.   Gather the ticks and throw them outside.   Then come in again and say 'Grand-father, close up the lodge.'   The stone will move into place.   Do as I say, for I have something to do with the sacred bundle upon the wall, for my skin is in the sacred bundle."   The next day Long-Tongue came back. As soon as he came into the lodge he said, "Woman, take some lice from my head and eat them."   The girl took Long-Tongue's head upon her lap and began to take the ticks from his head.   She would take a hack-berry in her hand, take off a tick, throw it to one side, then put a hack-berry into her mouth and crack it.   She kept taking off the ticks and throwing them away and cracking the hackberries.   When she had all the ticks off his head Long-Tongue fell over and died.   The girl went to where the ticks were scattered, gathered them up, and carried them to the entrance and said, "Grandfather, move."   The stone moved and she went out and threw the ticks away.   She went back into the lodge and said, "Grandfather, close up the lodge."   The stone moved and closed the lodge.   After a while Long-Tongue was alive again.   Early the next morning Long-Tongue said: "Woman, I am going far into the country. I shall be away for several days.   When I return I shall kill you."

The day before when the Raven was talking to the girl he told her that when Long-Tongue should speak of going a long distance for her to tell Long-Tongue to go first and kill a buffalo and bring all of it to the lodge so that she might make tallow from the bones.   The girl told Long-Tongue what the Raven had told her to say, and Long-Tongue said it was well and that he would do so.   She told Long-Tongue that she wanted to have something to do; that when she had nothing to do she became lonesome.   Long-Tongue went out and was gone but a short time when he returned to the lodge, bringing with him a whole buffalo. The girl began to skin the buffalo and to take off the meat piece by piece. Long-Tongue then said: "Woman, I am going now.   You will be busy with the meat.   Do not try to run away while I am gone, for I shall follow you no matter where you go, or how you go."   Long-Tongue went out and was gone.   The girl then made a big fire and began to make tallow.   While she was doing this the Raven came and said: "Here is now the chance for you to get away from here.   Make the tallow and I will tell you what to do."   The girl kept on making the tallow.   The

Raven went and took the sacred bundle down and untied it. He took from the sacred bundle the stones which the people used for smoothing their arrows. He also took a piece of flint out of the bundle and some white powder made from white clay, the arrow, and the flint knife. Then he told the girl to make three round tallow balls. The girl dug a hole in the ground and whenever she had tallow she threw it into the hole until it became full. Then the Raven told the girl to cover the ground in the center of the lodge with some tallow, and to put some on the sides of the wall, and some on the bundle and some on the stem grass that was lying about on the ground. After everything was covered with tallow inside of the lodge, then the Raven said: "Woman, it is time that we are going. Long-Tongue knows that you are preparing to run away. He will be coming, but we will try and get away from this place as fast as we can. You have a four days' journey to go to a certain place where the people will help you and save you. There is not an animal upon the earth that can overcome Long-Tongue; but there is one place where the people can destroy Long-Tongue. You must go to them." Then the Raven sat down by the fireplace and said, "Now put your arms over my shoulders, then wrap up the things that I have taken from the bundle and tie them upon your back." After she tied the bundle on her back she went and put her arms around the Raven's neck. Then the Raven began to call. He called four times. Then he flew out of the small hole with the girl on his back, and he flew a long distance.

At last the Raven became tired and he placed the girl upon the ground and said, "I will fly overhead and I will guide you to the place where you are going." The Raven told the girl to keep running to the east; that there was a place in the east which looked blue in color and that was where she was to go. The Raven told the girl to run as fast as she could and that she must not sleep for four days, because Long-Tongue knew that she was gone and that he was returning to his lodge. The girl kept running.

After a while Long-Tongue ran to the lodge and when he reached the lodge he spoke and said, "Woman, open up the lodge." He received no answer. Long-Tongue knew all the time that the girl was not there, and so he entered the lodge. He looked around and everything about the lodge was covered with tallow. Long-Tongue said: "That is one good thing that woman did. She put tallow everywhere. I like this tallow and I will eat before I think of going for her." He began to lick the ground. When he had licked all the tallow from the ground he then licked the tallow from the sides of the walls. As he ate upwards the opening at the top of his tongue seemed to grow. When he reached the top his tongue went out and licked the tallow from the walls. He licked all the tallow off of the walls and off of the ground and off of the stem grass.

After he had licked all the tallow off of everything he thought of the girl whom he was to run for. He started. He went out of the lodge and soon he found her tracks. He followed her and after a while he came in sight of her. Then he began to call her and said: "Woman, stop, return to the lodge with me, for there is no use for you to run. I am to kill you. I do not care if you run over this wide earth, I shall follow you until I kill you and then you will be no more. If you try to fly up into the air I shall follow you and kill you." The girl kept on and when Long-Tongue was close to her the girl remembered what the Raven had told her. She took the smooth stones from the bundle and dropped them upon the ground. As soon as she dropped the stones upon the ground the ground was covered with smooth stones. Long-Tongue said: "What a fine lot of stones there are here. I will gather them together. Then when I have caught the girl we shall come by here and I will make that girl carry these stones upon her back. I have no stones and so, while I have a chance, I will gather these together." Long-Tongue placed the stones in piles.

After he had gathered all the stones, he thought of the girl whom he was running after. He started to run again. The girl had gained on Long-Tongue, but again he was about to catch her. She turned around as Long-Tongue was about to put his hands upon her and took one of the balls of tallow and hit Long-Tongue upon the top of the head, so that the tallow spattered all over the ground. Some of the tallow got on the grass and weeds and when Long-Tongue smelled the tallow he said: "I am hungry. I will stop and eat of this tallow. I will kill the girl later." Long-Tongue stopped and began to lick the weeds and grass and when he had cleaned it all up he thought of the girl again. He ran on.

The girl kept running, but Long-Tongue soon gained upon her and was very near her again when she dropped the flint arrow-points. As soon as Long-Tongue came to the arrow-points he stopped and said: "I will stop and gather these things. I will put them upon my arrows. That girl shall carry them on her back when we come back." The girl ran as fast as she could, while the Raven flew overhead. As soon as Long-Tongue had gathered all the flint points he remembered again about the girl. It was easy for the girl to tell when Long-Tongue had started, for when Long-Tongue started there was a rumbling sound upon the earth so that people could hear it for many miles around. The girl heard this and so did the Raven. The Raven said: "Run as fast as you can, for he is coming." When Long-Tongue had almost overtaken her the girl took the arrow and stuck it into the ground and dogwood timber formed along the ravines. When Long-Tongue came to the timber he saw that the dogwood was straight and had no knots. He stopped and said, "I shall cut this dogwood and place it in piles so that the girl can carry them, for I want arrows." He stopped and cut and cut and thus gave the girl a good chance to get some distance away from him. When the dogwood was all cut and placed in piles, Long-Tongue thought about the girl and he began to run again. He gained upon the girl, and when he was about to lay his hands upon her, the girl dropped some sinew. She threw the sinew upon the ground and there was scattered over the ground many dead buffalo. Long-Tongue said: "This is good. I have my arrow-points, my dogwood for my arrows, and now I must have sinew with which to fasten these things." Long-Tongue began to take the sinew from the buffalo. When he had taken all the sinew from the buffalo he placed them in a big pile and said, "I will make that girl carry those things to my home." Then he remembered that he was after the girl, and he ran again.

Every time that he ran he turned into a rattling, rolling skull, so that the skull rolled upon the ground and made its teeth clatter and made a great noise upon the earth. The girl went on. Long-Tongue followed her again. He saw her and ran fast. Just as Long-Tongue was about to overtake the girl she dropped a piece of a feather. When Long-Tongue got to the place where the feather was he found many dead turkeys all around. He stopped and said, "I will take the feathers off of those turkeys and pile the feathers here and I shall make the woman pack them and I will have feathers for all my arrows." After he did this he thought of the girl and he ran after her again. This time the girl dropped upon the ground the flint knife, which made a gulch in the earth, so that when Long-Tongue fell into it he could not climb up on the other side, but ran back and forth.

The Raven flew over the girl and said, "You are near the place now." The girl looked up and she saw what seemed to her to be a mound. She went around the mound and she saw a man sitting outside of the lodge making a bow. The girl went to this man and said: "I come to you. Save me. There is a mysterious being coming who has been following me for several days. I am tired and weak." The man said, "Walk into the lodge." The girl went into the lodge and she saw another sacred bundle hanging up in the lodge. She went to where the bundle was hanging and sat down under the bundle. Long-Tongue finally climbed out of the gulch and began to chase the girl again. When he came to the lodge he saw the man sitting outside. Long-Tongue began to speak aloud and said: "Where is the girl that came by here? She is mine. I must kill her." The man paid no attention to Long-Tongue, but Long-Tongue kept on talking. All at once the man took hold of his stick, raised it up and said, "And why do you talk so loud around my place?" The man struck Long-Tongue on the top of the head, and the skull split in two. As soon as he removed the stick, however, the two pieces of the skull moved together again. The man then took a flint axe and hit one piece of the skull and knocked it to the west, and it flew up into the sky and became the moon. The man then struck the other piece and it flew up in the sky to the east and it became the sun. (That is why we have human pictures upon the sun and upon the moon.) The man said: "My girl, come out. Long-Tongue is gone. He will bother you no more. Make your home with us. I have some sons who are out on the war-path. Only the youngest of the brothers is here with me." The woman made her home with the man and the boy. A few days afterwards seven brothers came and they saw the girl. The father told them what had happened, then the brothers agreed that the girl should stay with them. The youngest brother was chosen to determine what relationship the girl should hold to them. He said, "This woman shall be our sister." All the brothers agreed and the woman remained with them as their sister. One day the men went into the lodge and opened the bundle. The woman saw an ear of corn in the bundle. She said: "Father, let me have this ear of corn. Let me put it into the ground, that I may gather more corn." The man would not consent. He said, "This is from Mother-Evening-Star and we can not let it go." But the girl said: "My mother is Evening-Star. I understand how to put this ear into the ground so that it will grow and we may have more corn." Finally the man gave his consent and she planted the corn. In the fall they had plenty. Again in the spring she planted more and the men knew that she would gather much corn. In the fall the woman showed signs of being pregnant. The old man was angry, but when the child was born a man visited these people who said, "I am the father of the child." He was North-Star. After the people found out that this woman had been with North-Star, they asked how it happened. The man said: "I was sitting upon the limb as a Red Bird singing. The woman came and while I was singing I lay with her." The woman then remembered seeing a red bird upon a limb some time before. Then the man said: "My daughter, we shall all go away now. You will go north with the child and your husband will go to the north and stand there forever. We shall go to the east and shall travel west. There the seven brothers will be, and in time I

shall join them.   Then your sister and brother will join us, so that there
will be ten stars instead of seven stars."   (These people in the heavens
are what is known as the Pleiades.)   "When the world comes to an
end then I shall join my sons.   My daughter will also join us, but while
we live upon this earth we shall be known as great warriors.   Although
we are birds, we are warriors.   We are the Hawks."

6. HOW EVENING-STAR'S DAUGHTER WAS OVERCOME.[1]

A long time ago the people had their village near a big stream of water
somewhere in the east.   The gods in the heavens came down upon the
earth in the west and each god gathered his animals, and then they began
to build an earth-lodge upon the earth.   Evening-Star sent her daughter
to rule over the lodge.   She also sent her four gods in the west and these
gods were to keep guard over the girl, for she brought a rains-wrapped-
up bundle.   Evening-Star, being the spouse of Morning-Star, kept the
things of Morning-Star in the bundle.   Among the things belonging to
Morning-Star was the war club.   The different stars which stand in the
heavens as gods were sent down to be stationed in certain places in the
lodge according to their stations in the heavens.   The spaces between
them were to be filled by different animals.   Evening-Star wanted
women to be higher than men, and so she sent her daughter to kill off all
young men who came to her, so that all women would do the same and
so overcome men.

When the people of the eastern village saw the new earth-lodge in the
west, they wondered who lived there.   They watched the people in the
west and tried to go to visit them, but the people in the west would not
have anything to do with the people in the east.   Several young men had
gone to the place and had seen the girl, and had tried to marry her, but
before they could get to the mud-lodge they were always killed.

In the east village was a poor boy.   As he grew up he wandered over
the country.   One night while he was sitting upon the hill a strange man
stood before him.   This strange man was painted red all over, and upon
his leggings were hanging scalps and eagle feathers.   His moccasins were
of buffalo hide with the hair inside.   He carried a club on his arm and
spoke to the boy, thus: "My boy, you shall see me again.   Take this

[1]Told by Big-Crow, a Skidi, the keeper of the Big-Black-Meteoric-Star bundle,
whose grandfather, Big-Knife, a Skidi brave, performed several sacrifices of human
maidens to the Morning-Star, and who was stopped by the whites in a similar ceremony in 1832.   This tale, told only during the intermission of a ceremony, teaches
the necessity of the Morning-Star sacrifice by pointing out the advantage which
the young man gained by conquering a certain maiden with the Morning-Star's
assistance.

and carry it with you. Go into yonder village and when you see that girl win her for yourself. I shall always be near you and will protect you." He gave the boy a moccasin and in the moccasin was the symbol of Morning-Star. The boy was told that when he should go to visit the girl he would meet obstacles. At each obstacle he was to throw the moccasin with the symbol of Morning-Star, and the obstacle would disappear.

The boy went home. He sent for an old man and told the old man to lead him to the other village, as he wanted to marry the girl in that other village. The old man led him and when they came to a certain place, the girl came out singing. She hit upon the ground with her war club, and there was a deep canyon in front of the boy and the old man. The old man looked at the boy and said, "What?" The young man stepped forward and dropped the symbol of Morning-Star into the deep canyon and the sides moved together and brought the symbol up, and the canyon was gone. They went on and again the girl came out. She struck upon the ground and there was a wide stream of water. The boy dropped the symbol into the water and the water disappeared. They went on and the girl came out again. When she came out she sang her song, and touched the ground with her war club, and there in front of the boy was formed a thick timber. The boy threw the symbol into it and the timber disappeared. Then they went up to the tipi. The girl had gone in and taken her seat in front of the men. The animals began to come out, but as each animal came the boy struck it with the symbol and so they all disappeared. When the old man and the boy entered the lodge the girl was told that she was to marry the young man. Then the girl said, "He must first go and get the baby-board for me."

The boy went north to a strange country, and began to cry. A strange man came to him, and he was the same man who had appeared to him before. He asked what he was crying about. The boy said, "Father, I am now married, but the girl wants a baby-board." The man said: "My son, you shall see me again. I will get the baby-board for you. I am Morning-Star. The baby-board which I shall get shall be adopted by your people and they shall always be under my protection. The child will grow to be a man or a woman." The man went off. He went to a lodge of animals and told the animals what he wanted. There was a certain lodge where the Beavers were, and these Beavers were making baby-boards, but fires were kept up by the Turtles, so that no one could go near enough to get a baby-board. When the animals heard what the man wanted, they called a council to see who would go and get the baby-board. Coyote stood up and said, "I will go and get the baby-board for you." He went, and when he entered the lodge of the Beavers and reached for the baby-boards which were hanging in a circle, sparks began to fly upon him. The sparks got so thick that he became scared and ran, and the fire seemed to follow him. He ran off to the lodge of the animals and told them. Then the Hawk went to the lodge and as soon as he flew into the lodge the Turtle stirred the fire and the sparks went up against the Hawk, the flames arose, and nearly burned the Hawk and he flew away.

Other animals were sent there, but they could not get it. The Magpie, the errand man of all animals, arose and said, "I will go." The Magpie flew to the lodge and flew down the opening at the top. He took hold of the baby-board and as he flew up the baby-board made noises and then the fire came up, but it was too late, for the Magpie was out. The fire followed the Magpie for some time until the Magpie became tired, then he gave the baby-board to the Diving-Duck. The fire still followed the Diving-Duck. When he came to the stream of water he dived and the fire struck the water and went out. The Duck came up and gave the baby-board to the man, who carried it to the boy. The boy took the baby-board to the tipi and as he entered one of the priests took the board, and put it in the west side of the lodge. The girl then spoke and said: "Now, you must get otter strings with which to tie the baby." The boy went. Another man came, and he helped the boy to get the otter strings. The boy took the otter strings to the lodge and they were placed in front of the girl. Then the girl said, "You must now get a piece of a robe to put upon the board for the baby to lie upon. Go south and bring the robe." As the boy went out he began to cry. After a while Morning-Star came and said: "My son, I have an arrow here. When we have reached the buffalo, we are going to kill one. I will go right up to the buffalo and you get to one side, shoot the buffalo, and kill it." They went toward the buffalo, and the buffalo came and charged. The boy stepped to one side and shot the buffalo in the heart. Then they took the skin off of the back and the boy took it to the lodge. The boy then got a wild-cat hide by the help of the Hawks. Then the girl told the boy to come to her bedside in the night; that he must stay outside until night.

The first night the boy started to enter the tipi he heard a whizzing sound. He knew it was a serpent. He touched it with the moccasin in which was the Morning-Star symbol, and the snake died. Then the girl said, "Stop; you can not come to me to-night. To-morrow night you shall come in." The next night he attempted to go in, but the girl touched the ground with the war club and two bears came and tried to kill the boy in the lodge. The boy waved the Morning-Star symbol at them and they were stunned. He then touched them and they were killed. Then the girl said, "You can not come." The next night the panthers came and the boy killed them also. The next night the wild-cats came and the boy killed them. Then the coyotes came, but they were willing to help the man. Then the next night the girl said, "You must not come." Then the boy went out during the day and cried and cried. He did not go that night, but all night he cried, and by morning as the Morning-Star came up he cried and right before him stood the man who had been helping him. "My boy," he said, "you are about to approach the bed of that girl. You have killed all bad animals. The girl herself is the only one now. Here, take this stone. That girl's vagina is like the mouth of a rattlesnake and has teeth. Take this stone when you are about to lie with her and rub the stone upon the teeth until you have broken them all up. Then she becomes a human being, and you can lie with her."

That night the boy did as the man had told him. After that the girl became his wife. Then in the morning Morning-Star came to the boy and said: "You have married this girl and you shall have two bundles. The girl's bundle shall be one and you shall make another bundle and place the Morning-Star symbol in it, and these two bundles shall be known as the Morning-Star bundles. When you went to get the girl there were two of you who went. You overcame all obstacles by my power. You will now learn the mysteries of heaven, the gods, the songs, and through that your people shall prosper and have good crops all the time. For my pay for helping you out in this way, you shall, from time to time, capture a girl from the enemy and offer her to me and then I will bless your people. All the obstacles that you met shall be represented in the ceremony. You shall represent each step that you took in gaining the girl until at last you shall come to represent the putting up of the baby-board. Then put the captured girl upon the scaffold and kindle a fire under her. All the children who are born from now on must have a baby-board with my picture upon the top, and shall have the covering of the buffalo and the wild-cat, and the otter-skin string shall be tied around the baby-board to hold the baby upon the board."

The boy and his wife went to his village and the woman carried the bundle with her. Then the gods who were Stars returned to their places in the heavens, and the animals which were present in the tipi went back into their dens in the timbers, rivers, and creeks.

7. THE DAUGHTER OF THE EVENING-STAR AND HER SACRED BUNDLE.

(See Abstracts.)

[Told by Woman-Ready-to-Give, a Skidi woman whose grandmother was formerly keeper of the second of the two Morning-Star bundles among the Skidi. This tale is presumably a variant of tale No. 6. It should be noted, however, that there are two Morning-Star bundles among the Skidi, and that the tale just referred to was told by one who represents one of these bundles, whereas the teller of this tale represents the other bundle. This story not only relates to the origin of a sacred bundle, but also relates to the construction of the earth-lodge of the Pawnee. It is especially interesting to note in this connection that, according to both tales, the earliest homes of the Skidi were not earth but grass lodges.]

8. CONTEST BETWEEN THE MORNING-STAR AND THE MOON.[1]

A long time ago the people had their village in a bottom. There was one young man who had his lodge in the hills. The people from the bottom could see him entering and leaving his lodge. Every day the young man left his lodge and went over the hills and in a very short time they would see him coming again with a deer, an antelope, or a buffalo upon his back. He would take the meat into his lodge and then would come out with it and scatter it all around.

One year the crops of the people failed. They became hungry. The people said, "We are to speak to that young man in the lodge and he may help us." But no one would go to his lodge, for the people had often tried to go to it but always found that there were snake dens all around it. In the village was a Spider-Woman who said that she knew his power; that she was going to challenge him, and if he beat her the people could have buffalo. Several of the men in the village went to the chief and told him that he ought to visit the young man and invite him to come and live with his daughter as his wife, so that the people might get something to eat. The chief said he could not go into the lodge of the young man. The people said, "Watch and as soon as he comes out and goes away from it you must meet him." The chief said that that was good. The chief walked out a long distance and watched for the young man. When the young man came out with his bow and arrows, the chief met him and said, "My son, I want you to come to my tipi and live with me as my son-in-law." The young man said that he could not do that, as he was in the lodge to feed the snakes. He said he would go and consult with the snakes and if they were willing he would let him know the next day at the same hour. The chief went home feeling happy.

The young man disappeared over the hills and in a few minutes came up again with a whole deer on his shoulder. He took the deer into the

[1] Told by Little-Chief, Chaui.

lodge, cut it up, and scattered it over the ground to feed the snakes. That night the young man told the Snakes what the chief had said. The Snakes said: "We are held here by the witch who lives with the people. If you overcome her and return her to where she belongs, then we can scatter out over the country and get our own food." The boy was glad, for he knew that he was now going to go back to his people. The next day he went out to hunt for meat for the snakes. He met the chief and he told the chief to go into the village and tell the men to come to a certain hollow and he would be there to meet them. When he reached the hollow he remained there. When he saw the people coming he made motions at the foot of a hill and there came out droves of buffalo. The buffalo ran along the hollow and the people with their bows and arrows killed them. The people went home with their meat and were made happy. The young man took his deer, went to the den of Snakes, and fed them.

The next day he turned the buffalo loose from the cave again. The people killed the buffalo, and they knew now that the young man was wonderful. On the third day when the people came to kill the buffalo the Witch-Woman came also. She said to the people: "Let the young man come. I want to challenge him." The young man came and the woman said, "If the buffalo come out again I will make them return to the cave, for I know who you are." When the young man tried to put the buffalo out the woman waved her robe and threw it on the side of the hill. There was a picture of the morning-star on the robe. The woman said: "I know you. You are the Morning-Star." The young man said: "It is true. I know who you are." The boy took his arrow and shot at the robe. When the arrow hit the robe the star disappeared and there on the robe was the picture of a new moon. The woman laughed and said, "So you know who I am?" The young man shot an arrow and when it struck the robe the new moon disappeared and there was a quarter of a moon. The woman laughed again. The young man shot another arrow and as it struck the robe there came a three-quarter moon. The young man said, "Now for the last time I will shoot my arrow at your robe." A full moon came upon the robe. The young man walked up to it and shot at the moon. The full moon fell upon the ground and turned into a spider. The young man killed the spider with his bow and arrows. He put the spider on the end of his arrow and shot up into the heavens. He said, "You must stay up in the heavens where you belong and not try to live with the people." The arrow went up into the heavens with the spider and the spider was left in the heavens as the moon. The old woman fell down and died.

The young man said: "My work is now complete. I will return with you." He turned the buffalo loose from the cave again and said, "All the buffalo will now come out from the cave and they will be scattered over the land." The boy went over the hills and another cave was found which contained deer, antelope, etc. They were turned loose. He brought one to the Snake den and then he returned to the heavens as the Morning-Star, leaving another boy in his place, who was given the mountain-lion quiver, bow, and arrows. The boy spoke to the Snakes and said: "You must now go all over the land. I must return to my people." The boy went into the village and there he married.

From that time on the people multiplied and had plenty to eat. They were saved from starvation by this young man, and because the spider-woman was killed the women gave birth. While the woman was among them the women did not give birth to any children. By getting her out of the way the people increased.

9. ORIGIN OF THE BASKET DICE GAME.[1]

When the creation was going on the gods made two images of man-kind out of mud, one a girl and the other a boy. In time they seemed to wake up. The bow and arrows were given to the boy, so that they could live by killing animals for food. The gods meditated as to their length of life—whether they should become old or live always—and whether they should have darkness to live in or light. The gods then sent animals and the gods said, "Let him kill one of these animals and whatever kind he kills let it be so." The animals went past the young man. Some were white and some were black, but he never shot until the last one came by. He shot this one through the heart. This was done in darkness. The last animal which was shot was spotted white and black. As the animal died it became day, so that the boy saw that the animal was spotted. The young man went on his hunting journeys in the forest. One night while they were sitting in their grass-lodge they heard singing just as if many people were dancing. It was continued all night. The next day the young man went into the forest, and there he found a lodge and a small field of corn. He did not enter the lodge, but returned to his wife. He brought her and as they approached the lodge a woman came out and invited them to enter. They entered the

[1] Told by Woman-Cleanse-the-People, an old Skidi woman, now the keeper of the Skull bundle. This tale is interesting not only for the fact that it gives the supposed origin of the well-known basket game among the Pawnee, but especially on account of the symbolism of the basket and dice as representing the seven stars and the moon, as well as the earth and its contents.

lodge and there at the altar sat four old men, who were daubed with ointment mixed with red clay. The woman who invited them was none other than the Moon, who had many children. All these children seemed to be girls. The dance began and they told the young man to learn the songs and to watch what they did, for in time he would do the same. He watched their movements and learned their songs. After singing then corn was brought in and they all ate. These two people received the seeds from the people who were living in the lodge.

After the dancing then different games were taught these people, and they got the basket game at this time. In their dancing the four old men who were singing were none other than the Wind, Clouds, Lightning, and Thunder. The woman who danced in the west was the Evening-Star and was the god of storms, whose permission they obtained in order to create. For this reason she stood in front of the four old men. She was dancing and had the basket representing the moon. The four other dancers were also women who were stars. These were supposed to be the daughters of the Big-Black-Meteoric-Star who stands northeast in the heavens, and this star was to give in time the medicine-men their bundles and mysteries. As they danced these four moved towards the west, for they stood in the east in line. Towards the last the four dancers on the east moved up and each dumped into the basket what he carried. There were two swan-necks and two fawn-skins. This ended the dance. The basket woman was the one who gave permission to the gods to make the earth, and that is why the basket is made out of willow, for the earth is filled with timber. In making this particular basket a knife must not be used, but water and mud are used to help make it. Everything was put in the earth, and what was not put in for mankind's power was afterwards given by the Big-Black-Meteoric-Star. These women put the swan-necks and fawn-skins in the basket, for they represented the four gods in the west.

In this ceremony these two people learned many things, and they finally got the basket and plum seeds, for the woman was afterwards told to get plum seeds and to put marks on them representing the stars. The basket was to represent the moon. This was done to remind them that Tirawa sent the stars in a basket (the moon), and that they fell to the earth so that they might teach these two people all they were to do upon the earth. The twelve sticks represent the twelve stars in a circle above the heavens who sat as chiefs in council. By moving the sticks they count and when done win the game.

Basket-Woman is supposed to be the mother of all stars and she is the moon. When these people, who were really stars, saw that the two people now knew what they must do in this life, they jumped into their basket and went up into the heavens again. The Spider-Woman said that the doctor's dance is the same and represents the moon, who gave knowledge to these people. She helped the Big-Black-Meteoric-Star to give the man power to cure the sick and to do mysteries. She sat in the southwest corner of the lodge and the people in the south called her sister, while the doctors in the north called her their wife.

10. THE ORIGIN OF A NEW BAND.[1]

A long time ago some people, Skidi or Pitahauirat, lived in a village in the north. They had many ceremonies and offered buffalo meat to Tirawa. In this village were many boys who played about in the timber, along the creeks. In their plays they held medicine-men's dances and imitated the medicine-men trying to do sleight-of-hand. Among these young men was one whose father was a medicine-man, and another whose father was a chief. The medicine-man kept the ceremony of the medicine-men, while the chief kept the sacred bundles, and also knew the songs and rituals that went with the bundles.

In the village was a young man who was poor and he did not go to play with the other boys. The medicine-man's boy and the chief's boy liked the poor boy, and they often went to his tipi and asked him to play with them. The poor boy always refused, but one time the two boys begged him so hard that he went to the place where they were playing. All the boys in the play took their turn in doing wonderful things. The medicine-man's boy took a willow stick and ran it down his throat. After they had all performed their tricks, the poor boy took the chief's son and the medicine-man's son aside, and said: "My brothers, you have been asking me to come and play with you. I can not, for I am poor. You boys are learning wonderful things from your fathers. My father is a poor man. He has no ceremony nor has he any sacred bundle. I am a poor boy, but since I have come this time I will come again. I want you to promise me that you will try to learn all the rituals, songs, and mysteries of the medicine-men. Will you promise me?" Both of the boys promised and they parted. After that the poor boy always played with them.

One night the poor boy asked the two boys if they had learned all that was to be known of the sacred bundles and the mysteries of the

[1] Told by Mouth-Waving-in-Water, a very old Kitkehahki medicine-man, one of the oldest of living Pawnee. While the tale apparently recounts a historical event, and is told as history, it especially is supposed to stimulate young men to greater deeds on the war-path, by encouraging them in the belief that possibly they also will become the founder of a new band.

medicine-men. Both of the boys said, "Yes, we know them now." The poor boy said, "Well then, my brothers, it is now time that we go upon the war-path." The boys agreed, and so the three boys went alone upon the war-path. For many days they went, until at last they came to a camp where there were three tipis. In this camp there was only one man and he was married to several women. The three young men attacked the camp and killed the man. The women made no resistance, for they were glad to get rid of their husband, who was cruel and had treated them badly. The three young men now stayed with the women and they began to teach them and their people how to speak their language. They took special pains to teach the boys and tried to make warriors of them. They took them on long journeys so as to teach them to endure hardships. As the three young men grew older, one of them took the boys with him and captured many ponies from the other people. They grew in numbers and captured many ponies. They kept moving their camp and attacking one village, then another, killing the men and saving the women and children. The three young men were careful to force their captives to adopt their language, and in this way they came to be one tribe.

After a time the three young men thought of their old homes and they were anxious to return and make offerings of scalps to the gods in the heavens. They moved the camp north, towards their country. They came to a valley with a stream running through it and a high hill was on the west side of the place where they made their camp. There the people stayed for several days. The poor young man went to the top of the hill and there stood for several days crying. At last the chief's son went up on the hill and begged him to come down and eat. He said: "Why do you stay upon the hill and cry? It is time that we return to our people and let them know what we have done. We have many scalps and our people will be proud of us. Besides we now have a whole village of captured people." The young man did not reply, but sat with his head down. At last the chief's son said, "Well, if you will not say anything, I will go down." The chief's son went down to the camp.

The next night the medicine-man's son went up to see the poor young man. He said: "My brother, why do you stand up here and cry this way? Look in yonder valley. We have many tipis. On poles in front of my tipi hang many scalps that I have taken from the enemy. In front of our brother's tipi also are many scalps. We have many women and children that we have captured. We also have many ponies. Come, let us go down and see our brother. Let us talk about going north to our country." But the young man said nothing, and so the medicine-

man's son left him. The two young men then determined to go together
to the poor young man on the hill and persuade him to come down.

In the night the two young men went upon the hill. One of them
spoke and said: "Brother, we have come up here several times, and
each time you have sent us away. Now we both have come up to ask
you to stop crying and come with us to take these captured people to
our people. Whatever you may request we both will grant. We do not
like to see you upon the hill here crying and starving yourself." The
poor young man said: "I am poor. I want to stay up here. If you
want to go home, go. I can not go home." The two young men said,
"No, we will not go home unless you go with us." "No," said the poor
boy, "I can only go home if you do what is in my heart." "Tell us,"
said both of the young men. "No, I can not," said the poor young
man. The two young men then begged the poor young man to tell
them what it was that was troubling him. The poor young man said,
"Will you do as I say?" The two young men promised. The poor
young man said, "Do you remember when we were boys that I would
never play with other boys, because they wore good clothes and I had
no good clothes? I saw chiefs who gave commands to our people. I
saw medicine-men who made people well, and also did many wonderful
things in their medicine-lodge. All of these things I saw. I saw the
priest go through ceremonies making burnt offerings to the gods in the
heavens. Do you boys remember how I asked you to go and learn
these things, one the sacred-bundle ceremonies, the other the medicine-
men's mysteries? Do you remember how I often asked you if you had
learned these ceremonies perfectly, and how you, my brothers, said,
'Yes, I know my ceremonies and songs and mysteries.' I then asked
that we might come out here where we could be alone and attack people who would travel alone with their families. We have captured
enemies. We have taken their scalps and their ponies. There is now
nothing that we want except to take all of these captives to our people.
Will you do what I wish you to do? If you earnestly desire me to be
with you, I will tell you my wish. I will then wipe my tears away
and my sorrow will go from me." "Speak," said the two young men,
"and we will do as you wish." The poor boy said: "We have conquered people. They are our people and their children are our children. Let us, my brothers, stay away from our people. Let this, my
brother, the chief's son, be the high priest, for he knows the songs and
ceremonies. Let this, my brother, the medicine-man's son, be the medicine-man, for he knows the mysteries of the medicine-men. Now,
brothers, let this poor brother of yours be a chief, for he has longed to

be a chief. Then let us stay away from our people and we will have a tribe of our own. These people will increase and we will teach them our language and our ceremonies. Will you, my brothers, do this?" The chief's son arose, took both of the poor boy's hands and said: "I like you more than a brother. I looked for you when we were boys and played around our village. What you have said I will do. We will stay away from our people and I will carry on the ceremonies, and the gods in the heavens shall receive the smoke from the scalps that we have taken." The poor boy then arose and said, "I thank you, my brother, for your friendly words. The gods overhead have heard your words and they will be glad when the scalps are placed upon the fire and the smoke goes straight up to heaven. Now," he continued, "what do you say, my brother? Will you also make my heart glad?" The medicine-man arose and said: "I am willing. We like you. I shall teach these people to do wonders in the medicine-man's mysteries and also shall teach them the ceremony and songs of the medicine-man. Then I shall teach them the different herbs and roots and what they are good for." The poor boy clasped both of the young men's hands, and said: "My brothers, my heart is filled with gladness. I can not speak to you of what is in my heart." He began to cry, and the two men could not speak, for they too were weeping. The night was clear and the stars shone bright in the sky. The three young men wiped their tears away and sat down, and the poor young man filled the pipe and they smoked together. The poor young man then said: "Look, my brothers, the stars are bright and they seem to speak to us as if they promised us success. Let us always remember that the gods in the heavens watch over us." They talked a long time and at last they arose and went down to the village.

The next morning the three young men sat in the tipi of the poor young chief. They agreed that the chief should take some of the young men in the village and go north to their old village and get seeds from the fields of their people. In a few days the poor boy chief selected some of the young men, and they started north to where their people had their corn-fields. It was in the fall of the year. The village had been deserted by the people. The men found some corn in the fields and picked up beans and squash seeds. They then started back to their new home. In the spring the people planted corn, beans, and squash. The chief's son got things together to make a sacred bundle. In the fall he went into the corn-field and found a white ear of corn with a tassel on top of it. He took this ear of corn to his tipi. Early in the spring a ceremony was performed and the corn and other things that were gathered were put in a wrapper and a bundle was made. A few years afterwards the other young man started up the medicine-men's dance. He taught young men whom he selected and he had many followers. The people increased and became numerous.

11. HOW THE PEOPLE GOT THE CROW-LANCE.[1]

Many years ago a number of men went on the war-path. On the way the leader of the war party told them that it would be the duty of every man to look out for a raccoon; that before they should get far into the country of the enemy they must make a sacrifice of the raccoon. For many days they traveled south. One of the men went off by himself. He came to a ravine. He traveled up the ravine. In the night he did not return. Early in the morning this man followed the ravine. By sunrise he saw a raccoon sleeping upon a tree. He took an arrow from his quiver and shot it through the side. The raccoon fell down from the tree. The man then pronounced it holy. He put the raccoon upon his back and traveled west. In the evening he came to the men in the main body of the people. When he came to the people he told them that he had the raccoon which the leader wanted. The leader was satisfied. He told the people that in order to have a ceremony they must find a country with thick timber. Scouts were sent out and after a while they returned and said that they had found a nice place. The people went to the timber and there they made the sacrifice of the raccoon. The raccoon was burned up. Some of the people in the crowd said that the burning of the raccoon was wrong; that they had never seen a raccoon burned; that it should have been roasted and eaten by the people. Some of these men being afraid returned to their country. The others went on.

Now, the man who made the sacrifice was one day sent out as a scout. The main body of the warriors had gone slowly and by noon had reached a high hill. They were seated upon the hill when they saw the man coming as if with good news. As he came over a hill, and went into a bottom land, the warriors on top of the hill heard shouting and yelling. Scouts were sent over to another hill to investigate and the scouts lay upon the hill where they could see the man and the enemy attacking him. The enemy killed the man and went away. After they were gone a short distance the scouts saw that they were not human beings, but that they were Crows and Coyotes. The scouts went back and told the leader what had happened. Some of the people said: "The people

---

[1] Told by Leading-Sun, an old Kitkehahki medicine-man. The tale relates the origin of the so-called crow-lance which is the standard of the Crow-Lance Dance, the ance itself being symbolic of the north wind, who is supposed to act in behalf of hunting parties in driving buffalo to them.

who went home told the trouble.   We should never have sacrificed the raccoon."   The leader of the war party went to the place and saw that the man was killed.   He felt of his body, but could find no bullet hole nor any wound.   He was not scalped, but there were scratches upon his body.   Then they took his robe and placed it over him and the war party returned to their village.

Now, when night came this man who was supposed to be killed thought that he heard some dancing.   He listened.   After a while he sat up and he saw people dancing around him.   When he looked at the people he did not know any of them.   There was one man who carried a lance and it was covered with crow feathers.   All of the dancers were painted black. They told the man to get up, and they went along until they came to the mountains.   There they took him from one place to another until they came to a hollow and there in the hollow stood a high tree.   The man was told to lie down under the tree.   He lay down and went to sleep. Early the next morning he woke up.   The first thing he saw was a number of Deer running around and jumping.   Then some one spoke from the tree where the Crows were and said, "Follow them if you wish." Then the man remembered the Crows.   Again the boy found Antelopes. They came to where he was, and the boy liked them.   He wanted to follow them and imitate them, but some one from the tree said, "Remember we brought you here."   Then the boy let the Antelopes go and remained at the tree.

The next day the Crows scattered out over the country.   The boy took his bow and arrows and went out and killed a young fawn.   This he brought back to the place where he was, built a fire, and cooked some meat for himself.   In the evening the Crows began to come back to their tree.   As soon as it was dark the boy lay down and he heard strange noises coming from the mountain side.   He wanted to go to the place, for he was sure that he heard singing, but some one spoke to him from the tree saying, "Go if you wish, but remember we brought you here." Four times the young man had a chance to follow some kind of animals, but the Crows held him back.   On the fifth night the Crows which had settled upon the trees disappeared and now there was singing inside of the mountain.   After a while one of the Crows came out and spoke to the man.   The man was taken into the side of the mountain.   There he found a big cave.   These Crows were seated around in a circle.   The lance was standing in the west, and it was covered with crow feathers. The Crow people began to sing songs.   At the end of each song all would imitate the Crow.   All night they danced and as dawn came they told the boy to lie down in the lodge, as they must go out.   The Crows flew

out and were gone during the day. In the night they came back and
the man heard them and he sat up. This time he danced with them.
For three nights they danced together. The fourth night they danced
and then the leading Crow said: "My son, to-day we part. We give
you this lance covered with our feathers. When you go back to your
people, start the Crow-Lance society. The one who shall carry the lance
shall be known as the priest. Any of the young men can take the lance
in battle who belongs to the society. The priest must carry the lance
on the march while hunting buffalo. The lance, as you know, is covered
with crow feathers. The Crow can see where the buffalo are in time, and
in that way the Crow will help you to find buffalo." The songs were
also taught to the boy.[1] The lance was given him and also the paint.
Then the Crow said that he was supposed to have been killed by the
enemy, but those who killed him were Crows and Coyotes.

The Coyotes and Crows came over the hills together and by their
crowing and barking they had scared the man to death. The Coyotes
wanted to eat him up, but the Crows wanted to take him to their lodge
and there teach him the dancing. If the Coyotes had had their way
they would have eaten the boy, but the Crows brought life to the boy
again and gave him the crow-lance dance. The people were to be taught
by the way in which the Crows and the Coyotes scared this man, that
sometimes they came in a body and scared them; that if the people
became scared they were killed; if they did not become afraid they
would not be killed.

12. THE ORIGIN OF THE PIPE-STICK CEREMONY.[2]

Many, many years ago the Skidi were few in number and lived somewhere in Nebraska. There was one young man among them who had
wonderful dreams. In one of his dreams he saw a water-monster coming up a big river. This monster which he saw in his dreams was a very
long one. The head was of immense size. Upon the head were hairs
growing out. On the top of the head stood something white, which he
believed was a soft downy feather. The head of the monster was of

[1] The music and text of the songs which form part of this and the succeeding
tales of this volume will be found in Part II.
[2] Told by Cheyenne-Chief, a young Skidi whose father, Pipe-Chief, was one of
the leading Skidi priests and chiefs. This tale relates to the origin of one of the
most interesting Skidi ceremonies, the pipe-stick or Calumet. This ceremony,
according to Skidi belief, as it exists in the other three bands of the Pawnee, was
borrowed from the Wichita. The tale also accounts for the decoration of the effigy
of the water-monster which is constructed on the inside of the lodge during the
dance of the medicine-men.

many colors. The young man woke up from his dream and for several days he sat in his lodge meditating whether to go to the big water he had seen or not. At last he made up his mind, and he went. For many days he journeyed to the northeast. At last he came to the big stream of water. The day was cloudy. He did not know where the sun was. While he was sitting upon the bank of the stream he saw the water spouting up. After a while he noticed that this water-monster of which he had dreamed was coming. The monster came up just as it did in his dream, and it dived back. Again it came up and went back. A third time it came up and went back. The fourth time it came up, remained for some time, and then went down into the water. The breath of the monster seemed to draw this man into the water. The man was afraid, but as he was influenced he ran toward the steep bank of the river. When he was near to the water he closed his eyes. He knew no more. When he opened his eyes the monster's head was at the south entrance. The man noticed that there were animals of all kinds in this place where he was. The monster said: "I came from the big waters to this place in order to bring you a message. I control all animal beings in the big waters. I have told them to speak to the people so that they can understand the powers which we have. In this lodge are different kinds of animals. This is an animal medicine-lodge. Here they will teach you the mysteries of all the animals. When you have gone home, make an image of myself and place it in your lodge. There you must stay by yourself, so that I may appear to you in your dreams and teach you the songs, and also my powers."

At this time the Skidi did not know that there were birds and eagles. After this man had been in the lodge, and the monster placed him on dry land again, it returned to its home. The man went to his home also. When the man was in his lodge he began to gather up a lot of willows and covering for the sea-serpent which was to be placed in his lodge. He killed several buffalo. Among them was one bull. He took the scalp from it, and stripped it, so that the sea-serpent would have hair, just as he had seen the serpent in the water. The hide was tanned, the hair taken off, and was dyed. This was for the covering of the head of the sea-serpent. The rest of the body was covered with mud. When it came to putting the feather on top of the head, the man did not know what to get.

In the night he had a dream. He saw a man standing near him. The man had mud all over him. On his face were streaks of red, blue, and yellow. On his head were scattered many soft downy feathers, and on the top of the head stood a soft downy feather about eight inches long.

The man said to the sleeper: "I am the Water-Monster you saw. I am a medicine-man. I am teaching you all the things that are to happen. I am teaching you many things which your people will have to do. The thing which you lack to place upon the head of the sea-serpent is a feather. The bird flies up in the sky, and I will teach you how to catch it. You must go upon some high mound, dig a hole on top of the mound just as if you were digging a grave; scatter green limbs over the hole; kill several rabbits, skin them, and place them upon the limbs. You must then crawl into the hole and lie there. First the magpies will come to taste of the meat, then the crows, then the bird that flies high in the sky will see these birds eating and it will swoop down and light, close to the place. It will hop around until finally it will get on top of the hole, when you must reach and grasp it by both legs. After this pull it into the hole and wring its neck after you have taken it in. That is where you will get the feather to place upon the water-monster." The next day the man went upon a high hill and for several days he worked around until he had the place prepared just as he was told. After he had placed the rabbits on top he got into the hole and lay there. First he noticed the magpies flying around, then the crows, and suddenly he thought he heard wind coming down from the sky. When this happened the magpies and crows scattered away. The eagle came close to the hole. When it was on top the man reached out, caught both legs of the bird and pulled it in.

For several days he lay there killing eagles. At last he took from the tail the one feather he wanted to place upon the head of the water-monster. The monster appeared again to the man in a dream and gave him a pipe-stem. It told him to string some of the eagle feathers and tie them upon a stick. He told him that he could use the pipe-stem and the eagle feathers in compelling other people to give him presents. The monster was not satisfied with what he had done for the man. He then told the man that he had killed some eagles. He told him to go over the country and keep on traveling until he should find the nest of an Eagle. The man went into the timber and looked and looked. At last he came to a big cottonwood tree and there he heard the whistlings of Eagles. He noticed that the mother was a Brown Eagle and that the father was a White Eagle. There were several young ones in the nest. The man looked up at the nest and cried. For a long time he cried and finally the Brown Eagle said to the man, "Why do you cry so?" The man said, "There is something that I want, and I want you to help me." The Eagle said: "Tirawa gave you a pipe. Take it and go. Tirawa will help you." The man continued to cry and the Brown Eagle told the boy that they could do only certain things for him; that although they represented the sky they could not help him. The man began to cry and cried for a long time. At last some one near him said: "I will be with the other people if they will help you. You see my skin has black spots all over it. My fur is blue. I represent the sky and the stars. I know what you want. I can cheat other people and I will now teach you how to cheat others also." He saw that the animal who had been speaking to him was the Wild-Cat. The Evening-Star then said: "It is well that we placed the Wild-Cat upon the earth, for he now helps to get presents from other people. I will give you an ear of corn and you will call this ear of corn mother. Although she looks dead, take the corn from the cob, place it in the ground, and it will live and bear again. You shall tie the ear of corn on to a stick. The stick must have a downy feather upon it to represent Tirawa." Near where the boy stood was a plum bush. This bush said: "My son, I will furnish you my timber for your forked sticks. You see I bear much fruit. Our kind of trees grow and bear." Above and close to the nest of Eagles flew the Wood-pecker. He said: "I will assist this man to make these sticks. When these sticks are completed the children who shall receive them shall sometimes ask for rain. If it is raining while the ceremony is going on, the children must ask of this man and the sticks that it stop raining. You must place my bill at the point of the sticks. I make my home in dry limbs. When it is stormy the lightning never strikes the place of my home. I have no trouble in raising my children." Then the Ducks flew overhead and said: "We will help. We place our eggs along the streams of water and they hatch. We have many children." After all these beings had spoken it was almost dark. The Owls hooted and said: "Take our feathers and place them upon the sticks. We will help the man to make his sticks." After all the animals had spoken, the four gods in the heavens spoke and said: "The Evening-Star has given us power to watch. If these people want rain they must sing songs and we will send it. If they want to stop the rain they must sing other songs." Then the man went home.

In the night he had visions of these different animals. They gave him songs. They taught him songs and he sang with them. While they were singing, as the sun came up in the east, he received a song from the Sun. The Sun said: "This you shall sing when you are passing around the circle of the lodge. 'The rays of the sun will enter the lodge. The rays of the sun are upon the lodge. The rays of the sun are moving about the lodge. The rays of the sun have covered the lodge.'" Another song was given. "The sun walks around the lodge. The sun moves about

the lodge.   The sun has covered the lodge."   In the night the man gave
some night songs.   "The night dreams have entered the lodge.   The
night dreams are moving about the lodge.   The night dreams have
touched the people.   The night dreams have covered the lodge."   "Let
the night dreams be.   The night dreams are coming.   The night dreams
have entered the lodge."   Then there were songs about the mother-corn,
the brown eagles, the ducks, the owls, and the wild-cats.   The man was
also taught that on the third night they must take a child and decorate
it in such a way that it would represent Tirawa.   The painting of the
child with the red paint about his face represented that the sun had
touched the child.   There was to be a mark upon the face of the child which
was to represent the picture of Tirawa.   At last the child was to be
placed on the nest of an oriole.   The two priests were to hold the child
up while the leader of the pipe-sticks placed the nest under its feet.   Then
the priests stood the child up on the nest.   This was to teach that the
child should grow up to be either a man or woman and that its life's pathway would be hard, but it would grow up, for the powers of Tirawa were
now upon it.   The oriole makes its nest high up in the trees.   The storms
never blow it away.   Snakes can not get to its nest, and its young ones
are always safe.   Then they finally dance, and the paintings and other
things are taken off from the child, together with the paw of a wild-cat.
Then the child is permitted to return home and the painting upon its face
must wear off.   The child must not be washed.

These are the things which were told me by my father.   The pipe-
stick ceremony came from heaven, from the animals, and from the water-
monster.

13. THE GIRL WHO MARRIED A STAR.[1]

A long, long time ago during the summer two girls were sleeping
on the top of an arbor.   As they lay there, one of the girls said "O
how I wish I had that star for my husband; I love that star."   That
night the girl went to sleep.   When she awoke she found herself in
a strange country.   She cried and cried to get back to her own country;
but when she found out that she was living with a man who was really
the Star that she loved, she was then happy.   The woman's husband
told her not to go away from home and not to dig in the ground.
He told her that she might dig wild turnips if she would be careful and

---

[1] Told by Curly-Hair, a young Kitkehahki, the nephew of Curly-Chief.   This
is a poor version of the well-known and widely disseminated tale which the
Arikara claim as their own.   It seems that the present version is somewhat mixed
with the story of Long-Tooth-Boy.   (Cf. tale No. 41.)

not dig too deep. After she had been with her husband for a long time, she gave birth to a child, and it was a boy.

When the child grew up and had become a good-sized boy, the woman went out to dig turnips, and she dug until she went too deep and her hoe went through. She then made the hole larger, looked down through, and there she saw the earth. The people were walking around and they looked like ants. She then covered up the hole and went home. A few days afterwards she told her son to tell his father to get many sinews for him. The man went hunting and from the backs of all the animals that he killed he took the sinews. Every day the woman would tell the boy to tell his father to get more sinew, until at last there was quite a pile. The woman sat down by the pile of sinews and began to make lariat rope from it. She kept on making the sinew rope for many, many days, until she had a big pile of it.

When she thought she had enough rope, she went and dug a big hole, then she took a long pole and laid it across the hole and tied the sinew rope upon the pole. Then she pulled up a little grass and covered the place and went home, for she did not want her husband to know what she was doing. As soon as her husband went with the other Star-men for their night's journey, she put the boy upon her back and tied another sinew string about the child and across her breast so that the child was tied fast to her back. Then she went to the hole and slipped down the rope. All night and the next day she slipped down the rope. On the fifth day, Star began to hunt for his wife. He went all over the country, and finally found the hole, and he looked down through the hole and there he saw the woman hanging, for the rope did not quite reach the earth. Star went and brought a round, smooth stone. He dropped the stone and it fell upon the woman's head and killed her, so that she fell upon the ground. The boy worked his way out from the rope and stayed around his mother, nursing upon her breast until she had been dead for some time.

A thunderstorm came and the boy ran for shelter. He came to a place that had a clean path, and he followed the path until he came to a tipi, and here was an old woman and her grandson, who was of the same age as the boy. They received him into their tipi, for the poor boy was glad to have a playmate. They stayed together and grew up together. One day the old woman told the boys not to go to a certain place; that there lived an animal that killed people. Little Star-Boy said, "Let us go to that place where grandmother told us not to go." They went. While they were going, a bear tumbled out of his den, bringing out much dust. The boys kept on going and the bear was about to kill them, when they hid by a rock that was close by the bear. While the bear was looking around for them, it had become cloudy, and as the clouds came over the place where they were, the lightning struck the bear and killed it. The boys arose, went to the bear and Star-Boy blew his breath into the mouth of the bear, and the bear's skin rolled off. The boy tied the nose and blew up the bear skin and then they led it to the old woman. They ran towards their tipi yelling and crying. The old woman came out, saw the bear and commenced to run. Then the boys laughed and said, "Grandmother, we have brought this bear to watch over your pumpkins; we shall stand it in the field, so that the wild animals will not come there."

In a few days the old woman told the boys that they must not go to a thickly timbered country; that there a monster lived. The boys went. When they came to the place they saw dust come out from a hole, but they kept on. The father of Star-Boy saw that he was in danger, and he sent the clouds, so that it thundered, and the lightning struck the big monster, as it came out from its hole, and killed it. The boys dragged the monster to their tipi. They scared the old woman with it, then left the monster outside of the tipi.

Again the boys were told by the grandmother not to go to a certain timbered country; that at the place were mountain-lions; but the boys went and killed the mountain-lions. The boys killed all the wicked animals in the country. The old woman, after gathering in her harvests, told the boys it was time to go back to their country, to tell the people that all the monsters and wild animals had been killed. They went back to their country, and the relatives of the boy took him to their home. Star-Boy told them that his mother had been taken up by Star, his father, who was one of the Star people in the sky. He was a great man among them. One time he disappeared. Nobody knew where he went; but they supposed that he went back to heaven.

14. THE GRAIN-OF-CORN BUNDLE.[1]

A man was roaming over the prairie. He came to a place where people had camped and there he heard a woman crying. The man went to the place where the crying came from, but there was no one there, and he did not know what to think. When he went home he lay down and in the night he had a dream. He dreamed that he saw a woman. The woman spoke to him and said: "I stay where the crying

[1]Told by Pretty-Crow, a young Skidi medicine-man, who it is believed obtained the story from his present wife, the widow of an old Skidi by the name of Wonderful-Sun, who was both priest and medicine-man. The tale relates to the origin of one of the bundles. It was told to emphasize the importance of economy in corn, and also to instill a reverential feeling toward corn.

came from, and I was glad that you hunted me and tried to find me. I am going to help you to find me, and also let you see me. As soon as the sun goes down and it becomes a little dark, I want you to go to the place where you heard the crying. I will be there, and there you shall see me and I will tell you some things that you do not know."

When the man awoke he thought of the woman he was to see that evening, and so he watched and looked over the country until the sun went down. He watched the women passing through the village, and as soon as the sun disappeared and it became a little dark he went to the place where he had heard the cry. As soon as he arrived at the place, instead of hearing the crying he saw a woman. The woman spoke to the man and said, "Look, look at me, for I am the one who was crying at this place." The man looked at the woman and he saw that she was a fine-looking woman. She said again: "Young man, when the people passed over this place while hunting buffalo they dropped me. I have been crying ever since, for you know that the people do not let a kernel drop from an ear of corn." Then the woman said, "Look upon the ground where my feet rest." The man looked and there he picked up a kernel of corn. This kernel of corn was speckled. "Now," said the woman, "pick me up and always keep me with you. My spirit is of Mother-Evening-Star, who gives us the milk that is in the corn. The people eat of us and have life. The women give the same milk from their breast when they have children and their children grow up to be men and women. You must carry me wherever you go. Keep me in your quiver and my spirit will always be with you." The man took the kernel up and the woman disappeared. The man went home and kept the kernel close to him all the time.

One day he went upon the war-path and tied the kernel to the quiver. When he had journeyed for many days the woman appeared to him in a dream and said: "The enemy is close by you. You are about to reach their village." The next day the man went out and before sunset he came in sight of a village. He sat down to rest and wait for sunset. As night came on he went down towards the village. Before he reached the village he came to a spotted pony. He got upon its back and rounded up several other ponies and drove them to where the people were. When they saw him coming alone with the ponies they were surprised. That night as he slept the corn-woman spoke to him and said: "Young man, take me. Spread some buffalo skins over me and cover me with a calf hide." The man did as he was told and the kernel of corn was put into a bundle and the bundle became a sacred bundle. The man told his mother to watch over the bundle and to care for it.

One day he went to the gambling grounds, and while there the mother opened the bundle and saw the kernel of corn. The woman picked it up and began to pray to it, and promised it to care for it, and also asked that she might have many children. Then she wrapped the bundle up and laid it away. When the young man came home he did not feel well and so he went to bed early. In his dream he saw the woman again, and this woman said: "I am Corn-Woman. Your mother saw me and asked many things. All the things that she asked of me will come true."

The young man became a good warrior. He brought home many ponies and scalps. He said, "In the tribe is a nice-looking girl whom I like." The Corn-Woman spoke to him in a dream and said: "I do not want you to marry for two seasons. When you have received my spirit and you understand me, then you shall marry. You must tell your mother to place me in a large hill of earth. When a stalk grows from the hill and you find corn upon the stalk do not eat it, but lay it away. Then the next spring tell your mother to plant some more corn and the next fall there will be a good crop and you will see how the corn has multiplied." The young man did as he was told. As the spring came the mother placed the kernel in a big hill of earth. In the fall she gathered five ears of corn. These she laid away until the next spring; then she planted much more corn.

About that time the young man married. The young man and his wife had many children, and their children had children, and thus they multiplied as did the corn. The man said to his mother, "Mother, you must never drop a kernel upon the ground nor into the fireplace, for the corn has life." The young man's first child was a girl. Corn-Woman appeared to the man in a dream and said: "I shall name the girl. Call her 'Woman-Carry-the-Leading-Corn,' because her father carried Mother-Corn upon his back when on the war-path." When Corn-Woman disappeared she told the man to tell his people, when they were ready to plant corn, to pray first to Mother-Corn and then to Mother-Earth. "When you have placed the corn in the earth then stand to the west and pray to Mother-Evening-Star to send rain upon the earth so that the corn will grow. Pray also to Mother-Moon, who helps give life to people, and she will listen to what people say. Never drop a kernel upon the ground, for Mother-Corn will curse you and your life will be shortened." Corn-Woman also told the young man that when the corn-fields were high, all the people were to take their children into the fields and to pass their hands over the stalks and then over the children. Thus the children would grow and bad diseases would go away from them. Corn-Woman also said: "When the tassels are out then watch.

There will be singing in the fields. Remember where the singing comes from. Remember that that is the sacred ear of corn. Take it from the stalk and take it to the old man, who will place it in the sacred bundle so that people will know that Mother-Corn did sing to her people." The Pawnee worship Mother-Corn, because she represents Mother-Evening-Star.

15. THE METEORITE PEOPLE.[1]

Many, many years ago, before the stars fell upon the earth (1833) there was a wonderful being in the land known as Pahokatawa (Knee-Prints-on-the-Banks-of-the-Water). This wonderful being had been killed by an enemy. He was cut up. The coyotes came and ate of his flesh. The birds also came and ate of his flesh. Some other animals came and ate of his brain. The gods in the heavens agreed to save this man and send him back to the people. The gods let the animals in the earth know that they wished this man to live again. They made all the animals go back to the place where the man lay and place the meat back where they found it. The birds were also told to do the same thing. When the birds and animals and insects brought back everything which they had taken away, they found that the brains were gone. They could not be found. The gods placed a soft, downy feather in the skull in the place where the brains had been.

After this man had made himself known to the people, he came to them from the sky as a meteor and would stay with them. Many times when the enemy were about to attack their village he came and warned them that the enemy were coming. The people were put on their guard, so that they were able to meet the enemy and overpower them. While he was with the people at one time he told them that something wonderful was going to take place in the heavens; that they must not be afraid when the meteors flew through the sky; that it was not time for the world to come to an end. "When the meteors fall," said Pahokatawa, "among them will be a large-sized one that will fall upon the plains. The thing will be the shape of a turtle and will have many colors." He said that the meteor would fall upon the earth and it would cause other meteors to light up and fly through the sky.

Many years afterward the Indian people had their tipis in a thick-timbered country near the banks of the Platte River. The stars fell from

[1] Told by Buffalo, an old Skidi medicine-man. The meteor people referred to in the tale are those under the special protection of the Morning-Star. The stone referred to in the tale is supposed to exist on a high, sandy hill in the western part of Nebraska, Lone-Chief, a Skidi, being the only one who knows of its existence; while the leggings worn by this Pahokatawa are still in existence among the Skidi and in the possession of Lone-Chief.

the heavens. The people became afraid, and began to mourn, thinking that the world was coming to an end. But the leader of the people said, "Remember the words of Pahokatawa." The people recalled the words, and they knew then that it was not time. They went out and tried to catch the meteors. Some of the old people, who are living now, remember the time, and say that the stars flew around like birds.

Two or three years after this happened, while the Pawnee were upon a buffalo hunt, two men were walking over the prairie, when they came to a barren place. There was no grass growing there and the men wondered why. It was a smooth, round place. In the center they saw a stone sticking out and upon this stone were many colors. They began to dig it out. It was the shape of a turtle. The legs and head and even the eyes were imprinted upon it. They went home and told the people. When Big-Eagle, the chief of the Skidi, heard of it, he told them that Pahokatawa had promised them a meteor. They went to the place with ponies and found the meteor. They placed it upon a pony. It was very heavy and the people could not carry it. There were only a few people who were allowed to see it. When this thing was taken into the village the people gathered around it and offered tobacco and smoke to it. Priests were sent for and they were the ones to offer the smoke from the pipe. This meteor was carried by these people wherever they went, the old people believing that it was part of the Morning-Star. They kept it with the Morning-Star bundle. When the people moved away from Nebraska into Oklahoma they placed the stone upon a high hill in the western part of the state. Lone-Chief, a Skidi, still living, was one of the party who took the stone upon the hill and placed it there. He thinks the white people have discovered it and taken it away. The people speak of this meteor as having wonderful powers about it. Whenever the warriors were about to go out upon the war-path they went to where this meteor was kept, offered smoke and prayers to it, and then they were successful in overcoming the enemy and capturing their ponies. The people believed that as long as this stone was present with them bad disease could not enter their camp.

16. BUFFALO-WIFE AND CORN-WIFE.[1]

There was a young man who would never go to herd the ponies, nor join war parties, as his companions did, but always remained at home. When he was about twenty years of age, he selected a hill and there he used to climb every day and sit upon a pile of stones, and look

[1] Told by Buffalo, Skidi. This variant of a well-known tale teaches reverence and respect for both the corn and the buffalo, and also explains the part played by the buffalo and the corn in the make-up of the sacred bundles.

around all day long. When he came back in the evening his mother would take a bowl of water and wash his face, and comb his hair. She was very proud of her son, for he was a handsome youth. After a while the people noticed that the boy would not associate with the other boys of the village, but spent all of his days alone on top of the hill, and they wondered why he did this. Some said, "He is looking for a girl to marry." Others said, "He must be a wonderful boy." Up to this time the people had not suspected that he was not of their family, and did not know that he had powers greater than theirs. He belonged to the Eagle family, and for that reason his mother gave him the name Without-Wings.

One day while he was sitting upon the hill, looking over the country, he heard singing from the west. He listened again and heard the singing on the east side. Finally the singing came closer to where he sat. After a while he looked and saw that a woman was coming from the east and singing as she came. He heard someone singing behind him and there was another woman coming from the west. The song they sang was:

> Without-Wings, even your mother looks at you and her heart beats.
> I look at you, Without-Wings, and my heart beats.

The woman from the east was Buffalo-Woman, and the woman from the west, Corn-Woman. Buffalo-Woman walked up to the young man and sat down on the right side of him. The Corn-Woman came up and sat down on the left side. Buffalo-Woman then said: "I know you have been thinking of marrying among your people, but what has been uppermost in your mind is that you want to marry Buffalo-Woman or Corn-Woman. I made up my mind to come to you. I came and I see this other woman here. I have brought you a pair of moccasins," and she placed the moccasins before him. Corn-Woman spoke and said: "What Buffalo-Woman has said is true. I also come and bring you moccasins." The young man was puzzled to know which moccasins to wear. While he pondered Buffalo-Woman took the right moccasin and put it on his right foot, and at the same time Corn-Woman took the left moccasin and put it on his left foot. Then each of the women took up her moccasin which was left. The young man spoke to them and said: "I take both of you. We will now go down to the village and we will go into my earth-lodge." The two women followed the man down into the village. When they approached the village they saw a woman playing outside of the lodge as if she were a young girl. She was the young man's mother. When she saw her son coming with two wives she ran into the lodge and put on an old, ragged dress.   Then the young man took his wives into the lodge.

The two women knew that they both loved the young man, and they also knew that his mother loved her son.   The mother was very glad to have the two women to live in the same lodge with her, and for a long time they all lived together.   After a while Buffalo-Woman began to show signs of pregnancy.   When her time was almost up she told the young man that she had to go out upon the prairie.   She went out and while upon the prairie she gave birth to a male child.   Soon after Buffalo-Woman came back with her child Corn-Woman began to show signs of pregnancy.   She told her husband that she had to go into the corn-field, but that she would return in a day or so.   She went into the corn-field and there she gave birth to a male child.   In a day or so she brought the child to their lodge.   They all lived together happily until the little children grew up and could walk.   The children were playing together and the two mothers were looking at them.   Buffalo-Woman gave her son a little black buffalo-horn spoon.   Corn-Woman's little boy wanted the black buffalo-horn spoon and cried for it, but the other boy would not give it up, and so to quiet her son, Corn-Woman gave him an ear of black corn.   When little Buffalo-Boy saw the corn he wanted it, but Corn-Boy refused to give it to him, and so they began to quarrel and fight.   Then the mothers became angry at each other, and before Without-Wings knew anything about it, Buffalo-Woman ran away with her boy.   After Buffalo-Woman and her child were gone, Corn-Woman wanted to go to her home.   Without-Wings wanted to go with Corn-Woman, but Corn-Woman told him that it would not do for him to go with her, and that he had better follow Buffalo-Woman. She told him that although he could not see her she would always be present with him and would help him.   When she said this she and the boy disappeared and they went back into the under-world.

Early in the morning Without-Wings took the shape of an Eagle and flew up into the air and flew towards the east.   He had not gone far when he saw a Buffalo cow and her calf.   Without-Wings flew above them all day, and in the evening the Buffalo cow turned into a woman and said that she was going to set up a tipi.   The woman set up a tipi and began to cook something to eat.   The calf turned into a boy and played about his mother.   Without-Wings then flew down, turned himself into a man and went up to the tipi.   Buffalo-Woman would not look at him, but the little boy ran up to his father and brought him something to eat and told him of their travels.   After they had eaten they all lay down and went to sleep.   Early in the following morning the woman turned herself and her son into Buffalo and went off, leaving Without-Wings asleep. When he awoke he looked around and found that there was no one near. He turned himself into an Eagle and flew into the air for a little distance, and there he saw the Buffalo and the little calf going through a thickly timbered country where they thought no one would come. The Buffalo cow did not know that Without-Wings was flying overhead and she and the calf went on until evening came upon them. Then the Buffalo cow turned into a woman again, set up a tipi and began to cook, and the calf turned into a boy again. Without-Wings came again. The woman would not notice him, but the little boy would go up to his father and give him something to eat. Early the next morning the woman and the child awoke, turned into Buffalo, made the tipi disappear, and left Without-Wings on the ground, as they had done before.

When Without-Wings awoke he found that the woman and the child had gone again. He turned himself into an Eagle and flew away, and as he flew he saw the Buffalo cow coming to a wide stream of water. The Buffalo cow swam and carried the calf on her back. The cow became tired, but she finally crossed the stream of water and then stopped to rest. After she had rested she said: "My boy, your father will never be able to cross that water. Now we will go on." She did not know that Without-Wings was flying above her. They went on, and when evening came again the Buffalo turned into a woman and put up her tipi. When she had the tipi up, and was cooking, Without-Wings came into the tipi. The woman was surprised, but she would not notice him. Early the next morning the woman and her son arose and she said: "We must hurry, my son, for we must cross some high mountains. When we have crossed these mountains your father can never overtake us, because he can not climb the steep mountains." They started and went across the mountains. When Without-Wings woke up he found that they were gone, and again he turned into an Eagle and flew up and saw the Buffalo and the calf crossing the mountains. Towards evening the Buffalo cow did not run quite so fast, and she told the calf that the next day they would be back to their home where their people were. As they were going over the mountains she told him that his father could not come that way; but that if he did come she wanted him to tell his father, that he had a grandmother who was very cruel and that she would kill him if he came farther.

In the evening, after they had passed the mountains, the Buffalo cow stopped and turned into a woman again. She put up her tipi and began to cook. After a while Without-Wings came down from the mountains and entered the tipi. The woman was surprised, but she would not look at him. The little boy gave the father something to eat. In the night, when they lay down to sleep, the boy left his mother and went over and lay down with his father. The father then asked the boy questions and the boy told him all about their travel. Then the boy said: "My father, when you come to our lodge in the village of the Buffalo be careful that the stone at the entrance does not fall down upon you as you come in. My grandmother is a witch and she kills all handsome men who come through that doorway. When you come into the door she will say, 'Now go and find your wife.' There will be many buffalo that look just like my mother, but I will be playing with some other calves, and I will run up to my mother and I will rub my tongue at the root of my mother's tail, so that you can distinguish her from the others. Then there will be gathered together a lot of little calves and I will be among them, and when you come to find me among the calves I will shake my left ear a little, and then you will take hold of me and say that I am your son. Then my grandmother will try to make you do some other hard things, but I will help you."

While the boy was telling his father all these things, his mother woke up, and then they all arose and walked together into the village. When they came to the tipi of the Buffalo cow she and her son went in. Before entering, Without-Wings looked inside and saw a big Bear ready to jump upon him. He spoke to the Bear and said, "Be still." When he said that, the large rock used for the entrance moved so that the entrance was wide open. Without-Wings started to go in, but the stone fell just as he was going through the entrance. As the stone fell Without-Wings turned into a soft downy feather, and as the large rock fell it brought the wind down with it, and the wind blew the downy feather inside before the rock could fall upon it. From the feather Without-Wings arose and the old witch was surprised to see him standing there. She told him that he would have to hunt his wife.

There were many other cows with his wife, and the witch did not think that he could tell his wife from the others. He went among the cows and selected his wife, for he saw the mark that his boy had promised to put upon his mother's tail. The old Buffalo cow then said: "Without-Wings must be tired. I want him to go into the sweat-lodge." The little calf asked Without-Wings if he wanted to go into the sweat-lodge, and he said, "Yes, I would like to go." The old witch brought the stones and put them on the fire so that they would be red hot. Without-Wings went into the sweat-lodge, and then the old Buffalo cow went and invited six bulls to come and lie around the sweat-lodge, so that the man could not get out. Then she went into the sweat-lodge. She took a large buffalo-horn spoon and dipped water from a bucket and poured the water upon the hot stones. The steam began to come down upon their naked bodies, and when it became too hot the man turned himself into a Badger and dug into the ground so that only his mouth and head stuck out of the ground. While the witch was grunting and making her medicine upon the hot stones, Without-Wings would call to her and say, "Pour some more water on the stones, old woman, for this is not warm enough for me." The witch thought that by pouring water upon the red-hot stones she could scald the man to death, but she found that she was getting the place too hot for herself, and so she asked that they get out of the lodge. They left the lodge and the man saw the Buffalo bulls around the sweat-lodge. When the bulls saw the man coming out uninjured they jumped up and ran away from the place.

A few days afterwards the old witch told Without-Wings that he must go after some wood, and she sent him to a place where there was a tree with an Eagle's nest upon it. It was a place where no one had ever been before, but Without-Wings went. When he came near to the tree where the Eagle's nest was, a storm began to brew in the sky right overhead, and the lightning struck all around him. Without-Wings spoke to the Eagles and told them who he was, and then the lightning stopped and the storm passed. He gathered the wood and took it to the old witch, who was greatly surprised, for she thought that the lightning would kill him, as it had all others who had tried to go there.

A few days afterwards the old Buffalo cow challenged Without-Wings to run a race with her. Without-Wings thought that she would run about forty or fifty yards, but when she explained the length of the race, he knew that she was going to run to the four world quarters. She said: "If you should beat me, then the people will be allowed to live upon the buffalo. If I beat you, the buffalo shall live upon the people." When they got ready to run the race, Without-Wings turned himself into a Magpie. When they started the witch had a cane, and this cane she pointed as far as her eyes could see, and then she was there. Again she pointed the cane as far as her eye could see and again she was there. In this way she traveled, going at a single step as far as her eye could see, and so she was far ahead of Without-Wings. He commanded the Badgers to dig holes all around so that she would fall into these holes while he would gain on her.

The Badgers began to dig and soon the witch began to fall. She fell so often that Without-Wings finally passed her and left her away behind. He continued running and finally he went all the way around the world and came back. When Without-Wings came back the witch also came back. She went to her lodge and spoke to the stone over the entrance, so that it would not fall upon her. Then she called the Buffalo and they came out from the earth. She tried to get the Buffalo away, but Without-Wings ran into the cave and chased them out, and so many came, that they seemed to cover the earth.

Without-Wings then came outside of the cave, and whenever he saw a Buffalo that he thought was no good he drove it back into the cave. There was one Buffalo that had two heads. Without-Wings drove it back into the cave. There came out some spotted Buffalo, and these Without-Wings did not like and so drove them back. He forgot, however, to drive back some of the white Buffalo which came out with the other Buffalo. When the earth was covered with Buffalo, the old witch pushed back the stone into the cave and closed it up. After that she tried to make love to Without-Wings. She treated him very kindly and she told him that he must not drink any poor, ragged woman's water.

One day while Without-Wings was walking around he saw an old, ragged woman coming with water. He thought he would get a drink, and after he had drunk from the woman's water, the village became excited, saying, "Without-Wings drank the chief's water." The woman who was bringing the water was the chief's wife. Then the chief became angry, and he began to dig up the earth and throw the dust up into the air. His body was nothing but bones, but he ruled over the village of Buffalo. Without-Wings fixed his arrow and went against the chief. He heard a mocking-bird singing, and it said: "There is an open place upon the chest of that bony Buffalo chief. If you shoot into that opening you will kill him. If you miss that hole then you will be killed." Without-Wings took aim and shot the skeleton Buffalo in the chest and killed him. Then the Buffalo had no chief. They told Without-Wings that they had no leader any longer and so they would form into herds and go their way. After they had divided into many herds and scattered, Without-Wings went back to his own people.

17. THE POOR BOY WHO MARRIED THE CHIEF'S DAUGHTER.[1]

There was a village of people. In the village was a boy who was very poor. He had no home. He was very dirty and had hardly anything with which to cover himself. When the people moved away from their village and went upon a hunt, this boy would always be left

[1] Told by Little-Chief, Chaui. This is a true tale related during the intermission of the ceremony, and presents all the elements of a hero tale. It especially teaches the poor boy the possibility of success through great effort, and also serves as a warning to maidens of the higher classes not to make fun of the poor boys.

behind. The boy would go through the village picking up pieces of sinew and pieces of meat which had been dropped by the people. These he ate and then followed on. When he would arrive at the camp he would enter some of the lodges for something to eat. The poorer class of people were very good to him, but the people who were well-to-do did not like the boy.

One day the boy decided that he would enter the tipi of the chief. As soon as he entered the tipi the chief's daughter spoke and said to the poor boy: "You dirty, good-for-nothing boy, go on out. I do not like you. I do not want you in our lodge." The father of the girl said to the boy: "You may be seated. When the girl cooks something to eat you shall have some of it." The girl was angry and refused to cook. She told the poor boy that if he wanted anything to eat he had to go for water for her. The poor boy went for the water. After the boy had eaten something from the tipi of the chief, he went through the village and slept at another place. After that, although the girl did not like the boy, the boy went to their tipi. She called him names and made him do things for her, such as carry wood and pack water. One time the poor boy, on entering the lodge of the chief, saw the girl by herself.

The girl saw the poor boy come, and she said, "You dirty, good-for-nothing boy, go on out of this tipi or I will get a stick and drive you out." The boy did not move. The girl picked up the stick, went up to the boy, and hit him upon the back several times. The boy ran out and went through the village crying. He went outside of the village and there he stood upon a little hill and cried.

The next day when the people broke camp there was left behind a poor, broken-down, crippled horse. This horse was a bay horse. It had been a very fine horse, but somehow the horse had its ankle unjointed and it had grown large. The horse became very poor, for the people who owned it never took any more care of it. This pony was left behind by the owners. The boy saw the horse, went up to it, and spoke to it. Then he took his robe and with his knife he cut his robe into strings, so that he had a lariat rope for the pony. He led the pony on. The pony could hardly walk. When he came near to the village he left the pony in the valley where there was good grass. He went into the village and there he remained. When it was daylight he went to where his pony was. For several days they traveled behind the people, but soon the pony began to gain, so that now it had flesh. At this time the boy was quite large, so that when he entered the village many people called to him to do work for them. He never would go near the tipi of the chief any more.

On one of the journeys, as the boy was leading the pony along, the pony said to him: "My son, I have taken pity on you. I unjointed my ankle so that the owners would give me up. There is nothing wrong with my ankle. This evening when we get to the village, tie me close to the village and walk toward the village. Go straight to the tipi of the chief and there you may sit down at the entrance. If the girl tells you to go for water, you must go. If she tells you to get wood, you get it. From this night on this girl is to think about you and she shall not rest until you have married her. I know she hates you, but that hatred will now turn into love." When they came to the village the boy left the pony outside and walked into the village. As soon as he saw the chief's tipi he walked fast. He entered the tipi and sat down. The girl said: "You dirty, nasty thing. What brought you here? Go out of this tipi or I will hit you with this stick again." Her father said, "No, do not drive the boy away from this lodge." Then she said, "If he wants anything to eat let him go and get some water for me and I will then give him some meat."

The boy went down to the creek and brought up the water. When he entered the lodge he placed the bucket of water close to the fireplace. Then he came out and went away without receiving anything to eat from the girl. The girl began to look for the poor boy, for she had some meat for him, but she could not find him. She kept looking around for the boy until at last she went into the tipi and picked up her robe and went out. Then she went from one tipi to another hunting for the boy. The boy was not to be found in the village. Then she went to where his pony was tied. There she found him lying down near to the pony. She went up to him and shook him. The boy told the girl to go away, that he wanted to sleep. But the girl put her arms around the boy and said: "Poor boy, do you know that I have been thinking about you? I have gone around through the village thinking of you and I could not sleep. I have been thinking of you all this time. Make haste. Let us get away from this place, for the people will make fun of me for marrying you, but from this day on you shall be my husband." The boy said, "You must go and get your awl, sinew, bow and arrows, and knife." The girl said, "I can get them." She went into her tipi and brought out the things which the boy wanted. They went down into a ravine where the timber was thick, close to the village, and there they remained.

The next day the people hunted for the girl, but they could not find her. After four days the people gave her up and they noticed also that the poor boy was missing. Some people said, "That poor boy must have stolen the chief's daughter." Others made fun of him. In a few days, however, the enemy attacked the village. The boy was spoken to by the pony. It said to the boy, "Make haste; we must go and join in the battle." The boy took the quiver filled with arrows, put it over his shoulder, got on the pony, and went to the scene. The people were already fighting. When the people saw the poor boy coming on his poor horse they made fun of him. But when the poor boy saw an enemy in the center he rode right into the enemy, and as he rode up against the enemy the people thought that his horse had fallen and that he had got up and got on a horse belonging to the enemy. But this was a trick of the poor pony so that the people would not recognize it as the poor crippled pony. After the boy had counted coup, and it seemed as if he had taken a pony from the enemy, he returned to the village and then to the hollow. Some of the men said, "I wonder where that boy came from?" After the battle the poor boy disappeared. In a few days the enemy attacked the village again. This time the boy went up to the village. He had red clay all over his body. The clay had been given to him by the horse. He got upon the horse and entered the line of fighters. There he killed an enemy and took his horse. Then he rode back into the timber where his wife was. He gave the pony which he had taken from the enemy to his wife. The people wondered what had become of the poor boy.

A few days afterwards the village was again attacked by the enemy. This time when he went into the fight the people knew him. He killed another enemy, took his scalp, and went to his place. The fourth time when the enemy attacked the village the boy remained in the battle. Then the people knew that it was the poor boy who had done all the killing in the other fights.

After the fighting was over, and the people had had three or four days' rejoicing for killing the enemy, the old man who was the crier for the people went through the village and notified the people that the next day they were to break camp and leave. The next day as the people were breaking camp the poor boy and the girl came out from their hiding place and entered the village. The boy was all dressed in buckskins and so was his wife. When the people saw the poor boy with the daughter of the chief, the young man who tried to marry her thought that her mind was not right because she had married the poor boy. When the chief heard that his daughter was married to the poor boy he was glad of it, for he said, "This poor boy is a great warrior and he has shown it in battle." After all the poor boy married the girl who hated him.

18. THE CANNIBAL WITCH AND THE BOY WHO CONQUERED THE BUFFALO.[1]

There was a lonely tipi upon a prairie, and in it there lived an old woman who was known as the Witch-Woman. There lived with her a poor boy who had great powers. They had four powerful dogs. One of the dogs, which was large and bob-tailed, was named Afraid-of-Nothing. The woman wore a black skirt which was made from black buffalo-hide, and black moccasins. About her waist she wore a piece of black buffalo-hide. The boy wore black moccasins and buckskin leggings. The hair of the buckskin was not scraped off, so that the leggings had hair on the outside. He had no shirt, but always wore a buffalo-robe that was painted yellow. The boy had a black bow with white bowstring. The bow had only four arrows, and they were all black. The boy was a great hunter. He killed many deer and buffalo. Once in a while the Buffalo came close to their tipi, then would run away. The old woman often said: "Grandson, go and kill a man for me; I can not eat the kind of meat you eat, for it is very tough; I am hungry and want to eat something tender; the human meat is so much like liver that I like it." The boy would go far into another country, and when he came to a village of people he would hide and wait. When a man came his way the boy would kill the man, throw him upon his back, and then would run. The people often pursued the boy, and when they had nearly overtaken him he would take one of his arrows and shoot. As the arrow flew, the boy and his load would disappear, for he sat upon the point of the arrow, so that the arrow carried him and his load. The people would turn back and the boy would safely reach the tipi of the old Witch-Woman, and she would eat the human flesh.

The Buffalo were aware that the old woman was eating human flesh and they became angry. They held a council and the chief of the bulls, who had a white spot on his forehead, said: "Let us bring the young man here and kill him, so that the old woman will have to stop

[1] Told by Curly-Hair, Kitkehahki. The story recounts the deeds of a wonderful boy who lived with Witch-Woman and overcame the buffalo, whereby man thereafter lived upon buffalo and corn and the buffalo no longer ate human beings. The story is supposed to be true. It also explains the origin of the Pawnee, an agricultural people, on the one hand, and other tribes, such as the Cheyenne, Arapaho, etc., the nomadic buffalo-hunting, warlike tribes, on the other. The story is frequently told by grandmothers to their grandchildren, both boys and girls, during the winter nights. It secures their interest in wonderful events, and inspires the hope in them that they too may some day roam over the prairie and learn the wonderful powers of some animal, and ultimately become great medicine-men. The Chaui have a version of this tale not represented in this collection, in which the four dogs of this tale are represented by the wild-cat, bear, mountain-lion, and wolf, which it may be noted are the warriors of the Morning-Star and the representatives of the gods of the four world quarters.

eating people." The Buffalo all said, "Nawa." It was decided to send two young Buffalo cows to the boy's tipi to tell him that the Buffalo wanted him. While the Buffalo were sitting in council, planning how they could kill the boy, the boy sat on a high hill, and kept swaying his head from right to left, and as he swayed his head he listened. All at once he arose and said: "Someone wants me." He went down to the tipi and said: "Grandmother, I am going on a long journey; is there anything you want?" The old woman looked at the boy, and said: "Look, my grandson; here is only a small piece of human meat for me. Go and kill four men and bring them to me, so that I shall have plenty to eat, and in the night I will sleep in the midst of the dead men." The boy was glad. He started at once and went to a village, where he killed one man. He carried the dead man to old Witch's tipi without any trouble. He went back to the village and killed another man, but some of the people saw him and went after him; but they were too late, for the boy had disappeared and had taken the man to his tipi. His grandmother was glad, for now she had two men. The boy went again to the village, and this time he found it hard to kill anyone, but finally he succeeded in killing a young man. He ran, the people following him.

When the people came close to the boy he took his bow and shot. Again the people lost the boy. He went home and told his grandmother of his narrow escape; but his grandmother said: "My grandson, you have but one more to kill; you may be gone a long time, and I shall use up my best meat in the meantime." The boy took courage and went back to the village. The first man he saw he killed, threw him upon his back, and fled. The people ran after him, but whenever the boy ran over a hill he disappeared, and came up on another hill. The people were so close to the boy that they could see that he wore deerskin leggings and had a yellow robe over his body and they thought that he must be a deer. The young man reached his tipi and threw down the dead man. He was angry and said: "Grandmother, I do not see why you want to eat people; I feel sorry for those people;" but the old woman said: "Grandson, go and kill one more for your grandmother and she will be happy." The boy said: "No; now I can go on my long journey. Tie up the dogs, and, after I am gone, untie all of them except Afraid-of-Nothing. Keep him tied." The old woman tied up the dogs and the boy went off towards the west.

For many days he traveled, but during all of that time he never saw any game, so that he was very hungry. Just as he was about to climb a hill he saw two Buffalo coming up on the top of the hill. The boy hid until the Buffalo came close to his hiding place, then he rose up and shot one through the sides, so that it fell and died. The other ran away to a ravine close by. The boy went to the dead Buffalo and cut into its back in such manner that he cut out one of the kidneys and was about to eat it raw, when some one spoke to him. The voice came from behind him and said: "Son, I am sorry you cut her in that way. Put back what you have in your hand, and be sure to put it in its place, then walk away and do not look."

The boy turned around and there stood a woman. The woman had a new buffalo robe over her. Her hair was not plaited. The woman said: "That Buffalo and myself came after you, and now you have killed her. Walk away." The boy walked away. The woman turned to the Buffalo, fell down, and pushed the dead Buffalo around until the dead Buffalo moved and rose up. The woman who had spoken to the boy was a Buffalo, the mate of the other. As the two Buffalo circled, one staggering, the other pushing, the boy looked around and there were two Buffalo going around in a circle. The boy stood and watched. After the Buffalo that was killed walked away. the other came and said: "It is all right now; go to yonder hollow and wait and we will come, for we want to talk with you."

The boy went to the hollow and waited. The two Buffalo went to another hollow; there they rolled upon the ground and turned themselves into women. Then they went where the young man was, and the two women sat down beside him. When they had seated themselves one of the women said: "We understand that you have wonderful powers. When you go and kill people and the people pursue you, you do something and you get away from the people. Is this all true?" The boy said, "Yes, it is true." The women said, "Tell us what you do." The boy said: "I will tell you. You see my arrows? When I am running from anybody, I shoot one of these arrows, and at the same time I sit upon the flint point, so that the arrow carries me far away, and the people lose me." "How many times can you do this?" the women asked. The boy said, "Four times, for you see I have four arrows." "What do you do when you have shot your last arrow and the people are still after you." "Well," said the boy, "I keep on until they are about to overtake me; then I throw this bow upon the ground, and I get away from them by traveling upon the bow, and when the bow stops, I stop." "How would they find you then?" "I hide in a fine meadow, where there is thick grass, and if they were to cut all the grass I should be in the center." "Now," said the women, "when they find you, then what?" "O," said the boy, "I run to a pond and hide there. If the people should throw the water out of the pond I would be in a mud hole, and there I would be killed." The women were satisfied. Then the two women and the boy arose and started to journey westward. When they were upon the prairie, the two girls said: "Young man, we came after you; will you go with us; will you keep up with us?" The young man said, "I will try." "Well," said the girls, "suppose we walk fast; can you keep up with us?" "Yes," said the boy, "I can." "If we trot, can you keep up with us?" "Yes," said the boy, "I can keep up with you." "If we run very fast will you keep up with us?" "Yes," said the boy, "I will keep up with you." The girls were satisfied, and said, "We will now set out for our country."

The girls started, the boy following. When they went out from the ravine, the boy saw that they were again Buffalo. He followed and finally ran and caught up with the Buffalo. One of them said, "See yonder hills; let us try and get to them by noon." The boy said, "All right." The three ran, the boy keeping up with the Buffalo. The Buffalo then tried to leave him behind, but he staid with them. When they came to the hills, the Buffalo again said, "Let us get to yonder mountains that you see far away." The boy said, "All right." The three ran again as fast as they could until they came to the mountains. The two Buffalo were then willing to rest, but the boy said, "Go on." The boy touched the Buffalo and they all started off again. They ran through the valleys and over the mountains. About midnight they were on top of a mountain. There they stopped. The boy lay down to rest, then the two Buffalo turned into girls again, and the two girls came and lay by the boy. The girls again questioned the boy as to how, if the Buffalo should run after him, he could get away. The boy told all the secrets of his traveling upon the arrows and the bow. He said: "The black arrows that I have are all little blacksnakes, the bow is a large blacksnake; the bowstring is the backbone." "Well," said one of the girls, "suppose the Buffalo were to run after you; what would you do when you first shot the arrow and the Buffalo did not find you?" "I would keep on." "Then," said the girl, "if I were there, I would say, 'Keep on; you will find him; he is still going on.'" "Yes," said the boy, "you could say that each time." "When the arrows have all been shot," said the girl, "what would you do?" "I would throw the bow upon the ground and get upon the bow, and stay upon the bow until the bow stopped traveling, in a broad meadow filled with thick grass." "What would the Buffalo then do?" said the girl. "Well, then tell all the Buffalo to surround the grass and eat it. When the Buffalo have eaten the grass, then choose one bull, who will go to the bunch of grass and let it blow its breath; I shall then jump out and run to a pond." "What shall I say then?" said the girl. "Tell the Buffalo," said the boy, "to drink out of the pond until they come to a small hole where there will be water. I shall be there. Let one big Buffalo come and let him blow his breath. I shall then jump out and the Buffalo will kill me. That is all."

The girls were then satisfied. They told of a wonderful bull with a white spot on his forehead, who was the leader of all Buffalo. Then they all slept. As the dawn came in the east, they arose and began to run. They went over high mountains and through valleys and again over mountains. The Buffalo then said: "You will soon see clouds of dust. It marks the place where our people are." They came to a valley, and as they climbed up the hill they began to see clouds that they knew were not rain clouds, but clouds of dust. When they arrived at the top of the hill, the girls said: "You may stay here; we will go down to our people and tell them that you have come." The boy sat down on the hill and watched the two Buffalo go down the hill. He saw at a distance many tipis, as he thought, and at a distance he thought he saw many Buffalo playing with sticks. While the boy was watching all these things, he saw many Buffalo gather together where the two girls were, and they seemed to be talking with the girls.

While he sat there someone spoke to him and said, "My son, where do you come from, and who has brought you here?" The boy looked around and saw an old Buffalo standing by him. The boy then said, "Two women brought me here." "Yes," said the Buffalo, "I know, my son; the Buffalo wish to kill you. The Buffalo are angry with you, for you have been killing people, and your grandmother eats them instead of eating the Buffalo. I am chief of the Buffalo who come from where the sun sets. I know you have not eaten any people, so I will help you. Come to where my people are." The boy followed the old Buffalo down the side of the hill, and he took him to his tipi. The bull then said: "My son, the first thing you want to do is to rise early to-morrow morning, and go to the pond in front of the tipi of the Buffalo with the white spot on its forehead. There you must dive four times, then come out. If you let White-Spot-on-Forehead get into the pond first, then you must die; but I am to help you and I shall fight with you." Early the next morning, before daylight, the boy was down to the pond, and dived four times, then came out. As the sun was coming up in the east, White-Spot-on-Forehead came out and went down to the pond to swim. When the bull got to the pond and smelled, he stopped, snorted, and said, "I smell a man in the water; I shall not swim." White-Spot-on-Forehead Bull did not swim. Between morning and noon the Buffalo began to gather on all the open prairie. The boy and his followers were on one side, while on the other side were White-Spot-on-Forehead and his followers. There they stood for some time. The Buffalo on one side were herded by the boy and the old bull, while the Buffalo on the other side were herded by White-Spot-on-Forehead. The Buffalo came together on each side as if to try to hook one another. The boy watched all the time so that he could send one of his arrows through the side of White-Spot-on-Forehead, but they did not come together, but scattered. The boy and the old bull went home. As they entered the tipi, the old bull said: "My son, White-Spot-on-Forehead challenges you to smoke with him to-morrow. You and the bull will each smoke. When you take a big puff of smoke, try to send it up a high, dry cottonwood tree. If the bull sends his smoke higher than you do, then you will be killed, and my people will also be killed. If you beat White-Spot-on-Forehead, you will take your bow and arrows and kill him." The boy listened carefully and he thought of what he would do. He thought of running away, and again he thought he would stay and see how things would turn out with him among the Buffalo.

Early the next morning the Buffalo gathered around the dry cottonwood tree. White-Spot-on-Forehead appeared as a man. He brought a large-sized tobacco pouch and a large pipe. As the Buffalo gathered, White-Spot-on-Forehead said: "Nawa, you, boy, and I are to smoke and see who can send the smoke the highest up this dry tree. If your smoke goes higher than my smoke, then you are to kill me, but if my smoke goes higher than yours, then I am to kill you." "Nawa," said the boy. White-Spot-on-Forehead put all of his people on one side, and the old bull's people went on the boy's side. White-Spot-on-Forehead said with a loud voice, "I now cut tobacco." All on his side said, "Nawa." Again White-Spot-on-Forehead spoke and said, "The bowl will now receive a coal." "Nawa," all said on his side. "Now I inhale smoke." All on his side said, "Nawa." "Now I send smoke up the tree." All on his side said, "Nawa." The smoke was blown at the base of the cottonwood tree, and it began to roll up the tree. All on his side kept crying, "The smoke is going to reach the top." Those on the boy's side kept saying, "The smoke fails to reach the top of the tree." All watched the smoke roll up the tree, and as the smoke was about to reach the fork of the tree it scattered.

It was the boy's turn. He took the pouch and pipe, cut the tobacco and said, "I now cut and mix tobacco with sumach leaves." All on his side said, "Nawa." Then the boy filled the bowl of the pipe and said, "I now fill the pipe." All on his side said, "Nawa." "I inhale smoke," said the boy. All on his side said, "Nawa." "Now I start the smoke," said the boy. All on his side said, "Nawa." The boy blew the smoke at the base of the tree, and as the smoke began to roll up the tree, the yelling and hallooing began.   White-Spot-on-Fore-head yelled, "The smoke will not reach the top."   The smoke rolled up the tree, went over the fork, and came down on the other side of the tree, and as the smoke scattered at the base of the tree, the boy's people made a rush at the others.   The boy jumped at his bow and arrows, and was about to shoot at White-Spot-on-Forehead, when the bull said: "Not yet, give me another chance; to-morrow we drink out of the pond, and whoever fails to drink all the water out of the pond shall be killed." The boy said, "All right."   When the boy went home the old bull said: "I will help you; White-Spot-on-Forehead will drink first, and he will drink all the water in the pond; then he will blow the water all back in the pond.   Take these horns I give you.   When your turn comes, you must put your arms into the water, holding a horn in each hand.   These horns will suck up most of the water, so you will not be obliged to drink too much water."   The next morning the Buffalo came together around the pond.   White-Spot-on-Forehead was the first to drink from the pond.   He drank all the water, leaving only mud-water.   The Buffalo threw up the water, and the pond was filled again.   There was great rejoicing on his side.   The boy went to the pond with the buffalo horns, one in each hand.   He knelt down on his knees and put his arms into the water.   His hands touched the bottom of the pond.   The boy seemed to drink the water, but the horns sucked up most of it.   The boy seemed to drink all of the water, for the pond was made dry.   There was now great rejoicing on the boy's side.   As soon as the boy had thrown up all the water, he jumped back, took his bow and arrows and tried to kill White-Spot-on-Forehead.   White-Spot-on-Forehead begged for another chance, and said: "To-morrow we select runners from our sides, and there will be a race."   The boy agreed.

Seven runners were selected on each side; three were short-distance runners and four were long-distance runners.   The old bull selected six Buffalo on his side, and the boy made the seventh.   These Buffalo went north for a long distance to the starting place.   They went over several hills until the Buffalo could not see the racers.   For a long time the Buffalo watched, and all at once a great shout was heard.   All the Buffalo looked, and there were the runners coming over a hill.   When the runners came over the second hill, White-Spot-on-Forehead's side gave a great shout, saying, "All our runners are in the lead."   This was true, for all of the boy's partners were behind, and the boy was the last to come over the hill.   The boy had on his yellow robe and also wore his buckskin leggings.   As the running Buffalo came to a long stretch of valley the boy lifted his robe over his shoulders, and then took the bowstring off from his bow. With the bowstring he whipped his legs, so that he could run fast. As he caught up with one of his Buffalo partners, he whipped the Buffalo's legs and the Buffalo was made to run fast. The boy kept whipping his legs until he reached another one of the Buffalo; then he would whip his legs. The boy caught up with all of his partners, and made them run fast by whipping their legs. The boy was now in the lead of all his partners, and they were running well. After a short time they passed the others, and were in the lead. White-Spot-on-Forehead's people were walking around, throwing dirt upon their backs with their hoofs and looking fierce, for they were ready to fight. Some of the bulls were locking horns as if beginning battle. Then they would stop and watch the hills. As the runners came up over the second hill a boy appeared, and not a Buffalo. This time there was great rejoicing on the boy's side. All of the boy's partners came over the hill first; then the others began to appear. As the boy came to the foot of the next hill he stopped, pulled out his bow, put his string on it, and as all of his partners came up to him he would tell them to stand by him. As the other Buffalo came up and tried to pass the boy, he would shoot an arrow through their sides and in that way he killed all of them. Then the boy and the Buffalo went over the last hill, and there the Buffalo were fighting. The boy ran among them and killed many. On his way through the herd of fighting Buffalo he came to where the old bull was fighting a young bull. The boy killed the young bull. White-Spot-on-Forehead's people were furiously enraged. The bulls began to hook one another. The boy's side were few in number and were overpowered.

The Buffalo started out after the boy. He ran fast, for his deer leggings gave him great speed. The deer's power gave out. Then the boy took his bow and one of the arrows and shot the arrow far away. He disappeared. The Buffalo stopped and hunted the boy, but could not find him. Someone said: "Where are the two female Buffalo who went after him?" Another answered, "They are coming behind." The Buffalo waited until the two girls came up. One of the Buffalo said: "What did he say he would do if we got after him?" One of the girls said: "Proceed; he is still going on ahead." The Buffalo again started and saw the boy far ahead. The Buffalo ran after him and when they were nearly up to him, the boy again shot an arrow and again disappeared. The Buffalo stopped and waited for the two Buffalo girls and asked them, "What did the boy say he would do?" They said, "Proceed; he is going on ahead." The Buffalo ran and again saw the boy.

They ran fast, but just as they came close to the boy, he shot one of his arrows and disappeared again. The Buffalo said to the Buffalo girls "What did the boy say?" Both girls said: "Proceed; he must be going on ahead." The Buffalo went on. Again the Buffalo saw the boy, and as they again came upon him he shot his last arrow and disappeared. The Buffalo girls came up and said, "Proceed; he is on ahead." The Buffalo went on farther and came close to the boy. The boy took his bow and threw it upon the ground and stood upon it. The bow turned into a blacksnake, which ran swiftly.

Again the Buffalo lost sight of the boy and said: "Girls, where will the boy be?" The girls said: "Keep straight on until you come to a fine meadow, where there is grass." The Buffalo ran until they came to a meadow, and the girls said, "Stop here." The Buffalo stopped. The girls said: "Surround the meadow, and let every one of us eat this grass, so that there will be only a bunch of grass left standing." The Buffalo all began to eat of the grass and came nearer the center as they ate. When they had eaten all but a little bunch of grass in the center, the girls said: "Now choose one bull who has a strong breath and let him blow his breath upon the bunch of grass, and the boy will come out from the grass." One bull was chosen and he went to the bunch of grass and blew his breath, and the boy jumped out from the grass, but disappeared at once. The Buffalo tramped and hooked at one another, until they saw that the boy was not there. Then they said: "Where will the boy be now, girls?" The girls said: "Go to the pond, and you will find him there." All the Buffalo went to the pond and the two girls said: "Now let all drink until the water is gone, for the boy is in the pond." All the Buffalo went into the pond and began to drink. They drank so much that nearly all the water was gone. The turtles came crawling up and fish lay upon the mud. There in the center was a mud-hole. The Buffalo chose another bull with strong breath. As he blew his breath the boy jumped and came upon the dry land. The Buffalo closed in upon him and again the boy disappeared. "What now?" said the Buffalo. The girls said: "We have killed him, for he has now used up all of his power."

The Buffalo went into the timber and sat under the shade of the trees. The boy was up in a tree. He was kept up the tree so long that he wanted to urinate. He was afraid that if he should get down from the tree the Buffalo would take after him, so he gathered up his robe and urinated in the robe. The boy held the water in the robe until it began to seep through, so that drops fell upon the head of a bull that was sitting under the boy. The drops kept falling and the bull looked up towards the heavens and said, "We killed a wonderful boy, and that is the reason raindrops are falling on my head. I do not see any clouds; this boy must have been a wonderful boy." While the bull was talking to himself the water had made a hole through the robe, so that it poured down on the head of the bull. The bull looked up and there was the boy sitting up in the tree. The bull rose, and grunted, as much as to say, "Here is the boy." Every one of the Buffalo rose and gathered around the tree. The Buffalo saw the boy and said: "We must get him this time, so that he will never kill any more men for food; but will kill our people. What shall we do to get the boy down?" One of them said: "Let us select five great bulls to run against the tree, and the tree will fall down and we will get the boy." Five large bulls were selected, who ran against the tree, and two fell dead at the bottom of the tree. Then the Buffalo said: "This will not do." One of the Buffalo said: "Let us hook at the ground with our horns and dig up the roots." They tried this plan, but their horns were broken off, so they gave it up. One of them said: "Let us hook the tree and take out piece by piece until we can get it down." One bull ran up and hooked the tree with his horn, so that the bark of the tree fell off. The others tried, and the bark came off easily. They kept on hooking and some of the Buffalo broke their horns, but they kept on until the tree became small at the base and began to quiver.

The boy became frightened and gave a loud yell. Again he gave a loud yell; then he waited. When he gave the yell the dogs at home began to run about, but they did not seem to know where the voice of the boy came from. The old woman, the boy's grandmother, also stood up and ran around. She finally went up to the bob-tailed dog and released it, and said, "Afraid-of-Nothing, your brother is in danger; lead us to where he is." The dog gave a loud yelp and ran west, the other dogs following, the old woman close behind them with a club. The dogs reached the Buffalo herd and the Buffalo felt them upon their heels, so that they began to run. Sometimes the dogs would bite their legs, so that they fell. The old woman, when she came up to them, hit the Buffalo with her club, and she killed many. As they ran past the tree, it fell down easily, so that the boy was not hurt.

When the Buffalo had all gone away the boy said: "Grandmother, cut up some of these Buffalo, so that we can get something to eat; and you, my grandmother, must eat this kind of meat and do not eat people any more." The old woman cut up some of the Buffalo and roasted the livers for herself. She said: "Grandson, this tastes like man's flesh. Hereafter, old women of my age shall eat liver, for it is soft and good." "Now, grandmother," said the boy, "we must go home, for there we must separate." The boy took his grandmother home. When they reached home the boy said: "Grandmother, you must go north;

take this sack with seeds in it and this hoe, made from the shoulder-blade of a buffalo. You shall plant these seeds, and whatever you raise in the fall always eat that. The dogs I turn loose; they may go where they wish. I will put on my leggings, moccasins, robe, and this lariat rope, made from buffalo hair, and I will go to the land of the Sun. From this time forth I shall be known as a great warrior." The old woman put her sack upon her back and went north. The boy, after putting his clothes on, put the lariat rope around his shoulders and went south.

In the meantime the Buffalo sat down in a valley and had a great council. "The people will live and they will kill many Buffalo and eat of our meat. White-Star-on-Forehead, who is our chief, shall make his home in the north and shall stay there. Henceforth we shall scatter all over the country. In all things we were beaten by the boy. In smoking the boy beat us; so the people will do the smoking, and they will send us only whiffs of smoke. In drinking of the water from the pond, the boy was given horns to help him drink the water; so from this time the people shall make spoons from our horns, and eat with them. In the running of the race the boy beat us; so that the people will always beat us in running and will kill us; and when the people are hungry we will seek fresh grass, so that they can find us. On hot days we will seek ponds to drink from, that the people may find us and kill us, so they can eat meat. When the people have multiplied, they will take pieces of buffalo robes and cut them up for the babies to lie on, so that the children will urinate upon our robes." Thus by the boy overcoming the Buffalo the people were to kill Buffalo. White-Star-on-Forehead was killed; so were the Buffalo girls. They were given a place in the north, where the three were to stand as gods and to send buffalo to the people. The old woman went north. Her descendants all had seeds, while the boy's descendants became warriors and never planted any seeds in the ground.

19. THE WARRIOR AND THE BLACK LIGHTNING ARROW.[1]

Many years ago several young men went on the war-path. They went into the western country, and for many moons they traveled until at last they became weary and discouraged, for they had gone to a mountainous country and there was no game or fruit to eat. They began to find fault with the leader of the war party, and to blame him for their misfortunes. At last he told them that if they would stay in

[1] Told by Sun-Chief, a young chief of the Pawnee whose father was a prominent chief of the Skidi band. The story describes the origin of a warrior bundle, the chief part of which was a wonderful, so-called, black lightning arrow. The story especially teaches obedience to the heavenly gods.

the valley he would go up on a high hill, and would pray to the gods to give him power and to help him to be successful in finding the villages of the enemy.   The other young men promised to stay in the valley while he went up onto the hill, and so he started.   His absence gave the warriors a chance to hunt through the ravines and upon the mountains, and they were successful.   They killed game and brought it into their camp.   In the meantime the leader of the war party was upon the high hill praying.   He went up on the high hill in the afternoon, and he stood there until dark, offering his prayers to the different gods in the heavens.   When night came he ceased praying and began to cry.   For three days and three nights he stood crying and asking help from the gods in the heavens.   The fourth night he noticed a dark cloud coming up from the west.   Then he cried louder.   After a while the cloud passed all over the sky and darkness overspread the earth.   The young man faced the west.   He had his robe over his shoulders, tied around his waist with a buffalo-hair lariat rope.   As he stood thus the lightning flashed and then it thundered, and as it thundered the boy fell over and knew no more.

In the morning he awoke, as he thought, from a deep sleep.   He found upon his breast a little black arrow about six inches long, with a point of the finest flint and shaft of black stone, and the end of stone so fine that it looked like feathers.   The young man knew that Lightning had given him this arrow, to let him know that he was to be successful in all his undertakings while upon the war-path.   The boy took the arrow and hid it under his robe and went down the hill.

The other warriors saw him coming and they were glad.   They seated him by the fire, gave him water that they had brought up in a buffalo bladder, washed him, and gave him some meat to eat.   After he had eaten he told the warriors that he had received something from Lightning, the wonderful god.   After he had eaten he sat down to the west of the fireplace and placed the arrow in front of him, then asked for a pipe and some native tobacco.   When he received the tobacco he arose, lighted the pipe, and began to smoke.   He stood west of the fireplace, and blew one whiff straight up to the sky, then four to the west, at the same time thanking the gods in the west for the arrow that they had given him. After thanking the gods he walked up to the arrow and gave it four whiffs, saying: "My brother, you came to me from the gods and I am thankful that you are with me.   I shall always carry you upon my body. If I neglect to care for you, then you may return to the gods."   When he had finished he dumped the ashes out in front of the arrow and waved his hands over the arrow four times.   Then he sat down.   He took a piece of the buffalo lariat rope and tied it upon the arrow, and then he placed the arrow upon his breast and tied the rope behind his neck so that the arrow hung from it upon his breast.

The young men then started again upon their journey, and traveled west until the night overtook them; then they made camp. The leader of the war party, the man with the arrow about his neck, had a dream during the night. He saw a man. The man had a buffalo robe around him and upon his face were streaks of white clay. Upon his legs were leggings with scalps hanging from the sides and also eagle feathers. This being told the young man that he was the god of all the warriors, and that he had given him the arrow so that he should always keep it with him, for it would bring him success. He also told the young man to go to the south side of the mountains and there he would find the villages of the, enemies. The next morning after they had eaten he told the warriors that they were to travel towards the south. They traveled south but a few days when they came to a village of Comanches. The young man then selected scouts to look over the ground and see where their ponies were placed. In the night the scouts returned and told their leader where the ponies were. Other men were then selected to go and capture the ponies. The men brought in many ponies, and the leader told all the warriors to get on the ponies at once and make a run for home.

It was night and they had only the north star to guide them, but they got out of the enemy's country safely. They traveled for many days and nights, and at last when they came into their own country they stopped and rested. The next day the leader of the party went up to one pony, cut some hair from the mane and tail, and strung it on a pole. This pole he placed on a high hill, and while he was on the hill he said to the god who gave him this arrow, "I am making you this offering of horse hair." He placed the stick in the ground and went down to the camp. The ponies were then divided among the warriors, and they went to their village singing their war-songs and giving the war-whoops. The people in the village arose and went out to meet the warriors. They told all that they had done, and of the wonderful arrow that the gods had given to the young leader.

The people waited a long time to see what the young man would do. They were anxious to see the wonderful arrow. At last it was told through the village that the young man with the wonderful arrow was about to go out upon the war-path. Many people went, even the old people, for they were anxious to see the arrow. When they had been gone three days and three nights from the village they made their camp somewhere upon the Platte River.   Then the leader was told by his scouts that there were some buffalo at a short distance from them. The leader, instead of sending others to kill the buffalo, said, "I will go and shoot, and if I kill the buffalo you people must come and skin and cut the meat."   He took the arrow from his neck and placed it in another man's hands.   As he went he thought of his arrow.   The buffalo were west, so that the young man looked towards the west always as he went to kill the buffalo.   As he raised up to aim at a buffalo he saw a dark cloud coming from the west.   He shot at the buffalo, threw down his bow, and ran to the place where the other warriors were, and when the warriors saw him coming they were frightened.   They thought that he had seen enemies, but when he called for the arrow they knew that something was wrong.   As soon as he took the arrow he told the people to get on top of him and to try to help him to keep the arrow.   The people drew around him and climbed on top of him as the dark cloud came rapidly from the west.   The lightning struck all around where the people were, and there was a great noise of wind coming through the air like the flapping of many large wings.   The man with the arrow at the bottom of the crowd called to the others: "Press down hard on me; the arrow is slipping from me."   The people began to pile closer on top of him, but somehow they rolled off, and as they rolled they pulled the man with the arrow over, and the arrow slipped through his hands.   It went back into the clouds and became a part of Lightning again.

The young man cried and mourned on account of the loss of the arrow. He stood for many days and at last he went to sleep.   The same man whom he had seen in his dream before, he saw in his dream again.   This man said: "I intended to make you a great warrior.   I did not make you promise me, but you made the promise yourself, and said that the arrow should always be present with you.   You broke your promise. The gods have taken the arrow back, but they will make you a great warrior anyway; but you will never become a chief.   Go.   Your party shall be successful.   You shall capture many ponies."   When the young man awoke he told the people that they were to continue on the war-path.   They went, and in a few days they found a village of enemies and there they captured many ponies.   After the young man lost his arrow he went upon the war-path only when the strange being appeared to him in a dream and told him that he would be successful.   If the being told him that a party would not be successful, he would always tell the men and persuade them not to go.   He became a great warrior, but not as great as he would have been if he had kept the arrow.   He was never made chief.

20. SPOTTED-HORSE; A BRAVE AND A CHIEF.[1]

A long time ago, when the Skidi had their village upon the Loupe River in Nebraska, a Skidi had a wonderful dream. He saw a man in his dream. The man had a robe over his body and the robe was turned out so that the man could see the drawings upon it. The robe had drawings of spotted ponies. The man also had around his shoulders a buffalo lariat rope. In his arms he carried a small bundle. This man spoke to the Skidi man and said: "Go and stand upon that high hill four days and four nights, and these things that I have here will be explained to you." The next day the man went upon the hill and mourned for four days, and on the fourth night the being appeared to the man in another dream and said to him that he had done as he told him to do, and said: "I give you this." It was a round thing which looked like a sun-glass. The being said: "Use this when you light your pipe, just before attacking the enemy. I will teach you how to make the pipe. The bowl must be of blue stone. The stem must be about seven inches long and is to have no hole through it. You must kill a certain animal that you will find in the southern country. Place these things in a bundle and call it holy-bundle, and carry this bundle whenever you go on the war-path." This man went home and a few days afterwards he found a blue stone and made the bowl for the pipe. This bowl was very small. He took a limb of ash and made a stem, not putting any hole through the stem. In his wanderings he found the thing that looked like a sun-glass. The man knew that this must be what the being told him he would find, and that he must light his pipe with it. He went on the war-path, and while he was gone he wandered away from the others and he found the animal that the being showed him in the dream. The animal was sitting upon a limb sleeping. The man took his bow and an arrow and shot the animal and killed it. He skinned it and carried it around while on the war-path. When they stopped for rest the man would pick up stones and rub upon the skin, so that it became tanned and soft.

When this man returned home he invited a few of his friends and told them of what he saw upon the hill. He told his friends that now he

[1] Told by Good-Chief, who at the time of his death last year was the oldest chief of the Skidi. His father, in turn, was in his time hereditary head chief of the Skidi and was the keeper of the chief's bundle. This tale is traditional history and is explanatory of the warrior's bundle, the most interesting feature of which was a small pipe with a holeless stem. When near the village of the enemy the owner held the filled pipe towards the sun, and attempted to smoke it. If successful it was an omen from the gods that he was to be victorious. If he did not succeed in smoking it the war party returned to their homes. The bundle differs from the ordinary warrior's bundle and is supposed to have had its origin from the sun.

had the things which were shown him in the dream, and that he wanted to try what he was told to do. The skin was spread, and the things were spread upon the skin. The skin was like that of a wild-cat, only the tail was long, and there were many horse-hoof prints upon the hide. The man filled up the pipe and went to where the ray from the sun was. He sat down and rested the sun-glass upon the bowl. He puffed with his mouth and the smoke was seen going up from the bowl, then through the stem, though there was no hole in the stem. "Nawa! Nawa iri!"(thanks! thanks!) the men said. After emptying the pipe, he wrapped up the bundle, putting some native tobacco in with the other things. A few days after this he invited some of his friends to come to his lodge. The men came to his lodge and they sat down with him. The owner of the bundle spoke and said: "My friends, some time ago, here in my lodge, I had a wonderful dream, and in the dream I saw a mysterious being. This mysterious being commanded me to stand upon the hill in the west; so the next morning I went up on the hill and stood there for several days. When I became hungry I saw the same being again, and it commanded me to do certain things and to find certain things. I also saw the being smoke a little pipe, which was lighted by the aid of the sun. I have found the things; here they are. I have tried the smoke after lighting it from the sun and am sure of being successful if I go out with a war party."

One by one, each man arose and stood before the owner of the bundle. "Nawa! Nawa iri! Take pity on us and allow us to join you, that the being who has taken pity upon you may also take pity upon us, for we are poor." The owner of the things spoke as each man passed his hands over his head and arms, and said: "My friends, I take pity upon you; but it is not I; it is these things before me, although they are dead, and the Sun who must help you." It was agreed to go on the war-path. The owner was the leader and carried the bundle. When they started the owner of the bundle went over on the east side of the main body of men. They made camp and the owner of the bundle came in from the east. In his journeys he went on the east side, so that people would not get in his way.

The man became a great warrior; he had many fine ponies, and with these ponies he killed many buffalo and took the meat to the priests' lodge. The meat was made holy and was jerked and dried. This man became a chief. He had no children and so he turned his bundle over to his wife when he died. She kept the bundle until a certain boy grew up who was related to the former owner of the bundle. The boy was taught how to carry the bundle and when to open it; and he was told to always walk all day on the east side of the company, and if anyone passed in front of him to turn back and go home.   As this boy became a man he took his bundle and went on the war-path with some other men, and was successful.   He changed his name from Yellow-Bird to Proud-Fox, for he was very proud because he had been successful in capturing ponies the first time.   He stayed at home but a short time, then went out again with another party.   He captured more ponies and changed his name again to Spotted-Horse.   This name he kept until one time when he captured many more ponies.   Among these ponies was a fine spotted horse.   This spotted horse seemed to be the chief of ponies.   He changed his name to Spotted-Horse-Chief.   While Spotted-Horse-Chief had that name men looked upon him as a great warrior.   Soon after he came back with many ponies, another party of warriors from the Sioux country came and captured many ponies from the Pawnee.   Spotted-Horse-Chief sat in his lodge and invited only a few of his friends.   He told them that he intended to go on the war-path; that he was going to try to get the ponies back.   The other men said that they would go with him.

The company started out very early in the morning.   When they had gone far from the village, they stopped to rest.   Scouts were on the hills, and they kept making signs to the company that some more men were coming.   The men arrived and joined the others.   They came to the Platte River and the ice had broken so that large cakes were floating down the river.   The leader with the bundle stopped on the east side of the company, and said, "Come, follow me, men!"   With all his clothing on he started to wade the river.   As he went where the current was swift he had to push away the cakes of ice that were coming down the river.   He crossed the river and stood upon the bank.   All of his followers were where he had left them, although he had commanded them to follow him.   He thought to himself: "Well, I wanted to come on the war-path alone; those men followed me; and there they are afraid to cross the river."   He then sang a warrior Coyote song.   When the men heard Spotted-Horse-Chief sing, they said: "It is true.   Spotted-Horse-Chief sat in his lodge planning to go out; we heard of it; our sisters and aunts fixed our moccasins, with pemmican and corn; we crawled up to his lodge and waited until he started out; then we followed Spotted-Horse-Chief. He did not ask us to follow him; now he asks us to follow him through this river.   He has crossed the river; he is a brave man; let us cross and follow him through the enemy's country."   The men all waded through the river, although the water was cold.   Cakes of ice were floating down the stream, but the men did not mind them.   They crossed the river and stood on the bank where Spotted-Horse-Chief had kindled a fire, so that the men might warm themselves. Spotted-Horse-Chief and the men then started on their journey south, all of the men going on the west side of Spotted-Horse-Chief. One day scouts came back and said: "Enemy's camp in sight; squat down!" The men obeyed. One man was sent to notify Spotted-Horse-Chief. He overtook him and waved a blanket at him. Spotted-Horse-Chief came to the company. He sat on the south side. He untied his bundle. He took the pipe, filled it with native tobacco, and took out the sun-glass. The men all looked at him. It was cloudy, but the sun came out as if to say: "I will come out and light your pipe." The sun came out and the smoke came out through the stem. The sun disappeared. Spotted-Horse-Chief then sang a victory song; he then stood up and spoke to his warriors: "My men, the gods in the heavens have looked upon us with favor; even the sun has blown his hot breath upon the bowl of my pipe; the winds helped me to draw my breath; the smoke passed through the stem without a hole. Think of the many warriors who have had success upon these prairies. The gods helped them and they will help us and guide us to success; we will get many ponies. Our names must be changed; you said the enemy saw us, but the gods will blind them; they will not see us. Each one of you now take your rawhide lariat rope, stretch it out, so that the gods will know that we have accepted what they have put in our way." Every man stretched his lariat rope in front of him on the ground. In the afternoon Spotted-Horse-Chief sent scouts to the village of the enemy. The scouts came back and reported that there was no stir in camp and that the enemy were driving their herds of ponies away from camp. After night Spotted-Horse-Chief selected men to go and capture ponies for him. These men went to the camp, found no ponies; then they went east of the village and found many ponies along a stream of water. These men drove all the ponies to where Spotted-Horse-Chief was and gave them all to him. Spotted-Horse-Chief commanded the warriors each to lariat a pony and drive them as fast as they could. They traveled four days and four nights without stopping to rest. When they did stop the men fainted and were sore, for they rode without saddles. Many ponies were captured and all the young men received new names and ponies.

After that whenever Spotted-Horse-Chief sat down to organize a war party many young men joined him. Spotted-Horse Chief in a battle with the Sioux was wounded and, although the men of the Buffalo Society doctored him, he died. The bundle, pipe, sun-glass, and skin were left with an old woman. This woman died at Pawnee Agency, Oklahoma, in 1879, and all these things were buried with her.

21. THE BOY WHO WAS GIVEN POWER TO CALL THE BUFFALO.

(See Abstracts.)

[Told by Thief, a Kitkehahki. The interest in this tale is chiefly in the lesson which it is supposed to convey, viz, that the gods of the heavens watch over the pregnant woman and protect the new-born child from harm and disease. The relating in the tale of the deeds of the young man who delivers his people from hunger, overcomes the enemy, and slays the monsters, furnishes of course the characteristic features of a hero tale. The connection of this story with the bundle is through the fact that the north wind, who assisted him in his search for food, ultimately gave him a bundle, and it is believed that through the rites enacted during the performance of the bundle ceremony the gods are moved to render similar assistance. Two additional versions of the tale are presented in Nos. 22 and 23.]

22. THE SON OF WIND, READY-TO-GIVE.[1]

The people were preparing to leave their permanent village and go on a buffalo hunt. While the women were putting their corn and squash into the cache holes and stopping them up, they saw that one of the most beautiful young girls of the village, who was helping them, was pregnant. She had kept her secret to herself for a long time, though she could not understand it, for she knew that she had not been with any man. When it was known, her uncles scolded her and tried to make her tell what man she had been with, but the girl would not say anything. Her father scolded her and drove her and her mother and the grandmother out of the lodge, saying that he would have nothing more to do with womankind. It was noised through the village that these people were outcasts and that nobody should have anything to do with them.

The people started upon their buffalo hunt, leaving these three women alone in the deserted village. They put up a grass-lodge to live in, and then went to several cache holes and opened them up and took corn and squash. After a few months the girl gave birth to a male child. The day that the child was born there was a great wind from the north. When the women found out that the child was a boy they were very thankful. The child grew fast and it was not long until he could walk. Then his grandmother made him a little bow and some arrows. As he grew older the grandmother made a larger bow and arrows. One day the little boy went into the timber, and while he was there a voice spoke to him and said: "My son, I am glad to see you. I am your father. From this

[1] Told by Yellow-Bird, the Chaui leader of the Buffalo Society, who died in 1904. This is the Chaui version of tale No. 21, and this tale, it is said, was told on former occasions during the performance of a Chaui bundle ceremony.

day on you must come to the timber and I will bring you something to eat. Take this bird home and roast it." The boy took the bird home and gave it to his grandmother. She roasted it and told him that he should eat only the head of the bird, and then he would have luck to kill many more birds. The body of the bird the grandmother ate.

The next day the boy went back to the timber and soon he heard a voice speaking to him. He looked about, but could see no one, but could hear these words: "My son, I am glad that you came. Take this rabbit home and let your grandmother cook it." A rabbit fell in front of him and he picked it up and took it home. The women did not question the boy as to how he got the rabbit, for they supposed that he was old enough to kill it with his arrows. They were thankful for the rabbit, for they had lived only on corn for so long that they were hungry for meat. They cooked the rabbit and ate it.

The next day the boy went back to the timber. He heard the voice speak to him again. It said, "My son, take this home and let your people cook it." A young fawn fell before him. He took it home and the women were glad, for they thought that the boy had killed it. Every day the boy went to the timber and each time he carried home larger game, until at last a buffalo was placed before him and he had to go and get the women to help him skin the buffalo and carry it home.

When the boy went back into the timber the next day the voice spoke to him and said: "Come with me." As soon as he said "Come with me," the boy looked and there stood a man. The man was painted with red ointment and had a buffalo robe over his shoulders. His leggings were of antelope skin, but the moccasins were made of buffalo hide with the hair inside. Over his shoulder was an otter-skin quiver and he carried an ash bow. The man took the boy far into the timber to a soft sandy place, and there began to tramp upon the soft ground. Then he said: "My son, remove some of the dirt where I have been stamping." The little boy began to dig into the earth with his hands, and there he found a rat's nest, and as he dug deeper into the ground he came to a rat's hole and there he found a big pile of ground beans. The boy gathered the beans up in his robe and took them to the women, and when they saw the beans they wondered how the boy could have found them, for they had been to the timber many times trying to find these beans, but were never successful.

The next day the boy went back to the timber. He saw the man again and went with him. When they came to a soft place in the ground the man told the boy to dig. The boy began to dig and he found many artichokes. He dug them up, placed them in his robe, and went home and gave them to the women. They were surprised, for they had tried many times, but could never find any artichokes. The next day the boy went back into the timber. The man spoke and said: "My son, I give you these leggings. I also give you these moccasins, and this robe that I have on. I also give you this quiver filled with arrows and the bow. From this day on you must kill your own animals for meat. You must go and tell the women where to dig these artichokes and beans. In the spring I shall return and shall teach the women how to plant the corn, squash, and beans. My son, I am your father. I am one of the gods and I stand in the north. My name is Ready-to-Give. When the people are hungry for buffalo, I blow my breath upon the land. My breath drives the buffalo to the people, and they slaughter many. The people made me angry, for they made you an outcast, my son, and so I have driven all the buffalo and game out of the country where they are traveling. The game and the buffalo will circle around and will come into this country. The people will roam over the plains for many years, and then they will think of you. They will think of your mother and the other women. They will wonder if you are still living. The people will be coming to open up their caches to get something to eat, for I shall make them hungry. Go to your mother and tell your mother that you have seen your father; that your father is the Wind which blows from the north, Ready-to-Give." The boy gathered up his things and went to the grass-lodge. When he entered the lodge he gave his things to his mother and said: "Mother, put these things away. I have seen my father. My father says his name is Wind, Ready-to-Give. It was he who was with you. The Wind touched you and you did not know it. He has gone, but he has promised to come back to help me kill buffalo and game, and in the spring he is to come back again to teach us how to put our seeds into the ground."

The women were astonished at the talk of the boy. When they wanted meat they told the boy to take his bow and arrows that he had received from his father and go out to the timber and kill some game. Whenever the boy went out a long way from home his father would meet him, and they would go together until they came to a buffalo herd. The boy would walk right in among the herd and would kill a buffalo, then the father and his son would skin the buffalo and cut up the meat, then they would carry the meat to the boy's home. After a while Ready-to-Give entered the lodge. The women knew him, and the mother of the boy gave him a seat close by. When Ready-to-Give spoke to the women, he said: "I shall be gone. I know where the people are. They are starving, but it is their fault. They made you people outcasts because this woman brought my child into the world. They will be coming back soon and they will bless my boy. They will pray to him and beg him for something to eat. My boy shall rule the people and he shall call the buffalo whenever the buffalo are not to be found, by saying: 'Ready-to-Give, blow your breath upon the land that it may touch the buffalo and make them to come to our village.' My son is now old enough to kill game. I shall have to go, as it is now winter and I shall have to stand in my place in the north, for it is my time to send food to people. You know where to go and dig artichokes and beans. The boy will not have to go very far to kill buffalo. I am gone." There was a noise of wind in the lodge, and there was a little dust from the ground which went up to the opening on the top of the lodge and with it the man disappeared.

After that the boy went to the timber, and sometimes beyond the timber, to hunt. Every day the boy killed three or four buffalo and sometimes three or four deer, so that the women had all they could do to tan the buffalo and deer hides, and to jerk and dry the meat. They made parfleches from the buffalo hides and in them they put the dried meat. When the women had many buffalo hides they agreed that they should make a tipi, for the grass-house was getting old and was not fit to live in. They scraped the hair from the hides, and made a fine large tipi. Then they made beautiful buckskin dresses.

In the spring while the boy was out hunting he met Ready-to-Give. They went home together. Ready-to-Give told the women that they should go into the bottom lands and clean them up; that he had brought corn and squash seeds and beans for them; that they must put them into the ground. He gave the white corn to his wife to plant, and the yellow corn he gave to her mother; the red corn and squash seeds he gave to his wife's sister, and the dark corn and the beans to the old woman. Then Ready-to-Give sat down and talked to the boy. He told the boy that he must make a bundle. He said: "You must carry home fire sticks and place them in the bundle. Then you must take some flint and place it in the bundle. When you have gathered the white corn you must place some in the bundle, for the white corn you shall always call 'Mother.' Then you must place a hawk skin in the bundle, for the hawk represents a great warrior. Next, you must gather some sweet grass, braid it, and put several strings into the bundle. This bundle shall be known as the 'Ready-to-Give bundle.' When you kill a buffalo bull in the winter time, place tobacco in its nostrils, and also place some at the root of the ears and upon the top of the head. Place this tobacco upon the head of the buffalo bull as an offering to the gods in the heavens. The gods will notice that an offering of tobacco has been made upon the skull, and they will know that their spirit is to dwell in the buffalo skull.   Then you must skin the head of the buffalo bull and take only the skull to your home.   Place the skull upon some high hill until the flesh is gone and nothing but bone is left.   Then take the skull and place it west and outside of the lodge, but when you are inside the earth-lodge place the skull on the west side of the lodge under the bundle When you have ceremonies place the skull to the north side of the fire-place, so that when the people are making offerings to the gods they will always remember to make a separate offering to the god who stands in the north, and who is always ready to send the people something to eat. I shall always dwell in the skull, for you now know that I am the Wind."

For many months Ready-to-Give remained, teaching his son the cere-monies of the bundle.   In the fall Ready-to-Give saw that the women and boy had plenty of meat, corn, squash, and beans to eat; then he said: "Winter is now coming and I must go away to my place.   The people are now thinking of returning to this place.   Have nothing to do with your uncles, for they left you behind to die."

One of the hunters made up his mind to go to the deserted village, for his children were starving, and he intended to open one of the cache holes to get some corn.   The boy had been away from their place hunt-ing.   When he came back with some meat he said: "Mother, there is a man coming toward our camp.   He is from our people."   The women said, "How do you know?" and the boy said, "My father told me."

Several days afterwards the boy told the women to watch, that the man was coming to their place.   The women watched and sure enough they saw a man coming over the hills.   He hunted around through the village looking for the cache holes, but he could not find any.   He climbed one of the lodges, sat upon the top, and looked over the country. He saw the smoke coming up from the timber, came down from the lodge, and walked down to the place where the smoke was coming from. When he came the women met him.   He was not one of their relatives, so they took him in, gave him something to eat, and when he was filled he said: "Women, who are you?   Where did all these things come from which I see around here?"   The women said, "Our son kills buffalo and that is why we have plenty of meat."   The women then told the man that they were the women who were made outcasts on account of the girl's condition.   The man remembered.   The boy was sent for.   He came into the tipi and sat down.   The man looked at him and he could see that the young boy had mysterious powers.   He had a soft downy eagle feather stuck in his hair.   His eyes looked strange. The boy said: "I am very sorry that the people left my people behind, but as you see now Tirawa has given me plenty. Though the people through me have plenty, they shall yet have more. Even though the people threw me away, yet they are my people. Tell them to come. Tell them I have plenty of meat for them. They shall come and they shall be my people." He told his mother to take some dried meat, wrap it up, and give it to the man, so that he could take the meat to his people. The man did not stay over night, but returned at once to the camp. When the people heard of the women and the strange boy and the abundance of food they traveled fast. When they arrived the man who sent the women away came and cried, and the boy went out and said: "I am now a man. Do not cry. You shall learn many things. Tell the people to come and make their home close by. Tell the women to come, so that these women may give them meat." The chief of the people then told the uncle to ask the boy to come and make his home with him; that he had a daughter who was old enough to be married, but the boy said, "No; I must feed the people first." He had the people make him a new tipi, and when they had finished it he hung the bundle which his father had promised him in the tipi, and placed the skull on the other side of the fireplace. Then he sat down and told the people, through the chief, that he was going to send for buffalo. On the fourth night he told the men to get on their ponies, go out, and surround the buffalo. They did and returned with much meat. The boy called the buffalo four times. After that he said, "I must go on the war-path." The boy went and came back with many ponies. Then the boy married the chief's daughter, and he lived until he was a very old man and then died.

23. THE MAN WHO CALLED THE BUFFALO.

(See Abstracts.)

[Told by White-Horse, the leading medicine-man of the Pitahauirat and the owner of the stone-man's medicine. This is the Pitahauirat variant of Nos. 21 and 22.]

24. THE WONDERFUL BOY.[1]

A long time ago there were no other people known in the world but the Skidi. The Skidi were living somewhere on the Loupe River. In the village were many people. Different games were given to the people. The women also had different games which were given to them. Among the games was a stick and ring game. There was one young man who was well-to-do, and who had many things to bet with the gaming sticks.

[1] Told by Good-Eagle, a Skidi medicine-man. This tale is somewhat similar to the preceding and may be considered as the Skidi variant.

Every day he was out where they played. In the evening he came home and entered his father's lodge. He gambled away everything he had. The boy gambled away buffalo robes, leggings, moccasins, and other things, so that he now had nothing. Ponies at this time were not known. In the night when he lay down he had only half a buffalo robe to cover himself with.

One day he went out to the gaming grounds and he lost many things, among them trinkets belonging to his sister and also her robe. The sister gladly gave them up. When night came the sister and brother had to lie together and over them was spread the half buffalo robe which the boy had not gambled away. When the morning came the father arose, and as he walked by the bed, he saw that the young man was sleeping with his sister and had only a half robe over them. He became very sad. He went out. When he returned to the lodge he became angry. He went to the bed, took the covering from the boy, woke him, and said: "My son, it looks very bad for you and your sister to lie together, and to have only this half of a buffalo robe over you. Get up, go to the gaming grounds, lose everything we have. When you have lost everything, then go away to some other place and never return." The young man jumped up and tried to cry. The sister caught him and said: "My brother, do not cry. What my father has said is true. He is angry with you because you have lost all my things. Some day I may get them back. Now, do not cry and do not go away from us."

The young man did not say anything. He did not go to the gaming grounds, but sat inside of the lodge all day. As night came he went to his sister and said: "My sister, fold up some dried meat and make it into a bundle. Tie several moccasins upon it, for I am about to start on a journey to a place I do not know. Take some arrows from my father's quiver and put them in my quiver. I shall now go." The girl said: "My brother, you must not go yet. Let me go to our uncles and see if I can not get several bear moccasins and a robe for you." She went and after a while returned with a buffalo robe, leggings, and several pairs of moccasins. The boy was glad. He put on the leggings and moccasins and with his bundle and quiver started west.

For several days he traveled without seeing any human being. At last he came to a village. When he entered he asked where the tipi of the chief was, and they showed him. The boy entered, and when he sat down the chief asked him where he was going. He said: "I am going west. Are there any more people in the west?" The chief said, "You will travel so many days and you will find more people." The boy started again and in a few days he came to another village. Here he was received by the chief, given plenty to eat, and was told to continue on his journey, as there were other people in the west. He came to the people; he was treated very kindly and meat and other things were given him. He was told to go on, as there were other people in the west. After a while this boy came to a village of people. The people were naked, had no bows and arrows, but had sticks. Every day the people went rabbit hunting and killed some, and lived on this kind of food altogether. The people looked wonderingly at the boy and asked him where he came from. They thought he was funny because he wore the leggings, carried a bow and arrows, and had a robe. They tried to keep him, but the boy said, "No; I must go, for I am going on a long journey."

After a while the boy came to some people and when he got into their lodge he found they had no mouths. They fed him with meat. He ate. They looked funny at him, for he ate the meat. When these people became hungry they put dried meat upon the pole and placed it over the fire. When it was smoking they would take the meat and place it against their noses and smell of it. When they were filled, they would throw the meat to one side. They talked with the sign language.

The young man left the people and went west. He came to other people who were very small, and these people had stones to throw. The stones were tied with strings and with these they killed their game. When they saw the boy with the bow and arrow they challenged him to shoot at a hide. The hide was stretched some feet away and a man selected to throw the stones. The stones were thrown at the hide and they went through the hide. The boy was told to shoot at it with his bow and arrows. He did this and shot through the hide. When they saw him shoot they thought it was wonderful. They began to examine the bow and the arrows. They kept the boy at their village so that he could teach them how to make the bow and the arrows. The boy taught them.

After several days he asked if there were any more people and they said that they did not know of any more. The boy said, "I shall now go on." He started. When night came somebody said to him: "My son, I will now let you know that you are beyond all people. It was I who brought you. I am the North-Wind. I shall take you now to the place where you are going. To-morrow we shall travel fast; towards the evening you will see a high peak. There you must go and you will see what the mound is."

The next day the boy traveled swiftly. Some time in the afternoon he saw a high peak in the distance. He ran towards it and in the evening when near to it he saw many eagle feathers strewn over the ground. When he reached the hill he saw that the point of the hill was a pile of eagles high up in the sky. The same voice said to him, "Take some brown eagle feathers, some downy feathers, and carry them with you to where we are going." They went on. They came to a steep bank and there the boy was told to lie down. Before the sun came up in the morning he was awakened by the Wind, who said, "Let us travel on." They went on. They came to a steep bank and there they stood, for at the bank the boy saw water. At some distance was a thick fog. Then the North-Wind said: "My son, although you do not see me I am always near you and I am always with you. I have been with you all this journey. I made you come to these different people and you have been treated well by them. I have kept them from killing you. We have come to the horizon. Here under the bank towards the south sits the Buffalo who controls this big water. Go. Stand upon the bank and throw the black eagle feathers to the Buffalo and say: 'My grandfather, I have come from a far-away country. I wish to take a look at you and ask your permission to let me go beyond this horizon.' The Buffalo will jump up from the edge of the water and will start on a trot some distance to the north and will come up on dry land. There you must give it some native tobacco and some feathers. The Buffalo will say to you, 'You must go beyond this horizon and when you have seen the people who live beyond, tell them that you have seen the people who live here and have my permission to pass on.' When they talk to you, and you return to me where I sit in the water, you must let me know and I will help you to take the Buffalo to your people." The boy did as directed, and when the Buffalo gave its permission for him to proceed, the boy thrust some feathers into the Buffalo bull's hair on the head and placed native tobacco upon its head. Then the boy said, "Grandfather, I must be going."

The Buffalo went along the path to the big water and went to the south and sat down in the water again. The boy returned to the bank. As soon as he got to the place the Wind said: "Take off your leggings, your moccasins, and the robe, and also your quiver; put them all in the robe, hold them in your hands, and wade into the water. From here I must now take you upon your journey." The boy placed his things in the robe and went into the water. When the water reached to his arms the Wind blew down, took him up, and carried him on for some time. At last the Wind said: "Here we are. This is the place where you want to go. Place your robe and things on the ground. You must go on the north side and the far east lodge you must enter. That is where the four gods in the west sit. There they will teach you many things. I will be in the lodge and they shall know that I brought you." The boy left his things and went on west to the lodge. When he came close he saw that there were three gardens—one on the north side of the entrance, which was filled with pumpkins; one on the south side with many beans; and one on the west of the lodge, which was a field of corn. When the boy entered the lodge they gave him a seat near the entrance, and the four gods in the west said: "Where do you come from, my son?" The boy said: "I came from a long distance." One of the four gods said: "We know. It was through us that the North-Wind brought you here. We know that you are a great gambler. You have lost everything you had. Look in the south of the lodge and there sits the South-Wind, who brings bad luck and is always in the way of some young man." The boy looked in the south and there sat an ugly-looking man. His skin was rough. He looked rather white. His hair was not brushed, but mixed up in every way. The god said: "That is the man who does harm to young men, and he is the one who goes to the earth and scares the Buffalo away from the people. Yonder in the north is the man who brought you to this place. You see his skin is like yours. The buffalo grease is on him. He is the good wind which drives the buffalo to the people. He has brought you here so that you may receive ceremonies and the seeds from us. We are representatives of Tirawa,[1] and you are in the home of Tirawa, but you can not see him. What we tell you will all come true." Then one of the priests said: "Errand man, you must go to the garden in the north and take a squash and bring it in." The squash was brought in, placed on the north side, cut open, the seeds taken out and placed near to the fireplace. The squash was cooked and given to the man to eat. When he was full they sang some songs which they were teaching the young man. After singing they sent another errand man out to bring beans into the lodge. They were put into a pot and boiled. These were given to the young man and he ate of them. Some of the beans were left over and not boiled. These were placed with the squash seeds. Again the priests sang. After singing they sent the other errand man and he brought in a small watermelon from the south side. It was cut open and the seeds were placed with the other seeds. The old priests sang again. Then they sent the errand man out for some corn. He ate some of the corn and some was left and placed with the other seeds. The priests began to sing again, and after the singing they took some dried buffalo meat, placed it in a pot, and boiled it. The young man ate of it, and he was then told that it was now time for him to go to his people, as his people were starving. In the first place he

[1] These four gods are Clouds, Lightning, Thunder, and Wind; they are often spoken of as the messengers of the evening star.

must feed them and then call the buffalo, for the people were now to kill them.

They asked the boy, on entering, if he had seen the Buffalo sitting in the water. They told him to return to the place and see the Buffalo again and it would speak to him. The gods began to sing, and after singing they said: "My son, it is now time for you to return to your people. The North-Wind will take you back. We now give you a buffalo robe, and in all that you want to do for the benefit of the people use the robe." The young man put the robe on his back and went out. He was told to put the seeds and things in the robe for the people. When he reached his clothes he took them up and started eastward. After he was gone a little way the North-Wind came and said, "We must go to a certain place." They went to a certain place. The wind then seemed to cover the boy up and they disappeared. The wind had told the boy to hold his things in his hands as he had done before.

After a while the boy was dropped into the water where the horizon touched the ground. It was like a fog. The water came up to his arms; he waded through the fog and finally reached the bank. Then the Wind said, "We must go now to the Buffalo." The boy dressed and went to the Buffalo. He threw down some feathers and asked the Buffalo to come up. He came up and stood on the bank, and said, "Grandchild, have you been to the place where the gods dwell?" The boy said, "I have." He told the Buffalo that he had the robe which was given to him by the people above and that the seeds were also given him. When the Buffalo saw the robe it was satisfied and said: "You have now all the power from me which I possess and the Buffalo people will go to your people. I now must return to my place." The boy put a few feathers again on the head of the buffalo and went on. The Wind then said to the boy: "We must go to the mound of the eagles. You must get all the feathers that you can." They got to the mound. The boy gathered many feathers, made a bundle of them, and then they went on.

They did not go to the different villages which the boy had visited, but the Wind took the boy on and at last they were seated on the side of the hill at night time. The Wind then told the boy to go into the village and to bring him blue beads, eagle feathers, paint, sweet grass, and native tobacco. The boy started to the village, but when he came near to it he smelt the people and could not stand it. He ran back to where the Wind was. There he remained with the Wind all night. The next day when the people went outside of the village they saw footprints of buffalo. They did not know what to make of it. The next night the boy attempted to enter the village again, and when he came near he could not go farther. He returned to where the Wind sat. The next morning the people saw the footprints of the buffalo close to their village. They followed the track, but soon lost it. The third night he tried again, but did not enter. The fourth night he went into the village and entered the lodge of his father. He went to his sister and said: "Sister, I am now here. Do not make any noise. Before you make fire waken up my father and tell him to go through the village and bring me blue beads, feathers, paint, sweet grass, and native tobacco." The father got up, went through the village, and brought all the things. The sister gave them to the brother and the boy said: "Sister, I will return. Watch." He took the things and gave them to the Wind. The Wind sent the boy back to his people.

As he entered the lodge he called for his sister, told her to make a fire, and she did so. When the father saw the boy he jumped out of bed and was about to put his arms around him. The boy stopped him and said: "Do not touch me yet. I know that my people are starving. They want something to eat. Go through the village and let them know that I have come back." The man went out and told the people that his son had come back. When the people heard it they went out and ran to the lodge of the young man. He told them that he had brought some things for them from the west. Then he told them that he knew that they were hungry and that he had hastened to come and feed them. He placed the robe in the north and then sat down. He said: "Now, my people, come to me one at a time and I will give you meat. You must take the meat home and eat it." The boy placed his hand under the robe and every time he took out his hands he had meat. The next day the people talked about it. At night he told the people again to come and get meat. The third and the fourth nights he gave them meat. On the fifth night he told the chiefs to send scouts to the hills in the northwest and there they would see buffalo. The scouts were sent out and as soon as they got on top of the hills they began to throw up their robes, which is a sign of good news. The people ran with excitement through the village. They saw the men coming down from the hill. They came into the village and said that there were many buffalo on the other side of the hills.

For several years there had not been a sign of buffalo in the surrounding country and now there were plenty nearby. The people went out and killed the buffalo. They took some of the buffalo to the lodge of the young man. There he sang the songs which he had heard in the lodge above. The people killed the buffalo four times. Then he told them that they must hunt for the buffalo themselves.

In the spring he told his mother and sister to plant the seeds which he had. In the fall when they gathered in their crops they did not have many to divide with other people. They planted again next spring and in the fall they had more. The boy divided the seeds among the people, giving a few grains to each family. In the spring they all planted and they had plenty of corn after that. They also had plenty of buffalo, and the people say that this is the way they got their seeds—it was through the man who was a great gambler.

25. THE BOY WHO PREFERRED WOMAN TO POWER.[1]

A long time ago, when the Skidi were living upon the Loupe River, there was a young man in the village by the name of Coming-Sun. One night Coming-Sun had a dream. Some one spoke to him and said: "To-morrow I want you to stand upon that high hill. You shall stand up there for four days and nights." He then awoke, and early in the morning he took his robe and told his friends that he was going up on a high hill and that they should not look for him. He went up on the high hill and cried all day and all night. The second day and night he cried, and the third day and night he cried, but did not see any signs of mysterious beings. The fourth day and night he staid there and in the night he stood and cried. When he felt weak, he lay down and some one came and said, "Stand up; I have now come." Coming-Sun stood up and there by him was a man who said: "I promised to take pity upon you if you would come to this hill. Now look in yonder valley." Coming-Sun looked, and he could see, as plainly as though it were day, a man come up from the ravine and go toward the spring. The mysterious being told Coming-Sun to run down and try to head off the man. Coming-Sun then ran down, but before he could catch up with him the man disappeared in the ravine. The man was dressed like a warrior; he had the otter on, with the hawk and mother-corn attached to it. As soon as the man disappeared Coming-Sun went back to the hill.

He again cried, and after a time he heard the same voice that had spoken to him, and he looked and there stood the man again. He said: "You can not run. You did not head off the man. Now look down

---

[1] Told by Roaming-Scout, the most learned of the Skidi priests living. The tale relates to a historical event at the time when a devout man known as Coming-Sun communicated with Pahohatawa, who gave him great power; so that he taught the people that Pahohatawa still lived, was one of the gods in the heavens, and that he should be worshiped with the other heavenly gods. By the fact that Coming-Sun lost his power by preferring woman, which he had been warned not to do, it shows that reverence for the gods and obedience to their commands is to be held higher than the desire for women.

in the valley." When Coming-Sun looked he saw some warriors driving ponies. The voice said: "Run as fast as you can and head them off." Coming-Sun ran down, and just as he was close to them the warriors drove their ponies into the ravine and disappeared. Then Coming-Sun went back to the hill and cried. The voice spoke to him again. He looked, and there was the mysterious being, who said: "You can not run. This time I want you to do your best to head off some of the people who are coming. Look," he said, "they are coming." Coming-Sun looked, and there was a great crowd of warriors coming with long poles with scalps upon them. Coming-Sun ran, and before he caught up with them they disappeared into the ravine.

Coming-Sun returned to the hill and continued to cry. It was nearly morning when the mysterious being came to him and said: "I will make myself known to you. I am Foot-Prints-upon-Bank-of-River. Have you no bag of medicine about you?" Coming-Sun said that he had not. The man said: "Why, look at me; I am a wonderful being; I am North-Wind, I am all kinds of birds, I am also all kinds of animals; even the grass and the trees; and here I carry a little bag of medicine upon my belt. Now, I give you this bag of medicine. I tried to make a warrior out of you, but you can not head off the warriors. I then tried to give you many ponies, but you could not head them off. I then tried to help you scalp the enemy, but you could not head them off. I will make you a medicine-man, and make you brave so that you can count coup on your enemy. Whenever you join a war party it will be successful, for you are among them and you have seen these things that I have shown you, but you can never be a leading warrior. Go to your home, for it is now daylight. Hereafter I shall visit you at night. Take this downy feather and wear it upon your head. When you want to call the buffalo put this downy feather upon a pole, and set the pole in the direction where you want the buffalo to come from."

Coming-Sun became a great man. He invited his brothers and told them where to go to capture ponies. They went, and he went with them, and whatever he told them came true. He prophesied many things and they came true. The mysterious being visited Coming-Sun each night, and each time brought him some things that were wonderful. One night he brought some buzzard feathers. If the enemy found the people, they were to stick the buzzard feathers on their heads in a circle, and the company of warriors were to stand in a circle and great clouds of dust were to rise, and they were to be covered up and hidden, so that the enemy would not find them. When the people saw the powers that Coming-Sun had, they asked him to call the buffalo. He placed his tipi apart from the others and he put the downy feather upon a pole and set it in the ground. He then told a company of men to go to a certain place and call buffalo. They went, and they found the buffalo as he had told them they would. Once a big drove of buffalo was brought by Coming-Sun, and the people killed them.

One night after he had been talking to the mysterious being in his tipi, a woman came into his tipi and told him that she was going to stay with him. While the woman was in his tipi, another young man came and took down the feather that he had upon the pole and carried it off. When he tried to call the buffalo he failed. The wonderful being came and told him that he was sorry that he thought more of women than of powers he was receiving from him, for he had made him a great medicine-man and a brave man. The being left Coming-Sun and went to other parts of the country and visited other people. Coming-Sun felt very sad and regretted his foolishness. In a few years he became blind and died.

26. BUFFALO GAMING STICKS.[1]

After Tirawa had placed men upon earth he gave them the game of ring and sticks and told them how to play it; he also told them that they were to sing certain songs before and after playing the game. It was evening when the first game was played. The next morning when they went to play they saw marks on the gaming field, but they did not know what the marks were. They took out the sticks to play and one of the young men went to the opposite end of the field to play. There he met a young woman, with whom he had intercourse. After a while she went away, and gave birth to a buffalo calf.

After a time a party went out on a hunt. As they traveled along they saw a snow bird. They shot at it with their arrows, but missed it. The bird flew on in front of them, and they came near to it and shot at it again, but could not hit it. They traveled all day, trying to kill the snow bird, but did not succeed. It seemed to be leading them on.

[1] Told by White-Eagle, an old Skidi and the owner of the Left-Hand bundle and the Skull bundle. This is a variant of the story of the origin of the buffalo game, other variants being found in the other bands. White-Horse, a Pitahauirat medicine-man, in his version claims that formerly a set of the gaming implements formed part of a sacred bundle and that the playing of these implements was supposed to bring the buffalo near to the village. This story may be told only in the lodge where sacred bundles are suspended, or upon the buffalo hunt. When told under the latter condition it is with the hope that their hunt will be successful, as was the hunt an account of which is presented in the story. It was believed that the relating of this tale would inform the spirits of the buffalo that they were talking about them, so that they would come and permit themselves to be slaughtered for the benefit of the people.

Night came and they could not see the bird, but in the morning it was there as before. They followed after it until all were tired out except the young man who had met the girl at the end of the game field. He continued to follow the bird until it led him to a ridge, where from the summit he could see a herd of buffalo approaching. He was tired and so he sat down and watched the thousands of buffalo approach. The young woman and her child, the buffalo calf, were among the herd of buffalo. The little calf was always crying for his father, for he heard the other buffalo calves cry for their fathers, and they came. One time he heard the bulls talking among themselves, saying, over and over, that his father must die, for they would not have him around. The boy's mother also told him that the bulls would kill his father.

The buffalo gathered around the young man, and the boy calf came up to him and told him that the buffalo bulls intended to kill him, but that he would save him. "The calves," he said, "will be placed in a row and you will be told to find your son among them. When you come around to look in our faces I will wink; then you say, 'This is my child,' and then they will not kill you." It happened as the boy said. The calves were arranged in a row and the bulls asked the young man to examine them. He walked around them three times and looked up and down the line, until he saw one of the calves wink. Then he said, "This is my son," and they did not kill him, but they put him to another test. They placed all the cows of the age of the calf's mother in a row. The calf ran to his father and said, "I will put a cockle burr on mother's tail, and when you see it, say, 'This is my wife,' and then they will not kill you." When the young man went to examine the cows up and down the line, he came to one with only one burr in her tail, and he chose her and said, "This is my wife." The bulls said to him, "You are all right; now you go home." In a few days he arrived at their village. There he told his people: "In four days the buffalo will come in great numbers; we will kill them and have plenty of meat, and fat with which to grease the poles for our game." Then they played the game and thanked Tirawa for the game and for the buffalo that he had given them. This was in the spring.

27. THE BOY WHO CALLED THE BUFFALO AND WENT TO NORTH-WIND.[1]

A long time ago, when the Kitkehahki lived upon the banks of the Republican River, they suffered from hunger one season. The crops failed, and they did not know what they were going to do for something to eat. The chief gave orders that they at once prepare to go west to hunt buffalo. The people began to hunt for their cache holes to get out their corn. They took everything out from their cache holes, and went west to hunt buffalo. They traveled for many days, but found no buffalo. At last they came to thickly timbered country, and there the chief told the people to make a permanent village; that they must live there. The people made earth-lodges for their village.

From the village scouts were sent out to see if they could find any buffalo in the country. Toward evening the scouts came and reported that there were no buffalo in the country, not even their tracks could be seen upon the ground. The people became hungry; the children cried for something to eat. The scouts were ordered to go forth into the country, but every time they returned they reported that there were no buffalo in the country. The people became scared, for it was winter, and the snow was on the ground and they had very little to eat. Some of the people had nothing to eat. The chief sent for the crier and told him to tell the men that he wanted several men to go out and hunt buffalo. The chief said, "Our people are now starving and you men must go out far into the country, even if you are gone several days."

Several men got together and said, "Let us go and be gone several days; it may be that we may find buffalo." Each man then asked his relatives to make moccasins for him. In one of the tipis there was a woman making moccasins. By the side of this woman sat a young boy. The boy was Coyote, and he played with the other children. The woman said: "These men are going far into the country to find buffalo. We are all getting very thin and weak, for we have nothing to eat." The boy sat looking at the woman as she made the moccasins. He lifted up his head and said: "Mother, make me moccasins. I want to go with the men and hunt buffalo." The mother began to make the moccasins. At the same time she doubted if the boy would go, for he was not yet a man; but when the moccasins were finished and the men ready to start

---

[1] Told by Mouth-Waving-in-Water, Kitkehahki. Told both during bundle ceremonies and while upon buffalo hunts, that the participants might meet with the same good fortune as was encountered in the tale. The tale, like all those which have preceded it, is supposed to be true, or to record an event which really happened, and like many of the preceding tales it is a spur to young men to hope to achieve something great, and also to hold the implements of the buffalo game in a spirit of reverence.

the boy joined them. The mother came to the boy and said: "My boy, come home at once, for the clouds are coming, and if it snows I am afraid you will get lost." The boy said nothing, but followed the men.

The men went straight west. The boy kept up with them for three days, but as they had nothing to eat he became very tired and hungry. In the night it snowed very hard, but the men kept on. The next day was clear, the sun was out, and the men went on. In the evening the boy fell behind, for he could go no farther, for he was now very hungry. He sat down to rest. The men did not wait for him. They went on. The boy saw the clouds come up from the west. The clouds he saw were snow clouds, and while he sat there it began to snow. Something dropped in front of him and he reached for it and picked it up. The thing was an artichoke. The boy ate the artichoke and felt better. While he was sitting down, someone spoke to him. The boy looked around, but saw no one. He heard a striking noise. The unseen being spoke again and said, "Do you feel better now?" The boy said, "Yes, I feel better." The unknown voice then said: "My son, it was I who gave you life. I left you alone until you should become this old. I made you come here. I am the Snow-Storm. I came with the snow and dropped you the artichoke that you have eaten. Now I am here. Look, and you will see me." The boy looked and there stood a man with a buffalo robe about his shoulders. The robe had snow upon it. He also had a fox-skin cap with a feather at the end of the tail. The wind blew and made the feather whip the robe, thus producing the noise that the boy had first heard. The strange man said: "Now, my son, I want you to go back to your people and ask them for certain presents that you must give me. These are the red paint, blue beads, black eagle feathers, and native tobacco. You must again scratch upon the earth and you will find artichokes. Take them home to your father and mother and let them boil and eat them. I have blown my breath upon you, so that you can travel as fast as I do."

The boy gathered the artichokes and started home. He did not seem to be traveling, he glided along so easily. Soon he came to the village and entered and went straight to his tipi. He woke his father and mother. He gave his mother the artichokes and told her to boil them. She put them in a vessel over the fire. The boy told his father to invite his relatives. When the relatives came into the tipi they were glad to smell the boiling artichokes. The boy spoke and said: "My friends, I came from a long journey. These things that you are about to eat were given to me by a strange being. Now, I ask you to give me the things that I shall name: Red paint, blue beads, black eagle feathers and tobacco.'' The people looked at the boy, and some of them whispered to one another, and said: "The things that he asks for are what the gods in the heavens like. Some god has taken pity upon him.'' After the relatives had eaten the artichokes they went out and brought in the things the boy wanted. The boy took the things and carried them outside of the village, and there he met the strange being. The boy gave the things to the man and he was glad to get them. He then gave the boy the fox-skin cap with the eagle feather on the tail. He said: "You shall be called 'Whipping-Feather.' In a few days you will travel as I do, and you will meet me driving Buffalo. Then you must tell the people to kill.'' They parted, the boy going home and the strange man disappearing.

Next morning the boy said to his father and mother, "Go to the timber and dig some artichokes.'' The old people did not like to go, but as they felt the boy had some kind of power they took a bag and hoe and went off; and as they dug along the sunny side of a bank they found a rat's path-way. They followed it until they came to timber, and there they found a pile of ground beans. When the parents came home with the beans the boy took them and placed them in his robe and told his father to go outside and tell the people to come and get a handful of ground beans. The man went and the women came with their sacks. The beans were given out by the boy so that all the families received some of them. The next day the boy went out by himself. He was gone but a short time when he came back carrying a deer upon his back. He took the deer and placed it under his robe. The boy then told his father to tell the people to come and get a piece of the deer meat. The people all came and each took a piece of meat, leaving only the ribs. These ribs were then put into a vessel and boiled. Then the chiefs and leading men were invited to the boy's tipi. After eating the ribs they all stayed in the tipi for several nights. The young man went off in the night and was gone for some time.

When he came back he told the chief to call in the crier. When the crier came in the boy told him to go through the camp and tell the people that there were some Buffalo close to the camp. Some of the young men were selected to go out to see if they could discover them. The men went out and as they stood upon the hills they saw some Buffalo bulls. They ran back to the village and told the young man and he told the chief to tell the crier to go through the village and tell the men to get their ponies and surround the Buffalo. The men went out, found the Buffalo, surrounded them, and killed all of them. After this killing the young man went out again. While he was gone on the prairie he met the strange being driving Buffalo. The boy and the strange being drove the Buffalo towards the camp. The boy then came to the village. He told the people that there were some bulls for them to kill again. The men went out and killed the Buffalo bulls. The third time the young man went out, and he again found the strange being driving the Buffalo. The young man went home and told the people that there were many Buffalo cows upon the hills. The men went out and there in a valley they found the Buffalo cows, which they surrounded and killed. The fourth time the young man went away and found the strange being driving Buffalo. The young man went home and this time he told the people to go and find the buffalo. This time the people found all kinds of Buffalo—bulls, cows, and calves. The people killed many and still there were many left. The Buffalo then scattered over the country.

The young man married. One day he called the people together and told them that the wonderful being had given power for him to be born; that when he was born the being watched over him; that at a certain age the being had driven all the Buffalo away; that the being had made him go a long distance to the place where he was; and that the being had helped him get the Buffalo. So the boy said, "I shall now go away to the being who is North-Wind." The boy went off and never returned.

28. THE MAN WHO MARRIED A BUFFALO.[1]

The people went on a hunt at one time and they found many Buffalo. Among the people on the hunt was a young man who did not like the women. He had several chances to marry some of the young girls, but he rejected them. One day the people went out to surround the Buffalo. This young man went with them. When the people ran after the Buffalo there was a bunch of about five Buffalo cows which broke away from the people, and the young man who disliked women ran after this bunch of cows. He ran these Buffalo into a mud-hole and one of the young cows got fast in the mud. The young man saw the Buffalo fast in the mud, so he jumped off from his pony, went into the mud, and lay with the cow. The young man went home and left the cow in the mud. After a long time the cow worked herself out from the mud and went away to the other Buffalo. It was then some time early in the spring.

Early the next spring the cows in the Buffalo herd began to have young calves. Among those who were to have calves was the cow

---

[1] Told by White-Horse, Pitahauirat. This is a variant of a story in which a man marries a Buffalo, has offspring, etc. The object of the story is to teach that human beings are related to the Buffalo, and it is believed that by relating the story it will cause the buffalo to come and offer themselves to be slaughtered.

which had had connection with a man. She had a little bull-calf. When the calf grew up it noticed other cows went with their husbands and the calves followed their fathers around. The calf asked the mother where his father was. The mother did not want to tell the calf, but he begged so hard that finally the mother said: "Your father is far away and can not see you." The calf began to cry, for he wanted to see his father, so the mother said: "We will go and see your father." They started and went towards the east. For many days they went east until at last they came to the village of the people. They stopped in a ravine. There the Buffalo cow turned herself into a woman and she turned the calf into a young boy. The woman had a fine buffalo robe over her and was a fine-looking woman. The boy had a calf robe with hoofs on it over him. The woman and the boy walked to the lodge of the man and there they sat down near the entrance. It was night. A woman came out and saw the woman and the child. This woman went to them and said: "Woman, what do you want? Do you want to see my brother?" for this woman was the sister of the young man. The Buffalo woman said: "Yes; I want to see the young man." The woman went into the lodge and said: "Brother, there is a woman outside who wishes to see you." The young man went out and there sat a woman. Her hair was not braided and he knew at once that she was not one of the tribe. The young man spoke to the woman and said: "Woman, do you want to see me?" The woman said: "Yes; I want to see you, for this boy is your son and I have brought him to you, for he wants to see you." The young man stood still and studied, for he had never been with any woman. The young man said: "Woman, I know no woman yet; you must be mistaken." But the woman said: "This boy is your son. Think and you will find out that you lay with me, and this is your son." The young man studied, but could not remember. The woman then said: "Do you not remember a long time ago, when you ran after Buffalo I jumped into a mud-hole? You came and lay with me." The boy then stooped down and took up the boy in his arms and said: "My son, my wife, I remember. Come, go with me into the lodge and see my father and mother and my sisters." The young man led the way into the lodge and said: "Father, mother, and sisters, this is my son and this woman is my wife."

When the old people saw the woman and child they knew that the woman and the boy were not human beings, and they would not touch the woman, but the boy they caught and caressed. The woman remained inside of the inclosed bed, for she did not want people to see her. Four days after this she began to be like other people. Then she told the old people to watch over the boy; that he was bad and might hurt some of the children. She meant that if the little boy should strike some of the children his hands would turn into a calf's hoofs, and they would hurt the children badly. The Buffalo woman also said: "Watch the boy closely. Do not let him fall upon the ground, for the boy will then get away from us." The woman meant that if the boy should fall down upon the ground he would turn into a Buffalo calf and would run away. The woman and the boy remained with the people and were happy.

Every day the young man went to where the people were playing with the gambling sticks. When the sun became hot and it was noon, the boy would take a bucket of water to his father. One day the young man went out to the gambling grounds and played with the sticks. He began to lose nearly everything that he had and he became angry. When the boy came with the water he stood to one side of the gambling grounds with the water, but the man would not go to his son to drink. The mother was sitting in the lodge. Something seemed to touch her. She arose and went out of the lodge. She sat down near the entrance and she saw her son with the water standing near his father. The man never went to drink and the woman became angry. The boy came home and his mother took him and went into the lodge. She took up her robe and that of the child and they went out. The grandmother saw them go out. She went right out and went to where her son was playing with the sticks. She called to him and said: "My son, stop playing. Come home. See, yonder go your wife and your child." The man looked, and when he saw his wife and child going away he threw down the sticks and went home. The young man entered the lodge and sat down. He asked for his leggings and moccasins. He put them on and went out. As he went upon the hill he saw the two going, not as human beings, but as Buffalo. He followed for a long distance. The calf would come back and jump around its father, and then would run again to its mother. In the night the Buffalo would sit down in a hollow while the calf would come and lie beside the father.

One day the calf came and said: "Father, are you hungry?" The man said: "I am." The calf said: "Father, strike me upon the forehead, not so very hard." The man hit the calf upon the forehead. As soon as he struck the head, pemmican fell from the head and dropped upon the grass. The man sat down and ate of the pemmican. When he had eaten enough he put away what was left. Then he went on again. The calf came to him again and said: "Father, are you thirsty?" The man said: "Yes, I am thirsty." The calf then began to paw into the ground. After a while the calf's hoof began to work out from the ground. The water began to come out of the ground. The calf started on and the man drank out of the hole. Thus the calf took care of the father, but the Buffalo cow never tried to help the man, for she was angry with him. When they had traveled for four days the calf came to his father and said: "Father, on yonder hills live my people." The calf went on. When they arrived at the hills the man saw in the bottom many Buffalo. He saw his wife and child run right through the crowd and disappear.

The next day the calf came to the father and said: "Father, my mother is angry with you because you would not come to me when I took water to you. My people are angry with you, but I shall stay with you. To-day you are to look for my grandfather. There will be put in line twenty Buffalo. They will let you pass in front of these Buffalo that are to be put into line and then they will let you pass behind. When you have come to my grandfather you will see my tongue mark upon his hips. As soon as you see that mark you must remember that I have made the mark. Then you must lay your hands upon the Buffalo and say that he is your father-in-law. If you fail to find my grandfather all the Buffalo will jump on you and kill you." The next day the young man was taken from the hill and placed where the Buffalo were. There were placed in line about twenty Buffalo and all looked alike. The young man went in front of the Buffalo, but he could not tell where his father-in-law stood. Then he went behind and saw one bull standing among them with a mark upon his hips, and he knew that the mark was made by the tongue of the calf. The man went up to the bull and said: "This is my father-in-law." The Buffalo were surprised and said: "He must be a wonderful man, but we will kill him anyhow."

Then the calf said: "My father, to-morrow you are to hunt my grandmother. You are to pass first in the rear and then in front. When you have passed in the rear and are going along the line on the front side, you will notice one Buffalo cow with two cockle burrs between the horns on top of the head. This is your mother-in-law. You must touch her and say that this is your mother-in-law." When this was done the Buffalo said: "This must be a wonderful young man."

Then the calf went to his father and said: "Father, to-morrow you are to hunt my mother. There will be several Buffalo standing beside one another. These Buffalo will all look alike, but when I play with my mother I shall put two cockle burrs on the end of the tail, and also two at the root of the tail. When you have seen these burrs you may know that she is your wife." The man passed along in front of the Buffalo that he could see her and then in the rear. He found one cow with the cockle burrs. He said: "This is my wife." The Buffalo said: "This must be a wonderful man."

After the young man had found his wife the calf came to him and said: "To-morrow you are to hunt me. There will be many calves placed in line and I will be among them. You are to pass down the line in the rear and then in front. When you are coming near where I shall be I shall wink at you. While I am winking at you, you will notice a cockle burr right over my eye. You must touch me and say that I am your son." Then the calf went back to the Buffalo. The next day the Buffalo were gathered together and they selected about twelve young bull calves, all of the same size, height, and color as the boy calf. They were placed in a line. The man went in the rear of the calves, then he went in front. The calf watched and as soon as he saw his father coming he began to wink at his father. The father looked at him and right over the eye was a burr. He knew at once that this was his son. He touched the calf and said, "This is my son," and the calf began to jump around, for the calf was pleased to know that his father had found him.

The Buffalo then agreed that the man should be with them always. Several Buffalo bulls got together and they ran up towards the young man as if to hook him, but when they ran against him they met another bull, for the young man had turned into a Buffalo bull. Then the people said: "We will send a drove of Buffalo to your village, for the people are hungry. We want you to bring some feathers, some native tobacco, blue beads, and clam shells." Twenty Buffalo were selected, and the young man, his wife, and son joined the drove and went towards the village. They traveled several nights and at last they came to the village. The twenty Buffalo squatted down in the ravine, while the woman, her child, and her husband turned into human beings and entered the village. The young man awoke his father and said: "Father, send for my uncles, and when they come in tell them that I want eagle feathers, native tobacco, blue beads, and clam shells." The old man went out and gathered up his relatives. When they were all together the people said that they would go and get the things. In a short time the people began to come in with the things. They gave the things to the young man. The young man then told the people that he knew that the Buffalo knew that they were starving for meat. He told them to go to a certain place in the morning and they would find the Buffalo there. He said that most of the Buffalo who had come with him were sitting in a certain place, and that the people were to kill those Buffalo and make them holy. He said that those Buffalo came to receive smoke, but they knew also that they were to be offered as a sacrifice to Tirawa. The young man, his wife, and child disappeared.

The next day the people were told that the young man had been there and that they were promised some Buffalo at a certain place. They sent several of the young men to the place to see. When they went they found the Buffalo sitting in a ravine. They went back and reported. The people got ready, went out, and surrounded the Buffalo and killed all the Buffalo. Most of them were sacrificed to Tirawa.

The young man took the things to the Buffalo people and they were thankful. Then the Buffalo people said: "You will now send more Buffalo." The young man took another bunch of Buffalo to the people and they killed this bunch, and the young man returned and received another bunch of Buffalo. Four times the young man brought Buffalo to the village. Then the Buffalo scattered over the country. One time when the people attacked the Buffalo they unknowingly killed the Buffalo who had once been a man. They consecrated him, and then they found out that he had been a man, because the hide that they took off had feathers all over it.

29. HOW THE WITCH-WOMAN WAS KILLED.[1]

There was a village of people and on the east side lived alone a Witch-Woman. She had no children. Sometimes she cured people when they were sick. At other times she was very mean to people and would let them die of disease. Sometimes she took some of her medicine, sat in her lodge, and threw the medicine into the air. The medicine would fly through the air and would enter into the people and kill them. On account of these tricks the people called her Witch-Woman.

In the village was a wonderful man known as White-Moccasins. A child was born in his family and it was a boy. The women in the village were very fond of this child. Each morning one woman would come into the lodge and pack the little child around on her back. After she became tired another woman would be ready to carry the child. Every day the child was taken out of the lodge, but the parents knew that it was safe. One morning a young girl came into the lodge and took the child out. After she became tired she gave the child to another woman. A woman came near where the women were. This woman looked at the child and went on. The women looked at her and they knew that it was Witch-Woman. They said nothing to the parents of the child.

[1] Told by Leading-Sun, Kitkehahki. The tale marks the end of the life of a group of supernatural beings who had been dreaded and feared and who were held responsible for many troubles, including sickness, etc. The connection of the story with the sacred bundle is not at first evident, but it is to be noted that the Witch-Woman was killed by the Hawk, who was the special guardian of the warriors, a skin of a hawk being always present in the warrior's bundle.

It seems that the old woman knew that the child was born under the protection of some minor god in the heavens. She disliked the child, and so one beautiful morning the old woman went to the creek, picked up a clam and said: "I want you to take my place as the Witch-Woman and travel with these people wherever they go. I will remain behind, for I want to take the child away from its parents." Witch-Woman blew her breath upon the clam shell. She turned into an old woman with a very wrinkled face. She was left in the place of Witch-Woman.

The next morning before daylight the real Witch went into the tipi of White-Moccasins. She took the little child upon her back and went out of the lodge. She went to the Witch-Woman and said: "You must remain here and if the people move away follow them. You are in my place. I shall go far away with this child, so that in time I may kill the child and it will never know that it had a father and a mother."

The Witch-Woman carried the little boy far away to where the sun rises. The people in the village missed the child. The parents went throughout the village hunting their child. Everybody turned out, but they could not find the child. The people all began to mourn. They mourned so much that some of them would tear down their tipis and move away. The people kept moving away from their village until only White-Moccasins and his immediate family were left behind. The people were now scattered all over the land.

The real Witch-Woman carried the boy far away. They came to a big water and stopped there. Here the Witch-Woman built a grass-house and made a garden. The boy and the woman remained in that place for a number of years. The boy grew to be large, and the Witch-Woman made a bow and some arrows for him. The boy went out hunting every day and brought in game. He believed that this old woman was his mother, for she called him her son. The woman saw that the boy had grown up and that he had many wonderful ways about him. She told the boy not to go far to the west; that wild animals would find him and devour him.

One day while the boy was out playing with his bow and arrows he saw a Crow sitting upon a tree. The Crow began to cry out and the boy heard what it said. The boy thought that the Crow said: "Boy, you do not belong here. Your people live west from here. Their village site is beyond here." The boy did not pay any attention to the words of the Crow, but the Crow said: "I saw that woman take you away. I know all about it. You do not belong here. There are many people out west where you belong." The boy paid no attention to this. The next day he went out hunting. When he came to a timbered country he saw a red Hawk sitting upon a limb. The Hawk made a screeching sound and the boy thought that the Hawk was calling him. He followed the Hawk. Whenever the boy looked at the Hawk, he thought he saw a scalp hanging down from its claw. The Hawk also seemed to carry a war club. Around its breast seemed to be a buffalo-hair lariat. The boy liked the dress of the Hawk, and when it made the screeching sound the boy followed it. The Hawk would fly from one limb to another, and when the Hawk saw that the boy was not coming it would fly towards him, circle around him, and fly west again. The boy saw that the Hawk wanted him to follow it, so he followed. After a while they came to a prairie country. They went over this prairie country, and after a while the boy saw the Hawk flying in a circle. Then he saw the Hawk drop something. When the boy went to the place he found the things he had seen. The Hawk then flew up into the sky and the boy sat down on the village site. He lay down, for he had come a long way and was tired. As soon as he went to sleep he heard the insects under the ground. They sang:

"Here lies the child of White-Moccasins.
Here lies the child of White-Moccasins."

The young man woke up and looked around, but could see nothing. He lay down again. Just as the dawn appeared the young man arose and stood on the village site. While he was standing there the whole village site seemed to say, "This is the child of White-Moccasins." He looked around for the voices. He went to the tipi poles and here the voices seemed to be. The fireplaces also said: "This is the son of White-Moccasins." The grass which had grown over the village site was speaking and saying that this was the child of White-Moccasins. Even the old moccasins which had been left behind were saying that this was the child of White-Moccasins. The boy stood still, looked around and said to himself: "I must be the child of someone else." He walked around through the village and still the voices came from every direction. Finally he went to one place and here was a clam shell. It said: "My boy, I was placed here by a Witch-Woman to follow your people and act as a Witch in her place. When the people broke camp I tried to follow them. The power which the Witch-Woman had given me was gone and I turned into a clam shell as you now see me. I called upon all the gods to send you back to this village site so that I could tell you where your people were. All the gods helped me. You have come. Take me up, follow this trail, and you will find your people. When you reach the first stream of water, drop me into it and there I shall remain." For some time the boy followed the trail and at last came to another village site. It was now dusk. When he entered the village site the voices came up from everywhere. The grass, the weeds, the insects, tipi poles, all shouted and sang:

"Here comes the son of White-Moccasins.
He was carried away from a village by the Witch-Woman,
This is truly the child of White-Moccasins."

The boy lay down and he heard the singing all around. It was kept up all through the night. The next day he followed the trail. If there was anything dropped by the people, a feather, a moccasin, a piece of sinew, a piece of an arrow, all these things sang the song he had heard at the village site. For many days the boy traveled west until at last he saw a village. When he came to the village everything seemed to sing about the child of White-Moccasins. As soon as the boy went into the village the people said: "Here comes the child of White-Moccasins." The chief took him into his tipi and asked him where he came from and who he was. When White-Moccasins found out that his son had arrived at the village he went to the tipi of the chief and demanded the boy. The chief said: "This boy is now in my tipi. He shall be my son, for I see that he has great powers." The boy said: "I can not do that, for I know that my father is living. The Crow was first to tell me of him. The Hawk led me to the village site from where I was stolen, and there everything sang of my father, White-Moccasins. The insects, the grass, the weeds, the trees, all sang to me of my father who was called White-Moccasins, and told me that I was his child. I shall go with my father." The chief said: "I do not mean that you shall be my son and remain with me, but I have a daughter who is old enough to be the wife of some-one. I call you my son because I want you to be my son-in-law." The boy said: "I can not do that, for I am too young." The boy told the people that on his journey he had picked up a clam shell, and that it had told him that the Witch-Woman had put it in the village in her place. He told them how he had taken the clam shell and placed it in the stream of water. The boy went back to his father and told him that instead of traveling west they would move to the south.

The boy had discovered that the people were starving, for they had not found any buffalo. Through the boy the people found many buffalo. When they had plenty of buffalo meat they talked of return-ing to their country. The people went back to their old home. When they reached the village the young man sat down in his lodge and invited several other young men to go with him on the war-path. Several of the young men joined him. He put the buffalo-hair lariat rope about his breast. He did not carry the scalp nor the war club. He left these in another bundle. He led the war party. They found the camp of the enemy, attacked the village, killed two enemies, took their scalps, and captured many ponies. When the war party returned to the village the people turned out to receive them. The chief then invited the young man to his tipi. The young man said: "No; I can not go there." When the young man had gone on the war-path four times, and was successful each time, he said to his father: "It is not yet time for me to take a woman for my wife. I have to make four buffalo holy and take them to the lodge of the priests. When I have done that I am ready to marry." The young man sat down again and planned another war party. He said: "My friends, I go towards the east, where the sun rises. I have an enemy there. I must kill her. If any of you wish to go with me you may." Some of the young men joined him and they went away. When they had traveled for some time they came to a big water and there they saw a grass-lodge. The young man told the others to remain behind, for he wanted to visit the grass-lodge himself. The boy turned into a Hawk and flew to the grass-lodge. When the old woman found out that the Hawk had visited her lodge she turned into an Owl. She remained in the lodge. The Hawk flew inside and with his right wing struck the Owl upon the head. Instead of the Owl being killed it turned into a Witch-Woman. The Witch-Woman laughed at the Hawk, but the Hawk jumped down to the ground and stood there as a young man. This time he had the club. He struck the woman upon the head, smashed her skull, and killed her. The young man now invited the other men to come. They took the old woman, placed her in a cache hole which she had dug, and buried her. The owl feathers, claws, and all her medicine bags they placed upon the fire and burned them. The warriors returned to their village.

Every time the young man went down to the creek he would hear the clam shells singing about him. At last the clam shells said: "We are ready to receive some of your people, and to teach them our power. We want some of your people to become medicine-men. We live in the mud. The mud in which we live has power to cure. We want to give this mud to the people." The young man at this time had a friend who went with him everywhere. He placed him on the banks of the water and told the clam shells to talk to the boy. The young man went home, and remained there. After a while the other young man returned and said: "I have some magic power now, so that I can do some wonderful things. If any of our people get sick I will doctor them." The young man was glad to hear this. He said: "It is now time that we go and hunt buffalo."

The people went on a hunt and while on this hunt the young man killed four buffalo and made them holy, so that they could be sacrificed to the different gods. After he did this he married the daughter of the chief. This young man became a great warrior, while the other young man became a great medicine-man. The young man then told the people that he was born under the protection of the sun; that this woman who was now killed was the last of the witch-women in the country. The young man then told the people that from that time on they must call him White-Sun; so he was afterwards known by this name. He did not become a chief. He was a great warrior and did not care to become a chief.

30. PURSUIT BY A RATTLING SKULL; THE PLEIADES.[1]

One time, while the people were on a buffalo hunt, they made their camp near a stream of water. A young girl in the village went off to gather some wood. She strayed and wandered around until she was lost and could not find her way back to camp. A Skull found and captured her and took her to its earth-lodge. When the girl was seated in the lodge, the Skull rolled up to her and told her that it had captured her so that she might wash it and keep it clean; that she was to eat the scales that came off from it, and if she did this her life would be spared. The girl was not allowed to eat anything but the scales from the Skull. The girl began to cry, but the Skull spoke and said: "There is no use for you to cry, for you are with me now, and you must begin to clean me."

The people missed the girl. They hunted and hunted for her, but they could not find her. For many days they hunted. At last the chief told the crier to cry through the village that they must break camp and move to another place. The people then moved away and gave up all hope of ever finding the girl. When they had been gone for some time the Skull spoke to the girl and said: "You must remain in this lodge. I am going far away." When the Skull was gone the girl began to cry. The Skull did not stay very long, but came back and rolled up to the girl and she had to take the scales off from it and eat them. Several times the Skull went off. Each time it came back in a short time. When the Skull found out that the girl would not leave, it told the girl that it was going to be gone for several days. The Skull rolled out and

[1] Told by White-Sun, whose grandfather was the leading medicine-man of the Kitkehahki. He was a famous story-teller. The object performing the magic flight in this tale is literally a rattling skull, and is not to be confused with the round individual mentioned in tale No. 5. This more nearly approximates the usual form of this tale among the plains tribes.

went off. After one day the girl went out of the lodge and went away out into the country, and stood upon a high hill and cried. A mysterious looking man came to the girl and said: "My girl, why are you crying?" She told him that a human Skull had captured her, that she was keeping its lodge in order, and that whenever it entered the lodge it rolled up to her and she had to take the scales from it and eat them, and that she wanted to get away from it and return to her own people. The man then said: "I can help you, but I can not do everything. After I have helped you all that I can, you must try and get help from someone else. Here is an arrow, a bladder, and a cactus. Take them and flee. The Skull will pursue you, but when it is about to overtake you first drop the cactus, then sing this song:

> My brother, the angry Skull is coming after me.
> Yonder it is coming over the hill-tops.
> My brother, the angry Skull is coming after me.
> My brother, the angry Skull is coming after me.

The animals in the country will hear you singing and will come to help you, and if they can not help you, keep going on. When the Skull is about to overtake you again, drop the bladder, but first you must put a little water in it. If the Skull still follows you, call, sing the song again, and the animals will come to your assistance. If they can not help you, and the Skull is about to catch you, then stick this arrow into the ground."

The girl took the arrow, the cactus, and the bladder. She then went down to the creek and put some water into the bladder. She began to run towards the northern country. In the meantime the Skull had gone back to its lodge and found that the girl was gone. Then it ran to the open country, saw her running and began to pursue her. After a while the girl saw the Skull coming over the hills. Then she began to sing. A Mountain-Lion appeared and took pity upon her. The Mountain-Lion asked the girl who it was that was coming after her, and when she said that it was a human Skull, he said: "I can not do anything for you, my girl. This Skull is a wonderful Skull. Go on. Some other animals are beyond here and they may perhaps help you." The girl ran on and soon the head came in sight again. When it was nearly up to her the girl dropped the cactus. As soon as she dropped the cactus the cactus spread out until there were many all over the ground, and the human Skull could not go over the cactus. Then the girl went on. After a while she turned around and saw that the human Skull had in some way rolled over the cactus and was rapidly gaining on her.

She began to sing the same song that she sang before. The Bear heard her singing, and came to help her. The girl told the Bear that a person was after her. "Who?" said the Bear. "A human Skull," said the girl. The Bear shook his head and said: "My girl, I am not afraid of anybody or anything but this Skull. It is wonderful and I can do nothing. Go on. Other animals are beyond here and they may be able to help you. I can not help you." When the Skull came in sight of the Bear, it began to call the Bear bad names. The girl ran on. The Skull continued to follow and just as it was about to catch up with the girl, the girl dropped the bladder with the water in it. When the bladder struck the ground and the ground gave way, there was a wide river with steep banks on both sides. The Skull saw many logs floating down the river and so it jumped upon a log and drifted down the river for a long way. The girl went on and met a Buffalo bull. The girl sang her song. The Buffalo listened, and took pity upon the girl and determined to help her, but when he was told that it was the human Skull that was after her, he told the girl to go on; that he could not help her. He said: "Go yonder. There are several brothers who live there. They may be able to help you." The girl looked around and there came the human Skull again. Just as the Skull was about to overtake her she stopped and stuck the arrow into the ground, and many thick, thorny trees sprang up, so that the Skull could not go through. Then the Skull turned and called the Buffalo names for helping the girl. The Skull worked around through the timber, and at last it blew its breath and a fire went forth from its mouth and burned the trees so that a pathway was made.

In the meantime the girl had found the lodge where the brothers lived, and she began to sing her song. Three little boys came out and listened to her. The youngest seemed to be about eleven years old, the other thirteen, and the oldest about fifteen years old. The boys had their quivers over their shoulders, and each boy carried a war club. They invited the girl into their lodge. The boys did not listen to the singing of the girl, for they had their eyes upon the human Skull. As the Skull came close to their lodge the eldest boy jumped out and with his war club struck the Skull so that the Skull broke into pieces. The girl was then told to come out and look at the human Skull. When she came out she picked up large stones and threw them upon the Skull and broke the Skull into many smaller pieces. Then she made a big fire, picked up the pieces of the Skull and put them upon the fire and burned them.

The boys told the girl that all their brothers were not at home, and that she could live with them until their older brothers came home.

The girl had some grains of corn in her belt, and also some squash seeds and beans. She took the brothers to the bottom land and made them clean a place, and there she planted some corn, beans, and squash. When they were planted the girl told the boys not to visit the field again until she told them to do so. Every morning the girl would go into the field and work. In the fall there was plenty of corn, squash, and beans in the field. The girl gathered corn and took it home and cooked it. The boys ate of the corn and they were satisfied. The girl then told the boys that she would have to cure some of the corn to keep for the winter. She took the boys into the corn-field and they gathered the corn while she made a big fire to cure it. After the corn was dried she gathered the squash and beans and told the boys that they must make a place for her to store away the corn, squash, and beans.

The boys dug a hole in the ground and there they stored away the corn, squash, and beans. In the winter the little brothers told the girl that their brothers were coming. The youngest ran and told his brothers about the girl. When the older brothers came, they said: "We shall have to send this girl away. What shall we do with her?" The brothers wanted to send the girl away, for it was not the intention that a girl should be among them, but the other three brothers said that the girl had given them corn, squash, and beans to eat and they could not very well send her away. They asked that they also eat of the things that she had. The girl prepared some corn, squash, and beans and gave them to the older brothers to eat. When they had eaten of the things they were satisfied. Then they said: "We will now decide what we shall do with this girl." They sent the girl out of the lodge, and then they began to talk about her. All the brothers left it with the youngest brother to decide what should be done with the girl. The little boy stood up and said: "We saved this girl from being killed, and in return she has given us plenty to eat. The girl has a right to be with us. I decide that she be our sister and that she remain with us." All the other boys said: "It is well. She shall be our sister." There were six of them and the girl made seven in the family.

In the night the girl found out that the boys disappeared. In the morning they came back. After a while the youngest brother told the girl that he and his brothers traveled through the sky in the night. After the girl had lived with them for some time the brothers decided to take her with them on their nightly journey through the sky country. At night she may be seen as the seventh star of the Pleiades.

31. THE POOR BOY AND THE MUD PONIES.[1]

A long time ago there were no horses. Dogs were the only animals that helped the people carry their burdens from one place to another. In those times there was a very poor boy in the village. He went from one tipi to another trying to get something to eat. Sometimes he was chased out, but at other times he was taken in and fed.

Once in a great while he would go into the lodge of the chief, and when the chief would see him he would feel sorry for him and sometimes he would give him moccasins; at other times he would give him leggings. Some people would speak against the boy and try to keep the chief from giving him any presents, but the chief would say: "Tirawa knows that this boy is living. As he is growing up he will watch over him and the boy may some day rule over us." But the people laughed at the chief for saying this.

The boy had a dream about ponies. He thought that two ponies were dropped down from the heavens and that they were for him. He so plainly saw the ponies in his dream that he knew their shape, and how their tails and manes looked. Often when the people broke camp and traveled along he would stay behind and would take mud and make ponies. Then he would place the ponies in his robe and follow the people. Before he would arrive at the village he would place the two mud ponies outside of the village. He would go into the village and go from tipi to tipi trying to get something to eat. Wherever he got a chance to stay over night, he would lie down in the tipi. Early in the morning he would go to where his mud ponies were. Then he would take the mud ponies down to the creek and pretend that they were drinking. He did this for many months, until the people had returned to their permanent village. Then he took the mud ponies down from where they stood, carried them a long way from the village, and stood them by a pond. He would go away and stay for a while and then return and make believe the ponies needed water. Then he would take them to where there was good grass and place them there.

One night the boy entered the lodge of the chief. The chief gave him something to eat and also a place to sleep. That night the boy had a dream. He thought that Tirawa had opened the sky and dropped two ponies for him. Then he thought in his dream that he heard Tirawa singing and he remembered well the song, for when he awoke he went out from the lodge and went up on a high hill, and there he sang the song.

[1] Told by Little-Chief, Pitahauirat. This is a variant of a well-known Plains tale and tells of the origin of the chief's society.

The people heard him singing and they wondered what the song meant. While the boy was singing, a mysterious voice said: "This song was given to you by Tirawa. Tirawa has given you a certain kind of a dance. You should become a chief. Go this night to where your mud ponies are and there you will find two live ponies." The boy went back into the village, to the lodge of the chief, and borrowed a lariat rope. He then ran to the place where his mud ponies were. When he arrived there he saw two ponies. The two ponies came to the boy and he caught both of them. The boy took the ponies to the village and tied them just outside of the village. He went into the lodge of the chief and told him that Tirawa had given him two ponies. Others, when they heard, said that the boy made the ponies out of mud, and that the mud ponies had turned into ponies, but the boy himself believed that Tirawa had given them to him. The people went out to see the ponies and almost worshipped them, for they were the first that they had ever seen.

The boy finally became the chief's son-in-law. He then went on the war-path alone upon one of his ponies. In a few days he brought back many other ponies. Then he sat down and sang the song that they had heard him singing on the first night.[1] The young men came from everywhere in the village to listen and be near him, for they knew that he was making up his mind to go again on the war-path. The young man led out a big war party and brought back many ponies. It was not long until he became a chief. He then started a society known as the Chief's Society and he was at the head of it. The songs which he introduced were the songs which he heard while on the hill. The songs and the dance were kept up by the Chaui and Pitahauirat. This dance became extinct in 1887 when Chief-Sun died. He was the keeper of the songs and the dance.

32. ORIGIN OF THE BUFFALO BUNDLE.[2]

A long time ago the Buffalo agreed to go to the home of the people. The leader of the herd was a bull who had white spots on him. The cow to whom he was married was also spotted white. On their journey the cow gave birth to a female calf, and the calf was the color of snow. The little white calf carried the sacred bundle. Each morning when they were about to start on the day's journey, the calf decided how far they should go. They came to a place where the people were, and they gave

[1] The words of this song have no meaning; the music will be found in Part II.
[2] Told by Mouth-Waving-in-Water, Kitkehahki. This story, as its title indicates, relates to the origin of the so-called Buffalo bundle. The story especially teaches that respect should be shown to the sacred bundle.

a certain number of buffalo to the people to kill. The people killed the buffalo and made many buffalo holy. They also captured the sacred bundle that the girl carried. When the bundle was captured by the people the buffalo were satisfied and agreed to go back to their country in the west.

During this time a young buffalo bull had taken away the white buffalo calf and had lain with it. When the Buffalo were about to return to their country the white Buffalo girl was missing. The Buffalo waited for the girl to come and decide how far they should go the first day. They called for her and she came up from a ravine where she had left her calf. She took her place and gave a command that the people should journey a certain distance. The Buffalo began to march and they journeyed for several days as the girl directed. Early one morning, just as the girl was about to tell the Buffalo how far they were to journey, there was a great noise from behind. The Buffalo turned and saw three buffalo bulls. In their midst was a poor little calf singing:

"I am hunting my mother.
My mother's name is White-Frost."

Then it sang again:

"I am hunting for my father.
My father is White-Bull."

The three bulls made fun of the calf and said: "You think White-Frost is your mother, and that White-Bull is your father!" but the calf went on through the herd singing until it reached its mother. The mother would not claim the calf, and would not let it suck, although it was apparent that she had a calf. The calf cried and said: "If you will not let me suck, I will turn your milk black and from this time on there shall be no more white Buffalo."

The calf returned to the village and turned into a boy. The little boy was given a home and lived with the people. He grew up to be a wonderful man. He then took charge of the bundle that was captured from the Buffalo. He told the people that when they killed Buffalo they must put fat upon the bundle, for the bundle belonged to Tirawa and the fat also belonged to him. The pipe and the raccoon penis went together in the bundle, for the pipe was used to give smoke to the gods, while the raccoon penis was used in offering the fat to the gods. He also told the people that when they should capture arrows from the enemy they should put these arrows upon the bundles, and when they made sacred pipe offerings they should use the enemy's arrows to tamp the pipe with, so that the smoke going to Tirawa would be offerings of the enemy; that they must never press the tobacco with their fingers, for if they did they would be offering themselves to the gods and would soon die.

33. THE LAST OF THE WHITE BUFFALO.

(See Abstracts.)

[Told by Thief, Kitkehahki. This apparently is only a fragment of the more extended story which the informant learned from his Chaui wife. Among the Chaui it is known that there formerly existed a ceremony, the altar of which consisted of four white buffalo skins.]

34. THE WIFE WHO RETURNED FROM SPIRIT LAND.[1]

Many years ago, when the people were in Nebraska, there was a young man who was well off and who had become a warrior when a mere boy. This young man was always away from his village on the war-path and he never cared to be with women. Every time he came to the village he would climb up on the mud-lodges and would look over the village and watch the girls who went to the spring for water. One time he saw a girl that he liked, and after that time he went down to the spring every day and tried to get a chance to talk to her. He met the girl near the spring several times, and he found out that she was the girl he wanted to marry, but he knew that he could not marry her until he had captured a certain number of ponies, and so he made up his mind that he would go on the war-path again and would try to capture some ponies.

He heard of a great warrior who was going on the war-path. The warrior invited several young men to come to his lodge, and he told them to get a dry buffalo hide for a drum and some drumsticks, for they were to sing coyote warrior songs. While these men were singing the young man in the village heard the singing and he knew at once that the warrior was going to lead a war party. The young man went to the lodge with his bow and arrows and moccasins, and joined the party. This war party went out and started towards the southern country to hunt the Comanche, for these people had many ponies.

The girl missed the young man, but she did not know that he had gone upon the war-path. She looked for him every day, and when she did not see him she was sad. She kept thinking of this young man until finally she became sick. Just as the people were getting ready to go on a buffalo hunt the girl died. The people took her up on a high mound close to the graveyard and there they dug a hole about two feet deep and then they set up two forks, one on the east side and one on the west side. They placed a pole across it and then put poles against this pole. Then they took the girl up there and placed her upon the platform, with

[1] Told by White-Horse, Pitahauirat. The tale not only illustrates, in a fairly complete manner, the belief of the Pitahauirat in the future land, but shows, like other tales already noted, the dire results of disobedience to the supernatural powers.

many presents of buffalo robes and all her dresses. They covered the place with grass and then with sod, so that the grave formed a little mound.

The people went on a buffalo hunt and killed many buffalo. While they were camped at one place they heard that certain warriors who had gone out were returning with many ponies. Among them was the young man. It was noised through the village that the young man had captured most of the ponies and had more than any other man. When he arrived at his father's lodge he sat down, and his mother began to tell him the news of the village. The mother, however, forgot to tell the young man that a certain girl had died. The next day she began to talk again and to tell the boy the news of the people, and she said: "My son, I forgot to tell you that a certain girl died in the village and was buried." The young man put his head down and the mother saw that he was sad.

The day before, the young man had mounted one of his best horses and rode around the place where the people dipped up their water from the creek. He did not see the girl, and so when he was told that a girl had died he knew that it was the one he liked. The young man lifted up his head and said: "Mother, fold up some dried meat for me and give me a new pair of moccasins." When he put on his moccasins he told his mother that he was going off again and that she must not worry about him, as he would return. The young man started towards the village. As soon as he started he began to cry and he cried all the way. When night overtook him he stood upon a high hill and cried. When he was tired he lay down and slept. He came into the country where the girl's grave was and there he cried again. He walked up the high hill on which was the grave and stood there several days and cried.

When night came he made up his mind that it would be better for him to go into the village and stay there over night. He thought that some of the people might be in the village and that they would give him something to eat. When he came near the village he noticed that there was one lodge where smoke was coming out from the opening at the top. He went to the lodge. He peeped in and saw a young woman sitting upon the ground facing west, so that he could not see her face. He kept looking in and he saw many buffalo robes and other things that the people had placed in the grave for the girl. After a while the young woman said: "You have been standing there a long time. Come into the lodge, but do not come near me. Sit down near the entrance." The young man seated himself near the entrance and she let him stay. The boy was thin and hungry, for he had had nothing to eat for many days. He sat there all night and the next day and all of the next night. The next night the young woman told the young man to come to the first post in the lodge. There he remained over night. The next night she told him to approach the fireplace, as there was a kettle on the fire. She told him to dip up some meat and eat, and when he had had enough to put the meat back on the fireplace. Every night the girl would invite the boy to move nearer to her. At last the boy went up to where she was sitting, but she told him not to touch her. She said that her dead relatives would not consent to have him touch her yet. She made him get into the bed and lie there. She told him that there were some things which were to happen and if he was brave and did not run away he might he able to keep her as his wife. She told him that she was not a real thing; that she might disappear at any time; but if he would do everything as she said, she thought that perhaps he would be able to keep her.

One night the girl told the boy to watch, as something was going to happen, and not to be afraid. In the night the boy heard drumming in the village. He also heard shouting, yelling, and singing. In the lodge there was fire in the fireplace and the fire never went out. The fire was kept up by the dead people. The fire burned low. When the drumming came near he heard a lot of little children running ahead of the drummers and they all rushed into the lodge. He heard the children talking and playing and they seemed to seat themselves around in the lodge. The drummers came into the lodge and the girl said: "When these people cease dancing here they will say that they have smoked and you must say 'Nawa.'" The invisible people came in and danced and after a while the leader of the dance said, "Now we have smoked." The young man said "Nawa." Then the children seemed to rush out of the lodge, though he could not see them; then the dancers went out. The next night the drumming sound was again heard, only a little earlier. The sound came into the lodge and the boy could see the feet of the children as they rushed into the lodge. Next came the dancing and drumming and as the dancers circled around the fireplace he could see their feet. They danced for some time and then the leader of the dance said, "We have now smoked," and the young man said "Nawa." Then he saw the feet of the children rushing out of the lodge and then the dancers left. Early the next night the drumming was heard again. This time when the people entered the young man could see their bodies. They kept on dancing and when the leader said, "We have smoked," the young man said "Nawa," and they went out. The next night the drumming came again and the dancers came in and he could see them plainly. They danced around the fireplace, and when the dancing was over the leader of the dance said: "Young man, when you first started from the village where your people are you began to cry. We knew what you were crying about. You were poor in spirit because this girl had died. All of us agreed that we would send the girl back. You can see her now, but she is not real. You must be careful and not make her angry or you will lose her. You have been a brave man to stay with the girl when we came in, but this is the way we are. You can not see us, but some time we can turn into people and you can see us, though we are not real. We are spirits. There is one thing you must do before this girl can stay with you. We have now smoked." They then went out. Then the girl said: "These people who were in here are all my relatives. They are anxious to help you to take me back, for they feel sorry for you. They have given you permission to talk with me and to be close to me, but we can not be together yet."

There was no more dancing, and no more affrights for the young man. Every day the young man went into the corn-fields of the people and found corn. He brought the corn up and they ate of the corn. The woman dished out meat to the young man. The young man began to gain flesh. One day while they were sitting in the lodge the girl said: "The people have decided to return to the village. They have started back. My uncles have started on ahead. Each of my uncles, four in number, has a little piece of buffalo meat and a piece of fat to place on my grave. They are now on the way."

Every day after that the girl would tell the young man where her uncles were and at what place they were now camped. One day she told the young man that her uncles were close to the village; that the next day they would arrive; that in the afternoon they would walk up to the grave to place the buffalo meat in the grave. "My uncles are now crying every day, for they are near my grave." The next day the woman said: "You remember what the leader of the dancers said about one more hard thing for you to do. To-morrow is the time when you shall have to do that thing." The next day the woman told the young man that he must use all his strength; that when the uncles should walk up the hill to the grave, they would go outside of the village and there they were to stand. When she gave command for him to take hold of her he must use all his strength to hold her, for when she saw her uncles she was going to try to disappear and to go from him. "Four times this shall happen and if I get away from you every time then you shall lose me. When we are out there and you get hold of me, you must call as loud as you can so that my uncles will hear you and they will come down and help you." The next day the girl told the boy to rise, that her uncles were now coming to the grave. They went outside of the village and when they stopped they saw the uncles of the girl going up to the grave. (The reason why the girl was trying to get away was because people were going to her grave and it was best that her spirit should not be troubled by human beings.)   As soon as she saw her uncles place the meat on the grave she said: "Pick me up quick."   The young man took hold of the girl and held her with all his strength, but the girl jumped up and down and the young man was thrown upon the ground and she got away.   While the young man held the girl he called at the top of his voice, but as the uncles were crying they could not hear his voice.   After the young man got up he went into the village and went into the lodge and there the girl was standing laughing.   She said: "Why, young man, you have no strength at all.   I am sorry to tell you that if I get away four times you shall never see me again, for, as I have said, I am not real.   Let us now go out again and you must use all your strength to hold me."

The girl and the boy went out of the village again and as soon as they were out she told him to take hold of her.   The young man then held her about the arms, put his legs around her body, and then began to call to the men to come and help him, but the men did not come.   The girl tried to get away and she did get away the second time.   The boy ran back into the village and when he entered the lodge she stood there laughing at him and said: "You are not strong.   Now we will go for the third time.   You must hold me just as tight as you can.   If my uncles hear you calling they will come and if they touch me then I must stay with you."   They went outside of the village again and stood there. The girl said: "Now catch hold of me."   The young man took her as before and he began to call to the men at the grave, but they would not come.   The girl began to jump up and down and she got loose again. Then the young man felt sorry and returned to the lodge.   There he found the girl standing laughing at him.   She said: "Young man, if you care for me and want me to stay with you, you must use more strength than you have shown.   This is the last time, and if I get away from you then I am gone and you shall never see me any more."

They went out, and before he could catch hold of her he began to shout.   About this time the men at the grave had stopped crying.   As soon as the girl gave command for him the young man caught her and jumped.   He put his legs around her and he reached out his hands and caught her hair so that her hair was twisted in his hands.   Then he shouted for the men to come.   She began to jump up and down.   Sometimes she remained up in the air for several minutes.   The boy hung on to her hair and down they would come upon the ground.   The men upon the grave saw them and they ran. The girl was up in the air as if swinging with the boy and the men ran as hard as they could. Among the men was one good runner. The girl came down with the boy and as they struck the ground this man reached them. He jumped upon her and the girl flew up again. When they came down again another man was there and he also hung to her and the girl went up and in a short time she came back to the ground and the other two were there. All took hold of her. When they had hold of her the girl took a long breath and said: "Uncles, you have held me. I will stay with you. I will not go away from you." Then she told them to let her loose, but the uncles would not let her go.

They went along, still holding her, towards their lodge. When they entered the lodge they saw her bed. The bed was covered with the robes which were placed in the grave. She told her uncles to go into the field and to bring her corn, beans, and squash, for she was going to eat, and that she should always be with them. The uncles would not leave her, so she had to go down into the fields with them. They came back with the corn and other things. She sat down and her uncles boiled some of the corn, beans, and squash for her. When she had eaten, she said: "I have eaten with you; I shall now stay with this young man." After that the girl told her uncles that they could stay four days and four nights with them, and that they must then return to their people.

After four days had passed, the men went into the field and gathered some corn, beans, and squash to take to their people. These men then started back to where the people were coming with the buffalo meat. They traveled for several days, and one day while they were journeying they met the procession coming. As soon as they met the people one of the uncles shouted and said: "My niece lives in the village with the young man who disappeared from our village." As soon as the people in the lead heard this they shouted back to others who were behind and so on until everyone knew. The girl in the lodge with the young man told all that the uncles had told the people, and she said: "They are nearing our village."

In a few days the people came to the village and instead of cleaning out their lodges and entering them the people went into the lodge where the girl and the boy were. The lodge was filled with people and when they saw her they knew that what the uncles had said was true. Then the people began to move into their lodges.

One night the girl noticed her mother looking closely at her. The old woman got up and took her hoe and went out. She went up on the top of the hill where the grave was and she began to dig into the grave.

When she had dug down she found the bones and all the things which were placed in the grave were still there, and she thought to herself, "Well, this can not be my daughter, for here she lies and all the things are here with her bones." When she went down and entered her lodge, the girl said: "Mother, I know what you have done. You do not believe that I am your daughter; but, mother, I am your daughter. My body lies up there, but I am here with you. I am not real, and if you people do not always treat me properly I will suddenly disappear." The woman knew that although her body lay in the grave, she was living with them as a spirit.

The young man was happy with his wife and for many years they lived happily together. Once in a while the young man would go on the war-path and would bring back many ponies. The woman gave birth and the child was a boy. The woman was not allowed to cook or to make moccasins for her husband, so that her relatives had to do the cooking and the making of moccasins for the young man when he wanted to go on the war-path. His son grew to be large, but the relatives of the woman never allowed him to touch the earth. They packed him upon their backs every day, and only when night came was the child allowed to lie upon the bed with his mother. As soon as it was daylight some of the relatives were there to put the child upon their backs. When one became tired packing the child, then another woman was ready to take him. The mother had told her relatives that they must not allow the child to play with other children, for in running around he might fall down, and if he did, it would be a signal for his disappearance.

One night the young man came into the lodge where his wife was, and he said: "My wife, I think it is time that I take another woman for a wife." The woman said: "No; do you not know that I told you a long time ago that I took pity upon you because you were poor in spirit and came back from Spirit Land to be with you? My relatives helped me to come back to you, and you promised never to take another woman for a wife." The man insisted upon taking another woman for a wife and he begged the woman so hard that she finally consented, although she had told her husband that if he should marry another woman, some day the new wife might get angry and call her a ghost-wife, and then she would know what was said about her. But she finally gave her consent for him to marry this other woman; so the man married another woman.

For several years they lived happily. One day the man went to the human wife and she gave him a pair of moccasins. The man put on the moccasins, but somehow they did not fit him, and he took the moccasins off and threw them away. Then the man went up to his ghost-wife and she had a pair of moccasins for him which her relatives had made for him. She gave the moccasins to him and he put them on and found that they were just right.

The next day he went into the lodge of his other wife and she saw that he had a pair of moccasins on that his ghost-wife had given him. She went up to him, took the moccasins off of his feet and threw them away. She said: "You threw my moccasins away and I will throw away the moccasins of your ghost-wife." The man became angry, took the moccasins, put them on, and returned to his ghost-wife's lodge. When he entered and was seated she said: "I know all that happened in the other lodge where your wife is. She threw away my moccasins and called me a ghost-wife. Now you see what I told you has all come true." The man became angry, spoke harsh words to his wife, and pushed her to one side. She said: "You must not do this; you must not strike at me. You know what I told you." But the man was angry and he struck at her. She said: "Do not strike at me any more, for you know what I told you. For one thing I am glad, and that is I have a child. If I had remained in the Spirit Land I should never have been allowed to have a child. The child is mine. You do not love my child. You let that woman throw away the moccasins which I put upon your feet." The man became angry again and struck the woman on the face. The woman said: "Do not strike at me any more." The man was angry and struck at her. She said: "I love my child. When I am gone I shall take my child with me." As the man lifted his hand to strike her again she disappeared and where she was sitting a whirlwind formed, and the whirlwind arose and went straight up in the lodge and whirled around and went out of the opening at the top of the lodge.

The man felt sorry for what he had done. The people scolded the man and he said nothing. He sat down near the fireplace and bowed his head. Towards evening he arose and went up on the high hill and there he stood near the grave crying, begging his wife to return to him. He cried and cried, and he stayed there upon the hill that night. The people took the child and put it to bed. In the morning they found the child dead. The people took the child up on the hill, opened its mother's grave, and placed the child there. Then the man cried all the more. For four days and four nights he stood there. The woman appeared to him again and said: "Always remember that when we die we live again. My people took pity upon you and I came to you. You struck at me several times. I am gone away from you. From this time on no more dead people shall come to our people, for you did wrong in striking me. Arise, walk down into the village and stay there.

Do not stay around the grave here, for you shall never see me, and I am not coming back to you." Then the woman turned into a whirlwind again and disappeared.

The man was broken-hearted. He stayed around the grave, and although the other wife came up he waved her to one side and would not listen to her. The man remained around the grave and would not eat anything, and so he starved to death. The people did not bury him beside the woman. They took him and buried him in another place. The woman went back to the Spirit Land with the child after the man died.

35. HOW THE WORLD IS TO COME TO AN END.[1]

Many years ago, when I was a little boy, I used to watch the old men sitting in the tipis, and sometimes in the lodges, rattling the gourds and singing. Several times I asked my father what the old men were singing about. My father would say: "Those old men are singing about Tirawa. When you grow up you will learn more about the songs of these old men." I was anxious to know more about the sacred bundle and the singing of the old men. When night came and I lay down with my grandmother, I said: "Grandmother, why do the old men sit in the lodges, rattle the gourds, and sing?" My grandmother then told me the following story:

My grandchild, many years ago, before we lived upon this earth, Tirawa placed wonderful human beings upon the earth. We knew of them as the wonderful beings or the large people. These people lived where the Swimming Mound is in Kansas. The bones of these large people were found upon the sides of the hill of the Swimming Mound. The old people told us that at this place the rain poured down from the heavens, and the water came from the northwest upon the earth so that it became deep and killed these wonderful beings. When these people were killed by the flood, Tirawa placed an old buffalo bull in the northwest, where the water had come in from the big water so that it overflowed the land. The buffalo bull was put at this place to hold the water back, so that it would not overflow the land any more. This buffalo was to remain at this place for many years. Each year this buffalo was to drop one hair. When all the hairs of the buffalo had come off then the people would not live upon the earth any more.

There were four things which Tirawa said he would do to kill the people, but he had promised that he would never send the flood upon

[1] Told by Young-Bull, at present the leading medicine-man among the Pita-hauirat and the owner of the Buffalo ceremony. The tale is interesting because it explains the Pawnee belief regarding the manner of the end of the world, at which time the south star, or god of death, reigns supreme.

the land any more. Tirawa said there were other ways of destroying the people on the earth. There were several ways of sending storms so that they would kill the people. There was one thing that Tirawa was not sure of doing, and that was sending fire from the sky to burn up the people. The gods in the heavens who were placed by Tirawa would have to sit in council and select a day when all things would end, and decide in what way all things should cease to be. We are told by the old people that the Morning-Star ruled over all the minor gods in the heavens; that the Morning-Star and the Evening-Star gave life to people on this earth. The Sun and the Moon also helped to give life to the people. The old people told us that the Morning-Star said that when the time came for the world to end the Moon would turn red; that if the Moon should turn black it would be a sign that some great chief was to die; that when the Moon should turn red the people would then know that the world was coming to an end. The Sun was also to shine bright and all at once that brightness would die out and the end would come.

The Morning-Star also said that the signs would be made; that as they gave life to the people they could also hold life back, for they had not the say as to when the world should end. The Morning-Star said further that in the beginning of all things they placed the North Star in the north, so that it should not move; it was to watch over the other stars and over the people. The North Star is the one which is to end all things. The Morning-Star told the people that the North Star stood in the north and to its left was a pathway which led from north to south; that when a person died they were taken by the North Star and they were placed upon the pathway which led to the Star of Death—the land of the spirits—the South Star.

The Morning-Star also said that in the beginning of all things they gave power to the South Star for it to move up close, once in a while, to look at the North Star to see if it were still standing in the north. If it were still standing there it was to move back to its place. The Morning-Star spoke to the people and said that in the first great councils when it was decided where each god should stand in the heavens, two of the people became sick. One was an old person and one a young person. They were placed upon stretchers, were carried by certain stars, and these two stretchers are tied on to the North Star. These two stretchers go around the North Star all the time.[1] The North Star continued to tell the people that whenever the South Star came up from the south it would come up higher; that when the time approached for the world to

[1] Ursa Major and Ursa Minor.

end the South Star would come higher, until at last it would capture the people who were carrying the two people upon the stretchers; as soon as the South Star captured these two people upon the stretchers they were to die. The North Star would then disappear and move away and the South Star would take possession of the earth and of the people. The old people knew also that when the world was to come to an end there were to be many signs. Among the stars would be many signs. Meteors would fly through the sky. The Moon would change its color once in a while. The Sun would also show different colors, but the sign which was to be nearest to the people was that the rivers and the creeks were to rise. The animals, such as otter, beaver, and others, were to drift down the streams. While they were drifting down these animals were to cry out and their cry was to be like that of people. When the people would go swimming in these streams of water, clam shells were to cry out to them, and when the people should try to get away from the clam shells some of them would get on their clothing, and when they would see the clam shells they would be in the shape of birds. They would be, however, clam shells and would cry out like babies.

My grandchild, some of the signs have come to pass. The stars have fallen among the people, but the Morning-Star is still good to us, for we continue to live. The Moon has turned black several times, but we know that the Morning-Star said that whenever the Moon turned black it would be a sign that some great chief or warrior was to die. My grandchild, we are told by the old people that the Morning-Star and the Evening-Star placed people upon this earth. The North Star and the South Star will end all things. All commands were given in the west and these commands were carried out in the east. The command for the ending of all things will be given by the North Star, and the South Star will carry out the commands. Our people were made by the stars. When the time comes for all things to end our people will turn into small stars and will fly to the South Star, where they belong. When the time comes for the ending of the world the stars will again fall to the earth. They will mix among the people, for it will be a message to the people to get ready to be turned into stars.

My grandchild, I remember one time when a man sat down and invited other warriors to go upon the war-path. As he took the things from the sacred bundle which he was to wear, he first filled the sacred pipe and offered the smoke to the different gods in the heavens and to Tirawa. Then he blew a few whiffs to the things which he was to wear. Then he was told by one of the priests that he must put on the things and go out of the lodge, so that the stars in the heavens would look down on him and that Mother-Corn would look down on him and give him power. The man was helped up by two other warriors. They walked out of the lodge with the man and there he stood with the pipe in his left hand. The otter-skin collar was upon his breast and the ear of corn was upon his left shoulder; the hawk skin on his right shoulder. The downy feathers were placed upon his head. As he stood outside of the lodge he looked around through the heavens and said, "Brothers, where is Mother-Corn?" The other two said: "The Moon has turned black. It was bright moonlight a little while ago and now it is dark." Then the three men went back into the lodge. When they entered, the two other warriors said to the priest, "The Moon has turned black." Other warriors went out to see the Moon and sure enough the Moon had turned black. The priest then said: "Leader, take the things off which you have upon you. Mother-Moon has disappeared in the heavens and it is a warning to you to stay at home. We know that the old people used to say that whenever the Moon disappeared and it was dark some big chief or some great warrior was going to die." But the warrior said: "No; I am dressed in a warrior's costume. Mother-Corn's path into the country of the enemy is plain. I will follow that path. The gods will look down and see me carrying the Mother-Corn and the hawk. They will help me to overcome the enemy." Some of the young warriors backed out and remained at home. Several of the great warriors and chiefs joined the war party. They went out and in a few days they met the enemy, who were on their way to attack the village. They were surrounded and only one man got away. He came home and told us that all of the rest of the warriors and chiefs were killed. This was one of the signs that the old people spoke of, and although they saw the sign plainly the men went out anyway and nearly all were killed. Now, my grandchild, go to sleep and think no more of what I have told you, for you are young yet and must not think about these things.

36. THE TALKING MEMBRUM VIRILE.[1]

When the Indians were upon the plains hunting buffalo, one young man was selected as a scout to look for buffalo. He went away off from the others, and as he climbed up a high hill he saw many buffalo in the valley. Then the man began to talk to himself about seeing the buffalo. He wanted to urinate. When he was through he held up his membrum and said, "Do you see them?" The man would hit his mem-

[1] Told by Thief, Kitkehahki. The interest in the tale is due to its moral teaching, which has added emphasis in the fact that the man who thus suffered misfortune was sent out from the priests' lodge to look for buffalo which were to be offered during the ceremony.

brum on the side and would again say, "Do you see them?" He kept on hitting it on one side and then on the other. After a while his membrum began to speak and it said: "I see them. I see them. I see them." The man said: "Well, that is enough. Do not say that any more." But it kept on saying: "I see them. I see them." The man saw that it would not stop speaking and he became scared. He went along to where he saw the people making their village. As he went down it kept saying: "I see them. I see them." He went into his lodge and sat down and it kept saying: "I see them. I see them." The people wondered what it was. After a while the man told them that when he was upon the hill looking for the buffalo he had asked his membrum to say that it saw the buffalo; that it had spoken and that it was speaking all the time. They tried in every way to make it stop speaking. After a while it said: "My mother-in-law must come and touch me and then I will stop." His mother-in-law went up to it, touched it, and said: "Please stop speaking," and it stopped. The next day the man was mad and ashamed and he left the village and went off and was never heard of again.

37. THE HERMAPHRODITE.[1]

There was a village and in this village lived a fine-looking young man. The young man never cared anything for women; but one night a young girl came to his bed and they lay together. After they had lain together for a while, the young man sent the girl away. He then went to a fine spring that was gushing forth from the side of a hill, and took a bath. Then he went home and lay down. That night in a dream he saw Spider-Woman sitting with her legs spread out, and a spring of water was coming out from between her legs. Spider-Woman told the boy in his dream that as he had come and washed after having connection with the woman, from that time on he should be like a woman. The boy woke up; he could not sleep any more. The next day the dream worried him, and for several days he felt as though he were sick, and he had a medicine-man come and wait on him. The medicine-man could not tell what was the matter. One time they sent for one of the medicine-men who, on examining him, told him that he was turning into a woman. The medicine-man told the relatives of the young man that he was turning into a woman, and that Spider-Woman was the cause of it; that the only way

[1] White-Sun, Kitkehahki. The common belief in the fact that springs take their origin from spider-women is emphasized in this tale. The teaching of the story is the warning given to young men not to bathe in springs after sexual intercourse—that is, while unclean. Not only must this be done for the good of the tribe, but also because the spider-woman, representing one of the supernatural earthly beings, must be treated with a certain amount of respect.

he could cure the young man was by having the relatives of the boy go to the creeks, springs, or any streams of water, and get the green moss from the bottom of the streams and bring it to him. The people went to the streams of water, but there was not any moss to be found. The medicine-man said: "Spider-Woman knows that I can cure the young man if I can get this moss; she has caused all this moss to disappear, so I can not cure him." When the boy heard that the medicine-men could not do anything for him, he was so ashamed that he committed suicide, rather than be half woman and half man.

38. THE SCALPED MEN.[1]

A long time ago some men went from their village on the war-path. The leader of the war party carried the sacred bundle upon his back. He carried the sacred bundle upon his back all the time and never offered any smoke to the gods in the heavens. Some of the warriors complained; they thought that they should offer some smoke to the gods on the way. When they came near to a village the leader took the bundle and placed it before him. He called the warriors and told them to be seated close to him. Instead of opening the bundle and offering smoke to the gods, he told the warriors that he had come to attack the village and to kill some of the enemy. When he said this all the other men agreed to attack the village. The leader got up, put the bundle upon his back, and led the warriors to the village. The scouts who had been out returned and reported that the village was a small one, but when the warriors attacked the village they found that instead of a few tipis there were many others in the valley. They were soon surrounded and all scalped but not killed. When the enemy left them upon the battle-field they all jumped up and gathered together. The leader was there with his bundle and they found that all of the warriors instead of being killed were only scalped. The leader then spoke to them and said: "There is not one of you who would want to go back to your people. Let us now go into a strange country and live there always." They all agreed to live away among the hills and there make their homes.

For many years the people looked for them to come home, but they never came. One day a man went hunting and as he climbed a high hill he heard people singing. He looked down in the valley where there

[1] Told by Bright-Eyes, a Skidi woman, who, at the time of her death recently, was the keeper of the Big-Black-Meteoric-Star bundle. The story is interesting on account of its expression of the belief, widespread among the Pawnee, that men scalped in warfare were not killed, but wandered off through the country, leading an independent existence, and as such were reckoned among the supernatural beings. Their home was supposed to be in the south, and occasionally, as noted in this and other tales, they conferred their magic power on some favored individual.

was a grove of trees, and there the warriors were dancing around in a circle. They were singing this song: "Scabs from the sore head drop." Whenever one scab fell off they all yelled, "There is the scab upon the ground." They sang this again and again. The man went down and saw that the warriors who were dancing were the same ones who had gone away upon the war-path and had not returned; that now they were scalped men. The man shot over them, so that they ran through the timber. He lost sight of them, but he knew they were living. He followed them up and at last he came to a big cave where their home was. The man was now afraid and did not go into the cave, but returned to his home and told the people that he had seen the men who had gone upon the war-path. He said that they were now scalped men and would never return.

II. TALES OF READY-TO-GIVE.

The tales presented in this group are known by the Pawnee as Ready-to-Give tales. They correspond to the group of tales in "The Traditions of the Skidi" known as hero tales. These stories, like those in the preceding group, are, as a rule, told during intermissions in ceremonies, and while some of them are considered as true and relating to events which actually happened, others are clearly recognized as of a fictitious nature. But in all the tales the hero, usually a poor boy, overcomes the enemy or dangers and thus benefits the tribe, or he brings the buffalo to the famishing village, or performs some act which is of general tribal benefit. Thus the hope is expressed that by the relating of the tales the corresponding amount of bravery and fortitude will be shown, but especially that some similar element of good fortune may result. The tales are known as Ready-to-Give, because Kawaharu, the god of the north, as explained in another place, is the especial patron of the hunter, and to him for success the hunters always appeal. Often these stories are told under certain circumstances while on the march toward the hunting grounds, at which time a grass-lodge is erected for the priests, and the girls of the village are encouraged to prepare a feast, when the priests sing and open one of the bundles. At such a time it is appropriate that tales such as these should be told. Thus in general it may be said that these tales as a group encourage heroic thoughts on the part of young men, because good fortune is desired to befall the tribe, and that through the relating of the tales respect is shown to the gods of the heavens and of the earth.

These tales fall into three natural divisions: Those numbered from thirty-nine to fifty are boy hero tales proper, and especially are explanatory of rites or ceremonies, and they are supposed to foretell or relate to things which are to happen. Those in the second group, numbered fifty-one to sixty-six, have to do with the calling of the buffalo. They are especially related during ceremonies by the priests, with the direct idea of bringing the buffalo nearer to the camp, because it was believed that the buffalo liked to be shown respect and often would voluntarily offer themselves to be killed in order that they might be offered to the gods. The tales of the third group, numbered sixty-seven to seventy-six, relate to the minor gods or wonderful beings, especially the witch-women and the spider-women. These had power over certain games. The upshot of the stories of this division as a whole is, that the witch-woman is transported to the moon, and the spider-women take up their abode in the sides of hills and become springs.

39. HANDSOME-BOY AND AFTER-BIRTH BOY.[1]

A long time ago the Indians had their village upon the Wide River. There was one poor boy among the people, but somehow this poor boy was liked by the chief's daughter. One day the girl was out with her ponies. On her way to the village she saw the poor boy going to the creek. She rode fast, caught up with him, and called to him. The boy did not want to talk to the girl, for he knew that if he were caught with her he would be either whipped or killed by the relatives of the girl. But the girl spoke to the boy and said: "I want you to come to my lodge to-night and sit in the entrance. I will be there to meet you." The boy said: "No; I will not go there. Your father might kill me if I were caught in his lodge." They separated.

That night the girl left her bed and went to the lodge where the poor boy stayed. The poor boy always had his bed upon the ground. The girl went to the boy's bed and they lay together. The girl begged the boy to sit up, for she wanted to talk to him, but the boy would not do it. After a while the girl said: "I know you think that you can not marry me, but there is a way for us to be married. I can take my meat bag and fill it with dried meat and fat. We can then go away to some far-away country and there we can live together." The boy became interested in the girl's talk. Then the boy said: "I have no bow and arrows with which to kill game." The girl said: "I will get my brother's quiver and bow and arrows." The girl then told the boy that she would see him out on the prairie the next day; that she would go for her father's ponies again, and there they would make arrangements to run away. The girl then left the boy's bed and went to her home.

The next day the girl watched over the village for the poor boy, but she could not see him. But while the girl was looking for the boy he was sitting on top of the lodge watching for the girl to go for her ponies. Some time in the afternoon the boy saw the girl go out from the village. The boy saw the girl catch one pony and ride it with the others to the water. After she had taken the ponies back to where she got them, instead of leaving them there she drove them over several hills. Then the boy went down from his lodge and went over the hills. He met her and they agreed to run away that night. The girl promised to be at a certain place in the village and the boy was to meet her there. They went home.

[1] Told by Woman-Newly-Made-Chief, Skidi, daughter of Scabby-Bull, a famous medicine-man. This is an interesting variant of the widespread tale generally known as After-Birth-Boy, the after-birth in this case not being thrown into the river but placed at the foot of an elm tree. Cf. Nos. 40 and 41.

As soon as it was dark the girl went to the place where she had promised to be and after a while the boy met her there. Then they traveled towards the south until they came to a big, wide stream of water heavily timbered on both sides. There they built a little grass-house. The boy would go out every day and kill game, so that they had plenty of meat. They were all alone, for the people were now far away.

The young boy had wonderful ways about him. When he came upon some wild animals or strange beings he got away from them and went back to where his wife was. For some time they lived together in the grass-lodge. At last the man told his wife that he thought it was time for them to build a small earth-lodge, so that he could make a strong entrance and fix it so as to cover the doorway at night and to prevent wild animals coming in. They began to build a small earth-lodge. At last the lodge was completed.

The man went hunting one day. He found a big buffalo bull and killed it. He took off the hide and took it home with him. The hide was stretched upon the ground and when it was dry it was very hard. This was then used to close up the entrance at night. For many years these people lived together here, and after a while the woman began to show signs of pregnancy. The man stayed close to the lodge and hunted. He did not go very far, for he wanted to be near to his wife.

One day the woman told the man that she would like to have some milk bags to roast on hot coals. She told him to try to kill a buffalo with a fresh bag. The boy went out and he could not find any buffalo near. He went far away over the hills and at last he found a herd of buffalo. He killed one of the cows, took the bag and some of the meat, and carried it to his home. When he entered the lodge he found that his wife was confined and was about to give birth. He threw the meat down upon the ground and ran into the lodge. He waited on his wife and after a while she gave birth to the child and it was a boy. Then the man took the after-birth, carried it out from the lodge, went into the timber, and came to a big elm tree. He dug in the dirt under the side of the tree and placed the after-birth there, and then went home.

Every morning after the man and the woman had eaten they would place some meat upon sticks which were placed near the fireplace so that the meat would be roasting. The child grew up. The man was very proud of it. The child began to crawl around. After a while it began to stand up and to walk. The child now had teeth and could eat meat. After a while the child got so that it played around inside of the lodge, and after a while it went out of the lodge and played. One day the man placed some meat around the fireplace upon the sticks. Then he went away on a hunt. He told his wife that he would be away for some time. The woman and the child were left in the lodge by themselves.

About noon the child came into the lodge and went to sleep on his mother's lap. She took the child, went to the bed, and placed it there. She covered the child with a robe. The child could not be seen if any-one entered the lodge. While the woman was sitting by the fireplace she heard strange voices outside of the lodge. She did not say anything, neither did she run, for she knew if they were enemies they would find her anyway and would kill her. If they were friends they would not kill her. When she heard the voices near by, talking in her language, she turned around and looked at the entrance.

After a while she saw a person come inside, then another and another, and after a while they all stood at the entrance. These strange people were very queer-looking. They had sharp elbows. On all their joints were long spines sticking out. At their heels also there were long spines. They had big eyes, and when they turned around the woman noticed that they also had another eye in the back part of their heads, so that these people really had three eyes—two eyes in front and one behind. Then they said: "The husband is gone. We can go in here and find something to eat. If she keeps quiet and does not call us bad names we will spare her. If she makes any fuss, or calls us names, we will kill her and take her to our home and cook her." They came in, found the meat around the fireplace, and they began to eat of it. While they were eating they would say, "Watch the woman, and if she calls us bad names we will kill her." They ate all the meat and then went away. The woman was watching them as they went away and she thought that all had gone out, but there was one that had not yet left, when she lifted up her hand and pointed at them and said: "The dirty, ugly-looking things, they have eaten up all my meat." As soon as she spoke the one behind saw her with his rear eye. He called the others and said: "The woman is calling us bad names and shaking her hand at us." Then they all rushed in, pierced her with their sharp elbows and heels, and carried her away to their place. These strange beings did not see the little fellow upon the bed or they would have killed him, too.

After the boy's mother was killed and carried away, the boy woke up, got down from the bed, and went to the fireplace. He began to eat of the bones which the people had left. About this time the father came in for some meat. He saw that the mother was missing; that there was blood upon the ground where she had been sitting, and he knew then that some bad people had come and killed her.

He followed the trail of the people and for many miles he followed their tracks until at last the tracks led into a thick timber. In the timber was a grass-lodge, and near it the leaves were all red. When the man was near to the grass-lodge he heard some one say: "Look into the pot, and see if the meat is done. It is nearly time for us to eat." The man then knew that his wife had been killed by these people and they were going to eat her. He had to slip away from the place or the strange beings would get him also and kill him. He went to his lodge, cooked some meat for the child, and then he placed the child upon his back and carried it around through the woods. For several days he stayed with the child. When their meat was about all used up the man thought to himself: "If I do not get some meat we shall starve. I must go and get some more meat." The man cooked some meat for the boy and told him that he was going on a hunt.

That afternoon the man brought in some meat. After he had placed the meat in the lodge he went into the timber. There he found a hollow log. This he took into the lodge and split it open. He began to clean out part of the log. He placed at each end of it a lot of tallow. He brought water in skins and placed the water in the hollow log. Then the man told the child that whenever he became thirsty he must drink out of the trough. The next morning the man filled the trough with water again. He placed some meat around the fire and told the child that when he got hungry to go to the meat and eat it and also to drink of the water.

One day when the father had fixed the meat and placed the water in the trough for the boy he went away upon the hunt. The child was alone in the lodge. Suddenly the child heard somebody singing outside of the lodge. After the song some one would begin to cry. The boy in the lodge was afraid. After a while a child appeared in the entrance. The song which the child sang was something like this:

"Handsome-Boy, your father loves you. He kills game for you and takes it to your lodge and you have plenty. Your father threw me away. My grandmother came and took me into their lodge. You eat meat all the time. I do not eat meat, but I eat things such as the ground beans, artichokes, grapes, and plums."

When the boy came inside he said: "Handsome-Boy, let us play." Then Handsome-Boy tried to get the other boy to enter the lodge with him, but the boy would not go in. The strange boy also remained some distance from Handsome-Boy. They played together outside of the lodge and all at once the boy jumped up and said: "Your father is coming," and he ran away and disappeared in the timber. As the boy jumped to run into the timber he said to Handsome-Boy, "Forget." Handsome-Boy would forget all about the strange boy and how he had played with him. He never spoke to his father about the strange boy. For several days the boy came and played with Handsome-Boy. Every day he would come closer to Handsome-Boy. One day they were play-ing in the lodge when the boy jumped up and said: "Your father is com-ing and I must go." The boy ran out of the lodge and the man saw him. This time the boy forgot to say to Handsome-Boy, "Forget." The man went into the lodge and when he saw that the meat and water were all gone, the father asked the boy how it was that every day the meat and water were all used up. Handsome-Boy told his father that a strange boy came to the lodge every day and before he appeared he sang and then cried. He said that in the singing the strange boy would say:

> Your father loves you, but he threw me away.
> He brings you much meat to eat.
> Grandmother gives me artichokes, grapes, and plums.

Then the man said: "What does the boy say?" Handsome-Boy said: "When we play he says to me, 'Your father loves you. He took me and placed me at the roots of a big elm tree.'" The man knew that that was where he placed the after-birth; that there must have been a child in the after-birth. He said: "My son, we must try to catch this boy, so that the boy can play with you all the time. I must go far away to hunt."

One day the man hid in the lodge, thinking that the boy would enter and he would be able to catch him. When the boy came, as soon as he reached the entrance he sniffed and said: "I smell your father. Your father is in the lodge." He then ran away into the timber. The man tried many ways to catch the boy, but he could not get him. The man took a strip of buckskin from the nose of the deer down to the tail. This he cut into small strings. The man gave the boy these buckskin strings and told him to tie them upon the boy's hair on top of his head. Each day the boy came in to play with Handsome-Boy. After they had played with the bow and arrows, eaten and drunk, then the strange boy would say, "Let me look into your hair and pick out the lice." Then Handsome-Boy would lie down and let the strange boy hunt the lice in his head. When the strange boy became tired, he told Handsome-Boy to look at his head.

One day while Handsome-Boy was looking for lice in the boy's head, he took the buckskin strings which he had and tied a bunch of hair on top of his head. He tied it very tight. While he was doing this the boy tried to jump up several times to run away, but as soon as the hair was tied fast Handsome-Boy said, "Come, father, come." Then the boy got hold of the mysterious boy and just as his father came the boy slipped away from him. He caught the buckskin strings, pulled them tight, and pulled out some hair from his head. The boy fell into the arms of the father. Handsome-Boy took the buckskin strings and the hair and placed them in the sacred bundle. After a while the strange boy was conquered. He said: "Father, I will stay with you. I am your son and Handsome-Boy is my brother." The boy stayed.

For many years these three lived at this earth-lodge. Every day the man went hunting. The two boys were now big and made their bows and arrows themselves. They made a sinew ring and tied it at each end. This sinew they placed in the dirt and shot at it. They were now big. They wandered over the timber. The father knew it. He was afraid they might come upon some wild beasts or strange people who inhabited the country.

One day when the father was ready to go out hunting, he said: "Now, my sons, you must not go to the river at a certain place, for at that place is a bull-boat. The bull-boat is stationed there. When a person enters it the boat starts across the river. When it gets into the middle of the stream where it is deep then the waves roll up and the bull-boat is upset and the person is thrown out into the water. As soon as the person gets into the water the bull-boat moves back to where it was upon the bank." The man went off on a hunt.

After a while the strange boy said: "Handsome-Boy, you know what your father said about going to that boat. Let us now go. He said we could go." Handsome-Boy said: "No; we must not go, for there is danger there." The two boys began to quarrel. One wanted to go and the other did not. At last the strange boy said: "Handsome-Boy, you are a coward. Give me my hair so that I may return to my grandmother." Handsome-Boy said: "No, brother I will not give you the hair and I will not let you return to your grandmother. I would rather die than to have you leave me. I will go with you." The strange boy was happy. They ran to the river and when they reached the bank they saw the boat. As soon as he saw the boat he ran down and jumped into it. Then he yelled to his brother and said: "Come, Handsome-Boy, quick; this is fine." Handsome-Boy ran down and jumped into the boat. The boat then started across. When it reached the middle of the river it began to roll up and down, for the waves became very high. Then Handsome-Boy became scared and cried. The strange boy said: "Watch me, watch me. You must do whatever I do." When the boat was about to upset the strange boy stretched out his arms and began to move as if he were flying. After a while the strange boy flew up, for he had turned into a goose. The other boy began to cry. The goose which was flying overhead said: "Do as I did, you coward. Move your arms. Fly up as I did." After a while Handsome-Boy also flew up and the bull-boat went down into the river, came up again, and went back to the bank. The boys flew over the dry land and turned into human beings again. Then the strange boy said: "Handsome-Boy you are a coward. When I tell you to do anything you must do it. If you do not do what I tell you, you will get lost and you will be killed."

They went home and told their father that they had ridden in the boat. The father said: "Children, I am glad that you did not get killed. I am glad that you came back. You must be careful in your wanderings over this country. There is one place where I do not want you to go. It is near the river. There is a steep bank there and at the bottom of the bank is the place where people do not dare to go."

The next morning after the man had gone away to hunt the strange boy said: "Handsome-Boy, you remember what our father said about going to that place. Let us now go." But Handsome-Boy said: "Father said not to go there." Then the strange boy said: "We must go." Handsome-Boy did not care to go. The strange boy said: "Give me back my hair. I must go back to my grandmother's." Then Handsome-Boy had to give up and go with the strange boy. They came to the steep bank and they looked down and there in the bottom were many snakes.

Handsome-Boy began to cry, but the strange boy said: "Oh, stop crying. Those things are nothing and we shall kill some of them and take them home to our father." The strange boy then told Handsome-Boy to sit down. He put his hands upon his legs and upon his feet. Then he said: "Now stand up." When the boy stood up he felt that his legs and feet were very heavy, for the strange boy had covered his legs with flint stone. Then the strange boy began to stamp upon the ground. When he started to do this the soles of his feet were like the skin of a horned toad. His legs were covered with the shells of a turtle. They walked down to where the snakes were and they stepped upon the heads of the snakes. When the snakes tried to bite them their teeth could not go through them. They killed four of the largest snakes with rattles on. These they took up on the hill and skinned them, leaving the rattles upon the skins. Then the strange boy said: "Handsome-Boy, we will place two of these snakes at the bottom of the doorway, one in the middle and one on the top. When we play we will run against the doorway. Then these rattles will rattle and it will sound nice. Our father, when he returns, will run against the door and the door will shake so that the rattles will make a noise and he will like it." They arrived at their lodge and placed the snakes upon the doorway. When the father came with meat he ran into the doorway and he heard the rattles sounding. He was scared. After he placed the meat upon the ground in the lodge he went and examined the entrance way and saw the snakes there. He was afraid. He said: "Boys, take these snakes away from the entrance. If you leave them on the doorway they will smell and rot." Handsome-Boy was willing to do this, but the other boy did not like to throw away what he had brought home for his father. After the snakes were thrown away they all went into the lodge and had something to eat. The man said to them: "My sons, I must say it, and I mean what I say, I do not want you to go to that high hill. The people who go there get killed by lightning. The animals who go there are struck by lightning. Now I ask you boys not to go there, because it is not an animal who kills the people, but it is the lightning in the heavens that does the killing."

The next day after the father had gone away the children began to play with their bows and arrows. All at once the strange boy threw down his bow and arrows and said: "Handsome-Boy, let us go to where father told us to go." Handsome-Boy said: "No; he did not say for us to go; he told us not to go there." The strange boy kept on. After a while the boy consented and they went. The hill was not a large one, but it was very high. When they reached the foot of the hill the clouds began to fly over the hill and they could see the clouds fall upon the hill. All at once the boys heard thunder, and then they saw lightning. Handsome-Boy was crying and telling the strange boy that they were lost. The strange boy said: "Stop crying. We must go there to the side of the hill where you see that high tree. That tree is hollow. There on the top of the tree is where the four wonderful beings live who send the lightning and who make the thunder." When they got to the tree the thunder began to sound and then lightning seemed to strike the tree, and the smoke caused by the lightning would come out at the bottom of the tree. The strange boy climbed the tree and got on the top. Then he reached down and he pulled out a human being. The human being was painted red. It was covered with a buffalo robe and a black lariat rope was tied around its waist. The boy held the human being by the arm and said: "So you are the wonderful being, are you, and what is your name?" The wonderful being said: "My name is Thunder." Then he said: "Now, Handsome-Boy, be ready to catch him." He then threw him down. Then the strange boy reached down again into the hollow log and he pulled out another. He held him up and said: "And what is your name?" This man was also a human being. He wore the robe and the red paint, but upon his forehead was painted the picture of lightning. He said: "My name is Lightning." Then he pulled out another. He also was painted. "What is your name?" the boy said. He said: "My name is Loud-Thunder." Then he dropped him in front of his brother. Then he reached in again. This time he pulled out another human being. He held him up and said: "What is your name?" This being said: "My name is Wonderful-Lightning." "So your name is Wonderful-Lightning? I have taken your lightning from you. You shall go to my home with me and you shall work there for my father." He dropped him down in front of Handsome-Boy and then the strange boy came down. When he got down he spoke roughly to the four beings. He took two of them by the arm and said: "Here, Handsome-Boy, you take these two and I will take the other two." Then they went to their earth-lodge and placed the four beings near the lodge. After a while the father came. The boys ran to him and said: "Father, we have brought Lightnings and Thunders, four in number, and they shall work for you." The father said: "Children, you have done wrong. They are from the heavens. They are not to be molested. You must take them back to the place where you got them." Then the strange boy said: "No; Tirawa did not intend that these things should be upon a tree always, where they could kill whoever came near them." Then the boy took one of the beings and said: "Now you must fly in the west. You must be in the west always and you shall be the one who shall thunder first early in the spring." Then he took one of the Lightnings and he said: "Go with the Thunder, and when the thunders first sound you must also lighten around the circle of the heavens." Then he took the other Thunder and said: "You must stand in the south, and you, Wonderful-Lightning, must go with this one. There will be times when you travel over the earth. The thunders will sound loud and the lightnings will be thick. Sometimes you will kill people." These beings were glad and they promised to do as the boy had said. They disappeared and were never to remain upon the earth any more. Now these boys had scattered the thunders and lightnings. The father of the two boys was now becoming afraid of them.

One day the father sat down with the two boys and he began to talk to them. He told them of the many wonderful places where he had told them not to go, but they had gone anyway and had destroyed those places. At last they had destroyed the gods and he thought that was too much. The man said: "There is but one more place where I do not want you to go. When I tell you not to go to a place, you go any-way. I will ask you to go to that place to-morrow." The next day the man cooked much meat and he told the boys that he would be away for some time and for them not to worry about him. Before he started he said, "Now, boys, go to that place, for there the people dwell who killed your mother." The boys heard what their father said. Then they went away to play. The father went off, but he intended to run away. He watched the boys. The boys never went to the place. Then he said to himself: "I told the boys to go, but they are not going. I do not understand them." Then the man tried to run away, but he found that the strange boy knew that he was trying to run away, so he gave it up. In the evening he returned to the lodge and here he found the boys. The next morning the man said: "Boys, I am going hunting. You must not go to that place." Then he went away on a hunt.

The boys took their bow and arrows and went away and played upon the ground. After a while the strange boy threw the bow and arrows upon the ground and said: "Handsome-Boy, you remember what our father said about going to that place. Let us now go and see what kind of people they are. Our father said they were the people who had killed our mother." Handsome-Boy would not go. He said that his father had said that they should not go there, for the people who were there were ugly and dangerous. But the strange boy said: "Let us go." Finally the boy gave in and they went. They started out on the run to the place. They kept running toward the timber. Once in a while Hand-some-Boy tried to stop, but the strange boy was so glad to go to the place that he kept coaxing the boy on.

After a while they got into the timber. They walked through the timber for some time. Soon they came to a place where the trees seemed dead. The leaves were yellow. They walked on until they came to an opening and there they saw a grass-lodge. They stood still, and one of the sharp-elbow people said: "Our grandchildren are here. They have come to visit us. Place the kettle upon the fire and put some water in it, so that we may boil some meat for them to eat." Handsome-Boy began to cry. The strange boy whispered to him and said: "Stop crying. If you cry these people will kill us. If you keep still they will not kill us." Then the people in the grass-house began to get ready to bring the boys in. The strange boy then told Handsome-Boy that when they were taken into the grass-lodge they were to be given seats on the north side of the fireplace. The sharp-elbow people were all to be sit-ting around watching them. The strange boy said: "When they get ready to kill us, then I will touch you. As soon as I touch you, you must reach for the kettle, place your right foot upon the rim, and do not be afraid of getting burnt. Then jump up. I will do the same. Then we will disappear and the sharp-elbow people will do the rest of the work necessary for killing themselves."

One of the sharp-elbow men came out and invited the boys in. The kettle was swung over the fire. The boys were given seats on the north side of the lodge. The sharp-elbow people began to question the boys as to where they lived and where their people were. The strange boy answered them. One of the sharp-elbow people said: "The water is boiling over the kettle. Be ready now to get the meat to put into the kettle." All the while the sharp-elbow people were touching one another to indicate that they were to jump upon the boys, kill them, cut them up, and put them into the kettle. When they were ready to jump on to the boys the strange boy knew it. He touched his brother and they both arose and said: "Grandfathers, we will now go home." The two boys stood up and placed their feet upon the rim of the kettle, and the sharp-elbow people ran to them, but the boys disappeared. The sharp-elbow people began to stick the sharp points of themselves into one another. The kettle overflowed with the hot water, so that when the sharp-elbow people fell down they were scalded. While they were striking the sharp points into one another, the two boys were standing outside laughing at them, for the sharp-elbow people became angry with one another and they fought and scattered the hot coals so that the grass-house was burned up. The boys could see them from where they stood. The strange boy then went to where the sharp-elbow people lay and he took the leader by the arm and told him to stand up. The sharp-elbow leader stood up. He touched him again and said: "You are now dead as a human being. You shall again take life and become a locust tree." Then he took the other people and placed them in different places in the timber as locust trees. Then he told them that people, when they saw the trees, would remember that they were once people with sharp elbows and had sharp spines all over their bodies. The boy also cut off four thorns before he turned them into trees, and he took them home and told his father that he had brought four awls for him. The man thanked the boys and gave them something to eat.

In the night the man could not go to sleep, for he was thinking of the wonderful powers which the strange boy possessed. He would say: "I am wonderful myself, but this boy beats anything I have ever seen. He has killed all bad animals throughout the country. Even the lightnings and thunders he has killed. These strange sharp-elbow people he has killed and they were the last to be killed. There are no other bad people. The next thing the boys will do will be to try to kill me. I had better run away." He had tried to run away when the boys started to go to the grass-lodge of the sharp-elbow people, but somehow the man found out that the power of the boy was watching him. He knew also that the boy knew that he was about to run away. Then the man came back to the lodge.

One day the father went hunting. He stayed for several days. When he returned he had a deer upon his back. He went back into the timber and brought another deer. He brought several deer and buffalo. Then the man began to jerk the meat and cook it. After all the meat was cooked he took some skin bags, brought up water and placed it in the trough. At this time the boys were away in the timber, so that for several days they did not come to the lodge. The man thought to himself, "This is a good time for me to go," so he went away. The strange boy said: "Handsome-Boy, our father has run away. He is afraid of us." Handsome-Boy, however, would not believe this. They went back to their lodge. When they entered the lodge the strange boy said: "Handsome-Boy, do you know how we got away from those sharp-elbow people?" Handsome-Boy said "No." Then the strange boy said: "When both of us stepped upon the rim of the kettle I said that we should turn into charred leaves, and as such we flew up and out of the opening. When the leaves were outside they came down upon the ground. When they struck the ground we were boys again. That is the manner in which we got away from the sharp-elbow people. Now let us find our father." Handsome-Boy said: "No; our father will come back." The strange boy said: "No; he is gone." Then the strange boy said: "Handsome-Boy, let us go to my home."

They went home and when they arrived at the elm tree the two boys disappeared and there they were in a lodge under the ground. The lodge was really a wood rat's nest. There Handsome-Boy found the bow and arrows and other things which the strange boy had taken away from him. The strange boy said: "Handsome Boy, this is where I received my powers. The wood rats are my grandmothers. They fed me with pecans, grapes, plums, and ground beans. I was never hungry. Here where we sit dwelt all the animal gods. Among them was one strange being who seemed to have lightnings in his hands, lightnings in his eyes, and lightnings in his mouth." He said: "This Lightning man spoke to me and said that there were some human beings who pretended to be lightnings from the sky; that they had killed many people; that it was time that they were taken away from this earth and power would be given them to stand in the heavens as thunder and lightning."

The strange boy again said: "Handsome-Boy, this is why I was not afraid of the thunder and the lightning which I captured in the hollow log on the side of that high mound." After they had been there for some time a woman came to the lodge with a black robe upon her shoulders and a black skirt. She gave the boys some ground beans and then she went away. The boys ate of the beans and then they left the place. The boys went through the timber hunting for their father. Every animal they met the boy asked if it had seen their father. The animal would say "No." The boy would look at it and would tell the animal that if it was lying to him he would kill it. The animal would say: "I have not seen your father. He did not go this way." The insects which the boys met were also asked if they had seen their father. The insects would say "No." When they met the bugs the boy would ask them if they had seen their father and the bugs would say "No."

They went all over the country, but they could not find their father. They finally went back into the lodge. A little Mouse came out from the side of the lodge. The boy asked the Mouse if it had seen their father and where he was. The Mouse said: "Yes; I know." The Mouse went from the fireplace to the wood mortar standing near the entrance. The boy went to the mortar. He picked it up from the ground and said: "Did you help my father to get away from us?" The mortar said: "Yes; I did." The boy threw the mortar away and said: "I shall not place you upon the fire so that you will burn up. The people will have use for you in the future." The two boys went to the hole where the mortar stood. They went into it and there they found their father's trail. They came to the under-ground world. They could see plainly. They traveled on. After a while they came to a big village of people. They went through the village asking people if they had seen their father. The people said: "Yes; he passed through here." They traveled on and on until they came to another village of people. They went through the village asking for their father. Everyone they asked said that the father had passed on through the village.

The two boys traveled on and after a while they came to another village. The strange boy said: "These people are very bad. We must kill them in the under-world. If our father is in this village they will not tell us. Now, Handsome-Boy, I want you to twist your head around." The two boys twisted their heads around and their heads rattled as if they were two gourds. Then the strange boy said: "Handsome-Boy, when we enter the village you must go through one way and I will go another. You must speak on the way and tell the people that if they look at you they will die; that if they do not look at you they will die anyway. If the people look at you they will die and if they do not look at you they will die just the same." The two boys started to go through the village. The strange boy started from the west side and Handsome-Boy from the east side. As each one went along he saw the people dying. Each said as he passed through the village: "Look at me or you will die. If you look at me you will die." When they reached the center of the village all the people had been destroyed. Then they went on. They came to a stream of water and there they found the tracks of their father where he had tried to cover them up.

The two boys crossed the stream of water and just as they were about to climb up the bank a strange being came out from under a rock and said: "Wonderful boy, I know you. You have great powers, but I am like you. I also have great powers. I will not let you pass here and kill these people as you have been doing. Your father passed through here, but you shall not pass." Then the boy looked at the strange being and said: "Very well; if you have power to kill me, go ahead." The strange being jumped at the boy and the strange being dropped away and began to beg of the strange boy not to kill him, and that it would let them pass through the under-world. This strange being was a Lizard. Then the strange being told the boys that their father had passed that way; that he tried to help the man, but as the boy had more power than he had he could not do anything. When the strange being jumped at the strange boy the strange boy had turned his legs into flint stone so that the strange being could not bite him.

The boys traveled on and came to a village. When they entered the village they were more cautious, for they knew that their father was in the village. They went through the village, twisting their heads as they went and their heads rattled like gourds. They killed the people. After a while they came to their father. They had already killed him and so they stopped killing the other people. Then the two boys took their father and carried him away up on a high hill, then went into the timber. They secured four dry willows, four cottonwood, four box-elder, and four elm poles. They took these poles up on the high hill. First they placed the willows at the bottom; then they placed the cottonwood crosswise over the willows; then they placed over these the box-elder; then they placed over these the elm. Then they set fire to it, and when it began to burn well they took their father and placed him on top of the burning timber, and as the smoke went up into the heavens the boys lifted themselves up in different directions towards the heavens.

What they burned this man for no one knows, and where the two boys went no one knows.

40. LONG-TOOTH BOY.

(See Abstracts.)

[Told by Thief, Kitkehahki. This is one of the many versions of the well-known Pawnee hero tale. It is not supposed to be a true story, but is told to the children that they may know that the animals have power to teach the people to do wonderful things. In the story is supposed to be an explanation of the Pawnee custom of erecting upon the pole the scalp of an enemy taken in war.]

41. LONG-TOOTH BOY.

(See Abstracts.)

[Told by Leading-Sun, Kitkehahki. This is another and much more complete version of the preceding story, though by the Kitkehahki it is regarded as a different tale.]

42. BURNT-BELLY AND HIS DREAMS.[1]

A long time ago there was a village of Indians. In the village was a wonderful man and his sister. They lived away from the village, always making their camp on the east side. In the village was an orphan boy who was very poor and nearly naked. Having no robe, he would sit close to the fire in order to warm himself and his belly became scorched, and so he was called Burnt-Belly. Some man took pity on him and gave him half of a buffalo robe with which to cover himself. He never washed his face nor brushed his hair. The little boy would go through the village, entering one lodge after another, carrying water and wood for the people. In this way he got something to eat.

Every evening he went into the lodge of the wonderful man. As soon as the boy entered the lodge and sat down near the fireplace, the young man would say: "Here comes my brother-in-law. My sister, you must feed your husband." The girl would laugh and would feed the boy. After the boy had eaten the wonderful man would say: "Boy, I hear people say that you are a great warrior, that you wear a war bonnet, and that you are now a handsome man. The people tell that you are my brother-in-law." The wonderful man would talk in this way to the boy so much that he would leave. The wonderful man said these things to the poor boy, for he was making fun of him.

One evening when the wonderful man was talking in this way to the boy, the boy went out from the lodge and went to the stream of water. He lay down upon the bank, went to sleep, and had a dream. He saw a fine-looking young man standing on the water. The young man wore fine buckskin leggings, fine moccasins, a fine shirt, a fine robe, and a quiver of otter skin with arrows and a bow. He had on his head a fine

---

[1] Told by Little-Chief, Chaui. Teaches the wisdom of refraining from making fun of the poor boys, for they may become great warriors or even chiefs.

war bonnet. This man said to the boy: "My boy, I feel sorry for you. You are poor; the people make fun of you and call you all kinds of names. They even make fun of you and say that you are to become a warrior and a chief. You see how I am dressed and that I stand here on the water. Before very long you are to dress just as I am dressed. You shall become a great warrior and shall marry the sister of that wonderful man. The wonderful man has dreams about the sun. In the dreams the sun told him to make a shield. Through this shield the young man thinks he is wonderful. In a few days a war party will start out and you must go to the lodge of this wonderful man and ask him for his shield. He will let you have the shield. You must follow the war party, and, although they shall try to send you home again, keep right on with them. I will protect you and will help you to overcome the enemy. When you have returned from this war party you must come down to this stream of water and I will speak to you again." The poor boy woke up, stood upon the bank, and prayed to the being he had seen in his dream that all might come true. He went back to the village and there he went from one lodge to the other trying to obtain something to eat.

A few days after the dream he heard that a party of warriors were going on the war-path. He went into the lodge of the wonderful man, and as he sat down the wonderful man began to tell him that he was to become a great man and that he was to marry his sister; that he was to become his brother-in-law. The boy did not pay any attention to it, but said: "My brother, I wish you would lend me your shield. I want to join the war party which is going out." The wonderful man sat for a while and at last said: "I will lend you the shield. You shall go and join the war party." He took the shield and gave it to the poor boy. The poor boy followed the warriors, who had already started on the war-path. When he caught up with them they scolded him and told him to return to the village, as he was too young to go with them. But some of the warriors who saw that he carried the shield of the wonderful man said: "Let him stay with us. If he gives out we will leave him. See, he has the shield of the wonderful man upon his back. It may be that he has wonderful power from the owner of the shield. It may be that the wonderful man has given him power to travel." They let the boy go with them.

A few days afterwards they reached the camp of the enemy. The warriors attacked the village. The young man went into the village, killed a man, and took the scalp. He returned to where the other warriors were. The scalp he gave to the leader of the warriors. When the fighting was done, the warriors found out that the only man who had killed an enemy was the boy and that he had also taken a scalp. They sat in council and said: "Let us not tell that the boy killed the enemy and took the scalp. Let us make the people think that some one else did this." When they reached their village the poor boy was not spoken of. He returned the shield to the owner. The women began to dance scalp dances and somehow it was learned that the poor boy alone had killed an enemy and taken the scalp. When the wonderful man heard the news in his lodge, he said: "They are making fun of my brother-in-law. The warriors did not say that the young man had taken a scalp." The boy continued to be a poor boy and went from one lodge to another.

A few days after his return from the war party he went down to the bank of the stream and there lay down. He went to sleep and had a dream. He saw this man again on the stream. He spoke and said to the boy, "My son, stay here on the bank of the stream for three days." The boy remained three days and when night came he had another dream. The fourth night the man on the water told him that he must wade into the water and dive four times; that he must walk out from the water and stand upon the bank for a short time; that he was to go to the lodge of the wonderful man; there he would meet the sister of the wonderful man with a bucket going to the stream; when the girl should return with the water, he was to ask her for a drink; then he was to go a short distance from the lodge and the girl herself was to follow him. The stream would say to him that he was the stream of water and the girl would be thinking of him. The next day he sat on the bank.

In the night he did as he had been told. He went into the water and dived four times. When he came out he felt strong. When he felt himself he found that he wore leggings, moccasins, buffalo robe, shirt, and quiver. He also had the war bonnet upon his head. He stood for a while and then turned around and went to the lodge of the wonderful man. Before he reached the lodge he met the sister and she stopped to see who the young man was. On her return with the water the boy met her again and talked a while and took a drink. She entered the lodge with the water. She could not rest. She went out and followed the young man. When she reached his side she told him that she wanted him to go to her lodge. The young man went with her and they sat down together in the lodge. Her brother was away at this time. In the morning when they got up from the bed her brother saw them. He was well pleased to have a brother-in-law. The young man was fine-looking had fine clothing, and a fine quiver of otter skin, with bow and arrows.

Soon after this the enemy attacked the village. The boy fought with them and drove away the enemy after killing several of them. After a while the young man himself led out a war party. They attacked the village of the enemy, killed many, taking many scalps and bringing home many ponies. When he brought the ponies home he began to give them away. The people wondered who this man was. The people would say, "What has become of Burnt-Belly." The boy stood up and said to the people: "We went on the war-path, we attacked the village, we killed many people, took many scalps and many ponies. The people are well off through it. You are anxious to find out who was the leader of this war party. It is the boy whom you all despised; the boy whom you called Burnt-Belly. It was this boy who led the party." Then the people knew at once that it was the poor boy, and when the wonderful man heard of the boy he said to himself: "All things that I have said to the boy have come true. It is wonderful. When he became my brother-in-law I would ask for Burnt-Belly." The people chose him for a chief and they knew him as a great warrior.

43. THE BOY WHO WORE A WOODPECKER CAP.[1]

There was a village upon the prairie with a stream of water running on the south side. On the west side were many little ponds and lakes. Upon one of the islands the people saw a strange being. This strange being was a little boy. He wore a woodpecker cap. Around the rim circle were many woodpeckers' heads. This little boy also had a quiver made of otter skin. The bow was of osage orange and it was black with age. The arrows were black and were feathered with the yellow feathers of a woodpecker. The leggings were made of antelope skin. Eagle feathers were tied upon the leggings, and here and there hung owls' heads. Every time he was seen upon the island in the night the people would hear the owls hoot about him.

One day the boy saw a strange woman swim across to the island where he was. The people in the village had never attempted to swim across the lake to the island, for there were many strange animals in the water, and people were afraid to swim across the lake. The woman came to the island where the boy was. The woman said: "My grandchild, it is now time for you to go among your people. I left you here upon the island so that the animals might take care of you and teach you their mysteries, and that some day you might be able to help your people. I have brought you an arrow. Whenever you want to cross the lake take this arrow, shoot it over the lake, and when the arrow falls

[1] Told by White-Horse, Pitahauirat. The practice of certain Pawnee medicinemen of wearing a cap or head dress bearing a circular band of woodpecker scalps is explained by this story. The moral of the story for children is that they should take care of their fine clothing.

upon the ground there you will stand. When you want to come back take the same arrow and shoot it over the lake and you will return to this island." The boy wore a buffalo robe which was not very large. Around the edge of the robe were many holes. The animals had given the boy many sweet-smelling weeds. These he tied upon the robe. The woman said again: "I came across this lake, for I am not a human being. I came over as a swan. I am not a woman. I am the Moon. I watch over the people and help them in getting food for themselves." As the night came the woman said: "Now do as I have told you about the arrow. Go across and come back. I am gone." The boy took the arrow in the night, shot it over the lake, and he was then across. He went into the village. The people ran out of their lodges and said: "Here goes the boy with the woodpecker cap. The owls are hooting about his legs." He entered one of the lodges. One man reached for his quiver, but as he reached for it he noticed that the black bow was not a bow at all, but was a black snake. Then he moved away and sat down. The Woodpecker-Boy motioned to a young woman to place his things upon a hook. She came and took the things and the snake permitted her. After he had taken off his things he sat down by the fire. One of the men then spoke and said: "Woodpecker-Boy, we are sorry, for we can not give you anything to eat. The people in the village are starving. We go out into the timber. We hunt for artichokes, ground beans, and pecans which the animals have buried, but we find nothing. We go out to hunt game, but we find none." The boy said nothing. He got up, went to his things, took his cap, and put it upon his head. He put on his leggings and moccasins. Then he took the quiver and put it over his shoulder. As he went out the people could hear the owls hooting upon his legs. Woodpecker-Boy went off into the timber and was gone nearly all night. He came back in the morning. Now, while he was gone he went into the timber and there he scratched around where the animals had hidden their ground beans, their pecans, and their artichokes. He also made images of raccoons, deer, and turkey. After he had done this he went around the timber and gave four yells. After this he entered the village.

Early in the morning the boy sat down and he told the man in whose lodge he was to send for the chief. The chief was sent for and he came. He sat down near the boy, and the boy said: "Chief, I am sorry for the people, but I can not do anything. I have been out to a place in the timber, and I have worked all night. Now, you go through the village and tell the people to go and surround the timber. Tell the women to take their hoes and bags and when they surround the timber and the chief gives the command they must run into the timber. Everybody must kill whatever comes in their way." The people went out to the place and they surrounded it. When the command was given them they rushed into the timber. Some women found nests of ground beans. While they were digging out these things their sisters came across raccoons. The men found plenty of deer jumping around through the timber. The people killed much game and dug many ground beans and artichokes. They brought the meat and everything home with them, and the people talked about Woodpecker-Boy. In the night the boy disappeared. The people asked about him. They wondered where he was. The chief wanted him, but the next day the boy was again seen upon the island.

Several days afterwards the boy returned. Again he entered the lodge where he was before and he told the people that he was going out to the timber, and that he wanted them to be ready in order that they might surround more game. The boy went over into the timber at night and returned early the next morning. The people surrounded the timber and this time they found larger game. When the people brought their meat home they talked about Woodpecker-Boy and said that he was wonderful. While they were talking about him the chief thought that it would be best to invite the boy to his lodge. The chief sent his servant to invite Woodpecker-Boy to his lodge. When the servant asked for Woodpecker-Boy the people said that he had disappeared. The next day he was seen upon the island again.

A few days afterwards the boy thought that the people were hungry and he crossed the lake again. For the third time he told the people to go into the timber. When they went they found buffalo. The men surrounded the buffalo and killed many of them. They carried the meat home and Woodpecker-Boy was again missing. The chief sent a crier through the village and asked the people if they had seen Woodpecker-Boy; the chief wanted him at his lodge, as he had decided that he should become his son-in-law. There were many men in the village who would have liked to be in the place of the boy.

In the village was a strange-looking man. He was always painted red, with a small robe upon his shoulders. He had bears' claws about his neck. This person had been watching Woodpecker-Boy. He went down late in the evening to where the boy always came across from the island. There he began to dig a hole. This man was a Bear-Man.

When the boy shot his arrow over the lake the arrow fell into the hole which the Bear-Man had dug. There the boy found himself in the hole. The Bear-Man came and said: "My son, hand up your clothes first. I will take you out of this hole. The chief is looking for you and I know by taking you out he will reward me." The boy took off his things and handed them to the Bear-Man. The Bear-Man put the things on. The leggings he put on and the owls upon it would not hoot. Then he put the robe on, but when he put on the cap the woodpeckers commenced to peck his head. He did not mind their pecking at his head for some time. When he put the quiver on his back he noticed that the arrows and the bow were snakes, and the snakes did not like it because the Bear-Man had them. Bear-Man went through the village with the boy's clothing on. Every time he took a step he would hoot like an owl, for the owls had stopped hooting for him. He was seen through the village and the people took word to the chief that Woodpecker-Boy was now in the village. The chief sent for him and when Woodpecker-Boy came he placed him in the lodge upon a cushion. He told his girls to sit with him. The youngest of the girls would not go. The two older ones went and sat by the supposed Woodpecker-Boy.

Several days afterwards this supposed Woodpecker-Boy tried to make it appear that he could do the same things as the other boy had done. He would disappear in the night and return in the morning. He would tell the chief to surround the place, and when the people would surround it there would be no game and nothing could be found.

About the fifth day the boy in the hole had begun to get hoarse from crying and yelling. He was also very thin and very weak, for he had had nothing to eat during all this time.

On the west side of the village lived an old woman with her grand-child. The grandchild went towards the lake shooting birds. He heard some one crying. He went to the hole and there the boy was standing. Woodpecker-Boy told the other boy to take him out. The boy ran to the lodge and said: "Grandmother, there is a poor boy in a hole. He is nearly starved to death. Let us go and take him out. He shall be my nephew. He shall call me uncle." The boy and the old woman went to the hole and there they found the boy. The woman pulled the boy out from the hole and took him home. She went through the village begging here and there for corn. Some people gave her a handful and others did not give her any. She went home and made mush for the boy.

Every day the woman and the boy would go through the village begging for some corn. After a while the boy became strong. Then he said: "Uncle, tell your grandmother to go and cut an ash tree and four dog-wood sticks and bring them to me." The old woman went into the timber and brought back the ash stick and the four dogwood sticks. The boy then began to make a bow and four arrows. When he made the four arrows he said: "I am strong now, uncle, so let us go into the timber." They went into the timber, but they did not see any game. When they saw a rat's nest, the boy shot at the nest and said: "Uncle, get the arrow and you will find a rat which I have killed." The boys took the rat home and the old woman cooked it for their supper. The next day they went out. In the timber they found a porcupine sitting on a limb. The boy shot it and they brought it home. The grandmother cooked it for their supper. The next day they went and they found a raccoon. The boy killed it and they took it home. The old woman cooked it for their supper. The next day they went out and the boy killed several quail. The following day they went out and the boy killed some prairie chickens. Another day they went out and the boy killed some turkeys. Then the boy told his uncle to save the turkey feathers, for he must make arrows. The next day they went out and they saw a young fawn. The boy killed it and they brought it home. The next day they went out and killed a deer. The next time they went out the boy killed an elk. The last time they went out the boy killed a buffalo. They came back and told the grandmother to go and bring the meat home. The grandmother brought the meat home.

Every day these boys went out and they killed game. Now they had plenty to eat. The old woman also had many skins and she built a fine tipi. The people saw the change in the old woman's place. Some of them went there and peeped in. They saw that the inmates were eating much meat, while the other people in the village were starving. Some people went to the chief and said: 'Woodpecker-Boy is in the tipi of the old woman. This man that you have here must be an impostor." The little girl, the youngest daughter of the chief, heard this. She went to the tipi and got some meat. She made her home there. Then Woodpecker-Boy told the girl that the man who was in her lodge was Bear-Man; that he had robbed him of his clothing and had thrown him into a hole; that he would not go to the chief's lodge until the man was killed. The girl got up and went to her lodge. She went up to the things which were hung there, reached for them, and the people inside did not say anything. Whenever anybody reached for the things the snakes would try to bite them. But this time when the girl reached for them the owls began to hoot and the snakes were glad, for they knew they were going back to their owner. She took the things to the boy, and the birds and the animals were glad to see the boy again.

The people rushed into the lodge of the chief to catch the man, but he had turned into a Bear and chased the people out. The people ran the Bear out of the village with fire sticks, so that the Bear became scared and turned into a bear again and went from the people for all time never to return to live with them any more.

After the boy had settled down and was strong again, he told the chief to send the people out into the timber. They went out and began to kill game and they found plenty of artichokes, ground beans, and game. When they brought in their meat the boy said: "This is the last time I shall do this for your people. It is the fourth time I have done it for you. Now you must move away from here and go far into the country, where you can find game for yourselves."

In a few days the people moved away from the village and went west, hunting for buffalo. They found the buffalo and killed many. After they came back from the buffalo hunt the boy gave them seeds to plant. The boy taught them to put the seeds in the ground, and after the seeds were put in the ground they were to hunt buffalo. The people learned how to plant corn in the spring, hunt in the summer, and gather their crops in the fall and then hunt again. The boy who visited the lodge said: "People, in your dancing you must wear my cap made of heads of woodpeckers. Then other people will know that there was a time when the Bear-Man wore my cap." The people had plenty to eat and were taught many things by the boy. Afterwards the boy disappeared, first singing to the poor boy who was now to take his place:

> Pa-oo! My uncle yonder came.
> You are now sitting high up in the top of a tall tree.

44. THE SHOOTING OF THE SQUIRREL'S NOSE.[1]

There was a village near a small stream of water. The chief's tipi was placed on the north side by itself. Close to the tipi was a ravine, and at the head of the ravine was a tall cottonwood tree which was forked near its top. On the east side of the timber was a little grass-house where there lived a poor woman with her grandchild. When the people went out to urinate they went to the grass-house and urinated on it. The old woman was not old from age, but she was poor and therefore was called an old woman. She took this little boy into her grass-lodge, for he had no home. She called him her grandchild. The boy wore half of a buffalo robe. This was the only bedding he had and it had a bad odor, for he often urinated on it. His hair was never brushed and he was always dirty.

When the children of the chief went out to play they went to the cottonwood tree and there they would scare a squirrel. The squirrel would

[1] Told by Leading-Sun, Kitkehahki. The story teaches that the daughters of chiefs should not despise the poor boys of the village, because ultimately they might become worthy to be their husbands.

run up the tree and when the children began throwing at it with sticks, other children came and joined them in throwing at the squirrel. The squirrel would run up the tree and would lie at the fork. When the children looked for it all they could see was the nose of the squirrel. This happened many times. Then the oldest of the girls said one day: "Father, let the crier go through the village and let him tell all the boys to get their bows and arrows ready, so that when we scare the squirrel up the tree they can shoot at it. Whoever shall hit the squirrel's nose and kill it shall become our husband. The skin we will use as a receptacle for our seeds." The chief sent for the crier and told him to cry through the village. He said that when his daughters chased the squirrel up the tree everyone must come with their bows and arrows, and whoever should shoot the squirrel upon the nose should marry the daughters of the chief. As soon as the young men heard of this they began to make bows and arrows. Every young man in the camp soon had bows and arrows. Everybody waited each day until the daughters of the chief went out to play, and as soon as they ran the squirrel up the tree the boys of the village began to gather around the tree and shot at the squirrel until sundown, and then they would give it up. This was carried on for many days.

Little Burnt-Belly-Boy, who lived with his grandmother, made a little ring. This ring was made of buffalo hide. He also had a bow and arrows, made for him by his grandmother. Every morning the boy would sit outside of the grass-lodge and would say to his grandmother, "Roll the ring out of the lodge." This the woman did, and when the ring came rolling out of the lodge the little boy shot at it. Then he would yell and run into the lodge. He would say, "Grandmother, go and see what I have killed." The grandmother would go out and there would find a young buffalo. The woman would jerk the meat and dry it in their lodge. After she would fill a parfleche with dried meat she would bury the parfleche under the ground. The bones were placed around the fireplace and were cooked in that way.

One day the boy told the grandmother that he was going over to shoot at the squirrel's nose. The grandmother laughed at the boy, but he went anyway. As soon as the young people saw that the boy was coming they laughed, pointed at him, and said: "Here is the boy who is going to shoot the squirrel on the nose." Everybody shot at the squirrel. The boy then stood up, shot, and hit the squirrel right on the nose. The boy ran to get the squirrel, but a man with bear claws around his neck picked up the squirrel and shouted: "I killed the squirrel." The boy picked up his arrow and with it several hairs of the squirrel, and when he went into his grass-lodge he said: "Grandmother, I killed the squirrel. Here it is." The boy handed the squirrel to the woman.

Now, when the man with the bear claws picked up the squirrel he took it straight to the chief's lodge. The squirrel which the man took was of brownish color and made no colors about the lodge. The squirrel which the boy had killed was of a bluish tint and it made the lodge bluish in color. The impostor married the two oldest daughters, while the youngest one would not consent to lie with the man, for she said that some one else had killed the squirrel.

One day the man with the bear claws promised the people buffalo. He told them to go out on a certain hill and that they would find buffalo there. When the people went they could not find any buffalo. Then he said: "It is because you do not give me the girl." The chief scolded the little girl and she ran away to the home of Burnt-Belly-Boy. She sat outside. She smelled the burning meat. After a while she slipped into the grass-lodge and sat down beside the woman. The woman knew her. She took pity on her and said: "Why did you not stay at home and become one of the wives of that man?" The little girl said: "No; I am the youngest, but I have more sense than my older sisters. I do not believe that the man killed the squirrel. I came here for I believe that this boy killed the squirrel. Now I know that it is true, for I see the squirrel skin here. I also know that this boy who stops here with you is a wonderful boy. I came and smelt this burning meat. I came into your lodge. Now I find that you have meat, and bones are roasting." The girl ate some of the meat which was being roasted. She was sent home.

The next day the boy sent his grandmother to ask the chief for the young girl. The woman went into the lodge and asked the chief if her grandchild might marry the little girl. The chief was angry and said: "She refuses to marry this man. I do not believe that she would marry your boy. I shall leave it with her. Daughter, will you have that dirty little boy in that grass-lodge?" She said: "Yes, my father; I will take him." The chief was angry, but when he saw that the girl was in earnest he gave his consent. The boy was brought to the lodge of the chief and he was given a seat near the entrance. The two older daughters made fun of him and their younger sister.

After the fourth day Burnt-Belly-Boy went away and when he returned he came as an eagle. When he turned into a human form his robe was covered with eagle feathers and his leggings were fringed with eagle feathers. He also wore an eagle cap. Upon the back of his buffalo robe was painted the sun. When the boy came to the lodge of the chief the two oldest sisters tried to leave their husband, but the young boy said: "No, you are married. Stay with your husband." Then Burnt-Belly-Boy told his wife to tell her father that in a day or so he would have the buffalo near, so that the people might kill them.

The next day Burnt-Belly-Boy asked the chief to have the crier tell the people to come with him. They went into a thick timber. There the people found skunks, badgers, raccoons, deer, rats' nests, ground beans, and pecans. The people returned to their homes with a great many things to eat. The two oldest girls were mad because their husband could not do these things. After the boy had helped the people to kill deer and other small game, he told them to go west and there they would find buffalo. The people went out, found buffalo, surrounded them and killed many. When the people returned they brought meat to the lodge of the boy to feast upon. After this the boy was given a new tipi. He brought his grandmother, placed her in there and he took his wife and lived with her in their new tipi. Always after that he lived away from his father-in-law.

45. THE ORIGIN OF THE CLAM SHELL.[1]

There was a village, and in this village was a man who was all the time hunting along the streams of water. One day, while around some ponds, he saw a young duck diving in one place and coming up in another. He watched it, and once in a while he would see the young duck take the weeds from the dry land and dive with them in its mouth. The man caught the young duck and took it home. He kept it for a while, but his wife told him to turn it loose. The man took the duck back to the pond and turned it loose.

The woman gave birth to a child, and the child was called Young-Duck. The girl grew up and as she grew her parents noticed that she had mysterious ways and liked to be around ponds and in the water. She was very proud. Her parents talked together, and the mother said: "Now, you see our child is like the duck, because you watched it and brought it here before our child was born. Let her have her way and be satisfied."

One day the girl came into the tipi and commenced to dig in the west part of the tipi. She made a hole about the size of a small bowl. She went out towards the ponds and stayed there for some time, and when

[1] Told by Bright-Eyes, Skidi. Apart from the story of the origin of the clam shell, as related in the tale, its interest is of a wider nature, because the clam shell was used largely by the Pawnee medicine-men, especially as a mortar in which to mix medicines as well as paints. The clam itself is regarded as a wonderful being, cleanly in its nature, although it lives in the mud. The moral of the tale is that widowers should not remain single.

she came back she brought some flag roots with tops on them, and some peppermints with their roots and tops. These she took to the hole and planted at the bottom of it. The next day she went to the hole and it had water in it. She told her mother to take a little wooden bowl, and to dip water from the hole and wash her face and head every day with that water. "I am to sit upon that pool," she said, "when I am not doing anything." The mother took the wooden bowl and dipped some water. She smelled of the water and it smelled sweet. She washed the girl's face and wet her hair with it. As she grew the girl became very pretty. Her hair was long, extending down to her knees. Every day her head and face were washed from the pool, and she sat upon it every day. She had dreams, and in her dreams a voice spoke to her and told her what to do. One day she went to the ponds, and when she came back she had a stick, about three feet long, with a hook at the end. She also had some long, dried, rawhide carrying-strings, with a head-band which was decorated very prettily.

One day the girls in the village went after wood and this girl went with them. The girls thought she was very pretty. They asked what her name was and she told them her name was Young-Duck. When they went far into the woods, she stopped at a dry cottonwood tree and told the girls to go and get their wood. There were about six or seven girls. They went and picked their wood, and while they were gone the girl lifted her stick and said: "Now grow long; stretch up to that dry limb and pull it down for me." The stick reached the limb. When she had pulled down enough to make a load, she trimmed the limbs and tied them up with her strings. She would then sit down and wait for the girls.

When the girls came they were surprised to see her wood all tied up. They went home together and the girl threw her wood all down near the entrance of their tipi and untied it. She then tied up her strings, then hung the stick and strings in the lodge. Her mother then went to get the bowl, dipped some water from the pool, and washed the girl's face and head. The girl then went to her pool and sat on it. The mother filled the little bowl with pemmican, which she had prepared for her daughter. This she ate very slowly. She did not talk very much.

After the girls had parted with Young-Duck, they talked about her and all agreed that she should lead them. Every day the girls came to her tipi and said: "Young-Duck, let us go after wood." "Nawa," she would say; then she would reach for her stick and strings. As she came out the girls would fall in line and she would lead them into the timber. Every time she came to a cottonwood tree she would stop and tell the girls to go on and gather their wood and take no notice of her.

She would then lift her stick and say, "Stretch and break that limb for me." This she did until she had plenty of them. Then she would sit down and wait for the other girls. When the girls came she would lift her wood on her back and lead the girls into camp. She was very neat, and her wood was always piled up in an even pile.

The boys of the village noticed her and tried to court her. A young man with game sticks brought his game near her tipi, so that she would notice him. Other young men passed by her tipi and shot their arrows, so that she would see how well they could shoot; but she would not look at them. In the night young men turned out with their flutes, but she did not listen. A dance was to be given in the village. On the morning of the dance she saw a Hawk sitting on a limb, and she knew him. "Yes; you may come and see me, but you must become a man." The Hawk went where the animals dwelt and begged them to transform him to a man. This was done; then he visited the girl and she knew him. She told her mother to tell her father that she would marry this young man. This was agreed upon and Hawk married the girl. The girl continued to sit on the pool of water, and when the girls came she went with them and gathered wood with them, and when she went home she piled her wood up in an even pile. Then the water was dipped, her face was washed, her hair was wet with it and combed. Then she would dip some water and wash her husband's face and head. After washing, she would sit on her pool, her husband by her. Pemmican was handed them in a bowl and they ate very slowly. Every day the girls came and Young-Duck went with them after wood. Her husband would go up on a high hill and watch them.

One day, as the girl returned home, she noticed a strange woman in their tipi, but she went on with her work. Her mother dipped water for her and she washed her face. When she had finished, she sat down on her pool of water, and pemmican was brought and handed to her and to her husband by her mother. The strange old woman saw all that was going on and she wished that she might marry the young man. She said: "I wish that I were in that girl's place, instead of having so many children to look after," and when she went outside she made up her mind to watch the girl; for she was a Witch. She went into the timber and cut a dogwood stick, about two feet long, whittled it down to a sharp point, and burned the point so that it was hard; then dried it.

One day she went into the timber where the girl generally gathered her wood. She hid in the brush, and after a while Young-Duck came. The other girls went on by, but Young-Duck stopped under the cottonwood trees. When she had her wood all tied up and ready to return home, she sat down on her wood to wait for the girls. She looked up

and saw the strange woman coming towards her. Said the old woman:
"My dear! My dear! You are my daughter. I have been looking for
you. You are so good and beautiful. Come and sit down by me."
The girl sat down and all at once the old woman took her sharp stick
and jammed it into the girl's ear, and thought she killed her. She blew
her breath into the girl's mouth, so that her skin, from her waist up,
came off. The old woman crawled into the skin, and put her own
dried-up skin on the girl. She then dragged the girl and threw her into
a stream. She hurried back to the wood and commenced to yell for the
girls, for she was hungry. This was something unusual. Young-Duck
would never call for the girls, and never yelled. The girls hurried back
and came to her, and they noticed that she looked very wild and did not
act like Young-Duck. They went home, and as the old woman got to
the tipi, she threw her wood down and went in and said: "Mother, I am
tired and hungry." This was also strange; for Young-Duck would never
throw her wood down, nor say that she was hungry. Instead of washing
her face and combing her hair, she went and sat upon the pool and said:
"I am hungry, mother; bring me something to eat!" The mother took
the meat to her and her husband, and she ate all the meat before the
man knew it.

At night the man suspected that something was wrong, for from the
waist down the old woman was her own self, and her legs were not round
like those of a girl. The next day the girls came as usual, and they went
after wood. As they went along, the old woman kept hallooing and
talking. The girls did not like it. They came to the tall trees, and the
old woman stopped. The others went on. The old woman took the
stick and raised it and said, "Hook that limb," but the stick would
not stretch. "Stretch," she said; "come, now, stretch," but the stick
would not stretch. She tried it on the north side, on the south and on
the west, but the stick would not stretch. She was afraid that the girls
would be coming, so she cut a lot of green willows and tied them, and
swung them on her back; then yelled for the girls to come. The girls
came with their wood and when they saw the girl with green willow
they said one to another: "Why, Young-Duck has never done this.
Listen, she talks all the time." They went home and the old woman
threw her wood down and ran into the tipi and said: "Mother, I am
tired, and my head aches." She then went to the pool of water, but the
water had dried up. That night she could not eat anything, but was
always jabbering and talking.

The next day she was worse, for the girl's skin was rotting and was
making her feel sick. It was noised around that Young-Duck was sick;

so medicine-men were sent for, but they could not help her. She would not let them touch her for fear they might find the false skin over her. All the medicine-men, one by one, were sent for, and none could help her. The young man, who all this time thought the woman to be his wife, felt badly. He said there was nothing now to be done; all the medicine-men had been sent for and they could not help her. "There is one more medicine-man that we have not sent for," said he, "and that is the man who lives in the west." He was sent for and he came. He entered the tipi and, although the people gave him a place by the woman, he squatted by the entrance. The woman had a bad color, for the skin over her was rotting. As the man came in, the woman saw that his face was painted black, and in his hand he held a black gourd. The old woman said: "You black-eyed Crow, I know you; you are going to find me out; I know you are going to find me out." The medicine-man sent the man after a bucket of water, saying, "Dip the water with a motion towards the west." This the man did and he heard some one saying:

Now, Hawk Chief, here I stand in the water.
I, Young-Duck, stand here in the water.

He heard the voice and knew it and looked all around, but could not see his wife. He went back to the lodge and told Crow. "Good," said Crow; "now you shall hear what I have to say." The old woman was now very sick, for she knew that she was found out. Crow sang this song:

Now, crazy old woman,
Your outer skin is rotten.
Crow flew and knows.
Crow flew and knows.

Crow kept on singing, for he was telling what the witch had done. Hawk went to the creek and stood around there in the night, and he heard a woman sing this song:

Here now stands Young-Duck.
Here now stands Young-Duck.
Yonder is Hawk Chief.

She sang several times and then disappeared in the water.

The boy went home, and Crow made the announcement that the woman was a witch and that she had killed the girl and had thrown her in the water. The people took the old woman out, and although she cried for mercy, they killed all her children. The boy went off to the water and listened and listened and listened for his wife's song again. He turned into a Hawk and flew up and down the creek, crossing over from one side to the other, hunting the girl. For four days he flew around, until he was tired and hungry. On the evening of the fourth day he lighted on a high hill to rest. He saw smoke coming up in the valley. He went to it and there he saw a tipi. He went in and there was a man, woman, and four girls, and his wife, Young-Duck, who had covered herself up so that Hawk could not see her. She had told the people not to tell him that she was there; so that when he asked about her they said they had not seen her.

The man kept asking and the youngest girl pointed to the place where she was lying. The man looked, and he saw his wife's feet. He reached for her, but she would not let him see her. He was glad to find her. She said: "You can not see me, for I am changed." The man insisted upon seeing her and she finally gave up. He saw that from her waist up she was an old woman. Her ears hung down. She told him that the old woman had bewitched her and that she was now changed, and would always live that way; and that he must tell her father and mother not to weep for her; and she also told her husband not to weep for her. She said: "You see what I am now. You will marry again some girl who will be good to you, but first you are to lift me up in the sky. Put me upon your back and fly high, then drop me. Then watch, and where I drop, fly there and find me and you will see what sort of creature I am." The man stayed near her all night. Although she was changed he did not care, for he had hunted for her and had found her. She was also very thin, for all this time she had eaten only ground beans. The next day they went out together and climbed the same hill that Hawk had rested on the day before. He turned into a Hawk again and the girl climbed on his back, and said: "Fly. You are strong; I am not heavy." The Hawk flew up in the heavens and gave a little turn, and the girl fell. The Hawk watched and flew where the girl fell; and there he found her, and she was a clam shell already open. The outside of the shell was rough, like the old witch's skin that had been on the girl. The inside was smooth and delicate like the skin of the girl.

46. THE POOR BOY WHO TURNED INTO AN EAGLE.[1]

In the beginning there were no people upon the earth. The stars in the heavens wanted to put people upon the earth and show them how to live. Morning-Star spoke and said: "Put two people down there on the earth among the animals, and see what they will do." The stars in the heavens agreed to put two people upon the earth. Moon agreed to send her woman down, and Morning-Star agreed to send his younger brother. The boy, although younger, called the woman his niece. The

[1] Told by Cheyenne-Chief, Skidi. The story points the moral that children, especially brothers and sisters, should not quarrel among themselves. The tale also foretells the sacrificing by the Skidi of a maiden.

stars carried the woman and the boy to the ground, and placed them near a stream of water. The stars gave corn, squash, and beans to them, and during the winter brought meat to them. The woman saved some of the meat and tried to save as much corn as possible.

When spring came she arose each morning and went to the bottom land and cleared a place to plant corn. One morning she put a few grains of corn into a dry bladder of a buffalo and tied the grains up and hung them on the wall and said, "My uncle, do not touch these, for they are seeds." The woman then went down into the bottom land and began to work, softening the ground and making hills for the corn. While she was working the little boy walked up and began to look for something to eat. He could not find anything, and so he climbed up and took the bladder with the seeds in it, untied it, and said to himself, "I will eat one of these grains of corn and put the rest back." He took one kernel and parched it on a hot coal and then ate it. He ate another and another until he had eaten all the seeds, then he hung the bladder up again where it had been.

The boy was young and lazy; his head was bushy, and his face and hands always dirty. When the woman came in and saw that her seeds were gone she kicked the boy and said: "Uncle, arise. What have you done with the seeds? I have worked hard, and here you have eaten up the seeds." She gave him a whipping, and he cried. Then the woman took some other corn which she had and began to pound it, for she was going to make some mush. The boy stopped crying, and began to sing:

> My sister, something is about to happen,
> My sister, something is about to happen.
> They will talk to you.
> Your seed corn; your seed corn is very fine.
> Something is about to happen;
> My toes are turning into eagle's claws.
>   *   *   *   *   *
> My feet are turning into eagle's feet.[1]
>   *   *   *   *   *
> My legs are turning into eagle's legs.
>   *   *   *   *   *
> My body is turning into an eagle's body.
>   *   *   *   *   *
> My nose is turning into an eagle's beak.
>   *   *   *   *   *
> My arms are turning into eagle's wings,

Then the boy gave one scream, threw his robe to one side, and the woman saw that her uncle had turned into an Eagle. She ran and tried to catch him, but the Eagle flew around the lodge and out of the hole at the

[1] The first five lines of the remaining five verses are the same as the first verse.

top of the lodge. She ran out following, crying as she went, "My uncle, my uncle, return to me, for I am all alone. Stay with me, and I shall not scold you any more." But the Eagle flew on and on. The woman began to cry, but still followed the Eagle. It flew on until it came to the lodge of the Badgers. The woman followed until she, too, came to the lodge of the Badgers. They took her in and said: "Why do you cry so?" and she said: "My uncle and I are alone. There are no other people in the world, and now he has turned into an Eagle. I want to catch him and take him back to our home." The Badgers said: "Let us help this woman, and get the Eagle for her." The Badgers dug a hole and placed this woman in it, and spread some limbs over the hole. They killed a Badger, cut the bowels open, and spread them out upon the limbs over the hole; then the Badgers all disappeared into their holes. After a while the crows, magpies, coyotes, and other animals came to the hole to eat of the dead badger. Soon a big flock of all kinds of birds came and flew around where the badger was lying, and then lighted upon the ground, and they said: "He is coming; he is coming. We shall have to wait until he tastes of the badger." After a while a great wind was heard above, and then a scream. It was the cry of the golden Eagle, which came and lighted near all of the birds. The Eagle looked around at all the birds, the magpie, and coyote and then sang: "I am not willing; I am not willing to taste of this animal which is cut open. Something is wrong; something is under that." Then the Eagle flew up, and as the Eagle flew up all the other birds flew away. Even the coyotes walked away. Once in a while they turned to look at the badger which was lying upon the limbs. After a while the Badgers came and said: "Woman, come out. We are powerless. We can not help you. You see what we have done, and your uncle knew that you were there."

Then the woman began to cry and she went on. All kinds of animals tried to catch the Eagle for the woman in the same way, but the Eagle would not eat of the dead animal and would sing: "I am not willing; I am not willing to eat of the animal." Then all the other birds would fly away. At last the woman came to a lodge of Elks. The Elks took her in and said: "Woman, it is easy. We can call any animal that we want. The Eagle is easy to catch." They killed one elk. They cut out its bowels and spread it out upon the hole. The fat looked very fine. The woman was placed in the hole, under the Elk. The birds came, and the Eagle came and it said: "I am not willing to eat of this meat. I am not willing." It flew away. The Elks were surprised. They were sure that the Eagle would eat of the meat. The woman began to cry. She went a long distance.

After a while she came to the home of the Buffalo. There were arbors and other places as if people had camped there. There was a creek on one side, and upon the side of a hill were many Buffalo. When the girl went to them they said: "We can help you. We know who this bird is. Although he is your uncle, he is not a human being. His only desire and wish is that he have human flesh. He is Morning-Star. Morning-Star is the chief of all the gods in the heavens. The other gods are willing that animals and buffalo meat should be offered to them, but Morning-Star wants human flesh offered to him. We might kill ourselves and place ourselves on these high hills near the streams of water, but he would know that we are trying to catch him. He wants human flesh. We will help you to catch your uncle, and you yourself shall catch him. Now watch. We will send big droves of buffalo into this stream of water. Many of them will get stuck in the mud and die. Others will drown. There will be many dead people. It will seem so, but they will not be dead. The animals and the birds in the air will all come together and they will want to eat of the buffalo, but they must wait for the golden Eagle. We will now take you. We will cut you open, and put your bowels on one side. Your breast shall be torn open. The golden Eagle will come and will want to eat the fat from your heart. When he lights upon your breast, and reaches for your heart, then his time has come. Then is the time for you to take hold of his legs. Then you shall have your uncle back." The Buffalo gave commands for the droves to run into the streams of water. Some went into the mire and into the mud and others were drowned. There were apparently many dead buffalo along the stream of water. Near the village was a little arbor and in this they placed the girl. They cut her open and put her bowels to one side. Her breast was torn open and she lay like one dead. The old buffalo went upon the hill and sat down as if they were sleeping. After a while the magpies came, then the crows came, and then the coyotes. Other animals came creeping. All kinds of birds came, and a large flock of eagles came and lighted upon the dead buffalo, but they dared not touch or eat any of the meat. After a while the birds screamed. Then a big noise of wind came, and the golden Eagle lighted upon the ground. It sat upon the arbor. It looked down and saw the dead person in the arbor. All the animals listened to the golden Eagle. He sang:

> I am now willing
> To eat this person lying there.
> I am now willing
> To eat this person lying there.

As soon as he had sung that, all the animals and the birds began to eat of the buffalo. The golden Eagle flew into the arbor, sat upon the breast of the girl, and looked under the breast for her heart. When it was about to reach for the heart the girl took hold of the legs of the eagle and she said: "Where is the heart that you shall eat? It is I, your poor niece, who has cried many days over the prairies and tried to catch you. I shall take you back and you must remain with me forever."

The instant the woman touched the legs of the Eagle, the Eagle turned into the boy again. He screamed and yelled and said: "My niece, I will return with you to your place. My niece, it shall be so. When the people are living upon the earth there will be a time when they shall capture an enemy and the captured woman shall be offered to the Morning-Star. But this offering shall not be made unless several buffalo shall be killed and made holy and offered to the gods as a sacrifice to the Morning-Star." When the woman and the boy went to their field, dark clouds came and covered them up and they disappeared from the earth, and they were no more upon the earth. The woman had returned to the Moon, and the boy had returned to the east to stand behind his brother.

47. THE POOR BOY WHO LOST HIS POWER.[1]

There lived in a village, that the people had deserted, a woman who was very poor. There lived with her a little boy who was known as Burnt-Belly. She loved the little boy. She went out into the fields and gathered corn, squashes, and beans for him. One day the little boy got his robe all white. The woman, though she loved the little boy, became angry and took a stick and hit him on the head. The boy cried; then she scolded him for crying. All at once the boy took the little white robe and wrapped himself in it, leaving only his head out. He then began to sing:

> Something fly towards me, my niece.
> Now my toes are turning to something,
> Are turning to handsome eagle's claws,
> Are turning to handsome eagle's claws.

Then he sang again: "My aunt, my legs shall turn into eagle's legs." Then he sang again: "My aunt, my body shall turn into an eagle's body." Then the woman turned around and hit the boy on the head, and said: "You will turn into an eagle!" The boy kept on singing and said: "My aunt, my arms shall turn into an eagle's wings." Then he sang again, and said: "My aunt, my neck shall turn into eagle's neck."

[1] Told by Thief, Kitkehahki. This story is similar to the preceding and points the same moral, viz, the value of obedience to the gods. It may also be regarded as a Kitkehahki variant of tale No. 46.

Then the woman turned around and said: "Turn to an eagle!" Then the boy sang again and said: "My aunt, my head shall turn into an eagle's head." Then he sang again and said: "My aunt, my nose shall turn into an eagle's nose." Then he sang again and said: "My mouth shall turn into an eagle's mouth." Then, as he sang, "My aunt, I shall fly up as an eagle," the woman turned around with her stick, ready to strike the boy; but he turned into an Eagle, threw off the robe, and flew up into the sky.

The woman cried and begged the boy to come back. The Eagle would not come back, but did not go far away. It stayed around where the woman was. The woman cried and cried, but the Eagle would say: "I will not come down, for you were mean to me." Then the Eagle would fly away, and when it came back it would tell the old woman that the people were coming. At last the old woman begged the Eagle so hard that it came back to her and turned into a boy again. The boy was older and was stronger than he was before he turned into an eagle. The woman had made a bow and arrows for him and was always careful not to scold him again. The boy took the bow and arrows and went into the timber to hunt. He killed rabbits and brought them to his aunt. After a while he learned to kill deer. Then he said: "My aunt, you must make me a strong bow and better arrows." The woman made them and the boy killed many deer, so that after a while the woman made a tipi out of the deer hides. She dried the meat and they had plenty to eat. When the people came with very little buffalo meat they found these people with plenty of meat and corn.

When the people came to the village the young man told his aunt that they must move into the timber and stay. They moved into the timber and the young man kept killing game. After a while the people visited this tipi and they found meat and dry hides around it. The chief was told about it. The chief invited the young boy and said: "Can you help us to get buffalo, so that we may also have meat?" The boy said that he could; then he went back to his tipi. He told his aunt that he was going to see the chief's daughter. She said nothing, for fear she might hurt his feelings. The young man disappeared as an Eagle and was gone several days. When he came back he said to his aunt: "I am going to take the people over the hills, for I have brought the buffalo for them. They will bring some meat back with them." The young man went and told the chief that he wanted the people to follow him over the hills. The chief told the people to go and so they followed him, and when they went on top of the hills they saw many buffalo. The people killed many buffalo and took the meat home. The boy was then told to tell his aunt to move his tipi up into the village. The young man told the chief that he could not do this, but that if they wanted to they could move to the place where he lived. The people moved into the timber and the chief then invited the boy and said: "My son, I give you my daughter to marry." The young boy said: "The chief is good, but I can not take her just now." The chief insisted and said: "The girl shall go to your home." The girl went to the boy's home and stayed all night. The next time the boy tried to get the buffalo he found that his power was gone from him, for he had lain with a girl and had no more power. If he had killed buffalo four times for the people he might have married and still kept his power; but before killing buffalo four times he married and so he lost his power.

48. THE FLINT MAN.[1]

A man went alone to a far-away country. For many, many days he traveled and at last he came to a prairie country. As he was going through the prairie country he saw something at a distance that sparkled. He went up to the object that sparkled, and found that it was a man made of flint. The flint man spoke to the man and said, "Nawa," and then spoke again and said: "Sit down and smoke with me." The flint man reached and took a pipe which was made from a stick, for there was no stone bowl at the end. The stone man filled the stick with native tobacco, gave it to the man, and told him to light it. The man began to smoke, and as the smoke got into his eyes, the stone man spoke and said: "You shall not see me for a while." The man looked to the place where the flint man sat, but could not see him. He again heard the voice of the flint man saying: "I can see people far away. I am made of flint, but I have powers from the gods to transform myself into anything that I want to be. Now I want to turn into a man."

The man looked and saw a man sitting in the place where the flint man had been. The man then said: "I shall give you power to turn into stone, and I shall also give you power to call the rain. When there is no rain, and the people need the rain very badly, then take this flint that I shall give you and lift it to heaven and then place it on the ground, sprinkle water on it, and clouds will form in the west, and the clouds will come and it will rain. You are poor, but I shall make you a powerful man. I shall now become a piece of flint, and shall go with you wherever you go. When you have returned to your people, heal the sick by placing me upon the pains. I will remove the pains and the sick will become

[1] Told by White-Sun, Kitkehahki. The tale illustrates the respect paid by the Pawnee to the flint which they used in arrow heads, knives, etc. It especially teaches, on the part of boys, respect for flint and the belief in general that flint had its origin from the powers in the west, especially in lightning.

well. Now I shall turn into a small stone. Take me and carry me to
your people. Smoke with me and talk to me and I will listen to your
prayers." The man who was sitting down turned into flint and the stone
grew smaller and smaller until it became a very little stone. The man
picked it up and he saw that on one side of the stone was the picture of
the sun; on the other side, the picture of the moon and several stars.

He took the stone home and placed it on the altar in the west of the
lodge. He invited several of his friends, and as his friends came in they
brought presents of black handkerchiefs and buckskin to make a covering for the stone. The man who found the stone filled his pipe and
gave four whiffs to the stone, four whiffs to the ground, and then dumped
the ashes in front of the stone. Then he wrapped a black handkerchief
about the stone, and then wrapped buckskin about it for an outer covering. The bundle was tied and placed to the side of the lodge.

The possessor of the stone heard of a wonderful being that lived close
to a big lake. He was told that the monster lay upon the banks of the
great lake, and killed all who came near. This man made up his mind
that he would go and visit this monster. He started, and when he got
close to the lake he saw the monster lying upon the banks of the lake.
He saw many human bones and skulls scattered around the monster.
As the man came nearer, the monster began to groan as if in pain. The
man went close to the monster and asked what the trouble was. The
monster said: "I have a pain in my back. If you will be kind enough
to step upon my back I will be thankful." The man said that he would
do so, but before he did he spoke to his stone and said: "My brother,
turn me into flint so that I may kill this monster." The man jumped
on the monster and as he jumped he saw several sharp bones sticking
up from the monster's back. Instead of sticking into the flesh of the
man, the bones broke as they struck him, for he had turned into flint.
After all of the bones were broken by striking against the man of flint,
the man walked to the monster's head and jumped until he had pounded
the monster's brains out with his flint feet.

The man went home and told the people that he had killed the monster which was upon the banks of the lake. The people went there and
found the monster dead. They cut the monster up, took fat and flesh
from different parts of its body, and mixed their medicines with it.

The man heard that in a certain part of the country there were seven
spotted calves that tried to kill people and were very dangerous. He
went to the place and saw the spotted calves sliding down a hill on sleds
strung together with buffalo ribs. When the spotted buffalo calves
saw the man coming they asked him if he would like to slide down the
hill with them, and he said that he would. They gave him a sled and

told him to take the lead and that they would follow. The man was suspicious of the spotted calves, and so he spoke to his brother, the flint, and asked him to help turn him into stone, as he thought the spotted calves were going to try to kick him to death. The man got into his sled, and the spotted calves followed him down the hill. They kicked him in every way, but they could not hurt him or even make a mark on his flesh. When they reached the foot of the hill, the man said: "Now it is my turn. You take the lead and I will follow." Then the man asked of the spotted calves why there were so many human skeletons at the bottom of the hill. They did not answer, but he knew that they were the bones of the people whom they had killed. They went up the hill again, and the calves got into their sleds and started down first. The man followed, and whenever he was close enough he would reach out and kick one of the calves. Whenever he kicked one it fell from the sled and was killed. By the time the man reached the foot of the hill he had killed all. He went to the village and told the people that he had killed the seven spotted calves. Some of the men went and skinned the spotted calves, and brought them to the village, so that the people knew that the spotted calves were no longer living, but that the man had killed them.

Several days afterwards the man was told that there was a certain being in the west who ate so much that nothing was left for the people, but if that being were killed or removed the people would then have plenty to eat. This man went to the place and when he arrived there he found a Buffalo bull standing upon a hill. When the Buffalo bull saw the man it grunted, rolled, and groaned. Then it hooked the earth; dug up pieces of earth with its horns. It ran towards the man, but the man had turned into stone. When the poor bull tried to hook him it only broke its horns on the hard stone. The man killed the Buffalo with his arrows. No sooner had he killed it than he found out that the bull was chief of all the Buffalo. He was frightened and went home. He told the people that he had killed the buffalo, and for them to make haste and prepare arrows, for they must try to kill some of the Buffalo. The man's father became frightened and said: "My son, what shall our people do to be saved? You have killed the chief of all the Buffalo. They will now come and try to kill us." The man went to work and took stones from the hillsides and placed them around the village, about three feet apart; then he told the people to stay inside. The stones grew and made a high wall around the village, with many openings, through which the people could shoot their arrows.

All at once the people saw a cloud of dust in the west reaching up to the sky. They then knew that the buffalo were coming. The buffalo came and in their fury they did not see the stones which encircled the village, and they ran into them and broke their horns and skulls against the hard wall. They became wild with excitement and began to kill one another. After that they ran in every direction and scattered all over the land. The next day the stones which were around the village had become small again and were their natural size. The people left these stones in a circle and went off to another country to kill buffalo. The stones were left in a circle, to remind the people that at one time one of their number had placed them in a circle to save his people from being destroyed by the buffalo.

Years afterwards the man lost the stone which he had in his possession. He tried to find it, but he could not, for some one had stolen it from him. The gods in the heavens were angry at him because he had lost the stone. They sent a rain storm from the west. He saw the storm coming and told the people that Lightning was going to take him and that he was to be placed in the heavens as one of the gods. The storm came and lightning struck the man and killed him instantly. The people were afraid to touch him, and so they let him alone, and moved away to another country.

49. THE TURKEY RITUAL.[1]

One day the crier ran out and shouted, so that all of the people in the village could hear, that there were a great many warriors coming to the village. When the people who were left inside the lodges heard that warriors were coming they all turned out. Even Spider-Woman, who had her lodge farther away from the village, went with them. The people went outside of the village to meet the great company of warriors. As they came near they saw that they were Turkeys. The old man shouted and said: "Everybody keep quiet and we will hear from these warriors where they have been." Old Gobbler began to sing:

> Yonder are acorns hanging upon the trees.
> Yonder are acorns hanging upon the trees.
> Far away by walking we will arrive.
> There where the blue clay lies under the earth.
> Yonder are acorns hanging upon the trees.
> Yonder are acorns hanging upon the trees.
> And that is why
> Our coats are shiny and oily.

[1] Told by Thief, Kitkehahki. This tale is similar to many others in which the buffalo voluntarily offer themselves to people for food. Besides the interesting references in the tale which afford explanations of certain rites, the story is interesting because it teaches the young men that a prophet is without honor in his own country. In other words, to obtain the favor of the young women they must go off into the enemy's country and perform deeds of valor. The paints referred to in the tale are supposed to be those found in the color of the turkey's coat.

Then the old man cried out and told the people what the Turkeys said: "These people have been where the blue clay lies under the earth, and that is why their coats are shiny and oily." Again the Gobbler sang:

> Yonder are acorns hanging upon the trees.
> Yonder are acorns hanging upon the trees.
> Far away by walking we will arrive.
> There where the red paint is buried under the earth.
> Yonder are acorns hanging upon the trees.
> Yonder are acorns hanging upon the trees.
> And that is why
> Our legs are painted red.

Then the old man cried out and told the people what the Turkeys said: "These people have been where the red paint is buried under the earth, and that is why their legs are painted red." Again the Gobbler sang:

> Yonder are acorns hanging upon the trees.
> Yonder are acorns hanging upon the trees.
> Far away by walking we will arrive.
> There where the white clay lies under the earth.
> Yonder are acorns hanging upon the trees.
> Yonder are acorns hanging upon the trees.
> And that is why
> Our coats are spotted with white.

Then the old man cried out and told the people what the Turkeys said: "These people have been where the white clay lies under the earth, and that is why their coats are spotted with white." Again the Gobbler sang:

> Yonder are acorns hanging upon the trees.
> Yonder are acorns hanging upon the trees.
> Far away by walking we will arrive.
> There where the yellow clay lies under the earth.
> Yonder are acorns hanging upon the trees.
> Yonder are acorns hanging upon the trees.
> And that is why
> Our mouths are painted yellow.

Then the old man cried out and told the people what the Turkeys said: "These people have been where the yellow clay lies under the earth, and that is why their mouths are painted yellow." Again the Gobbler sang:

> Yonder are acorns hanging upon the trees.
> Yonder are acorns hanging upon the trees.
> Far away by walking we will arrive.
> There where under the ground we found salt.
> Yonder are acorns hanging upon the trees.
> Yonder are acorns hanging upon the trees.
> And that is why
> We have dandruff on our heads.

Then the old man cried out and told the people what the Turkeys said: "These people have been where the salt lies under the earth, and that is why they have dandruff on their heads."

Again the Gobbler sang:

> Yonder are acorns hanging upon the trees.
> Yonder are acorns hanging upon the trees.
> Far away by walking we will arrive.
> There where rocks abound.
> Yonder are acorns hanging upon the trees.
> Yonder are acorns hanging upon the trees.
> And that is why
> Our feet are flat and rough.

Then the old man cried out and told the people what the Turkeys said: "These people have been where the rocks abound, and that is why their feet are flat and rough."

Then the old man told the people that the Turkeys were going to the land in the south where the rocks abound and where there were many acorns; that they wanted the people to know that there they would always live, so that the people could come there and hunt and kill them.

50. THE BOY WHO TURNED INTO A PRAIRIE DOG.[1]

There was a village upon the side of a hill. Near this village, towards the east, was a creek. Across the creek was a Prairie Dog town.

In the village was a little boy whose name was Black-Eyes. The boy was good-looking and everyone liked him. He grew up and was now a young man. He saw a nice-looking young girl in the village. Every day the boy stayed around the place where the people dipped their water from the creek. He waited there for the girl. One day the girl came. The boy talked to her, and she scolded him. The boy did not mind the scolding and followed her toward the village. Just before they entered the village she stopped the boy and said: "Boy, I want you to know that I do not care for you. I can never marry you and, I do not want you to talk to me any more."

The boy was sorry, and told his mother about it. While he was telling his mother about the matter he nearly cried. The mother told him not to cry, as there were many other girls in the tribe. The boy took his bow and arrows and said: "Mother, I am going." The boy went out from the lodge and traveled east. He crossed the stream of water and as soon as he got over to the other side he began to cry. His tears dropped on the ground. He entered the Prairie Dog town. In the center of the

---

[1] Told by Thief, Kitkehahki. The tale illustrates the breadth of the feeling of relationship on the part of the Pawnee to the animal supernatural beings, the relationship to the prairie dogs being brought out in this special tale, and for this reason the Pawnee told their children they live in earth-lodges, which they compare to the so-called prairie-dogs' lodge.

Prairie Dog town stood a young girl. The boy went there; she took him in and there they lived together in her lodge under the ground.

The woman hunted for her son. She traveled east. She saw his footprints just before he entered the stream of water. Then she began to sing:

> Yonder, truly, is my poor boy,
> His eyes like grains of black corn.
> Here and there are his tear-drops.
> Yonder, weeping, I go.

She crossed the stream of water, and as she did so she looked upon the bank and there she saw his tear-drops upon the sand. She began to sing again:

> Truly, he went along here, my poor boy,
> His eyes like grains of black corn,
> Here are his footprints.
> Yonder, weeping, I go.

She went on and she saw his footprints plainly. Then again she sang:

> Truly, he went along here, my poor boy,
> His eyes like grains of black corn.
> Here, across the stream, I see many marks of his tears.
> Yonder, weeping, I go.

The woman went into the village of the Prairie Dogs, and there in the center was a big hole and the footprints ended there. The woman began to cry. She cried for several days. In the day time she saw two Prairie Dogs come out from the hole where the footprints ended. After she had been there for several days she lay down and had a dream. She thought she saw a woman who was very young and beautiful. She was not tall. She was small and was very handsome. In the dream this girl said: "Woman, you must not cry any more for your son, for he is married to me. The girls of your people refused to marry him. He came to our village; I took him in and married him. We are living together and are happy. There is but one way by which you can get your son. Your son has forgotten all about your people. Go to your home. In his quiver there is one black arrow which the boy made himself and of which he thought a great deal. Bring that arrow, and lay it near the hole. You must then lie down."

When the woman awoke she went to her home and found the arrow of which the girl had spoken. She took the arrow, went back to the Prairie Dog town, and placed the arrow near the hole. In the morning the woman lay down near the arrow. Two Prairie Dogs came out. As the boy Prairie Dog came to where the arrow was he saw it, and jumped at it, and as soon as he caught the arrow the Prairie Dog turned into a boy again. The woman got up, took him, and said: "My son, I have been crying for many days, for I had lost you." Then the boy said, "Mother, we shall go home, but I must take my wife with me, for she is soon to bear a child." The boy then spoke to the female Prairie Dog, and she came to him. As the mother and son walked along, the Prairie Dog wife followed them, her belly nearly touching the ground, for she was pregnant. When they reached the village the little Prairie Dog wife rolled around in the dust, turned herself into a woman, and the three then entered the village.

The boy and the girl lived in the village for many years, and had many children. The boy became a great man. The Prairie Dog woman told the young man that he should never lie with a certain woman, because it was through her that he had gone away.

One time the boy was going from the creek to the village, when he met this girl. She spoke to him and he did not pay any attention to her. She continued talking and at last he stopped. She asked him why he never spoke to her. The boy told her why, and the woman said that she had been sorry that she spoke as she did when she really did not mean it. They went into the brush and were together.

On the way to his home the boy met his wife and all his children. She scolded him and said that she had told him not to associate with this woman; that he had not minded her. The boy begged with her, but it did no good. She kept traveling on until they crossed the stream. As soon as they crossed the stream the girl said: "Now go to your people and stay there. I am going to my people with my children." Then the girl and the children turned into Prairie Dogs. The boy returned to the village and he began to have bad luck. At last he died a broken-hearted man.

51. THE GAMBLER AND THE GAMING STICKS.[1]

Two young brothers lived in a village. The older wore yellow paint all the time, and always carried a cougar quiver with black arrows in it and a dark red bow. The younger boy was more quiet but more wonderful than the older brother. Not far from their village was another village, and many young men went there and never returned. It had

[1] Told by Beaver, a Chaui medicine-man. This tale may be regarded as a variant of No. 27, but it is not believed to be true, as is that tale, and hence is placed here. Still other versions were obtained from the other bands, especially two from the Kitkehahki, one told by Thief, the other by White-Sun. According to the first version the Gambler obtained his sticks from the Witch-Woman, and lost his power by the theft of his favorite ring by a buffalo, which had been informed by a traitor in his village. In the other Kitkehahki version, the brothers always dressed exactly alike. The Gambler's assistant is a little boy, who, however, warns the second brother of the futility of playing with the Gambler. This second brother obtains his magic gaming implements from buffalo skulls, to whom he prays on the prairie and which become live animals—a strong young bull and a cow rolling in the dust and offering themselves as javelin and ring; thus the chance of success would be greater on account of the tendency of the two sexes to come together.

been rumored that a gambler lived in that village and that all the men who had disappeared had played with him and had lost their lives by gambling them away after they had lost everything else; that this man's wife was Spider-Woman, and that she liked to eat people.

One day the older brother went off; he traveled east for many days. At last he came to a hill, and on one side of the hill there was a steep bank. Here the young man sat, looking at the strange village. A young man, errand man for the gambler, saw him. This errand man made it his business to watch and if any strangers came to the village reported to the gambler, who invited the stranger to eat with him. The errand man went and told the gambler that he had seen a strange young man and that he was fine-looking. The gambler sent the boy out to see where the stranger would stop. The young man on the hill arose and went to the village, and was invited to one of the lodges. The people told this young man that the gambler would be good to him and would invite him to eat with him, but they told him not to go.

While he was eating the errand man came and said: "I invite you to go to the tipi of the gambler, who wants to talk with you." The boy arose and went, thinking he had power to destroy the gambler and win from him. The gambler was glad to see the boy and gave him a seat near him, saying: "You must have traveled far. I shall give you the best I have for your dinner." The old woman whispered to the sky and said: "I shall have his head in the center, and I shall move other heads down." A wooden bowl was placed in front of the boy, filled with what looked like black corn. The boy ate, and as he ate, his power went from him, for he was eating human eyes. After eating, the man said: "Well, my son, may we play a little with the sticks?" The boy said: "I am tired; I will play with you to-morrow."

The next day preparations were made for the game. They went to the place and there they played. The gambler had many people on his side and the boy had many on his side. The boy lost everything he had. Then the gambler said: "I want you to put up yourself, and if I beat you I shall kill you; if you beat me you will kill me." The boy consented and they played. The boy lost. The old witch kept dancing around, while the game was going on, and yelling: "What a fine head he has! He shall be mine!" As the boy lost, the people ran away. The young man was taken to a place where the people were killed, and his head was chopped off. The head was taken into the lodge and the body left outside.

After a long while the people began to wonder why the boy did not appear at his home, and they asked for him through the village, but could no get trace of him. The younger brother sent birds out to see where the boy had gone. The Raven came back to him and said: "Your brother is dead. His head is at the gambler's lodge." The boy said: "I will at once start out to hunt my brother." The boy started, and as he went he brought all of his powers into play so that he could see well. He followed the steps of his brother, and where his brother had slept there he slept.

After a while he came to the bank where his brother had sat, and as he sat down he saw the errand man watching him. The boy said to himself: "I know you; I will fix you." He arose and went to the tipi where his brother had stayed. He was welcomed, for he looked so much like the other boy. The people told him that he would surely be invited to the gambler's, and they said: "He will offer you something to eat, and it will be human eyes. Do not eat them; tell him that you ate plentifully and do not care to eat any more, but if he does not object you would like to take the food to your stopping-place. If you bring the food, we will take it out and throw it away." The errand man came around and said: "The gambler wishes you to eat with him." The boy said, "Very well; I will go." The boy went, and as he entered the lodge the gambler told him to take a seat by him. They offered him the bowl of eyes, but he would not eat them. He said that he had eaten plenty. The young man was asked if he could play the game of sticks. He said: "Yes; I will play with you, but as I am tired I will put it off until the fifth day." "Very well," said the gambler. The boy told them that he wanted to take the bowl to his stopping-place, so that when he should become hungry he could eat it.

The next two days the boy spent around the tipi, for he was thinking of his brother who had been killed. On the third day he was invited again. The people with whom he stopped said: "This time he will try to feed you dried human ears. He will try to make you believe that they are pieces of squash." The boy went to the gambler's lodge. They were very kind to him and offered him the bowl of squash. The boy said that he was sorry, but he had eaten so much that he could not eat any more; but he was very fond of squash and wished that he could take it to his stopping-place. He arose and took the bowl of human ears with him. The people received the bowl and threw the contents away. The bowl was taken back to the gambler's lodge.

The fourth day came and the boy asked the man who was in the lodge if he could tell him of a place where there were buffalo wallows and bones. "Yes," said the man; "I can show you. You see yonder hillside? There is where the bones are. There the buffalo have been slaugh-

tered by people who did not take the bones home. They took only
the meat and left most of the buffalo on the prairie." On the fourth
night the boy went to the place, and there were many skeletons of buffalo.
He began to cry. He went from one to another set of bones and continued to cry. After a while he came to a set of bones where there was a
bull skull. Its horns were not smooth and were loose, and it seemed
very old. The boy stood at the head and cried. Then he sang a song:

> My father, my father,
> The reason I am crying,
> The gambler has requested
> That I play sticks with him,
> And I have no sticks.
> Give me sticks, father,
> Give me a ring, mother.

The old bull said: "My grandchild, I am very sorry for you and
we will try to help you. These are my children lying around here. We
have made up our minds to help you. I myself can not do it, for I am old
and can not stand the game, but there are some young bulls who will help
you, for we want to get rid of the gambler. Now go. The spirits of the
buffalo have all returned." The boy continued to go around from one
set of bones to another, crying as he went. At last he came to the skull
of a bull whose horns were sharp and turned in at the tops. Here he
stopped and cried and cried. At last the skull spoke and said: "My
son, what are you crying for?" The boy then sang, saying in his song:
"I am crying, for I am about to play sticks with the gambler, and I have
no sticks. Pity me! Help me! Give me sticks and a ring, so that I
can beat this gambler. We are to put up our lives." The young bull
said: "Very well, my son. We shall help you. I am the strongest bull.
I can fight a long time and never get tired. Now watch." The boy
watched, and buffalo came from different directions. They made a
bellowing noise and all ran and stopped where these bones were; then
they stamped and fought. At last these buffalo dispersed and he heard
one say: "There he goes!" The boy looked and the buffalo disappeared,
and there where the buffalo were he saw a stick. A voice came from
the stick and said: "I will be one to beat the gambler. Take me and
see that the point is burnt black."

Now the boy went farther, and he came to a skull of a young bull,
whose horns were yet straight. The boy then stood and cried. The head
moved and said: "My son, I will help you. I am young and easily
give out. I will be the white stick, and the man shall choose me and use
me. I will be the fine-looking stick; also very light. I will not try to
go after the ring, for I never had intercourse with any female. Now

watch and I shall move." Something moved. The buffalo had turned
into a playing stick, without ceremony, for it was to be the gambler's
stick. The boy picked up the stick and went to another set of bones.

Again he cried, and some one spoke to him and said: "Go over
yonder, for there are bones of a young woman buffalo who had just
learned to be after buffalo bulls. She can run and beat all the other
buffalo women." The boy went to the skeleton of a young female calf,
and cried and cried. He did not hear anything, so he threw the sticks
in front of the skeleton and then a female voice said: "I will help you, but
the bulls must come and turn me into a ring." The boy cried the harder
and sang: "Help me, my grandfathers. Give me a ring to go with
these sticks, so that I can beat the bad man who is killing people and
eating them." All at once there was a rush of buffalo bulls where the
boy stood. The buffalo stamped and bellowed, some saying: "I have
her; I ran my stick into her; I caught her with my legs." Others said
something else. The female buffalo spoke and said: "This is the way I
shall run to your stick, my boy." Now the female buffalo ran and turned
into a ring. The ring rolled and fell on the black stick and was on the
top piece of the stick. "Nawa," said the boy. (I thank you, my grandfathers.) Then the old bull said: "My boy, you can not see us, but our
spirits will be with you. You see many strings on the sticks. They
are many buffalo. Now take the sticks, put the ring on the black stick,
and hang them up in the lodge on the north side. Play first with the
gambler's sticks. He shall just about beat you, but just as he throws
his last stick you shall shoot his stick with your stick, and his stick shall
break. Then you shall use these sticks that we give you. Now go!"

The boy went home and put the sticks upon the side of the lodge
where he was told to hang them up. The next morning was the time to
play. The boy told the people to stay outside and sweep out the lodge
clean, and that no one should remain inside. The people went out and
the lodge was swept and the mats placed in order. Then the people
started out to the place where the man and boy were to play the sticks.
The gambler was already out with his sticks. The people divided and
some were on one side and some on the other. The witch woman was
at one end and already had a quirt made of bone, for she intended to hit
the boy on the head with it and kill him. Then the boy arose and sang:

> Yonder, from yonder I came,
> You challenged me to play.
> From yonder I came,
> Now rise, stand, play,
> For you are the gambler.
> From yonder I came.

They played first for the things they wore.   They picked up the sticks
and ran.   The gambler threw the ring.   The boy at once commenced
to lose.   The old woman danced, made fun of the boy, and said that his
head was what she was after.   The boy lost all his clothing.   Then the
man said, "Suppose we bet our lives now?"   The boy said, "All right."
They played and played, the gambler catching the ring every time, and
the boy losing.   The man had to hook the ring once more, and the boy's
life would be won.   As they started, the man threw the ring, then the
stick, and the boy took good aim at the man's stick and he hit it and
broke it.   The gambler wanted to put off the game, but the boy said:
"No; I am not tired.   I will either lose or win.   Bring another set of
your sticks."   The man said he had none.   The boy said: "I have a set.
You make one ring and I am beaten.   I do not want to go home.   If
my life is to go I am willing that I lose it at once."   The man then
sent his errand man, who was no other than Coyote.   He went to the
lodge, and as he entered he heard many buffalo, so that he got scared
and came out.   He came to the ground and said: "There are no sticks
in the lodge."   He was sent again, and again the buffalo scared him.
He ran away again and said: "There are no sticks there."   Again he
was sent.   He walked right in, and as he went towards the sticks, the
buffalo made a big noise, and Coyote ran and defecated in the lodge.
He went to the grounds and said: "I do not find any sticks there."
The boy then sent his errand boy, who was no other than Black-Bird.
He went out, and although the buffalo made a noise, he flew upon their
backs and got the sticks.   As soon as he got the sticks the noise ceased.
He saw much of Coyote's dirt on the ground of the lodge.   He took the
sticks to the ground.

The boy gave the gambler his choice of sticks.   The gambler chose
the white stick.   The boy knew that he would.   Before commencing the
game anew, the boy said: "Now let us bet all our friends, too.   If I
win, I have a right to kill all your people; if you beat me then you may
kill all my people."   "All right," said the gambler.   Away they went
with the sticks, the gambler throwing the ring.   They both threw the
sticks and the gambler hooked the ring, but the ring came off and went
to the burnt stick and sat on top.   The boy then took charge of the ring.
The boy threw the ring gently, then threw his stick.   The ring and stick
did the work.   The gambler had no chance.   At last the boy won all of
his property and everything that he had, so that he put his wife and all of
his children up.   The boy won them, and then the gambler put up his
own life.   When he saw that he was going to be beaten, he fell down on
the ground and said: "My leg is broken, and I can not go."

Then the boy stopped and sang:

> Come now, stand up,
> You are the gambler,
> Come now, stand up.
> Why do you sit down?
> You are the gambler,
> Come now, stand up.
> Now arise, stand up,
> Now arise, stand up.
> You are the gambler,
> You are the gambler,
> Now arise, stand up.

When the boy sang about the man being a gambler, he arose and said: "It is true; I am a gambler." Then he arose and again they threw the sticks. When they threw their sticks for the last time, the sticks and the ring turned into buffalo and ran away. As soon as the gambler was beaten the people who were on the boy's side took up their sticks and beat the gambler and his wife and children and the witch and Coyote until they were all dead. They all rejoiced because the wicked people were killed and could no longer put fine young men to death.

52. YOUNG HAWK HUNTS FOR HIS MOTHER.[1]

There lived in the country a Hawk, his wife, and child. The man was a great warrior. He never was at home. One time while he was away, and the child was gone, the woman disappeared. The boy began to cry and look for his mother. After a while the boy found a passage in the ground. He went into the ground and traveled in the under-world. He came to a village and stood near it. He began to sing.

> I am hunting my mother.
> Her name is
> Woman-Knows-Everything.
> Yonder village there.
>
> I am hunting my father.
> His name is
> Handsome Hawk.
> Yonder village there.
>
> My name is,
> My name is
> Young Hawk, who lives among the people.
> Yonder village there.

The people in the village turned out and said: "Listen to the boy singing." When they heard what the boy said in the song, they sent

[1] Told by White-Eagle. Skidi. This story explains the source of the power of certain hawks over snakes, and why they take their name, snake hawks.

a man out to tell the boy that his mother was not in the village. The boy traveled on and at each village he sang about his mother. At last the boy came to a village and he began to sing about his mother. The people said: "She is here."

Just about that time the father had returned to their lodge and he saw that the family was missing. He hunted them, and after a while he came to the same passage which the boy had entered. He followed up the boy in the under-world. Just as the boy started to go into the village the father came over another place. The mother was glad to see her boy. While the boy was sitting studying what to say, the father came in. Hawk went to his wife, touched her, and turned her into a Hawk. Then he touched his son and he turned into a Hawk. The father himself then turned into a Hawk. Hawk then caught the little snake which had taken his wife, flew off with it, and ate it. After this they became snake hawks.

53. THE DOG-BOY WHO MARRIED THE CHIEF'S DAUGHTER.[1]

The people were packing up, preparing to go hunting, when the wife of a man by the name of White-Moccasins gave birth. They found out that the child was not a baby, but a dog. White-Moccasins carried the dog through the camp and threw it into the creek. The little dog tried to swim in the water, but could not. A Clam Shell got hold of the dog and took it out of the water. The Clam Shell then sat near the edge of the water and listened to a song which the dog sang. After the dog was through singing, the Clam Shell began to sing. The dog looked to see where the song came from, but could not see anything. After a while the Clam Shell said: "I am singing." The dog looked around and saw the Clam Shell for the first time. The Clam Shell spoke again and said: "The people did you a wrong by leaving you behind. Your father, White-Moccasins, did not throw you away, but a witch woman threw you away. You were thrown into the water. I saved your life. You had better follow the trail of the people. As soon as you overtake them, tell them that you are the son of White-Moccasins. The people will be glad to see you, and will try to make you a chief. When you have caught up with them sing the song that you heard me singing." The Clam Shell then told the dog to look around. The dog looked around and he turned into a boy. Then the Clam Shell told him to look around again. He looked and there was a quiver. He told him to take the quiver and when he had the quiver, he told him to follow the trail to the village.

[1] Told by White-Sun, Kitkehahki. An interesting and abbreviated version of a widespread tale; teaches parents not to abandon their children.

The boy arrived at the village and began to sing:

> Yonder, behind, at the old village site,
> Is where White-Moccasins' child was left.
> Yonder the child was left, yonder.

When the people heard of White-Moccasins' son they were glad, and when the chief heard that it was White-Moccasins' son who was singing he invited the boy to his tipi. When the boy entered the chief's tipi the people gathered around the tipi to look at the boy. White-Moccasins came into the tipi. The chief spoke and said to him: "White-Moccasins, you did wrong to throw your child away. You told the people that your child was a dog, but we now find that he is a handsome boy. When you threw him away you threw away your own heart. He shall not go to your tipi any more, but shall stay with me." White-Moccasins said: "It shall be as the chief says," and the boy stood up and said: "I was thrown away. White-Moccasins did not treat me right. I will stay with the chief. I will herd his ponies and when he thinks the proper time has come, I shall marry his daughter." The chief was very proud of the boy.

Soon he called the people to come together to go on a hunt. The boy went with them. In the hunt the boy planned everything. They killed many buffalo, and when the people returned from the hunt they told the chief how the boy had been their leader, and how successful their party had been. After that the chief said: "My boy, you shall marry my daughter." The boy married the chief's daughter and they had many children.

One day the boy went off to the south. He walked up on a high hill and he saw standing there a black-tailed deer. When he looked again the deer was not there, but a young girl. The deer had turned into a girl. The girl said: "Boy, I want to warn you. White-Moccasins, your father, is trying to kill you, but it shall not be. Go to your home, gather the people, send for White-Moccasins, tell him that if he wants to kill you he will have to do it in open fight. When he tries to kill you, I will protect you. If he tries to poison you with medicines, I will be there to protect you." The boy listened to the girl, then he went home, and told the chief how he had seen a deer and how the deer had turned into a girl, and what the girl had told him. The boy invited many people, and among them he invited his father, White-Moccasins.

When the people had come, the boy stood up and said: "White-Moccasins, show your power. You may kill me if you can. I know that you are trying to kill me, and I will now give you the chance." White-Moccasins then stood up and went out. He gathered several

other men and then returned to the lodge. The boy said: "White-
Moccasins, you may kill me now if you can." White-Moccasins tried
to kill the boy, but could not. Then the boy said: "I will show you my
power." The boy waved his hand at White-Moccasins and White-
Moccasins began to pound his head upon the trees and everything that
came in his way. Then the people who were with White-Moccasins
jumped on the boy and began to strike him with clubs. The boy then
took his whistle and whistled. As the boy whistled, all of the people
about him fell dead. After a while he whistled again, and White-Moccasins fell dead.

54. SUN-RAY, WHO MISTREATED HIS WIFE.[1]

A man and his wife lived together some distance from the main
village. The man traveled over the country very swiftly and brought
home deer, buffalo, and all kinds of game. He would order his wife to
cook certain parts of the meat for him, then would give her only a small
piece of meat to eat. He abused her by throwing hot coals at her and
punching her with the fire sticks. The woman tried to get away from
him, but every time that she was about to go to her people her husband
would come, and before she knew it she would be hanging on his belt,
inside of a round rattle bound with hide and having a handle.

One time the woman ran to one of the villages, and there she told the
people that she was starving; that her husband was very cruel, and ate all
the meat that he brought to their lodge. She thought that she was safe
in the village, for she kept herself hid all the time. The people gave her
plenty to eat, and watched to see that her husband did not come.

Finally her husband returned from the hunt to the lodge, and when he
found that his wife was gone he traveled from one village to another, and
when he came to the edge of a village he took his rattle and pointed it
toward the village, moving around as he did so, and if the woman did not
appear in his rattle he knew that she was not in the village. Then he
would go to another village and move the rattle around, and if the woman
was in the village he would at once see her come out of his rattle; for the
rattle was made from a magic gourd, and whenever it was pointed towards
the woman she immediately appeared inside the rattle. Thus he found
the woman hiding in the village. When he returned with her to his home
he treated her very badly.

[1] Told by Thief, Kitkehahki. Formerly among the Pawnee there was a certain
society the members of which carried a peculiar rattle, open in the center, which
was supposed to have had power similar to the rattle described in the tale. These
rattles were painted yellow and were supposed to represent a sun ray twisted into
this shape. This society had its origin in the sun ray described in the tale.

One day the man went off on a hunt. The woman left the lodge and went to a creek. She cried around the creek. The Beaver came up and asked what she was crying about. She told them that her husband was very mean to her, and did not give her much to eat; that she wanted to get away from him. The Beaver then told her to stop crying and they would take her into their lodge. The woman was taken into the lodge of the Beaver and kept there for some time.

When her husband came to his lodge he found that the woman was gone. While he was hunting for her he happened to go down to the stream of water, and there he saw her footprints upon the sand. He took his rattle, moved it around the waters, and the woman, who was walking around in the Beaver dam, immediately appeared in his rattle, and he pulled her out with his string. He took her to his home, and when he woke her up he told her that there was nothing to be gained by trying to get away from him, for he could find her, no difference where she might go. The woman cried day after day and the man threw hot coals at her and told her to stop crying.

Again the man went out hunting and the woman determined to go off to another country. She went to a mortar, pulled it up, and turned herself into a Mole. She set the mortar pounder in its place again, then began to dig. She dug until she had gone very far, then came out of the ground. She took a little grass and covered her feet with it. She went to a far-away village. She went into a tipi in the night and lay down.

The next morning the people found her and they asked her where she had come from, and she told them that her husband had been very mean to her and did not give her anything to eat, and she was hiding from him. They felt very sorry for her and told her to stay with them.

Her husband returned to his lodge, and not finding his wife, went all over the country hunting for her. At last he found her in the strange village. He saw her in a tipi and he went into the tipi and stood by her. The people did not know he was there, for he had come in as a Sun-Ray. Before she knew it she was put to sleep and placed in the rattle. When Sun-Ray had done this he turned into a man. Then the people said: "You belong up in the heavens. You came and took a woman from this earth for your wife. You mistreated her and you do not give her anything to eat. It was very wrong." Sun-Ray was angry, and he took off his rattle and threw it down upon the ground and the woman woke up. He said to her: "Woman, you know that I find you wherever you go. These people are trying to take your part. I shall take you home and treat you as badly and even worse than I did before." Then he pulled the string of his rattle and the woman came out.

When he got to his home, he released the woman. For the first time Sun-Ray was sorry for her. He said: "Woman, I will let you go. I will take you to that village where you were and you may stay with the people. I shall return where I belong, and all the sun-rays will be together hereafter." Then Sun-Ray took the woman in his rattle, placed her on his belt, and traveled to the village and took her into the lodge where she had been. He told the people to take care of her, saying that he was going back to the sun, where he belonged; then he stood where he had entered the lodge as a sun-ray and disappeared.

55. HAWK SLAYS THE FIRE-KEEPER.[1]

A long time ago, when Tirawa created the world, he made one man to guard all the fire. His name was Fire-Keeper and his home was somewhere in the west. After a time Tirawa put people upon the earth. These people were descended from certain gods in the heavens, but the man in charge of fire did not like them. They were many, and had a village. On the west of the village was a stream of water which was so deep that no one could cross it. There were two young men who lived across the stream who were Hawk people. They were brothers and were wonderful beings. They wore coyote robes and carried war clubs all the time. They had a log across the stream, but they were the only ones who could cross the stream upon the log.

One day the older brother told the younger that he was going across the stream to get a wife, and so he left his younger brother and went across the stream. He went into the village and entered the lodge of the priest and asked for his daughter. The priest gave his daughter to the young man. Then he sent for all of the girl's relatives, except the Fire-Keeper, who was the brother of the priest's wife, to come to his lodge. Fire-Keeper was angry because they did not send for him, and he made up his mind to kill the young man.

The young man lived with his wife for many moons, until she gave birth to a boy. One morning he told his wife that he was going across the stream to see his brother. When he had crossed the stream and had

---

[1] Told by Thief, Kitkehahki. This is a bundle story, and is related to show the people that the gods of the heavens have superior powers to those of the gods of the earth. It also teaches the children to respect the bundles which come from the stars or the heavenly gods. The individual who had his tipi of living fire and tortured the Hawk is overcome, and the fire is carried back to heaven by the Hawk, who marries Mother-Corn. The pair represent respectively the Morning and Evening Stars. The bundle of the stars among the Kitkehahki has on it an owl which represents the power of the priest. It is said that when Mother-Corn married the Hawk she transferred to him all her power except her ability to make things grow again.

just stepped off of the log he was taken by some mysterious being. It was so foggy that he could not see the being. The being stripped the young man of his leggings, that were decorated with scalps, and his coyote robe, and took them and burned them. The young man tried to see, but he could not, for the being had burned out his eyes. He was carried off by the mysterious being and for several days was led along, until at last he was taken into a lodge and was told that he was a slave.

He was missed at his wife's place and the people wondered where he could have gone. One night the baby began to cry. The mother tried to quiet him, but he kept on crying. The mother thought that her husband must be across the stream with his brother. Said she: "I will take the child to his father, and when he takes him he will stop crying." She went to the stream and when she came to the log she was not afraid to cross it. She crossed and went to the lodge of the young men. She went into the lodge and saw only the younger brother. She asked where her husband was and the boy said that he had not been there. The girl said: "Take this baby. It may be that he will stop crying, for he is crying for his father." The boy took the child, but it cried the louder. The boy said: "Take the child, for I must go and hunt for my brother. I am afraid that some one has killed him."

The woman went out of the lodge to the crossing. Just as she was about to step upon the log she saw pieces of her husband's leggings. Then she looked around and found also bits of his coyote robe. She looked carefully and saw his footprints. She followed his tracks, which led toward the setting sun. She went on for many days, until at last she saw a big fire. She went to the fire, which was very bright, for it was night. She came to the fire and found a large tipi with a big fire in it. She peeped in and there sat a man at the west on the inside of the lodge, painted red all over. She knew him. He was her uncle. Again she looked, and close to the entrance sat her husband. He was burnt on different parts of his body and he was blind. The man in the west said: "Blind man, stir the fire. The fire is nearly out." The blind man went to the fire and took hold of his own war club and stirred the fire. The baby then began to cry and the woman began to sing:

> Uncle, you sitting there,
> Let him come out.
> Yonder the child was left, yonder.
> My husband sitting there,
> His child is crying;
> Ha-o-o, you sitting there.

The man spoke and said: "My niece, I want to kill your husband, for he married you without my knowledge. Stir the fire, you blind man."

The blind man again stirred the fire. The woman kept on singing till at last the man told the blind man to leave the lodge. The woman could not enter the lodge, for it was hot inside. The blind man came out and took his child, and the child stopped crying. Then the blind man said: "Go in and pick up my war club." The woman went in and brought the club, though it was half burned away.

She led her husband toward the east. For many days they went toward the east, until one day the blind man told his wife to lead him to a rocky place. She led him up a high hill. One side of the hill was very steep and rocky; the other side was covered with cedar trees. She said, "Here is the place. There are many rocks on the bank and at the bottom." "Put me on the edge of the bank," said the man, "and let my legs hang down." The woman obeyed. "Now," said he, "push me over, so that I shall fall over this steep bank." The woman would not do it, for she thought that he wanted to die because he was blind. The man kept on begging her to push him over the bank before the sun should rise. The woman would not do it. Finally the man said, "Throw me over; then you go around the bank and you will see me again and I will meet you there."

The man did not want to tell her what he intended to do, but he had to tell her that much or she would not push him over. After he had told her she pushed him over. Then she took up her baby and went around the bank. Before she came to the end of the hill she saw her husband coming up from a thick cedar tree. He had his coyote robe and also the scalp leggings. "I am here," he said. "Go to my brother's house and wait there for me. I am now going west to that being who burned my eyes out, and I am going to kill him. When some night you see meteors flying through the sky you may know that I have killed him."

They parted and the woman went to her brother-in-law's tipi and told him all. Her brother-in-law was glad, and said: "Let us now go to your people and let them know that you have come back." They went to her home. The woman then told her brother-in-law to go back to his home and wait for his brother. The boy went back to his tipi. One night the people saw fire flying through the sky, and the woman told them that her husband had killed her uncle, the Fire-Keeper.

When the young man approached the tipi of the Fire-Keeper, he was sitting at the entrance watching, for he knew that the young man had powers and he feared him. Instead of going to the entrance to attack him the young man turned himself into a hawk, and he flew into the top of the tipi, and flying swiftly downward struck the Fire-Keeper upon the head and killed him. Then the Hawk turned into a human being, and took the fire and threw it through the sky in different places, saying: "You shall do my bidding. Warriors shall carry you and you shall help to kill the enemy." All the stars then received light.

Then the young man went to the east. When he had journeyed all over the country the animals cried to him and said: "You have done good work. The Fire-Keeper is gone. He can not burn us any more." When he lay down in the night the owls hooted round him to let him know they were guarding him. On the way to his brother's, birds of all kinds gathered together upon a certain hill and waited for him. When he came there the birds one at a time spoke to him, and said: "You shall be always present with the people, for you married among them. You shall also be known as the Warrior-Bird. Your right wing you shall use as a club to kill small birds for yourself to eat." Hawk was satisfied with the sayings of the birds.

He returned to his brother's tipi. He went with his brother to the village. They told the father-in-law that when they died the people would place their skins in a bundle, so that young men might remember to carry the hawk and corn with them when they went out upon the war-path. The priests (owls) were always to remain at home to watch over the people.

56. THE SINGING HAWK.[1]

In olden times, when the Pawnee first went on a buffalo hunt, it was customary for most of the young women of the tribe to go to the priest's tipi and build a grass-lodge for him, for in the grass-lodge were to be held meetings by the old men of the tribe. A grass-lodge was given to the first people who were put upon the earth. Whenever a grass-lodge was completed it was customary for the young women of the tribe to take mush in wooden bowls to the priest's lodge, so that the old men would have something to eat while they sat in their lodge to sing the bundle songs and pray that the buffalo might be near.

It was in these meetings in the grass-lodge that the old people told wonderful stories about how the people called the buffalo, or how a coyote scared the buffalo toward a village. In their story-telling they also told of the being who stands in the north and with its breath sends the buffalo to the people. They told many coyote stories, for these stories, although not real, would have the effect of bringing them good luck and

[1] Told by Thief, Kitkehahki. This tale is of special interest on account of the song, which really represents a ritual formerly chanted after opening the bundle when on a buffalo hunt. The ritual, however, does not form an intrinsic part of any bundle ceremony. The tale was simply told along with the chanting of the ritual in the hope that it might draw the buffalo nearer the camp.

something to eat. It was in this meeting that this ritual was recited. The old man said that once upon a time the Coyote people—that is, the coyotes, crows, rabbits, foxes, magpies, hawks, eagles, and other animals— went on a buffalo hunt; that these birds and animals selected a Hawk to look for the buffalo. The Hawk flew towards the west and went around to different places where it was known that the buffalo generally stayed. Every time the Hawk would climb a high hill he would see only the prairies and no buffalo. He finally circled around towards the south, and then east, coming to where the people were, and there the Hawk found many buffalo. There he stood surprised, for he had gone a long distance in the country and could not find buffalo and here they were close to the people.

Then the Hawk went into the lodge where the birds and animals were and sang this song:

Now I climbed the hill and arrived at the top,
There where the streams of water shorten people's legs,
Where once great herds of buffalo started from,
Yet I saw nothing yonder but an expanse of land.
Only the expanse of land, only the expanse of land.

There where the elm trees are surrounded by hills.[1]
　　*　　　*　　　*　　　*　　　*

There where the hill stands in front of other hills.
　　*　　　*　　　*　　　*　　　*

There on the island hill where stand the cedar trees,
　　*　　　*　　　*　　　*　　　*

There at the point of a grove of timber,
　　*　　　*　　　*　　　*　　　*

There at the other end of the point of timber,
　　*　　　*　　　*　　　*　　　*

There at the place where one tree stands behind the timber,
　　*　　　*　　　*　　　*　　　*

There at the foot of the hills by the group of box elders,
　　*　　　*　　　*　　　*　　　*

There at the top of the hills where the skulls lie,
　　*　　　*　　　*　　　*　　　*

There where the mud covers the trails,
　　*　　　*　　　*　　　*　　　*

[1] The next twenty verses of this song are like the first verse, except the second line, which only is here given.

There where a group of trees stands by the water,
*   *   *   *   *

There where the ponies slip down hill,
*   *   *   *   *

There at yonder hill, the girls' hill,
*   *   *   *   *

There where the top of the hill is barren,
*   *   *   *   *

There by the earth-lodge at the foot of the hill,
*   *   *   *   *

There at the river banks by the swallows' homes,
*   *   *   *   *

There by the thicket of cottonwood,
*   *   *   *   *

There where the white clay is found,
*   *   *   *   *

There where the sand reaches the foot of the hills,
*   *   *   *   *

There by the group of black islands,
*   *   *   *   *

There on the hills where human bones lie buried,
*   *   *   *   *

Now I climbed the hill and arrived at the top,
*   *   *   *   *

There where the stream of water separates,
There on the island's point, where stands a tree clump,
Where once great herds of buffalo started from,
There I stood.

I stood surprised and rejoiced,
I stood surprised and rejoiced,
For there were the buffalo, like threads covering the earth.
There they were, there they were.

Thus in his song he told of the different places he had visited, how on climbing the hills he had found nothing but prairie. In the singing he mentions all the different places he visited and at last he comes to a place near the village and there he found the buffalo. This is why the people sing this song upon their hunt, that they may find the buffalo near and not far away.

57. THE BOY WHO MARRIED A BUFFALO.[1]

A boy and his sister lived by themselves. The boy traveled toward the south to get feathers; then he made arrows. He made one arrow red and another one black and the others plain. There was another village in the west, where the Buffalo lived. The daughter of the Buffalo chief came to visit the boy and his sister. The boy's sister saw some one coming to their tipi. Then the girl began to sing:

> Stand there, my brother,
> Some one is coming on the hill,
> There on the hilltops from where you brought your feathers.
> Pa-o-o, pa-o-o. (Cry of coyote.)

The boy stopped his work and said: "Whoever is coming, let him come." All at once a young Buffalo cow came into the tipi. The boy took his bow and arrows and shot at the Buffalo. The arrow did not go through the body, but the point curled under the hair and hung on the side of the cow. She ran outside of the tipi, and the boy followed, expecting every minute that the arrow would drop off. The boy kept on following the Buffalo until they came to box-elder timber. It was twilight. The Buffalo went into the timber. The boy followed and there he found a tipi. The boy lay down near the tipi and went to sleep.

Next morning, when the boy woke up, the Buffalo stood where the tipi had been. The Buffalo went east a little and circled around and then went west again. The boy became angry and called the Buffalo names. In the evening the cow went into a cottonwood grove. The boy went into the timber and there again was the tipi. The boy went into the tipi and there sat a woman all covered up with her robe. The boy sat down on the south side. When it was dark the woman gave the boy a calf robe and told him to lie down upon it. In the morning when the boy awoke the Buffalo stood by him with the arrow still in her hair. The boy crawled up to get the arrow, but the cow ran again. The boy followed. She went slowly and the boy kept following, expecting the arrow to drop. Towards evening the cow went into the weeping-willow timber. The boy went into the timber and again saw the same tipi. He went into the tipi and sat down on the south side. When it was dark the cow

[1] Told by Thief, Kitkehahki. This story is related during ceremonies by the old men to the children who may have entered the lodge; it especially teaches the boys to take good care of their bows and arrows and instills in them a desire to kill buffalo, that they may consecrate some of its meat to the gods of the heavens through the bundle. It also teaches young married people to be hospitable to strangers, especially those from distant countries, because they may thus be entertaining unawares supernatural beings of great power.

gave him a calf robe to lie upon. In the morning, when the boy woke up, the Buffalo was standing close to him. He followed her all of the next day until evening; then saw the tipi. He went into the tipi and saw the woman again. The woman called to him this time. The boy went and sat by her. The woman asked why he had no robe. He said: "I shot at a Buffalo and my arrow stuck upon the hair and carried the arrow away. I love my arrows and can not lose one of them." Then she reached and gave him the arrow. She said: "I am the Buffalo. You called me names. I will now take you to my people, for I love you and I want you to marry me." She reached behind her and produced some dried meat, which she gave to the boy to eat. After they had eaten he lay down with the woman and they slept together.

Next morning, when the boy awoke, he saw the Buffalo standing by him. Then they went together until they came to a place where sat an old, scabby bull. The boy had a bag of tobacco and he gave some of it to the bull. The bull was thankful. Finally they entered the village of Buffalo. Some of the Buffalo were glad to see the girl and the boy, and some were mad. The father of the girl, who was a chief, had a white spot upon the forehead. Her uncle had long horns. The long-horned Buffalo was mad and wanted to kill the young man. He made a dash at him and the boy shot him in the side and killed him. Then the father, with the white spot upon the forehead, attacked the boy, and the boy shot him also and killed him. All the Buffalo then became mad.

The young man then sang: "I want the ceremony of the Buffalo." The Buffalo ran about the boy and rattled their hoofs, but did not kill him, but the boy shot the Buffalo. Every time the Buffalo tried to kill him, he turned into a downy feather. Then the Buffalo said: "My son, we want some good smoke." The boy told them that he would give them tobacco, and to some of them he would blow whiffs of smoke. The Buffalo then told the boy to take a few Buffalo to the village and to have them killed. The boy took the Buffalo to the village to the people, and they killed them and sacrificed them to the gods. When the Buffalo were killed they returned to the herd and told that their meat had been put to good use and that they received smoke. When the Buffalo traveled toward the east the boy turned into a downy feather and rode upon the Buffalo. Finally the boy was turned into a Buffalo and lived with them and never returned to his sister. When the young man was turned into a Buffalo, soft downy feathers were stuck into the hair of his body. In one of their hunts the people killed the young man, took the hide off, and found the feathers stuck through the robe; and the people made the robe holy.

58. THE BUFFALO WIFE AND THE DISPERSION OF THE BUFFALO.[1]

In a certain village there was a young man who disliked girls and women. This young man was really not a man, but a blackbird. The women tried to catch him in the night, but he was always on the lookout, and escaped them. The girls tried to catch him, but he would not have anything to do with them. There was another village to the west of the first village, but this was not a village of people, but of Buffalo. Every day the young man painted his face with black streaks and made black streaks upon his leggings. He took a spear and shield and a quiver of mountain-lion, and mounted his fine white horse and rode around the village. Some of the people from the west villages came and said that in that village there was a girl who disliked men. The young man heard of her and wanted to go and see her. The girl also heard that there was a young man in the lower village who disliked women and she wanted to see him. The girl told her parents that she would like to go to the village to see the young man. Her parents told her to go. She walked toward the lower village and at the same time the young man left his village and went to the west to see the girl. There was a high hill between the villages and the boy climbed up the east side. As he came to the top of the hill he saw the girl walking up the other side of the hill.

When the young girl came up she spoke and said: "Where are you going?" The young man said: "I am going to the west to the other villages." The girl spoke again and said: "I am going to the lower village to visit the young man who dislikes women." She asked the young man where he was going. He said: "I am going to the other village to see the young girl who dislikes men." The girl dropped her head and answered, "I am that girl." Then she asked, "What is your name?" and he said, "My name is Streaks-of-Black-Paint-across-Face-and-Legs." The girl said: "I dislike men, but I like you." The boy said nothing and they separated, each going home. The girl told her people about the fine young man whom she had seen. The old Buffalo told her to go to the other village and bring the young man. The girl went back to the lower village and at dawn she stood on the little knoll at the north side and sang:

[1] Told by Thief, Kitkehahki. The tale teaches that the performance of deeds such as those which it recounts may prove efficacious in drawing the buffalo near the village so that the people might kill them. It also explains how the blackbird, because it married a buffalo cow, is allowed to perch on the backs of the buffalo without attracting any notice from them.

All you people in camp there.
Get wide awake all of you.
We shall see which one of you
Brought me down stream as his wife,
Brought me down stream as his wife.
Yonder we came, brought me down stream as his wife.

You spoke and said,
I have standing at my place a gray horse.
You brought me down stream as your wife,
You brought me down stream as your wife.
Yonder we came, when you brought me down stream as your wife.

Old Claw-Shield Coyote awoke and heard the girl singing, and said: "Old woman, that girl means me. You must not get jealous. Now listen. The girl sings and says that I ride a white horse. I must go and get my white horse, and I shall go out and get the girl and bring her to our tipi." The old man jumped upon his gray horse and went out. He asked the girl to come to his tipi, but the girl did not notice him. The boy was not in the village, so the girl went on to another village and there she stood on the north side again and sang. The young men came out. She sang as before.

Coyote had tried to fool the girl at the other village and failed. He got a number of cockle burrs and placed them upon the gray horse, and jumped on it so that the horse would prance because of the cockle burrs pricking it, and followed the girl to the next village. When Coyote rode up to where the girl was the handsome young boy was already there upon his white horse. Coyote went away angry and embarrassed. The handsome young man took the girl and placed her behind him on the horse's back. He took her to his tipi and they went into the tipi and sat down. The young man told his people to place corn before the girl for her to eat. The girl ate the corn. The people noticed that she had an elk dress on. After they had eaten, the young man took the girl upon his pony again and they went west to the Buffalo camp. They reached the Buffalo camp in the night. The girl jumped off from the pony and went to her father and said, "Father, I am married."

The father was glad. He then sent for the old Buffalo and the young man filled his pipe with native tobacco, and gave each Buffalo a whiff of smoke. The old Buffalo decided that eight of the Buffalo should be sent to the people. The eight Buffalo were sent to the people and they were all killed. When the Buffalo were killed, they were made holy and smoke offerings were made over their meat. The Buffalo were glad of this, and that night many more Buffalo went to the people. These Buffalo were also killed. The Buffalo knew that some of them were made holy and that the smoke offering had been made.

Again they sent many Buffalo, and they were all killed and many were made holy. Again a big drove of Buffalo was sent and among them was the girl with her husband. After she saw how the smoke offering was made over the dead Buffalo, they went back to the Buffalo village and the girl told her father what she had seen. The Buffalo were glad, and they sent a big drove of Buffalo. The people killed many. The Buffalo were glad of the smoke offering, so the bulls all agreed to lead their people toward the people, and this is the way the Buffalo scattered over the country.

This is why a woman must wear the elk dress during the ceremony, as did the Buffalo woman who came to the boy, when her husband makes a Buffalo holy. The people killed buffalo bulls twice, and twice did they kill buffalo cows. This is why we have four leading bundles and four particular posts in the medicine-lodge. This also is why, when the people made the eagle feather holy, they placed the feather upon the knoll, in imitation of the girl who stood on the knoll when she asked for her husband. All these things were taught the people that they might do them, so that the Buffalo would come.

The young man went back with his wife, and they stayed among the Buffalo people. For some cause or other, the girl Buffalo made the young man mad, for she scolded him and she said that he should always be with the Buffalo, but would never marry among them, and he jumped up and flew away. He was a Blackbird, and for this reason the Blackbirds like to be in the Buffalo herd.

59. THE POOR BOY WHO WANTED TO GET MARRIED.[1]

There was a village. On the east side of the village lived an old woman with her grandchild. They were very poor. The other people lived in fine earth-lodges, while these two lived in a grass-lodge away off from the village. When the people went out in the morning, they surrounded the grass-lodge and urinated there, and hence it had a bad odor. Every day the old woman went through the village begging. In this way they kept alive.

The boy was now very tall. One day he told his grandmother to make him a bow and some arrows. The woman made them. The boy played with the bow and arrows every day. One day he wandered from his lodge and went a short distance to the east where there was a

[1] Told by Cheyenne-Chief, Skidi. This story teaches that no matter how poor a boy may be, he may, by his own effort and by assistance, become a tribal benefactor.

high hill. Instead of climbing the hill he stopped and began to play with his bow and arrows at the bottom. The boy went to sleep. In his sleep he found himself under the ground with a fine-looking young man. This young man said: "I know that you are very poor. I have come to you to tell you that hereafter, every day, we, the Buffalo people, are to send you a Buffalo calf. When we think it is time to send you larger ones we will send them." Then this man spoke again and said: "I am the son of the Buffalo chief. His home is beyond the village where you see those red mountains. There is another opening there, and when the time comes we will make the Buffalo come out from the side of those mountains so that the people can kill them. Return now to your grandmother and to-morrow come back to this place, so that I can show you the opening about which I told you."

The boy went to his grandmother's lodge and did not eat anything for some time. He was thinking of what the strange man had told him. The next morning the boy arose and without eating anything he took his bow and arrows and went out to the place where he had been the day before. There he met the strange man he had seen. This man took him farther on until they came to the foot of the hill. On the side of the hill was a steep bank. The strange man said: "You must get behind this little knoll and you must watch closely, for there is to be a little calf come out from this bank. Where you see this steep bank, although it is covered, there is really an opening where the Buffalo can come out." The strange man told the boy that he must not look at the bank, but that he must be behind it so that he would not know just how the Buffalo came out.

They hid behind the knoll and after a while the boy heard some one coming. Then he heard the noise of hoofs rattling. After a while the strange man touched the boy. The boy looked up and there he saw a little calf standing looking at him. The strange man touched him and said: "Shoot it; shoot it, and be quick about it." The boy shot the calf with the arrow in the side and the arrow passed through the calf and came out on the other side. The calf gave one jump, staggered, bled in the mouth, fell over, and died. The boy was so glad that he jumped over where he had killed the calf, and when he was sure that he had killed it he turned around to see where the strange man was, but he had disappeared. The boy took the little calf home and placed it in the lodge.

Some time after that the old woman came, and the boy said: "Grandmother, I killed a little calf. I have it in the lodge." The old woman cried out and went to her grandson, passed her hands over his head, and said: "My poor grandson tells me that he has killed a calf. My poor boy, when you get strong so that you can go and hunt, then you can kill calves, deer, and other game for your grandmother." The boy took his grandmother into the lodge and showed her the calf. The boy took the arrow which the grandmother had made for him and said: "I shot it with this arrow. The arrow was sharpened and the sharp point burned so that it was hard." The grandmother was glad, and she at once skinned the calf, cut some of the meat up, and boiled it. While they were eating, the boy said, "Grandmother, you must not go begging any more. From this time on we shall have meat. The people will be coming to beg meat from you. Give the meat to those people who were kind to you and those who did not urinate on our lodge." Every day after that the boy brought a calf home, each time a little larger than the one he had brought home before.

Some time after this he began to get lots of buffalo, so that he had to get his grandmother to help him skin them and cut up the meat so that they could carry it home. Every day the old woman sat in the lodge and jerked meat. She also made some lariat ropes from the buffalo hide. The ropes she stretched across the grass-lodge on the inside, and she hung up the meat she had jerked to dry. When a lot of this meat was dry, she folded it up and placed it in parfleches which she had made from the skins.

One day when they were eating fresh meat, a young girl came into their lodge. The boy told his grandmother to give her something to eat; that her people had scolded her and she had come there to sleep. The girl ate some of the meat and she saw that the two had plenty to eat. She told the old woman that the people in the village were starving for meat; that the people in the village had hardly anything to eat. The old woman then took some buffalo meat from one of the parfleches and gave it to the girl, and told her to take the meat home and for her to eat the meat in the night by herself. The girl did not want to go to her home, but the woman begged her to go, and so she went.

A few days afterwards the boy went out and killed a big buffalo cow. The old woman and the boy skinned the buffalo, cut up the meat, and carried it home. After they had eaten, the boy went out to the opening on the side of the hill and there he met the strange man. The strange man gave the boy moccasins, leggings, a buffalo robe, an eagle cap, and an otter-skin quiver filled with arrows, and a bow. The strange being told the boy that he must go to his grandmother and tell her to go and ask some of the village girls to come and live with them. The boy went to the tipi and stood outside. He took his new bow and one arrow, and began to hit the bowstring with his arrow, and sang:

> Yonder, yonder, yonder.
> Yonder, yonder, yonder.
> Grandmother, to speak for me, go
> To the lodge of many maidens.
> Yonder, yonder, yonder.
> Yonder, yonder, yonder.

When he stopped singing, the old woman cried inside of the lodge and said: "My grandson, you know the people do not like us. You want me to go and ask many girls to marry you. I do not believe that they will have you." The boy began to sing the same song. While he was singing the old woman went out. Instead of her poor boy standing there, there stood a fine-looking young man with an eagle cap upon his head. He had on fine leggings, moccasins, a new robe, and a new quiver filled with arrows, and a new bow. She could not believe that it was her grandson. Then she asked if it were he, and he said that it was and he wanted her to go and ask the chief for his many daughters.

The old woman went to the lodge of the chief. She said, "I have come to ask for your girls for my grandson." The chief was lying down upon his bed. He got up and sat near the fireplace with his head down. He sat there for a long time. At last he lifted his head and said: "Woman, who is this grandson of yours that I should give him my daughters? Go to him and tell him that I will send my answer to him to-morrow when the sun is up high." The woman arose and went to her lodge. She told her grandson that he was to receive the chief's answer the next day. The boy then stood outside and began to sing again, saying:

> My grandson sitting here,
> Did climb and reach the hill tops,
> Yonder red hill tops.
> "Listen, grandmother," the people say,
> "Could your grandson find the buffalo
> By climbing yonder red hills?"

After singing he went into the lodge, sat down, and ate some meat. Just then the same girl who had been in before entered the lodge. She saw the boy's cap hanging on the side of the wall; also the leggings and moccasins. The boy wore the robe, and the quiver was hanging on the wall. The boy was sitting down eating. The girl spoke to the old woman and said, "Is that your grandson?" The old woman said, "That is my grandson." The girl then said: "Grandmother, I want you to know that I am the youngest of the chief's daughters. I have been here once before. I love your grandson and I want to marry him." The woman gave the girl meat and sent her to her home.

In the night the girl left her bed and went to where her father and mother were lying. She woke her mother and said: "Mother, take this meat and fat and eat it. Here also is a piece of meat and a piece of fat for my father. Give it to him and tell him that this meat and fat came from the poor boy who lives on the outskirts of the village. Tell my father that to-morrow he must send word to the poor boy and tell him that one of his daughters will marry him." The mother tried to scold her daughter, but the daughter said: "Mother, through this poor boy the people will be fed." The girl then went to bed. Her mother took the meat and fat and gave it to her husband. Now, these people had had nothing to eat for some time, and they were hungry. When the man ate of the meat and the fat he asked where it came from. The woman said, "Our daughter brought this meat from the poor boy's grandmother." The mother said further, "You must give your consent to let our youngest daughter marry the poor boy." The chief said, "It is well."

The next day the woman went back to the chief's lodge and there she sat down. The chief said, "Woman, go to your grandson and tell him to come to my lodge; that he shall now marry my youngest daughter." The old woman went to her grandson and told him that the chief wanted him at his lodge. The boy put on his eagle cap, his robe, his leggings, and his moccasins and went through the village. When the people saw him they wondered who the young man could be. He entered the lodge of the chief and he was given a seat near the entrance near the youngest daughter. The other girls who had been telling their father not to let them marry him, saw the poor boy and they were surprised. They also wanted to sit near the poor boy, but his wife would not let them come near. The chief told the boy that he was now married to his daughter. Then the boy told his wife to get up and go with him to his lodge. When they entered their lodge the boy told his grandmother to untie one parfleche of meat and boil it. The boy then sent word to the chief to come to his lodge to eat with him. The chief invited several other leading men. They entered the lodge, sat down, and were filled with meat. The chief then said, "My son, our people are very hungry." The boy said: "I know that. I shall try to see if I can get any buffalo in the country."

The next day the boy disappeared. He stayed away all day and re-turned at night. He said, "Chief, to-morrow go over these hills and you will see buffalo. Surround the buffalo and kill them." Early the next morning the chief sent criers through the village, telling the men to get on their ponies and to go out over the hills. The men went out and found the buffalo. They surrounded them and killed them.

Three times the boy brought the buffalo himself and the fourth time he led them out to the red hills. He stood upon the hill, waved his robe, and the buffalo came out from the sides of the hills. The people made a big killing and were satisfied. The people now had plenty of meat. After this the buffalo became numerous throughout the land, and the people did not need anybody to call the buffalo. The boy and the old woman went to live in the chief's lodge. The boy never married any of the other sisters, but remained with the youngest. They had many children.

60. THE BUFFALO AND RED-SPIDER-WOMAN'S DAUGHTER.[1]

Many years ago Red-Spider-Woman was at the center of the earth. She had many children, nearly all girls. She and her daughters raised corn, squash, beans, and tobacco. At this time the Buffalo were all in the north. The chief of the Buffalo people had a son whose name was Curly-Eyes. One day the chief held a council with his Buffalo, and it was decided in the council that there should be four Buffalo selected to go south to look over the country, for the Buffalo selected wanted to go to some other place. Among the four selected was Curly-Eyes.

The four Buffalo started south. When they came to the center of the land they found Red-Spider-Woman and her daughters. Curly-Eyes saw one of the girls and he fell in love with her. Red-Spider-Woman went into her fields and cut some tobacco and gave it to the Buffalo. The Buffalo went back to their country in the north.

When they arrived there Curly-Eyes spoke to his father and said: "We saw a woman with tobacco. She gave some of it to us. She has several girls. I love one of them and I want to marry her." The father said: "There is but one way for you to do, and that is for you to pay for her, so that we can bring her here. Then you can be married to her." So the Buffalo chief selected four more Buffalo to send to Red-Spider-Woman. When these four Buffalo came near the grass-lodge of Red-Spider-Woman they began to sing:

> Old red painted woman,
> We came here to ask for your daughter.
> We will give one valley full of buffalo.

The old woman came out and said, "You can not have the girl for one bottom-land full of Buffalo." Then the Buffalo returned home. The chief of the Buffalo, when he heard about this, said: "We will offer her more." Then the chief sent four other Buffalo and they went down to where the woman lived. When they came near to the lodge of Red-Spider-Woman they began to sing:

[1] Told by White-Sun, Kitkehahki. The tale explains the dispersion of the buffalo.

> Old red painted woman,
> We came here to ask for your daughter.
> We will give you two valleys full of buffalo.

The woman came out and said: "No, you can not have my girl." These Buffalo returned home and told the chief of the tribe what Red-Spider-Woman had said. The chief said: "I will select four more to go down there and they will also ask for tobacco for our people." So four more Buffalo were selected. They went down and when they were close to the lodge of Red-Spider-Woman they began to sing:

> Old red painted woman,
> We came to ask for your daughter and tobacco.
> We will give you half a land full of buffalo.

Red-Spider-Woman came out and said: "The tobacco you can not have; neither can you have my daughter for the amount of Buffalo you have promised me." These Buffalo returned home and told the chief of the tribe what Red-Spider-Woman had said. The chief said: "I will select four more to go down there and they will also ask for tobacco for our people." So four more Buffalo were selected. They went down, and when they were close to the lodge of Red-Spider-Woman they began to sing:

> Old red painted woman,
> We came to ask for your daughter and tobacco.
> We will give you a land full of buffalo.

The Buffalo went back and reported to the chief that Red-Spider-Woman had refused to give them either tobacco or the girl. The chief became angry and said: "Buffalo, we will now move down to where this Red-Spider-Woman is." All of the Buffalo moved forward and they began to travel south. For many years they traveled, and at last they came to the place where Red-Spider-Woman had her lodge. Curly-Eyes ran to the lodge, took out his girl, and the other Buffalo went and took away the other girls. They trampled her fields and her lodge. The woman ran and stood upon the prairie. She began to disappear and go into the ground. The Buffalo tried to kill her, but they could not. As she was about to disappear in the ground the Buffalo began to trample her and they killed her. She had just disappeared as she was killed. The chief of the Buffalo then said: "Red-Spider-Woman, you shall always remain under the ground. You had many powers. The root into which you have now turned will always have the shape of a human person. You will have curative powers and the people will dig you up for medicine."

From the root grows a vine with a little squash on it, and the Indians call this squash medicine.

After they had killed Red-Spider-Woman, the Buffalo scattered all over the land.   That is why the Buffalo were found all over this country.

61. THE SINGING BUFFALO CALF.[1]

There was a big drove of buffalo traveling among the hills when night overtook them.   They lay down upon the grass and slept.   In the night a buffalo calf had a dream.   When the calf awoke she let the buffalo know by singing.   She sang:

> Grandfather, I had a dream.
> The people are gathering to surround us.
> Truly they will surprise us.
> Truly they will surprise us.
>
> Grandfather, I had a dream.
> One spoke up and said,
> "They have dropped and are sitting down."
> Truly they will surprise us.
> Truly they will surprise us.
>
> Grandfather, I had a dream.
> Some one among us spoke and said,
> "The people are gathering to surround us."
> Truly they will surprise us.
> Truly they will surprise us.
>
> Grandfather, I had a dream.
> They drove you near the village,
> And then the playful boys killed you.
> Truly they will surprise us.
> Truly they will surprise us.
>
> Grandfather, I had a dream.
> Some one spoke and pronounced,
> "Mother holy," consecrating her.
> Truly they will surprise us.
> Truly they will surprise us.

When the buffalo heard the calf singing, they told her not to sing that way, but to go to sleep; that there were no people in the country.   But the calf kept on singing.   By daylight the people had already surrounded the buffalo.   They gave a yell and the buffalo all jumped up. The little calf that was singing ran away.   The calf's mother was the

[1] Told by Thief, Kitkehahki.   The calf giving warning to the buffalo taught the people that even children may know of the approach of the enemy or be aware of impending danger, and so they give heed and pay respect to the warning of children, just as they do to the warning of the old men of the tribe.

first to be killed and consecrated. The people killed many buffalo, and they ran many, together with the old bull, into the village, so that the boys shot at it. All came true as the calf had dreamed, and so from that time the buffalo always knew through dreams when the people were going to surround them. As long as there was one of their number to be consecrated to the gods, the buffalo were satisfied; but if none were consecrated, the buffalo did not like it and rose up at once and ran away, so that the people could not kill them.

62. THE BUFFALO AND THE DEER.[1]

Many years ago when the people were upon a Buffalo hunt a big drove of Buffalo would come down to be slaughtered by the people. On their way they would find a drove of Deer who also wanted to be slaughtered by the people. The leader of the Buffalo people became jealous and began to call the Deer names. He said: "Why do you come in our way? The people do not care for your flesh. They do not hunt you as they do us." Then the Deer replied and began to sing this song:

> Well, now, there you stand, yonder,
> With your large, dark eyes.
> Well, now, what then?
> Well, now, there you stand,
> With your large, dark eyes.
> Well, now, what then?

> Well, now, there you stand;
> They overtake you; they run you to earth.
> Well, now, what then?
> Well, now, what then?
> They leave your flesh on village sites for coyotes to eat.

> Well, now, there I stand.
> They overtake me; they run me to earth.
> Well, now, what then?
> Then they speak out,
> "Yonder deer I make holy."
> Well, now, what then?

Then the two contestants would return to their party and they would go on their way. The Deer became angry, and the next day while the people were on the march the Deer jumped up and ran among the people. The men ran after the Deer, and as they ran after it several said, "I con-

[1] Told by Thief, Kitkehahki. The story illustrates the reason for the Pawnee custom of invariably attempting to kill a deer in starting upon a buffalo hunt before they have reached the buffalo.

secrate that Deer to Tirawa." They killed the Deer and the people let the man have it who had consecrated it. The man took it to the lodge of the priest and there they consecrated the Deer to Tirawa by singing sacred songs. Several days after this the people found many Buffalo. They surrounded the Buffalo and killed many. Several of the Buffalo they consecrated to Tirawa, and so ever after that, whenever the Indians were upon the hunt, the Deer was first consecrated and then the Buffalo.

63. THE UNFAITHFUL BUNDLE KEEPER.[1]

There was a famine, and the people had hardly any corn or buffalo meat. The Buffalo were far away in the west at that time, but when they found out that the people were hungry for meat, the bulls sat in council and decided that the chief's daughter should lead the Buffalo to the village of the people. The Buffalo chief's daughter put the bundle upon her back and led the Buffalo to the village. She was called "Woman-Who-Carries-the-Corn-Ear." When they came near the village of the people, the girl divided the Buffalo into four herds. The first herd she sent to the south side and the people killed them. The next herd she sent on the north side and the people killed them. Again she sent another herd on the north side. The fourth herd she told to move towards the village, which was directly west. She remained behind with the bundle. Many of the last herd were killed and only a few escaped. During the chase the girl went into a ravine and gave birth to a calf. She left it in the ravine and went on to join her people, who were then returning to their home.

When the calf was left alone, the Wind came to it and sang a song to it, telling it that its mother's name was Snow-White, and that she carried the bundle with the corn in it; that her father's name was Young-Bull-with-Spot-on-Forehead. The calf learned the song and then started to follow the herd and find its parents. When it caught up with the herd it began to sing:

Something whispered and told me.
It was the Wind blowing, saying,
"Your mother, she is
White-Frost-Woman."
Thanks, thanks,
Thanks, thanks.

[1] Told by Thief, Kitkehahki. The story illustrates the importance of faithfulness and fidelity on the part of the woman who has in her keeping the sacred bundle. It also explains why some give birth to illegitimate children.

Something whispered and told me.
It was the Wind blowing, saying,
"Your grandmother, she is
Black-Frost-Woman."
Thanks, thanks,
Thanks, thanks.

Something whispered and told me.
It was the Wind blowing, saying,
"Your grandfather, he is
White-Forehead-Bull."
Thanks, thanks,
Thanks, thanks.

The people were astonished to hear what the calf sang, for they thought that the girl was still a virtuous girl. The calf kept on singing about its mother until the chief gave command for the herd to rest. The calf ran up to its mother and began to nurse; then the people knew that she was truly its mother, and so they made her throw down the bundle, for she was now a mother and not a virtuous woman, and so unfit to carry the sacred bundle. Then the chief of the Buffalo said: "The people who kill and live on us shall do the same. It shall not always be that a girl will give birth when she is married, but there will be times when unmarried girls of high birth will have children." Ever since that time some of our people have illegitimate children.

64. THE HUNGRY COYOTE.[1]

Coyote was out hunting something to eat when he saw many buffalo tracks. He was very thin, for he had had nothing to eat for several days. He sang this song:

Here, here it is (buffalo path).
Once it was that he watched me, did
Ready-to-Give, when I sat watching,
Waiting for them (buffalo) to come this way.
Here, here it is.

While he was singing he heard the beat of buffalo hoofs. He looked up and there he saw a young calf. Coyote said: "There comes my meat. I will kill the calf and eat him." As soon as the calf came up, Coyote said: "Why, here comes Round-Eyes, my grandson. And who told you to come this way?" The calf said, "My grandfather told me to follow this trail." Coyote said: "That is right. They know that I

[1] Told by Thief, Kitkehahki. The story is told to children who ask to dance when the songs are being sung. It explains the presence of many dead coyotes on the plains, and especially teaches children that when they kill game they should not look around to see what others are doing.

am sitting here, and they sent you. What did your grandfather say my name was?" asked Coyote. The calf began to sing:

> Now your name is
> "He-who-Lets-them-Pass-Unharmed."
> Now your name is
> "He-who-Lets-them-Pass-Unharmed."

Said Coyote: "That is my name. He told you right. And what is your name, little calf?" The calf began to sing:

> Now my name is
> "Poor-Pitiful-Calf."
> Now my name is
> "Poor-Pitiful-Calf."

"Oh, yes," said Coyote, "then you are poor. I feel sorry for you. And what else did your grandfather call me?" The calf began to sing again, and said:

> Now your name is
> "Takes-Pity-upon-the-Weak."
> Now your name is
> "Takes-Pity-upon-the-Weak.'"

The calf went by and began to run fast. All the time Coyote was talking the calf had to think what to do and what to say. He had gone some distance when Coyote began to think, "Why, I am hungry. Why did I not kill him and eat him? I am very foolish." Then he arose and began to halloo at Poor-Calf, but Poor-Calf was far away from Coyote. He kept on running. Poor-Calf disappeared and Coyote began to cry. He went to a hillside and lay down where the sun shone, and went to sleep and died. This is why we find coyotes lying on the side of hills. They die of hunger.

65. THE GATHERING OF THE PRIESTS.[1]

There was a Coyote village. These people made up their minds to open their sacred bundle. When they were about to open the bundle the young men jumped upon their ponies and went out to kill buffalo. As the old men sat down in the lodge with the bundle, the crier was sent through the village to let the women know that the old men were about to open the bundle and sing songs. When the bundle was opened a crier was told to go through the village and tell the women to bring dry wood to the lodge of the priests; also to bring some green willows upon which

[1] Told by Thief, Kitkehahki. The story illustrates the importance of women gathering wood for the priests' lodge and of girls preparing the mush for the priests' feast.

to place the meat. All of the women in the village went for dry wood and green willow branches.

There was but one girl left in the camp, and she was the youngest one. She took the pestle and began to pound some corn. She pounded the corn into a fine meal, and then boiled it into mush. After the mush was done she took it into the lodge where the old men were holding their ceremony. She placed the kettle inside of the lodge. The errand man received the mush and notified the priests that the youngest girl in the village had brought a pot full of mush for them to eat. All the old men thanked the girl by saying, "Nawa, nawa eri." The high priest then said: "The youngest girl in the village has placed a pot full of mush in our lodge. Before we eat of this mush we will sing a song." They took up their gourds and began to sing:

> Stir the mush.
> Well done, stir the mush.
> Youngest of our sisters,
> Well done, stir the mush.

The priests ate the mush and were grateful to the maiden who had prepared it for them. Other women brought the wood and the willows to the lodge. When the young men came back they did not bring any buffalo meat, and the old priests thought it very good for the young girl to prepare the mush for them. The bundle was kept open over night, and the next day the young men went out into the country again, and this time they killed some buffalo. Some of the meat was brought to the lodge of the priests, and when the priests ate of the meat they folded up the bundle, hung it up at the altar, and the priests then went to their homes.

66. THE MAN WHO SANG TO COYOTE.[1]

Many years ago, in the winter, when the Pawnee were living in their villages, a person going through the village in the night would hear laughing and singing in nearly all of the lodges. Being winter the women had plenty of wood piled up in the lodge, and the people felt that it was time to tell Coyote stories and to make the children dance while they were singing.

One winter, while the people were in their village, one young man went through the village entering one lodge and then another. He found that nearly all of the people in the village were telling stories about Coyote. The next day he went away from the village on a hunt. While

[1] Told by Thief, Kitkehahki. The tale illustrates the belief of the harm which may come from the promiscuous slaying of coyotes.

he was up in the hills he saw a Coyote coming out from a hollow. He pulled his bow to shoot the Coyote. He remembered that it was bad luck to shoot a Coyote, and he lowered his bow. He remembered also that the people were telling about Coyotes the night before. He stopped and yelled at the Coyote. He said: "Coyote, people talk about you nearly every night during the winter. Suppose you tell me a story. We are alone in the hills." Coyote stopped and sat down upon the snow. The man picked up a stick and ran to where the Coyote was sitting, threw the stick at him, and the Coyote began to run, never returning a bark. Then the man stood watching the Coyote as he ran and sang:

> That Coyote going along yonder,
> What is it he is carrying on his back?
> Truly I have tallow, thick tallow.
> It was killed
> On top box elder hill.

> That Coyote going along yonder,
> He has no stories.
> I have a story of the
> Whistling (scalp-man's) home in the Kiowa's country.

The man sang the song several times. As he did so the Coyote disappeared, and the man went home. After that the man was always lucky in killing game, and he always thought it was because he did not shoot at the Coyote.

67. HOW THE CANNIBAL SPIDER-WOMAN WAS OVERCOME.[1]

In a village there lived a boy who always wore his buffalo robe in a peculiar manner. The hair of the robe would be inside, only part of it showing where he lapped it over his shoulders. He was known to be a wonderful boy. Every once in a while it was reported through the village that a young man had gone into a country where there was another village and had never returned. In that village lived a Spider-Woman, who was all the time contesting with strangers in climbing an old cottonwood tree. The young man who wore the wonderful robe heard of Spider-Woman so often that he finally made up his mind that he would visit her village.

The young man started out to find it. He went through thick willows, and when he came to the edge of the village he saw a grass-lodge. He stood outside of the lodge. The youngest child in the lodge came out

[1] Told by Little-Chief, Chaui. The tale represents one of many forms of the contest between the young poor boys who became heroes and the Spider-Woman. It also explains why the woodpeckers make their homes in the tops of elm trees and the woodrats among the roots.

and saw the stranger. He entered the lodge and told his mother that there was a handsome young man standing outside. She said, "You must tell the young man to come into the lodge." The young man entered the lodge, and the woman gave him a seat. He placed his quiver in the west of the lodge on some bundles, and sat down on the seat. The old woman then said: "My boy, I am sorry that you came here, as Spider-Woman lives in the village and she takes the lives of young men. She has a person known as Eyes-Wide-Open who goes around and makes it his business to peep into all the lodges to see if there are any strangers in the village. He will come and see you and he will invite you to Spider-Woman's lodge. When she offers you mush to eat you must tell her that you have eaten plenty and that you are full and can not eat any more. The mush that she will offer you is nothing but human brains. If she offers you a bowl of black corn you must not eat it, for it is human eyes. If she offers you chopped squash you must not eat it, for it is human ears." While the woman talked to the boy she dished out some ground beans and placed them before him. While he was eating them, the entrance flap was lifted up and Eyes-Wide-Open looked in and said, "I came to invite the young man to eat with Spider-Woman." The woman whispered quietly, "You long-faced man, you ugly man, you are going to take this boy and try to kill him." The young man said: "Go; I am eating my supper. As soon as I am through I shall come over to the lodge of Spider-Woman."

The boy went to the lodge of Spider-Woman and she offered him mush to eat, but he refused, saying that he had just eaten and could not eat more. Then she said: "My grandchild, I should like you to come to-morrow and we will play a little. I want you to climb this tree with me." The young man said that he would come in the morning. He returned to the lodge of his friends and told the woman that he had agreed to climb the tree with Spider-Woman. He said that he wanted to get up early and to get something ready to eat in the morning, and he wanted all of them to go out of the lodge and leave him alone. The woman said, "Very well." In the morning the woman got up and cooked some more beans for the boy. The boy ate the beans and then told the people to go out, as he wanted to be alone. Then the boy took some white and black clay. He put the white clay all over his body and spotted it with black. He took from his quiver a bunch of red feathers and stuck them into his scalp-lock. Then he went out and told the woman that when Eyes-Wide-Open came, to tell him that he was ready to climb the tree. When the woman saw the young man she knew that he must be wonderful. She made up her mind that she would stake herself and her children upon the boy's winning, so that if the boy was beaten she and her children would all be killed. Eyes-Wide-Open came and said that Spider-Woman was ready.

The boy came out and the woman said: "My son, you wager me and my children. If you get beaten then we will be killed." The young man said that he would. He went to where Spider-Woman was and Spider-Woman said: "I am now ready to climb this tree. You climb the tree first." The boy said: "No, it is your game. You climb first and I will climb afterwards." The old woman said: "If you do just as I do you beat me. If you can not do as I do, then I will kill you and your people; but if you can do just as I do then you may kill me and my people. If you show that you can climb the tree better than I can you may kill me." Spider-Woman began to climb the tree. As soon as she reached a certain place the tree fell to the ground, and the old woman was thrown to one side and she stood there laughing. Then she told the boy to climb, and the boy said, "It is my time to climb." The boy went to the base of the tree with his robe over his shoulders. He began to sing: "I like to climb trees, for I belong in trees. I can climb up and down and the tree will not fall." Eyes-Wide-Open, who was standing at one side, heard the song, and he ran up with his club to the young man and said: "I belong on your side. I do not care to be with this old woman." Spider-Woman said: "Very well. You belong on that side and I shall kill you and place your skull among my other skulls." The boy continued to sing, and suddenly he threw the robe from him and the people saw that he was painted. The boy climbed the tree. When he reached the place where the tree was to fall, he began to climb down again. The boy reached the base and climbed up again, and when he got to the forks the tree fell down and the boy was thrown to one side and there he stood unhurt. The people ran to Spider-Woman and killed her and her people. They took them all over the country and placed them in ravines. Eyes-Wide-Open was also killed.

Then the boy said: "People, my work is done. I have killed Spider-Woman, who was always killing people and eating them. Let there be no more eating of human beings. This tree shall fall over and be no more." He went to the woman in whose lodge he had been and said: "Mother, if I had lost you would have been killed, together with your children. I overcame Spider-Woman. You and your children shall always live under an old tree, for you are mice. My people from now on shall make their houses at the top of a hollow tree and you shall have your house at the bottom of the tree." After he said this the people he had been with turned into mice, crawled under a tree, and made their

home there.   Then the boy said: "I am done.   My work is finished."
He flew up into the tree as a speckled woodpecker.

And so it is that we find the woodpecker's nests at the top of hollow
trees and the nests of the mice at the foot of the hollow trees.

68. THE WITCH-WOMAN WHO STOLE THE WONDERFUL ROBE.[1]

In a village a Witch-Woman lived with the people.   She killed many
handsome young men.   She also stole many things from the people, hiding the things which she took under her dress.   Sometimes she would capture a young boy and would turn the boy into some animal.   Sometimes
she would place them under the earth in the form of woodrats, moles,
or gophers.   She did so many bad things among the people that they
turned out and tried to kill her.   When they pounded her with sticks she
cared nothing about it.   When the people tried to cut her with knives,
the knives would not go through her flesh.   She laughed at them and
mocked them.   The people could not do anything with her.

They got together and decided to go to the old priests for advice.   A
man was sent to the priest.   He said to the priest, "I was sent to you by
the people for advice as to what we should do with this Witch-Woman."
The priest reached up, took down his sacred bundle, opened it, took out
a rattle, and began to recite rituals and songs which were given to the people by Tirawa.   At last he came to a ritual which told about the Witch-
Women through the country; that they were to be done away with by
young men from different parts of the country.   Then the priest stopped
singing, wrapped up the bundle, and hung it up.   He told the man to go
and tell the people that the Witch-Woman was not to be present with the
people always; that Witch-Women belonged to the earth and in time
they would be placed upon the earth.   He told the man also to tell the
people that certain young men would come into their village who would
be the ones to do away with the Witch-Woman.

Early the next spring a young man came to their village.   This
young man was not known to the people.   The buffalo robe which he
had over his body had stars and dark clouds painted on it.   Paintings of
lightning in the clouds, the sun and moon were also upon the robe.
Flocks of swallows and also gadflies were painted on the robe.   The boy

[1] Told by Leading-Sun, Kitkehahki.   This story is told to children to teach
them to be careful not to meddle with objects of a ceremonial or religious nature
or with objects which did not belong to them.   Closely corresponding variants of
this tale were found in all four bands of Pawnee, the one given here being the most
complete.   The songs which accompany this version were obtained from Thief,
also a Kitkehahki.   In another version of this tale, obtained from the Chaui Old-
Woman, Coyote was substituted for Witch-Woman.

lived with the people for some time.   One day he was challenged by the
Deer family to run a race.   These Deer, it seems, represented the old
woman.   She was trying to do away with the young man.   It seems that
the old woman was suspicious that the boy was from some god in the
heavens.   The boy went to the races and ran with the Deer and overcame them.   The boy went to his tipi, picked up the robe, covered himself with it, and went on.   The old woman saw the robe and said: "What
a beautiful robe.   It must be a fine robe.   It will make a pretty skirt for
me.   I must have it even if I have to steal it."

One day the boy went to where the men were playing with the gambling sticks.   As he sat down one of the men challenged him to play with
the sticks.   While they were playing a false alarm of an attack by the
enemy was given.   When the men ran to where the alarm was given,
the old woman went to the robe, picked it up, took her dress off, and put
the robe under her dress.   She went away.   When the men discovered
that there was no enemy in sight they returned to the playground.   The
boy missed his robe.   The old woman was standing at one side of the
village watching him.   As soon as she saw that the boy was looking for his
robe she made faces at him and said: "Young man, you will never find
the robe.   The robe is now my skirt and it shall keep me warm.   You
shall never know where it is."   The young man went through the village
from one tipi to the other asking for his robe.   The people had not seen it.
At last he went up to the Witch-Woman and asked her if she had seen
anything of his robe.   She said: "No, I have not seen your robe."   At
the same time she made faces at the young man, saying to herself: "You
will never find the robe.   I now have it for a skirt."   The young man
went through the village again.   He stood in the west, then walked through
the village, singing:

> I am hunting a robe.
> My painted robe I am hunting.
> The heavens are painted upon it.
> Attention!   It is among the people.
> Attention!   It is among the people.
> Attention!   It is among the people.

When the old woman heard this she began to clap her hands and said:
"The robe must be a wonderful one, but you shall never again have it
in your hands, for the robe is my skirt."   The boy sang again:

> I am hunting a robe.
> Who picked it up?
> Flocks of swallows are painted upon it.
> Attention!   It is among the people.
> Attention!   It is among the people.
> Attention!   It is among the people.

When the woman heard it she said: "It must be a wonderful robe, but you shall never have it again, for I now have it for my skirt." The boy continued to sing:

> I am hunting a robe.
> Who has picked it up?
> Dragon-flies are painted upon it.
> Attention!   It is among the people.
> Attention!   It is among the people.
> Attention!   It is among the people.

At last the boy began to sing:

> I am hunting a robe.
> Who has picked it up?
> The lightning is painted upon it.
> Attention!   It is among the people.
> Attention!   It is among the people.
> Attention!   It is among the people.
>
> I am hunting a robe.
> Who has picked it up?
> The thunders are painted upon it.
> Attention!   It is among the people.
> Attention!   It is among the people.
> Attention!   It is among the people.
>
> I am hunting a robe.
> Who has picked it up?
> The winds are painted upon it.
> Attention!   It is among the people.
> Attention!   It is among the people.
> Attention!   It is among the people.

The Witch-Woman heard this song and she said: "Do you think I am going to be blown away when I have more power than you have?" The boy cried again. As he finished he blew with his breath from the west to where the woman stood. Then he cried again and this time clouds were seen coming from the west. Clouds blew over the land. When the boy cried the fourth time the old woman took the robe off and threw it down and said: "My grandchild, there is your robe. You must not let the storm blow me away." Just about that time the wind caught the old woman and whirled her up into the heavens as if a whirlwind had struck her. It began to rain all over the land. On the side of a hill was a ravine and the rain seemed to stop there. Suddenly the wind, where the woman was, seemed to go on, and the woman was brought down again, and she was blown up on the side of the hill at the head of the ravine where it was now muddy. There she was sunk into the mud.

She opened her legs so that when she struck the ground the mud flowed about her and she began to urinate. The boy saw this. Then he said to the people: "The Witch-Woman shall be no more. She shall stay in the side of the hill and there will flow from that place a spring. In time she shall either turn into a spider or a black-tail deer. She will fool the people by her wonderful ways." The young man then went to his robe, picked it up, shook the water from it, and placed it upon his shoulders. He said: "My work is done. I go now to where I came from. I represent the north wind. From this time on whenever you see a flock of snowbirds you will see some white speckled ones among them. Remember that I was one of them—the one who killed the old Witch-Woman." The boy pulled the robe over his head, covered himself, sat down, suddenly turned into a speckled snowbird, and flew away to the north. The people then knew why the buffalo robe had paintings on it, for the snowbird is speckled with black.

69. HOW THE CANNIBAL WITCH-WOMAN WAS OVERCOME.[1]

A young man wandered away from his village. He came to another village and when he entered it he was taken in by the chief of the tribe, and Eyes-Wide-Open, a Coyote, came and invited the boy to eat with a witch-woman. The boy was told to eat nothing that the witch might give him, as it was all human flesh. The boy went, and the witch offered him something to eat, but the boy would not eat. The witch said, "My grandchild, I want to play a game with you," and the boy said: "Tell me what it is. Perhaps I shall play with you." The old woman said: "To-morrow I should like you to go down to the creek with me. We will both dive and whoever shall come up first from the water shall be beaten." The boy said that he would dive with her. She said: "If you come up before I do, then I take your life." The boy went home and told the people. The next day, early in the morning, Eyes-Wide-Open came and told him that the old woman was ready. The people all went down to the stream. The boy and the old woman went into the water and waited until they were in the middle of the stream and then dived. In a few minutes the boy came up. When the old woman heard the shouting and calling by the people she knew that he must be up, and she came out of the water and took the boy to her home and cut off his head, and placed his head among the skulls that she had. She told Eyes-Wide-Open to watch through the village for some other young men.

[1] Told by Little-Chief, Chaui. This tale is a variant of No. 68, in which the Beaver assists in conquering the Witch-Woman.

The boy had a brother at home who was the very image of the one who was killed. He went to the village hunting for his brother. When he arrived, Eyes-Wide-Open invited him to the lodge of the old woman. When the boy entered he saw his brother's head among the skulls. The woman said: "My grandson, I want you to dive with me to-morrow. If you come out first, I will take your life. If I come out first, you shall take my life and the lives of all my people." The boy then said: "I am willing to do this if the chief and his people will be on my side." The old woman sent Eyes-Wide-Open to the chief and asked him if he and his people would be on the boy's side. The chief said that he would.

That night the boy asked the chief where the old woman had her place for the diving. The chief told the boy where the place was. The chief went home and left the boy at the place. The boy then stood upon the banks of the water and cried. A little Beaver came up from the water and asked the boy what he was crying about. The boy said: "I am crying because I have to dive with the old woman. This woman has killed many young men who visited the village." The little Beaver then told the boy to stay there, as he was going to see his father and mother. The little Beaver dived and went into his lodge and told his father and mother that there was a fine-looking young man upon the bank crying because he was going to dive with the old woman. The father said to the young Beaver, "My son, what can we do for this boy?" The young Beaver said: "Let us take pity upon him and help him, so that this old witch shall be killed and there shall be no more of her kind in the land." The Beaver said that he would. Then the young Beaver was told to go and invite the boy.

The little Beaver came out of the water and said, "My brother, follow me, and then whatever I do, you do also." The Beaver dived into the water. The boy followed, and he soon found himself in the lodge of the Beavers. Then the Beavers told the boy that they had decided to take pity upon him and were going to help him kill this old woman. The Beaver then told the boy that when he should dive, he should select the place on the west side, and as soon as he dived he should swim up to the lodge and enter it. There they would keep him as long as the woman remained under the water. The boy was thankful. The old Beaver said to the young Beaver, "Lie down while I cut your leg off." The young Beaver lay down and his leg was cut off. It was placed in a pot and boiled, and after the meat was cooked they took it out and fed the boy with the meat of the leg of the Beaver. When the boy ate of the leg the old Beaver took the bone of the leg and threw it outside of the lodge into the water; then the old Beaver said to the young Beaver, "Go and bring your leg back again." The young Beaver went out, dived into the water, and when it came back it had its leg on again. The boy was told to go home and to be ready to dive with the witch the next day. The old Beaver then gave the young man blue mud with which he was to daub himself all over. The boy went home and went to bed.

Early in the morning Eyes-Wide-Open came and said, "Young man, the old woman is ready to dive with you." Then Eyes-Wide-Open cried through the village and told the people to go down to the stream of water; that the young man and the old woman were going to dive. When they arrived at the water the boy selected the west side and the old witch stood on the east side. They walked down to the water, waded in, and when they reached the middle of the stream they dived. As they dived the boy swam under and reached the lodge of the Beavers and entered it. As soon as he entered the lodge of the Beavers the old Beaver said: "My son, lie down and I will cut off your leg and boil it for your brother to eat." The young Beaver lay down, his leg was cut off, put in a pot, and boiled. Then the old Beaver told the boy that while the pot was boiling he must lie down and sleep. The boy lay down and slept. The man told one of the Beavers to swim towards the bank and to watch and see when the old woman should come out from the water. The Beaver swam to the bank and sat under the grass which hung over the bank. The Beaver watched and watched.

The old woman and the boy had dived in the morning. It was then in the afternoon and neither of them had come up. Towards evening the old woman thought to herself: "The boy must be drowned. I must come out of the water." The old woman jumped out from the water. She began to straighten out her hair, and as she reached the bank she said: "The boy died under the water a long time ago and we must hunt for his body." The people on the boy's side said, "No, we must wait until the boy comes up from the water." The Beaver came into the lodge and said, "The old woman is now standing on the bank." The Beavers awoke the boy, gave him meat and he ate, and then the old Beaver threw the bone out of the lodge into the water and told the young Beaver to go and bring back the leg. The young Beaver went out, dived into the water, and when it returned it had its legs again. Then the boy was told to go out of the Beavers' lodge, to swim to the middle of the stream and then jump out. He did so. When the boy came up from the water there was a yell from the side of the boy, and the people began to kill the people who were on the side of the old woman. The people on the old witch's side were all killed. The old witch was killed on the side of the bank and tramped in under the ground, and as the people stepped upon her belly they made the water run from her genital. She was left there, and that is why we have springs near the banks of the streams of water. If the young man had not beaten the old woman in diving there would still be witches in the country, and they would be killing people.

70. THE GIRL WHO CALLED THE BUFFALO.[1]

In a certain village, where Coyote and his wife were living, the people became hungry. Coyote's name was "Shield-with-Buffalo-Hoofs." His wife, who was Spider-Woman, had around her waist a tanned buffalo skin. Hoof-Shield went hunting every day, and when he returned, being hungry, he would call his wife, and say, "Old woman, let me cut a piece from your dress that I may eat it, for I am very hungry." The old woman would let Hoof-Shield cut a piece off from her dress every day. Finally the woman objected, for she had but a small piece left to cover herself with. She scolded Hoof-Shield and told him that he ought to hunt like other men.

One morning Hoof-Shield told his wife that he was going hunting, and as she arose he cut a piece from her dress and ate it. He then started on a hunt. He went far into the country, but found no game. He kept on until one evening he smelled burnt beef. He followed the smell for four days and at last he came to a high hill. He went upon the hill to look about, and from a thick timber in a valley to the south he saw smoke rising. He could also see the tips of the tipi poles. As he was very hungry he went to the place. When he reached the tipi he heard no stirring around, and so he stopped. A woman inside spoke and said: "Why do you stand outside? Come in." He raised the entrance flap and entered. Matted sweet grass was spread all around the tipi. At the west of the fireplace sat a pretty young girl. Hoof-Shield said to her: "My granddaughter, I came from a far distant country where the people are starving, and I am starving. I want something to eat." The girl said her brothers were not yet there, but that he should have something to eat as soon as they came. He looked around in the tipi, but could see nothing to eat. The girl said: "My brothers are now coming."

There was a peculiar noise in the sky and presently a Bald Eagle came through the tipi and sat down by the girl. The Eagle looked around and said: "Why, grandfather is here. I know he is hungry.

[1] Told by Thief, Kitkehahki. The tale teaches children that they should always be on the lookout for something to eat, and that they must have higher aims in life than pushing girls in a swing. The fact that the coyote, magpie, and buffalo are associated together teaches that whenever one or other of these animals is seen the other can not be far off.

He shall have something to eat." Coyote could see nothing. Presently another Eagle came. This time it was the White Eagle, who said: "Ah, grandfather is here. I know that he is hungry. He shall have something to eat." Coyote looked around, but he could see nothing to eat. Another Eagle came through and it was the Black Eagle. "Ah," said he, "grandfather is here. He shall have something to eat." Coyote could see nothing to eat. Another eagle came through, and said: "Ah, grandfather is here. He shall have something to eat." Coyote could see nothing to eat. Another bird came swiftly through, but said nothing. This bird was a Hawk. Another bird came, which was a Crow. The Crow looked at Coyote and scolded him. Next came a Magpie; then all kinds of birds came in and flew around the tipi in flocks. The Bald Eagle said: "Sister, we must send you off to get the Buffalo, so that our grandfather can have something to eat." The Eagles took the girl outside of the tipi. Coyote was told to go along and look on. The Eagles took the girl to the south side of the tipi and there two rawhide lariat ropes hung down from the sky. The Eagles placed her upon the lariat ropes. She was then swung and flew away toward the west. She disappeared while the Eagles were all saying, "There she goes. She is now coming back." After she was gone, they said, "Crow, kill two Buffalo for our grandfather, while we take the girl into the tipi." The girl came back upon the ropes and the Buffalo were running behind her raising a great dust. The Eagles took the girl and carried her into the tipi. The Crow flew among the Buffalo, and as it said "Caw" over a Buffalo, it fell dead. The Crow killed two Buffalo and then the Buffalo went back west. The birds all scattered out, flying away to the different trees. The Eagles stayed with the girl and they told the Coyote to skin and cut meat up for himself. Coyote skinned the Buffalo and cut up the meat, eating as he cut. He stayed several days until he was stout and fat. Then he thanked the girl and told the Eagles that he had children who were starving. They gave him the meat that was left. He packed the dried meat and started for home.

When Hoof-Shield reached home he fed his family, and then told the old woman to cut up a lot of dried meat and boil it. He then went to the chief's tipi and invited him and some of the leading men to come and eat with him. They came in, and they were surprised to find so much dried meat. In a few days the meat was all gone. Hoof-Shield went again to the girl's home. Again the birds helped him to get meat, but the Crow scolded him for coming. After the girl had been swung and Buffalo were killed for Hoof-Shield, the Eagles spoke to him and told him not to bring anybody. "For," said the Eagles, "we know you, and you may lose our sister by bringing some one else." Hoof-Shield again went home and fed the people.

One day as he was getting ready to go to the place again, a friend came up to him and said, "My brother, where do you go? Let me go with you. My children are starving." Hoof-Shield told the other Coyote to stay at home; but he begged so hard that Hoof-Shield finally gave in and took him with him. They went a certain distance, and then Hoof-Shield said: "Do you now smell anything?" The other Coyote snuffed and said: "Yes, I smell burnt meat." Hoof-Shield then said that the smell came from afar off, but that it was from the place where they were going

They went on until at last they came to the tipi. The girl told them that her brothers were scattered out and that they would not be home for some time. "But," said Hoof-Shield, "we are hungry and we want something to eat. Take pity on us. Let us swing you. My brother will kill the Buffalo while I take you into the tipi." The girl consented. She climbed into the lariat swing and they swung her. She traveled far into the sky towards the west and disappeared. Hoof-Shield would say, "Do you see her?" The other Coyote would look and say, "No, I can not see her." Then Hoof-Shield would say, "I see her. She looks very small." When Hoof-Shield saw clouds of dust he said, "I see the girl coming with the Buffalo." The two stood watching until they saw Buffalo coming. They were so many and so thick that the two Coyotes became scared and ran into the tipi. The Buffalo ran past the tipi, then circled and ran back toward the west with the girl. Hoof-Shield then said, "We have done wrong; let us run away, for she has brothers who are wonderful and they may kill us." They ran away and returned to the village.

In a day or so Hoof-Shield went again to the girl's tipi. He stayed at a distance, for he did not want the brothers to know that he had lost the girl. He saw the birds flying in different directions, and so he knew that they were hunting for her. When the brothers came into the tipi, they found their sister gone. Then the Eagles sent the Magpie to tell all the birds to come to the tipi. The birds came. Some were in the tipi and others flew around the tipi, so that they looked like a big black thing in the sky. The birds were told that they must find the girl, whether she was in the sky or upon the earth or under the ground. The birds all flew in different directions, and towards evening they came back. Hoof-Shield went down and entered the tipi. When he entered, all the birds turned upon him and said, "Have you seen our sister?" and "Where is she?" Hoof-Shield told the birds that some one else might have been there and lost her. The Crow looked sharply at Hoof-Shield and said, "You are the one who lost our sister and you must help to return her." Hoof-Shield said he would do the best he could; that he would get some of his friends to hunt.

The next day the birds were again sent out. They were told not to return that day unless they should find the girl. They flew away and in the evening they began to come in, but they had not found the girl. There was one bird that did not return that day. It was a Blackbird. The next day the Blackbird came in and said, "The Buffalo are playing with the girl." There was then a noise, for the birds were glad to know that their sister was alive. The next day they selected an Eagle, a Hawk, a Crow, and the Blackbird to go where the Buffalo were playing with the girl. They flew away to the west until they came to the place where the Buffalo were playing with the sticks. The birds looked down and saw the Buffalo throwing the ring and throwing sticks at it. They knocked the ring around until the birds were mad, for they knew that the ring was the girl. They called it names, but when they hooked it they would say, "I have had connection with her."

The birds went back to the tipi and reported to the other birds the treatment the girl was receiving. The animals also came into the tipi. Coyote then said, "Bring some pine juice and spread the stuff all over me." The animals went and got some pine juice. This they spread all over Coyote, except his feet. Coyote told them to put plenty of the juice on each side of his neck, so that his neck would look as though matter were running from it.

Then animals and birds were chosen to go with Coyote to rescue the maiden. Coyote was to be leader; the Badger came next, for he was to dig holes for Coyote to run through; then came the Rabbit and the Fox. Among the birds selected were the Prairie-Chicken, Crow, Blackbird, Magpie, Hawk, and Eagle. They went on together. The Blackbird told them where to go. When they had gone a certain distance the Badger was told to dig for the Fox. The Badger made the hole. Then they went on, and again at another place the Badger dug another hole for the Rabbit. They went on until they were near the place where the Buffalo were, and then the Badger dug again for Coyote. The birds and animals then stopped, but Coyote went to where the Buffalo were playing with the sticks and the ring. Coyote went up and sat around where they were playing. Some of the bulls made fun of Coyote and he pretended that he was sick. Coyote went close, and one young bull came up and scolded him and was about to hook him, when others said: "Let the poor Coyote alone. He is nearly dead. Can you not see the matter on each side of his neck?" So the bull let Coyote alone. The ring rolled close to Coyote and Coyote opened his mouth as though he were gaping, but he spoke to the girl and said: "I am here, granddaughter. Roll up close to me the next time." The next time the Buffalo rolled the ring it went straight to Coyote. There was an uproar. The Buffalo all grunted and ran after Coyote. Coyote gave the ring to the Rabbit, who ran with it, while Coyote went into a hole. The Rabbit ran on until it came to its hole, then gave the ring to Fox, who was there. The Fox ran on with the ring, and when he came to his hole he gave the ring to the Prairie-Chicken, who flew on. When the Prairie-Chicken became tired, it flew to a muddy pond and lit on a tree. Many Buffalo ran into the muddy pond and could not get out on account of the mud. The Crow took the ring, the Buffalo still following. The Crow became tired and gave the ring to the Blackbird, who flew right over the Buffalo. The Blackbird became tired, then gave the ring to the Magpie, who flew on. The Magpie became tired and gave the ring to the Hawk, who flew on. The Buffalo still followed. The Hawk became tired, then gave the ring to the Eagle, who took the ring and flew up into the heavens. The Buffalo saw this, and said: "Let us now scatter all over the land, so that we will be killed by the people." So the Buffalo scattered out over the land. The Coyote never went back to the village. The girl was taken back to the tipi and she was told to go to her people. She went to her people and here she told them that they must select a girl every year to be holy and then the Buffalo would come to the people.

71. WOOD-RAT-WOMAN WHO WISHED TO BE MARRIED.

(See Abstracts.)

[Told by Coyote-Standing-in-Water, the wife of a Skidi priest. This is the Skidi variant of No. 45. This tale is told to children to teach them that when they grow up they should marry the girls of their choice; especially that they should not marry old women and thus not be able to rear a family.]

72. THE WITCH-WOMAN WHO WISHED TO BE MARRIED.

(See Abstracts.)

[Told by Thief, Kitkehahki. This is a variant of No. 71.]

73. THE BASKET GAME, OR THE WOMAN IN THE MOON.[1]

In olden times there was a Spider-Woman upon the earth. She had several daughters and they lived by themselves. They had a garden and raised corn, squash, and beans. People went there to get seeds from the old woman, but instead of getting seeds from her they were challenged to play the dice game. This dice game was not the one in which they used a basket and seeds. They sat down upon their feet and jumped up and down. While they were jumping, storms were called by old Spider-Woman, so that the people froze and were beaten. Spider-Woman killed many people this way and she had many skulls around her grass-lodge.

There was a village where lived two young men who seemed to have wonderful powers. The people in this village told these two young men that there was a Spider-Woman in their country; that she was killing the people; that they would like to have them go and visit her. One day the older of these two boys said, "Brother, let us go where that woman is." The younger brother said, "We will go." They started for the place. For several days they went, and at last they came to a corn-field. Here they stopped. They saw a grass-lodge. They also saw the skulls around the lodge. They saw one girl standing outside of the lodge. They went up to her, and as soon as she saw them she said: "Boys, you must not come into this lodge. My mother will see you and she will kill you. You must return to your own home." The boys said, "We want to go in." The girl said, "If you go into the lodge you must not eat what the woman offers you, for the food will be human flesh." The boys then said, "We will go away for a short distance and we will come back and go into the lodge." The boys went away behind the corn-field.

When they saw that the girl had gone into the lodge they went away from their hiding place and approached the lodge. The other girls came out and the boys saw that they were very ugly. The girls ran back into the lodge and said, "Mother, here come two fine-looking boys." As they approached the lodge Spider-Woman came out and said, "My grandchildren, I have been looking for you for a long time." Then she said to herself, "These boys have come to see my daughters, but they can not have my daughters, for I shall kill them." She called them to her and said, "My grandchildren, you must come in and have something to eat, for you look hungry." The older boy said, "Yes, we are, for we have been on the road for some time." They entered the lodge. Before

[1] Told by Fox, a Skidi warrior. During the telling of this story the children squat down, placing their hands upon their knees and jump about, imitating the moving of the dice in the basket game. Next the boys sing and the women dance. The belief among the children is that their dancing, which now imitates grasshoppers, may carry the evil spirits up to the moon.

going into the lodge the older boy untied a sack of medicine and gave some of it to his younger brother, telling him to eat it. Then he took some of it and ate it himself.

They went into the lodge and sat down. Spider-Woman kept mumbling to herself as she dished out some mush for the boys. As the bowl of mush was placed in front of the two boys, the girl they had seen before watched them and shook her head to let them know that they must not eat. But the boys ate of the food anyway. They ate everything which was in the bowl. The older boy knew that they were eating human brains. After they had eaten up the brains, the older boy said: "Grandmother, we must go out for a little while. We will be back again." The old woman was afraid that the boys would run away and she begged them not to go.

The boys went out, and after they were out of sight of the lodge they sat down and began to vomit what they had eaten. After they had vomited what they had eaten they returned to the lodge, and when Spider-Woman saw them she said: "Why, this is strange. I gave human brains to these boys with poison in it and here they come walking into my lodge again. I must feed them again and give them stronger medicine." She began to dish out something again that seemed to be black corn, but which in reality was human eyes. The older boy took the little sack of medicine again and put some of the root into his mouth. Then he passed it to his brother, and he also took some of the root. The wooden bowl of human eyes was placed before them and the boys began to eat. After they had eaten all there was in the bowl the older boy said, "Grandmother, we must go out for a little while." The two boys got up and went out. After they were out of sight of the lodge they began to vomit everything they had eaten.

When the boys returned to the lodge and Spider-Woman saw them she knew that she could not poison the boys with her medicine. She said, however, "I will kill them." She told the boys that they could remain with her all night, as the next day she wanted to play the basket game with them. The older boy said, "Grandmother, I like that game and we will play." The boys lay down upon a bed on the ground, while the old woman placed her girls near the entrance, and she made her own bed near the entrance, so that she would know if the boys left the lodge.

The next morning the old woman fed the boys with some squash, but the boys found out while they were eating it that it was not squash, but human ears. After they had eaten they went out and vomited everything. When the sun was up high the woman said, "The sun is high; let us now play the game." The older boy said, "Very well."

The boys went out of sight of the lodge and when they returned they had white clay over their bodies and also over their faces. They had little black streaks extending downward from their eyes. They got down on their feet and the old woman began to sing. Now, close to the place where they were jumping up and down there was a steep bank where the old woman would jump up and down with people and there she would push them over. They would fall over this steep bank and be killed. Now, it was at this place that they were jumping. The old woman began to sing about the storms, the snow, the blizzard, and the black clouds. Then she saw that she could not kill the boys by the windstorms. She then changed her song, and the storms disappeared and the sun came out. When the snowstorm was there where they were dancing the two boys turned into snowbirds. When the storm was gone and the sun came out the boys turned into larks. The old woman saw that she could not do anything with the boys. Then she gave up and said: "Let us go into the lodge and I will give you my daughters. I will also give you something to eat." The older boy, however, said: "No, we must keep up this game. Let me do the singing now and you dance." Then the boy began to sing:

> I like yonder coming,
> I like yonder coming,
> The blizzard and snow drifts, yonder coming,
> Yonder coming, far away.

> I like yonder coming,
> I like yonder coming,
> The stormy clouds, yonder coming,
> Yonder coming, far away.

> I like yonder coming,
> I like yonder coming,
> The stormy black clouds, yonder coming,
> Yonder coming, far away.

As he sang these songs it all happened. The blizzard came and the woman nearly froze to death, while the boys jumped up and down like snowbirds. But as she had power to bring the snowstorm she did not freeze. Then the boy changed the song and said, "I like it when comes out and it gets hot."

> I like yonder coming,
> I like yonder coming,
> The boiling heat, yonder coming,
> Yonder coming, far away.

The sun did come out, and it was boiling hot. The old woman began to cry out and say: "Let us stop. It is getting too hot." The old

woman tried to stop, but she could not, for some unknown power was
making her jump up and down and she was being lifted from the ground.
Then the boy sang:

> I like yonder coming,
> I like yonder coming,
> The swarm of grasshoppers, yonder coming,
> Yonder coming, far away.

> I like yonder coming,
> I like yonder coming,
> The swarm of grasshoppers now arriving,
> Yonder coming, far away.

As he sang the song a swarm of grasshoppers flew down and began to
circle around the old woman. They flew all around her and under her
feet, and they began to lift the old woman up. The boys kept on
singing:

> I like yonder coming,
> I like yonder coming,
> The swarm of grasshoppers upwards flying,
> Yonder coming, far away.

Spider-Woman begged the boys to stop singing, but they did not
listen to her. Spider-Woman tried to fight the grasshoppers with her
hands, but she could not keep them off. Finally she took her dress off
and she began to whip at the grasshoppers. At last she gave out and the
grasshoppers carried her up into the sky. When they arrived at the moon,
they placed the old woman in it, and there she was left to stay for all
time. That is why we see something hanging from the moon. It is the
old woman's dress. The grasshoppers then flew from the moon to the
sun and there they swarm around the sun. This is why we see a swarm
of grasshoppers flying around the sun in the summer time.

74. THE GIRL, SPIDER-WOMAN, AND THE BALL GAME.[1]

A man and his niece lived alone far away from other people. The
man was lame and could not move around very much because his feet
and his knees were swollen. Notwithstanding his lameness he would
disappear every day. The girl did not know where he went or how.
Sometimes he never came back until late at night, and she grew provoked at him. She told him that he should stay at home, and that he
should not go so far away; that if she got into trouble he could not run to

[1] Told by Sun-Chief, Skidi. The story especially serves as a warning to the
children not to wander far away from home lest they be captured by some supernatural being of vile influence.

help her. The uncle told the girl that he would be near to help her if she needed him.

One time while her uncle was gone a strange being came to the girl. Before she could cry for assistance, she was taken up by the wind and was carried to a far-away country. There she saw Spider-Woman, who told her that she had been brought there to play a game of twin balls with the people. The girl began to cry and the Spider-Woman went away. A little girl came to her and asked her why she was crying. The girl said, "I was taken away from my home and I am here all alone." The little girl told her to stop, crying saying that she would take her to her home. The girl went with the child and when they entered the lodge the girl found that there an old woman with many children lived. This woman was Wood-Rat and the children were young Rats. They told the girl about Spider-Woman who was challenging everyone who came that way to play twin balls. The girl told Rat-Woman that she did not understand the game; that she had never played it. Just before sunset the errand boy for Spider-Woman came and invited the girl to eat with Spider-Woman.

When the errand boy was gone, Rat-Woman told the girl that Spider-Woman was going to place something before her to eat. That the things which would be placed before her would look like black corn, but in reality were human eyes. She was told to say, when Spider-Woman told her to eat it, that she could not eat anything because she had already eaten enough and was not hungry. Rat-Woman also told the girl that she would challenge her to play the game of twin balls. The girl went to Spider-Woman's home and found many human bones scattered around near her place. When she entered the lodge she heard Spider-Woman whispering to herself: "She is fine looking. Her head shall be placed before all of the other skulls which I have in my lodge." Spider-Woman placed a wooden bowl filled with human eyes for the girl to eat, but the girl would not eat. She gave as an excuse that she had eaten at the other place; that she could not eat any more. She asked Spider-Woman to let her take the wooden bowl home, as the people at home would be glad to eat of it. Spider-Woman let her take the wooden bowl with her, hoping that she would eat some of its contents later.

The girl took the wooden bowl to the home of Mother-Rat, and when she received the wooden bowl she threw the stuff out and then gave the bowl to one of her children to take back to Spider-Woman. Mother-Rat then told the girl that many a young man had lost his life by playing twin balls with Spider-Woman. She said, "She will surely challenge you to play with her before daylight." The girl went out in the night and cried upon the high hills and through the timber. She asked every bird that she saw to tell her uncle that she was taken far away, and that she was about to play a game known as the twin-ball game and that she needed his help. The birds did not seem to listen to her. Then she went back to Mother-Rat's home, and there remained for the night. Before daylight the errand boy came and invited the girl to Spider-Woman's lodge. The girl went, and when she entered the lodge Spider-Woman gave her a seat near her, and told her that she had a game known as twin balls and that she wanted her to play with her. The girl accepted the challenge, but told Spider-Woman that she would have to wait four days, as she was looking for her uncle. When the girl went back to Mother-Rat's home, she told her what Spider-Woman had said. Mother-Rat cried and said, "She will surely kill you." That made the girl sad, so she went out upon the hills and cried.

In the meantime the uncle of the girl had come back to his lodge. He found the girl missing. He took a bundle down that was hanging in the lodge, opened it, and from there he took out twin balls. He placed the twin balls upon the ground, and put his feet upon them. Then he hit his ankles with the stick that he carried. As he hit his ankles with the stick he would make a motion as if throwing the twin balls into the air, and when he lifted the stick he flew through the air, and when he let the stick fall to the ground he would drop. In this way he went into the southern country looking for his niece, but he could not find her. Then he traveled in the same way in the western country, but could not find her. Then he traveled the same way in the northern country, but could not find her.

When he went back to the place where they had their lodge, a little bird was sitting upon a limb and was singing. The man could hear the bird singing, and listened. The bird sang: "I know where your niece is. She is about to play the twin-ball game with Spider-Woman, who will kill her if she defeats her." The man said to the bird, "Lead me to the place where my niece is." The bird flew towards the east. The man stood upon the balls and began to strike his ankles with the stick. Then he lifted the stick up into the sky and the balls flew up with the man. The bird came to the timber. When the man arrived at the timber the bird began to sing, "Now you can hear the voice of your niece crying." The man stopped and listened, and he heard her cry. This was in the evening. The man then ran to where she was crying and he found her. He told her that he had come to protect her; that she would kill Spider-Woman, for she should use her own twin balls. The man said to the girl: "On the day when you shall play with Spider-Woman, I shall be close by. I shall blow my breath upon the strings that hold the twin balls together and shall wear the string out so that it will break. You shall then say, 'I will go and get my twin balls and we will play.' "

When the day that was set for the game came, her uncle told her to take his stick and to hit him several times upon his ankles where they were swollen. The girl did as she was told by her uncle; then she went to play the game of twin balls with Spider-Woman. Spider-Woman threw the twin balls up and the girl tried to catch them, but she could not. When the girl touched the string she noticed that it seemed to be giving out, and so she made up her mind to catch the balls with her stick. She did not get the best of the old woman, but she knew that the stick was cutting the string, for she remembered what her uncle had told her. When the old woman was about to win, the girl caught the balls and threw them, but the string parted and the balls separated. Old Spider-Woman then wanted to stop playing, so that she could fix her twin balls, but the girl insisted that they finish the game, as she, too, had twin balls. She told her uncle, and her uncle put out his feet and she began to beat his feet. After a while she noticed the twin balls coming out from under his feet. She took the balls and went out and began to play with the old woman again.

The girl won all the games they played and won all of Spider-Woman's people, and at last she won Spider-Woman herself. The people who were with the girl rushed on to the old Spider-Woman, killed her, and burned her. When the old woman was burned she was seen to jump from the fire into the grass in the form of a spider. The girl went home and told her uncle all that had happened. Her uncle told her to whip his ankles and to place the balls at his feet. By so doing the man took possession of the twin balls again. The man then said: "This is the way we get rid of Spider-Women. We shall not have such persons among the people, but the people will have sickness such as I have, so that they will have to walk with a crooked stick for support." And so that is why the people have rheumatism.

75. THE BOY WHO KILLED THE CANNIBAL WITCH.
(See Abstracts.)

[Told by Thief, Kitkehahki. This story is told to children to teach them that when roaming over the prairie they should not marry strange women, because the strange women are spider-women and have a bad influence. It also teaches the children that birds are good friends, that they help to destroy evil spirits and exist on earth for this purpose. The story also encourages the children in their desire to help slay the evil spirits. The lark especially was to be respected and esteemed, because the lark it was who led the boy to the lodge of the gods in the west, where he received a sacred bundle and instructions, at which time also the people were promised the buffalo. The larks, in their song, speak in the Pawnee tongue, "I am not afraid."]

76. THE WITCH-WOMAN AND HER HOME.[1]

In a village was a hunter. One time he went east hunting. After a while he came to a grass-lodge. The Witch-Woman came out and met him. She invited him into her lodge. When he was seated she placed something in a wooden bowl for him to eat. The man was hungry and he ate what was in the bowl. In a little while he became very sick and died. The woman cut his flesh up and hung it up on poles. She took his head into her lodge and placed it there.

About four days afterwards the dead man's wife thought it strange that her husband did not come home. She sent her son to look for his father. The boy was about thirteen years old. He traveled east in about the same direction which his father had taken. After a while he came to the grass-lodge. There he saw human limbs hanging on poles. The Witch-Woman came out and said: "My grandson, I am glad you came. Before I give you anything to eat you must first dance. If you dance longer than I do, then you conquer me. If I dance longer than you do, then I conquer you." The Witch-Woman went in. She took a piece of string and made a hole through the man's left ear, ran the string into it, and tied it there. At the other end of the string she made another opening in the right ear and tied it with the string. She then placed the head upon the boy's breast. She put the loop around his neck. Then she began to sing for the boy:

> Dancing with his father's head,
> Dancing with his father's head,
> Walking he came, walking he came.

She continued singing. The boy was dancing all this time. The Witch-Woman was also dancing. The Witch-Woman finally gave in and was about to kill the boy when several men came to the place. They took the old woman, killed her, and saved the boy. The Witch-Woman was put into a fire and burned. She burst while in the fire and something flew up and rested upon a tree. When the people examined the thing it was found to be a croaking tree frog. The boy took it home and told the people that it was the Witch-Woman who had killed the man and that she was now dead; that when she was placed on the fire she burst open and a frog flew up on the tree. They discovered in this way that the woman had turned into a tree frog.

[1] Told by Bright-Eyes, Skidi. The story conveys a warning to hunters when away from home not to stop at strange habitations.

III. THE ORIGIN OF MEDICINE CEREMONIES OR POWER.

The stories in this group correspond to the group in the Skidi volume under the heading "Medicine," and are supposed to be true. They explain rites or ceremonies of the medicine-men, or the origin of the medicine powers of the individual medicine-men. With these tales are many songs, the publication of which, however, is reserved for another place. These tales are not told on ordinary occasions, and never except on payment of objects of value or of money. The tales, therefore, are considered as private property and belong either to a group of medicine-men controlling a medicine ceremony, or to individuals, who naturally possess the story of the origin of the medicine power which they use in their practices.

---

77. THE MEDICINE-CHILD AND THE BEAVER MEDICINE.[1]

When the Skidi band of Pawnee were living upon the Loup River, the other three bands lived near the mouth of the Platte River. A child was born in the Skidi village. As the child grew, he developed many mysterious ways and acted peculiarly. He would not play with the children, but stayed at home and played "medicine-man" by himself. He would wander off to creeks and to the timber and stay for some time.

One day as he entered his mother's lodge he heard some one groaning. He sat down by the fireplace and watched. A woman was sick. The boy arose and asked that he be allowed to put his hands upon the woman and see what the trouble was. He slapped his hands upon Mother-Earth, then rubbed the palms together, then laid them upon the woman, where the pain was, and the pain left her. The woman told the older people what the child had done. The people were astonished, for the child did not know anything about medicine. After that the boy was looked upon as a medicine-man, but he did not make a practice of curing people. It was only at times when mysterious influences came upon him that he went to sick people and treated them. Every time he treated a patient, the patient recovered, and so all were seeking to have the boy heal their sick.

[1] Told by Beaver, Kitkehahki. Beaver inherited this story from his father, who was the keeper of the Beaver medicine, the origin of which this story explains. The skin of the Beaver, which is supposed to have given the power, is that of an albino and is still in possession of one of the Kitkehahki medicine-men.

The people, on their hunts, met the other band of Skidi, who were living upon the Loup River, and they told them of the wonderful boy, who was yet a mere child, but was healing people and curing them of their diseases. The Skidi men who were told about the boy went home and told their band that the lower band had a medicine-child who was wonderful and who had power to cure. The most powerful medicine-man decided to visit the boy and see what powers he possessed, and to find out whether his power came from the animals or from the gods in the heavens. He told his wife that he wanted her to go with him to the lower villages, and they went. At last they came to the three lower villages and the man asked where the medicine-boy lived. The people told him, and he and his wife went to the boy's lodge and entered it. The boy was there. He arose, took a buffalo robe, opened it, and spread it out on the west side of the lodge. He then placed two pillows and asked the man and his wife to take their seats upon them. They took the seats offered them. Then the young man called upon his women relatives to boil some meat for the visiting medicine-man and his wife. The women prepared a meal and offered the food to the man and his wife and they ate, and when they had had plenty, they passed the wooden bowls to the women who had offered the meat to them. The man then reached for his tobacco pouch, which was a skunk skin, and from this bag he took out a little pipe, filled it up with sumach leaves and tobacco. He lit the pipe, passed it to the young man, and the young man took the pipe from the old man and smoked. The boy passed the pipe back to the old man, who smoked and emptied the ashes out of the pipe upon the rim of the fireplace. Then the old man spoke to the young man, saying: "My friend, I came here to make friends with you. I came to stop here with you for several days, and to talk with you about the mysteries of a medicine-man. I am a Skidi, and I have heard of your success in curing people, and I thought I would come and sit up at nights to talk with you." The young man felt honored by this visit, for it seemed that his own people were jealous of his success in curing people. The old Skidi medicine-man spent one whole night and part of the next day in telling where and how he received his powers. When he had finished, he ate, and then said: "My friend, we will now leave you. We will go to our village. I shall think about you and I shall make you another visit. If you can make me a visit some time, come. I shall be very glad to have you visit me." The old man and the old woman arose and went out of the lodge and returned to their village.

After a time word was again sent to the young man that his Skidi medicine-man friend was coming, and his wife with him. The young man spread the robe again in the west side of the lodge and put two pillows upon it. When his visitors came in he motioned them to take their seats. They sat down. The women prepared the meal for them and they ate. The old Skidi began to continue his story about the mysteries of the medicine-men, and the young man listened. For two nights they sat up, and the third day. Towards the close of the third day the Skidi man stopped telling about his mysteries, and he and his wife arose and left the lodge and went to their village. The Skidi medicine-man made several visits to the young man and he continued to tell his story.

Once he visited the young man and took him presents of a buffalo robe, a pipe, eagle feathers, and some other little things. Word was sent to the boy that the old man and his wife were again coming. The old man and his wife, upon entering, placed the gifts that they had brought to the young man in front of him and said: "My friend, I have come to you this time, and bring these gifts to you. I now wish to hear your story, why you, though you are yet young, should know the mysteries of a medicine-man." The young man accepted the gifts and laid them to one side. He told the old man to continue his story, as he was very much interested. They sat for three days and three nights, and upon the fourth day the old man stopped and told the young man that he now thought it was time for him to tell him something. The young man told the old man that he had no powers whatever; that he had not seen any mysteries in the heavens, nor had he been taken into the animals' lodges; that if he had cured people, it must have been through a power that he did not know was present with him, for he had no roots or herbs to give patients, and that in reality he was not a medicine-man, and that he would like very much to have the old man continue. The old man was enraged by this turn of things, for he had expected a long story that he might learn how the boy had been taken into the animals' lodge, and what powers he possessed.

On the fourth night, as they were sitting, the old man reached for his skunk bag, pulled his pipe out, filled it up, and handed it to the young man. The young man lighted the pipe, smoked it, and passed it to the old man, who smoked a little and passed it back to the young man to smoke. As the young man was emptying the ashes from the bowl of the pipe, he fell over for want of sleep. The old man woke the boy. The boy sat up and the old man said: "You are now very sleepy and tired out. We shall leave you and go home. I am glad we have talked, and some time we shall come again to see you."

The boy lay down by the side of the fireplace with his robe wrapped around him. From that time on he felt a peculiar sensation in his stomach.   As the days went by and several months passed, the young man felt larger, as if his stomach was growing.   He knew then that the old Skidi man had done something to him.   He told his relatives of his condition.   The time came for all the tribes to go hunting.   The young man told his people that he was going off, that he was pregnant, and that he was no longer fit to be in the village; that he was going to leave the village entirely and go off and die in some unknown country, so that the people would never know that he was in this condition.

He took some meat and went off and left the village, traveling south. The people left their village and went west on a buffalo hunt.   The young man went south toward the Platte River.   He then traveled toward the west, following the Platte River.   He did not eat anything all this time, for he felt very much ashamed and he did not care to live. When he came to the hills, he went into places where he thought wild animals would find him and kill him, but none came.   He finally went across the Platte River to some rocky hills.   He was very weak, his stomach was prominent, and his limbs were thin and his face also.   While he was upon this hill he heard peculiar noises in the distance.   He followed the noises, and, as he reached the ridge of a high hill, he looked down on the other side and saw a tipi.   The tipi was very large and looked new.   He went down the hill to the tipi.   As he approached the west side, somebody within said, "Do not come near our tipi."   But the boy went on.   When he came close to the south side, somebody commanded him to stop where he was or he would be killed; but he went on and was not killed.   When he came to the entrance, he was again commanded not to enter; but he lifted the door flap and the voice said, "Do not come in, for we shall eat you up if you do."   But the boy went in.

Everything in the tipi was quiet.   The boy threw aside the robe that he had upon him and told the people in there that he was ready to be killed; that he was in great trouble and that he did not care to live.   "Look upon me and you can see what my trouble is," he said.   On the west side sat little men, and other men were sitting in a circle around the tipi, and on the south side a peculiar-looking man sat who was dressed differently from the others.   He had white clay streaks upon his face, and over him were hanging black lariat ropes, decked with downy feathers, and a war club was tied to the ropes.   These people said that they were sorry not to be able to do anything for him, for they did not have the power to grant what he wanted.   "But," they said, "we will leave it to the two errand men who are sitting by the entrance to decide whether the animals shall help you or not."

There was a Raccoon on the north, and a Muskrat on the south of the entrance, and they were the errand men.   The Muskrat arose and said that he was going to leave it all to the Raccoon.   The Raccoon arose and called on the head medicine-men, but reminded them of his errands, his willingness to do their commands, and said: "This is a poor man. I feel sorry for him.   He stands there with a large belly like a woman. I ask you to cure him and make him well and to give him power to become a medicine-man."   All the animals said, "Nawa."   But they could not do anything for him until the other lodges had been notified. The four little men in the west commanded the man in the south to take this man to the animal lodge under Spring-Hill.   The man in the south rose up, sat down in front of the unfortunate boy, and told him to get on his back and close his eyes.   The boy closed his eyes and the animal flew up and out of the lodge towards the southwest.   He flew for some time and then lighted on a high hill.   He told the unfortunate boy to look, and when he looked he saw the same man who brought him there.   After the man had rested, he sat down again and told the boy to get on his back.   The boy obeyed and the animal flew again, and when he lighted he told the boy to open his eyes, and he did so.   He was in the lodge of the animals and there the man sat among them as a Hawk.

The Hawk spoke up and said that the animals from the other lodge had sent him there with the boy to ask the animals of this lodge to help him; that the two errand people had given their consent.   "Very well," they said, "we are willing to help this man, but we can not do it here."   At the entrance of the lodge was a Buzzard on the south side, and a Magpie on the north side.   They were the errand men of this lodge.   The animals left it with these two to decide whether they should help the boy.   The Buzzard stepped up and said that he would leave it all with the Magpie.   The Magpie felt sorry for the unfortunate boy, for he was very thin and had had nothing to eat all this time, and he was big in the belly.   The medicine-men all said, "Very well."

They sent the Magpie to all the other animal lodges.   The Magpie went to all the lodges and went to the lodge at Pahuk last, for there was the lodge that was really at the head of all the other lodges.   The animals of that lodge told the Magpie that he must fly to the different lodges and invite some of the other animals to come to the lodge at Pahuk, for there the boy must be made well.   They also instructed the Buzzard at the Spring-Hill lodge to carry the boy upon his back to the lodge at Pahuk. The Magpie flew up the stream and stopped at the different lodges, and at each lodge he said that the lodge at Pahuk had sent him to say that this lodge should send some of their animals to Pahuk, where they were to cure the boy.   Each lodge that the Magpie visited selected its own animals and sent them to Pahuk. At the lodge of Spring-Hill he told them that the lodge at Pahuk had decided to do as the errand people had requested them, and were going to take pity upon the boy; that they must send their representatives down to the lodge, and that the Buzzard, who was errand man, was ordered to carry the boy to the lodge at Pahuk. The Magipe told them to send the Buzzard at once down to Pahuk while he went to visit the other lodges. The preparations were made for the Buzzards to carry the boy down to Pahuk, which was very, very far away. One of the Buzzards stepped out in front of the boy and told him to get on his back and to close his eyes. The boy climbed on his back and the Buzzard flew up. The three flew close together, two flying right under the one with the boy on his back. They flew for a long distance and then lighted upon a hill. The next one carried the boy, and they flew on, just the same as before, and they came to another high hill, and they lighted. Then the third one carried him, and they flew just the same as before, and they lighted upon the steep bank of Pahuk and left the boy upon the bank.

The Buzzards went into the lodge, and when the boy became conscious, he was sitting in the lodge of the animals. He saw the four little men whom he had seen in the first lodge sitting in the west. He also saw the man who first carried him to the Spring-Hill lodge sitting among them. He saw many other kinds of animals, and also the errand men who had come from the different lodges. The errand men stood up and spoke to the different animals, asking them to help the unfortunate boy, saying that it was their wish to do so. While they were talking the young man had gone to sleep. When he woke up he looked around him and there were all the animals; the four little men he had seen before sat there as Ground-Hogs. The leading medicine-men, who were Beavers, requested the Otters to take the boy and cure him; but the Otters said that they could not help the boy. The leading medicine-men asked the Bears to wait on the boy, but the Bears did not give their consent. They asked every animal in the lodge, but all failed to help the boy. The leaders then asked the Ground-Hog people if they would help the boy. They said, "Yes, we will help him." The boy was put to sleep and placed on the south side of the center of the lodge. The leader of the Ground-Hogs walked over to the fireplace, around the boy, then asked the errand man to bring a bowl of water and set it at the feet of the boy. The animal went around the bowl of water and then dipped his nose into the water, and worked his jaws; and when he swallowed he gave a leap, then a somersault, and then vomited up a bone. All the other Ground-Hogs did the same thing. Each went around the bowl of water, dipped his nose into the water, and when he lifted up his mouth commenced to work his jaws; then he leaped, turned a somersault, and vomited up a different bone from any that the others had vomited.   These four kept going around the bowl of water, each dipping his nose and working his jaws, turning somersaults, and throwing up different bones of the baby that was in the boy.   At last they worked and worked, but in vain.   They could not do any more.   Finally they went over to the Bears and asked them for help.

The Bears were willing to help.   They went up to the young man, and the youngest of the Bears took his smallest claw, stuck it into the boy's belly, and cut it open, taking the meat out and throwing it to the little animals.   The Bears and all the medicine-men rose up and all the other animals rose and made a great rush to the boy and each animal worked his power.   The Bears picked him up and carried him around. Finally they healed the wound.   Then they stood the boy up and pushed him around until he finally walked; then they seated him on the south side.   The boy looked at himself and wondered if he was himself. The animals then told the boy that they were through with him; that he should go above their lodge and subsist on whatever he could in the daytime, but at night he must always return and they would have their mysterious performances, which they intended to teach him.

The boy was taken out of the lodge and placed on dry land.   He went through the timber, found artichokes, dug them up, and ate them. He went on, found plums, and ate them.   He went to the place where the people had their village and earth-lodges, and there he found a knife and some other material, such as sinew.   Then he went to the timber and cut an ash tree and made a bow; then he cut some dogwood and made blunt arrows, so that he had a bow and arrows.   He went through the timber, killed game, such as rabbits and birds, and ate them.   In the night time he would return to the lodge of the animals: The animals would take him, and each animal would play sleight-of-hand upon his body, at the same time teaching him.   They kept him there for a long time.   When fall came they told him that the tribes had returned, and that they were living in their own village.   They called him one night and told him to go to his village and enter it in the night, and then to go to his lodge; and that there he would find his father and mother, who believed that he was dead; that he should wake them and tell them that he wanted two parfleches filled with dried meat, and a number of robes and much tobacco.

The boy went out of the animals' lodge and went towards the village, and he found that the people had returned to their village.   He went through the village to his own lodge and entered.   He went to the bed of his mother and woke her up.   When she awoke she acted as though she were dreaming, but the boy told her that she was not dreaming; that he was really there.   She arose, made a fire, woke the old man, and told him that the boy had come back.   The old man arose and sat by the young boy near the fireplace.   The boy told his father to go and call his relatives, saying that he wanted to get several presents from them, and that he wanted to take these presents to a certain place.   The father did not ask any questions, for he knew that the boy was going to take the presents to some animals' lodge.   The man went out and called his friends in.   When he told them what was needed, they all rose, went out, and brought the things that the boy had instructed them to get, and the gifts made a great pile.   The people were glad to see him.   His uncle offered to help carry all the things to the place for him.   The young man told his uncle to bring a pony, put a saddle, and parfleches, one on each side, and then the other gifts, on its back.   Then they traveled.

When they came close to Pahuk, the young man told his uncle to take the things off from the pony's back, and then he sent his uncle back home.   The boy went to the edge of the bank and saw what looked like feathers on the waters, and he heard peculiar noises in the water.   He rolled both the parfleches down into the water, one at a time; then he threw the gifts down; and after the gifts were all thrown down, he jumped over the steep bank into the water, and found himself in the animals' lodge; and there he saw the two parfleches of meat inside, and the gifts.

The animals were thankful for the presents that had been thrown into the water by the boy.   There were so many animals in the lodge that they did not all receive presents, so they sent the boy out again and he went to the village and asked for more presents and took them to the animals' lodge.   Then he received more instructions as to how he should kill his enemies.   The four little men told him that they were the animals who killed people or animals by simply making movements of the jaws; that they were going to ask him to kill the smallest one and skin it, but to leave the skull in the skin.   The boy killed the smallest one, skinned it, leaving only the head part in the skin, and set it out to dry.   When it was dry he picked up stones and rubbed the hide, so that it became soft.   They told him that since he had this in his possession, he would have the same power that they had; if any of his enemies tried to poison him, all he had to do was to go down to the creek and think of the man who was trying to kill him; that he should take his hide, dip its nose in the water and pull it up, and when he should see a piece of liver in its mouth he might know that it had killed the man.   All the different animals talked to him and told him of their mysteries, their roots and herbs, their way of curing, and their sleight-of-hand. At last they said, "Go now to your people, take these things with you, and teach other people about our mysteries."

The boy went to his lodge, and the next day it was announced through the village that the lost young man, who had been known as the medicine-child, had returned. At last the other Skidi band heard that the young man who had been lost had returned. The old man who had bewitched him heard of it. For several days he thought of what he should do, for he knew that he had poisoned the young man, and knew the young man had come back. He was sure that the young man must be wonderful. So one day he told his wife that he wanted her to gather up her medicine-bags, her robe, and several other presents; that he wanted again to visit his friend who had returned. They started and they went to the lower village, and as they walked through the village they met a man, and they asked where the boy's lodge was. He pointed out the lodge to them, and they went in and placed the presents down in front of the boy, and the medicine-man told him that he was very glad that he had come back; that he had returned to have some more story-telling. The young man said that he was willing. The old man sat down and talked and talked, and then he said, "I must be going home." The old man and the old woman went home.

In a few days the young man made up his mind to visit the old man. He went to the Skidi village and asked for the old man's lodge. The lodge was pointed out and he went to it. The old man was glad to see him, and the old man sat up all night with him, talking about the different mysteries. The old man filled up his pipe and put in the same medicine as when he poisoned the boy before. The young man knew what the old man was doing. He smoked the pipe, but would not swallow the smoke, but would blow it away. The old man became tired, but really was not tired, for the young man had had the pipe. The young man mixed up tobacco and some of the other roots and sumach leaves, so that on smoking from the young man's pipe the old man became very sleepy. The old man was anxious to get rid of the boy, but the boy stayed all night. The next day in the afternoon the young man was invited by the chief to eat with him, and as the boy entered the lodge the chief came to meet him and passed his hands over him and said: "My son, I am glad you have come back. We all understand that you were in a bad condition. I give you these presents—a buffalo robe, feathers, and other things. I want you to return the poison that the old man gave you and kill the old man, for we are all afraid of him." The young man said that he knew nothing of the different bad medicines. After the boy had feasted with the chief, he went to the old man's lodge again, and there sat and talked about the mysteries of the medicine-men. The old man became very sleepy. The young man told him to go to bed, for he was going home.

The young man left the old man's lodge and went directly to the creek. It was winter and the creek was frozen. The young man took a long pole down to the creek and he broke the ice that had frozen that night. The young man took out the little animal he had, dipped it in the water, and saw the water stir. After a while he went up to the round place where the ice was broken, and in the edge of it lay this little animal, with a piece of liver in its mouth. It was towards morning. He saw blood on the ice everywhere, and on the water where the ice was broken he saw pieces of entrails from the old man. The boy took up the animal and went home. The wife of the old man arose and made a fire, cooked breakfast, and went to the bedside of the old man to tell him that his friend was missing. The old man did not move nor talk, and his head was covered with his buffalo robe. The old woman went and uncovered him and found that he was dead. His stomach was drawn in. The old woman gave a loud scream, and told the other people in the lodge that the old man was dead. Some of the people did not know how he came by his death, but the chief suspected the young man. The Skidi took the old man and buried him, burying with him all his medicine-bags and other things, and everybody was glad to get rid of him. The young man went home and slept, and when he waked up there were several people in his lodge who told him that his friend had been killed; that somebody had bewitched him; but the young man said nothing.

The medicine-men met in their lodge. The young man went in, took a seat among them, and danced with them. The people liked his dance. They met in their lodge again to do sleight-of-hand. The young man went in, was given a seat, did some sleight-of-hand that was better than any that the other old medicine-men were doing, and so at last he was acknowledged the leading medicine-man. This particular dance was known as Kurapira, Medicine-Child dance.

About this time the Potawatami Indians were visiting the Pawnee. They looked on at their sleight-of-hand performances. They were awed by the mysterious doings of this young man. The sleight-of-hand performances were over, the Potawatami had been entertained, presents of robes and other things were given them, and they were ready to go home. Before they started, one of the Potawatami turned and said, "Make us a visit, and bring that young man with you; we want very much to see him and get acquainted with him." A year went by and the Pawnee did not go.   Finally the Potawatami sent another invitation to the Pawnee village, inviting the Pawnee to their village and asking that they be sure to bring the young medicine-man.

The Pawnee started on the journey to the Potawatami country. When they arrived, the Potawatami received them and were very good to them.   The young medicine-man noticed one man who was particularly attentive to him.   In the ceremonies that they had, the man wore an otter hide, which the young medicine-man knew was a witch.   At other times the man wore a bear robe over his body.

One night the Potawatami attacked this young medicine-man by throwing his medicines at him.   The boy put on his medicine and then made motions with his hands, as if to catch something in the air.   When he caught something he would place it on the fireplace, and the people would gather around and examine it, and there would be the sharp bones of the skeleton of a sunfish.   When the war chief asked for the final ceremony, the Potawatami gave this medicine-man one pony and several gifts—such as pipes, robes, otter and beaver skins.   In the night the young medicine-man told his friends to lie in a circle around him, for he was sure that some one was trying to bewitch him, and to have their ponies close by the tipi.   All lay down, and late in the night the young man heard some one groaning outside, and all at once he saw some one in the entrance who kept crawling, crawling, crawling, until he came to him, then with a movement of the body and the flourish of an eagle wing, he turned as if satisfied and went out of the lodge.   The young medicine-man arose, took up his medicine, followed this strange person up to his lodge, went into the lodge, and found the Potawatami just taking off his robe and talking to his wife.   The young man took the skin of a mole, swung it, and threw it out at the Potawatami.   Then he gave four groaning sounds, stamped his feet, and went out.   The young medicine-man went back to the lodge where the others were, woke them up, and said, "Now, let us go."   The other men arose, mounted their ponies, and started.

When they were outside of the village, the young medicine-man told the other men that somebody had bewitched him; that he was already bewitched; that he wanted them to ride just as fast as they could, so that they might reach the stream, and when they reached the stream they were to go right into the water; and that as they went through the water, the thing that was in him would try to climb out; and that as the thing stuck its head out of his mouth, they must, by a quick motion of the hand, catch the head and throw it away; if they were afraid to pull it out, then he must die.   They whipped up their ponies and traveled fast. They finally came to the stream and the man was beginning to get sick. They went into the stream, and as the boy went through the water, he kept repeating: "It is coming up. It is coming up. Be ready as soon as the thing sticks its head out of my mouth to pull it out." When the water came up to his neck he told the others to watch; that it was coming. As soon as they saw the thing stick its head out of his mouth one of the men grabbed it quickly and threw it on the bank of the river. The young medicine-man fell down and disappeared in the water as the thing was taken out of him. In a little while the young medicine-man stood up and said, "He is dead."

It was then early morning. They unsaddled their ponies and let them graze around while they cooked a little breakfast for themselves and ate. Then they took the animal that was lying on the bank and burned it up. The young medicine-man told the others that they must not tell the other party about his vomiting up this animal; but that they should tell about the death of the Potawatami. While they were on the bank of the creek, their friends came from the other side of the creek and said that when they left the Potawatami village there was a great commotion, for one of the Potawatami had died early that morning. The other people knew that the young medicine-man had thrown up the animal about the same time, but they said nothing. Then they all marched back to their homes together.

The people had gathered their corn and were about to go on their winter hunt. On that hunt they killed many buffalo. Then, in the spring, they went to the other villages, planted their corn, and again went hunting. That time the young medicine-man told his relatives to have the men kill buffalo and dry the meat; that he wanted to give them a medicine-men's sleight-of-hand ceremony. The meat was brought into the medicine-men's lodge where the young medicine-man was with the many young men, to whom he was teaching the mysteries of medicine. At that time many wonderful sleight-of-hand performances took place. On the last day of the final ceremony, before daylight, the young medicine-man went to the timber with some other young men, cut down a cottonwood tree, and dragged it up to the lodge; and there they set the cottonwood tree in front of the lodge, so that it would always stand there and would grow. The sleight-of-hand performances continued and the young medicine-man did many wonderful things. When he put the tree outside of the lodge, it was the most wonderful thing that had ever been done; so that the other medicine-men had to keep quiet and had to acknowledge this young medicine-man as the leading medicine-man.

When the ceremonies were over, the people began to get ready to go hunting again, for it was in the winter time. They went hunting that winter and killed many buffalo, and in the spring they returned to their village to put in their corn; then they went hunting again. While they were hunting, it was rumored that the young medicine-man would have his medicine-man's dance again. They killed many buffalo and dried meat for that purpose. Upon their return the young medicine-man called the men to his medicine-lodge again. For three days they had sleight-of-hand performances in the earth-lodge. On the third night the medicine-men were told that the next day they were to make preparation to go down to a certain pond that was close to the village; that the young medicine-man had given instructions that all the medicine-men should make their lodges around the pond; that they were to make a kind of beaver lodge in the center of the pond; that the medicine-men would go down there on the fifth day and do their sleight-of-hand at the pond, so that the people would see them openly. The medicine-men went to the pond on the fourth night, and there they cut the willows, cottonwood, box elder, and elm, and made lodges around the pond, in the water. After that was done, the people made a great beaver lodge in the center of the pond. Just about daylight the young medicine-man took a cottonwood tree that they had brought from the timber and swam to the beaver lodge, and there he placed the tree in the center of the lodge. In the early morning the people heard yelling and shouting at the pond. They went down there, and they found the medicine-men hard at work. Then they commenced to exercise their magic powers and to perform sleight-of-hand tricks. Some of them took sharpened willow sticks, with the leaves at one end, and stuck the willows through the cheek of another man. Others took pieces from the cottonwood tree and swallowed them, and then they would pull them up again. At last, in the afternoon, the young medicine-man stood in the west with a dead loon, and he set the loon free in the west, and the loon flew around the pond and back to the man. The young medicine-man said: "Now the loon has gone around the pond, and all the medicine-men will now leave the pond. First bury your limbs and the things that we have been playing with in the water. We will now go to our lodge and eat; then we have done with our ceremony." The medicine-men all went back to the lodge, ate, and were dismissed by the young medicine-man.

Years afterward this pond was visited by some men who gave presents of robes, tobacco, beads, and feathers. They all saw that in the center of the pond where the young man had planted a tree there was an island. The young medicine-man lived to be an old man, and in his old age he gave his son his beaver that he used in his medicine ceremonies and told him to keep up the ceremony, for he himself was getting old. His son learned his ceremonies and the old man died.

78. THE ORIGIN OF THE LOON MEDICINE CEREMONY.[1]

A long time ago when the Skidi were living on the Loup River, in Nebraska, there lived a poor boy.   The boy had no relations and had to go from one lodge to the other for food.   When he had grown to be a good-sized boy, the chief's son, who had become very fond of him, asked him to come into his lodge and live with him.   The chief's boy gave the boy moccasins, leggings, and a robe, and a lariat rope made out of buffalo hide. He told the poor boy that he could look after their ponies, and that it would be his work to water them.   The poor boy took care of the ponies so well that the chief's boy's relations were glad to have him stay with them, and they gave him many gifts and were always kind to him. In a few years the two boys grew to manhood.   The chief's son was so devoted to his companion, who had grown into a handsome man, that he made up his mind that he would keep him in his lodge, and that he should sleep with him in his own bed.

In the tribe there was another chief who had a beautiful daughter, and the chief's son courted the maiden.   It was understood through the village that he would marry the girl, for she showed him every favor. If she happened to be in the fields working, and the young man came to the field, she threw down her hoe and went to meet him, and her mother or aunts who were with her would take up the hoe and carry on the work, so that she could talk with the chief's son.   If the chief's son came to their lodge in the night, her relations did not object to her going out to meet him, for it was understood that he would in time marry her.   The chief's son, knowing that the girl came to him whenever he wanted her, decided that he would not marry her, for he had never asked her to marry him, neither had he ever asked her parents to let him marry her.   He tried to think of some excuse that he could give for not marrying her, but he could not think of any.   Finally he made up his mind to have his poor friend lie with the girl and then he could accuse her of faithlessness and refuse to marry her on that account.

One night the chief's son went to the lodge of the girl and asked her to meet him at a certain place a short distance from the village, for he wished to talk to her.   She promised to meet him in a little while at the

[1] Told by Buffalo, Skidi.   The story, besides reciting the origin of one of the medicine ceremonies of the Skidi, conveys the moral that women should be true to their husbands.

place. The girl went back into her lodge, and the chief's son went to his lodge and called his friend out, and the two boys went outside of the village. The chief's boy told the poor boy to lie down in the brush and hide, and he obeyed. As he lay down he heard some one coming, and so he kept quiet. The girl came. The chief's boy met her. They sat down close to the poor boy in the brush; then the chief's son began to talk to the girl about whom she should marry. The girl told him that he was the only one who was going with her, and that it was understood in the village that he was to marry her and that she would never marry anyone but him. The boy told her that he would marry her only on the condition that she would do as he was going to tell her to do; that he wanted her to lie with his friend, the poor boy, and that if she would do that he would take her as his wife. The girl objected and said that she did not care for the poor boy, and that, even though he wanted her to lie with him now, the time would come when he would not like it and would always be reminding her of it. The chief's boy begged and begged for her to do what he wanted, but she would not do so. At last he jumped up and went away and left her. She went home. Then the chief's boy came back to his friend and said, "You see I have been begging for you to lie with that girl, but I could not get her to do it and so we will go home."

Several days passed and the chief's boy formed another plan. He went to the girl's lodge and asked her to meet him outside of the village again that night. She promised to come. As soon as the girl promised to come, the young man went back to his lodge and called the poor boy out. They went outside the village and the chief's boy gave his leggings to the poor boy, and also gave his robe and the wampum beads that he wore about his neck. The chief's son said, "Now, when the girl comes out to meet you, do not speak loud, but whisper. Go to the brush yonder and lie down with her. After you have lain with her and she finds out that it is you, then tell her that you want to take her to a far-away country. Go south and travel for about four days, and I will come on horseback and hunt you up. Then I will bring you back to the village."

The poor boy dressed himself in the clothes of the chief's son. The real chief's boy remained behind, while the poor boy went to the place the girl was to come. After a while the girl came and the boy met her. They walked on until they came to some brush. They sat down and whispered a long time, and the poor boy whispered to the girl and told her that he had made up his mind to marry her. The girl, thinking that he was the chief's son, gave in and finally lay with the poor boy. After the poor boy had lain with the girl he sat up and told the girl to sit up and listen to what he had to tell her.   He pulled the robe away from his face and said: "Girl, I am the poor boy.   My brother, the chief's boy, has deceived you.   I know the way he talked here to you and I know just what he wanted you to do.   I care for you and I want you to be my wife, and that is why I did not come right out and tell you who I was. You are disgraced because a poor boy has lain with you.   You do not care to go back into the village.   I am willing that we go south, and there I will try to make you happy."

The girl said that she would go; that she did not want to go back to the village, as the people would make fun of her, especially the chief's son. The poor boy, instead of going to the place where the chief's son was sitting, went direct to the lodge of the chief and took a quiver filled with arrows and a bow and a knife.   Upon his belt he put a horn and flint stones with which to kindle a fire.   After he had gathered these things he went to meet the girl.   He told her to go to her tipi and to bring her sinew and awl, and her robe.   He waited outside while the girl went in and brought the things; then they started upon their journey to the south.   During the day they rested, and in the night they traveled again.   The boy went out and killed game, so that they had something to eat.

After the fourth day the girl's relations became uneasy about her. They hunted her through the village, but they could not find her.   At last they sent a woman over to the chief's lodge to see if the chief's boy was there.   She saw him and went back and told that he was there.   In the night the woman was sent back to see if the chief's boy would go out of the lodge, thinking that he might have left the girl outside of the village and would go to her.   The woman went and watched all night and saw that the boy never left the lodge that night.   The next day the girl's uncle was told of her disappearance, and he was also told the chief's boy was the only one who was courting her.   The uncle of the girl went to the chief's lodge and he found the chief's boy lying upon the bed.   He told the chief that the girl was missing, and that they thought that his boy had taken her.   The boy sat up and said that he had not seen her for several days, and that she was not with him.   Several men were sent through the village to see if any young man was missing.   These men went into every lodge and counted all the young men.   At last they came into the lodge of the chief.   There they counted the people and found one person missing.   They knew that the missing one was the poor boy, and so they asked if the boy had been there for the last few days, and the chief said that he had not.   The people then knew that the poor boy had taken the girl away, and some of them threatened to kill the boy if he should ever return, for a poor boy had no right to marry the daughter of a chief.

The poor boy and the girl traveled far to the south and never thought of returning to their home. Some mysterious change seemed to have come over them, and they forgot all about their home, and were happy alone with each other. At last they came to the Platte River. Instead of crossing the Platte River they went down the stream to the east. For many days they traveled until they came to a swampy country. Then the boy knew that they had come to the place that was known as Pahuk. He went into the thick timbers and he saw many lakes and ponds. Then he returned to get his wife, for he had decided to make their home in the forest near one of the lakes. He cut timber and made a grass-lodge for himself and his wife. When the lodge was completed the young man went off into the timber and found many birds and animals.

Every day he went hunting and brought back some game, so that they always had plenty to eat. One day while the young man was gone his wife went down to the pond to get some water. Just before she came to the pond a Loon flew up from the bank and lighted not very far away. She knew that there must be a nest close by. She went to the edge of the water and looked for the nest, but she could not find it. She gave no thought to the Loon for many days. One morning before daylight she got up and went down to the pond for some water. When she arrived at the edge of the pond she heard the noise of young birds. She hunted and she found them. There were two little Loons. She tried to catch them, but they swam into the water. After that, every morning she arose early and went down to the pond to try to catch the little Loons. One morning she slept longer than usual and after a while she heard sounds like the voices of children. She touched her husband, woke him up, and said, "Do you hear people talking outside?" He listened and then said, "Yes." The voice said, "I wonder why our mother does not come for water." The woman remembered the Loons. She arose and went out and saw the little Loons walking down toward the pond. She went down to the pond and there she saw the Loons playing in the water. They swam to her and she picked them up and carried them to her lodge. There the little Loons played about. After that the Loons would come every night and the woman would lie with one and the man would lie with the other. Early in the morning the Loons would wake up and make a noise, so that the man and the woman would wake up; then they would say, "It is morning; it is time for us to get up, for we must go down and take a swim in the water." Then the woman would get out from her bed and go down to the pond with them. The Loons would swim; then the woman would go back to the lodge and the Loons would follow.

One night while they were lying together the Loons spoke and said: "Father, you are now our father. This woman is our mother. She can not have any children during her lifetime, but we will give you and her power so that you can doctor the sick and make them well. They will give you many presents for doctoring them. We want you to follow us down into the pond. Let our mother stay here and you go with us." The woman remained in bed, while the man followed the Loons to the pond. The Loons struck the pond and made a great noise. The man, standing upon the bank, saw in the center of the pond something like sparks of fire coming up from the water. Then he heard a great noise. After a while he saw two kinds of water fowl swimming around in a circle and the two young Loons were in the lead. As they swam around the pond there were two big swans on each side of them, and they were flapping their wings on the top of the water, making a drumming sound. As the birds circled around, two little Ducks swam to the center of the pond and there they began to form a downy feather. First one of the Ducks placed a little downy feather in the center, and then the other one placed a downy feather upon it, and then they swam around the downy feather in the center and all at once it seemed to grow, and it began to change in appearance until it looked like an earth-lodge upon the pond. All at once the other fowls went to it and each took a piece of the downy feather. When everyone had taken a piece the downy feather was gone. Then all at once the noise of the fowls ceased and the fire died down. After a little while the young Loons came up and they said, "Father, let us now go home." They went to their grass-lodge and lay down. In the early morning the little Loons went down to the pond and swam around the pond until the woman went down, and then they followed her home.

For several years they lived at this place. The young man killed all kinds of game, so that they had plenty to eat. One day the Loons asked the woman, "Where are our people; where do they live; where do we come from?" The woman told the Loons that their home was far away. The Loons then said, "We wish to go to our people, for we want to be with them always. My father has been taught the mysteries of the water fowls, and so he shall start a medicine dance among his people." One of the Loons then told the man that he should go and try to capture ponies from the enemy. The man said that he would go. His wife made several pairs of moccasins for him, and then he started. Every day while he was gone the Loons would fly up in the sky to spy around, and then they would return and tell the woman that no enemies were in sight. One day the Boy-Loon told the woman that he was going to go and hunt for his father. The Loon flew up and was gone for several days. When it came it told the woman that her husband was coming with many ponies. In a few days the man came back with many ponies.

The Loons were anxious to go back to the people, and so they told the man and woman that they wanted to go back to their people. They started back to their village. The woman carried the Loons in her lap as she rode one of the ponies. For many, many days they traveled, and at last they came in sight of their village. The man looked down into the village from a high hill and he saw some one sitting upon the lodge of the chief. He called his wife to drive up the ponies and they went down into the village. The people were frightened, for they thought that they were enemies. It was four years since the man and the girl had run away from the village. When one man rode up and saw the woman coming with the Loons sitting in her lap, she told him that she was the girl who had disappeared many years ago. She said that she and the poor boy were coming. The man went back and told the people that the poor boy and the girl were coming; that they had with them two Loons and that he believed that they were wonderful. The poor man sent the woman to her father's lodge, while he went into the lodge of the chief's son. He gave several ponies to the chief's son, and told him that he had been to the wonderful land of Pahuk, and that the water fowls had given him and his wife two Loons. He said that he wanted to make a present of this Loon to the chief's son. The chief's son was glad, and he invited the man and the Loon to eat with him. The Loon walked through the village and the people laughed at it, for it was a strange sight to see a water fowl walking through a village. When they went into the lodge, the Loon was rather shy, but the chief's son was so good to it that the Loon sat by the chief's son. The poor boy went back to his wife's lodge and there he remained.

After a while the poor boy gathered a number of warriors and said, "We will go upon the war-path." A few young men joined, and they went. They found the camp of the enemy, captured many ponies and brought them home. The chief's boy seeing this, made up his mind that he would lead a war party, and he sent for the poor boy to assist, and so the poor boy and the chief's son led a war party together and they carried one of the Loons with them. The Loon guided them and protected them. They found an enemy's camp, attacked the village, killed several people, took some scalps, and captured many ponies and returned home victorious.

In a few days the chief's boy wanted to go again, and so another war party was formed. One night when they had been gone for several days the Loon was sitting at the foot of the bed of the wife of the poor boy. A young man from another lodge thought of the young man's wife. He thought to himself: "Her husband is gone far away. I shall go and lie with his wife and he will know nothing about it." He went into her lodge and crawled into her bed. She tried to make him leave, but he remained, and after she had consented he felt something at the foot of the bed and he kicked it and said, "What is this thing sitting here?" He kicked it and the Loon jumped from the bed and began to make a loud noise. The woman then scolded the young man and told him that he had done wrong, for he had hurt the Loon's feelings and that it might tell her husband. The young man jumped up and ran out of the lodge.

In a few days the war party returned without ponies. The warriors told how on a certain night the young man had jumped up and said, "Something has gone wrong; we must return to our village." When the young man returned he found that the Loon was sick. The young man remained near the Loon and cared for it, but it grew worse. The woman was scolded and was told to leave the lodge and never to return again. The young man every night when he lay down placed the Loon by the head of his bed. The Loon spoke to him and said: "Your wife allowed a man to come to her bed and let him stay with her. When the man was here he kicked me from the bed. I am very sorry. I am going to die. My spirit is broken, but when I am dead, take off my skin and throw the flesh into the waters. Keep the skin. My spirit shall remain with the skin and I shall be with your people and shall speak to you in dreams. My father, the poor boy, knows how they are to use me in the medicine-lodge. Do not destroy my skin." In a day or so afterwards the Loon died. The young man skinned the Loon and threw the flesh into the water, and hung the skin on a high pole. In a few days the other Loon died and it was also skinned.

In the summer time when the medicine-men had their ceremony the poor boy started the Loon Dance. The two Loons were carried by two errand men and all other animals followed—that is, each medicine-man who represented an animal followed. After the dance was over, the Loons were placed in a sacred bundle, and these were carried by warriors when upon the war-path. When the medicine-men had their ceremonies they took the Loons out and stood them in front of the medicine-men, remembering that those two Loons taught mysteries and the wonderful ways of the animals to the people. They also taught the people the use of the different roots and herbs for sickness. Thus the poor boy, through these Loons, became not only a warrior but a great medicine-man. A few years after the Loons had died the poor boy taught all that he knew to the son of the chief, for he was also broken in spirit. He finally died and all the mysteries of the medicine-man were left with the chief's son.

79. THE LIGHTNING'S MEDICINE CEREMONY.[1]

A long time ago the Kitkehahki had many ceremonies, but they did not have any medicine-men's ceremonies. In one of their villages on the Republican River was born a girl baby. She had a birthmark upon her forehead. Some said, "It is the picture of the Moon." Others said, "It is the picture of some Meteor or Star." As the child grew people noticed that her actions were peculiar. In the daytime she stayed in the lodge most of the time. At night she went outside and either stood near the entrance or went upon the top of the lodge. She always looked at something in the heavens and sometimes seemed to be counting the stars. Her mysterious ways surprised the people. Her aged father said, "Let the friends and relatives of this girl let her alone." She was given full freedom to run around through the timber or anywhere she wanted to go. When she became older her parents kept her inside the lodge.

In olden times it was customary for the old people to make for their daughters mats from rushes, and a pillow from the hide of a calf that was only a year old. The hair was left on the hide, and the pillow was sewed up with sinew and the hair of buffalo was put inside. Whenever there was a rainstorm the mats and pillows were rolled up and placed upon the beds. During the day they were used around the fireplace in the lodge. The old people made the mats and a pillow for the girl, who was growing into a beautiful young woman. The girl understood how to take care of her pillow and mats; also her buffalo robe.

One day when the people were sitting around the fireplace, all at once the girl jumped up and said, as she started to go outside, "Mother, I believe there is going to be a rainstorm." The men looked at one another. The women all said, "It will not rain, for it is clear; there are no clouds." As the girl was returning to the lodge it thundered. The girl then said:

[1] Told by Good-Food-in-Kettle, a Kitkehahki woman, who claims to be descended from the family mentioned in the story. This is considered one of the best of the Kitkehahki stories, and recounts the origin of a certain medicine ceremony. It especially taught the people that the stars in the heavens can send one of their number to the earth to teach their ways. The supposed meteor which struck the girl, as related in the tale, was found and was in the possession of the family for many years, but was lost.

"I knew it was going to rain. Do you all hear that?" The people arose and went out and stood facing the west, where great dark clouds were rolling. The girl did not go out, but sat down upon her pillow by the fireplace with bowed head. The people came in and began to roll up their mats. They spread them upon their willow beds and lay down under them, for they knew that the lodge was not well covered with grass and dirt, and that it would leak. The girl still sat by the fire. Once in a while her father would throw the mat back from his face and look at the girl. She sat with bowed head, now and then looking up at the hole in the top of the lodge where the lightning flashed repeatedly. After a while she arose and went out of the lodge, but soon she returned to her place by the fire. At last she pulled her mat over by the northwest post; then she placed her pillow by the post and lay down. The rain was now pouring down. The old man watched his daughter and saw that now and then she would stick her head out from the robe. As she stuck her head out the lightning flashed, and it thundered very sharply. Smoke filled the lodge. All the people were stunned.

When the father of the girl came to, he looked about and saw fire on the side of the lodge where the lightning had struck. He went to where his daughter lay, and saw smoke coming from her head through a round hole. He raised her head and saw that the pillow also had a round hole through it. He removed the pillow and there in the ground was another hole, and smoke was coming from it. The man then cried and said, "People, arise; my daughter has been killed by lightning." The people arose and gathered around the place, although they were afraid to go near a place where lightning had struck. The father began to dig into the ground where the lightning had struck, and kept on digging into the ground until he touched something with his fingers. He kept on digging until he dug the thing up. It was in the shape of a woman. It had a head, shoulders, and body, and was of many colors. The man showed the thing to the other people and he told his wife to get a piece of tanned buffalo hide. This was brought, and then the downy feathers were taken from the body of an eagle and they were placed at the altar. The father brought in some cedar limbs and placed them upon some live coals. He made tea from cedar nuts and poured the tea into a wooden bowl. A flint was placed in the wooden bowl, and the scent of the skunk was placed in the tea. The father then took some live coals and placed them by the wooden bowl; then he placed some cedar limbs upon the live coals. The people were then told to wash with the tea; then to place themselves over the burning cedar limbs, so that the smoke would pass over their bodies. Each person's face was smeared with the mud where the lightning struck the ground; then each went where the stone was placed and made a prayer. The father was the first to go to the stone. He spoke and said: "Father, yonder lies my daughter. You took her life. I will not cry, for in place of my beautiful daughter you came, and are now in her place in my heart. You are from the heavens and have taken my daughter. Keep the power that you had while you were in the heavens. Give me and teach me your powers, for from this time on you shall be my father." Then the man left and the other people came and talked to the stone. After all this the lodge was swept and the people washed themselves. After the lightning struck the girl the clouds disappeared and the sun shone brightly.

The next day the father invited his male relatives and told them that the lightning had struck his daughter. He told them that it was not a flint, but was an object the shape of a human body. The men sat around in a circle while the girl was laid out where she had been killed. The father told the other men that he did not know whether to take the stone and bury it with the girl or to keep it at the altar in the lodge. The pipe was filled and given to one of the men. The man lighted the pipe, then arose, walked to the stone, and blew a few whiffs to it and said: "Father, smoke; you shall be one of us; you have taken one of our daughters, but we know you are from the heavens and have great powers. You shall remain with us." After smoking, the man passed the pipe on. He then took the stone and passed it over the body of the girl; then placed it again in its place. Every time a pipe was smoked, the ashes were placed before the stone. After the smoking was over, each man reached and lifted the stone. Although it was small it was very heavy, and so they called it "iron stone."

The people began to make preparations to bury the girl. She was taken up on a high hill and a grave about two feet deep was dug. Two forks were set at the head and foot of the grave. A pole was then laid in the forks. Poles were then set upon each side and the girl was set inside. Grass was placed on each side, then dirt. The father talked to the people and said: "I do not mourn, for I believe that the gods in the heavens favored my girl and that they have taken her. Let us go home and think that the gods have taken her." The people all went home, but the father stayed around the grave and at last went to sleep.

In a dream he saw his daughter. She stood up and he saw a bright star upon her forehead. Her hair was plaited smoothly, and on the back of her head were eleven eagle feathers all strung together so that they looked like a moon. The girl spoke to her father and said: "My father, the gods have favored me; I am now staying by the moon. I am not among our people, but am among the gods. The stone in your lodge was a god, and was in the heavens. The lightning did not kill me; it was the stone that fell from the heavens. Stay not around this place longer, for I am to turn to stone and will not be able to hear you if you speak to me. Go home and make your bed on the north side of the stone. Let your pillow be near the stone, for it will speak to you when you are asleep. It is a god. When you speak to it, it will listen to you. The other gods will favor you in many things, for one of their number will be present with you."

The girl disappeared; then the father moved and opened his eyes, but for a long time could not see, for the light about the girl had dazzled his sight. At last he could see plainly, though it was night. He went home and told his wife that he had seen their daughter and that she had told him to lie by the stone. The woman said, "Husband, do what our daughter told you to do." The father made his bed by the stone and laid down. While he was asleep he saw in his dream a man standing at the head of his bed. This man said: "My son, I liked your daughter. I came to her and killed her. I lost my place in the heavens. I am now here with you. I am one of the gods. Keep me at the altar, and do not let people come around where I am; keep them away. Cover me with the hide of a buffalo; in front of me make a little hole, and in this hole pour water, so that you will have fresh mud to put upon my body. You see I have the soft downy feathers upon my head. You did right when you put downy feathers upon my head. See, my robe is turned with the hair outside; my face is daubed with mud; red paint is around my mouth. I hold in my right hand something like a gourd rattle; in my left I hold an eagle wing; you see I am a medicine-man. To-night I will tell you that I am not the Lightning; I am a god. Your daughter is gone. I now take her place, and I will from this time on teach you to be a medicine-man. I stood high up in the heavens. I know where the animals' lodges are, but these animals' lodges will be, after I have opened the entrance, in the earth. It will be through my power that you will understand all of these things."

The next day the father sat up, but neither ate nor drank water. He went out to the creek and took a bath; then he went into the lodge again and picked up some mud from the holy place. He laid his hands upon the stone and said: "My father, my heart is glad, for I saw you last night. This mud I put upon my head and face. I will now go out upon some high hill; there I will stand and fast. If it is your wish that I fast and mourn let me know while I am there." The father then went out of the lodge and went west. At the first hill he came to he stopped and began to cry; he stayed there until night, when he fell asleep. He dreamed that he saw the same man, and that this man told him not to mourn or fast; that some time in the future he would be told where to go and where to stay; that then the animals' lodge would be opened to him. The man did not stay upon the hill any more, but went home. He lay down by the altar and did not dream anything.

For several days he lay by the altar without dreaming. One rainy night the man lay down by the altar where the stone was, and while it rained and stormed he slept and dreamed that he saw a man who represented the stone, who told him that the time had come when he should go to a distant place where the animals' lodge was. The man awoke; the rainstorm had passed. The man went out and stood upon the lodge and cried.

He stayed upon the lodge until there was another rainstorm; again he dreamed, and this time he dreamed that he saw the strange man again, who said: "To-morrow you must leave the village. Go to the place that is known as Swimming-Mound upon the Republican River. Your people you shall take with you, and also the stone. When you have reached the mound, place the stone upon it; take your place upon the south side of the stone, facing north. Once in a while walk around the stone in a circle, so that the grass will be trampled down. You will stay upon the mound until a rainstorm shall come. When it thunders, watch upon the banks of the Republican River; wherever the lightning strikes upon the banks, there go. Carry the stone with you. There you will find a clump of trees upon the bank. There you will see that the lightning has struck many times. The dirt shall have been moved away, and there you will find a hole; crawl into this hole and place the stone at the entrance. Go through the entrance and you will find that it will become larger. As you go through the entrance you will notice that the passage will lead you under the Swimming-Mound. As you approach the animals' lodge you will hear all kinds of mysterious noises. You will hear the noise of rubbing on the sacred stick of the animals. When you hear this, sit down and you will see an animal coming from the animals' lodge. The animal will pass you and will go to the entrance. As the animal comes to the entrance and sees the stone, it will stop. It will then return, pass you, then enter the animals' lodge. The animals will then find a way to remove the stone from their lodge entrance. While they are meditating over this, appear. The animals will see you and will make a request of you to remove the stone. Tell the animals to give you their power; that you will then remove the stone. As you stand upon the hill, do not care for the mysterious voices that you will hear."

The man awoke. It was nearly morning. He took his pipe, filled it, and smoked. He gave a few whiffs to the stone, then laid the pipe down and laid his hands upon the stone and said: "Father, I dreamed about you. I saw you as a man. You have told me to go to the Swimming-Mound. May all that I saw in my dream come true, for as soon as the sun appears I shall move with my family to the Swimming-Mound. I will do as you have said. Father, take pity upon me." He then took his pipe and emptied the ashes by the stone. Then he rubbed his hands over it, saying, "Father, let all these things that I saw last night come true." Before the sun was up he roused the women and told them to cook some dried meat. The women began to cook, sitting on the east side of the lodge. The man sat on the west side with bowed head and with the robe wrapped around his legs. When all the people were seated around the fireplace the man spoke and said: "My kinfolk, make preparation to move away to the Swimming-Mound upon the Republican River. My father has spoken to me in a dream." The young men were told to go and drive the ponies from the hollow in the hills. After breakfast the women began to put their things into the cache hole near the entrance. Saddles were placed in the hole, having been made ready to be put upon the ponies. Nothing was said to any of the other people in the lodges. They put their saddles, their meat, corn, tipi, and everything they needed upon the ponies' backs. By daylight they started in a southwesterly direction.

For many days they journeyed until they came to the Republican River; then they followed up the river. When they came to the Swimming-Mound the man told the women to pitch their tipi in the river bottom. Then he took the stone, folded in his buffalo robe, and went to the mound. As he walked up he noticed that there was no wind, but as soon as he had made a place upon the hill for the stone the wind began to blow up on each side of the mound. The man thought that the mound was blowing its breath upon the stone. Then again he thought that the animals of the mound were sending the wind to blow off from the stone all smells of the people. The man then stood up, as he had been told to do. In the night he heard strange noises coming from the mound. It sounded like the rubbing of sticks, and drumming. The man had no fear. He stayed all night. By morning the wind ceased. He stayed upon the mound all day and neither ate nor drank.

The second night he again heard strange noises, and whistling. He soon heard what sounded like a strong wind. He looked, and there was a big drove of elk around the hill. He closed his eyes and said, "Father, shall I listen to these animals? Are they to give me power?" Then he began to cry. He fainted and fell. He saw a man stand by him. This man was painted with red paint. His head was decked with small downy feathers. He had in his right hand a whistle, made from a reed; he also had over his shoulders an elk skin, and he said: "My son, you see that I am a great man. All these Elks do what I say. Leave this place, for this is our home and we do not like your presence here. If you leave, I will give you this robe and whistle, and I will give you great power. This stone before you came from the heavens. Remove it also, for it draws lightning and will kill many of my people if left here." The man recovered and stood up again and cried. When the sun rose, the man saw the strange man standing in front of him, and he knew it was the Elk.

The man again stood all day on the mound and cried. By noon he saw many Eagles flying overhead. They lighted around him, and he saw another man with his head decked with soft downy feathers and his body covered with clay. The man said: "My son, leave this place. Take the stone with you and we will give you great power, for I control all of these birds that you see. This mound is our resting place. The stone resting there is from the heavens, and if it stays upon the mound there will be rain here all the time. Some of my birds will be killed." The man awoke and the birds disappeared. That night he stood by the stone. In the night the strange noises began again. The man seemed to hear people singing and making a noise like that of a flock of geese. Then he looked toward the river and saw fire coming up from it. As he stood and watched he thought he saw all kinds of fish, beaver, mink, and other animals swimming around. He seemed to know that these animals, too, wanted him to take away the stone. The man did not pay any attention to all this, but closed his eyes and began to cry the more. He did not look toward the river any more.

The next day as the sun rose he saw many colors. As the sun rose higher he saw these colors everywhere. He rubbed his eyes, then looked again and saw these colors. They were like many rainbows. Then he looked at the stone and said, "The same colors I see everywhere" (meaning the stone). All day there were many, many colors everywhere.

When night came the man began to get frightened. He began to tremble and think to himself: "What am I afraid of? I have been here all of this time. What can I be afraid of?" He was about to leave, when a green light seemed to shine from the stone. This attracted his attention. He looked at the stone and said: "Father, make me brave. Let me not leave you for fear of the animals." His fear went from him. He began to cry again, and while he cried he heard strange noises again. He did not pay any attention to them, but soon he heard a loud noise which seemed to come from the timbered country. He became scared and trembled. He thought, "Must I run?" Again he looked at the stone and he saw the green light, and again his fear went from him. He heard the noise again, and as it sounded louder and nearer he opened his eyes to see what the thing was that was making it. He thought that it was a white-legged horse. When he looked at the stone again, he saw that it gave a bright light. Then the noise stopped, and there stood before him a man. The light shone so brightly from the stone that he could see the man plainly. The strange man had a bear robe over his shoulder. Around his ankles were bears' claws. His face was painted red. From his mouth two tusks stuck out, and when the strange being breathed different colored dusts seemed to cover the stone; but the stone's light seemed to dispel the dust. The strange man then said: "My son, upon this mound is my lodge. I live here with many of my children. I go and kill all kinds of animals and people. You come here upon this mound with the stone, and I do not like it, for the stone is from the heavens. It will bring rain and lightning, and it will kill my children." The man closed his eyes and cried with a loud cry. The light went out. The strange man turned into a Bear and trotted away. The strange noise continued all night. The morning was cloudy. All day the clouds seemed to roll as if in madness. They rolled about in the heavens, but there was no lightning or thunder. The man thought that the time was near for it to thunder, and that his dream was to come true. So he took new courage.

Towards evening he looked and saw another, darker cloud coming from the west. He heard sharp thunders and saw lightning that seemed to be making its way to where he was standing. He heard drumming, the rubbing of sticks, the sound of geese, and the howling of coyotes and bears. The clouds from the west seemed to come rapidly, for he now heard thunder overhead. He tried to close his eyes, but the flashing of the lightning opened them. Soon the rain poured down. A noise went by the man that sounded like a hailstorm. Presently his eyes were opened by the lightning. Then it thundered. He thought he saw the lightning strike the ground, for there was fire and smoke upon the bank of the river. Again and again it lightened and struck at the same place. Soon the storm seemed to encircle the man and the lightning struck him down. The storm passed away, and the sky cleared; the man lay stunned. As he lay there he saw a man whom he knew to be the Stone-Man. The man said: "My son, all I have told you to do, you have done. The animals who dwell upon this mound wanted to scare you away. These animals have never been friendly with people, but they have delighted in killing and eating them. Now they shall talk to you in their lodge this very night, and they will give you great powers. Arise, take me and carry me to the place where I told you to see me. You know the place where the bank was struck many times by lightning. There the entrance to the animals' lodge has been opened to you. Go through the entrance to the animals' lodge and stay near the animals' lodge; they will call you themselves. They will ask you to remove me. Do not listen to them. When they have taught you all their secrets then you may come and pick me up and carry me back to your tipi. Place me outside at the west. Hang up the things that the animals shall have given you."

The man arose and walked to the bank of the river. There he saw where the lightning had struck the bank. He even saw a tree. He went to the tree and beyond there was a hole. He went into the hole, and at the very entrance smoothed a place with his right foot where he placed the stone. He then crawled into the hole for some distance, until it began to grow larger, so that he could stand up. He went on until he heard the noises of drumming and of many Geese. At last he came to where the animals were. He sat down. He heard great noises and saw a small animal coming from the lodge, which was lighted by a big fire. The animal came and passed him and he saw that it was a Mink. The Mink went on to the entrance. In a little while it came back and ran past the man. As soon as it went into the lodge the drumming and noises ceased. In a little while there was a great noise among the animals, but there was no drumming. The man hearing the noise of the animals became scared and lay low.

For some time the animals continued the noise, and when the noise ceased a man came forth, who, when he saw the man who had brought the stone to the entrance, sat up. He said to the stranger: "My brother, the animals have sent me to you. They want me to tell you that they want you to remove the stone at the entrance." The stranger said: "My brother, how did you get in here? Why are you here?" The animal man said: "I am a fire-maker for the animals. I do not care to be among our people any more. There is another man here who is also a fire-maker for the animals. Will you go away and remove the stone?" "No," said the stranger, "I will not remove the stone until the animals have taken pity upon me and given me the ceremony of the medicine-men." The man went back to the lodge and for a time there was silence in the lodge. Again the man came and said: "My brother, the animals have agreed to take pity upon you, for you can remove the stone. They are afraid to touch it. The stone is from the heavens, and the

animals are afraid of it.   Come in where the animals are and they will see
you.   When you go in you must cry and be meek.   Ask the animals to
help you and they will do so."   The stranger arose and went with the
messenger into the lodge.   All the animals arose and walked around the
fire.   Then all was dark and the man could not see what was going on.
When he could see he found himself lying on his back at the south
and inside of the lodge.   He arose and began to cry, and as he cried
he talked.   When he stopped crying he was told to stand west of the
fireplace.   He looked on the ground and saw several things that looked
like pieces of ice.   The man came and said: "These things were taken
from your stomach by the animals.   You will now take them into your
mouth.   As you receive them in your mouth stamp your feet, then they
will go down into your stomach again.   You are now to possess power
to mesmerize and to throw things into people's stomachs."   The man
took one of the things and put it into the stranger's mouth.   He
dropped one at a time into his mouth and told him to stamp his feet.
The man did so, and as each was dropped the thing seemed to melt away
in his mouth, and as he stamped his feet on the ground the thing disappeared and returned to his stomach.   When this was done the man at
the entrance told the stranger that he now had power the same as all of
the animals had.

The stranger was then given a seat near the entrance.   He looked
around and saw all kinds of animals sitting around the circle.   One of
the men at the entrance was a scalped man; the other who had talked to
the stranger gave him an account of his life.   He said: "In my youth
I knew nothing; my mind was not good and I used to run at random
through the village.   Once in a while I knew what I was doing, but one
time when I seemed to be out of my head some strange being came to me
in a snowstorm and led me away, and by some mysterious agency took
me into the animals' lodge.   The animals cared for me and cured me.
Before my birth my father killed a black-tail deer, so that when I was
born I always acted crazy.   Now that I am well I always want to stay
with the animals and wait upon them."   The strange man was kept
in the lodge for several nights and was taught sleight-of-hand performances.   He was told, among many other things, that when he should
build the animals' medicine-lodge he should kill several snipe and cranes
and take their skins to hang inside the lodge.

When the animals had taught him all of their powers they told him
that he must go out and bring in the stone.   The man went out and
brought in the stone and set it upon the west side of the lodge right in front
of the leading animals who were known as the Big-Medicine-Animals.

One by one the animals went to the stone and blew their breath upon it. The last to go was Skunk. Skunk said: "My son, I know lightning. I get my power from it. I can also make rainbows in the night." The Skunks gave the stranger power to cleanse people from the lightning shock.

After all the animals had given their breath, they said: "Take the stone with you. The power from the heavens and the animal power you shall have with you. This lodge shall be known as the Stone-Medicine-Lodge. When you decide to have the animals' ceremony and perform the mysterious rites of the animals' lodge, you shall set the stone in front of the altar. The other altar shall be of cottonwood and willows. Place the dead Beaver that we shall give you upon the second altar." The medicine-men's power to do sleight-of-hand and songs were taught the strange man. When the animals had finished teaching him he was told to go home and bring them some tobacco, a black silk handkerchief, and a shell. He was also told to take the stone with him to his home. He was given many animal skins and soft downy feathers. He took the stone and placed it into the feathers; then he was guided out of the lodge, and it was evening.

The man went on to find his camp. He could see clearly in the night. He came to his tipi and went in with the stone, which he set at the west side; then he hung his skins on the tipi poles above the stone. He lay down and went to sleep. In the morning one of the women arose and made a fire. She saw the things hanging upon the tipi poles, and also saw the stone and the man. She woke up some of the other women and pointed to where the man lay. The women were glad when they knew that he was back. They cooked some corn. They knew that the man would make an offering. He awoke and went out, taking with him his pipe and pouch. He went up on a high hill and filled his pipe, and said, "Now, Father Sun, you shall smoke." The man filled the pipe and held it in his hand until the sun came up in the east, then lighted the pipe. He drew a few whiffs, then held the pipe, stem towards the east, where the Sun was coming up, and said: "Father, smoke, and make true all these things that I have heard and seen. The heavens took my daughter. She is dead, but I think she now stands in the heavens as a star. Give me your power so that I may understand mysteries." He emptied the pipe and passed his hand over the pipestem, then made motions with his hand toward the Sun. He went home and took his seat by the stone and other sacred things. He again filled his pipe and smoked, giving a few whiffs to the stone, then a few whiffs to the things that were hung upon the pole.

The people lingered at Swimming-Mound for some time. The man disappeared nearly every day, and when he came home he brought roots and herbs. The man told the people not to pay any attention to him, for he would be taken care of by the animals. One day he went off and did not return for some time. When he did return he could not understand the people. He was under the influence of some mysterious power. When he went away the next day, the women watched him. They once saw him appear as a deer, then as a coyote, and again he flew like an eagle. They learned that by mysterious power he was guided to where there were herbs and roots which he dug up. For many days he was under this influence. When the man recovered, he said, "It is now time that we go to our people." The women brought their ponies and packed their things upon them; then they all started for their home in the east. Each night, after the people had pitched the tipi, the man placed the stone in the west and hung the things upon the pole. Then he sat down and smoked. After he had smoked and eaten, he sang songs that the women had never heard. He kept up the singing nearly all night. At last they came to the village.

The people were glad to see them and gave them many presents. In the night the man invited his male relatives and told them all that he had gone through, what he had seen in the animals' lodge and what powers he had received. The man told his friends that he came after presents and native tobacco. The men soon gathered the things and gave them to him. He thanked them and went out, leaving the lodge. For some time he did not come in. When he did return he told the people that the animals had received the presents and were glad to get the smoke. He then told his friends that he wanted them to help him to build a lodge that winter; and they agreed to build a medicine-man's lodge.

In the fall several men went and cut the forks for the circle in the lodge. All of the timber was cut and brought to the village and piled up. The women brought elm-bark strips to tie it with. These strips were tied and hung up to dry. Willows were also brought and piled up. The people all went hunting buffalo. While on the hunt, winter set in. The people were successful; they found many buffalo and brought much meat home. Then the man invited his male relatives to his lodge, where he taught them the songs of the medicine-men. The men liked the songs. The man told them about the lodge that they were to build, and the men looked forward to the time when they should build the lodge.

Early in the spring a place was selected in the center of the village for the new lodge. Ten forks were set in a circle to support the poles. The lodge was completed at about the same time the corn was planted.

The corn came up. The people began to get ready for a hunt. The old men held their bundle ceremonies to secure from the gods success in hunting. When the man heard that the chiefs had given orders for the people to get ready to go on the buffalo hunt, he sent for his relatives. When they were seated in the lodge he told them to kill several kinds of snipe and crane, for he wanted their skins. He also told them to kill many buffalo, so that much meat would be dried and used in his new ceremony. With these instructions in their minds the people went on the buffalo hunt. It was summer, and they did not go very far before they found many buffalo. Much buffalo meat was brought to the man's lodge.

In the night the man invited the chiefs and braves of the tribe, and when they were all seated he said: "We are seated in my lodge. The young men are roasting some ribs by the fire. What I have in my mind the chiefs and braves must know. My daughter was killed by the heavens, and the thing that killed her is here with us." The man rose and took up the stone and placed it in front of the chiefs and braves. "I have talked with this stone in my sleep for a long time, and now I have done all that it told me to do. I was placed upon Swimming-Mound and stayed there for several days. By the help of this stone I went into the animals' lodge. The animals taught me many wonderful things and also taught me their songs. They also told me to have sleight-of-hand performances in my lodge that you have helped me build. Now, my friends have killed many buffalo; you see the meat in front of my lodge. The meat will be jerked and dried, put in parfleches and kept for the sleight-of-hand performances which we shall have for our people. When we return to our village corn will be plentiful as well as meat. We shall have plenty to eat while we give the sleight-of-hand performances. I want the chiefs and braves to know that I will have something that will be new to our people." The chiefs and braves were glad to hear what the man had to say; they now knew why so many men took meat to this man's lodge. After they had eaten, they went home.

When all of the people had returned from the hunt to the village, preparation was made to have sleight-of-hand performances. The women went to their fields and gathered corn to cure, and fires were made everywhere to roast the corn. After the corn was cured the man sat down in his lodge. He sent for some of his relatives, from whom he selected two young men to act as errand men; the other men were seated. The two errand men were told to put their robes over their bodies, with the hair outside; then they were told to take eagle wings and brushes of wild sage and sweep out the lodge. When the lodge was swept out the man told the errand men to get some wild sage. They brought the wild sage and piled it up in the west, inside of the lodge. The man then placed the skin of a beaver upon the wild sage and put the stone in front of the beaver. The rest of the wild sage he spread around the circle of the lodge. Other men came in with the skins of birds. Two sticks, one of which extended from the head to the tail, and another which crossed the first stick and supported the wings, pierced the birds. The two sticks were bound at the crossing by means of a sinew string. The birds were hung up in the lodge; one was hung up in the west, another in the north, another in the east, and another in the south. There were other smaller species of snipe that hung around the lodge. There was something wonderful about these birds, as the medicine-men saw and heard afterwards.

The two errand men were told to get dry ash wood and four dry ash limbs. The first was a large timber, from which the bark was peeled and in which notches were made. The small limbs were shaved down smooth and were about the length of a man's arm. The pole with the notches was placed in front of the altar, and the sticks were placed across the pole. Old medicine-men also took part, so that there was a great company of men in the lodge. The medicine-men's wives brought in many kettles of corn. At each meal a parfleche was untied and dried meat placed by the fireplace to be cooked. Those of the medicine-men who had learned secrets of different animals or heavenly bodies, came into the lodge and begged that they be allowed to take part in the ceremonies. The man thanked them and told them to come and select their seats in the lodge.

When all things were completed the man placed two water drums in front of the altar. A procession was formed inside the lodge. The man then told the men that they were to go into the timber to cut young cottonwood trees and willows. The cottonwood trees were to stand one on the west side of the altar, one on the north side, and another on the south side, and two were to be set near the entrance. The willows were to be placed about inside of the lodge so that there would be little lodges around within the lodge; the other procession started toward the timber. As they went along the man yelled and grunted at them and threw them down. Sometimes when they arose, the men vomited corncobs; sometimes a piece of stick or a piece of root. They kept on going until they came to a creek. Then the man began to wave his eagle wing, and all the men ran into the water and began to swim. The man told them that they must wash clean, for they were to do many wonderful things, and that they must wash themselves every day. After they had washed, they went into the timber and cut two cottonwood trees which were to be carried by the two errand men.   The other two cottonwood trees were cut, and two other men were selected to carry them.   Willows were cut, and the other men, according to their places in the lodge, carried them.   The two errand men were placed in the lead; then followed the willow men; then, last of all, came the two men with the cottonwood trees.   The man then headed the procession.   As they neared the village the man began to wave his eagle wing and shout and grunt.   Every time he shouted and grunted the men fell to their knees.   This was to show the people that each man had power in his stomach that was being taken from him.   The man also did this to find out to what animal clan the men belonged; for the only time the people could tell what clan the men belonged to was when they were wounded, for then they would imitate the animal of the clan to which they belonged.

When they came to the lodge they stopped in front of it, and a song about entering the lodge was sung.   The march was resumed and they went four times around in a circle, then entered the lodge.   As they went in great noises went up, for as they circled around the fireplace each man imitated his kind of animal.   Four times they went around the fireplace, then the two errand men stopped, one on the north side and the other on the south side of the entrance.   The others went to their places under the willows.   The other two men stopped west of the lodge. At the altar sat only the four singers; the rest of the space was filled with willows which were so arranged inside the lodge that each animal group had a booth or lodge of its own.   Then the men went out after their animal skins, medicine, and paints.   Meat was served to the different men, and preparation was made for the rubbing which belongs to the powers of the stone and symbolizes several thunderings at one time. The next day each man was told to go out upon the hills to mourn, sleep, or do anything, then eat wild sage and take a swim; then rub the wild sage over his body.   They were neither to go home nor to touch a woman.

This new lodge of the medicine-man had not yet the cedar tree.   On the next day, when all the men got together, they sang, and in the night the owner sang.   At daylight the owner arose and called the other men to follow him, as many as wished to go with him.   They went far into the country and came to some cedars.   Those who followed were told to remain at a distance.   The owner went alone, while the other men sat down and waited.   After a time they thought they heard many cubs and they were about to run when they heard the man coming with the tree.   He did not let anyone go, for he wished to keep secret the way he got the cedar tree.   When the cedar tree was brought to the village there was great rejoicing.   The cedar tree stood on the south side of the lodge where the

Bear family was. This was the only cedar in the medicine-lodge. In the night the medicine-men did many wonderful things. The owner of the stone and ceremony was among the first who, through the powers of the stone, made lightning. The fire was put out, so that it was dark in the lodge. The medicine-men stood up on the west side of the fireplace; a dyed and tanned buffalo hide was waved through the air, and then the stone was waved by the owner in front of the hide, while several of the other men squirted water with their mouths upon the stone. In this way lightning was made. Others performed sleight-of-hand tricks.

The first night of the sleight-of-hand performances, the leader placed the water drums in front of the altar; then he spoke and said: "All put mud, downy feathers, and animal skins on your bodies. We want now to throw up the animal power from our insides. We want the people to see these powers." The owner and the three men ran around the fireplace, each taking up a handful of ashes and throwing them up to the four world-quarter gods. They stood in a line, and as each stamped with his feet he fell to the ground, face downward. The things called "powers" were seen sitting upon the ground. The men left them lying there and went and took their seats in the west. Now the drums were taken up and the men began to sing. Each man came out from his willow lodge and danced. When they stopped singing, all of the men fell to the ground and in a few minutes all was quiet.

As each man revived, he went and stood in front of his willow lodge. The owner told the errand man to place a wooden bowl of water west of the fireplace. The owner and the other three then went to the powers, which looked much like ice or glass. The owner was the first to pick up this. He held the power up with his thumb and finger so that the people could see it, then he dropped it into the water and lifted it to his mouth and swallowed it. He then stamped his feet on the ground and beat the sides of his body with his palms, then stood up straight and said, "Now, medicine-men, this power that I have within me I shall keep. I shall not throw it up any more." The other three men went through the same movements, which were then repeated by the other medicine-men.

Night after night they performed, until all the people became interested. Other medicine-men who had never before taken part came into the lodge and asked permission to take part in the ceremony. One night, just before they began their sleight-of-hand performances, a warrior of distinction walked in and stood in the lodge and said: "Medicine-men, I came to ask your permission to take part in your ceremonies. I wish to perform some sleight-of-hand tricks, and I wish these brother medicine-men to see me perform them." All of the medicine-men said: "Nawa, it is well. Let our brother come and play in this lodge." The warrior then said: "For three days I will make preparation, and the fourth night I will come and perform." The warrior then went out. He was known as a great warrior. He had gone into the enemy's country and had captured many ponies, for it was an easy thing for him to bring ponies home. His face was always painted red upon the forehead, and when he appeared at the medicine-lodge his mouth was daubed with clay, which extended toward his ears; and white clay was about his eyes. He had a little soft downy feather on top of his head, and a downy feather stuck in his scalp-lock. His hair was covered with white clay. He had a robe about his shoulders, and a belt with eagle legs filled with native tobacco about his waist; and he wore an otter collar with an ear of corn on it.

One day after going to the lodge, he went through the village and saw a boy who was very poor. He said to the boy: "Come with me to my lodge; I have something to say to you." The boy followed the warrior to his lodge, and when they were seated a bowl of soup with dried meat in it was placed before him and he was told to eat. The boy ate, for he was very hungry, and after he had eaten the warrior said: "Boy, I want your help. I am about to perform in the medicine-men's lodge. Will you help me and perform with me?" The boy arose, walked to the man, and passed his hands over the man's head and said: "You take pity upon me. I am poor, and I will do whatever you wish me to do." In the afternoon the two went off into the hills. They came to a high hill, and on the side of this hill they dug until they came to some sticky mud, which they took up and carried to the warrior's lodge. The next day the lodge was swept out. The boy was told to make mud ponies and to make them as nearly perfect as he could. He began to make the mud horses, and he made four, all of the same size and build. When the boy finished a pony he set it in the rays of the sun that came through the hole in the lodge.

On the fourth day, when he had completed the four ponies, they stood in the rays of the sun; and the boy sat by them, moving them as the rays of the sun moved around the lodge. The warrior told the boy that they were now to try the sleight-of-hand tricks. He sang and danced round. The magic worked and the warrior was satisfied. In the night they went to the lodge. The warrior, with the assistance of the boy, made the mud ponies walk around the lodge. The warrior sang, and every time he moved his robe the ponies trotted. When he stamped his feet the ponies stopped. The warrior was satisfied. The medicine-men wondered, for the warrior was not a medicine-man. The spectators were impressed and they gave many presents to the warrior. After the performance the warrior told the boy to gather up his ponies and to go with him. The boy gathered the ponies and placed them in his robe. They went out of the lodge toward the creek, and when they got to the creek the warrior told the boy to throw the ponies into the water. When the boy had thrown the ponies into the water, they went home. The warrior never after this was known to have a pony. His power went from him and he became a poor man. Whoever it was that had given him the power had become displeased with him for throwing the ponies into the creek. He should have stood the mud ponies upon dry land in some cave. This ceremony of sleight-of-hand performance lasted several days, but finally it was over. Ever after that the people made great preparation for this ceremony. The participants were known as "medicine-men," or "stone-medicine-men."

One summer the people went out hunting. The owner of the stone went and took the stone with him. It was now covered with skunk's hide, a handkerchief, calico, and cotton. The coverings were offerings the people had made to it. When they reached the head of the Republican River they were attacked on all sides by the enemy and were finally driven into a small ravine. One of them while out saw that all of his people were about to be killed, and rode east to the camp of the Potawatami. He went to their chief and told him that his people were surrounded by the enemy. The chief sent for the medicine-man and told him to select twenty young men, with their medicine-bags, and have them mounted on horses. The young men were selected and started. Soon they came to the place where the Pawnee were surrounded and were about to be killed. The twenty men rode in a line, and the enemy saw them coming and turned upon them. Ten Potawatami stepped forward and shot. Each shot brought down a man. The enemy rushed at them, but the other ten men went forward, took aim, and again each shot brought down a man. The other ten men had reloaded and they went forward, for the enemy had again made an attack. Again ten of the enemy were killed. The other ten went forward to meet the enemy. Finally they came to the dead bodies of the enemy. They took out their knives and cut out the hearts from the bodies and put them into their medicine-bags. Then they dipped blood and spread it upon their faces. They also rubbed some of the blood upon their guns. The enemy watched them and became scared. They let the Kitkehahki alone and turned upon the Potawatami, who kept making every shot count. Finally the enemy retreated. The Potawatami kept on after the enemy and saved what few Kitkehahki were left. The owner of the stone was alive. He went to the place where he had packed his pony to look for the bundle with the stone upon it. He could not find the bundle; it was lost. All the people who knew the Stone-Medicine-Men's ceremony have died and the ceremony no longer exists.

80. THE STONE-MAN MEDICINE-LODGE.[1]

Tirawa created a man and woman and put them upon the earth. They had two sons and many daughters. When they grew up each of the two sons took a wife. Then the old man, who was called by his children Man-from-the-East (Pitahauirat), said: "I have one lodge. We can not all live in this lodge. Let us make another lodge to the right, where my older son will live with his family. Then let us make another lodge to the left of us and there my younger son will live with his family. The tipi to my right, with all the other tipis which shall be placed about it in the future, shall be known as Leading-Village (Chaui); and the tipi to the left, with all other tipis that shall be placed about it in the future, shall be known as Small-Village (Kitkehahki). The old man taught his two sons the bundle ceremonies and gave them bundles that were something like the original bundles which he had kept. These bundles were known as Kawarakis.

The family of the son who placed his tipi to the right made its village somewhere near Nemaha, Nebraska. The other family went farther south and made their village near Little Nemaha, Nebraska. The other families stayed behind and they increased very rapidly. The old man said to his sons: "Your two lodges must face the west, as mine does. As your families increase, you must make more lodges and they must all face east." Again he spoke and said: "Your descendants, my oldest son, shall communicate with the animal gods. They will teach you the mysteries of the different herbs and roots that are under the ground. You shall be a great medicine-man. You, my younger son, shall understand the stones that are set in many places over the land. The stones will teach you their mysteries, their power, and their strength. My people who remain here with me shall know the sacred things that belong to Tirawa, and we shall be known as "Tirawa people."

The two sons went their ways, and the old man with his family remained where he was. The Kitkehahki went south; the Chaui went west; the Pitahauirat stayed east. The Pitahauirat were known to be a people who were favored by Tirawa. The Chaui were known to be a people watched over by the heavenly gods. The Kitkehahki people had many

[1] Told by Good-Food-in-Kettle, Kitkehahki. This tale, while recounting the origin of a certain medicine-lodge and certain migratory movements, is in part a hero story.

bundles. They understood the powers of the stones. They knew where there was a stone god, and this stone god used to talk with the people and made them famous among all other people. Among the Chaui there grew up a young man who disappeared, and when he came back he was a wonderful young man. Among the Pitahauirat was a man who acted curiously and had many names. They called him the Cheat-Coyote, or Crow-Feathers. He stole things from many people.

One time, when the three bands came together to make an offering of buffalo to the gods, Crow-Feathers saw Animal-Boy from the Chaui band. This young man was dressed in fine buckskin leggings and moccasins. Crow-Feathers wanted these clothes and determined to have them. One time Animal-Boy went out in the timber. He met Crow-Feathers, who dared him to turn into some kind of animal. The boy at first would not do anything, but finally consented. He took off his leggings and moccasins and arose and flew like an eagle. As he flew over Crow-Feathers' head, Crow-Feathers said: "Be an eagle always. Do not come down any more." The boy then flew around and around, but could not turn into human form again. Crow-Feathers took the leggings and moccasins and went home. The boy was missed, and after a long search he was given up for dead.

There was a poor man and woman who lived east of the village. They had no tipi, so they had to make a grass-lodge. As the woman gathered some grass, a bird of some kind flew downwards and fell into the bunch of grass. The old woman looked into the grass and there lay a baby boy. The woman ran and told her husband that she had a baby grandchild. The two wrapped the baby in old skins, but they were so poor that they had nothing to feed the child. They lay him by the fire. The next morning the child was larger. As days went by the child grew taller. In a few days he was of considerable size and ran around. One day he ran to the man and said: "Grandfather, make me a bow and four arrows, so that I may play with them." The old man made the bow and arrows and the boy went out to the timber to try and kill game. He could not kill anything with the little bow and arrows, so he told the old man to make him a larger bow and larger arrows. The man made them and gave them to the boy. Now the boy asked the old woman to make him a spider-web ring. The old woman cut up a piece of her robe and made the ring. The boy hung the ring outside the grass-lodge. The next day he arose early and played around the lodge, calling for his grandmother to awake and get the ring and roll it for him, so that he might shoot at it. "Well," said the old woman, "I will roll it." She rolled the ring inside the lodge, and the boy shot at it. The arrow went through the ring and the boy said: "Get your knife, grandfather, and skin the buffalo." When the old man looked at the place where the ring had been, there was a dead buffalo. The old man gave a grunt of satisfaction and began to skin the buffalo. He cut up the meat while the old woman laid the bones around the fire to roast.

They did not throw any of the meat away, for they were poor and hungry and had not had any meat for a long time. When the meat was gone, the boy asked the old woman to roll the ring, and he shot and killed another buffalo, and he continued to kill a buffalo every day, so that they had more meat than they needed. The old people recognized that the boy was wonderful, but none of the other people in the village paid any attention to him, for he continued to run about through the timber ragged and dirty. No one recognized him for the Animal-Boy who had disappeared some time before, but he was the same boy. When he had disappeared, the animals took him to their lodge and gave him great powers. Then he returned to the people as a poor boy.

Among the Kitkehahki was a man who had gone very far into the west, where he found a man of stone. This man of stone spoke to him and said: "You shall be called Stone-Man. You shall be a great warrior; arrows will not go through you." The man returned to his people, and he treated them so badly that they tried to kill him, but they could not. The people were hungry, for there was a certain animal that scared away the buffalo by its howling. This animal was known as the red fox. The chief gave out orders for his people to try and kill this fox. They tried in every way to kill it, or catch it, but they could not. The chief told the crier to go through the village and tell the men of the village that whoever would kill the red fox should marry his oldest daughter. The crier went through the village telling the people what the chief had said. The little boy at the old woman's, who was now called Belly-Boy, said: "Grandmother, I shall kill the red fox and I shall marry the chief's daughter." The old woman nearly cried. She laid her hands on the boy's head and said: "My poor boy thinks he is going to kill the red fox."

The boy prepared himself and went out. He wandered over the prairie until he came to some timber. There he found some men fixing timber to trap the red fox. Everywhere he went he found men fixing some kind of trap to catch the fox. Burnt-Belly went home, and said: "Grandmother, all the men are out fixing their traps to catch the red fox. Crow-Feathers is out and I know he is going to take my fox away again. I will make my trap near our place, so we can watch it. Go with me, grandmother, and cut a long elm pole. Then put a sinew string at the small end. Dig a hole and set the pole in it. Then make a kind of hole in the ground where the loop of the sinew string will be. Lay a piece of stick across, and place the bait on there. When the fox bites the bait it will get caught and will swing in the air." The old woman went out and fixed the trap as she had been directed by the boy. Then they went home. Burnt-Belly could not sleep, for he was thinking of his trap.

Early on the next morning he went to the trap and there was the fox. The fox swung up and down, so that the boy jumped around as he tried to pull it down. At last he caught the end of its tail and went up and down with the fox. Finally, the hairs came out of its tail and the boy fell to the ground. As he stood up, some one struck him on the side of the head and said: "Get out of my way! This is my red fox. I am going to kill it and take it to the chief's tipi, and I shall marry the chief's daughter." The boy looked at the hair in his hand and he found that he had the whole hide of the red fox. He was satisfied, and went home. The man who had struck him was Crow-Feathers. As Burnt-Belly entered the lodge of his grandmother he said: "Grandmother, I have here the red fox. Crow-Feathers tried to take it away from me, but I have it here." The old woman took the fox hide and hung it up on the grass-lodge.

Crow-Feathers took his fox home, and when the chief saw it he was glad, and gave his daughter to Crow-Feathers. The fox was tied to a long pole and the pole was set in the ground. Each day the people went to Crow-Feathers' tipi to see the fox. As the people came near the fox the hair came off from it, and it fell to the ground. The hairs were not red, but of a bluish color. The people said: "Why, the fox is not red." Still the buffalo did not come anywhere near the village, but the boy had his bow and arrows and ring. Each day his grandmother rolled the ring and he shot at it, and there would always be a buffalo lying in the place where the ring fell. The old man would skin the buffalo and the old woman would jerk it and dry it, throwing nothing away. Crow-Feathers was married to the chief's daughter. Everybody talked about it, for the people were hungry and they looked to Crow-Feathers to help them in some way.

One day Burnt-Belly said: "Grandmother, take a roll of pemmican and go and visit the chief's tipi. Sit down at the entrance and when you get tired, arise and drop the pemmican. The people will see it, and the chief will see it, and he will call you back. When he calls you back and wants to know what the thing is, tell him that it is a piece of fat, with which you grease the boy's eyes." Burnt-Belly went off, knowing that his grandmother would go to the chief's tipi. The old woman did as she was told, and when she dropped the pemmican, the people were astonished, for they did not think the old woman could afford to have any meat. When they called her back, she told them that the thing was fat to grease her grandchild's eyes with. "But," said the old woman, "if you want, you may grease your lips with it." The old woman went home. The chief had a younger daughter left, and he told the girl to follow the old woman home and see what she had at her house. The girl went, and peeped into the grass-lodge. She saw the real red fox hanging up on the side of the lodge, and it made the lodge red. She also noticed many parfleches filled with buffalo meat piled up around the lodge. The boy was sitting by the fire, warming his belly. The girl did not enter the lodge, but she went home.

When the old woman returned, the boy told her that the chief's younger daughter had been there to see him. The old woman nearly cried and said: "Why, my grandson, you must not think that you can marry the chief's daughter. I will go and see what the girl wanted." The old woman went out, and saw the girl just as she entered the village. When the old woman came in, the boy said: "Grandmother, I want you to take a parfleche and lay the red fox upon it and carry it to the tipi of the chief. Tell the chief that the poor boy sends the meat and the fox to him. Tell him that I want the younger daughter for my wife." The old woman went to the chief's tipi and set the meat and the fox in the entrance, at the same time saying: "My grandson sends these things to the chief. Let the chief hang them by the other fox, and let the people see them. Also let the chief gather his friends and feed them with this meat, and, as they eat, let them send for my grandson, and let my grandson sit by the chief's daughter, that they may eat together and become husband and wife."

The chief listened to the old woman's words and was glad. He sent for his friends and told them to look at the red fox. The people were astonished, for they saw that the lodge looked very red. The chief, after he had eaten some of the meat, said: "The poor boy shall sit by my daughter, and she shall be his wife. Send word to my son-in-law, that my new son-in-law may live in his tipi with him." The boy came and sat down by the girl. The chief spoke again and said: "My boy, this day you shall be my son-in-law. You shall live with my other son-in-law." That day the boy told the girl to go with him. They came to a pond. The boy washed and came out, a fine-looking young man. He had a cap made from woodpecker's feathers, and his robe had many stars upon it. They went home and entered the tipi of Crow-Feathers. They made their bed at the north side of the tipi, while Crow-Feathers had his bed in the south part of the tipi. In the night Crow-Feathers peeped, and he saw something strange happening. There seemed to be sparkling of fire going up from the robe of the young man. There was some kind of power upon the robe that made it look like many lights. The next morning Crow-Feathers saw that Burnt-Belly was handsome and dressed very fine. Crow-Feathers tried to imitate him in dress. His wife was mad at herself, for when Burnt-Belly first came to their tipi his wife asked her sister if she could pour some water into her bowl, so she could wash, and the sister refused. The next morning the older sister said: "You may take my bowl and let your husband wash his face in it." The younger girl refused and said: "I have my own bowl for my husband."

The next day Burnt-Belly went off through the timber and caught a woodpecker and took it home. The next morning he told his wife to follow him, for he was going to his grandmother's to eat. He placed the woodpecker upon the top of his head. As they went on, the woodpecker flopped its wings and whistled. Crow-Feathers saw that the boy had a woodpecker and so he went out into the timber and somehow he caught a woodpecker and took it home. In the night Crow-Feathers saw the sparkling upon the young man's robe. He grunted and with the branch of a tree he struck the bed of hot coals. Then he threw the coals upon his robe. Early in the morning he found that he had burnt his robe, but nevertheless he took the woodpecker and tied it upon the hair on top of his head and said to his wife: "Let us go out; the people ought to see my power." Crow-Feathers went out and the woodpecker began to peck his head. It pecked it until it began to bleed and the blood ran down his face. His wife ran up to him and said: "You are being hurt. Take the bird off and let it fly away." The girl took the bird off and it flew away.

One day Burnt-Belly told the chief to tell the crier to tell all the young men to tie their ponies close by, for some of them were to go out and look for buffalo. There was joy throughout the camp and the men staked out their ponies. Early in the morning there were several men selected to go out and look for buffalo. They were told to go to certain hills. They went to the hills, but they saw no buffalo, and so they came back. The young man then told the chief to tell the crier to go through the village and make known to the men that they were to go to a certain place, for the men had brought news that buffalo were sleeping in the valley. The men got upon their ponies and gathered at the chief's tipi. The chief led them out. Crow-Feathers was glad, for he went, while Burnt-Belly stayed home.

The men went out to the hills and when they were upon the hill the men who had gone out said: "It is here that we were and we saw no buffalo." While they were talking, Burnt-Belly came up. "Look," said he, "yonder in the valley you will see buffalo. Surround them and kill them." The men looked in the valley and there they saw the buffalo.

The chief divided the men so that some went on the west side and some went on the north side and some went on the south side and the others stayed where they were. As soon as the robe was thrown up in the air, the men rode towards the buffalo. The buffalo rose and ran, but the people came from all sides, so that the buffalo ran around in a circle, so that all, even those who had poor horses, got a chance to kill a buffalo. Crow-Feathers was among them. He found one buffalo, and he chased it around until at last he wounded it. It was then nearly dark. Finally he succeeded in killing the buffalo, and he found that it was a poor, thin bull, unfit to eat. Nevertheless, he was proud of his success. He skinned it and took the meat home. He felt very proud, for he thought that he had killed a buffalo, and that Burnt-Belly, being afoot, would not kill any. As soon as the people surrounded the buffalo, Burnt-Belly ran, and when he came to a fat cow he pulled its beard and then went on. From the sides of some he pulled hairs, and the hairs became hearts. From the beards of others he pulled hairs, and they became tongues. He came to one cow that was very fat. From its tail he pulled some hair and these became the whole buffalo.

The boy was first to get home. He told his wife to fix a place for him to put the meat. Branches of trees were spread out and the boy began to reach from under his robe and to take out meat, hearts, and tongues, and place them upon the branches. When he had taken out all, there was a large pile of very fine fat meat. In the night came Crow-Feathers. He began to take the meat off from his pony's back. As he entered the lodge he saw the boy's fine meat, and he asked the boy's wife where it came from. She said that her husband had brought it. "But," said Crow-Feathers, "how did he bring it?" His wife told him that the boy brought it in his robe. After this, Crow-Feathers tried to kill the boy, but the animals took care of him, and one morning Crow-Feathers was found dead in his bed.

The people then knew that the boy had wonderful powers, except one man, who was the Stone-Man. One day the girl went out to the creek for water, and on her return she found the Stone-Man waiting for her. She tried to pass him, but he would not let her pass. Stone-Man said: "If you will give me a drink from your bucket I will let you pass." "No," said the girl, "I can not let you drink from my bucket, for my husband will find it out." She said she would tell her husband, but Stone-Man said he did not care, and took the vessel from the girl's hand and drank from it. The girl went home and told her husband what the Stone-Man had done. The boy said: "I know that he is my enemy. He is going to try to starve all of us. I will go after him and see what I can do. I may kill him and I may not. He is a wonderful man. If he has animal power I will get the better of him."

The boy took his bow and arrows for the first time since his marriage. He went among the hills, and there sat the Stone-Man. As Burnt-Belly went near the Stone-Man he said: "My son, do not try to harm me." The boy took an arrow, put it upon the string, and shot at Stone-Man, but the arrow flew back; and every time the boy shot at the Stone-Man his arrow flew back. The boy went home. The animal power seemed to go from him and he was sad. Stone-Man also was sad. At last he made up his mind to live among the people. He had his tipi taken down, and packed up his ponies, and then he went west with his wife. He traveled far until he came to a hilly country where there were many stones. He found a round place where hot water bubbled up, and he lay down near this to rest. By his power he made the buffalo go west, so that the people could not get any meat. He and his wife went to work and made an earth-lodge. When the lodge was completed, he went out and brought into it a fine stone that he had found upon the hills. This stone he placed at the west, inside of the lodge. He went out every day, killed buffalo, and brought home the meat, and the woman jerked it and dried it. Out of the skins they made robes and parfleches, and the woman placed the dried meat in the parfleches, and tied them up. After a time a girl baby was born to them. The mother died, so that there was left only Stone-Man and his daughter.

Among the other people the wonderful boy lost his wife. She died, and then he went away from his people. The people became dissatisfied, for there were no buffalo in the country and they were hungry. The chief gave orders for the young men to travel through the country and see if they could find any buffalo. They went in pairs into different parts of the country. Two young men went directly west for many days. At last they could get no farther, for they had nothing to eat. They climbed to the top of a high hill, then they lay down and looked toward the west, and in the distance they saw an earth-lodge. They knew by the earth-lodge that whoever lived there must be a Pawnee. They arose and went towards the lodge. When they came near they lay down and waited until sunset; then they went to the lodge and listened. They heard a man talking. They knew that he belonged to their people and so they went in. As they were entering the lodge the man said: "My daughter,

some one is coming into our lodge. Sit up and we will see who it is."
At the entrance there appeared two men who looked very thin, for they
had had nothing to eat all the time they had been out. Stone-Man
greeted them with, "Nawa," and pointed to the side of the fire and told
them to be seated. After they were seated Stone-Man asked them many
questions, for he wanted to know what had become of Animal-Boy.
Stone-Man was told that Animal-Boy lost his wife and then disappeared.
Stone-Man uttered a grunt of satisfaction. He said: "Daughter, fix
something for these men to eat, for they have brought us news from our
people." The girl placed a pot upon the fire, then put some dried buffalo
meat in it. The men ate till they were filled; then they lay down by the
fire. While they were resting, they heard strange noises in the lodge,
and when they moved to find out what the noise was, Stone-Man spoke
up and told them to lie still and not move.

In the morning the two men were given something to eat; then Stone-
Man told the girl to give each a parfleche filled with dry meat. He
then said: "Now you must go to your people. Tell them I am here
and there are many buffalo here, and that I will give them something to
eat. Tell them that I have a lodge here and that I do not get hungry.
Now you may go." The young men put the meat upon their backs
and went home.

When they reached home, the young men told of the man in the west,
and of many buffalo near the earth-lodge. The chiefs met in council and
it was agreed to go to the place. Thus the Kitkehahki band went west,
and with them some Chaui. When they got to the lodge, Stone-Man
came out and told the people to make their camp south of the lodge.
Then he told all of the men to come to his lodge, to get some meat. The
girl brought the meat out and placed it on the ground. The men came,
and the chiefs and leaders divided the meat. Stone-Man was all the
time looking at the young men, for he wanted to select a husband for his
daughter. At last he saw a handsome young man. He made up his
mind to get the young man for his son-in-law.

The next day Stone-Man called all of the men to his lodge. When
the young man came, he said to the men: "I have a daughter. I want
this young man to marry her." The chief spoke up and said: "Leave
it to the young man; if he is willing, let him marry her." The girl was
standing outside of the earth-lodge. She was dressed in fine buckskins
and she had a yellow robe over her shoulders. The young man saw her
and he liked her. He stepped forward and said: "I will go to your
lodge, and I will do as you command me to do." Stone-Man said: "I
am satisfied. Now I give you a handful of buffalo. Go west and you

will find the buffalo." Stone-Man took the young man home and gave him a seat by the side of the girl in the lodge.

In the night, the three sat around the fireplace, and Stone-Man began to talk to the young man and tell him what was expected of him. The young man did not understand what he wanted and so he did not say anything. At last Stone-Man told the two to go to bed. When they lay down they had to lie still, for whenever the boy moved Stone-Man would grunt and say: "Why do you move? Lie still." They had to lie still all through the night. When the girl tried to tell the boy something, Stone-Man knew it. When he found out that the boy had no power of any kind, he said: "My son, although you lay by my daughter, you are not married to her. To-day we are to play the hoop game. We must play inside of the lodge." Now, at the south of the lodge it was dark and there was a hole from which a hot stream issued. No one knew what this was except Stone-Man. They began to play the game. The ring was rolled and the sticks were thrown. Every time that the young man threw his stick, Stone-Man began to grunt and tried to trip him. As they ran from north to south Stone-Man began to grunt, and when they came to the south end of the lodge he threw the boy into the hole. A few days afterwards Stone-Man again invited the men to his lodge. He selected another man to be his son-in-law. He treated this young man as he did the other one, and he, too, was thrown into the hole where the boiling water was. He did this to many other young men. Every time he took a son-in-law, he promised the people buffalo.

In his wanderings Animal-Boy was told by the animals where the people were and what was being done to the young men of the tribe. The animals promised the youth protection and they told him to go to his people. Animal-Boy traveled west until he found his people. Animal-Boy arrived just as the men were going into the lodge of Stone-Man, and so he went with them. He stood among the men, and when Stone-Man saw him, he said: "I want the young man with the woodpecker cap upon his head." The boy went with the Stone-Man, but first asked permission to take two of his errand men. Stone-Man gave him permission. As they entered the lodge, Stone-Man said: "My son, I want you to send one of your errand men to tell the chief that there will be many buffalo near the camp by daylight." Animal-Boy sent one of his men to the chief. The people were glad to hear it. In the night, when the people had all gone to bed, the girl said: "I think I know you. I hope you will kill my father, for he has killed many young men." Animal-Boy spoke and said: "I am afraid that I can not kill your father, but the animals are with me and with their help I may kill him." As the boy said this, Stone-Man grunted and said: "Do not stir or move, my children. Lie still. Do not talk."

The next day Animal-Boy went out with the men and killed a buffalo and brought in the meat. Stone-Man was angry and scolded Animal-Boy. In the night he said: "My son, you are not yet married to my daughter. If you will go and get me some plums, you may have my daughter." It was winter, and all the plums were gone. "The plums," said Stone-Man, "must be all whitish, and they must have no specks." The boy went to bed with the girl, and the girl tried to talk, but Stone-Man would say: "Daughter, do not move nor talk." In the morning the boy said: "My wife, your father asked for plums. I shall go and get them for him, for I want you to be my wife." The boy put his robe over his shoulders and started south. After he had gone a long distance he stopped and sang:

> My father, Grizzly Bear;
> My father, Cinnamon Bear;
> My father, White Bear;
> My father, Black Bear;
> Help me! Help me!
> I want some plums for my father-in-law.
> He thinks that I can not get them.
> Come, my fathers, help me!

The Grizzly came, but could not find any plums; the Cinnamon Bear came, but could not find any plums; the White Bear came, but could not find any plums; but when the Black Bear came, he said: "My son, I am from the south where the plums stay upon the trees nearly all winter. Do not cry; I will get the plums for you. Come, let us go where there is a plum bush." They went, and when they came to the side of a hill, they found a plum bush. The Black Bear went under the bush and growled. Then he said: "My son, spread your robe over the plum bushes. Now shake the bushes." The boy did as he was told. He heard something dropping upon the ground. He looked, and there under the bushes were many plums. He selected only those that had not specks or spots on them. The plums were made by magic power and so they were nearly all good. The boy took the plums home, gave them to his wife, and said: "Take these plums to your father. I hope that he will like them." The girl carried the plums to her father and gave them to him. Stone-Man was surprised, but as he picked them up one by one he said: "This one is no good; I can not eat it." He kept throwing them away until he did not have any left.

That night Stone-Man told Animal-Boy to get him some of the finest timber, with no crooks or knots in it, and to make him a fine bow and arrows out of it. Again the boy went out; this time to the southwest. He came to hilly country with swamps in the bottoms. There the boy cried and called upon the animal gods to help him to get the bow and arrows. The boy called upon the Mountain-Lion for the bow. The Mountain-Lion came and said: "Stop crying, my son; I have a bow here that is wonderful. The wood is imitation of ash. There is a long sinew on the back of the bow. It is not the sinew of buffalo. The sinew is from my tail. The bowstring is also sinew from my tail." The boy was glad to get the bow. Then he went to the bottoms and there he stood crying, "My father, listen to me. When I was among the animals, far away, the rushes, flag roots, and other weeds that grow in ponds promised me aid when I needed it. Have them give me arrows of different colors, four in number, and let them be straight." Some one close by him spoke and said: "Spread your robe upon the rushes. Shake the robe, then take the robe off and pull up four stems of rushes. Take them and put them inside your robe. Throw the robe four times upon the ground, then open the robe and you will find the arrows you are looking for." Although the boy could not see who it was speaking, he did as he was told. When he had thrown the robe four times upon the ground, he opened it and there were the four arrows. One arrow was red, one white, one yellow, one black, and they were all fine arrows The boy then went and stood among the rocks and stones. He began to cry again, and again he heard a voice that spoke to him and said: "Place the arrows in your robe, then pick up the finest stones you can find; place these stones with the arrows, roll up the robe, and throw them on the ground four times." The boy did as he was told. When he opened the robe, the arrows had the flint stones upon them. The boy was glad. He went home and gave the bow and arrows to his wife, and said: "Give these to your father." The girl gave the arrows to her father. Stone-Man said: "How crooked these arrows are; the bow is not a good one. I would like to have the finest feathers of swift hawks upon these arrows; and I would like to have the finest gray wolf for my quiver."

The next day the boy went out and cried. A swift hawk came and said: "My son, do not cry; we know what you want. See, a whole flock of swift hawks are flying overhead; they will drop you their finest feathers." When the boy looked up he saw many hawks flying overhead, and soon the feathers began to fall. The boy picked up the feathers and took them home. Again he went out and cried. A wolf came and said: "My son, we know what you want. See over yonder hill are coming wolves. I will give you four wolves, for your father-in-law wants four hides instead of one." The wolves came, and the four leading wolves were chosen. They stood side by side and the boy spread his robe over them and shook the robe. When the boy removed the robe, there were four wolf hides. The boy went home with the wolf hides. He gave the wolf hides and feathers to his wife and said: "Give these to your father." When Stone-Man received them, he said: "These are fine. This quiver, bow, and arrows shall be hung up in the southeast, inside the lodge. I want another quiver full of arrows and a bow, so that I can hang it up in the southwest of the lodge. Then I want another quiver to hang up in the northwest. Then I want another quiver to hang up in the northeast. Then I will be satisfied."

The boy took the errand man into the timber, and there they made the other bows and arrows. They took the bows and arrows to the lodge. When they came back they tanned the wolves' hides and made them into quivers. The quivers were then presented to Stone-Man, who was astonished. "Wonderful man! wonderful man! my son-in-law." Many other things he asked of the boy, but with the aid of the animals the boy supplied all of his demands.

At last, Stone-Man said: "My son, to-morrow we shall play the hoop game. We will see who wins. If you lose your life in the game, all the people shall turn into stone. If I lose, the spring in my lodge will bubble up, and the people will always remember that this was my home." Animal-Boy went out in the night and cried. The animals came to him, one by one, and promised him aid. The Otter came and gave the boy a piece of root, and said: "Keep this in your mouth, for Stone-Man will try to put you into the hole where the boiling water is." The boy went into the lodge and lay down. Stone-Man grunted and said: "Now, children, lie still and be good children; to-morrow we shall play with the sticks." The girl took courage and said: "I hope you will kill my father, for he is very bad; he has thrown many young men into that boiling water." The boy said nothing, but moved away from the girl.

The next day Stone-Man took the sticks and ring down. He laid the sticks in the south side in the lodge and called the boy. The boy went. They took up the sticks and Stone-Man picked up the ring. They ran towards the north. The ring was thrown, then the sticks. They picked up the sticks and again they ran, this time toward the hole of the boiling water. After they ran back and forth several times, Stone-Man grunted and pushed the boy towards the hole. When Stone-Man touched the boy and pushed him, the boy fell, struck the edge, and slid across the hole with the quickness of an otter. Several times Stone-Man pushed the boy, but he escaped every time. One time the boy turned into a real otter; then Stone-Man said: "I am beaten, so we will quit." They sat down and the girl gave them something to eat. In the night Stone-Man said: "The people shall live. I intended that they should all turn into stones. I would very much like to have you, my son-in-law, drive to me a four or five year old buffalo, so that I can chase it around my lodge, or let it chase me around my earth-lodge. I have four quivers and many arrows."

It was night, but the boy arose and went out of the lodge and went west. He came to the place where he thought the buffalo were. He stood up and cried, and said: "My father, I am in need of your help. This man who lives in the lodge wants me to drive him a buffalo that will fight with him." Then he cried again. The boy opened his eyes and there by him stood a man. His hair was long, his face was dirty, and he wore a robe that had horns upon it. The man said: "My son, I am the leader of all these Buffalo. The man who lives yonder is Stone-Man. I will take you where the stone is that gives him the power he possesses. Come with me." The boy followed the man and they came to a plateau. There, on the top, was a stone. "This is the stone," said the man. "Now take many hard stones and throw upon the top of this stone until you break off many small pieces. Then take more stones and throw them on the sides of the stone, and you will take the power from this stone and the man." The boy did as he was told, and it took him all night. "Now," the man said, "let us go back to where the Buffalo are, and we will select one for you to run to the lodge."

It was daylight when they reached the herd. The man uttered a loud cry, "Ho! Ho! Ho!" The Buffalo all stood up. They came and surrounded the boy and the man. A young Buffalo that was low and had thick wool all over it came up. "This," said the man, "is the Buffalo that you are to take. It has great powers; its horns are of flint, so that when it fights the man it will kill him. Follow it. It will lead you to the lodge. When the bull gets to knocking pieces of stone from the man, let your errand man pick them up and pound them to dust; then let your wife pick up the pieces of stone and throw them into the boiling water." The boy followed the Buffalo. Some time in the afternoon they reached the lodge. Stone-Man was sitting upon the lodge, watching the boy running the Buffalo. Stone-Man stood up and said to himself: "He is a wonderful young man; but I will kill him after I kill the Buffalo. He will never marry my daughter."

The Buffalo ran around the lodge and stood on the north side with its tongue out, as if it were winded. Stone-Man went down from the top of the lodge and went in. He took down one of the quivers, took the bow out, pulled the string, and found it all right. He ran out to the place where the Buffalo stood, grunting. The Buffalo ran and the man shot at it. Instead of the arrow going through, the point became entangled in the hair. Stone-Man shot at it many times, but did not kill it. He shot all of the arrows from the first quiver and then he told his daughter to bring the next quiver. He continued to shoot at the Buffalo, but could not kill it. He used all of the arrows from the second quiver; then he called for his daughter to bring him another quiver. This quiver did not have many arrows in it and they soon gave out. He called for the fourth quiver. This quiver contained the four arrows that were colored. They were not real arrows, for they were made of rushes. The Buffalo knew this, so it sat down with its tongue out. Stone-Man grunted and ran up to the Buffalo, but the Buffalo took no notice of him. He shot it, but the arrows had no effect. Stone-Man shot the last arrow; then he ran and passed the Buffalo. The Buffalo jumped up and hooked the Stone-Man, and a piece of stone fell from the man and went through the air whistling. The man kept grunting, and the Buffalo kept hooking him and knocking pieces off until it had Stone-Man down. The errand men of the young man came and threw rocks at the man until they shattered him in pieces. The girl came and picked up the pieces and threw them into the boiling lake. As soon as the pieces fell into the lake, the steam came out and filled the lodge and went out from the top of the lodge. These people ran to the camp.

They stayed there until the next morning; then they went back to the lodge and they found that it had turned into solid stone, but still retained the shape of an earth-lodge. This is why we have geysers in the west, hot boiling water coming out from the ground.

The young man took his wife home, and the people went back to the east and made a village somewhere upon the Republican River. The young man started the animals' lodge among the Kitkehahki, and performed many miracles. Even the woman, the Stone-Man's daughter, took part. She had men shoot her with spiked arrows, but they dropped from her body. In the ceremony of the medicine-men, the Animal-Boy would place at the foot of the altar a stone that was supposed to have dropped from the Stone-Man while the Buffalo was throwing him around. The daughter picked it up and kept it. This is the reason why the animals' lodge among the Kitkehahki was known as the Medicine-Stone-Man-Lodge, although the young man was the one who gave the animal ceremony to the Kitkehahki. This stone was kept by the descendants of these two people, Animal-Boy and Stone-Man's daughter.

One time the Sioux attacked the Kitkehahki while they were on a buffalo hunt. The Sioux ran these people into a ravine, and here the keeper dropped the stone, rather than have the enemy capture it.   The keeper was killed.   The stone was never found, but there were other men who had learned the ceremony, and to this day the ceremony is still kept up by the priests.   Songs are still sung about Animal-Boy—about his wanderings and his wonderful doings.   This boy died of old age and left many children who were taught the ceremony by their mother.

81. THE FOSSIL GIANT MEDICINE-LODGE.[1]

In olden times when the medicine-men began to have their performances there was a society known as Stone-Medicine-Men.   They began to get ready to have their ceremony.   These people were called Stone-Medicine-Men, for at the altar sat a large white stone, so it seemed to the people; but when I was taken into the lodge to be taught the mysteries of these medicine-men I found it different.   The old man to whom I gave presents, so that he would teach me, told me to sit down with him in one of the lodges of the animals—that is, inside of the earth-lodge.   He did this because he wanted me to hear the story which he had to tell about this stone which was placed at the altar.   The old man told me this:

Many, many years ago, when our people lived upon the Republican River, we used to go hunting in the western part of what is now Kansas.   Upon our journey on one of these hunts we stopped near a place where there was a big mound known as the Swimming-Mound.   Here one man went upon the hill and into the timber.   There he wandered until he became tired, when he lay down upon this high mound.   While asleep he saw a man standing near him.   The man was of large stature, and spoke to him in his dream and said: "My son, I have come to you.   Many of my people were drowned here in this place, and here our bones rest.   The people make light of our bones when they find them.   I will now tell you that when you find some of these old bones they have curative powers.   Upon the south side of the hill you will find a bone.   That is a bone of one of my thighs.   Take it, wrap it up, and my spirit will be with that bone and I will be with you and will give you great power."   The man awoke, looked around, but could see nobody.   Then he went to the side of the hill and there sticking out he found this supposed stone.   The man began to dig out the bone.   When he got the bone out it was the thigh bone of a giant.   Upon the bone were carvings of a woman and a man.   On one side was the carving of a skull, at another place bow and arrows, and

[1] Told by Young-Bull, Pitahauirat.   This tale is of what is commonly known as the Stone-Medicine, owing to the fact that the fossil used on the altar was believed by outsiders to be a large stone.   By the medicine-men themselves, however, it was regarded as the bone of a great giant.

around the thigh were several stars. Around the joint was carved the sun, and at another place the moon was carved. The man took the thigh bone home with him and placed it in a buffalo robe and hung it up in his tipi.

Once in a while the keeper of the thigh bone had a dream of this man, and it taught him how to hold the ceremony and where to place the bone. Sometimes when this man was asleep he would hear singing. Then somebody would say: "Listen carefully to the song which you hear, for they are your songs. You must learn them and sing them in your ceremonies." The man would listen, and after a while he got so that he could sing the songs himself. Several years afterwards he was told by the person he saw in the dream to have a ceremony. The man sat down in his lodge and invited several other medicine-men to sit down with him. He placed a young buffalo robe in front of the altar, and placed some calico upon the robe. He put the thigh bone upon the calico. When the other men entered, he seated them and began to sing about the thigh bone. Every time he mentioned the thigh bone in the song he spoke of it as a stone. The people began to call these people the Medicine-Stone-People.

When I approached the altar in one of the ceremonies to pray to it, I saw the pictures upon the thigh. I also found out that instead of a stone it was a bone which we had before us. The man who was the keeper of the thigh bone became a very great man. He never rode on horseback when upon the war-path, for he had the strength of a giant. He killed a buffalo with one shot from his bow and arrow and carried the meat upon his back. This man became a great medicine-man. In all his doctoring, instead of giving herbs and roots to the sick, he took the dust from the bone, gave it to the people, and it cured them. Many years ago the people were visited by a disease known as smallpox. It was very bad. All those people who went and touched the thigh bone did not get sick. All those who took sick and drank of tea made from the thigh bone became well. The people thought that this must be a wonderful stone, and they never knew what it was until some of the men gave it presents in order to come close to the owner and found out that it was a thigh bone instead of a stone. These medicine-men who belonged to this society have all died. There were no descendants, and the whole ceremony and everything connected with it are lost.

82. THE SQUASH MEDICINE.[1]

A long time ago, before ordinary people were placed on the earth, Tirawa put upon the earth a race of giants, who were given great power. These large people went out into the country and when they killed a buffalo they carried it easily. They were not afraid of wild animals, for they had great power. They were not afraid of the gods in the heavens, for they felt that they themselves had the same power. Early in the morning, when the sun rose in the east, these people would turn out and call the sun names and make fun of it. When they heard the thunder in the west they would call it names. They would turn their backs to the timber and show the utmost contempt for it. When Tirawa saw the people doing these things, and saw that he had not done right by making these large people, he said: "I shall now destroy them. They make fun of me, and they make fun of my minor gods. I have tried to punish them and I can not do it on account of the great power which I gave them. Although I shall destroy them, the earth will receive them and they shall turn into big roots, and when I have placed the smaller people on the earth they shall dig the roots and use them for sick people."

Then Tirawa sent the rain on the earth. The rain did not pour down very hard. The buffalo in the west seemed to have moved from its place and the waters broke through and everything was covered with water. There seemed to be more thunder and lightning from the heavens. Where the water rushed upon the land the people were washed away and were left on steep banks and other high places. Where the people were not destroyed they stood upon the land and the earth seemed to become soft and these people sank down. While they were sinking they were covered with lightning and clouds. This was done, because when they sank down into the earth some power should be left in them so that their remains would become medicine. The people who were washed away did not turn into roots, but their bodies were lodged in banks and other places. Tirawa promised that when the small people should be on the earth they should find these bones of the large people and that the bones should contain curative power for the sick.

Many years afterwards when the small people were put on the earth the Big-Black-Meteoric-Star came to a man in a vision and told him where to find the roots; that these roots should be dug up from the earth; that they were made from a large people who had been destroyed on account of their wickedness; that the roots should not be dug where they

---

[1] Told by Buffalo, Skidi. The tale explains the origin of certain root medicines which came from giants.

were very sensitive; that the roots contained power; that if dug, the odor of it would get onto the people and they would not like them on account of the odor, for it was something like that from a person's armpits. The Big-Black-Meteoric-Star explained all that had happened to the large people, and how they had turned into roots; that the roots were the large people who had been on the earth and had been destroyed; that before digging they must sing songs and give an offering of smoke from the pipe, so that they would not become angry at them and so that they could easily dig them. The songs were taught to the people by the Big-Black-Meteoric-Star. The smoke offering was also explained by the Star, who told the man to go and dig for roots; that in digging he must dig up the whole root; that it was in the shape of a human being; that if it was a man it would have a root upon it, but if it was a woman it would have none. The curative power of the root was also explained.

After the Big-Black-Meteoric Star had talked to this man about the root, it disappeared. The man knew that the root was one that the people were afraid of; that when they saw the vine, they moved away and would not go near on account of the odor which they might receive from it. Some had tried to dig the roots, but they had received the odor and would have nothing to do with them. They thought that the roots meant evil fortune to the people who received the odor. One day they saw the man who had had a vision sitting down near a plant. The people ran away from the place, and it happened that the people were making their camp close by. This man sat down near the root and began to sing songs. When the men in the camp heard the songs they knew that they were entirely new ones. Some of the men went and sat down near the man. After a while several men came and sat down with the man. The man then said to them that the Big-Black-Meteoric-Star had spoken to him. He told the people that he was going to dig the root; that he was told to dig it, as it had power to cure the sick. The other men were afraid, but when the man began to sing they knew that he must have learned the songs from some one other than a human being. After this man was through singing he filled his pipe and stood near the plant. He gave a whiff in the east to the Big-Black-Meteoric-Star. Then he knelt down and gave four whiffs to the place where the vines grew from the root. He said, "You, our father, our mother, I ask you to permit me to remove you from where you now stand." As he spoke he noticed water oozing from the top of the root. By this he knew that the root had given its consent to be removed. While he knelt, he said: "I thank you. I am to remove you, so that you may remain in the medicine-man's bundle, and I am to use you for the sick." When he saw the water coming from the top he remembered what the Big-Black-Meteoric-Star had told him; that if instead of the water coming out it had burst and air had escaped, he would know from that that the root was angry and that it was turning its odor upon the people. Then they must allow it to remain under the ground, for there was no use in digging it, as it would yield no curative powers.

When the Indians heard the man thanking the root, they all were thankful and they jumped up and went to where the man was kneeling. There they placed their hands near the root and all thanked it. After this the men sat in a circle west of the root. Women were sent for, and they came with their hoes. One of the women stood in the west, another in the south, another in the east, and another in the north. The man filled the pipe again and went to the woman in the west. He lighted the pipe, knelt down, and gave four whiffs to mother-earth, saying: "Mother-earth, we are about to dig into you. We do this to remove father or mother, whatever it may be, which is to remain in our medicine bundles. Allow us to remove it, for we do not want you to take any of the power which it contains. This root was one of your children. You received it when Tirawa destroyed it. You were good in receiving the root so that we may now take it, when you permit us, and use it among our sick people." The woman in the west began to dig; then the woman in the east; then the woman in the north; then the woman in the south. The west represented birth; the east, the power when they grow to be men and women; the north, chief or warrior; the south, the South Star, where they are received when they die. For a long time the women dug, until they finally came close to the root. As they took away the dirt from it they saw that the root was in human form. At last they took the whole root out and placed it on the west side of the hole. The women then put back the dirt into the hole and covered it. The man then arose, took the root and placed it in the center of the circle of men.

He then sat down, filled his pipe, lighted it, and gave a whiff to the east to the Big-Black-Meteoric-Star; then straight to heaven to Tirawa; then four whiffs in the west to the gods who sat there and who sent the rain-storms, thunder, and lightning upon the earth; then to mother-earth who received the giants after they were turned into roots. Then he knelt down by the root and gave four whiffs to the head; to the right arm one whiff and also to the left hand; then to the feet; then went back and gave one whiff upon the stomach upwards to the head. When he dumped the ashes he placed them at the feet of the root. Afterwards he passed his hands over the pipe-stem and said: "Father, you are now with us. The gods taught us how to remove you from the earth. The earth was willing for you to be removed. You let us know by the water from the top that you were willing to be removed. We removed you from the earth so that we might use you to heal the sick. We are not to place you near the sick. We are not to place you near the entrance of our lodges where people will step on you. We are to place you in our medicine bundles and we shall feel that your spirit and power is with us always. Take pity on us and help us to cure the sick." Then the man said, "Help me to carry this root into my tipi."

Word had been sent to his people that the root was to be brought to their tipi. The tipi had been swept out and new mats placed on the ground. The root was placed on the west side of the fireplace, and there the people sang songs. While they were singing, other medicine-men came in and sat in the lodge. When they were through singing the man filled his pipe again and gave a few whiffs to the Big-Black-Meteoric-Star, then one to the root, and gave a few whiffs to the head, and said: "I am now about to cut you up, so that these medicine-men who have entered may be allowed to break pieces off of you, so that they may have some in their bundles. Do not be angry because they are near me. Take pity on all of us and help to drive away diseases from the camp." Then the man sat down and said to the medicine-men: "From what part of the root do you wish a piece?" Some said they would take a piece from the arm; some said they would take it from the feet, ankles, or knees. The man himself took the part around the hips. He also had the chest, for nobody had chosen it. The man then said: "Now, the root is divided among us. Its power is with every medicine-man in the tipi. Let us think of it. Let us not treat it roughly, but hang it upon the wall where the children and the women will not touch it. Every night let us give it a few whiffs of smoke so that it may remember that we believe that it has wonderful power. Each of us will now go to our place and there pray to the root and put it away." All of the medicine-men left.

That night the man had a dream, and he saw a woman clothed with a black dress and covered with soft downy feathers. This woman had in her left hand a clam shell. In her right she held powdered root. She sang a song, then she took some of the root and dropped it into the clam shell, which contained water. Then she said: "When you are doctoring a sick person sing this song, hold the shell and the dust of the root; drop it into the shell; when you have finished singing give it to the patient and he will become well." When the man awoke he reached for his pipe, filled it, lighted, smoked, and said: "My mother, I shall do as you have told me in my dream. Let your spirit always be with me in my dreams, so that I may learn your powers, and I shall always be ready to offer you smoke in the night." So it was through the root and the songs he learned from the woman, who was none other than the root itself, that this man became a great medicine-man.

83. THE ORIGIN OF THE GEESE MEDICINE.[1]

A long time ago, when the Pawnee were living in Nebraska, there was a young man in the village who was very handsome. This young man had several ponies and joined many war parties. Whenever he returned to the village he would sit around at the place where they dipped water from the river so that he might see the girl he liked. Whenever the girl came she dipped her water and ran away from him. He determined that he would win the girl in some way, but that he would try to court other girls and in this way he would finally be able to marry the girl he loved. He would put on his robe and go through the village in the night. Whenever he saw a girl he would try to talk to her, but the girl would run away.

He did this for many years and at last he found out that the girls did not like him. He went to his home one night, sat down, filled his pipe, and smoked. While he was smoking he thought of all the young men in the village and how well they were liked by the girls. He determined to go and stay with a certain young man who was ugly in appearance but whom the girls liked.

That night the young man went to the tipi of the homely young man. He stayed with him for several nights, and one night while they were sitting and smoking the young man asked the homely young man how he managed to be liked by the girls of the village. The homely young man told him that he possessed a power given him by the antelope. The young man then begged the homely young man to let him know this secret. The homely young man told the boy that if he were in earnest he would take him to a certain place and leave him there alone. The young man then said he was willing to go with him. They got some meat and corn and went toward the Missouri River. There the homely young man tied the young man around the waist with a lariat rope and told him that he had to hang over a steep bank. The homely young man

[1] Told by Buffalo, Skidi. It is the belief of the informant that possibly this tale is the Arikara version of the origin of a medicine which corresponds to the Loon medicine of the Skidi. It is claimed that many years ago an Arikara woman who married into the Skidi was the owner of a medicine bundle which contained two geese, and that she brought the story with her. It is possible, however, that the story is a part of the Skidi mythology. Apart from the explanation afforded of a ceremony, the story teaches boys that no matter how good looking they may be, women would have nothing to do with them if they were proud. It also teaches the necessity of undergoing great hardship before admission may be gained to the medicine societies.

tied one end of the lariat rope to a tree, and said to the young man: "Now you are poor. Do not be angry. You must cry." The young man was put down over the bank, and the homely young man went off. The young man hung on the bank for several days. Every night he noticed fire in the water, which was caused by the animals that were swimming in the water.

The fourth night the young man fainted. When he regained consciousness he was in an animals' lodge. The animals spoke to him and said: "Young man, we have taken you in. We know that you are poor in heart. We know that the girls among your people dislike you. We also know that you went to a young man for help. The animal who took pity upon this homely young man was the Elk. The Elk has control of this lodge. It was the homely young man's place to come into this lodge, for he promised to come here, but you have taken his place. What we tell you, you must tell him." The animals began to tell him what he must do, and gave him great powers. The fifth night, just before dawn, the young man found himself lying upon the bank. He sat up; and while he was thinking of the time that he was in the animals' lodge, some one touched him on the shoulder. He turned around and looked and there stood the homely young man. The homely young man then said: "My brother, I have built a big fire, and I also have cooked some meat for you. Let us go and we will eat." They went to the fire and sat down and ate together. The young man then told the homely young man all that he had seen in the animals' lodge, and said: "All these things that I have learned belong to you. I will tell you all these things." The homely young man was glad, for the young man had been honest with him. When the young man told him these things, the homely young man told him that he was going to give him the power that he himself possessed.

They went home, and when they were seated in the homely young man's lodge he took down his sacred bundle, unwrapped it, and took therefrom a flute. He then took some red paint and a piece of root and four strings of elk hide, which he handed to the young man, saying: "These things are yours, my brother. When night comes, put the paint all over your body, take a little piece of this root and put it in your mouth. Then take this flute and go around the village and blow it. The women and girls will come to you. Be careful not to take any women who are married, or any young girls, for it will make trouble for you. Go now to your home and place these things in your lodge." But the young man said: "My brother, I will not go to my home. You are now my brother, and I wish to remain with you." The homely young man then said that it was well. When, after a while, the homely young man was gone, the young man put the paint upon his body, put the little root into his mouth, and then he went out and blew the flute around the village. The women came out, and he saw that they were not the ones that he wanted. That night he did not take any woman to his home, but went into the homely young man's lodge. The second night he painted and went again around the village with the flute, but did not take a woman home with him. The third night he did the same, but did not take any woman home with him.

The fourth night he went around and the girl whom he loved came. He did not notice her, but went on. She followed him into the lodge of the homely young man. Before daylight the young man tried to get the girl to go to her home, but she would not go. She stayed with him all day and the next night, and the homely young man came and said: "My brother, this girl's parents are looking for her. I am afraid they are going to make trouble for you. I told you not to take any young girl into your lodge." The young man said: "My brother, I am not going to give up this woman. I am going far away where I shall not be troubled." The young man left all of his things and told the young girl to go with him. They left the lodge and went toward the east. For many days they journeyed toward the east. The people found out that the young man was missing and they knew that he had taken the girl, so they hunted all over the country, but could not find them.

One day the young man and the girl came to a swampy country. As they were wading through the ponds the girl saw two young Geese in the water. She picked them up and said, "My husband, I wish to take these young Geese with us, and I shall call them my children." They went on, and when they had gone a certain distance the young man said, "We will rest here." They made a grass-lodge in the timber, and there they lived some time. Every day the girl would take her young Geese to the pond and let them swim around and eat; then take them back to their grass-lodge. The young man went out every day and killed deer and brought meat to their lodge. When they had much meat and the Geese were growing to be large, the girl told the young man that they had better go farther into the timber, for there were no large ponds near by and she was afraid that her Geese might stray away, for they were now very large. They left and went farther south. They came to a large tract of timber and there made another grass-lodge. The girl would stay with the Geese, while the young man would go hunting. The girl would talk to the Geese as if they were human beings.

In the winter time the girl would make moccasins for the Geese and they would walk around in them. She had planted the corn that they had taken with them, so that they had corn to eat as well as dried meat.

One day while the young man was gone, one of the Geese spoke and said, "My mother, why are we so far from everybody?" The woman replied that they had run away because they had been threatened with death. The Goose spoke to the girl and said, "Mother, you tell our father that we want him to go south, for there are many people, and he can capture ponies and we will watch over him and get him back to this place." When the boy came home she told him what the Goose had said. The young man then spoke and said that he would go, and the next day the young man went south. After about four days one of the Geese said: "Mother, I will follow our father and I will find out if he is well." The Goose followed him and was gone several days. One day the Goose came back and said: "My mother, our father is well. He is near the enemy's camp."

In a few days the Goose told the mother that he would go again and see where his father was. He again flew away and was gone for many days. One day he came back and said, "Mother, our father will be here in a few days with many ponies." The young man came back with many ponies. Then the Goose said, "Mother, tell our father that we must return to our people." The mother told the young man, and he said, "We will go." They started upon their journey. The Geese flew overhead, and when they saw any buffalo they came back and told the mother to tell the father to go out and kill the buffalo. The young man would go out on the pony and kill buffalo; then they would make their camp. The young man killed so many buffalo on the journey that they had much dry meat. The Geese flew on one day and came back and said, "Mother, we have seen our people's village." They went on and came to the village in the night. The young man made their tipi outside of the village.

In the morning the young man told his wife to cook meat. He went and invited the homely young man, who came, and the young man told the homely young man to go and invite as many people as he wanted. Among those invited was the father of the girl. When the people came into the tipi they saw the Geese sitting at the entrance. They ate much meat and returned to their homes, and said that the young man who had disappeared with the girl had come back with many ponies and much meat. They also told the people that they had two Geese with them who acted like people. The father of the young girl invited the young man to his tipi and told him not to think about the time that he was ready to take his life, for now he was glad that he had come back with his daughter as his wife.

The young man always had his tipi on the south side of the village, and always had the homely young man in his tipi. For many years they lived together, still keeping the Geese. Finally one of the Geese became sick and died. The other Goose spoke one day and said: "Mother, my brother is dead. I must now go to my people. You shall give birth to only two children, who shall both grow up to be men, though one shall die, while the other will live to be great." The Goose flew away and disappeared.

The young man was allowed to pitch his tipi among his people. In years afterward the girl gave birth to a boy, and years after she gave birth to another boy. These boys grew up until they were young men; then one of them became sick and died. The other became a great warrior and was known as a brave man among his people. The people tried to make him a chief, but he refused, telling them that he was only a medicine-man and not a chief. This young man started the Geese society among the Pawnee, and did many wonderful things. The father and mother both died of old age and the young man became the leading medicine-man. He had many children, and he also died of old age. The people said that it was through the power of the gods that he had lived so long.

84. THE WONDERFUL BOY WHO KILLED HIS FATHER.[1]

A long time ago while the Kitkehahki were upon the Republican River they gave many medicine-men's dances. They once had a ceremony of sleight-of-hand performances which lasted several months and many people from other bands came to see the ceremony. There was one who came from another land who did many wonderful things. The leading medicine-man went home one day and told his wife that he did not like to have the stranger perform, for he had done many wonderful things that his medicine-men could not do. While the leading medicine-man was talking, his fourteen-year-old son came up and sat down by him. The father told all the wonderful things that the stranger did. The boy did not say anything until his father left the lodge; then he said: "Mother, I want you to go to the field and find two squashes with long necks. I want you to help me perform in the medicine-men's lodge." The mother said: "My son, how can we do these things when your father has not said anything about the secret of their mysteries. I know that he has not taken you to the medicine-men's lodge, for you are too young." The boy said, "Come, mother, we will go together to the fields."

[1] Told by High-Eagle, Kitkehahki. The tale relates especially to the origin of certain sleight-of-hand performances and is told at the conclusion of the ceremony. The story also is told that the young men may strive to emulate the boy of the tale and so obtain the pity of the animals.

The two went to the fields where they came to a creek, and the boy told his mother to bathe. She went into the water and bathed. While she was bathing she heard the noise of a swan. She looked around and saw only her boy. The boy did some tricks that surprised his mother. He performed these tricks to let her know that he had some wonderful power. They left the creek and went into the field. They found the two squashes and took them home.

When they reached home the boy told his mother to enclose a place near the entrance in the medicine-lodge, so that people might not see him do things that he was about to do. The enclosure was made. The boy told his mother to bring in the squashes. The boy took his knife and cut both of them in two. He told his mother to take out all the seeds and to clean the inside nicely. As soon as the squashes were cleaned the boy placed in them soft downy swan feathers. He made some mysterious movements and put the squashes together so that they were solid. He then told his mother to take the seeds and bury them west of the village. The boy left the squashes in the enclosure and went away. In the night, when everybody had gone to witness the performances of the medicine-men, the boy and his mother performed several wonderful tricks in their own lodge. The mother saw her boy do these things and thought to herself, "When my husband sees these performances he will embrace his boy and will be glad."

The boy said, "Mother, we will now go to the medicine-lodge and do these things." They each took a squash and went to the medicine-lodge. Those who were looking on at the performances gave way to them and they entered the medicine-lodge. The boy stood up and said, "Medicine-men, help me; I want to perform a little." Everybody was glad, even the boy's father, though he thought the boy would fail, for he had not given him any power. The medicine-men arose and stood around the boy and his mother. The boy began to sing. He ran to the crowd of spectators and invited anyone who would, to assist him. Two young men came forward. They were given knives, and with these knives cut the squashes in two. When the squashes were opened they found soft downy feathers in them instead of seeds. The boy then took the squashes, put them together, and they were solid again. He thanked the two young men and said, "Help me once more." The mother went and brought in a bowl of water. The boy began to sing. His mother placed the squashes upon the ground. As he sang he ran around the fireplace, took a mouthful of water from the bowl, then went where the squashes lay and sprinkled them. He continued to do this until there was a pool of water. The boy now ran around and started off, and the two squashes began to make a noise like swans. They were swans and they followed the boy. After a time the boy went up to them, laid his hands upon their necks and caught them, and they were squashes again. He picked them up and gave them to his mother. They went out of the lodge and went home.

There was rejoicing in the lodge. The medicine-men thought that the father must have taught the boy how to do the wonderful things, but it was not so. The only man who did not seem to take pleasure in the boy's performances was his father, who with bowed head sat in the west. He thought within himself: "I thought the stranger very wonderful, but now my son comes, a mere child, and he performs greater things, and the things he does are not mine, and I have no knowledge of them." Next day the boy and his mother took the squashes and dumped them into the creek. People told throughout the village the wonderful things that the boy had done. Nearly every day they talked about the boy. His father hastened the ceremony of the medicine-lodge to a close, for he did not feel right in his mind.

The ceremony was over. An old man cried through the village, telling the people to store away their corn and other things and to get ready to go on a buffalo hunt. The people began to dig cache holes; others, who had them, cleaned them out. All this time the leading medicine-man never spoke to his son nor asked him to come near him. On the buffalo hunt he began to speak to the boy and called on him to help.

One time when they were surrounding buffalo, the medicine-man told his son to stay by him and to follow him if he should run after a buffalo cow. When the run was made the boy watched his father, and when he saw him running after a buffalo cow that seemed to be getting away from him he followed, until they had gone away out among the hills by themselves. The father then whipped up his pony and soon overtook the cow. He shot at it and it fell into a ravine. The boy caught up and they began to skin the buffalo. The father looked up and said, "My son, I must go up on the hill and look around, for we are in the enemy's country and they may be coming." The father climbed the hill, and as he went he thought of the wonderful things that the boy had done in his medicine-lodge and his heart was filled with envy. He reached the top of the hill, then turned and looked at his son for a moment, and then shot an arrow at him. The boy turned and started to run, but when he saw that it was his own father who had shot him, he fell to the ground and died. The man went to his son and made sure that he was dead. He picked him up and threw him into a tributary of the Republican River. He went back to the buffalo, cut the meat, packed the pony, and went home. He turned the boy's pony loose. The man reached home in the night and at once inquired for his son and was told that the boy had not come home. A crier was sent through the camp to ask if anyone had seen the boy. No one had seen him. Some people said: "We saw him follow his father." A search was made, but the boy was not found.

The man mourned for his son and pretended that he had met death by being thrown from his pony. Some men went and hunted over the ground where they had surrounded the buffalo. They did not find the boy and so they all gave him up for dead.

On the night of their return to their permanent village the boy returned to his mother. He woke her up and told her to keep still and give no alarm; that he would stay with other people for a few days and then send for her. The mother felt of her boy and she was sure he was alive. The boy went to his uncle's lodge and there he stayed. In the morning his uncle saw him and was glad. It was noised through the village that the boy had returned. His father heard of it and sent for him, but the boy would not go to him. Again his father sent for him and offered him all his medicine bundles, but still the boy would not go to him. The father tried to get his wife to help him get his boy back, but the woman would not do anything, for she now suspected that her husband had killed their own child.

The boy sent for his mother. His mother went, and the boy said, "Mother, do you want me to tell you where I have been?" She said, "Yes, tell me all about it." The boy said, "Mother, father and I ran after a buffalo cow, and I caught up with him as he killed it. After we had begun to skin it my father went up on the hill to look around for the enemy. The next thing I knew an arrow had gone through my body. I looked around, and there was my father. I fell over and died. Later I found myself in the animals' lodge at Swimming-Mound, for our swans had taken me there. The animals took pity upon me and brought me to life. Here are the scars upon my body where the arrow went through. The animals kept the arrow. They told me to come home. I want to kill my father." The woman said, "Kill him, for he did wrong."

The boy took from his bundle a bone from the sunfish, placed it in the palm of his left hand and blew his breath upon it, and the bone was gone. The boy said: "Mother, father is struggling, for I sent that bone straight to his heart. Go now, mother, for he is dead. I will come home when he is buried." The man died, and everybody said the boy was right. The boy grew up and was a great medicine-man. He told of the animals' lodge at Swimming-Mound. Men used to go there and cry, but they were never received by the animals.

85. THE MEDICINE-MAN WHO KILLED HIS SON.[1]

A long time ago the Pawnee held their medicine-lodge ceremonies and performed sleight-of-hand. While they were performing a ceremony the wife of the leader of the medicine-men spoke to her son, who was now about thirteen years old. She said: "My son, it is now time that you were in the medicine-lodge where all these acts are being carried on. Go to the medicine-lodge. When you have entered, walk up to your father, place your hands upon his head, pass them down over his body, speak and say, 'My father, I want you to take pity on me. I want you to accept me in this lodge. I have one pony and I now give it to you.'" The boy went to his father and did as his mother had told him, but his father refused him, and would not admit him into the lodge. The boy went back and told his mother that his father had refused him. The mother did not know what to make of it. She said: "Take these presents to your father, place them before him and tell him that you want him to take pity on you." The boy went, but the father again refused. The boy returned to his mother and told her what his father had done. Then the woman said: "Once more you shall go. Take this pipe filled with native tobacco, place it in his hands, and tell him that you wish to become a member of the medicine-lodge." The boy went into the lodge and placed the pipe in his father's hands, but his father refused to light the pipe and returned it to the boy. The boy went home and told his mother that his father had refused. The mother then said: "It is strange that your own father should do this. He is the leader of all the medicine-men and he rejects you. You shall go to him for the last time. Take this vessel of corn which I have boiled, and this dried meat into the lodge. When he sees this surely he can not refuse." The boy took the corn into the medicine-lodge. He again went with the dried meat and put it in front of his father. His father still rejected him. The boy went home to his mother. As he sat in his mother's lap he cried and said: "Mother, I do not see how I can meet my father when these ceremonies are over. I can not understand why he refuses me." Then the mother said: "Boy, you must not cry. Your father is not the only medicine-man. My father was also a leader in a medicine ceremony. To-day, for the first time, your father shall know that I understand some of the mysteries of your grandfather."

The woman took her sacred bundle, untied it, and took therefrom a skirt which had been dyed black. Upon this skirt were scattered soft

[1] Told by White-Horse, Pitahauirat. This story may be regarded as the Pitahauirat version of the preceding tale. The story teaches that the father should not refuse to admit his own son to his medicine ceremony.

downy feathers. She also took therefrom a buffalo hair robe, which was also covered with soft downy feathers. She unbraided her hair. She took from the bundle a ball of mud. This she spread all over herself. Then she spread some of it all over the boy. She took a buffalo robe from the bundle and placed it on the boy's shoulders. She then took her own robe and put it upon her shoulders. Then she tied up the bundle and put it away. She took the boy by the hand and they went to the medicine-lodge. As they entered the lodge, and the woman's husband saw them, he bowed his head instead of looking up, and never said a word. The woman and the boy seated themselves on the north side near the entrance. Other medicine-men gave them this place. In the afternoon, when the grand procession of medicine-men was about ready, she daubed the boy with mud and downy feathers. She went to her tipi, opened her bundle, and took from it two gourds with round necks. These she took into the lodge. When everybody had marched out, the woman began to sing about the diving ducks. The boy was imitating the ducks. They marched outside in a circle four times and then entered the lodge. The medicine-men were surprised at the way in which the woman was carrying on, for she was the wife of the leading medicine-man, and these songs which she was singing were not the songs of any of the men who were within the lodge. After the performance was over the woman was told that if she wanted to do sleight-of-hand performances, she could do so that night. She told them that she was not going to do any sleight-of-hand performances at night. She said she wanted to do it in the daytime and that she wanted to do it the next day at noon.

That night the medicine-men began to do their sleight-of-hand performance and kept it up until daylight. The woman asked the medicine-men all to join in and help her. Her husband would not have anything to do with her. He tried to discourage the others from doing anything, for he did not know that the woman understood any of these performances. When all the other medicine-men agreed to help the woman she told them that she wanted them to march down to the creek. She and the boy were in the lead, and the medicine-men followed, singing for them. They arrived at the creek. The woman jumped in with the gourds in her hand and held the gourds under the water. Then she brought them up from the water and the gourds had turned into soft downy feathers. She turned them loose and the soft downy feathers drifted down the stream. She waved her hands at the downy feathers and they turned back and came upstream to where she was. Then she took hold of them, pulled them down under the water, and when she took them out they were gourds again. The people were shouting, for they were glad to see this woman perform when her husband had refused to aid his boy. The boy was now given the gourds. Then the woman began to sing and the men helped her. The boy was told to jump into the water with a gourd in each hand. When he jumped in he waved the gourds under the water and his mother told him to release them. The boy released them under the water, and after a while they came up and there were two ducks instead of the gourds. They swam around in the water, and after a while they returned to the boy, who caught them, and they turned again into gourds. When the boy came out from the water with the gourds the medicine-men were so glad that this had happened, that they began to mesmerize one another. They began to mesmerize the woman, but she had too much power for the men. When the medicine-men went into the lodge they told what the woman and the boy had done. The boy's father was still sitting in his place with his head bowed, for he was angry. He could do many things, but none which could equal that of turning gourds into ducks. He was jealous.

The medicine-men often spoke of the power of this woman and her child. Wherever the husband went after that the people spoke of his wife and boy as being wonderful. People thought they were doing a good act for him, but they were not, for the man was angry with the woman and her son. After the performance of the woman and the boy they returned home. They never went to the medicine-lodge again. After the ceremony was finished, people began to make preparation to go hunting. They surrounded the buffalo several times. Once when they surrounded the buffalo the medicine-man took his son with him. They went far from the other people. After they had left the others far behind, the man turned to his son and said, "So you and your mother will outdo me in sleight-of-hand performances." He took his bow and arrow, shot the boy in the side, and threw him into the river. Then the man went home.

When he arrived at his home his wife said, "Where is my son?" The man said that he did not know. Then the woman and the man went through the village hunting for their son. As the boy was not found the woman began to mourn. The father also began to cry. From that time on the boy was dead to them. Many years afterwards the boy's father married another woman and no longer lived with his first wife, the mother of the boy.

After the boy was thrown into the river the water took the boy's body downstream until it came to an animals' lodge. Here the body was stopped, but the animals said: "It is not our place to touch him. If we are to bring the boy back to life he must be taken to Pahuk."

The boy drifted downstream. On the one side was the Beaver, and the Otter on the other side, the Mink heading the procession. Other animals swam behind the body. They came to Pahuk and the boy was taken in. He was placed upon the ground in the lodge. The arrow was taken out, and the boy was brought to life through the powers of the Beaver and the Otter. Then the animals said: "We know he killed you, but we wish you to return to your people. You must go back to your people now and tell them that we want native tobacco, eagle feathers, blue beads, and sweet-smelling grass."

The boy went home to his lodge and there he found his mother. He woke her up and said, "Mother, I am here." The mother got up, cried, and said, "And this is the way my son used to do when he was living and now he comes to me always only in dreams." He said: "No, mother, it is true. I am here. Do not make a noise. Go to my relatives and tell them I am here and I want native tobacco, eagle feathers, blue beads, and sweet-smelling grass." The mother touched her boy, made a fire, seated him, and then went through the village. The people opened their sacred bundles to get the blue beads and other things which the boy wanted. These things were brought to the boy and placed before him. Then the boy thanked them and said: "My relatives, I go from you. You shall see me again." The boy left and was not heard of again for some time.

One night he came back into the lodge and awoke his mother and said, "Mother, I am here." She got up, caught him, and made a fire. People knew that he had come back. For some time the boy remained with his mother. The father would come and visit them, but the boy never had much to do with him.

One night the boy sat down with his mother before his sacred bundle, where he kept the things which had been given him by the animals. He said, "Mother, I will now tell you my story. Mother, my father shot me with one of his arrows and killed me. If he had left me upon dry land I should have died, but he picked me up, carried me to a stream of water, threw me in, and said, 'Animals under the water, I give you this boy for you to eat.' The animals took pity on me. If you want father to live he shall live. If you think he ought to die because he did me wrong, then take this little water-dog down to the stream, dip it into the water, and if when you take it out there is a little piece of liver in its mouth, you will know that the people down at Pahuk have eaten up the insides of my father. If you dip this little animal's nose into the water and there is no liver, then you may know that what I tell you is not true."

The woman took the little animal and went down to the stream of water. She dipped the animal's nose into the water, and when she took it up she saw a little piece of liver in its mouth. She could see the water heave, for the animals were in the water moving around. When the water was stirred the woman could see pieces of entrails in the water, and also blood. She went back to the village into her lodge. The boy took the animal and placed it near the fireplace, gave it some smoke and tobacco, and then put it back in the bundle. After that the boy became the leader of the medicine-lodge and taught the people what the animals had taught him and not what his father had taught him. The people knew that the boy was a wonderful boy and that he had been taken into the animals' lodge at Pahuk.

86. THE CHIEF'S SON WHO RECEIVED THE ANIMAL POWER.[1]

A long time ago the people had their village upon the Republican River. In the village was a fine-looking young man who was a son of the chief. The young man was very kind and was good to everybody. There was a man who became very fond of the chief's son and one day he came to him and said, "I would like to talk with you and take you to a far-away country." The boy, suspecting nothing, promised to go with the man, and so they prepared for their journey and started. They traveled for many days until at last they came to a place known as Pahuk. They went to a steep bank and sat down. The man began to tell the boy that there had been stories told about this wonderful place, and that he had brought him there because he wanted to tie a rope around his waist and let him down over the steep bank to pick up some eagle and wood-pecker's feathers which were upon the bank. The man put a lariat around the boy's waist and let him down the steep bank. When the boy reached the bank he began to pick up the feathers. He then looked up to tell the man to pull him up, but the man was not there and there were no signs of him. The boy cried for help, for he was in trouble. On the journey he had become pregnant, and gradually grew larger all the time until, when he was upon the bank, he knew that he was about to give birth. Then he cried and yelled and called to the man to pull him up, but the man had run away and left the boy hanging on the side of the steep bank so that he would die. The boy cried until he was exhausted and then he went to sleep.

[1] Told by White-Sun, Kitkehahki. The story teaches that it is impossible to deceive the animals. Especially does it illustrate the dire consequences befalling one who betrays a friend.

The animals came out from under the bank and found the boy. When they saw him they said, "Let us take pity on him," and they carried him into their lodge. When the boy awoke he saw all kinds of animals and birds, and he was surprised. The Buffalo was the first to speak. He said: "Let us help this poor boy. We know what the trouble is. He has been bewitched." All the animals agreed, and the Elk was the first to stand up and run towards the boy. The Elk jumped over the boy, and when he jumped over the boy the other animals saw blood in the Elk's mouth. Then the Buffalo ran and jumped over the boy and there was blood in his mouth. Each animal took his turn, and then they all ran busily about in the lodge. The dust rose towards the sky, so that the boy could not be seen. The Bear came to where the boy was and stopped. The Bear screamed, then took one of his claws and cut the boy open. He took out the bones of the child, threw them away, and healed the wound. The boy was then told to sit up. Then the Snake came and said: "My son, I am bad. I kill people. I can kill you by spitting upon you. I give you this bone. Strike the enemy with this bone that I have given you and it will kill them." The Buffalo came and said: "I will teach you something. Take this whistle." Upon the center of the whistle was painted a buffalo skull. "When you get into trouble, whistle and I will be with you. I will make you brave so that you shall get out of trouble." Then the Bear came and said: "My son, I can kill people. Look at me." The Bear at this time was on his four feet and when he arose there was a great dust. When the dust passed by, the Bear blew his breath and the dust came from his mouth. He told the boy to take a little dust and put it into the sack. It was to be used as a paint to put upon the sick people and upon the wounded. Then a Buffalo cow came and said, "I can kill people." She made a great dust about the boy. Each animal taught the boy some mystery; then they told him that he must return to his people. Before they let him go they told him that they must teach him some sleight-of-hand performances. The Eagles taught the boy how to fly. The Ducks taught him how to swim and dive. The animals then said that the boy was hungry and that they wanted to feed him. They sent the Crow into the west, and the Beaver into the north, and the Otter into the east, and the Hawk into the south, to bring food for the boy. While these animals were away to get something for the boy to eat one of the animals spoke to the boy and said: "We know what the man did to you. He tried to poison you. He tried to make you like a woman. We have taught you great mysteries. If you desire you can bewitch him." After the animals came back with something to eat, and the boy had eaten, the leading animal of the lodge, who was a Beaver, said: "My boy, it is time to go home. The animals will show you the way. The Owl, Buffalo, and two Crows will be the ones to lead you to your home. They will stop outside the village. Enter the village, but do not let the people know that you are there. The next day after you arrive, take the man who tried to poison you to the river and swim with him. Our animals will go up the stream and they will bewitch him." When the Beaver finished speaking, the Crow came near to the boy and touched him and the boy found himself outside of the lodge of the animals. Then he was told to try to fly, and he arose in the air and flew like a crow.

They left the boy just outside of his village. In the night the boy went into the village to the lodge of his father and spoke to him. The father did not believe that his son, whom he had mourned for as dead, could have returned. He made his wife make a fire and then he saw that it was his son and he was glad. The next day the people heard that the boy had returned. They came from all directions to see the boy and to give him presents. Then the boy sent for the man who had injured him, and when the man came the boy picked up a bucket and said, "Come with me down to the creek." When the boy was dipping water the other man touched the water. As soon as he touched the water he was dragged under. The man disappeared and was never seen again. When the boy came up he told the people that the man was a witch, but for them not to be afraid, as he had disposed of him and that he would never return to trouble them.

87. THE THUNDER-BIRD CEREMONY.[1]

A long time ago when the Kitkehahki lived upon the Republican River, near Swimming-Mound, there were two people who were half women and half men. These two people once took up their hoes and sacks made of buffalo hide and went to a place where there had been artichokes. They found none and so they went farther down the river until they came to a bank where there were many artichokes. One of the hermaphrodites straightened up from digging artichokes and saw a man sitting near. He showed no sign of fear, but went on digging. As he dug he whispered to his companion: "There is a man sitting near

[1] Told by Mouth-Waving-in-Water, Kitkehahki. The ceremony described in this tale is sometimes known as the Elk medicine, because of the great feather appendages placed on the bird which stands on the altar and which bear a superficial resemblance to the antlers of the elk. The ceremony is no longer given by the Pawnee, as none of the medicine-men who belonged to this society are now living.

us. I will continue to dig around, and suddenly I will straighten up, walk around the bank, and hit him upon the back of his head with my hoe; then we will kill him." His companion said: "Go at once and do as you have said. I will keep on digging." The one who first spoke straightened up and walked around as though he were looking for artichokes. When he came around behind the stranger he took his hoe and struck him behind the head, and the man fell. Then he called for his companion and they killed him. They took up their sacks of artichokes and ran home.

When they reached the village they told the people that they had killed a strange man and that the man lay along the bank where they had dug artichokes. The men did not believe them, but notwithstanding they went to the place and there they found the strange man. The man had on a robe with the hair side out. His face was painted with blue mud and red streaks of paint. His hair was roached and covered with soft downy feathers, and a long downy feather stuck through his scalp-lock. His head was covered with blood, so that every man who came to the place thought the man had been scalped and would not touch the head. The people removed his robe and saw around his shoulders a black hair lariat rope. Some people said, "He must have been a warrior." Others said, "No, he is a wonderful man." They all went home and had war dances and in the night the women gave scalp dances.

Two or three days after the man had been killed, an old man took the hand of his grandson, who was four or five years old, and led him to the place where the dead man lay. When they got there the man gave the boy a stick and said, "Now, grandchild, strike the enemy and count coup on him." The boy struck the man, and then he saw the long downy feather upon the dead man's head. He said, "Grandfather, let me take the downy feather from the dead man's head." The old man took his knife and cut the scalp-lock where the feather was stuck in, and then gave the stick to the boy to carry to the village. When they got to their lodge the boy placed in front of it the pole that had the scalp and the downy feather attached to it.

The next night the boy in a dream saw the man who was daubed with blue mud. The downy feather was in his scalp-lock. The man said: "My son, I came to your people to talk to them, and they killed me. I am not a man; I am Thunder-Bird, the bird that flies away up in the heavens. Look at me." The boy looked, and there just where the man had stood was standing a tall bird. This bird had long legs and its bill was very long. It was like a crane. It opened its wings and the boy saw upon its breast the downy feather that the man had had in his scalp-lock.

The bird turned back into a man. Then the man told the boy that he was going to tell him something wonderful; that he must keep the downy feather, for as long as he kept it his spirit would be with him. The boy awoke and he lay awake for a long time, thinking of what he had dreamed. In the morning he went out and there upon the lodge was his stick with the scalp and feather. After a time the boy threw away the scalp, but the feather he kept, for he knew that it was not that of an eagle but of a crane. As he grew up he carried the feather with him.

One time while on a buffalo hunt, the boy hung the feather near his tipi. He dreamed again of seeing the man and he said: "My son, let us go through thick timber near here; I want to talk to you. Take me to the timber. Place the feather upon some limb and go on through the timber." The boy awoke, and did not wait to eat, but went out of the tipi, took down the feather, and went into the timber. He left the feather as he was told to do in his dream. He went on into the timber, and as he came to a pond he saw a man coming through the reeds and brush, who every once in a while turned into a crane, then back into a man. The boy said, "This is wonderful! I wonder what it is." He stopped and looked and saw that it was the man he had seen in his dream.

This mysterious being came close to the boy and said, "My son, we will now go into the timber." They went into the timber to a place that seemed to have been cleared for a purpose. At the west was the altar. There stood a large bird, with downy feathers on the top of its head. The bird was dead. In the east was an unknown animal. Another bird was in the south, known as Bird-That-Never-Moves. The boy was seated at the west behind the bird. The man then began to teach the boy a ceremony, and then he taught him some sleight-of-hand tricks. For several days they sat together, and the mysterious man told the boy that the people had gone on; that they had given him up as dead. Then he told him to go on home.

The boy started for home and carried with him the things that were given him by the mysterious man. The boy did not seem to get tired, but ran faster every day. One night he saw the camp, and so he went on, walking very slowly. He heard a man crying upon a high hill, and went to the hill and saw that the man was his father. He slowed his steps until he was close, and then he said, "Father, stop crying; I am here." His father looked and saw his son standing before him. He tried to put his arms around the boy, but the boy told his father not to touch him for a while. They went on down to the camp, and there close to the village was his mother, crying. The father told the boy to wait while he went and told his wife that her son had come back. The man went up to his wife and told her to stop crying, that the boy had come back. She stopped crying and they went to the boy. The boy told his mother that she must not touch him. They went to their tipi, and the boy told his parents not to let other people know he had come back. The next day the people saw the boy with his parents and wondered about him. People from the next camp came into their tipi and tried to find out where he had been, but the boy would say nothing. When the people found buffalo, the boy told his father to kill many, so that they could have plenty of the dried meat. The man knew that the boy wanted dried meat to take to the medicine-man's lodge. He told his relatives what the boy wanted, and they killed many buffalo and dried the meat. They suspected that in time the boy would work wonders. When the people had killed many buffalo and all their families had plenty of dried meat, they turned back to their village.

After they had arrived and the people had settled down, the medicine-men began to prepare for their wonderful ceremonies. When they were all ready the boy unwrapped his little bundle and said: "Father, I must go into the medicine-lodge. I want to perform sleight-of-hand tricks." The father went out and told his relatives what the boy had said. They came into the boy's lodge and brought many presents that were to be presented to the medicine-men. The boy arose with his buffalo robe wrapped around him and his face daubed with blue mud. He put his little bundle upon his left arm and started for the medicine-lodge. His relatives followed him with goods, buffalo robes, blankets, and dried buffalo meat. The boy went into the lodge and stood in the center, while the man who carried the goods and meat stopped. The young man spoke to the medicine-men and said: "Medicine-men, I am a young man. I have come into your lodge that you may give me a seat among you. I want to perform, and have brought my friends with me who have with them goods and meat." All of the medicine-men said, "Nawa." The leading medicine-man gave him a seat in the south. The goods were then placed near the altar, and the meat was placed near the entrance. The boy did many wonderful tricks, so that the people wondered, for his people were not medicine-men. Towards the last of the ceremony the boy turned the downy feather into a large thunder-bird. He also made a skull, which was placed in the east, while the thunder-bird stood in the west. He then made a crane, a bird that stands by the ponds and lakes and looks at the sun. This was placed at the south with three things in the lodge that the boy had made. At last he made them disappear. Then he stood up before all of the medicine-men and said: "Medicine-men, my tricks are ended. You have seen me perform. I have a ceremony that I want to perform, but I want a lodge first. I want three things to be placed there when the lodge is done—the skull in the east on the north of the entrance, a sun crane in the south, and a large crane in the west." The medicine-men were glad to hear what the boy said.

After the ceremony the boy's relatives went to work and gathered poles and forks, and the lodge was put up. A buffalo skull was brought out and placed at the northeast entrance. In the south was placed a sun crane; and the young man himself placed the large crane at the west. This crane had soft downy feathers upon the top of its head, but it also had feathers standing on its head like deer horns. The people called this particular ceremony the "Elk dance." They saw many wonderful things performed by the boy. After the boy had finished his tricks the ceremony was ended. He did not allow any others to perform any sleight-of-hand. The lodge was never inhabited until the boy died. Then the birds and skull were removed.

88. PROUD BOY AND THE ANIMAL MEDICINE.[1]

The Kitkehahki were to have a great bundle ceremony known as "Karipiro." This ceremony was the greatest of all and lasted four days. The people invited the Chaui and the Pitahauirat. These two bands were far away, so that runners had to be sent out for them. When all the people had gathered together it was time to go after the tree that formed the center pole of the ceremonial lodge. The priests opened the sacred bundles and sang the rituals explaining why they were to get the tree. When the priests came to that part of the ritual that spoke of the tree, the people—men, women, and children—arose and started for the timber, which was about four miles away.

Among the boys who went out for the tree was one who was called Proud-Boy. At that time he was not proud. Among the girls was one whose father was one of the leading men from the Pitahauirat. The boy noticed the girl, but the girl did not notice him. When they neared the timber, young warriors were sent through the timber to find a suitable tree. They came back with news that the enemy was in the timber. Then an old warrior was selected to go and defend the tree. This man sneaked through the timber and sat in a position to pounce upon the enemy when he approached. The people on horseback rode into the

Told by Overtaker, a Pitahauirat who is one of the owners of the Buffalo ceremony. It is possible that there are certain Comanche elements in this story, as the narrator formerly lived among the Wichita where he came in contact with the Comanche. The story in the main, however, is purely Pitahauirat. Apart from the explanation offered in the story, it teaches that a man should not steal the wife of another man.

timber and brought news that the enemy was alone. The enemy kept going nearer to the place where the man was concealed. At last an attack was made and the man killed the enemy. The tree was found and a young girl was selected to cut the tree first. Then the warriors assisted her. As the tree fell there was great shouting by the men, and the women gave their war cry. The tree was then taken up by the men on horseback. Other men rode alongside, so that when the men who were carrying the tree became tired they might take their places. A command was given for the men, women, boys, and girls to run to the village. The winner of the race to the village was to become holy, and red ointment was to be put on his body. If the winner was a woman she lived with the priest until the season was over; if a man, he wore a holy robe and was anointed by the priests during the whole season. In the race, Proud-Boy ran near by the girl, but he could not keep up with her, for she was a swift runner. Everybody was present when the tree was carried into the village and set in place. Proud-Boy wore his paint and fine clothing all the time, for he was always on the lookout for the girl. His clothing consisted of a buffalo hide string, about two feet long and about two inches wide, which was tanned on one side and had hair on the other side. The ceremony was performed, visiting tribes returned to their homes, and the Kitkehahki were left alone in the village.

That summer the Kitkehahki went buffalo hunting. They killed many buffalo. The young men in the tribe consecrated many buffalo and took the meat to the lodge of the priests. The meat was jerked, and it was decided that they were to have another ceremony, similar to the one they had had before. The Kitkehahki returned to the village, and early in the spring a runner was sent out again to invite other tribes to the ceremony. The tribes came together again. Proud-Boy watched for the girl. He saw her. She was dressed in beautiful garments. She had a buckskin skirt, and her dress was of young buffalo calf skin, tanned and dyed black. Her leggings were of buffalo hide, and young calf hoofs were hung down the sides of them. Her moccasins were also black buffalo hide. The boy went home and told his father that he thought it was time he had something to wear. His father gave him a piece of buckskin and a buckskin string to tie about his waist. He was disappointed, for he wanted leggings. He went to his aunt's and she made the boy a pair of elk moccasins. The boy painted up the best he could, and as he dressed he said to himself: "I have laid away my buffalo string. I am getting to be a young man."

The ceremony was performed. Again the people went many miles away to get the tree. Some rode horses and others walked. Proud-Boy

stayed around where he could see the girl. After they had found the
pole and given it to the men on horseback to carry, a command was
given for the people who were on foot to race to the village. Proud-Boy
ran near the girl until she went ahead of him. He lost sight of her, but
he kept on, and when he reached the village he saw the girl sitting by the
priests; and he at once knew that she had won the race. Some said the
girl had not won fairly, for they had seen some one carrying her on horseback. Because there was some doubt, the people agreed to go after
another, so that the race might be run again. When the girl's father
found out that the race was to be run again, he went to the priests and
asked that the race be put off until the next day. The priests agreed to
this. The girl was sent home. Her father took a small calf robe and
painted the inside red. "This," he said, "my daughter, you shall wear
to-morrow in the race."

The next day a crier went through the village to tell the people to get
ready to run. The girl had on only her black skirt and black moccasins,
and the calf robe over her shoulders. She looked beautiful, the boy
thought. They went near the timber; then a command was given for
the people to run. They ran. People on horseback rode on either side
of the procession. Proud-Boy ran as fast as he could. He did not try
to get near the girl, for he wanted to run his best. Finally he began to
give out. Then he saw to his right something red, waving or floating in
the air. Proud-Boy looked, and it was the girl. The red calf robe was
tied about her shoulders and with her left hand she held her skirt. The
boy held his breath, for he saw that the girl was passing everybody, even
some men whom Proud-Boy knew to be good runners. Proud-Boy ran
on with all of his strength, and as he ran he watched the red robe. When
Proud-Boy saw that the girl passed everybody and was in the lead, he
gave a war whoop and fell exhausted. When he arose he said: "Now
I know that she beat them all. This day I call upon the heavens to
help me make her my wife. I shall go upon the war-path, capture
ponies, kill the enemy, and take a scalp; then I can claim her. I shall
give many ponies for her, and the head priest shall lead me to her lodge.
My father thinks I am still young, but I feel that I am now a man." All
this the boy said as he walked to the place where the priests were seated.
He saw the girl seated in front of the priests. The priests were satisfied;
for as one of the priests arose and anointed her body with the holy
ointment, they all sang. As the pole was being raised and put into the
hole, and as they were shouting and crying to the gods, Proud-Boy,
although not yet a warrior, stood among them and shouted. His cry
was really a petition to the gods to favor him and to help him to win

the girl who was now sitting before the priests.   The singing was kept up by the priests for one whole day and one whole night.

The next day the girl was taken to the lodge of the priests and there she had to live.   Her parents then had to live with these people, although they belonged to the Kawarakis, a band of the Pitahauirat.   The girl had to sit under the bundle all of the time.   She did not like this, for she wanted to go out and play with the girls, but the old man spoke to her and said: ''You have holy ointment upon your body and you yourself are holy.   You must sit still, for if you should go out and make any noise, the winds would hear you and would not send buffalo.   If you play you will make a noise upon the ground that will scare the buffalo away, and the gods in the west would hear the noise and they would think that the people did not want cool days in the summer, nor rain.''   So the girl lived with the old people and became the keeper of the sacred bundles.   Proud-Boy would go at night and peep into the lodge to see the girl.

The time to go on the buffalo hunt came.   On the journey she had to carry the sacred bundle upon her back.   When the journey was ended the bundle was placed upon the sticks and she sat down in front of it.   Proud-Boy would pass by many times before the bundle was taken into the tipi and hung up.   When this had been done, the girl had to go and sit down under the bundle.   The people had not gone very far when they found many buffalo.   The men went out and surrounded the buffalo.   They killed and brought the meat to the priests' lodge, where the girl was.   The tongue and heart were boiled for the girl and this was all she ate.   When the people had killed many buffalo and had plenty they went back to their village.   As they neared the village, scouts were sent on ahead to see if the corn, beans, and squash were good.   The runners went, and when they came back, they brought corn, beans, and squash and reported good crops.

When the people entered the village, corn, beans, and squash were gathered, and the priests gave a ceremony, so that the girl might be washed. The priests met, the bundle was opened, and sweet-smelling grass was put upon glowing coals that were now placed in the southwest of the lodge. The contents of the bundle were waved over the smoke and were again placed upon the wrappers.   The girl was taken to the smoke and a ritual was recited while the holy ointment was removed from her.   The eyes of the gods were wrested from her after the ointment had been removed, so that she became the same as any other girl.   Before telling her of her freedom, the high priest took some wild sage and dipped it into a bowl of water.   With this he made motions about the girl, but did not touch

her. Then she was taken by her grandfather, who took some fresh fat
from the holy meat and greased her with it. She was told to be seated on
the north side of the lodge. When the singing was all finished, all offerings of meat and corn were first given to the girl, then to the others. The
girl was given meat, then the priest took her by the hand and placed her
by her grandfather, who, after the ceremony, led her home.

At this time Proud-Boy told his father that he wanted to marry the
girl. The girl was now known as Yellow-Corn, for the reason that she
represented Mother-Yellow-Corn. The father spoke and said: "My
son, you can not marry Yellow-Corn. You have not walked over this
earth to the enemy's camp, you have no scalps over your tipi, you have
no ponies staked out around our tipi, you have not brought in any small
game, and you can not yet shoot the buffalo under the shoulder." "I
know," said the boy, "but my father is a great chief. He can give many
ponies for his son. He has men who will kill buffalo for his son. My
father has many scalps. What more do you want?" But his father
said: "My son, you can not have Yellow-Corn, for you have made no
sacrifice to the heavens; the heavens have not seen nor received your
smoke. Do not think about marrying Yellow-Corn. You shall marry
when I think best." The boy was sad.

That winter he was not the same as usual. His grandfather made him
bow and arrows and he wandered about over the country. In the spring
his people had many ceremonies, but the other tribes were not invited.
The following winter the people went on a buffalo hunt and brought
much dried buffalo meat back to camp. In the meantime the boy grew
up, but he was not the same boy that he had been. He sat about his
father's lodge with his head down, until he went to his bed. He did not
care to play with the boys nor to listen to the talk of the old men. The
next spring some people came from the other tribe and told that Yellow-
Corn had married the greatest warrior in the village. The boy heard
it. He was angry. He would not speak to anybody. His mind was
disturbed. He threw away his bow and arrows. The robe that had been
given him he laid aside. The leggings that had been given him he gave
to his mother.

Again the time came for the people to go hunting. They went north
to the Platte River, where there was thick timber and hills. The thick
timber was full of owls and birds of all kinds and many wonderful animals. On the side of the hills were holes, and the people said that they
were the homes of the water-dogs, which possessed magic power. One
morning Proud-Boy awoke and went to the timber. He came to the
timber. He came to the homes of the water-dogs, and while he was there

the people broke camp and went off. Proud-Boy's people looked for him, but could not find him. Some of the people said that they had seen him going towards the timber, and the father said, "My son must have been eaten by wild animals in the timber." The people began to mourn for Proud-Boy, for they thought that he must be dead.

Proud-Boy went through the timber. Now and then he came to a hilly place thick with cedars on the side of the hills. There the water-dogs dwelt. In the timber he saw many wonderful birds. The magpies came close to him and all kinds of birds flocked to him, and the owls hooted, although it was daytime; but Proud-Boy did not hear or see the birds. His mind was always on the girl he loved and he thought of her constantly. He came to a thick willowy place and there he saw a girl, whom he thought to be the girl he loved. He ran to her and threw his arms about her neck; then he found it was a black-tail deer. The deer jumped up and threw him to the ground. He stood up and looked about. For a time he felt dazed; then he cried. While he was crying, he heard the owls hooting close by him. Then he heard a bear, then a mountain-lion roaring close by him. He felt afraid and a shiver ran over him. He said: "Kill me, for I no longer care to live. The one I cared for is gone from me." Again he heard some strange sounds. The screech-owl hooted so near him that it made him sleepy and he lay down and went to sleep. Towards evening before sunset he awoke. The birds were sitting all around him and one said: "My son, we take pity upon you. You are poor in heart. We have nothing to give you except the root that you see in the center. We all eat it when we are sick. We all eat it when we are wounded. Take a piece of it. Carry it with you and we will always be near you."

Night came, and the owls and the water-dogs came to him and gave him great powers. Towards morning, when the birds were flying around in a circle, singing their songs, a Buffalo came and said: "My son, you shall have a robe. My power is the Sun. When you get a robe, paint upon it the symbol of the Sun; and if you should ever be killed, have the robe thrown over your body and all these birds and animals will come and wake you from your sleep. Through life the Sun will always shine upon you and warm you." The Buffalo went off and the boy went to sleep again. He found himself in the animals' lodge. The Bear came to him and said: "We are of four kinds, Grizzly, Cinnamon, Black, and White Bear. I represent the Grizzly and the Cinnamon Bear. I give you power to have a spirit like mine. You shall conquer the enemy. You shall know about the different roots and herbs, so that you can make medicine. When you go to your people, have them make a tipi for you, so that you may live by yourself. When you have the tipi finished, draw my picture, the Cinnamon Bear, on the south side of the entrance, and draw the Grizzly Bear on the north side of the entrance. We will guard your tipi always." The Mountain-Lion said, "Have my picture by the Cinnamon Bear and instead of drawing me with the fore legs upwards, draw me as I stand now, only with my mouth wide open." The Buffalo said, "Have pictures of us all around the tipi." The Eagle said, "Have my picture at the back of the tipi." The Owls spoke and said, "Have our pictures one on either side of the Eagle; the Black Owl on the north side, the Red Owl on the south side." Then all of the other birds said, "Put us upon your tipi, too." The Buffalo arose and said: "My son, when you go among your people and kill your first Buffalo, let it be a Buffalo bull. That bull will be me, and my spirit will be with you always. Take only the scalp of the Buffalo and leave the horns on it. Hang the scalp upon a pole at the head of your bed. Now return to your people." As Proud-Boy arose, the birds flew up into the air and the animals ran in different directions through the timber.

Proud-Boy then went to the place where the camp had been and found that the people had gone. He followed their trail for three days and three nights. When he came near the camp of his people he waited until it was dark; then he went into the camp and found his father's tipi. He entered it and sat by the fireplace. He spoke and said, "Mother, I am here." His mother arose and kindled the fire. When it blazed up she saw by its light that her son was sitting there naked, with only a pair of moccasins on. She made a noise as if to cry, but Proud-Boy said, "Mother, do not cry; I am here." His mother made a big fire, then woke her husband. When the father saw his boy he did not say anything, but remained in bed. The mother prepared some meat for him, then spread a robe upon the ground and told him to lie down.

The next morning Proud-Boy was gone, but he returned before the people started off, and went with them. When in camp he would dress up in a beautiful robe, leggings, and fine moccasins. He carried in his right hand an eagle tail for a fan. His face was painted all the time. He stood around where the boys were playing, but would never play. When he talked, he told of some great deeds that he was going to do in battle, and sometimes he said that he wanted to fight somebody. Frequently he went to the playgrounds on horseback. His horse sometimes had red paint on its nostrils, on its shoulders, and on its thighs; also at the root of its tail. At other times the horse was painted green, yellow, and black, and occasionally white. Proud-Boy often rode past the boys at play, holding his eagle fan up to his face, so that he could not be seen. While the boys were playing he would ride among them and command them to stop making a noise.   Then he would tell of how he longed to fight in battle; of how he would kill and take a scalp.   After he had boasted this way he would ride to his tipi, get off of his pony, and turn it loose.   The children would go home and tell how Proud-Boy acted and what he said, but the people did not pay any attention.   The children then gave him the name of Proud-Boy.   Still he came every day, either riding or walking, to the place where the boys were playing, and continued to boast.

The people killed many buffalo while out on the hunt.   After they had dried the meat they turned eastward and started to their village. When they came to their village they had many ceremonies of thanksgiving for their successful hunt, and they offered the tongue and heart of many buffalo to the gods in the heavens.   They did not have to go on the hunt the following winter, for the buffalo came in droves to their village.

During the winter Proud-Boy asked his father to kill a young buffalo bull and to take its scalp, leaving the horns upon it.   The father killed a bull and brought home the scalp, which was tanned and fixed up as the boy directed.   He also asked that several buffalo be killed to make him a tipi, for he wanted to live by himself.   The women sewed together the tanned skins, and while they worked Proud-Boy went through the camp and selected men whom he had heard were good at drawing pictures and asked them to paint his tipi.   The men came, and the tipi was spread upon the ground to be painted as Proud-Boy directed.   The first picture drawn was that of the Cinnamon Bear, which was at the outside of the entrance to the southeast.   The Bear was painted standing, with its fore legs upward.   The Grizzly Bear was drawn upon the northeast side, north of the entrance.   The Mountain-Lion was then drawn next to the Cinnamon Bear, with its mouth wide open.   Buffalo were then drawn all around the tipi.   Then the Eagle was drawn on the west side at the top of the tipi.   Then the Owls were drawn, the Red on the south side of the Eagle and the Black on the north side of the Eagle.   All kinds of birds were drawn all over the tipi.   When this was done, Proud-Boy told his father to select women to go out and cut cedar poles for the tipi. Women were selected and the poles were brought and prepared.   The tipi was then folded and put away.

In the spring, the Kitkehahki began again to make preparation for the big ceremony.[1]   They left their permanent camp and selected a

[1] In the race there was a willow stuck by the place where the old men stood, and whoever should come out first was to take the willow and stick it in the ground, thus marking the center of the circle in which to hold the ceremony.   The one who did this received presents, though he did not keep them, for they were offered to the gods.

place upon the Platte River to hold their ceremony. Runners were sent out to invite the other tribes to come and take part. While the people were waiting for the different tribes, who could be seen approaching in the distance, the boys were playing games. Proud-Boy joined them and talked in such a way as to make the boys believe that he was a great warrior. That night he ordered his mother to put up his tipi. The tipi was put up. Dirt was piled around the circle of the lodge. Inside the lodge, at the west side, was also piled dirt, so that there was a mound. By the mound was placed a cedar tree. At the head of the boy's bed was hung the buffalo scalp. Upon his bed the robe was spread. It had a picture of the sun and all kinds of birds upon it.

After the lodge was completed, Proud-Boy took his pony and painted the nostrils, the shoulders, the hips, and the root of the tail with red clay. He tied some eagle feathers to the tail and the mane. He dressed in his robe, leggings, and moccasins, took his eagle fan, and rode to the place where the boys were playing. As he rode among them, he said, "Boys, I am going to watch the people as they enter the village, and when I see the girl that I love I am going to take her home with me." As the tribes approached from all different directions and entered the village, Proud-Boy mounted his pony and rode to the place where they entered the village. He watched one tribe as it passed, but he did not see among all the people any girl that he cared for. Then he rode back to the place where the boys were playing their games and told them that he had not seen the girl he loved among the people. The next day another tribe entered the village. Proud-Boy arrayed himself and his pony as he had done the day before. Then he rode among the boys and said, "Boys, I am going to watch the people come, and if I see the girl I love I shall take her home with me." Proud-Boy rode to the entrance of the village, and there he sat straight up on his pony, holding his eagle fan over his face. He watched and watched until all had passed, but the girl did not come. He went to the boys and told them there was no girl that he liked among the people who came that day. The next day another tribe came from the east, and again the boy arrayed himself and rode among the boys and said, "Well, boys, I am going again." He went and watched as he had done before, but he did not see the girl he was looking for. He did not go to his home, but rode around the village. In the village he saw all of the people crowded around his tipi. They did not go near it, but admired it from a distance. They thought that it was a wonderful tipi, and they marveled at the pictures, for it was the first tipi with pictures upon it that was ever seen among the Kitkehahki. Some said: "Proud-Boy must be a wonderful boy. It may be that the animals took pity upon his spirit and gave him great power when he was in the woods for several days."

While Proud-Boy was listening to what the people were saying, he saw at a distance some people coming with pack ponies. He rode to the entrance of the village and waited until they came up. As they came nearer he saw that there were only two people, an old woman and a young girl. He watched them as they approached. The girl looked up at him and he saw that she was Yellow-Corn. He dashed out to meet her, and as he rode he felt a great happiness. He did not speak to Yellow-Corn, but turning to the old woman he said: "I love your daughter. I have come to take her with me. May she go?" The old woman looked at the young man and she remembered that his people had always treated her daughter well. She said, "Yes, she may go." Proud-Boy put Yellow-Corn upon his pony's back and the two rode off. As they came near the place where the boys were playing, he made several grunts, so that the boys would notice him. Then he took the girl to his tipi.

When they reached the tipi, Proud-Boy helped Yellow-Corn from the pony and turned it loose. He led her into the tipi. She sat down upon the robe and looked around at the mysterious things in the tipi. Proud-Boy went out and told his mother to bring some food. His mother came and placed before them a wooden bowl of pemmican and water. She then went out and Proud-Boy and Yellow-Corn ate together. While they were eating, Proud-Boy spoke and said: "Yellow-Corn, did you know that I cared for you? Did you notice me in all the ceremonies? Did you know that I tried to be near you in the race? Did you know that I was angry and sad when I heard that you were married to some warrior? I went off, and while I was gone I got these things that you see. I did not bring you here that you might eat and then go back to your mother. I brought you to my tipi to stay as my wife. You are the first woman to enter my tipi, with the exception of my mother, who brings me my food." The girl said: "I knew that you loved me. I saw you many times, but, as you know, women have not the right to say whom they shall marry, and so I had to marry the man who was chosen for me. It will be best, Proud-Boy, that I go to my mother's tipi. This is the first time that I have been separated from her. As you know, I have a husband, who is a great warrior and is not afraid of anybody. He has killed many enemies and brought scalps and counted coup. He will soon come home, for he has been gone for many moons." The boy said: "Proud-Boy knows all these things, but Proud-Boy learned to love you and brought you to his tipi, and here you are to stay. He is not afraid." The girl at last consented to remain.

After Yellow-Corn's mother had put up her tipi, she began to look for her daughter. She went to different tipis and at each place she was told that Proud-Boy had taken her daughter to his tipi. She asked where Proud-Boy's tipi was, and she was told to go to the other village, that there she would see a tipi that had pictures of birds and animals upon it. The mother went and saw the tipi. She entered and said: "My son, I have come after my daughter. She is married and we are expecting her husband to come any day. He has been gone for many moons. He is a warrior and has many brothers who are not afraid of anybody." But Proud-Boy said: "Mother, this girl has been in Proud-Boy's mind since the first time he saw her. Now Proud-Boy has brought her to his tipi. She is now his wife, and if your son-in-law comes home and gets angry Proud-Boy will take care of himself. Return home, for Yellow-Corn shall make her home with me." The old woman arose and went home. The next day the old woman went and again asked for her girl, but the girl refused to go, for she was happy with Proud-Boy. Ceremonies were performed, but Proud-Boy and Yellow-Corn remained in their tipi all the time, and never attended. After the big ceremony there were other dances, but these two never went.

One morning some one yelled and said: "There is a straight smoke going up over the hills to the south. It is the smoke of some warriors!" People went out of their tipis and saw the smoke. Then men riding fine horses and holding in their hands long poles, with scalps upon them, were seen coming over the hills. They were a victorious party of warriors. Men, women, and children ran to meet them and to learn of their deeds. Some one yelled and said: "These are the warriors who went out some time ago. They have killed people and taken their scalps and ponies." Proud-Boy knew what was coming, so he told Yellow-Corn not to be afraid; that he would take care of her. When the victorious warriors came into camp, Yellow-Corn's husband was told that his wife had been carried away by Proud-Boy and that she was living with him. The warrior said nothing, but went to his own home, not to the tipi of his wife's mother. Apparently he did not care because his wife had left him. His brothers came into the tipi where he sat and they said: "Brother, you are a great warrior. The chiefs call you brave. You make war on the enemy and bring home many scalps and ponies. You have made buffalo holy. Your smoke went to the heavens. You are anointed by the priest. The heavens and the gods know you. Will you let Proud-Boy take Yellow-Corn from you, and he a young man who has never yet killed a buffalo, and who has never walked over this earth to attack the enemy in his own camp? Let us get our bows and arrows and kill both

Proud-Boy and Yellow-Corn. Then, my brother, you will be looked upon as a great warrior and you can marry some other woman. Come, my brother." This is the way these warriors talked to their brother.

At last he gave in and promised his brothers that he would help kill the two. The news was spread, and Proud-Boy's father was told that the brothers were planning to kill his son. The father told his boy, and Proud-Boy said: "My father, I am a young man, but I have a strong heart. Tell our people not to fight for me. Let them come and kill me. I will not run. When they have killed Yellow-Corn and me, take us into my tipi and lay us side by side on my bed; then spread my robe over us. Then leave the tipi. You will see us again." The man looked at his son and wondered if he could come to life again.

In the evening the news that Yellow-Corn and Proud-Boy were to be attacked the next day was spread throughout the village. That night Proud-Boy took the root that had been given him while he was in the timber, and ate of it, and gave some of it to Yellow-Corn. Then he said: "Yellow-Corn, will you stay by me? Will you be killed with me?" She said, "Yes, it is all right. I will die with you." Then the boy said: "Yellow-Corn, do not be frightened, for we shall come to life. It is now time that people should know who I am."

Early in the morning Proud-Boy arose and went out of the tipi. It was a clear day and the birds were singing. He called Yellow-Corn and said: "Bring the buffalo scalp. Let my father, the Sun, look upon it." The scalp was brought out and hung outside of the lodge. Proud-Boy told his mother to cook nothing for them. His father was out watching. Proud-Boy and Yellow-Corn went into the tipi. Proud-Boy painted Yellow-Corn and gave her some root to eat. Some people in the village yelled and said, "The warriors are coming!" The boy and the girl seated themselves in front of the buffalo scalp. The men came and rode by them and around them, shooting at them with arrows. Two of the men had guns and these two were the ones who shot and killed them. The other men rode their horses over them. The people ran from their camp to see the dead Proud-Boy. His father told the men to put up their bows and arrows. They obeyed and rode off.

The father and the mother took the dead bodies and laid them upon Proud-Boy's bed, and then covered them with the painted robe. The entrance to the tipi was then closed. The people stood afar off and watched. They said: "The parents do not cry, and the bodies have been taken into the tipi. There must be something wonderful in the tipi." When the Sun was near noon, the people saw a straight dust going up from the tipi. They pointed to the dust. There were noises in

the tipi. Mountain-Lions and Buffalo were bellowing, Birds were singing, and Owls hooting. There was a great dust coming out from the top
and sides of the tipi. The noise ceased and the dust went away. The
news went through the village that wonderful things were going on in
Proud-Boy's tipi. Some people said, "We understood the animals and
the birds took pity on Proud-Boy and gave him power." Again the
dust was seen and the noises heard. The news of this was taken to the
men who had killed the boy and the girl. The warrior said: "I am sorry
that I killed the boy. I knew that the boy was wonderful when I heard
that he had a wonderful tipi, but it can not be helped now." The
noises continued for a time, then subsided. When this had happened
four times and the dust had settled, Proud-Boy came out of the tipi and
said: "Mother, prepare food for us, for we are hungry." This was in
the afternoon. The mother boiled some meat and fed Proud-Boy and
Yellow-Corn. The news went through the camp that Proud-Boy and
Yellow-Corn were alive, and the men who had killed them heard of it.
The next morning the young man said: "Father, you see my bow and
arrows, my shield and spear? I shall not use them to fight against these
men; but before the moon disappears every one of them shall die."

The next morning the young man sat in his tipi and took from under
his bed a water-dog. This he pointed toward the village of the men.
When the sun was high the leading warrior was found dead in his bed.
Every day after that a man died until all of the men who had anything
to do with the killing of the boy were dead. The people knew why the
men had died and did not question. They said: "Let us make Proud-Boy
our chief." But the boy said: "No, I can not be chief. I will be a
medicine-man. I will cure people of their sickness. I will teach my
people to do wonderful things. My wife will wait on the women, for she
will know how to prescribe for them." From that time Proud-Boy was
a great medicine-man. All the people painted their tipis in imitation
of his.

89. THE BEAR MEDICINE-MAN.[1]

Many years ago when the people lived near Fremont, Nebraska, a
little boy wandered away from the village and went into the thick timber.
There he found many Magpies. He tried to shoot some of the birds, but
he could not hit them. He finally ran after one. It would fly up and light

[1] Told by Little-Chief, Chaui. This story is generally related during the Bear
ceremony. It is also related outside of the ceremonial lodge to children, and is
especially supposed to inform the poor boys that the bears are their friends, and
that they could count on securing mysterious power from the bear family if they
approach them in the proper spirit.

on a limb a short distance away. The boy thought that he could surely kill it. Every time he shot at it, it would make a screeching sound. In following the bird the boy could almost make out that it was calling him whenever it made the screeching sound. In the evening the bird seemed to lead the boy to the lakes where there were many bulrushes and cane-brakes, etc. The boy would then pay no more attention to the Magpie. He went into the ponds and dug up artichokes and stems of bulrushes and ate them. Then he would lie down in a pile of dried rushes. The next day the Magpie would return and the boy would follow it and try to kill it. The boy did not know that he was lost. For four days and nights he wandered through the thick timber and over the ponds.

One night the boy had a dream. He saw a man standing before him, all painted black; he had a big bunch of feathers on the top of his head. The man said: "For several days you have been trying to kill a bird. You have followed it from one place to another. That bird is the errand bird of the medicine-lodge of the island. I have come to tell you that I am that bird. You must return to your people and after several years you must come here again. The people are looking for you and they think you are dead. You will find me in this timber again when you come." When the boy woke up he found that the sun was up high. As he started he saw the Magpie. He followed the Magpie through the timber and at last they came to the edge of the woods and the boy then saw where he was. He returned to his village, and it was told throughout the village that the boy who had been lost had come back. The boy told his parents that he had wandered over the ponds and was taken care of by the birds.

It happened at this time that the Skidi made their village near to these Chaui. The Skidi were great medicine-men, but they were jealous of other people who became medicine-men. Among the Skidi was one leading medicine-man who seemed to understand all the powers which the animals possessed. He was known to be a wizard. This man was known to have killed a number of men. He also was known to visit the graves and there dig up human ears, hands, and hearts. These, it was said, he used in killing other people. The people were afraid of him. When he invited anybody to eat with him they knew that they had to eat some part of a human body.

Now this Skidi heard of the little boy. He invited him to his tipi. The boy entered the tipi of the Skidi, and when he sat down he was given a pipe to smoke. After he had smoked, a wooden bowl was placed before him filled with mush. The boy ate of the food which was in the bowl. After he had eaten, he went to his home.

A few days afterwards the Skidi broke camp and went away. The boy thought to himself that it was time to return to the timber. When he went into the timber he found the Magpie again, and when the Magpie saw the boy it flew from one limb to the other, making a screeching sound, and the boy could see that the Magpie was glad to see him. The Magpie led the boy around through the timber. Finally it came to the boy in a dream and said: "Something is wrong with you. I will hasten now to take you into the lodge of the animals, for you must not remain in your present condition." The next day the boy woke up and followed the Magpie around until they came to a pond. Here the boy lay down to sleep. When he woke up he found himself at another place. (A song was taught the boy to be sung in the medicine-man's lodge, where it tells of his lying down to sleep in one place and waking up in another.) The boy lay down again and he dreamed that he was lying upon the fireplace in the lodge of the animals. With him in the lodge was a Turtle.

When the boy woke up he found himself at another place. Then he began to dig into the earth. He found canes and bulrushes growing all around. When he went to sleep again he saw a man covered with mud. Fire came from his mouth and eyes. He said: "My son, you have been lying upon my back for some time. I moved around. You found yourself at different places, but I was moving around. I am the Turtle. I am the fireplace of the animal lodges. I will tell you one thing which you can do to try my power. Make a bow out of an ash tree. Then take a cane and sharpen it. Put soft downy feathers upon the cane and put downy feathers upon the bow. When you want to do any sleight-of-hand jump out from the animals' lodge. Run around the fireplace with the bow and reed arrows. When you have gone around four times, then stand in the west, facing east. Take aim, shoot at the turtle in the back, and the turtle, which is the fireplace, will move away.[1] This is all I can tell you now. You are not well and the animals in the lodge know of it. They can not help you, for there is nothing that can be done for you." The boy woke up and wondered why the Magpie and Turtle had spoken to him in that way. When the boy went through the timber he found the Magpie. The Magpie came to the boy and sat in the tree. It said: "My brother, you are not well and you are in trouble. This night I shall ask the animals in the lodge to take you in." The Magpie went away. The boy woke up and looked around. After a while he saw in the ponds sparks of fire. Then he heard something

---

[1] The fireplace in the ceremony of at least one Skidi medicine-lodge is shaped and painted like a great turtle.

like a drum and then yelling. Sometimes he would see many sparks of fire going up. He thought he saw many animals swimming through the ponds and coming nearer to him. The boy had this time strange sensations running through him. He thought his hair stood up; then he fell over and knew no more.

When he awoke he was sitting by the fireplace. He looked around and he saw all kinds of animals sitting in groups in the lodge. The Beavers seemed to be the leaders of the medicine-men in this lodge. He saw the Magpie sitting on the south side of the entrance. These two were the errand people for the lodge. The Magpie then flew up and around the lodge. It stopped at the entrance and stood there. This was all as the boy had seen it in his dreams. Black mud covered his body. A big bunch of Magpie feathers was upon his head. He said to the animals: "My brother feasted with a man who had animal power. He fed him with scrapings from a buffalo hide. He mixed this stuff with white clay and some kind of medicine. When the boy ate this there was a little ball of clay formed in his stomach. That little ball of clay has been growing until now it is large." For the first time the boy heard this. He felt strangely about his stomach, but had not paid any attention to it. The Magpie continued and said: "Animals, I wait upon you. I carry messages for you. I have never asked anything of you. To-day I come to you with a poor heart. I ask you to take pity upon this brother, so that he may live." The Magpie sat on a limb near the entrance of the lodge.

When the animals heard what the Magpie said there was great shouting all over the animals' lodge. Each animal made a noise, so that there was much noise in the lodge. When the noise died away the Beavers asked the Magpie what he meant, and the Magpie said: "I have told you. This boy has a ball of clay in his stomach and that ball is growing within him. If that ball of clay is not removed it will continue to grow until he will burst and die." Then the Beavers said: "Animals, we have before us a human being. He is in trouble. We will first visit him and see if we can remove this ball of clay from him." There was great shouting, much noise and singing. The Beavers went to the boy. They jumped over him several times. Then they turned on the boy and squirted water all over him. They touched him with their mouths and made grunting sounds. After this they went to their places and the leader said: "Animals, it is hard. We can not do anything for the boy." All of the animals failed to help the boy. Then they decided that the boy should go to another animals' lodge which was farther up the Platte River. The Magpie said, "I will take him there."

The next day the boy found himself upon dry land, and for the first time he noticed that there was a heavy weight in his stomach. The boy saw the Magpie and followed it. For several days they traveled until they arrived at the banks of the Platte River. There the boy lay down and went to sleep. He was awakened by a great noise. He sat up, looked around, and again he saw fire in the water in different places. Sometimes it was like a lot of hot coals coming up in the water. At another time, when he saw these hot coals in the water, it seemed as if something were blowing through the fire and the sparks scattered out. The boy had a strange feeling. He was again knocked over, and when he woke up he was in the lodge of the animals. He saw the Magpie sitting there. The Magpie said: "My brother here was taken into the lodge at Pahuk. They could not do anything for him, so they sent him to this lodge and I came with him." When the animals looked at the boy they said, "If the lodge at Pahuk can not do anything, we can not do anything."

The Magpie took the boy out again and they went to another place called Spring-Mound, on the banks of the Republican River. The boy was placed on the ground where the spring was. He was taken into the lodge. Most of the animals in the lodge were Catfish, Mink, Raccoons, Otters, Beavers, and a very few birds. They could not help the boy here. He was now weak. When this lodge failed to do anything for him, the Magpie told the boy to follow again and they would go to the lodge at Pahuk. The boy walked back. The ball of clay had grown larger, so that now his stomach protruded. He became very weak and thin. When he walked he had to use his bow for a cane. He was nearly dead, so he decided that if he got to Pahuk he would lie down upon the place where the Turtle had been. If he died there it would be well. Just as he reached the banks of the river he found he could go no farther. He fainted and fell.

The Magpie entered the lodge, and the animals with their power took the boy in. The Magpie again begged the animals to help the boy. The animals said that they could not do anything, but that there was one animal who was classed with the animal medicine-men; that he controlled all the lodges of the animals; that he it was who carried the war club; that he could do many wonderful things; that if there were any of the birds who were willing to go for this being, to speak. They said, "If this animal does not help the boy, then nothing more can be done." The Magpie flew up and said, "I will go for that being." Then there was a great noise again throughout the lodge, for they were glad to think that the Magpie should be willing to help the boy. The Magpie went out from the lodge and it was gone for some time. When it went back to the lodge it flew around and said: "Animals, he is coming. I carried presents to the being and it received them and promised to help the boy."

For some time afterwards the boy noticed a great dust coming in at the entrance. After the dust had settled the boy saw that the being was a Bear. The Bear was given a seat on the north side of the lodge so that it could look at the sun. The leader of the lodge said: "Father, our errand man brought a human being into the lodge. He made a special request as an errand man that we take pity on this boy. We have failed to help him, for the thing which he has in his stomach can not be destroyed, because it is a stone and it is hard. We have called upon you to help us." The Bear then said, "If the boy will promise me one thing I will remove the trouble and cure him." The Bear said to the young man, "When I cut you up, I want to eat a piece of your liver." The boy told the Bear that it was all right and that he could have a piece of his liver. The Bear then stood on his hind legs and began to strike upon his breast. All at once it cried aloud, rolled in the dust, and then stood up again. While the Bear was going through this performance the boy was told to lie down. The Bear jumped at the boy and looked at him for a long time. The Bear began to blow its breath upon the boy until he became unconscious. Then the Bear took its right paw and with the least claw it struck the breast of the boy and tore him open. The Bear reached into the stomach of the boy and took out a large round stone. This he threw to one side. Then the Bear put its head into the boy's breast. When it lifted up its head it had a piece of liver in its mouth. After the Bear ate the liver, it began to scream and yell, and it jumped on the boy and blew its breath upon his mouth and nostrils and upon the opening. The animals saw the opening closing up until it was closed and well again. The boy lay there as if he were dead. The Bear jumped to one side, and cried out for the animals to put life into the boy. The animals could not make the boy alive. Then the Magpie flew up and begged the Bear to restore him to life. The Bear jumped at the boy and blew its breath upon his nostrils and mouth until he began to move. The Bear took him up in his arms, hugged him, and then he began to breathe. The Bear jumped away from the boy and the boy stood up. The Bear ran around and the boy followed. After they stopped running, the Bear said, "My son, from now on you shall have the power to cut people open and to eat their liver." This had never been done before. The animals then began to teach the boy their powers. They sent him home and the people were surprised when they saw him coming.

The boy had great power. He did many wonderful things, and the people talked about it. The news reached the Skidi. The Skidi man again invited the boy to his tipi. This time the man would not eat with the Skidi. They talked about old times and the boy told the man that he had tried to poison him, but that the animals had taken him into their lodge and cured him. The boy opened his hand to the man and the man saw a bear claw there. When the boy closed his hand and opened it again, the bear claw was gone and the man fell over dead. Instead of the Skidi mourning for this man they thanked the boy for killing him.

The boy became a great medicine-man. It was through him that when they had their medicine ceremonies he called a live bear to visit them in their lodge. It was also through him that the Bear-Men used to cut people open and eat their liver. This boy also belonged to the Deer society. At one time the medicine-man and the Deer family were about to quarrel over their power. This young man spoke to them of taking away their fireplace. They knew then that he had power to make turtles around the fireplace move away. That would take away their power also. The medicine-men yielded to him. They were afraid that in doing some of the animal powers they might kill one another and that the Deer family might not be able to heal their people.

This boy became a great medicine-man, and he took the name of Smoking-with-the-Bear. Every day before the sun came up he went out of the lodge, sat upon it, and watched the sun as it came up. Sometimes he filled his pipe and smoked to the sun and to the bear. He taught his son his mysteries, and especially the secret of cutting a man open. This secret died when Medicine-Sun died, for he was the last of the bear family who learned the secrets from this boy.

90. THE BEAR MEDICINE.[1]

Many years ago the Pawnee went on a buffalo hunt. They followed the Platte River. When they had journeyed many days they came to a rough country where the people found cedar trees and they knew they were getting into a dangerous country; for the country was filled with wild animals, such as grizzly bears and mountain-lions. Among the people was a man, his wife and son. The man was poor. He had but one pony to pack his tipi and other things upon. The boy was handsome. Every time the Pawnee made their camp, the chief's son would

---

[1] Told by Medicine-Sun, a Skidi priest and medicine-man who died last year. The idea in relating this story is the same as in the preceding story. It further teaches the value of friendship among young men.

visit the poor boy in his tipi and they would sleep together. For many nights the chief's boy slept with the poor boy in the poor boy's tipi. The chief's son then coaxed and coaxed the poor boy to go to his tipi, but he would not go.

On one of their journeys they came to a mountainous country, to a place called Mountains-Covered-With-Seeds. The camp was made on the south side of the mountains. The people found many buffalo, and they killed them and brought the meat home, jerked and dried it. They camped for several days at this place while they were drying the meat, and the chief's son stayed with the poor boy all the time. The poor boy's father had gone with the party to kill the buffalo, but had not killed any himself. Some other men called him to help skin and cut their meat, and they gave him some. When he came home the boy felt ashamed because his father had not killed any buffalo. While they were at this camp the father had told the boy that men did not dare go into the mountains where the cedars were, and if they did they never came back; for there were mysterious animals among the cedars that killed people, even horses and ponies. The boy listened to all that his father said, and one night he was thinking about the place, although the chief's son lay beside him talking to him and playing with him. He waited, and as soon as the chief's son went to sleep the boy said to himself: "I will now go and be devoured by those mysterious animals in the mountains." So the boy left his bed and went out. He threw his blanket away and went towards the mountains, and as soon as he began to climb the mountains he began to cry. He climbed to the top of the mountains through the cedar timber, and on the other side he saw a ravine running up the mountains. He followed this ravine and crossed a little stream that was running down from the mountains, and on the other side he found a trail that was much like a human pathway. He followed this path until he came to the place where the mountains met and there he found a hole. He thought to himself: "This is what I came for; I shall now enter this den, and if there is a wild animal in there he can devour me. I am poor in spirit all the time when I am at home. My people are poor. The chief's boy is well off, he likes me, he likes to stay in my tipi, and I always feel bad to have him with me, although he likes me."

The boy went into the den and he found that it was the home of the Bears. There was sleeping on one side of the cave a mother Bear; in another place were three or four young Bears. The boy sat down and the cubs came to him and played with him. After a while one of the Bears went and awoke the mother, and said: "Mother, there is a boy in our lodge." The mother woke up and saw the boy sitting there playing with her children. She felt sorry for him, and spoke to him and said: "My son, I am sorry you came into this den. This is the den where a powerful Bear lives; he is the largest Bear in the country and has wonderful powers, given him by the Sun. See, yonder in the corner are skeletons of human beings, even horses and ponies, that he has brought in here for us to eat. He has taken the things that the people wear and brought them here. You can see them hanging upon the wall yonder. He has wonderful powers and he does mysterious tricks with the things that are hung up there. I am very sorry you have come and I am afraid you will never go back to your people alive."

The boy said: "Mother, I am poor. I came seeking your place; I have found it. If your husband comes and kills me, it is all good and well; I shall be eaten up, but I shall be thankful, for I am poor in spirit all the time when at home. I am poor, so I might as well be dead." The mother Bear rose up and said: "He is coming; I can hear him running. He smelt your tracks. There, take the little Bear in your arms. Hold tight to him. If he tells you to turn the little Bear loose, do not obey him, for he thinks a great deal more of that little Bear than of the others. It may be that he will spare your life for taking the little Bear in your arms." The boy took the little Bear in his arms, and the Bear came tumbling into the hole, spread his paws down upon the ground and then upwards, and exclaimed: "What! What! What! I smell a human being." He called his wife and said: "Where is the man?" The Bear saw him. He ordered the boy to turn the little Bear loose, and said: "How dare you hold my child in your arms! Turn him loose or I will kill you!" But the boy would not turn him loose. The Bear ordered the boy to turn the little Bear loose many times, but he would not pay any attention. At last the little Bear said: "Father is not going to kill you; he is going to take pity on you, for he thinks much of me. I will ask him to spare your life." The little Bear asked his father to take pity upon the poor boy, as he had come to them, and as he had played with them, saying that he wanted to keep the boy in the den with them. The Bear grew calm, but before he quieted down he had been exhaling different colored dusts. When this breathing of dust ceased, the boy knew that the Bear was no longer angry; so he turned the young Bear loose. The Bear went around the lodge and sat down.

The Bear told the boy that he had killed many people, some of them hunters; that many had shot at him, but that the arrows dropped off from his shaggy coat, and that he had killed them and brought their guns and things into the den. The Bear also told the boy that he was the leader of all the Bears; that the Sun communicated with him directly, and that he was the son of the Sun. He said: "I shall take pity upon you, my boy, for I want you to go back to your people. Let them know that they must not come around my den and try to kill me, for they can not kill me. I also want you to go into the lodge of the Bears and take your place on the north side of the lodge, so that you will always face the south. I shall also teach you to do sleight-of-hand."

The Bear began to sing and he turned the cubs into human beings, and also the mother Bear; then he turned himself into a man. All the time he continued to sing Bear songs. The Bear took a bow and arrows, ran up to the boy, and shot him in the side with an arrow. The arrow fell back and did not pierce him. The next time the Bear ran up to the boy and blew different colored dusts upon his side; then he went back a few paces and shot at the boy with an arrow, so that the arrow went through the boy and he fell over. The Bear and his wife and children all got around him and worked over him until they restored him to life. All these things they taught the boy. For several days the boy sat in the Bear's den, learning the secrets of the Bear. The Bear spoke and said: "The people have been killing many buffalo; they have remained several days; now they are about to continue their journey and I shall let you go; but remember that you are one of us now, and that you must visit me once in a while." They sang another song, and father and mother seized the children, tumbled them over several times, and they were turned into Bears again. Then the woman was seized by the man himself, and she turned into a Bear. Then the mother Bear and the children fell upon the man and he was again turned into a Bear. Now they went around the boy, took hold of him, and he was turned into a Bear. They ran around in their den a certain number of times and then rested. The boy was caught again and turned into a human being. Then the Bear took him to the place where the cedar tree was standing. The Bear reached up in the tree, took down one bear claw and strung it on a string of buckskin, and put it around the boy's neck. The Bear now told the boy to put his breath into his, and that now he had the different colors of dust in him, which were very curative; so that when he went home if anyone was wounded, or if there were sores on anyone, all he had to do was to touch his sides with the palms of his hands, blow his breath, and the dust would come; for it was the spirit of the Bear that had been given him; and if the people should make him angry, it was now possible for his canine teeth to come out as did those of the Bear, so that he must be very careful among his own people. The Bear also said: "Now, I have given you my power; you are my son. You shall

live to be an old man, and when I die, then you are to die.   When you
go hence and the people have returned to their village, you must come
to a certain place upon the Wonderful River (Missouri).   There under
a certain steep bank is an animals' lodge, where you will stand until
you are taken in.   There you will learn to be a medicine-man, for I have
control of that lodge.   Go now, my son, to your people."   When the
boy left the cave it was night.   He went to his home and lay down.
The next morning the father and mother got up and saw him lying there;
they also saw that he had a small bundle.   They knew that this bundle
meant something, so they took it and wrapped it up in a robe and hung
it up on the side of the tipi.   The next day the chief's boy came to his
tipi and was glad to see him again.

When the people had dried their meat, they broke camp and started
back to their permanent village.   They were attacked by the enemy.
The boy did not join them, but the people had success in driving the
enemy away; but one man was brought home wounded.   The different
medicine-men in the village were sent for to wait upon the man.   They
waited on him, but he seemed to grow worse.   The poor boy visited the
wounded man.   Some of the medicine-men who were waiting on the
man were singing, when the Bear spirit in the poor boy took hold of him,
and he jumped up, going close to the wounded man, and then to a ray
of the sun that was shining in, and there he stood in the sun's ray and
poured forth from his mouth different colored paints.   He then turned
to the wounded man and blew his breath of dust upon the wound.   The
dust seemed to enter the wound, and the man felt better.   The boy
became quiet and took up his robe and left the lodge.   The wounded man
cried, "Go after the poor boy, and let him wait on me again."   The boy
was sent for, and when he came in the other medicine-men, who waited
on the wounded man, sat on one side and gave the patient up to the boy.
He went through the same performance, and after he had finished he sat
down, and the wounded man said, "My son, come every day to treat me;
you shall have several ponies and several robes."   The young man came
and cured the wounded man, and it was noised through the village that
the boy had cured the wounded man.   The last time he waited upon
the man he sang a song about the Bear, and the people said that the
young man must have been taken into the Bear's den.   He sang to tell
the people that he had cured the man.   The presents were taken to his
lodge, and the robes and other presents were brought in, while the ponies
were tied outside.

The boy went into the lodge and asked the people to sweep it out
and put the mat and other things in order, saying that he did not want

any of them to stay in the lodge, for he was going to have a ceremony of his own. The women swept out the lodge, spread the mat on the ground and went out. The boy was then alone. He took down his bundle, and took therefrom the bear's claw and four downy feathers, each having a different color. He laid them upon the ground and went out to the place where the ponies were tied. He first put his hands into the mouths of the horses, went back into the lodge, and passed his hands over the bear's claw and the feathers. This was a sign of thankfulness to the Bear who had taken pity upon him; for he had never owned a pony, and these were his first. After this performance, he filled his pipe and sang a song, calling the spirit of the Bear to him. The boy smoked the pipe, and after smoking went out and told one of the women to go and bid the chief's son come to his tipi.

The poor boy went back into the lodge, sat down, put another cushion on the mat, and as the chief's son entered the young medicine-man motioned him to take a seat on the cushion that he had placed there for him to sit on. The chief's son saw the things spread out in front of the poor boy, and he knew then where the boy had gone when he disappeared. The chief's son now arose and put his hands over the poor boy, and told him that he was glad he was back, and that he now knew that the poor boy had been among the Bears, and that the Bears had taught him the mysteries. He begged the poor boy to teach him. The poor boy said: "No, I can not, my brother, for your father is a chief, and you can never know these mysteries. You must be kind and good to the people, for some day you will be a chief. To have the spirit of the Bear you must kill people and take scalps, and this I do not want you to do. I sent for you, for I have been treating the wounded man. I do not want the people to know my power, but when I went to visit the wounded man the spirit of the Bear overcame me, for the people who were waiting upon him were not doing right by him. I have cured him. The people know my power, and you, who have befriended me, ought to know of my power before anyone. I possess it, it is in me, but I can not explain it to you. Now it is time for me to wrap up the things in the bundle and hang them on the side of the lodge. Now, my brother, I have several robes which I received for waiting upon that wounded man. Take your choice." The young man took one robe which had pictures of a pipe upon it, for these things belong to a chief. The poor boy took the chief's boy outside, untied one of the ponies, and handed him a rope. Said he: "This, my brother, is yours; take it home, use it for your own, but come back to-night and stay with me." The chief's boy was very thankful. He took the pony to the chief's lodge, went in, and found his father sitting there.   The boy said: "Father, the poor boy is possessed of wonderful animal powers.   I am glad that when he was poor I was his friend, for now I shall try to learn the mysteries that he knows."   The old chief spoke up and said: "Nawa iri (it is good); I am glad to hear the words you have spoken.   Take your robe, your pony, and your things, and make your home with the poor boy.   Let him teach you all these things; then I shall know that you are learning. Visit us once in a while, so that we may know that all is well with you." The boy went back to the lodge of the poor boy and said: "I have come to stay with you, my brother.   My pony may stay with your ponies.   I shall look after the ponies, and we can be together always.   My father wishes us to visit him sometimes at night, but he wants me to be with you all the time."   The boys remained together in the poor boy's lodge, and the poor boy would sing the Bear songs which had been taught him. For a long time they were together.

Once the village was attacked by the enemy.   The people went out to fight, but the poor boy stayed in his lodge, untied his bundle, put the bear claw about his neck and the feather upon his head, and painted his body with red paint, making two black streaks downwards from his eyes.   Then he took only a few arrows and a bow and went out.   The chief's boy watched him.   The poor boy attacked the enemy and he killed a man.   He went from there close to the line on the enemy's side, and they were shooting at him, but the arrows and bullets seemed to drop off from his body.   He attacked another enemy and killed him. Then the enemy's line was broken.   They came home with many scalps and the whole village was in an uproar, singing and dancing victory songs in honor of the poor boy.

In the battle, as the poor boy attacked the enemy, the chief's boy watched the battle and saw the poor boy rush in the midst of the enemy and kill them, and he was thankful that the poor boy was his friend; and in his heart he said: "My friend is a brave man.   How I wish that I had the courage that he has; but then he has told me that I must not kill and so I must be satisfied."   The people talked about the young man and asked him to enter their Bear dance ceremony, for all the people recognized the fact that he possessed wonderful powers.   The boy joined in the Bear dance and was finally made leader of the Bear dance ceremonies. As the poor boy grew to be a man, so did the chief's boy.   The chief's boy kept begging the poor boy to take pity upon him and give him the same powers that he possessed; but the poor boy said: "No, I can not."

Winter came, and the people began to talk about going on the buffalo hunt.   The poor boy and the chief's boy got ready to go with the hunting party. They departed, and the poor boy said that the chief's boy should do all the killing and bringing in of the buffalo, and when he saw certain meat he would tell the chief's boy to prepare it for him, for he was going to put it to a special use. The people journeyed west and they found many buffalo. In one of the killings the chief's boy had killed a young buffalo cow. The poor boy told the chief's boy that this meat should be his; that he was going to ask his mother to jerk the meat, dry it, and put it in one of the parfleches by itself. The meat of the buffalo cow was jerked, dried in the sun, pounded, piled up carefully, and then put into a parfleche and tied up. When it was tied up, the poor boy told the chief's son that that was his meat.

Towards spring the people went back to their permanent village. As summer came, the poor boy told the chief's boy that he wanted him to go with him to the northeast, to a certain water known as Wonderful River; to bring his pony, saddle it, put the parfleche on the saddle, and several robes for their bedding. They started toward the northeast, with one pony that carried their things. They traveled for many days until they came to the Wonderful River. They went down the river, and after a while they came to the place that the Bear had told the poor boy of. "Now, my brother," said the poor boy to the chief's son, "this is the place we were bound for; be brave and do as I tell you. Do not retreat, for I wish you to have powers different from mine." The young chief said that he would be brave. They lariated their pony at some distance from the river, put their things upon its back, and went to the steep bank of Wonderful River. The poor boy untied the parfleche and cut the meat in small pieces. Then he took from his bundle a lariat rope made of rawhide. He tied a rope around the body of the chief's boy and another to the boy's legs; then he lowered him over the steep bank and brought him up again, so that the poor boy knew the lariat would work. Then he put all the meat in the parfleche again, and tied it up and put it on the back of the chief's boy; then he gave him a sharp stick. He let him down the steep bank to the ledge in the middle of the bank. There he told him to set the parfleche and his stick. Then he pulled up the chief's son again, put him upon the bank, and said: "Now, my brother, you are poor in spirit; I, too, was poor in spirit when I made up my mind to go to the den of the Bears; they took pity upon me because I was poor in spirit. Now if you want to possess some powers, make up your mind to go through this and try not to draw back; I am to place you under the bank here, and you are to hang there, and as the different birds come to you, feed them, put meat upon the sharp stick that I have given you and hold it out from you, and they

will come and eat; then put another piece of meat on and feed all the
birds that come to you. If they take you into their lodge, well and good;
if you are not taken into the lodge within four days, then I shall draw
you up and we shall go home, for then I shall know that you are not
favored by the animal gods. I shall leave you now, shall go a long way
off for four days, and on the fifth day I shall come back and see if you
are still there." The chief's boy said, "Very well, I shall do as you
have told me."

The boy went to the timber, cut two dogwood sticks of good size, then
came to where the chief's boy sat. He trimmed down the sticks, which
were about six inches long, and sharpened them at one end. He told
the chief's boy to sit down with his back toward the sun, saying that he
wanted the sun to look upon him so that the sun would tell the Bear that,
instead of the poor boy being there, he had put down another man in
his place. The poor boy said: "Have courage, so that you can receive
the powers from the animals." The poor boy took hold of the skin on
the back of the chief's boy, first on the left side, taking it between the
first and second fingers and the thumb, then running the stick through
the skin, which protruded through the fingers to the backs of them; then
he did the same on the right side of his back, running another stick
through the skin. The boy then got up and took out another lariat
rope that had ten soft elk hide strings at the ends. These strings he tied
on to the sticks. He let the boy slip down the bank and hang there;
when the boy reached the ledge where the parfleche and the stick were,
the poor boy then tied the other end of the lariat rope to a tree. He
looked down and saw the chief's boy; he saw that he grasped the sharp
stick and that he could reach the meat. The poor boy waited until
towards evening upon the bank. The chief's boy was crying. In the
evening the poor boy noticed the birds coming down the stream from the
west. He also noticed that some of the birds went to the chief's son
and received meat from him. The poor boy saw that his friend was
favored by the animals, so he left him and went away and hid in the
timber. He stayed there for several days, wondering what had become
of the boy. On the fifth day, the poor boy went down to the place.
The boy was gone. The poor boy was satisfied that the animals had
taken him, so he went off. The poor boy stayed around close to the
bank for several days. When the chief's son had remained four or five
days, then the poor boy commenced to sleep on the bank.

One morning, while the poor boy was sleeping, something seemed to
touch him. He woke up and saw that it was morning. He lay down
again, and again some one touched him. He looked up and saw that it

was nearly day, but that no one was about. The third time he was awakened; but the fourth time, when he awoke, he looked to the east, and the sun came up. As the sun came up the boy looked upon the bank, and there stood his friend. The chief's boy had on leggings that had deer hoofs upon them; in some places were bear claws; in some places pictures of birds. He had upon his body a robe which was decorated with sweet grass and other sweet perfumes. He had a bundle under his arm. The poor boy arose, and said, "My brother!" Both embraced and said, "I am glad to see you again." The chief's boy said that he would tell the poor boy of all the mysteries he had seen when they went home; that they must hurry and get to their home. So they went to their pony, put their things on it, and started home. The chief's boy put his bundle in the poor boy's lodge.

The next day the chief's boy told the poor boy to go with him to his father's lodge, and they went. They sat down and the father was glad to see them. The boy's sisters and other relatives were also glad to see him. The chief's boy said: "My father, this boy and myself went to a strange country. This boy has taken pity upon me; he let me go down into the animals' lodge, under the Wonderful River. There I found the animals in a circle. They taught me the powers of the medicine-men. This poor boy was not selfish; he let me receive this power which was for him. The animals have requested that I take them presents of native tobacco, some feathers, some beads, and some meat; get them for me, my father, for I must be going back." The father arose, passed his hand over the poor boy, and went out. He visited the different lodges of his relatives and they brought much meat, many beads, and much tobacco. The boys received the presents and they again made the journey east to the Wonderful River. The chief's boy disappeared, carrying the presents with him and coming back the next day. They then went home.

In the fall, when the people had their medicine-men's sleight-of-hand performances, these two boys went into the medicine-men's lodge. The poor boy took his seat facing the south, as directed by the Bear. The chief's boy sat by him. Before the ceremonies were opened, the chief's boy stood up and said, "Medicine-men, I want to select a place to sit." The medicine-men all said, "Nawa." The boy went around the fireplace on the west side, then to the east on the north side of the entrance. Here, at this place, was set up a cedar tree, and at this place no one of the medicine-men sat, for it was a place alone for the man who had been taken into the animals' lodge and understood their mysteries. When he took his seat there, a great noise was made by the men throughout the lodge. As the young man took his seat behind the cedar tree he came out and appeared again, and there he stood with his robe on, covered with blue mud and downy feathers. The medicine-men knew by his appearance that he had the powers of the animals. They noticed also that all around the bottom of the cedar tree were downy feathers. The old medicine-men performed sleight-of-hand that night. The two boys did not do any sleight-of-hand for the first two nights. After the third night, the poor boy did feats which the other medicine-men could not do. The next night the other young man did some wonderful things, and after that the people acknowledged the two young men as the leaders of the medicine-men. The chief's boy became the leader of the Medicine-Men's dance. The other boy became the leader of the Bear dance. The chief's boy became chief, for he was powerful. The other man was a brave, and they were both medicine-men, with great power.

The poor boy told the chief's boy that, no matter where he was or how healthy he was, as soon as the Bear should be killed or die from old age, he also was to die; so the chief's boy knew that when the time came for him to die, he could not help himself. One day they were sitting in the lodge and the man grunted. He took up his robe with the bear's claw on it, embraced his friend, and went out of his lodge. Then the people went out and they heard the screams of Bears. The poor boy disappeared and was never heard of again. Before he disappeared, he had taught many Bear songs and the ceremony to the people. The other man mourned for the poor boy for some time, but he knew that he had to die and so he stopped mourning. He kept up the Bear dance and the people liked him, for he was the chief and a medicine-man as well. He married and had many children. He taught his children the mysteries of the medicine-men, and they, too, became great medicine-men. The father died of old age, but before he died he taught his children all the mysteries that were given him in the animals' lodge; and to this day the same ceremony that was carried on at that time is carried on by the Pawnee.

91. THE BEAR MEDICINE AND CEREMONY.[1]

Many years ago there was a little girl among the Skidi who had mysterious ways. As she grew up she did not like to have her nails trimmed, and one time when she had them trimmed she nearly died. Before her birth her father had killed a bear, and this bear's spirit had entered the child, but no one knew it. She grew up to be a woman and was married

[1] Told by Medicine-Sun, Skidi. The story is interesting because it teaches that women might obtain medicine powers from the bears and make use of this power in practice of medicine.

to a famous warrior. She had a child, but it died. She again had a child and it died. Again she had a child, a boy, and he grew up to be over ten years old.

One time the Skidi went on a hunt and they took the boy with them and tied him on a spotted pony, for they wanted him to ride. When they returned to the village they found that the boy's father had gone out with a war party. The boy became sick; the mother was frightened and she sent for the best medicine-men in the camp. They came, but their medicine and power could do no good and the boy died. The mother dressed the boy, took him up on a hill and dug a shallow grave for him; then she made a kind of a house over the grave. The mother stayed by the grave several days and nights and grieved, for she had lost every child she had. After a time she became afraid, for there were many bears and mountain-lions in the country, and so she went home.

The people moved their camp and went toward their permanent village. The woman went with them, but she was in mourning. She had cut her hair and had gashed her arms and legs with a knife, so that she was in great pain. Several days afterwards some warriors overtook the people, and told them they had seen a grave and asked who had died. The people told them that the woman had lost her boy. They said that somebody had robbed the grave or else wild animals had opened it. The woman heard it. She arose and started for the place. She found her son's body exposed; the clothing gone. She cried and cried, and then she made up her mind to stay there and die. She reburied her boy, then sat down by the grave. She cried all day, all night, and again the next day, the next night, and so on. On the fourth day she became frightened. In the evening she looked around for a place where she could stop over night. She saw at a distance a thick timber with many cedar trees. She went to the cedars, and among them she found a large cedar with its limbs spreading and drooping so that the branches touched the ground. She crawled under the branches and there sought protection.

Some time in the night she heard a noise that sounded like a donkey braying. She listened, and heard it again and again. She was frightened, but she thought, "I might as well die here." She heard the noise again; this time nearer to her, and she recognized the growl of a Bear. The Bear spoke and said: "Do not be afraid; I know you are under the cedar tree; I felt sorry for you and so came after you. I and my wife have taken pity upon you, for we know you grieve because every time you have a child it dies. Arise and come with me." The woman arose and followed the Bear. The Bear once in a while gave a loud grunt, and wild animals moved out of his path. He led the way through a valley, then up a hill. There the woman saw a very steep bank, and on the bank was a cedar tree. The Bear slid toward the tree and disappeared. The woman followed and disappeared, too. In another moment she saw that she was in a Bear's den. The den inside was like an earth-lodge. On the south side of the lodge lay the Bear's wife, with her paws on the ground and her head resting upon her paws. The Bear made a peculiar noise, and six cubs came from the north side of the den and sat down. The Bear again made a peculiar noise and his wife sat up. She looked at the woman, who sat by the entrance on the south side. The Bear spoke to the woman and said: "I took pity on you and asked my wife to help you, and she has promised that she will. Now the first thing we shall do for you is to give you a promise, and if you do as we tell you, our promise will be good. Run after our cubs and you shall have children equal to the number of cubs you catch." The woman arose and ran after the cubs. The cubs looked so clumsy and big that she thought she could catch all of them. She ran after them, but she could not catch a single one. She was giving out, but she did not give up. She kept on running until the youngest Bear gave out and fell behind the others, and the woman reached out and caught it by the legs. She held it in her left arm and ran again until she succeeded in catching another, but as she then had two Bears she could not run any more, so she gave up trying. The Bear told her that the two Bears were hers and that she could take them home. Then he blew his red dust breath into her face, then his yellow breath, then his black breath, and then his white breath. When this was done, the Bear said: "If a man is wounded you must blow these different breaths into the wound and he will feel better and soon get well. Now my wife will teach you something."

The female Bear went up to the woman, put her fore legs around her neck, and then coughed up a piece of powdered cherry. The woman ate this. Then the female Bear coughed another substance, and this time it was a piece of powdered hackberry. The woman ate this up. Again the Bear coughed up something, and this time it was powdered bull-berry. The woman ate it. "Now," said the Bear, "you are prepared to doctor the sick; when you have blown the different breaths upon the sick, you can cough these different powdered berries and give them to the sick and they will at once feel better." The Bears kept the woman in their den, teaching her many mysterious things. At last the male Bear said: "It is time for you to go home. Take this red paint of mine and this red downy feather. Give them to your husband and tell him that I gave them to him." The female Bear said: "I give you my yellow paint and my yellow feather; take them; they are yours. When you doctor, put the paint upon your person; put the feather upon your head. We want you to make a tipi and have it painted. Tell your husband to get many tanned buffalo hides, sew them together, and make a tipi. At the bottom of the tipi paint a yellow circle, on the middle of the tipi paint a black band, and above this paint red. On the west side put a picture of a cedar tree resting upon the black ground. The cedar tree will be the tree that you see on the side of my den. On each side of the tree in the center will be owls. They are two owls who are friendly to us, who come and guard our entrance. Take these two young Bears to your home. If you want to kill them when you get home, do so and make casks of their skins so that your children can crawl into them. The Bears will come back to us after they are killed."

The woman took the two young Bears and started to her home. The least one was very gentle; the other one was somewhat wild and did not like the woman. On the third night the wild Bear strayed off and never came back to the woman. The next morning the woman got up and took the little Bear in her arms, and when she became tired she put him down on the ground and he followed her. At last they came to the village. The Bear did not want to go into the village, for he was not used to the odor of people. The woman picked him up and carried him on her back into the village. It was noised around through the camp that the woman had come back and that she had a young Bear. People did not pay any attention to the story. In the night the woman had a dream. She saw the female Bear, who said to her, "Have the little Bear killed; do not be afraid; he will come back to me."

The next day the woman told one of her brothers to kill the little Bear, and he did so. The woman tanned the skin, then took the yellow paint and painted it on the inside. She then put the yellow-painted feather on the head of the bear skin. The bear skin was hung up on a pole outside of the lodge, so that the sun could cast its rays upon the skin. The skin was to hold the spirit of the Bears, so that the spirit would be present with the woman. Every time the woman was touched she made a grunting noise like that of a Bear. Every morning just as the sun came up in the east she was always sitting there with the yellow downy feather on her hair, painting with the yellow paint. She also had the bear hide. As the sun came up she would rise and go into the lodge, put her things in a bundle and hang them up. Her husband came home. She did not tell him where she had been, nor did she tell him about the Bear. The man noticed that the woman made grunting sounds in the night and thought that she must have been with the Bears. The people were careful how they talked to her, for they knew that she acted like a bear.   The woman herself began to realize that she had the spirit of a bear, and she knew why it was that, when a young girl, she became very sick when her nails were cut.

One day the enemy attacked the village.   She gave the red paint to her husband to put all over his body, and also gave him the red feather to tie in his scalp-lock.   He went out and fought and was very brave.   The enemy's arrows did not seem to have any effect upon him.   When the battle was over, the people brought in one man who was badly wounded. The wounded man's folks sent for some of the best medicine-men in the village, but the medicine-men said, "We can not do anything for him." The man gave the grunting noise of a bear, so the relatives said, "Let us send for the woman who grunts like a bear."   The people sent their errand man to the woman.   The man went to the woman's tipi and went up to where the woman sat, and, passing his hands over her, said, "Have pity upon me and the relatives of the man who was wounded and is dying."   She sat still for a while, then said, "I will go."   The errand man passed his hands over her head again and thanked her; then went back to the wounded man's lodge and told the people that the woman was coming.   The woman sent word to the wounded man to be patient, for she was coming.   She also sent word that the women should sweep out the lodge and that the men should burn cedar limbs in the lodge, and that the man should be placed on the south side of the lodge.

All these things were done.   A tipi was now put up to the west of the woman's lodge.   She took her husband into the tipi, carrying her medicine bundle with her.   When they went in she untied the bundle, and for the first time her husband saw the things that she had in it.   She took her skirt off and wore a piece of tanned buffalo to cover her waist. She painted her body with yellow paint and took the yellow feather and put it in her hair.   She then painted her husband with the red paint and put the red feather in his hair.   She then sang a song to call the Bears to help her.   The Bears had told her to sing the song, and promised that if they heard it and decided to help her, she would find on the next morning cedar limbs around her tipi.

The song she sang was this:

Some one spoke and told me.
Yonder shall come, yonder shall come.
That my father stood where I now stand.
Yonder shall come, yonder shall come,
Yonder shall come, yonder shall come,
Yonder shall come, yonder shall come,
Yonder shall come, yonder shall come.

> I am now imitating the Bear,
> I am now acting like one.
> Yonder shall come, yonder shall come,
> Yonder shall come, yonder shall come,
> Yonder shall come, yonder shall come.

This song she repeated several times. All the time she was grunting and making a noise like a bear, so the man was made to feel like a bear. They sat in their tipi all night singing bear songs. In the morning the man filled his pipe; then they both went out. As the sun came up from the east, the woman inhaled power from it, and the man smoked to it. Then the woman and the man gathered some of the cedars and they started for the wounded man's lodge. The wounded man's relatives were anxious to have them to come, for the wounded man was getting worse.

As the woman and man went through the village they sang another song. When they entered the lodge they sang a third song. Then the woman went around the lodge by way of the north, then to the south, where the patient lay.

She stood on the east side of the lodge and blew her breath; there was no color to her breath. Again she went around the lodge and blew her breath. Again and again she went around the lodge, then told the people to remove the robe and to bare the man's wound. She looked at the wound, then blew her breath at it, and her breath was yellow. The breath went straight to the wound. She went around the lodge again and stood on the east side and blew her breath again. It was red and went straight to the wound. Again she ran around the lodge and stood on the east side and blew her breath, and this time it was black, and it went straight to the wound. The last time her breath was white, and it went straight to the wound. The wound seemed to become fresh and the blood began to flow. She then went to the man and blew different breaths into him. The spirit of the Bear within the woman was roused. The woman began grunting and raising her hands. Some of the people said, "The bear's teeth are coming out." Her husband took the cedar limbs and tapped the woman on her back until she quieted down. Some limbs of cedar were put upon the coals, so that the smell of burnt cedar and smoke was all over the lodge. The woman and the man then went home. Four days afterwards the woman went through the same performance. She never gave the man any medicine, but the man's wound began to heal. The third time she went through the performance, and the fourth time. The wound was healing rapidly and the wounded man was getting well.

One day the man sat up in his bed and talked to his relatives and said: "My people, this is a wonderful woman; ever since she doctored me I have felt good. In my sleep I see her as she is, naked with only a covering about her waist, the yellow feather tied to her hair, in her right hand a cedar limb, in her left hand the young bear hide; on her left side a she cinnamon bear is walking. She and the bears come to my bedside and walk around me; then they are gone." The wounded man continued: "Now, my friends, I want to know how many ponies and how many buffalo robes you are going to send to this wonderful woman, for I now feel well. I am a little weak, but I feel that I can walk around and the wound will not hurt me." His friends told him that they were to send many robes, seven parfleches filled with dried buffalo, and five head of ponies. The wounded man was not satisfied, for he had made up his mind to make himself poor in heart before her, so that she might take pity upon him and give him the spirit of the Bear.

The woman learned the thoughts of the man in her dream from the Bear. One day the woman and her husband went to the lodge of the wounded man, and she told the wounded man not to worry about her pay; that she was satisfied with the pay, and that from that day the wounded man was to become a member of the Bear society. The man arose and thanked the woman by passing his hands over her head, then down over her arms, saying, "You have taken pity upon me. I was wounded very badly; I could not see; it was all dark to me." The woman told the man to sit down. Then she went around the lodge and stood in the west, facing east. She called the wounded man to her. He went to her and she stood him in her place. She then ran around the lodge, slapping her side as she went around. Then she staggered and caught the wounded man, pulled his head to hers, so that their mouths met, and she put some pounded cherries into his mouth and told him to eat. He ate. The man became well. His relatives sent robes, and parfleches filled with meat, upon ponies to the woman.

Another ceremony took place. As the offerings were brought, the robes and parfleches were taken into the tipi, and the ponies were tied outside. The woman took her medicine bundle, emptied it, and placed the young bear hide on the west side of the fireplace and the feathers and the paints on each side of the Bear. She next took some native tobacco, went out to the horses, put her hand in each horse's mouth and wet her hand with the horse's saliva. She rubbed the native tobacco with this. Then she went into the tipi and stood on the west side of the fireplace. She offered a little of the tobacco to the sun, and set the tobacco on the edge of the fireplace; then she offered a little more to the west, where the sun sets, and that was also placed by the fireplace. Then she offered a little more to the southwest, to the home of the Bears; this was placed upon the ground, southwest of the fireplace. Now she went to the bear hide and placed the native tobacco upon its nostrils, passing her hands over the head and down the body. She made another preparation of tobacco and horse saliva. She took it out and placed it on the southwest side of the tipi, for this was a special offering to the Bear. The woman then told her husband to fill his pipe and smoke, and to give one whiff to Tirawa, four whiffs to the sun in the east, and four whiffs in the west to the setting sun, and four to the southwest to home of the Bears. The ashes were dumped out southwest of the fireplace.

When the man had finished the smoke offering, he called his errand man to take the ponies to the other herd of ponies that were grazing upon the prairie. The man returned to the tipi, and as he sat down the woman began to tell him how the Bear came to her and how he took her to their den. Her husband was glad to hear the story, so the woman taught him all the songs she had learned from the Bear. The people now knew that the woman had wonderful powers.

Several years afterwards she gave birth to a son, and this son grew and was never known to be sick. Years afterward she gave birth to a girl. These two children grew. The woman gave birth to several other children and they died. She knew that they would, for she caught only two young Bears, when she was told to catch as many as she could.

On one of their buffalo hunts the man killed many buffalo and the woman tanned them. She had many, so she made a tipi. After the tipi was completed, she sent for the wounded man and some of her own relatives, and she had the tipi painted as she had been told by the Bear.

In the Bear ceremonies and dances the woman was sent for, because she was one of the leading persons in the Bear dance. On the buffalo hunts the woman always had the man possessed of the Bear spirit; so if he was attacked by the enemy he could fight and would not be afraid of the enemy; for the arrows and bullets could not go through his body. "But," said the woman, "if they should happen to strike you on the hands you will surely die." On one of these hunts the men had gone to attack buffalo, and the women and children had gone to a creek near by and made camp. As the men attacked the buffalo and scattered out, the enemy attacked them. As the shouts and shooting were heard, the men left their dead buffalo and ran their ponies toward camp. In this way the Skidi gathered together and they fought the enemy; but the enemy was more numerous and the Skidi had to run. The last to run was Bear-Woman's husband. He fought bravely and was wounded in several places on the body, but he kept on fighting. The Skidi were run into a pond. Then the enemy turned their ponies and gave up the chase. As the Skidi crossed the pond, Bear-Woman's husband began to give out. "Tell my wife that I am going to die; tell her that I was not possessed with the Bear's spirit when we were attacked; tell her I fought hard, and as I have many wounds I must die."

Word was sent to the woman and she went through the camp asking the women if any of them were sick with blood. The man's own niece came forward and said, "I am sick." Bear-Woman took this young woman with her to where the men were coming with her husband. The women got there too late, for the man had died. The woman began to mourn for her husband. Many days and months the woman continued to mourn for her husband. As her children were growing up, she commenced to teach to her boy the mysteries of the Bear. Her tipi was always decorated.

The fame of her powers reached other bands, and once a Chaui came to her tipi and placed before her a parfleche filled with dried buffalo meat and many robes and two ponies. He placed his hands upon her head and begged her to teach him the mysteries of the Bear. He sat down in the lodge. She sat for a long time in silence. At last she spoke and said: "You are trying me; you want to see if what you have heard is true. I do not do the things that you have heard I do, for these things are done by other powers. I believe in these powers. You will doubt them and doubt me. I will try you, and if I see that you are not poor in spirit I will stop." This Chaui man proved to be a believer in animal power; so the woman taught him the mysteries of the Bear. The Chaui man was so good that the woman gave him her Bear dance. His tipi was also painted like the woman's tipi.

The Chaui man stayed with this woman for many years. He hunted and killed buffalo and game and brought them to the woman's tipi. He also cared for her children, and clothed them with the finest of buckskin. In the fall, after the hunts, the woman joined the medicine-men's lodge, and sat with the Bear family, on the south side. She did not join the Bear family who sat in the west, and who were the Grizzlies, for these were the ones who caught men in the doctors' lodge and cut them open with a bear's claw, and pulled the liver through the opening and ate it. This, the woman said, she was not told to do. In her sleight-of-hand she made a plum tree grow from the hard ground, inside the medicine-men's lodge; then she would shake it and many plums would fall from the tree. Many wonderful things she did in the sleight-of-hand performances. Most of these things she taught to her own son.

Many times, while on a buffalo hunt, the woman would find cedar limbs around her tipi. She would tie them into a bundle and pack them around until the people who belonged to the Bear family came and asked for some of the cedar branches. She would give them away, but never threw them away.

This woman lived to be very old. When she died, the son took her place and became one of the four leading dancers in the Bear ceremony. The woman before she died gave a name to the Chaui man, and that name was Carry-the-War-Club-in-Anger. Her son she named Wonderful-Sun.

Her teachings are now kept by Seems-Like-Chief. He is a young man, but has in his keeping a bear's claw that the woman was supposed to have, and also has a young bear robe which is decorated. This dance is still performed each summer by the descendants of this Chaui.

92. THE BUFFALO POWER AND THE WILD HORSE DANCE.[1]

A long time ago there was a big village upon a river, and in this village lived a chief who had become famous for traveling to many places and capturing many ponies and killing people. All of the other chiefs looked upon him as the big chief of the tribe. When he gave orders they were carried out at once. This chief had many wives, the youngest of whom gave birth to a boy. The chief cared for this boy and talked to him, telling how he had become a great chief. The people looked to the son to become chief some day and fill his father's place without having to go on the war-path. As the boy grew up he thought that his father did not like him, because he talked so much to him about what he should do to become a chief, to fight in battles, go on the war-path, and capture ponies. The boy made up his mind that as soon as he should get a chance he would join a war party. The first war party he found going out, he joined. The war party failed and had to return home unsuccessful. The young man wanted to go on another war party, and so he would stay out at night, visiting different lodges, to see if there was any war party going out. Whenever he found a war party starting out he joined it. The parties that he joined were unsuccessful. They met obstacles, were seen by the enemy, were run after, sometimes surrounded, and often some of the warriors killed. The boy, however, always managed to escape. If the war party happened to capture many ponies, they were overtaken and the ponies taken from

[1] Told by Roaming-Chief, Chaui. The story especially points the moral that a chief is not necessarily a great man, and especially that, if he proves to be lazy, people will have no respect for him.

them. The warriors began to worry, and they finally found out that when the young man was with the party it met hardships, was found out by the enemy, and driven away. Other war parties that the young man had not joined were successful and brought home many ponies. After these facts were recognized the warriors were careful to conceal from the boy their departure from the village, and if he followed and caught up with them the warriors told him to return home; and they called him all kinds of names, but still he would follow them. Finally all of the warriors would turn back home, for they knew there was no use going farther. The whole village grew to dislike the boy and he came to be known as Poor-Boy.

At length the boy's father heard what the warriors thought of his son. He became angry at his boy, called him all kinds of names, then told him that he should go upon the war-path alone. His father and mother both were angry at their son and ashamed of him. The boy became very sad. He would sit day after day, wishing that the enemy would attack the village, so that he could ride one of his father's ponies right into the enemy's lines and be killed; but the enemy never appeared. Once or twice he was about to commit suicide. All at once he made up his mind to go away from his village, so that if he was found by the enemy he might be killed; and if not found by the enemy he might meet some wild animals and be killed by them; and if not killed by the animals, he might starve to death.

One evening the boy went to his mother and said, "Mother, can you give me one or two pairs of moccasins and a little something to eat?" His mother said, "No, my son, I can not give them to you, for there is no use of your trying to join war parties." The young man said, "I am not going with any war party, but I am going alone." His mother gave him two pairs of moccasins, one pair filled with parched corn and the other pair filled with pemmican. In the night the boy put his leggings and moccasins on and a covering robe over his shoulders, took his quiver, slung it over his shoulders, took a piece of buffalo hair lariat rope and tied it around his waist, and hung his moccasins from it. He started out and went directly west. Each day he took a very little of the meat and a few kernels of corn. The farther he went the more he ate, until at last he had eaten all he had. He kept on day after day. He was very hungry and very thin, so he could walk only a very short distance; then he had to stop and lie down, for his strength was leaving him.

One day he felt dizzy. He could not see very far and he knew that he must be dying. At a short distance there was a hill. He made up his mind to go to the hill and lie down upon it, so that if he should die the birds would find him, and the people, seeing the birds fly over the hill, would come to it and find his body and would know that he was dead.

When he reached the top of the hill he saw a big lake in a valley and things that looked like people standing around the lake. He did not lie down, but went down to the lake to wash his mouth. He stooped over and drank some water, cleansed his mouth, washed, then sat down by the lake and spoke with a loud voice and said: "This is a good place for me to die. You gods who may have control of this place, let me die here." He then took off his moccasins, his leggings, his robe, and everything that he had on. He spread the robe, put all the other things in a row and tied them up, stood up and said: "You animals who have control of this lake, I give you these things, for I am about to die. I have no further use for them," and he threw the bundle into the lake.

He sat down and he thought he had gone to sleep, for while he was sitting there he saw two clouds of dust coming up from the west. The first cloud was made by two wild horses, one a black horse and the other a gray. The two horses ran around the lake, one on each side of it; and they came to the boy and stopped. Both looked at him; then they turned and ran back from whence they had come. The other cloud of dust came and there were two buffalo, and they circled around the lake to where the boy was sitting, stopped on each side of him and looked at him. Then the buffalo returned from whence they had come. The boy thought he woke up. He saw the dust again. This time the horses were together, and the two buffalo were together, and instead of stopping on each side of him, they ran over him, so that he was rolled over. The horses and buffalo went back from whence they had come. The boy sat up again and saw a big drove of buffalo coming. The buffalo ran over him and trampled him, and he thought that he was killed.

Somebody touched the boy, and he sat up. He was in a big lodge under the lake. He looked around on the north side, and saw that the men of that side were all decorated with paint and feathers and imitated Horses. On the south side the people wore the Buffalo tail upon their backs, and were Buffalo. The leader of the Buffalo spoke and said: "My son, we know that you are very poor. The people do not like to have anything to do with you, for you have been very unlucky in all your undertakings, and the people grew to dislike you. We knew this. We sent for you. All the men that you see on my side are the Buffalo that you saw attack you. All the men that you see on the north side are horses that you saw when they attacked you. We had to do this in order to bring you into our lodge. We made up our minds to take pity upon you and give you certain powers, so that you may become a great warrior, and finally become a chief. We wish to make a medicine-man of you and you must start a dance among your people known as the Buffalo and Wild Horse dance. There are your things in front of you. Put the things upon you and sit among us. Before we do anything for you, we wish you to go home and let your father and mother know that your are alive, for they are mourning over you. We also want you to go after presents for us. Now, I want you to look at me and you will see that all these Buffalo on the south side are my children. Now that you have been taken into my lodge you shall die of old age, but you shall also have many children. Now look at me." The boy looked on the south side and there sat an old bull whose skin was bare of hair, on account of old age. There were a few hairs on his head; the rest of his skin had no hair. The bull said: "My son, you have heard me ask my children to take pity upon you, and they have consented to do so; but first bring me native tobacco, blue beads, a black silk handkerchief, and brown eagle feathers." The Horse then spoke and said, "My son, look at me." The boy looked, and there sat an old black Horse. It had only a few hairs on its mane and tail. The black Horse then said: "My son, my children have taken pity upon you; but first get me native tobacco, sweet grass, black buffalo lariat rope, eagle feathers, and paint." Then they set the boy west of the lodge, and all the Buffalo and the Horses arose and ran to the boy, and as they gathered around him he disappeared.

When the young man came to, he was sitting by the lake as he sat before. He saw to his right something standing up like a Horse, that spoke to him and said: "I am going to your home with you. I am the black Horse that you saw on the north side that was so poor, old, and thin." The boy then arose and started back home. In the evening the black Horse said, "My son, I eat the grass. You must eat as I do." The boy ate a few bunches of grass and was filled. Each day the horse circled around the boy, and this was done to take the tired feeling from the boy. The Horse and the boy traveled fast. One night they came to a village and the Horse stopped and told the boy that it was his father's village.

The boy went into his village and found his father's lodge. He entered the lodge and woke up his mother. She screamed, but the boy spoke to her. He told his father that he was there. The old man kindled a fire. The boy told his mother and father that he had come, but that he had not come to stay; that he had to go back, but that he wanted his father to go through the village and tell his brothers that he wanted tobacco, blue beads, a black silk handkerchief, sweet grass, and brown eagle feathers. He told his mother to go and get for him tobacco, sweet grass, a black lariat rope, brown eagle feathers, and paint. The boy told her to go to her brothers and get these things. His father and mother both came into the village with the things the boy wanted. When the boy received the presents, he told his father and mother that he was to go away for a short time, and would return in a few days. The boy carried the presents out to the Horse. The Horse circled around him and hit him with his tail, to give him speed. The boy and the Horse started back to the lodge of the Buffalo, and before daylight they arrived and were taken into the lodge.

The Buffalo and the Horse put the feathers upon their heads. The Horse gave the boy a spear, a shield, and a black lariat rope. The Buffalo gave him buffalo wool and some mud and told him to use it upon his body in battles. The boy was taken out of the lodge again. He went home.

The first chance he got he called upon a certain poor boy that had been his friend when he had fallen into disfavor with all the village. He took this boy and they went upon the war-path alone. In a few days they found a village and the two captured many ponies. Among the ponies were three that were very fine—one black, one dun, and one gray. When they came near the village the boy kept the black and the dun ponies, and the gray he gave to his friend.

Several times the two young men went out, and each time they were successful and captured ponies and brought them home. Other warriors sneaked around to find when these young men were going out, for they went out secretly. The boy became a great warrior. When the village was attacked by the enemy, the young man sat in his lodge and told stories in an unconcerned way. When he thought it was time to go out to help his people, he took the dun horse, put the paint upon it, put the paint upon his body, and took the shield and the black lariat rope and spear. He placed the black lariat rope about his waist and jumped upon the dun horse and went out to battle. He rode between the foes and all the time waved his spear while the enemy were shooting at him. Again he passed through the lines and shook the spear at the enemy, and when he saw that they were frightened he commanded all his people to attack. When his people made a rush at the enemy, they gave way and his people slaughtered many of them. His father saw all of these things that he had done and was well pleased. He spoke to him and told him that he must marry. There was another chief who had only two children, a boy and a girl. To their place the boy was sent to marry the girl. They were married, and in a few years they had children, and the boy became chief of the tribe.

There was another young man, who was also of high birth, who became very jealous of the young man, for the young man had married the girl whom he wanted. The jealous boy went to the girl's brother and told him many bad things about his brother-in-law, so that the brother also wanted to harm his sister's husband. The married boy told his brother-in-law that of all the Horses he had, he must not ride the dun Horse or the black Horse when hunting. The brother-in-law stayed in the tipi one day and told his father that he wanted the dun Horse for his own use, but his father told him that he could not have the dun Horse, for it belonged to his son. The boy left the tipi, went out, bridled the dun Horse, and chased Buffalo. As he came up with one bull, it turned around and hooked the Horse in several places; then it hooked the boy in several places and killed him. The owner of the dun Horse was staying in the tipi, when the black Horse neighed. The owner of the dun Horse then said to his father-in-law: "Go and bring your boy, for he is dead. A Buffalo has killed him and my Horse." The old man did not believe it. He went through the village asking everybody if they had seen his son, and if anybody had come in with the news that his son had been killed. Nobody seemed to know.

The old man and the old woman went out and found that the horse was still living, but that the boy was all cut up. They took the boy home, mourning as they went along, and just as they came opposite the village the owner of the dun Horse sent word to the old people to take the body of the boy around the village and place it on the east side. The old man knew that the young man was going to perform a miracle; that he was going to try to bring his boy back to life. The owner of the dun Horse then told the people that they must all keep quiet and fasten their Horses tight, so that none of them could get away. That night they heard the Horses neigh and snort; then there was a rumbling noise. All the horses in the village seemed to jump up and run and were scared; but the owner of the dun Horse had placed guards around the village to keep the people still. The neighing of the Horses was kept up; also the rumbling noise. One of the men followed the noise around and found out that it was the black and the dun Horses that were running to the body of the young man. Just as the sun was coming up in the east, the two Horses ran over the young man and touched him. The horses went on the south side of the village and there stood panting.

All through the night the young man sat up. He awoke his wife; told her to prepare a meal by boiling some of the fattest buffalo meat. After the meat was boiled down, the owner of the dun Horse told his wife to go to their brother and touch and shake him and tell him to arise from his sleep and come, for he had slept too long. The woman went and touched her brother, told him that he had slept too long, and that it was time for him to get up. The young man sat up and said, "I have slept too long." Then the young girl hugged her brother and said, "My brother, you were killed." Then he remembered chasing the Buffalo. He went to the tipi and ate.

The people would not believe that the young man had brought his brother-in-law to life, and they said that the young man was not powerful. One time when he led a war party out they were seen by the enemy, and just as the enemy were about to overtake them the young man, owner of the dun Horse, took the lariat rope from his shoulder, and called the men together to stand by him. He put the lariat rope over his shoulder, and a storm came down from the heavens and covered the enemy, and they went off in different directions, but around where they were it was clear. The owner of the dun Horse told them that he was the one who had caused the storm. They captured many ponies and went home.

At another time many different tribes joined together to kill these people, for they had heard that they had a wonderful man among them. The tribes attacked the village and the people went out to protect their village and fight, and after a while the young man came and fought with them. He saw that the enemy were numerous and that his people would be killed if he did not prevent it. He went to the east end of the battle lines, jumped from his pony, took his spear and swung it over his head. He dropped it in the center of the battle line. As the spear fell upon the ground, a noise was made in the ground, and the earth opened up and his people stood on one side and the enemy on the other side, so that the enemy could not attack them any more. The people then knew that this young man had great powers; but still the jealous young man kept on talking to the brother about him.

At another time when a battle was going on, the girl's brother got on the dun Horse, went out, and fought the enemy. He knew very well that the owner did not want him to ride the horse, for he had told him so. The owner of the dun Horse spoke to his wife and said: "Your brother has been trying in some way to cause my death. He has succeeded at last. You see me now for the last time. My father, the Buffalo, told me that I would have many children and grow to old age, but my brother-in-law has done wrong; for both of my horses must not fight in the same battle, but one must fight at a time. I go to battle for the last time. Keep this black lariat rope for your own. Our children will grow up. Let them carry it upon the war-path, for it has great powers. These things that are used in the Buffalo dance, keep. Save them for our children, for they contain much power." The young man took his spear and shield, mounted the black Horse, and went into battle. He rushed right into the enemy's lines, was knocked over and killed, and the black Horse that he was riding was also killed. His brother-in-law upon the dun Horse followed him and he also was killed, and the dun Horse was killed. The enemy ran and the people were victorious. When the battle was over, the people called the brother-in-law all kinds of names for the way he was doing; for it had come to their knowledge that it was on account of the boy riding the dun Horse that the other young man with powers was killed. The girl kept the lariat rope, and when her children were grown, she gave it to one of her sons, who grew up to be a medicine-man, and always danced the Wild-Horse dance.

93. THE ORIGIN OF THE BUFFALO CEREMONY.[1]

A long time ago the Kitkehahki made their village upon the Republican River. On the south side was a place where the men played with the gambling sticks. Here every morning the young men went who had the sticks, and they called for the other young men to come out and play. There was one ring that belonged with the sticks and other men had rings of their own. These they kept until they themselves played the game. There was a young man named Howling-Fox who liked to watch the others play the game, but never played himself. He went out every day and sat on the northeast side of the playground. One day while the men were playing with the sticks, Howling-Fox, who was looking on, heard a peculiar noise under the ground where the men were playing. He watched and listened. The noise went towards the east. In the evening the noise went back toward the west, but he could not see anything.

After the men finished their game they went home, and Howling-Fox arose and went with them. That night he had a dream. He dreamed that he saw an evil one standing by him, who said: "My son, I want to speak to you. I know you have heard my footsteps. I walked by where the men were playing with sticks. To-morrow remain on the

[1] Told by Mouth-Waving-in-Water, Kitkehahki. This may be regarded as a variant of several tales already presented relating to the so-called buffalo game. In this story, however, the man becomes a medicine-man through the power of the ring, and the story may be, therefore, properly regarded as belonging in this group. It is said that the story is told in such a way that the people should be on the look-out to keep the pipe filled, in order that those in the lodge might smoke during the pauses in the relation of the story.

grounds and I will be there to talk to you." The man woke up. He had been dreaming. He arose, put his robe about his shoulders, went to the creek, and washed. After eating his breakfast he dressed, took his pipe and tobacco bag, and went to the grounds. He sat down on the northeast side of the playground as usual, and filled his pipe. After smoking, he watched the men play. In the evening when the men finished their game, they went home, but Howling-Fox sat still and waited. After everybody had gone, he saw a woman coming towards him from the west.

He arose and went to the woman, who said: "Well, do you know me? I have been to your lodge to talk to you." The man said: "Yes, I know who you are. You are not human. You are a Buffalo, for I saw your tracks on the ground." The woman sat down and told him to sit down. She then said: "My son, I have been all over the country looking for my daughter. I have seven children and they are all bulls but one. My only daughter is missing. I have traveled all over the country hunting for her, but can not find her. The other day when you were sitting yonder I came by and you heard a rumbling under the ground. You wondered what the sound meant. I came in the night and went to your lodge and spoke to you. You saw my footprints upon this ground. You are wondering what I am here for, but I have told you that I have been all over the land looking for my daughter. I found my daughter's tracks upon this ground where the men play the sticks. I want you to find my daughter and return her to me. I will make you a great man. I will give you powers so that your people will never become hungry as long as you live. My daughter runs around on this ground once in a while, for some man has her and only uses her in the game when he plays with the sticks. She was killed and her genital was taken from her and made into a ring, but she came to life again and is now in the care of some man. When you go home, go to the different men who have these rings. Bring them to me to-morrow night. When I have seen them I can tell where my daughter is. Bring also a stout string with you. I must now run away, and you must go."

The Buffalo woman ran away and Howling-Fox arose and went home. He lay down and slept. When he awoke the sun was high. After he had eaten breakfast, he went to the different lodges of the men who had rings. He went into one of the lodges, passed his hands over the man's shoulders, and said: "My brother, I want you to take pity upon me. I want you to let me have this ring. If this is not the ring I want, I shall return it to you. If it is the one I want, you will be well paid." The owner of the ring said, "I will let you have the ring." The man took the ring from his sacred bundle and gave it to Howling-Fox. Howling-

Fox went to another man who had a ring and begged it of him. The man was about to go to the playground, and had the ring on his wrist. He took it off and gave it to Howling-Fox, who thanked him and went on to another lodge. The man in this lodge was seated by the fireplace. Howling-Fox told him what he wanted, and the man was glad and gave his ring willingly to Howling-Fox. He went home with the rings, and as he entered he told the women to brush out the lodge. Then he asked all the people to leave the lodge. When they had all gone out, Howling-Fox placed the rings west of the fireplace, then took his pipe and filled it with tobacco, which he lighted. He blew a few whiffs to the heavens, then to the ground, then he blew one whiff to each ring. As he dumped the ashes onto the fireplace he said: "My mothers, I did not know how you are made, but now I do, and I also know that you live. Help me, I am poor in spirit. I hope that one of you is the one I am looking for." Howling-Fox then took the rings and placed them under his pillow. He went out and told the people to enter the lodge.

As the people went into the lodge, Howling-Fox went up on top of the lodge and sat down. He watched the men playing the game of sticks. Towards evening he saw all the men go home from the playground. Howling-Fox then went down from the lodge and entered it. He took the rings from his pillow and went out to the ground. He sat down on the north side and placed the rings in front of him. He filled his pipe and smoked. The sun had set and it was dark. Howling-Fox placed the rings on the north side of the grounds, near the place where he was sitting. He waited, and after a while he heard a rumbling noise. The sound seemed to come from under the ground. As it came nearer he could hear hoofs rattle. He stood up and went to the rings. The noise came closer and closer and at last Howling-Fox saw a dark form approaching. The form disappeared, and Howling-Fox heard a noise that he knew to be that of the Buffalo rolling upon the ground. When the Buffalo stood up, Howling-Fox saw that it had changed into a woman. The woman came to him and said: "I am here. I am glad that you have brought the rings. Let us now go to them." They went to the rings. There were three of them. The middle one had a blue bead upon it instead of the white bead. The woman went up and said: "This is my daughter. She shall go back to my people and the bulls shall play with her. You have the string; now tie the ring." Howling-Fox did as he was told. The woman spoke again and said: "My son, from this day forth I shall look after you, and when you are in need of meat I will come and tell you where you can get it. I must now return to my people, for they are far away. My daughter will return with me.

Her grandfathers, the old bulls, will decide whether she shall remain a ring or whether she shall become a Buffalo again. My son, you will see me in your dreams. I will come to you and speak with you. Take this piece of mud. It has my power, and with it you can cure people. This mud you must spread across your mouth. When you go to the sick you are to blow your breath, and the smell that is in the mud will reach them. Now take the ring and string and tie the ring fast upon my head, so that it will not fall."

Howling-Fox took the ring and string and tied the two parts on opposite sides of the ring. He placed the ring upon the top of the Buffalo's head and with the strings tied it very tightly to the Buffalo's horns. The Buffalo snorted, for she was satisfied. She ran toward the west and was soon out of sight. The man lingered around the grounds and repeated over and over to himself, "So I really have seen a Buffalo, a wonderful Buffalo." As he looked to heaven, he said: "Thanks to you in the heavens! I am a poor man. I had not seen anything so wonderful. I thank you."

Howling-Fox went home and lay down. In the morning he took two of the rings and returned them to the owners. He went to the man whose ring was gone. He laid his hands upon the man's head, passed them over it, and said: "My brother, your ring is gone. Ask nothing about it. I have one pony. You shall have it in place of the ring. I shall let you know more about the ring in the future, and I shall again pay you." The owner of the ring was satisfied and said: "My brother, it shall be as you have said. If there is anything wonderful I want to hear from you again." Howling-Fox was satisfied and went home.

In the fall all the people went toward the southwest on a Buffalo hunt, but there were no Buffalo to be found anywhere; not even bulls. They went far into the southwest and the people began to complain, for they were getting hungry. The chief kept giving commands for the people to go south. One time when the people had made a camp, Howling-Fox went out of the tipi and met a woman who spoke to him and said: "My son, I am here. I am the woman who was with you and talked with you. I know the people are starving. You know what I promised you. Now I come to tell you that I am here to help you call the Buffalo. Tell the chief that you want them to stop going south, and that you want them to go northwest." Howling-Fox had to be careful how he talked to the chief, for the chief was hard to please. He asked his friend for meat. She gave him dried meat, which he had the women boil. He then invited the chief, and when the chief came in, Howling-Fox said: "Chief, I present to you this dried boiled meat for you to eat. As the people are hungry and we are still going south, let us go northwest. Let the chief give me the lead. I may help the chief and his people." The chief was glad to hear what Howling-Fox had to say. He went out and gave orders to the crier to go through the camp and cry out, that Howling-Fox would give orders where they were to travel and how far they were to go. The crier then went to Howling-Fox, who told him to tell the people that they were to travel northwest.

The people broke camp the next morning and went northwest. They made short journeys, for the people were very thin and weak. Several days they went, until they got to the Platte River, where they made their camp. In the night Howling-Fox went out and again met Buffalo-Woman, who said: "I came from afar. There are no buffalo here. Let the people make an earth-lodge, and let its entrance be in the west. There you shall sit, and I will come in and visit you. In four days I shall return here. I shall want at that time eagle feathers, blue beads, and native tobacco." The woman disappeared and was gone, and Howling-Fox went into his tipi. He had some boiled meat that he had kept. He sent for the chief and told him that he wanted an earth-lodge built. Some of the people began to help build the lodge. There were other people who complained and said, "We ought to be traveling, so that we could find Buffalo." But the people went on with the building of the lodge.

The fourth night Howling-Fox went out and met Buffalo-Woman, who said, "Go now and get the things I told you that I want." Howling-Fox went and brought the things and gave them to her. She was glad to get them. She said, "My son, go with me and carry these things that you have brought me." They went over the hill. She found a buffalo wallow and began to roll in it and turned into a Buffalo. Howling-Fox then ran along beside the Buffalo and they went on till they came to some Buffalo bulls. Howling-Fox took the feathers, native tobacco, and other gifts and tied them on the horns of the bulls, who were pleased. The bulls turned upon the cow and she became a woman. She said: "My son, the bulls are pleased. They promise you some Buffalo in a few days. They also give you power to call the Buffalo. They are glad you found my daughter and returned her to me. Now we must start back to your home, for it is very far to your people." The woman went up to Howling-Fox and covered him with her robe. She began to blow her breath. The wind seemed to blow. Howling-Fox did not move nor try to look. At last the wind went down. The woman turned him loose from her robe and said: "Here we are, my son; go to your tipi and sleep. As soon as the lodge is finished, you must meet me there. I will go and prepare the inside of the lodge for you." Howling-Fox entered his tipi and lay down.

In the morning he invited the chief. When the chief entered the tipi, Howling-Fox said: "I have been away, my brother. In a few days your people will find plenty to eat." The chief was pleased, and he ordered the lodge to be finished. After the lodge was completed, the chief notified Howling-Fox that the lodge was finished. That night Howling-Fox went out to the place where he was to meet the woman. The woman told Howling-Fox that she had brought some bulls with her for the people. She went to the new lodge with Howling-Fox. She entered the lodge, which she was glad to see. She told Howling-Fox that she was going away and that she would come again. She told him how to fix the lodge, for she was to bring her father, the chief of all the Buffalo. She said, "I want my father to receive the native tobacco and eagle feathers from you." Buffalo-Woman then went away. The next day Howling-Fox sent word to the chief to tell all the people to keep away from the lodge. Howling-Fox had a big fire made in the fire-place and stayed in the lodge by himself. Towards evening the fire went out, and as night came he took up ashes and scattered them around the fireplace, so that they completely encircled it and extended on through the entrance.

In the night Howling-Fox left the lodge and met Buffalo-Woman. Soon another Buffalo came; it was the bull. He sat down in the west. Howling-Fox then filled the pipe and lit it. He blew a few whiffs to the place where the bull sat. After he had finished smoking, the bull grunted. Buffalo-Woman spoke and said: "My son, my father is satisfied. He says that you are to tell the chief and the people that they shall kill some Buffalo; that the Buffalo are thankful for the return of the girl." The bull went out and another came in for smoke. The man filled his pipe again and gave a few whiffs to this bull, who promised Buffalo to the people the next morning. The bull left the lodge and another came in. Howling-Fox stayed up all that night, making smoke for the bulls that came into the lodge.

Early in the morning Buffalo-Woman gave some dried meat to Howling-Fox. Howling-Fox invited the chief and the crier. The crier put the kettle over the fire that he had made. He then cut up the dried meat and placed it in the kettle. The chief was surprised to see the hoofprints upon the ashes that were scattered upon the ground. He was more than surprised when Howling-Fox placed the dried meat before the crier. When the meat was cooked, the crier went after the braves, who, when they reached the entrance of the lodge, were surprised to see Buffalo hoofprints upon the ashes. When they were all seated, the chief addressed them and said: "My people, you have come into this new lodge. You see hoofprints of the Buffalo. You can see that they were not put there by men. You can see the meat that we are about to eat. This brother of ours will tell us what the Buffalo said." Howling-Fox told the men to eat, which they did, for they were very hungry. After they had eaten, Howling-Fox told the chief to send three or more men over the hills to look for Buffalo. The chief sent three men at once over the hills. The men went, and when they were upon the top of the hill they looked all around the country, but they could see nothing. They came back and reported to the chief, saying, "We have seen no Buffalo." Howling-Fox said, "Go again upon the same hill and look down the hill."

The men went back to the same place on the hill and looked down at the foot of the hill. There was a ravine, and in this ravine there sat several Buffalo bulls. The three men then went on the opposite side of the hill and threw up their blankets for a signal that there were Buffalo. Then they went down the hill into the camp. They entered the lodge. The pipe was filled for them. Each gave a few whiffs to the sky and the ground as a thanks offering. When the pipe was emptied, the leader of the three told where the Buffalo were. A crier was told by the chief to cry through the camp and let the men know that they were now to attack Buffalo. The ribs, tongues, and hearts were to be brought to the lodge. The men made preparation, for each wanted to kill a Buffalo for his family. The men all gathered together near Howling-Fox's lodge. Howling-Fox went out and said: "Men, you are to kill many Buffalo. When you bring them home, do not let the women pound the head with an axe to get the meat out. Let them get the brains out at the neck joint by boiling them out. As you run the cows, there will be one cow to run out. This cow you shall not kill, for she is a messenger for our people." The chief led the men upon the hill.

A man was selected to make motions with his hands for the different companies to move and make the attacks on each side. The surround was made. A sign was given by the chief, a rush was made, the Buffalo rose from the ground and tried to run, and the people began to kill. Everyone saw the Buffalo cow that was not to be killed, and they let her go. They killed many bulls and everybody was given meat. As the men skinned the Buffalo they found the eagle feathers and native tobacco upon their heads. Each man who had killed a Buffalo then knew that Howling-Fox had had something to do with their coming. Each man as he entered the camp rode up to the lodge and cut out the ribs, tongue, and heart as they had been told to do. Howling-Fox stayed at the lodge with the chiefs and braves to receive the offerings.

The people were happy. They had plenty to eat. It was known through the village that Howling-Fox brought the Buffalo. The people gave him many presents and many ponies. After the first killing, the people killed four more times; then the Buffalo passed the camp and went east. Howling-Fox told the chief that they had plenty of dried meat and that the promise of the Buffalo had been fulfilled and that they must move east to their permanent village. Howling-Fox did not go east with his people, but stayed behind in the old camp. Buffalo-Woman visited him during the nights and taught him Buffalo dance songs and gave him the Buffalo ceremony. Howling-Fox went back to his people and started the Buffalo dance. In the dance he always wore, upon his left arm, a ring that he had taken from a Buffalo cow. He sent for the man who had owned the ring, and gave him presents of Buffalo robes and one pony. Then he taught him the Buffalo ceremony and the songs. Howling-Fox soon died, and the people said it was because he had given out all of his secrets to the other man.

94. THE BUFFALO MEDICINE DANCE.[1]

The people were upon a buffalo hunt and had made their camp in a valley. The holy lodge that held the sacred bundle was in the center of the village. While they had their camp in this valley a buffalo bull attacked them. The people pursued the buffalo, but he ran right into the holy tipi where the bundle was hanging up, and tore the tipi all to pieces. The people sent for a man who understood the spirit of the buffalo, and when he saw what the buffalo had done he told the people that something was going to happen. In the afternoon dark clouds came in the west and it began to rain and storm. The wind blew so hard that it picked up one woman and blew her away. After the storm was over a drove of Buffalo came near the village and one of the Buffalo spoke and said: "People, you shall have your things again. You shall have the buffalo skull, the drums, and gourds." So the things which were carried away from the sacred lodge were brought back and placed in the lodge again. Then the drove of Buffalo went away.

The Buffalo who had spoken to the people came again and invited some of the Buffalo medicine-men to go with him into a country where

[1] Told by White-Sun, Kitkehahki. This story is told to show that when buffalo attack a village it is an omen of bad luck; especially is it believed that a storm will follow.

the Buffalo were. The medicine-men went, and far away from the village they came to a steep bank. There the Buffalo ran away and told the medicine-men to do the same thing. The men followed the Buffalo and they entered the lodge of the Buffalo. When they entered the cave, they first came to deep water. The people went into the water and kept walking in it until they entered an animals' lodge. There they saw on one side a Bear, and on the other side a Buffalo. The Bear and the Buffalo began to do sleight-of-hand. After a while these men saw other animals sitting around. As the animals did the sleight-of-hand performances, they arose, blew their breaths, and as they did so, soft downy feathers fell from their mouths. One Buffalo stood up and took a reed whistle and swallowed it. Afterwards he threw up feathers instead of the whistle. Then he said: "People, I give you this ceremony. You must have a Buffalo skull and give presents to the skull, for the spirit of the Buffalo will be in the skull, and the skull will give you dreams so that you will know what to do in the Buffalo ceremony." The people went back to their village, and they performed the ceremony, and the first song that they sang was the song which the Buffalo had taught them.

95. THE WOMAN AND THE BUFFALO DANCE.[1]

The people left their permanent village to go upon a hunt. Only a young woman who was with child was left behind. The people were angry with her because she would not tell with what man she had been, and so they had gone and left her alone. She had not been with any man, and did not know how she had come to be pregnant. She gave birth, and she and the child stayed alone in the deserted village. One night the child began to cry. The mother tried very hard to stop the child from crying, but he would not stop. At last she took the baby in her arms, threw him upon her back, and started west, not knowing where she was going.

She finally came to a high hill, and as she was ascending the high hill she found a Buffalo bull sitting in a hollow. She stopped, for she was scared. The bull said, "Nawa. Why are you carrying your baby?" The woman said, "My baby is sick and has been crying for some time." Then the bull grunted and the smoke came out of his mouth. The bull spoke and said: "Woman, I will give you a root, but I want you to be careful how you give it to the child. The child will get well. I will

[1] Told by White-Sun, Kitkehahki. In this story a woman receives power from the buffalo and becomes a medicine-woman.

doctor him myself." Then the Buffalo said: "Let him nurse. Now place him upon the ground." Then the Buffalo bull began to roll in the dust on the ground. When he stood up he said: "Woman, take up the robe which I have made while I wallowed. Place the baby in the robe, and put some of the dust all over the child." When the woman had done this the child stopped crying, and then the bull began to bawl, and after a while three more bulls came. The bull spoke and said, "Let us doctor the baby," and the other bulls said: "Everything has been done for the child which could be done except to blow breath upon him. If you want us to blow our breath upon the child we will do so." Each bull went up to the child and blew his breath upon him. Then one of the bulls took a large piece of wool from his back and placed it upon the child. He told the woman not to be afraid; that her son would get well. While they were all standing around the woman and the child, a Buffalo cow came. She lay down and the Buffalo bull told the woman to let the boy lie beside the cow. The mother placed her child by the cow. After a long time the cow spoke and said: "The child is now well. He has had sleep." The boy crawled around the bulls, and the bulls awoke and they doctored him. By daylight the boy was strong and well. Then the Buffalo gave the root to the woman, and the Buffalo bull said: "When the boy is sick, take this root and pound it and give it to him. The disease and the medicine will fight, and when pains come out upon the sick one, take him down to the creek and wash him. Be not afraid of wild beasts, for the root will scare them away."

The woman took her boy and went off, and on the way she saw a snake. The woman, having the root, passed by the snake, and when she passed she looked back and saw that the snake had died. Every time that the child became sick the woman washed him in the river and he became well. After a while a man came to the village where the woman and her boy lived alone, and said: "Let me live with you. Let me be your husband." The woman said, "I will let you live with us." Soon the man learned about the wonderful medicine that his wife had, and saw her power to cure the sick, and he was glad that he had come there and married her. He asked her to tell him how she had received the power, and she told him about her sick child and how the Buffalo had pitied her when she was alone and in trouble, and had saved the life of her boy, and had given her medicine that would always keep disease and danger away from him. When the man heard the story he wanted to go and see the Buffalo and thank them for what they had done. He and the woman and boy started west and soon came to the Buffalo. The Buffalo bull who had first helped her, came and spoke to them again. He said: "You must dance the Buffalo dance as I teach it to you. You know that the Buffalo roll upon the ground. Imitate me and do the same thing." Then the Buffalo stood up and threw himself down and rolled upon the ground, and when he arose he said: "Take that which is upon the ground. You shall use it in the ceremony as a rattle." Upon the rattle was the picture of a buffalo skull. "This rattle you must also shake before sick people." The Buffalo rolled again and made a whistle. At the end of the whistle was a shell hanging down which was the shape of the moon. There was another shell tied to the middle of the whistle. Then the Buffalo said: "When you doctor, put medicine upon the patient. Take the whistle and blow upon it near him. When you have whistled, look about you and you will see my shadow. If you see my shadow then you may know that the patient will get well. If you do not see my shadow you will know that the patient is to die." Then the Buffalo said: "I have many children. You shall have many children, too. They shall grow up to be men and women. Always take care of the rattle and the whistle." After this the Buffalo bull disappeared. Then the man and the woman went home with the boy. As the boy grew up the man taught him what the Buffalo had said. The man became a great medicine-man and gave the people the Buffalo dance.

96. THE BUFFALO MEDICINE DANCE.[1]

A little boy went out upon the hillside to play and there he saw an old, lean Buffalo. The boy went to the Buffalo and talked to him and called him his grandfather, and said: "You are getting old and can not stand much now. You can not travel as you once could." All at once the Buffalo looked up and said: "My grandchild, I have lived a long time upon this earth. I am now very old. I am glad that you take pity upon me. Your people kill my people and eat them. I have come many times with my people, but somehow your people have never killed me. Now, my grandchild, before I die I want to speak a few words to you. I have some things that I want to give you." The boy went and cut a lot of grass and brought it to the Buffalo and fed him.

After he had eaten, the Buffalo said: "Look at me. Whenever you want to see me, take this, smell it, and you will see me." The thing that was handed to the boy was a little ball which the Buffalo bull had carried in his stomach and which possessed magic powers. "With this

[1] Told by White-Sun, Kitkehahki. In this story a boy receives power from the buffalo and becomes a great medicine-man.

I shall make you a great medicine-man. I shall give you the Buffalo dance." The Buffalo then gave the boy a whistle and some roots. "These roots you shall give to wounded people when you doctor them. When I am dead take my tail and a piece of my scalp, dry them, and use them for yourself. Whenever you see a place where there are many buffalo, where the buffalo bulls have made their water, take up the mud, place it in a buffalo bladder and keep it. When you are about to dance, take a small piece of this ball which I have given you and chew it. Then take a little of the root and chew it. Then take some of the mud from the ball and put it upon your face and more upon your nose and more upon your body. When the medicine and the ball have reached your stomach then your spirit shall turn into a Buffalo spirit, so that when you dance the people who are looking on can not help but be under your influence and they will give you many presents. You shall do the same thing when you are doctoring a wounded man. Sickness I can not doctor. When a person is wounded, then you can doctor, but when he is sick from disease, you can not."

The boy went back to the village and told his father all that the Buffalo had said, and gave him the things which the Buffalo had given him. These things which the boy received from the Buffalo were made mysteriously by the Buffalo. They were not handed to the boy, but the boy picked them up when the Buffalo spoke to him. When the father heard of what the boy had seen, he asked the boy to take him to the place where the Buffalo was, and there they found that the Buffalo had died. Then the boy told the father to take off the tail for him and also a piece of the scalp. The boy stayed around near the Buffalo for several days. His father knew where his boy was, so he did not worry about him.

Several months afterwards the people had their medicine ceremony. The boy took his things and went into the medicine-lodge and did just as the Buffalo had told him. He put the Buffalo robe over his shoulders when he danced, and it changed into different colors, and the people all wondered and gave the boy many presents. After the dancing was over, many medicine-men spoke and asked where he had learned the dance. The boy told them that the spirit of the poor Buffalo had taught him, and so they called his dance the Buffalo dance.

97. THE BUFFALO GAME MEDICINE.[1]

In the early times a man lived among the people who knew about the trees and the herbs. He wandered about with the animals and they taught him many strange things. One night while he was sleeping out under the open sky some one touched him and he awoke. He looked around to see who it was, but did not see anyone. He looked up in the heavens and he saw, as if they were drawn there, two sticks lying side by side and a ring between them. They were stars and were in the west. He looked at them a long time, and wondered what they meant; for people had never seen anything like them before.

He went to sleep again and a young man appeared to him and told him that it was he who had shown him the ring and sticks in heaven, and that he wanted him to make two sticks like them and to get the ring from the Buffalo cow. "You must throw the sticks through the ring and so try to catch the ring. Play with the sticks in the west part of your village, for the home of the buffalo is in the west. Never play in the east, for diseases are in the east. From the south comes death. From the north come enemies to your camp. Go make a bow from ash wood, take two dogwood sticks, shave them down and make arrows; sharpen them at one end, then hold them over the fire so that they will harden. You must then kill two young buffalo bulls; have the women tan them, and then cut them into long strips so that you can wind them around the body of the sticks which you shall prepare. Then go to the timber, and when you come to an ash tree sing this song:

> Some one said,
> "Sticks standing in the ground,
> Here they are standing,
> Yonder are they standing."
> There coming, coming yonder.

"Go through the timber until you come to a straight ash covered with something like soft feathers. It will be a peculiar stick. Darken the enemy's sight by making a motion as if to cut at the bottom of the tree on the north side. Then make a motion on the east side, for you must cut the diseases. On the south side make the same motion to cut death. Then cut on the west side of the tree. Although you cut it, it shall have life. Light your pipe, give a few whiffs to the heavens to remind us,

---

[1] Told by Yellow-Bird, Chaui. While this story is somewhat similar to several others which relate to the ring and javelin, or buffalo game, it belongs to the medicine group, because the individual in the story was taught how to make the sticks, which in this case had their origin from a constellation in the sky, and how to use them in sleight-of-hand performances in the medicine-man's ceremony.

the gods of the heavens, that we gave you the sticks and rings, and then we will hold the spirit in the sticks. Then give a whiff to the base of the tree, dump the ashes and bury them. After the smoke offering, cut the tree down. Repeat the ceremony before a second tree, then cut it. Trim the trees, and from them cut two sticks the length of your body, for they shall represent men. Then go to two other trees, perform the same rites and cut down the trees, trim them, and cut two sticks shorter than the first two, for they shall represent buffalo with one horn. Although the sticks shall represent men, they shall have the spirit of a buffalo with one horn who is in the west. Shave the sticks down, splice them, take sinew that you took from the buffalo and bind them. Kill a cow; do not eat the flesh; but take the skin from about the vulva. You must lay her head toward the east, so that when the buffalo come from the west they will note the absence and follow your camp. Be sure and play in the west always. Now go home and do these things. I will be there to teach you further."

The man went home, called his friends together, and they went to the timber and did as he directed. He kept the sticks together, and when they went on a hunt he killed the two young bulls and made sinew. The sticks were then spliced together and tied with sinews. On the head parts were made marks for ears; marks were made for the hands and legs and one horn. Then the thin sticks, four in number, were placed across them where the hands and legs were to be. They were tied at the top and the other ends were spread open. The front part represented the Sun, and the hind portion the Spider-Woman or the Moon. They were the ones who first played in the heavens, and, as the Sun lost, the Moon gave the game to man. A smoke offering was made and everything received a whiff. Then the wrapping was done; the front leg was put with the thing on it, then one of the hind sticks was put on for legs; and last of all the hind stick was put on for the horn. The front part was then fixed with some dried hide to represent ears, and the two notches were eyes. One stick was burnt at the head to make it black, to represent darkness or north; the other was white, to represent day or south.

The people then went on another hunt and the man who had had the dream killed a buffalo cow. He cut the ring from her and then left her lying with her head toward the east. He took the ring home. He dried it and rubbed it, then bound it about with strips of tanned buffalo. One night he had another dream, and the strange man who appeared in his dreams gave him a white bead, which was to be put on the ring and which was to represent the star itself. He fastened the bead to the ring and the next day he invited some of his friends to go to the west part of the village to learn the game. The sticks were carried by men, while the ring was carried by his granddaughter, for the ring was now a granddaughter to all men, and should be spoken of as such. The people went out with the man to the west side of the village, where they found a place where there was only buffalo-grass.

They sat down, the man filled his pipe, and after smoking to the sun, the moon, and the stars, he went to the ground and gave whiffs of smoke to the ground; then to the ring and the sticks. He then dumped the ashes—a little on the center of the ring and a little on each of the sticks, where the heads were supposed to be. "Now, my friends, the sticks were given me from above; we shall play. The crowd must divide into two parties, so that we will be in pairs; so that when two throw the ring at the sticks, the other two will be there to take them and pierce the ring with the sticks. We shall count one hundred and twenty, or as many as ten fingers and ten toes on six persons. If you ring at the head, you count three persons. If you ring at the hands or legs, you count two persons. If you ring at the horn it will count six persons, and you will win. We shall have two sticks—one long one and the other short. The short one will count one person if it reaches the bead. If it does not touch the bead it will count just the hands. The long stick will count ten if it reaches the bead. If it reaches just the ring it will count five. There are other measures that will be added afterwards. Now we play, and the side which loses must bring wood and kindle fire and boil the meat; the other side will offer a piece of heart and tongue of the buffalo to the gods in the heavens and to the buffalo."

The playing was commenced with great rejoicing, and when one side lost, wood was brought, fire kindled, and meat put in the kettle and set on the fire. When the meat was all cooked the man took a piece of heart and tongue and offered it to the sun, moon, and stars. He then took some fat and rubbed it on the sticks and ring, and then upon himself. The sticks and ring were then taken home and tied to a pole, which was stuck in the ground.

That night the man had another vision. The same being came to him and said: "Now you have seen the game, I am now to give you another ring. This ring you will get from a calf. You must be by yourself and you must pray to Tirawa, for it will be not from Tirawa, but to remind you that he gave you the buffalo, the sticks, and everything that you have. On this ring you must put a blue bead, which will represent Tirawa. The ring will represent the earth. The white bead you must carry on the war-path. In doctoring, you will use no herbs or roots if the sick person has played the sticks. Go straight to where they are playing, and as they come with the sticks and the ring, go where the ring stops, and in the center take some dust, go home, and let the man smell the dust; then rub it over his head, arms, and legs and he will get well."

As the tribe increased, other people prepared meat and had the game. Young boys saw the game and they made sticks and rings and they had a game of their own. But this particular man did a sleight-of-hand. He took the black stick into the medicine-man's lodge, and after passing it around for examination he took it and put his mouth on the end, put the bowl of a pipe that was lit at the other end, and drew the smoke from the bowl. The stick was passed around and no hole could be found.

98. THE LOST WARRIOR AND THE SINGING BUFFALO MEDICINE.[1]

There were many warriors who were on the war-path, and as they were going into the Cheyenne country they were overtaken by the enemy. One man slipped off from his pony and hid in the thick brush. The enemy passed him and went on after the others. The man came out from his hiding place and went on towards home. He thought that he was lost. He cried and called to all the gods in the heavens and to all the animal gods. Just a little before daylight, as he was climbing a high hill, he heard some one singing. He went on and when he had climbed the hill he heard the singing coming from the east. He looked and saw a Buffalo cow running towards him and snorting as she came. The man was frightened, but the Buffalo said: "Do not be afraid. I was singing as I loped along over these hills; you heard the song, and I will teach it to you and you will start up a dance that will be called the Big-Warrior dance." The Buffalo and the man sat down together on top of the hill and they looked toward the east.

As the sun came up the Buffalo galloped off towards the east, singing the same song:

> There coming, coming yonder,
> There coming, coming yonder,
> There coming, coming yonder,
> There coming, coming yonder,
> There coming, coming yonder,
> There coming, coming yonder,
> There coming, coming yonder,
> The buffalo is coming, coming yonder.

[1] Told by Thief, Kitkehahki. The story teaches that when traveling over the country one should be attentive, because at such times the animals might desire to teach them songs to be used in medicine ceremonies, etc.

The man learned many mysterious things from the Buffalo, and the Buffalo gave him power to travel without growing tired and to capture many ponies. The man was told to sing the song at dawn as the Buffalo had done. The man returned to his home, and when the dawn came in the east he sang the song about the Buffalo coming with good message to the man. After that the man when on the war-path always had success in capturing ponies.

99. THE BUFFALO MEDICINE WAR SHIELD.[1]

One time a boy went upon a hill and looked down upon the village and saw many young men talking to young girls. He had tried to do the same thing, but the girls did not seem to care for him, though he did not know why. While he was thinking of the different girls to whom he had tried to talk, and who would have nothing to do with him, he began to cry, for it seemed that none of these girls would ever have him, and he had no one to love him or make a home for him. As he continued to think he arose and left the place where he was and went to another hill farther from the village. There he stood upon the high hill and began to cry. While he was crying he called to the gods in the heavens and said that he cried because he had no woman to love him, not even a sister. After a time he stopped crying and wandered away, and was gone for one winter. No one knew where he went.

In the spring he came back again, but when he was close to the village he made up his mind that he would not enter it, for he had no sisters nor relations where he could go to make his home. He climbed a high hill, and looking about he saw a big herd of Buffalo not far away. The boy ran after them, and as they crossed the ravine he saw among the Buffalo a woman. The boy called the woman and she stopped. Then the boy said, "Woman, I am all alone; I would like to marry you." The woman said that she was willing; that he could be her husband. Then the boy went with the woman to the place where the Buffalo were. When they reached the Buffalo, the uncle of the woman came and spoke to the boy and said, "I want a scalp and some blue beads to give to the Buffalo." The boy went back to the village and entered the chief's tipi. He told the chief that he had come after scalps and beads, and that he wished that he would give them to him. The chief sent a man through the

---

[1] Told by Big-Crow, Skidi. This story relates to the origin of a medicine war shield, the power of which, however, is finally taken away from the owner because he disobeys the injunctions placed upon him and does not keep the taboo.

village, who went to different sacred bundles, opened them, and took scalps and beads out of the bundles. The boy took these things back to the Buffalo camp, and gave the beads and the scalps to the Buffalo.

The Buffalo were very proud of their presents and in return they gave the boy a small shield. The Buffalo said, "You shall wear this shield in battle upon your left shoulder; never upon your right shoulder." The boy then took his wife and they went back to his people.

Two days after they arrived in the village it was attacked by enemies. The man threw the shield over his left shoulder and went into battle. He was very brave, and killed so many people that the warriors talked much about his deeds. Again the village was attacked. The man again wore the shield over his left shoulder and rushed into the midst of the enemy, killing more than any other warrior. Again, for the third time, the village was attacked. The man threw the shield over his left shoulder and rushed out to fight, and he killed more men than he had before. The fourth time the enemy attacked their village. In the excitement the man forgot what he was doing and he took the shield from his left shoulder and placed it upon his right shoulder. In a little while he was wounded. He was taken to his tipi and left there to die.

A Buffalo bull came in the night, stood at the entrance and made water, and then went off. In the morning the boy arose and went out, put his hands into the mud made by the bull's water, and smeared it upon his face and nostrils. He went back into the lodge and lay down. Suddenly many Buffalo began to roll about in his lodge, but nobody could see them. There was a great dust in the lodge, but the people outside could see nothing but the dust flying out of the lodge. The boy rolled out of his bed and fell in the dust. The dust seemed to whirl around, and as there was much wind in the tipi the boy was thrown about, and after a while he was rolled out of the entrance. He lay outside in the dust for a while, then rolled back into the tipi, and when he rolled back he had turned into a Buffalo. Again he went out of the tipi and rolled in the dust outside of the tipi. He went back into the tipi, and when he came out again the people saw that he was a man again and that he had a buffalo robe upon his shoulders.

He was known as a wonderful man ever afterward. The Buffalo had taught him never to put buffalo horns or buffalo hoofs into his fire, for when he did he would die. This was a secret which he kept to himself, and did not tell anyone. One time, some one, through carelessness, threw a buffalo horn spoon into the fire and he died.

100. THE MAN WHO MARRIED A DEER.[1]

A long time ago when the Skidi lived near what is now Fremont, Nebraska, one young man went out upon a hunt. He went over the hills and finally came to a place that is called Pahuk, where he stopped to rest. In the afternoon he went into a swampy place in a dogwood thicket, and there sat down to eat. While he was sitting there he thought he heard somebody coming. He looked in the direction from which he had come and there he saw a woman coming. He recognized the woman as one whom he liked, and when she came near he went up to her and took her into the thicket. The man gave the woman something to eat, and after they had eaten the woman jumped up and hugged the man. The man finally lay with her. When they arose, the woman became a black-tail Deer and ran off. The man knew at once that he had been deceived by the Deer. He was angry at himself, and he determined that he would kill the Deer. He shot at it several times, but each time as he shot the Deer it would shake itself and the bullets would drop to the ground. The man then tried to go back to his home, but the Deer followed him until he finally gave up trying to go. He followed the Deer to a swampy place until at last they came to a big thicket. Here the Deer stopped and turned into a woman and told the man that he would have to live with her. The man stayed with the woman and the woman finally transformed him into a Deer.

They wandered over the country for several years until one day the woman gave birth to two young fawns. Always, in the meantime, the woman had been teaching the man the wonderful ways of the black-tail Deer. The man was able to transform himself into a Deer at any time, and then change to a man. After an absence from home of about three years, the woman asked him if he would like to return to his people. The man said that he would. Then the woman told him that she was going to take him back to his people; so she led the way and the man and the fawns followed. When they approached the village, the woman told the man that the people were having their yearly medicine-men's ceremony; that he must go straight to the medicine-lodge and let the people know that he had returned; that she could not enter the village for a time, but that when the medicine-men had consented to let him enter their lodge he must return to her and the fawns. The man went

---

[1] Told by Buffalo, Skidi. Like a similar story, it teaches the people, especially the young men, to be careful of strange women they may encounter while upon the prairie. Such women, according to the tale, are most likely black-tailed deer which have transformed themselves into women, and the influence of these deer upon men who cohabit with them is so great that they often become crazed and die.

into the village in the night and entered the medicine-men's lodge. When the medicine-men saw him enter the lodge they greeted him with a great noise. The man then begged that he might do some sleight-of-hand performances. The medicine-men consented and the man went back to the Deer and the fawns, and when they were about to start the Deer turned into a woman and the fawns into children, one a boy and the other a girl. The man then took the woman to his home, and when he had taken her and the children into the lodge they had to put up an extra buffalo-hide tipi for them, because the odor of the people was offensive.

When they had been there several days, the woman and the children became accustomed to the odor of the people; and the woman told the man to get ready, that she wanted to go to the medicine-lodge and do some sleight-of-hand performances. The man put a lot of white clay all over his body, and the woman spat at different places on his back, thus making the black marks. The woman and children were painted in the same way. The man then took them into the medicine-men's lodge and they were given a place nearest to the entrance of the lodge, behind the cedar tree. The medicine-men then all agreed that this man should do the sleight-of-hand performances that night, for they were anxious to see what powers he had. The man and the woman asked the medicine-men to lend them deer antlers. The antlers were lent them and they began to sing. While they were singing, the man would take the antlers and place them upon his head, and the antlers would remain there. He would then ask some spectator to take them, but they were fastened. When he would reach for the antlers they would come off. He then threw the antlers to one side and went to the place where the children were and brought out the boy. He placed a young fawn skin over his back and they began to sing. The little boy began to jump around and after a while turned into a Deer. When the Deer began to jump around in the lodge the woman began to make a noise like that of a deer. The man then went to the fawn, and as he placed his hand upon its head it turned into a boy again. When they had finished doing these things the man spoke to the medicine-men and said, "Brothers, I and my wife have performed a little sleight-of-hand for you, and every night we shall come and continue our performance." The medicine-men greeted them with yells in imitation of different animals. The woman and children then left the lodge and went to their home. Every night they did a little sleight-of-hand, and when the medicine-lodge dance was over the medicine-men met together in the medicine-lodge and invited the man to be with them. In this meeting the medicine-men all agreed that he should be their leader; that he was possessed of more powers than they were.

For a number of years the man lived with the people. One day the woman said to her husband: "I must now go to my people. My children are with you. They know of our ways, and whatever they may not know, teach them, for I can not remain with you any longer." Before the man could say anything, the woman went out of the lodge, changed into a black-tail Deer, and ran away. The man saw her go. He stayed with his people and cared for his children, but he was always unhappy. The children grew up and both married. The boy possessed great powers as did his father. When the man saw that his children were happy he took his quiver, bow, and arrows, and went into the woods and never returned to his people.

101. THE DEER DANCE.[1]

Many, many years ago a man wandered away from the village and was for many years upon the mountains. While he was there he lay down upon a high mound and went to sleep. He had a dream, and in the dream he saw a man standing near him who had black paint over his body. He had a buffalo robe around him. This man spoke to him in the dream and said: "My brother, I came for you. I am the messenger in a Deer dance which is being carried on at the foot of the mountains in a cave. You must go to that place, for the people there are anxious that you should take part in our ceremonies. The ceremony they wish to give you, so that you can take it back to your people."

After the man was through speaking he started off. He spoke again and said, "You must go in the direction I go." When the man awoke he looked around to see if he could see the man. Instead of the man he heard some one speaking to him from the sky. He looked up to the sky and there he saw a Raven flying around, and it was this Raven who was speaking to him and telling him to go to the place. The man did not pay any attention to the Raven. He felt queerly. He wanted to leave the place. He was scared. All at once the Raven flew down past the man and spoke to him, telling him to do as directed in his dream. As soon as the Raven spoke to him and told him which way to go, there was a great noise in the distance. After a while he found out that the noise

[1] Told by Roaming-Fox, a young Pitahauirat man, the keeper of the Deer dance in his band. The story serves as a warning to young men when away from home to be as alert as possible, as they, too, might be taken into a similar lodge and receive mysterious power.

came from the top of a high mountain. As he went to the top of the mountain the noise kept going from him until it stopped. The boy went to a certain place and there the man was standing at the entrance to the mountain. He said: "My brother, do you remember me? It was I who came to you in your dream. When I saw that you did not care to come I came to you as a Raven. When I saw that you would not listen to me I gathered a lot of Ravens and placed them upon the hill and told them to make a great noise. They did this and you followed the noises. You thought they were people, when they were not. Now you are here. The Ravens have entered the place and we will enter also." When they went into the cave the boy saw all kinds of animals and birds. The Elk people were the leaders in this dance. From the south side came the rattling of the gourds and then a song. When the boy looked again all the animals and birds in the cave had turned into people. They were painted after their animal and bird kind. The boy noticed that the Elk were painted red and wore elk hoofs upon their wrists. They also wore elk teeth upon their breast, strung on a buckskin string. Each one of these Elks had a whistle. On the north side were the Jack-Rabbits and Ravens. The Raven people were painted black. The Jack-Rabbits were painted with white clay. On the south side were the Foxes and the Coyotes. These two sets of people were also painted with white clay. There were all kinds of birds in the cave as well as animals. These people began to dance.

The first song which this man heard these people singing in the cave he thought was very fine. The people in the cave began to eat the red beans which grow in the south, and they gave the man some of the red beans to eat. After a while he became sick, for the beans were very strong. He fell down and lay there as if he were dead. While he lay there he went into the heavens, where he saw Tirawa. Tirawa was sitting in an earth-lodge. He held a bow in his left hand and bunches of wild sage in his right hand. When the man saw him, Tirawa placed the wild sage upon the ground and waved them, and many red beans rolled out. Tirawa spoke to the man and said: "You must go to your people and teach them this dance; and also teach them how to drink and eat these beans, so that they may see me, too. You must now return to the cave." The man stood up as if he had been asleep. He danced a while with the people, and then as daylight was coming the people turned into animals and birds again and began to go out of the cave. At night these animals and birds came back and again they had the dance. For four days this man stayed in the cave learning the mysterious ways from these people. On the fourth night they danced all night, and the animals and birds told

the man that he must go to his people.   The man went out of the cave
and went east to his people.

On the way he made a song which he was to sing at the opening of
his ceremony.   The song is about the Raven-Man who first spoke to him.
The second song which went with the other song was about the Raven-
Man going away after telling him to go to a certain place in the mountains.   He also made up two more songs about the Raven flying overhead
and flying downwards.   He also made up two other songs about the
Raven crying to him and a great noise being made at a distance.   He
made up another song about the Ravens making great noises upon the
top of the mountain.   Then he made up two more songs about when he
first entered the cave and heard the singing of the animals.   He made
up a song also in which he says, "The song which the people sang was
fine."   The song which went with this latter song says: "The song was
fine as I heard it at a distance."[1]   The man started the ceremony among
the people.   It was known as the Deer-Dance or Elk-Dance, and these
songs are the first which they sing to show the people where this man
got his dance.

102. THE WOLF-WARRIOR.[2]

A company of warriors were out on the war-path.   One man was
separated from the party and could not find it again.   He climbed a
high hill and as he neared the top of the hill he heard a song.   The song
was like this:

> Here and there over this earth,
> Here and there I have traveled.

The man looked around for the singer, and there on top of the hill
sat an old Wolf on his haunches with his body erect.   He was looking
towards the heavens and singing.   He sang the song several times, and
the man heard the song and recognized it as the Wolf-Warrior song.
The wolf was old, his hair had fallen, and there were few hairs upon his
head, paws, and the end of his tail.   The Wolf saw the man and said:
"Come, my son, I want you to see me.   This is my medicine that you

---

[1] The import of the songs are as given above.   They consist of endless repeti-
tions of the same lines.   The music will be found in Part II.
[2] Told by Thief, Kitkehahki.   This relates the origin of the individual power
obtained from a wolf by which a man became a fast traveler and a great warrior.
The story serves as a reminder to old men that before dying they should transmit
their power to young men.

see before me; although I am old I eat a little of this root and it makes me strong so that I can walk a long distance without growing weary. You can take the root, powder it fine, mix the root with white clay so that it will become dust, and when you are on the war-path and are very tired, take the pounded root and snuff it up your nose, and the tired feeling will go from you and you can travel fast. When you go home kill a wolf and make you a robe; then kill two more wolves and have moccasins made; have the front paws upon your moccasins, the hind paws back on your heels. Always wear the moccasins and wolf robe when you are on the war-path and want to travel fast. Do as I have told you and you shall become a great warrior and you shall have long life."

The man answered the Wolf, saying: "My father, you are a wonderful being. Tirawa watches over you and has given you long life. Give me long life, my father; make me a great warrior and I will keep the things you have told me. I will always have my tobacco bag filled with sumach leaves mixed with tobacco, so that I can smoke to you." The Wolf then said: "My son, lie down by me to-night. I am dying of old age; by the time the sun comes up and looks upon me I shall be dead. When I am dead, cut my nose and then cut a strip up the scalp about the length of the forefinger to the wrist. This you must dry and wear upon your scalp-lock, for this nose shall be my spirit, and if you keep it you shall live to be old and you shall not die until your skin is wrinkled and you have only a few hairs left upon your head. Then give these things to your children and tell them about me, so that they will take care of my things." The man sat down and the Wolf began to howl again and raised his head towards the heavens. As he kept on howling, the man listened and he heard a song. He heard it so plainly that he could sing the song:

> Often when the sun is high,
> Then I despise myself.

This song was to belong to the man, for he was to get old like the Wolf. The Wolf kept on howling, and that night the man lay down by the Wolf. As darkness came on, the Wolf crawled nearer to the man and sat down by him, and so the Wolf and the man slept side by side. The Wolf's power was transferred to the man through the medium of a dream. Towards morning, when the first morning star, "Wolf-Star," came up, the Wolf sat up and gave one big howl, then lay down again. At dawn the man awoke and saw that the Wolf was still sleeping. He sat up, faced the east, and waited for the sun to come up from the horizon. As its first ray shot across the land, the Wolf lifted up its head and looked at the sun, gave a howl, and as the sound died away the Wolf died. The man went up to where the Wolf lay and spoke to him, with deep feeling, and wept. He remained upon the hill several days, and one night the Wolf came to him in a dream and said: "My son, take the nose off from my body and keep it, as I told you. Do not stay upon the hill any more, for the Sun, my father, who gives me my power, has given me permission to follow you all the time. When I last cried, it was a cry to the Sun, for now the Sun has helped me to pass out of this world to our home, to a place unknown by man." When the man awoke, he looked about him and saw the Wolf lying there. He took his knife out and laid it on the ground. He took some sumach leaves and tobacco and placed them inside the nostrils of the Wolf. After this, he took his knife and cut the nose with a piece of the scalp on. He left the Wolf on the hill; for the Wolf in the dream had told him that he should leave his body on the hill. The man took the things that he was to take with him, the root and the nose of the Wolf. The man did not go to join the war party, but went on home.

When he reached home, people asked about the others who were with him. He told them that he was lost from the others and had not seen them any more, and so he had come back home. The people called him a coward and said, "You should have remained with them." The man did not say anything. Days went by. The man was always absent from the village. While he was gone one day, the war party came over the hills as if to attack the village. They were on fine ponies that they had captured from the enemy, and each was singing his victory song. As they approached the village men went out to meet the victorious party, while the women and children climbed the mud-lodges to see the victorious war party come in. Some of them had white clay all over their bodies, and others were painted black with prairie grass that they had burned, to let the people know by the smoke that a victorious war party was coming. When the men came home the people told them that they did not go out to meet the man who had come home alone. The warriors then told the people that they thought the man had strayed off and perhaps been killed by the enemy, for he had never been seen by them again. Wolf-Man returned to the village when he saw the war party approaching, and listened to all they said, but remained silent.

The summer passed. In the fall when the people were gathering their corn, another warrior of distinction sat in his lodge and invited a few of his friends to join him, telling that he intended to go out among the Comanche. Wolf-Man heard about the war party, and he stole away from home and joined the party. There were good warriors in this party, so Wolf-Man was not so prominent. When they reached the enemy's country he made up his mind that he would scout on ahead. Every morning when the war party began to journey, Wolf-Man would remain behind. In the evening he would be the last to come to camp, and he would tell of all he saw farther south, where the other scouts had failed to go. Most of the warriors did not believe him.

One day he stayed behind, but when he did travel he went far beyond the others. He turned back, and on his way the other scouts saw him. They were surprised, for these scouts had started out before anyone. Wolf-Man went to where the main company had made the camp. The two scouts reported carefully all they had seen and they also told that they had seen Wolf-Man coming from a long distance in advance of them and that he had a report to make. Wolf-Man then told how he walked and passed the other scouts and how he had gone a long way from the scouts. There were no signs of any enemy, so Wolf-Man recommended that they go southeast to the land of the Osage. The two leaders were glad to hear the man speak. The next morning, before daylight, he was told to scout on ahead. The man went out, and before daylight he was back, for he had seen Cheyenne and Arapaho breaking camp.

The company hid until noon; then they came out from their hiding place and followed the trail. The trail was plain. They could see the enemy making camp. They could also see where they were taking their ponies. After night scouts were sent to capture the ponies. Wolf-Man was one of the six scouts selected. He went with the men, but finally went away from them to the place where the leader was, with the other young men. As he drove the ponies up, the leader came and met him. "All these ponies I give you," said Wolf-Man. The leader thanked him and said, "This day you shall be known among our great warriors as the Man-Who-Has-No-Leader." Wolf-Man went back to camp and found more ponies, brought them to the leader, and again he gave them all to him. The young men surrounded the herd of ponies. Each man had his lariat rope trying to rope a pony. Everybody was told to catch his pony and to drive the herd. Most of the men caught ponies and got on them. While the men were riding and driving the ponies they saw Wolf-Man walking, sometimes running, and he did not seem to get tired. The leader, when he divided the ponies, let Wolf-Man take his choice of all. Wolf-Man took one pony. The leader divided the ponies so that even the young men who for the first time had gone on the war-path received a pony, and every one of the warriors had a pony. As they neared the village the leader started a prairie fire and made the young men take the burnt grass and paint their faces black.

The people in the village saw the smoke. Soon they saw the warriors coming over the hills on ponies and singing their victory songs, and
they knew that it was the war party which had gone out. When the
warriors were in their lodges, they told of Wolf's-Man's wonderful
endurance in walking. After that when a leader wanted to go on the
war-path he invited Wolf-Man. Wolf-Man was always ready to go.
He was the leader of scouts. The war party always came back successful,
for they had Wolf-Man with them.

Among the warriors was a famous leader who determined to go on
the war-path. He sent for only the best men in the tribe, and Wolf-Man
was among them. This party of warriors started out for the Mexican
country, for in that country they could capture mules and fine ponies.
Before starting, Wolf-Man had a wolf robe made. He also had moccasins
made from wolf hide. The nose and scalp of the wolf he wore on his scalp-
lock all the time, and he wore the wolf robe and his wolf moccasins.
When the company had gone far south into the enemy's country, the
leader found two men who seemed never to grow tired, and yet they
traveled farther every day than the others. They soon were recognized
as leaders of all the scouts. They were sent out in different directions
one day, and when they were far away from the others they met. There
were no enemies in sight. They could see no sign, and so they started
back to the place where the leaders were with the other men. As they
journeyed, both seemed to be equal in endurance. Wolf-Man's companion
said: "How do you travel so fast? You must possess some power."
"Well," said Wolf-Man, "I will let you know. See my moccasins? They
are made of wolf hide. I wear them on my journey; when I near the
camp, I take them off. I also use this dust in my buckskin sack. Take
some and snuff it up into your nostrils." The other man took the dust
and snuffed it. The tired feeling wore off and he felt like walking a
long distance. They went on for many miles, and then Wolf-Man said
to the other man: "Have you no guardian nor helper? I have told
you my secret, now tell me yours." The man reached for his scalp-lock
and took from it a small root. This he broke and gave to Wolf-Man,
and said, "Chew; swallow." Wolf-Man took the root, chewed it, and
swallowed the juice. He felt as though it were morning and he had not
been traveling all day. As he swallowed the juice from the root he felt
relieved from hunger, for the root tasted like fat. Wolf-Man said, "This is
wonderful; who or what animal gave you this root?" The man answered
and said: "This root I got from a Horse; the Horse did not speak to
me, but I had a dream, and the Horse told me in my dream that I must
go with him and he would show me the Horses' root. I followed the

Horse and he showed me the root; I dug it up and tasted it; I knew how it tasted; I woke up. The next day I went out and found the root, and dug it up and tasted it and it was the same, and so I kept it." Wolf-Man did not say any more, for he had found one man equal to himself in traveling. Wolf-Man also knew that the man did not tell all of his story.

When they reached camp they told the leaders where they had been, and it was hard for the leaders to believe them; for it was a journey of several days to the place where they said they had been. These two men were the ones who found a Mexican village and took from a corral many ponies and mules, giving them to the leader. The leader thanked them.

After this trip Wolf-Man made friends with the other man who could walk fast. They became old and were often invited by young warriors to tell their war stories to them. Wolf-Man outlived the other man and came to Oklahoma in 1872. He was then a very old man, but still a good walker. He had a son whom he took pains to teach his secrets and songs. One night after the old man had given all of his things to his son, he lay down in his earth-lodge and waited through the night for the first ray of the morning sun to come, for he knew that when it came he had to die. The ray came through the lodge and rested on the old man. He gave one cry and died, as the wolf had died, of old age.

103. THE COYOTE AND WOLF MEDICINE.[1]

A man was walking along and he met Coyote. Coyote spoke to the man and said, "How would you like to smoke my pipe?" The man thanked Coyote and told him that he would like to smoke it. After the man had smoked he returned the pipe, and then Coyote said to him: "You have smoked my pipe and so I will not catch you and kill you, but will take you to my people. I want my people to know that you have smoked my pipe. They will be glad to see you and will give you great powers." They went on, and after a while they met many Coyotes and Wolves. When the Coyotes and the Wolves saw Coyote with the man, one of the Wolves called to the other Wolves and said: "All be seated. Let us hear what these people who are coming have to say." When they were seated Coyote stood up and said: "This man is my brother. He smoked my pipe. He came with me to make you people a visit. Let us take pity upon him and make him a wonderful man." The man was frightened, for the Wolves came close to him. Then the man was told to look. He looked and saw many Coyotes, old and young. The Coyotes

[1] Told by White-Sun, Kitkehahki. The moral of the story is about the same as that of the preceding.

began to roll in the dust; then they came to the man and gave him roots and told him that the roots were good for the sick. Then one of the Coyotes arose and said: "We will give you this root and if any man is bitten by a mad dog give this medicine to him. He will then get well and not go mad. The other medicines are good for the urine and for pains."

A Wolf stood up next, rolled in the dust, then arose and gave to the man a whistle, and said: "I give you the whistle. When anybody is sick, use this whistle and the person will be made well." Then another Wolf arose and said: "I give you this bone with which to kill people. You must kill people, consecrate them, and give them as an offering to the gods." Then a Coyote arose and said: "I go around in the night and no one sees me, and I get things to eat. This bone that I give you to use as a club represents me." Then another Coyote stood up and rolled in the dust. He gave the man a piece of bone with the skull of a Coyote on it. This Coyote said: "Take this bone. If anyone attempts to poison or bewitch you, lay the bone on your forehead and you will kill them. My power is in the bone." The man spoke and said: "This is enough. I thank you. Wolves and Coyotes, I am glad." Coyote took the man back to the village. "When you get home," he said, "take this whistle. Blow it before you get home. Blow hard and we will hear it; all the Coyotes and Wolves will hear it." The man did as he was told and heard the Coyotes howl in the distance. The man arrived home. After several days he heard of a man who could not make water. He went to him and doctored him until he was cured.

104. THE SCALPED-MAN MEDICINE.[1]

A long time ago a war party went to the Comanche country to capture ponies. The warriors captured so many ponies that they began to organize another party as soon as they arrived home. The second party had anything but the success of the first party. It was surrounded, attacked, and lost many ponies and the lives of some of the bravest warriors. They ran in terror from the enemy, and many of the wounded fell by the way, unable to go farther. Among these was one man who was wounded in the leg. He managed to keep up with the others until night came and they camped. During the night his wound grew worse, and at daylight

[1] Told by Sun-Chief, Skidi. The belief in scalped people has already been referred to. The tale teaches that travelers away from home should not be afraid of these scalped people, because they have the ability of conferring power. The story is also interesting because it shows the existence among the Pawnee of the power of ventriloquism.

when they were ready to break camp and start on he was not able to go with them. Some of the men went out and killed a few buffalo, jerked the meat and made it into a bundle, which they placed at his head. Others brought water and fire sticks for him and did all that they could to make him comfortable, then they left him, promising to let his people know of his condition as soon as they could, so that they could come to his rescue.

The war party had not been gone long when the wounded man heard many voices, and he became frightened for fear the enemy were upon him. Soon he heard some one laugh, and a voice that sounded so near that it was speaking in his ear said: "I just wanted to scare you. It was only I who made all of that noise." The man looked everywhere, but he could see no one. The next morning he saw some of his meat had been stolen during the night, and he thought that surely the enemy had followed him. When night came he again heard many strange voices, and the next morning he discovered that more of his meat was gone. He became very much frightened and cried aloud that whoever was stealing his meat should come and kill him, for he would rather be killed than starve to death. For reply he heard only some one laugh. For several evenings he continued to hear voices, now near, now far away, and each morning he discovered that more of his meat had been stolen. Finally his last piece of meat was stolen and again he called out for the person who took it to come and kill him. For reply he heard only some one laugh, and then suddenly Scalped-Man appeared before him and said, "If you will come to my home, I will heal your wounds and care for you." The man was not afraid of Scalped-Man and said that he would go with him, for he knew that he would die if he stayed where he was. Scalped-Man took him upon his back and carried him to his home, which was in a big cave.

There in the cave were heaps of wild sage spread upon the ground. Close to the fireplace was a buffalo skull with presents of blue beads, eagle feathers, black silk handkerchiefs, and wampum about it. Back of the skull was the pile of meat that the man had lost, and many other parfleches filled with dried meat. Many buffalo robes were scattered through the cave, and on one of them Scalped-Man placed the wounded man. He looked about for an opening, but could not see any, and he could not tell how they came in.

Every day Scalped-Man would leave the cave and be gone for a long time. Before he returned, the wounded man would always hear many voices crying out, and giving war cries, and then all at once he would hear a laugh and then Scalped-Man would appear in the cave. He would tell the man that it was he who was making all the noise, but the man could not believe him for a long time, but at last he was convinced. While Scalped-Man was away the man thought that he heard his own father and mother crying and calling his name, and then other people crying and calling to him. He became so excited that he arose for the first time and tried to walk. He was so sure that his father and mother had come and were looking for him, that he started to go to them and cried out to them, but he could not find the entrance. While he was running frantically about, trying to get out, Scalped-Man called and said, "Get back there; the people will see you and take you away from me," and he appeared before the excited man and began to laugh. The man asked him if he had seen any of the people who were calling him, and he said that he had not. After a while he told the man that it was he who made all the noise that sounded like the voices of his people. The man refused to believe Scalped-Man at first, but he began to cry and call and made his voice sound like many people talking, until he convinced the man. Then he offered to give him the power of making the many peculiar sounds.

Every day he taught him, and he learned so rapidly that soon he could make sounds so well that he could fool Scalped-Man just as he had been fooled by him. Scalped-Man also taught him sleight-of-hand performances, and gave him a white downy feather and covered his body with white clay. He put many coats of clay over the wounded leg, and the soreness went away and the wounded man was healed. Then he blew his breath upon the eagle feather and put it in the man's hair, saying: "Keep this and it will give you power, for it stands for me. I am a spirit and I travel like the wind and I run fast. When you want to run fast like a spirit, put this downy feather in your hair and spread clay all over your body as I have done, and then you can run. If you fight with the enemy, spread the clay all over your body, and when you want to run fast, spit upon your hands and wet the soles of your feet or moccasins, and then you will be as swift as the wind. Break wild sage and carry it with you, and the pieces will turn into arrows at your wish when you are fighting. Now, I have taught you all that I know and have given you all the power that I have. In return I ask only that you do not mention me to the people or ever tell anyone where I live. If you do I shall know it at once, and though I move to some other place, I will punish you for telling." Scalped-Man then embraced the man and told him that in a few days his people would come to see if he were living or dead, and so he would have to return to his old camp in the cave where the men had left him, so that his people would find him there.

The people did come and found him in his own cave, and they were surprised to find him a well man. He asked for some blue beads, native tobacco, a black silk handkerchief, and some eagle feathers. These they gave him, and in the night he went to Scalped-Man's cave and gave him the presents. The man came back to his people and they returned to the village.

When they arrived, the Medicine-Men's ceremony was in progress, and on every night the different medicine-men were performing some sleight-of-hand performances that were taught them by different animals. The man went at once to the medicine-lodge, and asked that he be permitted to do some sleight-of-hand. The first thing he did was to throw his voice in different directions so that there seemed to be many people speaking, when really there was only he. Medicine-men were all surprised and they called him the wonderful man, but other people who had heard that this man had been living with Scalped-Man, called him Scalped-Man.

While they were having the Medicine-Men's ceremony, a cry was given that the enemy were about to attack the village, and the men rushed out to meet the attack. Among the enemy was one who seemed to have power to make the arrows go to one side or the other and not pierce him, and to ward off blows so that he could not be wounded. The people began to be frightened by his power, and cried for more help. The wounded man, who had become a medicine-man, was in the medicine-lodge. When he heard the cry he arose, covered his body with white clay, put the downy feather in his hair, hung an eagle-wing whistle about his neck, then took in his left hand some pieces of wild sage and in his right a small war club and started forth. He blew his whistle, and as he blew it he ran so fast that he seemed to be carried by the wind. He saw that his people were retreating before the enemy, and so he ran around and attacked them from the rear. Some of the men turned and tried to shoot him, but the arrows went to the right and left of him. The wonderful man, who also had power to escape arrows, ran to attack him, but the man raised his small war club and hit him a blow on the head that felled him, and he rolled over dead. As soon as he fell dead, the enemy gave way and became frightened. The man rushed into their midst and struck another, and another, until he had killed many, and then he turned back and went into the medicine-lodge. When the rest of the warriors returned to the village, they spoke of a certain man who was so covered with white clay that they could not tell who he was, but they all talked of his great bravery. He became a great medicine-man and warrior, and though he fought in many battles he was never injured.

After he had lived a long time he committed suicide. Something told him that his friend Scalped-Man was gone, and so he did not wish to live any longer.

105. HOW THE PAWNEE GOT THE EAGLE DANCE.[1]

Many years ago while the Pawnee lived near Nemàha, Nebraska, the people agreed to remove their village on west to the Republican River. When the people reached the place where they were to make their new village, there was a man among the people who wandered away. The relatives of this man did not know where the man went. The people kept on building their village and in about two years it was complete. Here the people remained for some time. When summer came they moved west to hunt for buffalo. When they had gone far, the man who was lost came into their camp. He wore a buffalo robe about his body, the hair outside, and covered with soft eagle feathers. His head was covered with soft downy feathers, one soft feather being stuck into his scalp-lock on the top of his head. The people looked at him with wonder. On account of the way he was dressed and covered with eagle feathers they knew that he must have been to some animals' lodge, or to some other mysterious place. He did not join the people on their journey, but waited until everybody had passed, and then he followed.

When he would reach the village he would sit down on the south side and remain there. Sometimes he went to where the men were playing the javelin game. He would sit down on the south side of the field and remain there alone. He would never allow any man to come and sit with him. When the people had gone a long way through the western country, the man disappeared again. After several days the man came back to the camp with many more eagle feathers. He tied the eagle feathers in a small buffalo robe and hung the robe up in his tipi.

When the people saw the bundle which he brought back they were sure that he was a wonderful man, and that he must have wonderful ways. The people killed many buffalo and returned to their village. The man who was lost went with them, taking his sacred bundle. The people looked upon him as wonderful, but in reality he had no powers of any kind. He found, however, a wonderful place and brought things from that place to his home. He was anxious to learn more about the wonderful place he had found, and so he went to the place whenever he

[1] Told by Young-Bull, Pitahauirat. Apart from the story of the origin of the Eagle dance, the tale is similar in the moral it points to No. 86. Here also the lesson is taught that a young man should not mistreat a member of his own tribe for his own personal benefit.

was not watched by other people. When he would reach the place he would find many eagle feathers scattered over a high hill, and before gathering them up he would stand on the top of the hill where a soft downy feather seemed to be placed. There he would stand and cry. He heard no strange noise, neither was he put to sleep in order to be taken into the lodge of the animals, and he knew all the time that he received no power from anyone. He would stop crying, gather the feathers and take them home. The first feathers he found he placed all over his robe.

At this time, when the people had their village upon the Republican River, this man decided to learn what was in the hill where he found so many eagle feathers. He studied and thought what he should do for the animals that were in the hill. At last he made up his mind. One evening he went out where the children were playing and there he found his nephew playing with the other children. This little boy thought a great deal of his uncle. He used to follow him around through the village. When the boy saw his uncle he ran up to him and asked to be taken home. The man put the child upon his back and carried him off. When they were gone many days the man told the boy that they were going to a wonderful place. When the boy was taken away, the parents looked for him all through the village, but they could not find him.

After a while the uncle came back, but the child was not with him. Then the people knew that the child must be lost. The uncle, upon reaching the wonderful place with the child upon his back, saw many feathers scattered over the hill. He went up to where the downy feather was, stood there, and cried. As he cried he took the child from his back. He placed the child upon the downy feathers and said: "To whatever being is in this place, I now give you my nephew to devour. For this present I want you to take pity on me and give me the power which you possess, and teach me why these feathers are scattered over this hill." As he let the boy go, the boy dropped into a hole, for where the soft downy feather was placed was really an opening for the eagles to fly in and out. As the boy fell into the hole the man began to cry, and although he cried for several days he saw that he would receive no powers from anybody. He began to walk around and pick up the feathers. Afterwards he went home.

When the boy was dropped into the hole all the Eagles in the den gave a whistling sound, jumped up, and looked at the boy. The Eagles began to talk among themselves and say: "This is wrong. This man who has been visiting our place has stolen his own nephew and has placed him in our den in order that we might feast upon him. He has given us this boy. The man who has been visiting us has received from us many feathers. We were arranging a time when this man should be allowed to come into our den. Instead of waiting until we should arrange for him to come, he has stolen a child and has given it to us. This child has a father and a mother. The father and the mother are hunting for the child, and they are mourning at this time for the child. This father and mother love their child." Then one of the Eagles said, "See, on the east side of our den are seated our father and our mother." All the Eagles looked to the east in the den, and there sat two old Eagles. Their feathers were worn off. They looked very old. Then the Eagle who was speaking said, "We will leave it to these two old people to tell us what to do with the boy." The two old Eagles then began to stir around, stretching their wings and their necks. The old man Eagle said: "The man in his haste to learn our power has stolen this boy and thrown him into our den to learn our secrets. We had promised to help this man, but since he has stolen this child we will let him go and will not give him any powers. Let the child remain with us. I give you my power and my consent to turn the boy into an Eagle." All the Eagles in the den jumped up and screeched, for they were satisfied with what the old Eagle had decided. The child was now told to sit up. The Eagles flew around in the den, for they were very numerous. All these Eagles were descended from the two which were now old. The Eagles flew around in the den and also around the boy. Then the Eagles flew in a flock around in the den and surrounded the little boy. When the Eagles flew up, there were many feathers scattered around the boy.

Again the Eagles surrounded him. This time they covered him with soft downy feathers. The next time they flew around the boy and surrounded him. When they flew away the arms of the boy had feathers upon them. Again the Eagles surrounded him, and when they flew away the boy was not there. They flew around the den several times and then placed the boy on the south side. When the Eagles had flown away the boy sat there as an Eagle, for he had been turned into an Eagle according to his age. The boy tried to fly, but as he was still young and his feathers small, he could not fly. Every day the Eagles flew out of the den and went over the country. In the afternoon they would return to the den with all kinds of meat and animals and drop them into the den. The boy and the other young Eagles would surround the meat and eat of it. When the young Eagles had eaten the meat from the bones, and the old Eagles had returned to the den, the bones were taken out and dropped over the country. For some time the boy remained in the den, for he could not fly out. The boy was being taught by the old Eagles the power which he was to have. The old Eagles kept telling the boy how bad the man had been for dropping him into the den.   They told him that in time he was to help to kill the man for what he had done.

For some time afterwards the boy was told to try to fly out of the den.   He flew up and out of the den, but the other Eagles remained with him to watch over him and see that he did not go back to the people. In the evening the Eagles, together with the Eagle-Boy, came back to the den.   For several months the boy flew out, but was always watched by the other Eagles.   After a while the Eagle boy went off by himself and always brought in a badger or a prairie dog, or sometimes he would bring fish which he had taken from the creeks.   These things he placed before the old Eagles.   The boy found out that the old Eagles were very fond of fish and he would bring more for them.   One day the boy Eagle went out and brought in a small-sized deer.   When the old Eagles saw that the boy brought the deer into the den, they knew that he was now strong.

In the night when all the Eagles were gathered together in the den, the old Eagle said: "It is now time for this young Eagle to return to his people.   We have given him powers which we possess, and he must go among his people and be good to them.   But before he goes to his people I wish to be satisfied, for I want to eat of the man who brought this boy and threw him into our den."   The Eagles all screamed and said: "Our father has spoken well.   We will go and bring this man, so that the Eagles may eat of him and then our father shall also eat of the man.   Our brother here knows his uncle.   He will take us to where he is and we will catch him and bring him to this den."   That night it was planned to go and catch the man and bring him into the den.

The next morning, just as the sun was about to come up, the Eagles began to fly out from the den.   They joined the Eagle-Boy up in the sky When they had all left the den the Eagles could be seen flying in the sky. After all had come together they flew to the east where the people had made their village.   The Eagles flew up high into the sky, so that the people could not see them.   The Eagles flew over the village, and there on the south side of the village the men were playing with sticks.   There on the south side sat the man who had stolen the boy.   His robe was covered with eagle feathers, and the boy knew him at once.   The Eagles flew around once or twice overhead where the man sat.   Then the Eagle boy flew down and all the Eagles swooped down with him.   The men who were playing sticks saw the Eagles fly down toward the man in a funnel-shaped line, and when they saw that the Eagles took hold of the man and lifted him up from the ground they knew that something was wrong.   The men ran from the gambling grounds into the village.

There was shouting all through the village.   The people came out and watched the Eagles as they bore the man up into the sky.   The Eagles twisted the man around until they finally unwrapped his buffalo robe. The robe dropped down to the ground and the Eagles took hold of the man's flesh by the arms and legs.   They flew away with their burden to their den, but instead of flying through the hole into the den with the man, they dropped him from the sky into the hole.   He fell upon the ground in the den and was killed.   The Eagles now flew into the den and placed the man in front of the two old Eagles.   They ate of him for several days.   When he was eaten up and there was nothing but the bones, the Eagles all came together and took bone after bone out of the den and scattered them over the earth.

After the Eagles had carried this man off, the people broke camp and went away from that place.   From that day to this the people have called this site "Place-Where-the-Eagles-Carried-a-Man-Off."

Several years afterwards the Eagles turned the Eagle-Boy into a man, and when the Eagles saw that he was quite a young man they were satisfied to send him home again.   The Eagles all came together and agreed that the boy should return to his people.   The oldest of the Eagles, except the two old parents, told the boy to kill him and remove his skin, leaving only the head in the skin, and to take the body out of the den and throw it away.   He told the boy that by doing this his spirit would be with him always; that the spirit of the Eagle would always be with him to help him in anything he undertook.   The old Eagle said: "My son, I should have given you my feathers, but you see, as I stretch my wings, that my feathers are worn off.   You shall grow to old age just as I have grown, and all your children and all who shall have received the powers which I possess shall grow to great age."   The old Eagle then took one claw from his right leg and gave it to the boy and told him to wear it when fighting with the enemy.   The Eagle also gave the boy a soft downy feather for him to wear in battle.   The old Eagle then commenced to scratch with its claws in the earth.   Then he told the boy to place the dirt in a little buckskin, for it was the paint that he should put upon his body when in battle.   The Eagle reached behind and took therefrom a bone whistle, which was from the wing of an Eagle.   He said: "When you have spread this paint upon your body, and you have the soft downy feather upon your scalp-lock, and you do not feel that we are near you, put this bone in your mouth, whistle, and our spirit will be with you."   The old Eagle promised the boy that in sickness the Eagle would be sent to watch over him and help him to wait on people when they were sick and cure them.   The old Eagle also said: "When you have been with your people for some time you must get an Eagle-wing fan. That wing will have our power and our breath, so that in waving that wing over a sick person we will breathe over them. The sickness will go from them and they will become well. After you have been with your people for some time you must kill a young fawn and from the fawn skin you must make a rattle. The rattle you will use when you sing for sick people. In shaking this rattle over them it will arouse the animal spirit in them. The sick will try to imitate our kind and they will be made well." The old Eagle then selected other Eagles to fly with the boy to his home. At daylight ten Eagles flew out of the den with the boy. They flew toward the south where the village was located upon the Republican River. When they came near the village the Eagles flew down to the earth. They alighted upon a high mound. They told the boy to go to his people; that they would watch over him and take care of him. The Eagles flew around the boy Eagle and he turned into a young man. Then the Eagles flew away.

The boy went toward the village. When he entered the village he looked into the different lodges, and at last he came to one lodge where he saw his father and mother sitting by the fireplace. They were all scarred and had their hair cut short. All these years they had mourned over their lost child. The boy entered the lodge and said, "Father, I am here." The man looked and saw a young man with a buffalo robe with many Eagle feathers upon it. He thought this was the same man who had been carried away by the Eagles. The boy said, "Father, I have come back to remain with you." The father saw that the boy was now quite a young man. He jumped up, caught his son in his arms, and said, "Woman, come, our son is here." The woman came and cried, but the young man said: "Do not cry, for I am here now. Take this bundle and place it at the altar in the west."

It was then told through the village that the boy who had been lost had returned. The people began to come in. The men sat in a circle around the fireplace. The boy told how his uncle had found a wonderful place away from the village; that the wonderful place was a mound covered with Eagle feathers; at the top was the entrance, but it was covered with soft downy feathers so that the hole could not be seen; that his uncle had gone there and gathered the feathers; that he had placed these feathers upon his robe; several times he had gone to this place; that the people looked upon him as a wonderful man when in reality he had no power at all. He told that his uncle was in a hurry to learn of the powers of the Eagles and had thought that by giving something to the wonderful place he might receive powers. He decided, therefore, to steal the boy and give him to the birds, so that the birds might give him powers. He said that he came into the village and carried him to the wonderful place. The boy said: "When the man stood by the entrance he cried and gave me to the birds. 'To you, Eagles in this den, I give my nephew as a present. Take pity upon me and give me your powers.' " The boy continued and said: "I remained in the den for many years. The Eagles did not eat me. Instead, they took pity on me and I flew into the sky, looked over the country, and I saw you, my people, traveling around. I remained with the Eagles until it was decided to take the man up, so that the Eagles would receive him in their den and eat him. I came and helped, and we carried the man up into the sky and down into the den and the Eagles ate him up. Now you understand why the Eagles took the man up into the sky."

The boy remained in the village for some time. A war party was got up and they went into the country of the enemy. The boy did not follow them. Soon after this the boy told his people that he was going to follow the war party. About four days afterwards the boy disappeared, but as he did so he turned into an Eagle and flew away to the warriors. He saw them, flew down, turned into a young man, and went into their camp. The men were surprised when they saw him. Before morning the boy went away. As the warriors continued on their march they saw the boy coming over a hill. He told the warriors that the enemy was near at hand. Scouts were sent out to look over the village, and they came back and said, "We must attack the village, for there are only a few tipis." The warriors began to put on their war costumes. Some put on war bonnets, some spears, and some carried shields. Others were naked. The boy sat down, took some clay and spread it upon his body. He placed a bone whistle upon his breast. He put a soft downy feather in his scalp-lock. In his right hand he carried a club. The club he did not have when they first saw him, but afterwards they discovered that it was the claw of an eagle.

When they attacked the village the boy was the first to go into the village, so that when a man came out from a tipi he struck him with his war club and killed him. Again he came through the village and struck another man and killed him. Then he went through the village and took two scalps. These scalps he tied upon his club and then went away from the fight. After the fight the warriors returned. The boy said, "Leader, I give you these scalps, but I want two small pieces, one from each scalp, to hang upon my eagle claw as a gift to the old Eagle." This was promised him. After all the warriors came back the boy told the leaders that he was going to his home. That night the boy disappeared. He had turned into an Eagle and had gone home. The next day the boy was found in his lodge, and when he was asked about the warriors he told his father that he had been with them, that they had attacked a village, and the warriors had acted bravely and had taken some scalps. The people who heard the boy telling this to the father went through the village and told the people what the boy said. The people made fun of the boy. They believed that the boy had gone out and had never overtaken the warriors, but had returned.

In a few days the warriors came over the hills singing war songs and shouting the name of the boy, telling how he had first attacked the village; that he had killed two and that he had also taken two scalps. Then the people believed what was said of the boy. After that, whenever the boy sat down before going on the war-path, other young men came and sat with him. They knew that he had great powers. They followed him, and he was successful in conquering the enemy and capturing ponies. He always had upon his body the white clay which was given him by the Eagle, the whistle, and the downy feather. The enemy tried to kill him, but they could not hit him and so he was never killed. After he became a great warrior he thought it was time that he should enter the Medicine-Men's lodge.

One summer the people went on a buffalo hunt. In the fall when they came back to their village, and the medicine-lodge was cleaned out and the medicine-men were to have their ceremonies, the boy thought he would do something. When the lodge was all ready, the Eagle-Boy went into it. When he entered the lodge the leading medicine-man got up, went to him, and asked him what he wished to do. Eagle-Boy said, "I have come into your medicine-lodge to act with the medicine-men." The young man was given a seat in the northwest, for the medicine-man knew that the den of the Eagles was in the northwest. When his turn came to do some sleight-of-hand, he took the whole eagle skin which he had, ran around the fire three or four times, and threw the whole eagle skin west of the fireplace, and there sat a live Eagle. The other medicine-men, as soon as they saw this, got up from their seats, took their pipes filled with native tobacco, went up to the live Eagle, and offered native tobacco and smoke to the Eagle. When the young man went up again to the Eagle he ran around it several times, and as he reached his hands toward the Eagle, the Eagle's life seemed to die away. The boy caught the Eagle and it was the skin of the Eagle again. The boy performed many sleight-of-hand tricks, and after this he was looked upon as a great medicine-man. When anybody was sick he was sent for. He went, taking with him the Eagle wing and the rattle. He sang songs

about the Eagles, and waved the eagle wing over their bodies where the
pain was. The pain would leave them.

Eagle-Boy became a great medicine-man, a warrior, and finally a
chief. He became very old. Then he handed the story, the eagle skin,
and everything that went with it to his son. These talismans have
been handed down until at the present time Hawk, of the Pitahauirat
band, is the keeper of everything—the whistle, the rattle, and the white
clay. He now dances the Eagle dance. In the medicine-men's dances,
Hawk sings the song that was taught the boy by the Eagles when they
carried the boy's uncle up into the sky. There is another song sung when
the boy was transformed into an eagle. There are also other songs which
go with this story.

106. THE DOG MEDICINE.[1]

A boy was going along when he came to a hill, where he sat down to
rest. After a while he saw a Dog coming, but he did not notice the Dog
closely. After a little time the Dog came and sat down near him, and
spoke to him and said: "Listen to me. I have something to tell you.
I am sorry that I am here. People do not take care of me. You have
had hard times in the village. I saw you coming away because the
woman whom you wanted to marry scolded you. I know that you want
that woman and by my help you shall have her. You must go south, for
the people have gone into the southern country."

The young man went south. He found the village and remained
there, and as the Dog had taught the boy a song, the boy sang in the
night. The girl he wanted to marry came, and he told her to go with him,
and she consented. They traveled far, until they came to the place where
the Dog was sitting. The Dog was glad to see them and said: "Tell me
of your marriage. You must call me brother all the time." The boy
told how he had gone into the village, and how the people were glad to
see him. He told how at night he went out and sang a song and the girl
came to him. The Dog then gave the boy a buffalo robe, an eagle wing
for a fan, a bone whistle, and a gourd. The Dog said: "Whistle when
you want me. The bone whistle you must use in your medicine ceremony. I will give you many children. I have taken pity upon you,
for you had a great desire to have children. I am going to teach you
how to be a medicine-man." The Dog blew his breath and the smoke
came out of his mouth. Then he gave the man some roots and taught

[1] Told by White-Sun, Kitkehahki. The story teaches that even dogs should not
be mistreated, for they also have powers which it is possible for them to bestow upon
the people.

him what they were good for. The Dog then said: "You must dance the Dog dance, and when you are having the Dog dance, whisper to me and I will listen to you." The Dog continued: "I have also given you a pony. This pony you shall capture when you have gone on the war-path. You will know it, for it shall have the picture of a star upon its forehead. It shall be a wonderful pony, for it shall not be a real pony, but myself. Go home to your people and dance, and at once start upon the war-path. Carry the things which I have given you. I will make my home upon these hills and when you have returned come to this place."

The boy went home, and in the evening he called several young men to sit with him in the lodge and smoke. While they were smoking he said: "Brothers, I want you to go on the war-path with me. How many of you will go with me?" All the young men who were in the lodge said that they would go. The war party started out before morning, and were far away from the village when it became daylight. For several days they went south, and at last they came upon a village of the enemy. The young man selected several scouts to go into the village and to drive the ponies from the village when they found them. The ponies were brought, but the young man did not see one with a star on its forehead, and so he was dissatisfied and started into the village himself. On the way he saw a pony tied close to the entrance of a tipi. When he saw the pony and saw the white spot upon its forehead he knew that it was the pony that the Dog had promised him. Instead of reaching down to untie him from the post, he took his knife out from the scabbard, cut the rope, and led the pony out from the camp. When he had reached the place where the young men were, they traveled towards home. For several days and nights they traveled without sleep. At last they stopped to rest and sleep. When they had had a little rest they began to journey again and they went into their village. The boy gave all the ponies that he had away except the one with the white spot. When the boy had eaten and rested a little, he jumped upon his pony and went to the place where the Dog was. The boy found the Dog at the place where he had left him. The Dog told the boy that he had the pony which he had promised him, and said: "In a few days your people will have a medicine ceremony, and you must go into the lodge and dance with them." The boy returned to the village, and while he was there it was noised through the village that the people were going to have the Medicine-Men's ceremony. The boy went into the lodge and asked that he be permitted to dance. The medicine-men gave him a seat, and when his turn came to dance, he sang a song which the people had never heard before. The boy was painted with red ointment all over his body.   There were many downy feathers upon his head, so that when he danced it seemed to the people as if sparks of fire were all around him.   The people gave him many presents.

After the dance the people talked about the boy and some believed that he was a medicine-man.   In a little while a man took sick, and his relatives went for the boy to doctor the sick man.   The young man selected three men to go with him who were to help him sing.   When the boy began to sing Dog songs, he jumped up and ran, and he spat out a small dog hide close to the sick man.   When the dog hide was spread open there was a picture of the moon upon it.   The boy spread the dog hide upon the patient and the patient went to sleep at once, and in a few days he awoke a well man.   The boy went to his home, and the relatives of the patient sent him many presents for his pay.   The boy afterwards started what is known as the Young-Dog dance among the Pawnee.

107. BURNT-BELLY AND THE DOG.[1]

Many years ago the poorer class of the Pawnee lived in grass-lodges. The well-to-do people lived in earth-lodges.   Among the Pawnee at this time was an old woman who lived on the outskirts of the village with her grandson.   He sat by the fireplace all day long and so his belly began to turn black from burning.   In those times a poor boy had only half of a buffalo robe with which to cover his body.   When he sat by the fire he placed his belly towards the fire with his robe upon his back.   One day the old woman and the boy went through the village picking up kernels of corn which people had dropped.   They found a little Dog outside of an earth-lodge.   This Dog was brown in color.   The boy picked up the Dog and carried it home.   Whenever the grandmother made mush the boy would divide with the Dog.   The Dog grew up very fast, so that it was now quite large.   At night the Dog would disappear.   When it returned it would bring dried meat mixed with fat.   The old woman did not like the Dog much at first, but when it began to steal meat for them she liked it and made it lie with the boy.

One time when the boy and the Dog went to bed, the boy saw the Dog in his dream.   The Dog told the boy that it was now time for him to go upon the war-path; that he must listen to him; that he would protect him and keep him from being caught.   Several days after this dream the boy decided that he would go.   He told his grandmother to make him a pair of moccasins.   When the moccasins were finished he

[1] Told by Leading-Sun, Kitkehahki.   The moral of the story is the same as that of the preceding tale.

started with his Dog and went south into the country of the enemy. For several days they traveled and finally came to a village. The Dog entered the village and brought out a bay pony. The pony was very thin, and had big lumps on its heels. The Dog told the boy to get on and to return home. The boy got on the pony and returned home. When they reached home with the pony the grandmother was very proud. Soon after this the people went to hunt.

At this time the son of a chief began to take interest in the boy. When the chief's son came to the poor boy's grass-lodge he rode a spotted pony with a fine saddle, and he himself was well dressed. Burnt-Belly did not have any saddle on his old pony and did not have any clothing. Both of the boys were good riders and they would get on their ponies and ride before the people. When they camped the boy would go to the chief's tipi. While they were there, if the Dog came, the chief's son told the people not to scold it.

One time while these boys were together, Burnt-Belly asked the chief's boy to give him four or five spiked arrows and a bow. He said he wanted to go with the people when they should surround the buffalo. The chief's boy got the arrows for Burnt-Belly. When the time came for the people to surround the buffalo, Burnt-Belly was there with the chief's son. The people made fun of Burnt-Belly, but he never said a word. When the people surrounded the buffalo, and word was given for them to run, Burnt-Belly got among the buffalo before anyone else. He shot and killed one. He shot and killed another and then he started back. The chief's son came to him. He had killed nothing. Burnt-Belly gave the chief's son one of his own buffalo. Burnt-Belly took the meat to his grandmother and she was thankful. The chief's boy came to his grass-lodge and there they slept together.

Again the Dog came to the boy in his dream and said, "You must go on the war-path again." This time the chief's boy followed him. They were gone only a few days when they found the camp of an enemy. This time they each took two ponies and went home. After they reached home the boy was told by the Dog that he had enough ponies and that it was now time for him to kill an enemy. The Dog gave red paint to the boy; also owl feathers. The Dog also gave a bone whistle to the boy. The Dog told the boy that the Sun was his father, and that the red paint was to show that the Sun was protecting him; that the Dogs had a father in the heavens who sat near Tirawa; that he was one of the children. The young man got ready to go on the war-path. The chief's son came and said, "We will go together." They went into the country of the enemy and were gone for several days.

When they found the village of the enemy, they went in at night and killed one or two people and took their scalps. They returned home. The people then discovered that it was Burnt-Belly who was taking the son of the chief away on the war-path. On the hunt Burnt-Belly killed many buffalo, so that now his grandmother had a fine tipi. The Dog said to the boy, "Four times you shall come with scalps into the village and then you must get a woman for a wife." The boy went upon the war-path four times, and each time he returned with a scalp. At this time he was recognized throughout the village as a great warrior. He went and asked for a girl and the girl was given to him. He married her. The young man was sorry that he had married, for the chief's son wanted him to stay single so that he could follow him on the war-path.

Some of the young men kept after him and asked him to go on the war-path. At last he consented. When he consented to go on the war-path, the Dog came to him and said: "Go. I shall watch over your wife while you are away." The young man went. The party captured many ponies and killed one or two of the enemy. They returned to their village. On the way the Dog met them, wagging his tail. The man knew that all was right; that his wife had behaved herself well.

Many times the young man went as a leader of the warriors. Once while the young man was on the war-path another young man decided that he would visit the young man's wife. He went into the lodge where the girl was. The Dog was on the bed. When the young man came close to the bed the Dog growled. The woman began to kick the Dog. When the man got into the bed he kicked the Dog out. The Dog went out of the lodge and went to the lodge of the grandmother. When the young man came back with the victorious party the Dog did not come to meet him. The boy was hurt, for he knew that something was wrong. He went to where the Dog was, and the Dog came to him. Then the young man took the Dog out of the lodge, went up on the top of a high hill, and there they sat down. The people in the village saw the young man sitting with the Dog. Man after man went up on top of the hill with a pipe to try to get the man to smoke, so that he would come back into the village.[1] The boy refused to smoke, for the Dog had told him all that had happened. Finally the chief's son came with his pipe. Burnt-Belly said: "My brother, it is too late. I can not go down with you. Had you come before any of these other people, I could have gone down with you. But, my brother, I shall always sit upon the hill with my Dog. When you are upon the war-path, come up, let me know what you want, and it may be that I can help you. See, I am turning into

[1] A common method of healing a breach of this nature.

stone." The boy and the dog turned into stone and there they sat upon the hill. The people believed that their turning into red stone was the origin of red sandstone in the country.

108. THE EAGLE AND THE SUN DANCE.[1]

Many years ago when the people had their village upon the Platte River, there was a young man who thought that he was poor. He began to compare himself with other young men who had ponies, buckskin leggings, beaded moccasins, and ear-bobs in their ears. He had none of these things, and he felt so sorry for himself that he got up and walked away from the village and went up on a high hill and there began to cry. He stood there for several days, and on the third night he thought he heard drumming at a distance, but he was not sure. The fourth night, however, he heard the drumming very plainly, and knew that it came from the river. He started towards the river, but as he approached the drumming ceased, and so he went back upon the hill. He began again to cry and again he heard the drumming coming from the river. The boy went there three times, and each time the sound ceased as he approached, but when he went the fourth time not only did he hear the drumming but also whistling and something flying overhead. He looked up and saw a bald-headed Eagle. The Eagle spoke to the boy and said: "Have you heard the drumming and the whistling?" and the boy said, "Yes." Then the Eagle said: "I have come to take you to the drumming."

The Eagle flew into the timber, returned and flew around the boy, and then went back into the timber. The boy followed him to the timber, and there he found all kinds of birds sitting in a circle, and he saw two big Swans in the center beating their wings and making the drumming sound that he had heard. The Eagle spoke to the boy and said: "Now, look and see how these people are dancing. I give you this dance. You can see that every bird is whistling. It is their noise." Then the Eagle again said: "When you dance you must dance for four days and four nights. For four days you were out and the fourth night you found this dance. Three times you came to the river, and you never found anything, but on the fourth night you found the birds dancing. When you are dancing you must not eat, neither must you drink anything. You must fast when you are dancing, for when you were hunting

[1] Told by Cheyenne-Chief, Skidi. This is to be considered, of course, as only a fragment of the tale of the origin of the Sun dance among the Skidi. The ceremony itself has not been held for over thirty years.

this dance you ate nothing, neither did you drink." Then the big white Swans in the center spoke and said: "My son, we are leaders of this dance. When you go home our spirits will go with you. You shall from this time on dream of this dance and dream of all that you are to do and then you will have the ceremony. You shall always give this dance at the time when the Buffalo bulls get upon high hills and stand there, for it was at that time that you found the birds dancing in the timber." When the Swans had finished, the Owls circled around and began to sing. The man learned the songs which were sung by the Owls, and then he was told to go home and start the dance.

When the young man started the dance he had visions, so that he knew clearly the rites which he was to perform. After the first dance the boy knew the ceremony and gave many Sun dances during the summers.

109. THE SKELETON-MAN AND THE SUN DANCE.[1]

A long time ago a man and his wife went off from the village on a hunt. They came to a thickly timbered country, and there made a little grass-house. Every day the man would go hunting, while the woman would stay in the house. One evening the man came home and brought meat with him. They sat outside of the grass-house and cooked the meat on coals. While they were cooking the meat they heard somebody coming from the timber. The man told the woman to go into their lodge, and the woman went in. After a while the man entered also and they lay down. The man took his bow and arrows and placed them beside him and put his knife under the mat. Soon he heard a noise and so he reached for his bow, and called, "Who are you?" As he spoke, the being, who had entered, turned into a skeleton and dropped to the ground with a rattling of bones. The man told the woman to get up and to put the bones into a robe and to place them somewhere in the lodge, but the woman was frightened and would not do it. Then the man gathered the bones in his arm and placed them in a corner of the lodge. As he lay them down a voice whispered to him and said: "I am Knee-Prints-upon-the-River-Banks." Then the man began to cry.

The next day the man sent his wife home, for she was frightened. When she reached her village she told the people what had happened, and they made fun of her. The people said: "You should have remained with your husband." This mysterious being called to the man as soon

[1] Told by Big-Crow, Skidi. This tale is also a fragment of the Skidi origin of the Sun dance.

as his wife was gone and said: "I come to smoke with you." The man filled his pipe, lighted it, and handed it to the mysterious being and he heard only one whiff, and then the mysterious being whispered and said: "Fill the pipe again; I did not get enough smoke." The man blew his breath into the pipe and there was nothing in it. Then this mysterious being spoke and said: "I control all the animals and the birds. I will now give you a dance which will be known as the Whistle dance. If you will stay here I will teach you just what to do." The man remained with this mysterious being and he learned the ceremony of the Sun dance.

This ceremony was known only to Pipe-Chief, an old Skidi priest, who is now dead.

110. THE WOMAN WHO WAS BEWITCHED BY A FOX.[1]

A long time ago, when the Kitkehahki lived near Nemaha, Nebraska, something wonderful happened. My grandmother did not see it, but her grandmother told her. One day some women went out to gather wood. While they were gathering dry limbs, one of the young girls strayed away. She came to a tree that had been broken by wind. The hollow trunk of the tree lay upon the ground. Some mysterious power prompted her to look into the hollow log and there she saw a child. The child had a very small face and scarcely any hair, and its arms were very thin and its finger nails were long. The child looked at the girl and reached out its long, thin arms to her. The girl was so frightened that she did not know what to do. She stood up and looked to see where the other women were, but she could not see them. She looked into the hollow tree again and there was the child grinning and making motions with its hand as if calling to her. The girl was so frightened that she could not run. Her scalp seemed to draw up in a knot upon the top of her head. Again she looked, and the child was still there. This time the girl noticed that the child had yellow paint all over its face, and black paint close to the hair. The girl ran to where the women were gathering wood. She told them that she wanted them to go and see the child. The women went. They looked into the hollow tree, but no child was there. The girl was disappointed, and she began to scream. The scream was that of a fox and the women saw a fox running from them. Something was exerting a mysterious influence over the girl. She wanted to run to the fox, and she screamed and yelled like a fox.

[1] Told by Good-Food-in-Kettle, Kitkehahki. The moral of this story is similar to that of No. 101, except that in this case women are warned to be careful of the animals they encounter while away from home, especially in the timber.

The women held her. The wood they had gathered they put upon their backs and went home. On the way the girl became very wild.

When they reached home her uncle, a medicine-man, was sent for. As soon as he entered he said that the girl must have seen one of those wonderful little people. "It is human; it has wonderful powers; it is not a fox," said he. The man ordered some live coals to be placed upon the ground where the girl was held down. He untied his medicine bundle and put some herbs upon the live coals. The smoke came up and the women placed the girl over the smoke, so that she could inhale it. The man then prepared some medicine, which was given to the girl. She began to vomit, and she threw up white clay mixed with fox hair. Then the man began to draw upon her body with his mouth. In this way the hair was taken from out her limbs, arms, legs, and body. Smoke was again placed before the girl, and she began to get better. The man then told the people that if there were any more hairs left in her body that they would in time break out. That is what is called undoing the bad medicine from animals. When the woman became of middle age she complained of a pain in her wrists. There was a breaking out, and when the white clay came out she began to get well. She lived to a good old age and had many children.

111. GHOST-MAN WHO BECAME A WHIRLWIND.[1]

A long time ago there was a man who lived in graveyards. He would never stay at home. One time he came into the village, and while walking through the village people saw whirlwinds about him. The whirlwinds came up by him and disappeared. People said that the man must be a ghost. He once heard of a man who was very sick, for a ghost or whirlwind had surrounded him and wanted to take his spirit away. Ghost-Man went and asked that he might attend the sick man, and he was given permission. Ghost-Man sat down by the sick man, picked up dust and threw it up in the air. This formed a whirlwind which enveloped the man and he became well. Ghost-Man went home and claimed no pay.

Other people were affected by the same sickness, and Ghost-Man went and made them well. Once a man was taken sick because he had dreamed of dead people. Ghost-Man went to him and, instead of

[1] Told by Big-Crow, Kitkehahki. Apart from the fact that the story gives expression to a belief in ghosts, it especially teaches that people should be extremely careful when seeking the services of a medicine-man.

throwing dust in the air, he whirled himself around and turned into a whirlwind, which enveloped the sick man and made him well. Instead of turning back into a man, Ghost-Man fell down to the ground a skeleton. The people were scared and ran out of the lodge. The man who recovered stayed in the lodge, gathered up the bones, and buried them.

Ghost-Man made a mistake when he turned himself into a whirlwind. This is why we call whirlwinds "ghosts" or "spirits."

112. THE MAN WHO WENT TO SPIRIT-LAND.[1]

A young man lived in a village where there was a beautiful girl. He loved the girl, but he could not win her, for he was poor and unknown. At last he determined that he would become rich and famous so that he could marry the girl. He went on the war-path with two or three other young men and they captured many ponies, which they drove into the village. When the ponies were divided, the young man selected a little brown pony, which proved to be a good runner. When he rode the pony he was able to surround and kill buffalo. Again he went on the war-path with several other young men. They found an enemy, killed him, and the young man counted coup. They then went back home and women danced in honor of the young man's success. The young man then thought that he might win the girl. He asked for her and her relatives allowed him to marry her. In a few days the young girl became sick and died. She was buried, and the young man stayed around the grave and cried.

One night somebody spoke to him and told him to leave the grave, for his wife was dead and he could not see her. The young man paid no attention to the voice. Every night the mysterious being came to him, and one night he said: "Do you want to see your wife?" The man said: "Yes." The mysterious being told the man that he could take him where his wife was if he would be brave and not get scared at the things that would happen. The young man promised to be brave. The mysterious being said: "I will take you, but you must travel alone. You must travel toward the south. You will not see me, but I will now and then speak to you to let you know that I am with you." The young man started and traveled for many days. Several times he thought

[1] Told by Thief, Kitkehahki. The story is said to be related not only to children but to adults. It illustrates the belief in a future world and explains the origin of the Whistle dance which is still retained by the Pawnee. It especially illustrates the bad effect of the wrongdoing of the young man who, after he had recovered his wife from Spirit-Land, did not take care of her but paid attention to another woman.

that he had been fooled and was about to return, when the mysterious being spoke to him and said: "Keep up your courage; keep right on." The young man went on.

One dark night he thought that the ghosts were upon him and that they were in his way, but he kept on until he saw a bright tipi. When he came close to the tipi, somebody inside spoke and said: "You must not come into this tipi." But the young man went in and found an old woman sitting on the south side of the tipi, and he saw wild sage spread all around. The woman asked the young man what he was there for. He said: "My wife died some time ago; I miss her, and I am hunting for her." The woman said: "The journey is hard, but I will let you go. From here to Spirit-Land all is darkness. You will come to a stream of water that is black, and across this stream of water is a log. If you can cross over this log you can enter Spirit-Land. If you fail to cross it you will die. I will now give you these mud balls that you must carry. When you enter into Spirit-Land the spirits will be dancing, and among them will be your wife. You must sit down and watch the dance, and whenever your wife passes, you must throw one of these mud balls at her. The fourth ball with which you hit her will remind her of her people still living, and they will remind her of you. She will then know you are there and will come to you. When she comes to you, go to the mud balls and pick them up, for by means of them you will return to your own country." The woman told the young man to start, and that on his way back he must visit her, for she was going to give him a certain dance.

When the young man left the tipi he went on until he came to the log across the black stream. When he stepped on the log and found it was unsafe, somebody spoke to him and said: "Keep your courage." He walked until he came to the end of the log, then he jumped off. He went on until he came to the village. There all was light. On the south side of the village men and women were dancing around in a circle. Among the dancers was his wife. When she came around where he was sitting he threw one of the mud balls at her and hit her. She again came around and he hit her again. Again she came around and again he hit her. The fourth time she came around, and he hit her again. She looked at him and came to him and wanted to know what he was doing. She said: "It is sad, but I can not return with you." But the man begged and said: "You must go with me." She told him to wait, for she wanted to go to the village and gather some of her things. She came back and stayed with him for some time. Finally she made up her mind to go with him. They went back and all was light. They crossed upon the log together. They went on until they came to the old woman's tipi. The old woman then gave them something to eat and kept them there for some time. She taught the young man a certain ceremony known as the Elk dance. She gave him a whistle and some red beans and told him that when he returned to his people he must give them the red beans to eat, so that they would receive power to communicate with the dead spirits. She then told the young man to take the four balls with him on the journey home, and whenever they became hungry to throw one of these balls away and it would turn into a buffalo. "Then," she said, "you must cut up the buffalo and jerk the meat and dry it, so that you can carry it with you. When the meat gives out you must throw the next mud ball and it will turn into a buffalo and you must kill it. Cut up the meat and dry it and carry it with you. When you have used all of the meat, throw the third ball, and when you have used the meat from the third ball throw the fourth ball." They started on their journey and did as the old woman told them to do. With them the mysterious being traveled, as he had promised the young man that he would. When they had thrown the last ball and killed the last buffalo, the mysterious being said: "Now I must leave you. I took you to the Spirit-Land, and you have your wife and also the ceremony. I am the Wind. Your village is now but a short distance away." Then the young man and the young woman went on and they finally reached home.

The man and his ghost-wife lived happily for some time, but when the young man started up the Elk dance the women liked it so much that they came to him and wanted him to marry them. The ghost-wife had told the man that she did not want him to have anything to do with other women, and when he disobeyed her she became sick and died again, and this time she died for good. The man cried at her grave as he had done before, and the Wind came to him and told him that there was no use of his crying; that the woman had come back to him and that he had not treated her right. The young man went into the village and taught some friends his ceremony, and after he knew that his ceremony was known, he wandered off and died.

113. THE SPIRIT WIFE AND THE WHISTLE DANCE.

(See Abstracts.)

[Told by White-Horse. This tale is the Pitahauirat variant of No. 112.]

114. HANDSOME-BOY.[1]

Many years ago, while the people had their villages upon the plains, there was born a male child who was called Handsome-Boy. His parents were very careful with him, and kept him hidden most of the time in an enclosed place upon the bed in their earth-lodge. They were very proud of their son and always kept him clean and clothed him in the best clothing that could be found in the village. Once in a while the boy would be allowed to go out and play with the children. After a while he grew up to be a handsome young man. His father was very careful not to talk with him about the war parties that went out, and not to let him attend the dances given to the victorious warriors when they returned with ponies and scalps, for fear that he might want to go on the war-path. He was all the time closely guarded, but whenever he went out he overheard people talking about the war parties.

One night after most of the young men in the village had gone on the war-path he did not sleep, but lay awake thinking of the other young men who had gone on the war-path, and wondering why his parents would not allow him to go. Some time after midnight he heard a woman near his bed. The boy asked the woman what she wanted, and the woman said: "You ought to know why I am here." The boy said: "I know not what you mean." The woman kept on telling him that he knew why she was there. At last the woman spoke plainly and said: "I came to lie with you." The boy said: "No, you must go to your home; I do not care to lie with you." The woman jumped on the young man, and the young man became angry and struck her and kicked her so that she fell from his bed. The woman became mad and said: "Young man, I came to lie with you and you will not lie with me. You are not a great warrior that women should come and try to be with you. You are only a boy whose name is Handsome-Boy. You have won no great name by your deeds. The young men of the village are now making the earth ring with their shouts as they start forth on the war-path, and here you are lying asleep. I do not care if you do not wish me to lie with you. I hope that the women of the tribe will have nothing to do with you whatever, for you do not go on the war-path, neither do you know how to kill the buffalo. You stay inside of the lodge day after day and night after night." The woman went out from the lodge.

The boy lay there and thought: "This woman has told the truth. I may be handsome, but I do not gain anything by lying around here and permitting my parents to pet me. To-night I must be a man and go

[1] Told by Little-Chief, Pitahauirat.

forth through this country to the camps of the enemy and make for myself a name." He got up from his bed, put on his leggings and clothing, took his quiver with bow and arrows, and went out to catch his ponies. One was a bald-faced bay horse; the other was a mouse-colored horse. He got upon the back of one of the horses and led the other one away. He traveled for many days over the plains. At last he stopped to rest and began to make camp, when he found out that he had forgotten to bring anything to make fire with. He killed game, but ate only kidneys and some other things that he could eat raw. He thought that he was going to die of hunger.

One night he lay down and he had a dream, in which he saw a man standing near him, who had on a fine pair of leggings that were fringed with human scalps and trimmed with eagle feathers, and he had the bear claws about his neck. The man spoke to the boy and said: "It is now time that you know who I am. I stand between the people and the spirits. From this time on I will take charge of you and I will make a great man of you. I want you to go towards the southwest until you come to a high hill. I have placed something for you upon that hill."

The next morning the boy mounted one of his ponies, and led the other pony to the high hill. He sat down upon the hill and there he saw human beings coming up from a stream of water. These beings looked like eagles, but they walked around like men. The boy thought to himself: "That man whom I saw in my dream must have meant these people. I will go to them and see what they are." He put his hands upon the ground to support himself in rising. As he did so he touched something, and he picked the thing up and looked at it and he found that it was a flint knife. He took it, for he did not have a knife about him and he knew that it was what the man had promised him in his dream. He put it in his belt, mounted his pony, and went towards the water. Before he arrived at the water he saw a drove of buffalo. The boy killed a buffalo and with his knife skinned it. He made camp and remained at that place for several days while drying meat, so that he would have meat to eat when on his other journeys. While there he again saw the mysterious being in his sleep. The being told him to go to a certain place, and there upon another hill he would see two sticks that he must take and rub together and fire would come from them.

The next day the young man traveled and traveled until towards evening he arrived at the place. As he neared the top of the hill he thought that he saw fire-flies go from one weed to another, but soon he saw that they were sparks of fire. When he came to the place the boy found a weed in the center of a bunch of other weeds. This he took and also another of the same kind.   Then he placed one stick across his flint knife and another one on top of it, and began to rub.   The place was sandy and he picked up sand and threw into the hole where he was rubbing. He continued to rub, and after a while fire sparks began to drop out. A little later he picked up some dried grass and placed it near the place where the sparks were falling.   He kept on working until the grass blazed up.   Then he placed dry limbs upon the burning grass and soon he had a fire.   He went out and killed game and brought the meat to the fire and roasted some of it, and ate it.   He was thankful for the knife and the fire sticks.   He placed the fire sticks in his quiver and went on.   He came to a village of Prairie Dogs, and when he was lying there he dreamed again and saw this mysterious being again, who said: "You must go and kill several buffalo and you must remain here at this place until I tell you when to go away."

The young man awoke.   It was then daylight and he went and mounted one of his horses and rode to where he saw a drove of buffalo. He rode among them and killed one buffalo with his bow and arrows. He took the meat to where he had his things, threw it off from the horse, and began to jerk it.   He gathered a lot of wood and piled it up near the meat.   Then he took his fire sticks again and made fire.   When he had made the fire he roasted the meat and ate it.   After he had eaten he jerked the rest of the meat and placed it out in the sun to dry.   There he remained for a number of days.

One night he lay down and went to sleep, and while he was asleep he heard many people dancing and singing, and he could hear the people shouting and saying: "Handsome-Boy has killed an enemy!   Handsome-Boy has scalped an enemy!"   When he awoke it was dark and silent all around him.   He lay down again and had another dream, and he saw the mysterious being again.   The being said: "My son, to-day you are to find an enemy.   You are to fight with him.   You are to overpower him and kill him.   You must take his scalp, and dry it and keep it, for some time you will want it to hang upon your leggings."   After this the boy woke up and he looked around and it was still in the night.   He lay down again and went to sleep.   He heard singing and dancing, but the singing was close to where he was and the people were shouting: "Handsome-Boy has killed the enemy and has taken the scalp."   They continued to dance and the boy raised up, looked in the direction of the singing, and he saw the people.   Then he arose and walked over to where the people were.   As he came near he saw that they were not people, but Prairie Dogs that scattered and ran into their holes as he approached. The boy then went to his place and took some native tobacco from his quiver. He took it to the Prairie Dogs' holes and placed it there, telling them that he was well pleased with their singing and dancing. He told them that he only wished that it was true that he had killed an enemy. Then he said: "I offer this tobacco to you so that you may help me if I should meet any enemies."

After placing the tobacco in the Prairie Dogs' holes he returned to his place and he went to where his ponies were tied. He mounted one of the ponies and rode it towards the north where he could get up on some high hills to look around and see if there was an enemy. As he climbed a high hill the sun was coming up, so that he could see a long distance. As he looked towards the north he saw a man coming. The man was on horseback and was all alone. He then rode back to where his quiver and blankets were. He took some paint that he had dug from the earth and painted the horse with it; then he put some of the paint upon himself. He took his bow and arrows and rode out to where the man was coming. He met him, and the man shot and showed fight. They rode up to each other and began to shoot arrows at one another. After a while Handsome-Boy shot an arrow into the man's side. He fell from his horse and Handsome-Boy jumped off of his horse, took out his knife, and took the man's scalp. He took the lariat which was tied around the dead man's belt and led the pony to where his stopping-place was. He took a long pole and tied the scalp upon the pole and put the pole in the ground. He sat there all day. In the night he went to bed. Just a little before daylight he heard dancing again. He knew that the dancers were Prairie Dogs and he did not bother them. By daylight the dancing ceased. Then the boy went and placed some more tobacco in the Prairie Dogs' holes. The next night he had a dream. He saw the mysterious being, and it said: "In about three more days you are to see hard times. You are to have a hard time with some enemies who are coming this way. Do not be afraid, for I will be near you and protect you."

Three days afterwards he had another dream. He saw the mysterious being, who told him that he must start out towards the east. He told him that on his way he would meet the enemies, who were coming. The boy went the next day as he was told, leaving two of his ponies behind. He went over several hills, and as he was going over the last hill he saw some men coming towards him on horseback. The leader, being on a fast pony, was coming a long distance ahead of the others. The boy, instead of running, jumped from his pony and took his bow and arrows. As the man approached he saw that he had a spear and intended to spear him. The boy ran towards the man, and as he drew near, the man's horse became scared and threw the man off. The boy ran and shot him three or four times, then took his war bonnet off and tied it upon his saddle. The other men then came up and surrounded him. The boy did not watch his pony, for it followed him wherever he went. He killed several others, and finally the enemies became afraid of him and left him. The boy went to work and took scalps from the other men. These he took to his camping-place.

That night he had another dream and saw the mysterious being again. The being told the boy that he must go north, and there upon the prairie he would see a pile of dirt and there would be a hole there; he must go into the hole; that although it would be a long journey he wanted him to go through this cave; that he would learn something there. When the boy awoke he knew that he had been dreaming.

He took the enemy's horse and turned it loose. His own ponies he took care of, saddled one of them and led the other one. Then he went north over the prairies. When he came to a prairie country he saw at a distance a big mound. He went to the place and he saw that the dirt was fresh just as if it had been dug recently. He saw that there was a hole in the ground. He looked down into it and saw footprints of a little child. He went to the south side of the hole and there he tied the ponies and placed his things in a pile, leaving only the breech-cloth which he wore. Then he went to the hole and entered it. He went far inside, and he saw that the farther he went the larger the hole became. He still saw fresh footprints along the pathway which he saw in this hole. As he walked through this passage-way he made up his mind that he would go to the end to see what was there. He began to run, and he ran and ran, but came no nearer to the end. Sometimes it circled around and then again it was straight. He crossed several streams of water which were running through this passage-way. After a while he heard whistling. When he reached the place from where he heard the whistling he saw a little human being about four feet high. This being was daubed all over with mud, and had an eagle-bone whistle which he whistled. This being spoke to the man and said: "You may pass. I will talk to you when you come by here." Then the boy ran on and on. All at once he saw that it was beginning to grow light at the other end. When he got out at the other end he looked around and he saw his ponies grazing around and his things there. He saw also a village of people and several men came to meet him. These men said: "Why, this young fellow has come, but he is not dead. He has come to us in body." One of them said: "My nephew, you have come and you shall enter our village, for we know that you are wandering over the country and the person who is watching over you brought you here." So they took the young man to the edge of the village and stood him up. Then they brought some coals and placed them on the east side of him, on the south side, on the west, and on the north. Then they placed wild sage upon the hot coals, so that the boy stood in the center where the four smokes went up. After the smoke died out the uncle came and touched him with wild sage. Then he took one stem of wild sage and took the leaves off and rolled it into a ball. He gave it to him and said, "Eat, and swallow the spit, for you must not spit anything out." Then they took the boy into the village and they gave him many things to eat.

After four days the uncle said: "My nephew, it is now time for you to leave us, for you are not dead, but the being who has been watching over you made you come here. Since you have come here you know now that the people who die come to us through this passage. It is very good for a young man to die in battle. Warriors find the road here easy and are gladly received, but the people who die upon their sick bed have a long and hard journey. The people who commit suicide never enter this entrance. If they do enter, the person who watches drives them back. Now you must go. It is not time for you to come to stay." They placed the hot coals again as at first, and placed the wild sage upon the hot coals and the young man stood in the center of the smoke. After the smoke died away they took wild sage and rubbed it upon him and told him to go, and to return to his people, as it was not right for him to wander over the country. They said he was to tell them of the journey he had taken. The boy entered the passage-way and began to run again. When he reached the little being who was in the way, the being spoke to him and said: "You will stop a little while." He saw the little being there as he had seen him before, but when he closed his eyes and opened them again there stood the man concerning whom he had been dreaming. He had on the buffalo robe, and the leggings with the scalps and eagle feathers. Then he knew him. The man said: "Do you remember me?" and the boy said: "I do." Then he said: "I am the one who has been taking care of you, and it is I who brought you here so that you could go to where the dead people are. You have seen them with your own eyes. You have seen some come in covered with blood. They were the people who died on a sick bed. I am the Wind that blows. I shall always be with you, so that in fighting with the enemy you need not be afraid, for they can not kill you. I give you this mud and I give you this downy feather to put upon your head. When you go to battle, if the enemy shoots the downy feather, you will die. I give you also this whistle which I have and you must blow it in the battle. You must go out of this entrance, and as soon as you go out I will guide you to your people;

you must return to your people." The boy left the wonderful being and ran with the things which were given to him. He ran for a long distance until he finally came to the entrance of the cave. He looked for his pony, and he saw it there again; also his other things. Then he put the saddle on his pony and started north.

Night came and the wonderful being came to him in a dream again and told him to continue traveling on to the north. The next day he went on again until night overtook him. He lay down to sleep and the being came to him again in a dream and told him that the next day he must cut little pieces from each scalp; that he must string these pieces of scalp on a string and must wear them on his breast; that he would in time have scalps all over his leggings and all over his breast, and then he would be known as a great man. The next day the boy did as he was told. He had several scalps, and he cut little pieces from each one and put them on a string and wore them upon his breast. He continued his journey, and when he lay down to sleep the being came to him again and said: "My son, your people are near at hand. I forgot to tell you that your father and mother have adopted another boy in your place, and that they think of him and love him just as they did you. They thought that you were dead. When you reach the village of your people and see your parents caressing the other boy, you must not get angry. You have been to the Spirit-Land and you must not show resentment." The boy went on, and the next day, some time in the afternoon, he saw the village. Just outside he met a boy, and the boy asked him who he was, where he was from, and where he belonged. He said: "I belong to your people. I have been away. I am a warrior and I am just returning." The boy then said: "Warrior, let us go into the village and go to my lodge. My father and mother will be glad to have you with us. After you have been with us a few days you may hunt your people and go to them." The young warrior was glad.

They entered the village and went to the boy's house and he was kindly received there. They gave him plenty to eat and a good place to sleep. The people who had seen him enter with his scalps and war bonnet came and asked about the warrior who had arrived in the village, and invited him to the Crazy-Dog dance to dance with them. Handsome-Boy said that he would go with them. While there he saw his father and mother, but he thought: "I will stay here to-night and to-morrow I will go to them. I will give all these scalps to my father." The next morning Handsome-Boy's mother came and invited the young man to bring the stranger to their lodge, for they wanted to see him. Handsome-Boy hastened to go to his father and mother. He did not wait for the other boy, although he was invited to take him. When Handsome-Boy entered the lodge of his father he saw the boy who now took his place lying upon the bed. Handsome-Boy walked towards the bed and started to sit down at the foot of the bed, but his mother and father both called to him to keep away from the bed, and told him to sit down at another place. Handsome-Boy moved away from the bed and seated himself upon the ground. His feelings were hurt, so that he did not let himself be known to his parents.

After the sun was high up, two men went through the village inviting the young men to go to the Young-Dog ceremony. When the two men entered the lodge of the boy, they invited the boy and the stranger to come to their ceremony. The two young men went to the ceremony and there they were told to take seats on the south side. When the ceremony began a young man on the north side was selected to act as a brave for the dance, and Handsome-Boy was selected on the south side.

Just as the people were about to dance, an alarm was given that the enemy was about to attack the village. When they went out to fight the enemy, the dancers scattered out to their tipis and there they took their ponies and their weapons and went out to fight. Handsome-Boy mounted his pony and went out with the others. Just as he entered the battle he met the young man who invited him to stay with him at his home. Handsome-Boy told him to follow him wherever he went and to stop fighting whenever he stopped. Handsome-Boy went into the thickest of the battle with the other boy behind him and made a dash through the line of the enemy. He killed one enemy, and the boy who was following struck the enemy and counted coup. Then they went back to the line. An enemy was killed in front of every battle line, and Handsome-Boy rode up and struck each enemy and counted coup. The other boy, following him, also struck the enemy. Again Handsome-Boy made a dash at the line of the enemy. This time he routed them, selected his man, killed him, jumped off his horse and took his scalp while the boy counted coup on the enemy. Handsome-Boy then stopped, but the people saw him and recognized him. The enemy was routed and overpowered, and Handsome-Boy and his companion had killed many and taken many scalps.

That evening when the fight was over, Handsome-Boy went to his new home, where he was received with great honors by the people who lived in the lodge. The old people rejoiced that the young man came to their lodge, for it was by his help that their son had counted coup. In the evening the women came and asked for the scalps. Handsome-Boy told a woman to untie a certain bundle. Upon untying the bundle the woman took therefrom several old scalps.   She gave these scalps to the women, together with the fresh ones.   The women then went to one of the lodges and there they started a dance known as the women's Scalp dance.   The women started out from their lodge and went straight to the young man's lodge, and there they danced and shouted, saying: "The young man killed the enemy, took scalps, and counted coup."   The shouting was the same as he had heard when he was out upon the plains near the Prairie Dog town.   The young man gave most of his presents away to the women who were dancing.   The women danced nearly all night, going from one place to another.

The next morning when the sun was high the two men from the Crazy-Dog ceremony came again and invited the young men of the lodge to go to the ceremony.   The two young men went, and when they were seated Handsome-Boy was again selected on the south side, to act as a brave and to ride his pony around the dancers.   He arose and left the tipi of the dancers and went to his lodge.   He caught his pony and painted it with red paint and then he painted himself.   He put the string of scalps about his neck and put the war bonnet that he had taken from the enemy on the prairie upon his head.   Then he went to where the people were having the dance.   When he arrived he noticed a gray pony tied in front of the tipi where they were to have the dance.   The horse was tied to a spear stuck in the ground.   This was to show to the people that the person who stuck the spear into the ground would give the pony to any warrior who would kill with the spear several enemies in the next battle.   If a man among the dancers was willing to undertake to kill the enemies and thus avenge those who had been killed in battle, he was to dance up to the spear and take it up from the ground.   The dancers came out into the open air and went through the village dancing from one tipi to another.

While they were dancing, the other brave who was selected with Handsome-Boy to be a leader rode among the dancers and told all of his deeds.   He told of his killing one of two enemies and scalping him. When the young brave told his story there was great shouting.   Handsome-Boy rode among the dancers and began to tell his story.   He told that when the young warriors went over the prairie upon the war-path he was left lying upon his bed, and in the middle of the night a woman had come to his bedside; that he had driven the woman away and then she had called him names and made fun of him because he was not a brave warrior, and so he decided at once to start upon the war-path. He said: "I arose from my bed and made up my mind that I would go upon the war-path, and I went at once.   I was upon the prairie for many years, and one day I met an enemy.   I fought the enemy, killed him, and scalped him. His scalp is upon my breast at this time. Another time about forty or fifty warriors attacked me. I killed their chief, took his war bonnet, and also scalped him. The scalp is upon my breast. I have returned to my own people and now I am here with you. You saw me fighting the other day and so I will not speak of that myself. I am the young man whom you called Handsome-Boy." The old men shouted and sang for joy. The old women cried, sang, and danced for joy. The father and mother came. They tried to take him to their lodge, but he motioned them away and said: "Father and mother, you have one in my place. You pushed me away from his bed. Keep him. He is as good as I am. I have a new father and mother and a brother. I will make my home with them."

After the dance was over Handsome-Boy and his brother went to the lodge of his father and said: "Father, I have come for my ponies." The father said that it was well, and so the two boys went for the ponies. When they brought up the drove of ponies, the boy divided the ponies into two bunches. One bunch he left for his father and mother, and the others he took for his new father and mother.

In a few days it was noised about that the enemy was seen in the country and the people began to watch. When they came and attacked the village Handsome-Boy went to the lodge where the spear was stuck in the ground. He took it up and rushed into battle and killed four with the spear. Each time he took the scalp and hung it upon his belt, so that when he went to the lodge of the mourners he took four scalps from his belt and gave them and the spear to the people who were mourning. He then went to his lodge, and the people brought the pony which was tied in front of the ceremonial lodge, and it was given to him. Handsome-Boy gave the pony to his new father. The father then said: "My son, it is now time that you take a woman for your wife." A young girl was selected for him; he married her and they lived many years. They had one child. The child was a boy. The woman was very mean, but the father put up with all her bad doings.

At one time the people went on a hunt. The young man was selected to lead the people on the hunt. The mysterious being appeared to him in a dream and told him where the buffalo were and how to find them. The next day he sent out scouts to look for buffalo, and they found a large herd. The people began to realize that the young man was a wonderful man. His wife was always away from their home, and whenever she came home she told her husband that a certain young man had tried to approach her. Every few days she kept telling him this, and then she would say: "What would you do if you were to find me with some man?"

Handsome-Boy would say: "I could not do anything, for it is not in me to strike anybody." This was because the spirits had told him while he was there that he should never strike anybody.

One day his wife was telling him how a certain young man had followed her around, but Handsome-Boy did not take it up nor try to hurt the young man. His wife became angry and began to call him names, and even tried to strike him. Handsome-Boy went off from the village and lay down with his face upon the ground and wept. For some time he lay upon the ground. After a while some one came and stood near him. Handsome-Boy said: "Sit down, whoever you are." A beautiful girl sat down by him and said: "Handsome-Boy, I have come to you. I have come to be with you and to take you to my lodge to be my husband." Handsome-Boy told the girl that what she said was good and that he would take her for his wife. They waited until after dark; then they went into the village. The girl took Handsome-Boy to her tipi that had been put up outside for her. She told him to lie upon the buffalo robes which were spread upon the ground while she went to tell her mother to cook some dried buffalo meat for him. As soon as the girl told her mother that Handsome-Boy was in the tipi, she began to cook something for him and the old man jumped up with his tobacco and pipe and went into the tipi where Handsome-Boy was. The old man was glad to have Handsome-Boy for his son-in-law. He told him that he was glad that his daughter had selected him for her husband. He filled the pipe and they began to smoke together. After a while the woman brought in buffalo meat and placed it before Handsome-Boy. He ate of the meat and passed the wooden bowl to the old woman. The old people knew that Handsome-Boy and their daughter wanted to be alone and so they left and went into their own tipi. Handsome-Boy and the girl remained in the tipi for four days and four nights.

On the fourth day the child of Handsome-Boy began to cry for his father. The people did not know where Handsome-Boy had gone. They hunted for him throughout the village, but they could not find him. Towards evening the boy cried for his father and pointed in a certain direction. The mother, seeing the child pointing, went in that same direction until she came close to a tipi. The child pointed to the tipi, and the mother peeped into the tipi and she saw her husband there with another woman. She took the child home, gave it to his grandmother, and said: "Take this child to a certain tipi. His father is sitting there and you may let him take the child." The old woman took the child to the tipi where his father was. She entered the tipi and put the child into the lap of the father. The father was glad to hold the child.

The child stopped crying. The young woman took the child and put it upon her back and carried it around; then she gave him back to his father. The child's mother came and went up to her husband and struck him several times and called him names, but he did not do anything or say a word. Then she said: "I will now kill you and our child." She took out a knife, and just as she was about to stick the knife into the child Handsome-Boy's new wife struck the woman back of the head with a club and threw her to the ground. Some men ran into the tipi as the woman fell to the ground. One of the men hit the woman with a club on the head and killed her. Handsome-Boy did not say a word; but the people had heard of the meanness of the woman and knew that she was a bad wife and mother. They said that they were glad that she was dead because she tried to kill her own child. Nothing was done to the woman who struck her, and Handsome-Boy married her.

For several days Handsome-Boy sat in the tipi with the child in his lap. The chiefs of the tribe came into the tipi and sat with him to watch and guard over him, for they knew that his spirit was hurt. The chiefs would talk to him and say: "You are the ruler of these people. Cheer up and do not feel downhearted." Handsome-Boy at last spoke and said: "Chiefs, it is well that you are the chiefs. It is wrong that I should be a chief. I have taken many scalps and killed many people. You have given me the whole tribe to govern, but I can not do it, for when I try to tell the people what to do they will say that a woman hit me on the side of the face and will laugh at me and not obey my commands. I will not be a chief." He went to the home of his brother. He told the father to make a certain kind of leggings. The leggings were to be made of buckskin with the scalps hanging down on them, and an eagle feather every inch between the human hairs. He also had the ring of scalps completed. Each scalp counted the dead that he had killed. Handsome-Boy went into his tipi with his new wife. He arose and went out, having the leggings on, and he was never heard of again.

If he died or was killed no one knows, but the night before he went he sat down and called the people together and told them that he had been to the Spirit-Land; that he had seen many of their relatives, and he told them how they must live and how good it was to die in battle. He told the people what the spirits had told him to tell them. Then he said to the people: "This is why I can not strike our people, even if it be my own wife. When it comes to an enemy, then I can strike and kill." The next day after this happened he went out and disappeared and never came back. This is why the Pawnee, in their secret ceremonies, wear leggings with scalps and eagle feathers for decoration.

115. THE WEEPING CEDAR TREE.[1]

In olden times a war party went out to the west to find the enemy. For many moons they traveled. At last they came to a rough country. There they made a camp. In the night these warriors heard a woman crying. Three warriors were selected to find the woman. They went in the direction of the crying, which became fainter as they drew near to it. They went away, and again the crying was heard. They followed the sound again and all came to a cedar tree. It was the cedar tree that was crying like a woman. When they found it was the cedar tree that was crying, one of the men said: "Warriors, let us go home." They would not listen to the man, but continued their march. The man would not go with them, but lingered behind, for he was afraid to go on the war-path after he had heard the cedar tree weeping, for he thought it was a bad omen. The next day they were attacked by the enemy. The lone man looked on from a distance. All were killed, so the lone man went home and told the story.

116. BIG TURTLE.[2]

In olden times a warrior borrowed the warriors' bundle, for he was going to leave his country to capture ponies or to kill people. He took the bundle to his lodge and invited other young men to join him. The young men came into the lodge where the leader was sitting with the bundle in front of him. As the young men came into the lodge they were told to sit around the fireplace in a circle. A pipe was filled and lighted, and the men smoked to the gods in the heavens to insure their success. When the pipe was empty the leader spoke to the young men and said: "I am about to go into the enemy's country. If any of you want to go you had better get ready, for I am going to start in the morning." The young men all went out and returned in a short time with their bundles of clothing and food and their moccasins. They left the lodge in the morning and started out for the enemy's country. For many days they walked.

One day as they were walking along a deep ravine the warriors saw a big Turtle moving along. Two mischievous young men climbed upon the Turtle's back and said: "Let us ride the Turtle." They jumped up and down, but all at once they found themselves stuck fast upon the

[1] Told by Big-Crow, Kitkehahki. This is presumably a fragment of a longer tale which relates the origin of some medicine-lodge.

[2] Told by Curly-Hair, Kitkehahki. The story is told to the children so that they may not make fun of any animals on the earth.

Turtle's back. The young men were scared and called out to their leader. They said: "Something wonderful has happened to us; we are fast." The leader said: "I can not go on without you, so I will get on also." The leader stepped upon the Turtle's back and he also became fast. The other men climbed on, and they, too, became fast. The leader told the youngest of the warriors to stay upon the ground; to go home and tell the people what had happened. The young man followed them until at last the Turtle came to a big water and disappeared under it with all the warriors. The boy saw the Turtle go into the water, and as the men were disappearing under the water the leader of the warriors spoke to the boy and told him not to cry, but to go home and tell his people that a big Turtle took them into the water; that whenever he should want to go upon the war-path he should come to the place, and that they would talk to him and tell him where to go to capture ponies.

The boy remained for several days around the water. One night he had a dream. He thought he was under the water and there he saw the other men in a lodge under the water. The leader of the warriors spoke to him and said: "You must go home and tell the people that we are under the water, but that we are living." The next day the young man went home. He told the people about the Turtle taking the people into the water. Some people believed it and some did not.

Some time afterward the young man went to the place and there he remained for a while. He was finally taken into the water and there he saw different kinds of animals, and the Turtle was the leader of the other animals. The boy was taught many mysteries, and he was then told to go home. When the people saw the boy doing many wonderful things they did not like it. All the people gathered together and said: "Let us go to the water where the Turtle took the people." The people moved to the place, and when they reached the water they made their village near it. They took their skin buckets and began to dip the water and throw it to one side. For many days the people dipped the water. At last they got to the bottom of the water, and there they found the skeletons of the men who were taken into the water by the Turtle. They could not find the Turtle, and so they gave it up. After this was all done, the animals did not like the way the people did and they took the power away from the boy.

IV. COYOTE TALES.

The tales of this division may be related at any time and upon any occasion except during the summer, at which time it is said that the star known as Fool's-Coyote would inform the Snake-Star, who in turn would inform the snakes, who would bite the teller. These stories are not true. Some of them, as may be noticed, are unquestionably episodes of longer tales. They teach especially the ethics of tribal customs and beliefs; in a word, they form a code of living. They are generally told at night in the winter, the special object, other than that noted, being to furnish amusement and to pass away the time. Many of the stories are accompanied by songs, during the singing of which the children dance to the time of the singing. Thus the tales are supposed to free the children of bashfulness and shyness.

Many of the tales have certain elements of the culture hero, or at least in many of them there is some element which may serve to encourage the poor boys and girls and to arouse in them ambition.

The tales might be considered as forming two groups, Nos. 117 to 142 forming the first group and referring to Coyote. The second group, Nos. 143 to 148, consists of animal tales proper, but differ from the tales of the first group only in the fact that some animal, or other animals than coyotes, enters into the composition of the story. Notwithstanding the fact that the coyote individually plays no part in this second group, they also are known as "Coyote tales."

----

117. COYOTE AND THE SCALPED-WOMAN.[1]

Coyote was traveling over the hills one day when he saw a Scalped-Woman sitting on a hillside. He saw that matter was running from her head. He commenced to make fun of her and said: "It looks as though mush were running over the top of the pot." The woman said: "You

----

[1] Told by Thief, Kitkehahki. The story is told to teach the children about a certain class of people who lived on the earth and were human beings, but as they were scalped they did not live with the people. They had animal power and could teach many mysteries to the people.

are making remarks about my head." At the same time Coyote was wondering how he could manage to have connection with this Scalped-Woman.

He said: "I am talking about a pot. When my grandmother puts meal into the boiling pot the mush overflows." After a time Coyote yelled and said: "I did mean you." Scalped-Woman jumped up and said: "I will kill you." She ran after him. Coyote went over the hill and changed himself into a queer-looking man. He had on his chin a little buffalo grass, so that his chin looked as if he had whiskers like an old man. Near him was a patch of tobacco. The woman came up and saw him standing there, and said: "You tobacco grower, did you see Coyote pass by here?" Coyote pretended that he was a man and mumbled to himself. The woman said: "That man can not understand. I guess Coyote went on by." She went on over the hill.

Coyote-man turned into Coyote and called after her: "I did mean you." Scalped-Woman started after Coyote again, and almost caught him. Coyote ran over the hill again and stood there, a warrior, with great powers. He had jointed grass that looked like feathers stuck up around his head. He sang a song about the grass warrior:

> This grass I walk around
> When I walk around,
> Grass I have as I start out as a warrior.
> This grass I walk around
> When I walk around,
> Grass I have as I start out as a warrior.

Scalped-Woman said: "Warrior, did you see a man pass by here?" Coyote kept on singing as if he did not know her, but she continued to question him. Finally Coyote said, impatiently: "Why do you talk to me? I will shoot you with these arrows. Do not talk to me any more." The woman went on. After she had gone over the hill, the warrior turned into Coyote again and said: "I did mean you." Scalped-Woman started again and was about to catch him. Coyote crawled into a hole in a rocky place and came out on the other side. Scalped-Woman crawled in after him and became fast. Coyote raised her dress and they had connection. Then the woman began to kick. She said: "Let me get out, so that we can do it right." Coyote kept on and Scalped-Woman got loose. She went up to Coyote and hit him with her hand and said: "You are a rascal. You are now my husband." They went off and lived a while together; then Coyote pretended that he was going on a hunt. He went off and never came back.

118. HOW A WITCH-WOMAN WAS KILLED BY COYOTE.[1]

There was an island. Upon this island lived a Spider-Woman. She killed many people. Coyote happened to come that way, not thinking of the Spider-Woman. He was going through a timber, and just as he came to the edge of the timber he saw Spider-Woman coming at a distance. The place where he was was thick with timber, there being many young willow trees. Coyote sat down and wondered what he should do to gain the friendship of Spider-Woman. Coyote took hold of his membrum and began to play with it. Soon it became hard and he stuck it out from the timber. He kept moving it backwards and forwards and Spider-Woman saw it. She stopped, gave a yell, and laughed. Then she began to sing:

> Yonder I see it with my eyes,
> Yonder I see it with my eyes,
> You, yonder, moving back and forth from the bushes,
> Ugly red thing, O!

She continued to sing, and after a while she began to dance. Then Coyote moved faster and the old woman began to sing and dance faster. Spider-Woman thought it so funny that she continued to dance until she finally gave out, dropped down upon the ground, and died. Then Coyote went on about his business.

119. COYOTE MARRIES HIS DAUGHTER.[2]

In a village there lived a Coyote, his wife, one daughter, and several sons. They went off on a hunt, and while they were away the old man became sick. He told his wife that he was going to die. One day he became worse. Then he sang:

> Well, now, there she comes, yonder;
> Old woman will have a happy time.
> She who was my wife,
> As they make a gurgling noise.

After he sang, the old woman sang a song and said:

> Old man's membrum, crooked
> Like the handle of a dipper.
> Yes, I shall miss it.

---

[1] Told by Bright-Eyes, Skidi. The story is told to teach the young girls not to be like the spider-woman who danced when the Coyote acted as he did; that only half-crazy women could do as the spider-woman did. A woman who becomes morally bad can do anything. The people tell this story to keep their girls from doing wrong.

[2] Told by Thief, Kitkehahki. This story is told to teach the young men that when they marry, and have children, they should never think of marrying their own daughter, for it is very wrong.

Then the old man said: "My wife, when I am dead dig a hole and place my body in the hole, but leave my head sticking out, for you know that I was very religious and always looked to Tirawa for assistance. When you see a man making arrows, when the other people have left their village, then you may know that he is a chief. If he should ask for my daughter let him have her. When they have killed buffalo and you see a man coming with only the tongues and the hearts, then you may know that he is the chief, and if he asks for our daughter let him have her." Coyote died and was buried just as he wanted to be. His wife and children gathered up their belongings and went and joined the other people.

In the meantime Coyote crawled out of the grave and said: "Now my wife thinks I am dead. I must fix myself up so that I can deceive my wife and marry my daughter." He ran into the village and he stayed close to the grass-lodge where his family lived. The next morning when the people broke camp he sat down in the midst of the village site and there began to make arrows. When the old woman and her children started out they went past Coyote who was making arrows, and the girl said: "Mother, that looks like our father." The old woman said: "Come daughter, this is the chief and we must not trouble him." After the woman and the children were gone Coyote got up and followed them. When they reached the village the girl saw Coyote going through the village. The girl was sure that it was her father, and when he entered a lodge close to their own she went up to the lodge and peeped in. She saw a man sitting inside who looked like her father, the only difference being that this man had but one eye.

While they were here in this village the people went out, surrounded the buffalo, and killed several. The old man went to the killing and begged several people for tongues and hearts. Then he came to the village and went past the lodge of his own family. When he heard his children talking about the man with the hearts and tongues upon his back he stopped. When he turned around he looked at the children, but he had only one eye, for he had closed the other one to make the children believe that he had but one eye. He said: "Children, take these to your mother and tell her that the chief wants her to eat them." The children took the hearts and tongues to their mother. The mother made a big fire and was cooking the hearts and tongues when Coyote came into the lodge. He had but one eye. He said: "Woman, being the chief of this village, I have looked through the place for a girl to marry me. I like your girl the best. I have come to ask for her." The old woman said: "You shall have my daughter, for her father wished that she should marry a chief." When the old woman placed some heart and tongue before the old man and the girl, the old man forgot himself, for he was happy thinking that he was now married to his own daughter. The little boys who were playing whispered to their mother and said: "Mother, that looks like our father. Both of his eyes are open now." When the old woman looked at Coyote she saw that he was her husband. She picked up a club, went up to Coyote, and said: "Old man, I am glad that I found you out before it was too late." He begged and begged, but the old woman brought down the club upon his head and smashed his skull. The boys jumped on their father, kicked him around, and dragged him out. The next day when the people began to break camp, the women and children joined them and left Coyote upon the ground. They did not bury him.

When the people see a dead coyote lying upon a village site they say: "This coyote must have tried to marry his own daughter and was killed."

120. COYOTE AND HIS TWO WIVES MEET WONDERFUL-BEING.[1]

One fine, bright morning Coyote arose and awakened his two wives. When they had eaten their breakfast, Coyote said: "We will now go into the land where the sun travels (meaning the south); there we may find some other people, and we will live with them. We are all alone in this country, and I am afraid that the giants may find us."

They started out and traveled into the southern country. When they had been traveling for several days they came to a brook of clear water. There they stopped to rest. There was a high hill on the south side of the brook. While they were resting, one of the women looked up on the high hill and there she saw Wonderful-Being. She pushed the other woman and awoke her. Then she awoke her husband. They all stood up. Both of the women said: "He will kill us; let us run away." But Coyote said: "Let us not run away, but do as I tell you. Put your robes close to your bodies and then the strings around them. Then pick up those pebbles along the brook and throw them into your robes, so that when you jump up and down the stones will rattle and make a peculiar noise." The women did as they were told.

Wonderful-Being came close to them and said: "What are you people doing and where are you going?" Coyote had told the women that

[1] Told by Buffalo-Come-to-Drink, one of the oldest of the Kitkehahki and a medicine-man. This story is told to the people so that they shall have fear of the giants, and to let the children know that in olden times the giants were upon the earth and were destroyed by the Evening-Star.

as soon as he began to dance, for them to dance. He thought that Wonderful-Being was going to crush them and throw their flesh away and keep their skins for his own use.

Coyote paid no attention to the Wonderful-Being, and Wonderful-Being again spoke to him and said: "Do you not hear what I say?" Coyote paid no attention to Wonderful-Being, but all at once began to jump up and down, and then he sang as follows:

> Here we stand, old woman,
> Truly that looks like the man,
> The wonderful man we killed,
> Whose membrum you struck and counted coup,
> Whose membrum you struck and counted coup.
>
> Here we stand, old woman,
> Truly that looks like the man,
> The wonderful man we killed,
> Whose membrum you struck and counted coup,
> Whose membrum you struck and counted coup.

He kept singing and repeating the same words over and over again, and as the three kept jumping up and down the stones in their robes began to rattle. When the Coyote stopped singing, then the two women began to sing, and said: "Old man, does not this Wonderful-Being look like the man we killed yonder? Must we kill him, so that you, old man, may count coup on Wonderful-Being? Shall we kill him? Shall we kill him?"

When Wonderful-Being heard the rattling of the pebbles, he did not know what to make of it. Then from what he heard of the singing he thought that he was going to be killed. Wonderful-Being began to move backwards and they kept up the singing and dancing. After Wonderful-Being went over the hill he turned and ran. Coyote went up on the hill and saw Wonderful-Being running away. Then he called his wives and they ran from the place. When they tried to rest, Coyote would speak to them of Wonderful-Being, and again they would jump up and run. Coyote would tell them how easily Wonderful-Being could have killed them if he had just tried. They kept on running until at last the older woman of the two fell over and died. The other one went on with Coyote and they came to a rocky place and there they made their home.

This is why we find coyotes in rocky places and also why we find dead coyotes upon the prairies. Whenever a coyote gets scared it runs and never knows when to stop until it falls down and dies.

COYOTE TALES.

121. COYOTE TRIES TO FOOL THE RAIN-GODS.[1]

Coyote traveled over the prairie for many days. He could not find any water and so he almost died from thirst. When he could go no farther he sat down upon the ground and looked to the heavens and said: "To you four gods in the west I give my tongue and my heart and the best parts of my body if you will send me a little rain." At once clouds formed in the west and a rainstorm came. The rain began to fall and pools of water soon formed over the prairie. Coyote then drank and felt refreshed. It still continued to rain. Then Coyote said: "You gods in the heavens, I did not ask you for so much rain. What shall I do if I give to you my heart and tongue and other parts of my body? I can not get more and I need these things in my body. I will not give them to you. I take back all that I promised you." New clouds came from the west and it began to lighten and thunder and the rain poured from the sky. Coyote tried to run, but the water was so deep that he had to swim. Then suddenly a hailstorm came and hailstones struck Coyote upon the head and killed him.

When people go over the prairie and see a dead coyote upon the ground they say: "This coyote fooled the gods and the gods killed him."

122. COYOTE AND THE PRIESTS.[2]

The people went hunting; among them were Coyote-Man, Fox-Man, and Rabbit-Man. There was also among these people a woman who was called Spider-Woman. On the journey these four were always in the lead, and if they saw any buffalo they reported the fact to the priests. One time these men and this woman were sent out. They saw many buffalo. They returned to the priests' lodge and reported many buffalo. The next day the people turned out and surrounded the buffalo.

When the people had many buffalo and were returning home, Coyote-Man took the meat he had to the priests' lodge. Fox-Man, seeing that Coyote-Man went there, also took his meat to the lodge of the priests. Rabbit-Man also took his meat there, because the other two had done so. Spider-Woman, seeing the men take their meat there, also took her meat to the lodge of the priests. The priests took up their rattles and sang songs about these people bringing the meat to their lodge:

[1] Told by Leading-Sun, Kitkehahki medicine-man. This story is told to teach the children that although they may be in dire distress they must never offer themselves up to the gods.

[2] Told by Thief, Kitkehahki. This story is told to teach the children that when they grow up they should always remember the priests and their bundles; that when they kill a buffalo they should take it to the lodge of the priests so that the meat might be offered to the gods in the heavens.

Alone she came with her pack strings,
Alone she came with her pack strings,
The daughter of Claw-Shield,
This has the young woman done:
Alone she thought of
The wonderful old men.

Alone she came with her pack strings,
Alone she came with her pack strings,
The daughter of Brave-Fox,
This has the young woman done;
Alone she thought of
The wonderful old men.

Alone she came with her pack strings,
Alone she came with her pack strings,
The daughter of Jack-Rabbit,
This has the young woman done;
Alone she thought of
The wonderful old men.

Then the errand man went through the village asking women to bring their pack string to the priests' lodge and to go after wood for the priests. Coyote's daughter came with her pack, Fox's daughter came with hers, Rabbit's daughter came with hers, and Spider-Woman's daughter came with hers.

123. COYOTE WHO CALLED HIMSELF "DRAGGING-THE-STONE."[1]

There was a village of Coyotes. The people in the village heard that there was another village of Coyotes east of them. One Coyote decided that he would go and visit the other village. He started, and after a while he came to the village. He looked around and he saw the Coyote-men playing with gambling sticks. He thought to himself: "Now, if I go into the village these people will kill me. I must plan some way to make these people afraid of me." He reached the edge of the village and he shouted: "People, I come to visit your village. My name is Dragging-the-Stone." The people were all frightened. Some said: "What kind of a man is this who has such a big name as Dragging-the-Stone!" They all looked at him and were afraid of him. Coyote was dressed like a warrior, and he had a quiver filled with arrows and a bow. He then walked through the village in an unconcerned way and went to where

[1] Told by White-Horse, Pitahauirat. The story is told to teach the young men that when they go on the war-path, if they should happen to meet enemies, not to be scared but to be brave; that no matter how much frightened they are they must not show it to the enemy.

the men were playing with the gambling sticks. There he sat down by himself and watched the game.

After a while a young man came to where he was sitting and said: "Dragging-the-Stone, the chief of these people invites you to eat dinner with him." Dragging-the-Stone looked up at him and said: "Has not the chief a mouth to eat the things he has to eat? Tell him that Dragging-the-Stone says that he does not care to sit with him to eat." When the young man returned and told the people what Dragging-the-Stone had said, they said: "This must be a wonderful man." In a little while another man came and said: "Dragging-the-Stone, the giant, the wonderful being, invites you to come and eat dinner with him." Dragging-the-Stone then said: "Has not the wonderful being, the giant, a mouth? He shall eat alone of the food that he has prepared for me to eat. Tell him I do not care to go and eat with him." When the man reported to the giant, the wonderful being, what Dragging-the-Stone had said, the giant said: "He must be a wonderful man. He must be either equal to me or more wonderful than I in power." After a while another man came and said: "Dragging-the-Stone, the bravest man in the village here invites you to eat with him." Dragging-the-Stone looked at the man and said: "The brave man has a mouth. Let him eat what he has. I do not care to eat with him." When the brave man heard what Dragging-the-Stone said, he was afraid, and he told the people that this man must be a wonderful man.

Towards evening, after all had stopped playing with the sticks, Dragging-the-Stone got up and went to the poorest lodge that he could find in the village where lived an old Coyote and his wife, and he made his home with these people. Everyone in the village was afraid of Dragging-the-Stone, and none went near him. The old Coyote told Dragging-the-Stone that there was a wonderful being in their village; that when people killed buffalo this wonderful being went to the fattest buffalo and told the people that he was going to have the buffalo, and they had to let him have it, for he was bad and either killed them or blew them away. Dragging-the-Stone said: "I wish to meet this wonderful being, for I do not like him to be robbing the people of their meat."

One fine, bright morning an old man began to cry through the village asking certain men to go out into the country to find buffalo. He sang as follows:

> Hurry, bring your bow and arrows.
> You, Coyote, of the Claw-Shield,
> You are to look for buffalo,
> You are to look for buffalo.

> Hurry, bring your bow and arrows.
> You, Brave-Fox, who angry go through ravines,
> You are to look for buffalo,
> You are to look for buffalo.
>
> Hurry, bring your bow and arrows.
> You, Jack-Rabbit, who hold high your bow and arrows,
> You are to look for buffalo,
> You are to look for buffalo.
>
> Hurry, bring your bow and arrows.
> You, Raven, who shout at the people,
> You are to look for buffalo,
> You are to look for buffalo.
>
> Hurry, bring your bow and arrows.
> You, Old-Woman, always contrary,
> You are to look for buffalo,
> You are to look for buffalo.
>
> As for myself, I never lag behind,
> I never lag behind,
> I never lag behind,
> I never lag behind.

The first one called was a young Coyote; he came with his bow and arrows. The next one was Brave-Fox; he came with his bow and arrows. Then Jack-Rabbit and Raven were called; they came with their bows and arrows. And lastly old Coyote and Old-Woman-Coyote were called. The old woman said: "Dragging-the-Stone, do you hear them calling my old husband and me to look for buffalo?" He said: "Yes." The old man and the old woman took their horses and joined the party which was going to hunt for buffalo. They went off, and in a little time the people saw these people coming back. They went into the lodge of the chief and said: "People, on the other side of the hills are many buffalo. We must at once prepare to surround the buffalo." Everybody began to get their horses to go out to surround the buffalo. The old woman said: "Dragging-the-Stone, would you like to go?" and he said: "Yes." The old woman said: "I have a horse that you may ride if you wish." Dragging-the-Stone took out some red paint and painted the horse, put some eagle feathers on its tail, painted himself, and jumped upon the horse and rode among the people.

When the people saw Dragging-the-Stone coming among them to be one of the men to surround the buffalo, they pointed at him and spoke about him and said: "Here is Dragging-the-Stone. We will now find out how wonderful he is." The people were becoming excited and their horses were jumping up and down getting ready to run. Dragging-the-Stone was riding the old woman's horse, and it was jumping up and

down and was very unmanageable. After a while Dragging-the-Stone
felt something coming up from the back of the horse. He kept on
riding until the object went into his body; then he jumped off and examined it and found that it was the horse's penis. Dragging-the-Stone
then took his bow and arrows and shot the horse and killed it. The
horse was the property of the old woman, and when the old woman
wanted to be with men, she rode upon this horse. Dragging-the-Stone
went on, and he came to a man who had killed a buffalo. The man who
killed the buffalo came up and said: "Dragging-the-Stone, I will give you
this buffalo." Dragging-the-Stone thanked the man for the buffalo.

After a while other people came, and they began to skin this buffalo.
While they were skinning they saw the giant coming. When he came
he said: "People, you may go away from this buffalo. This is my
buffalo and I am going to have the meat." The people then looked
towards Dragging-the-Stone to see what he would do. Dragging-the-
Stone told the people to continue skinning the buffalo and not to listen
to the giant. After a while the giant said: "I am going to have
the meat of this buffalo." Dragging-the-Stone said: "You are not.
This buffalo is mine." They began to quarrel and the giant became
mad. Dragging-the-Stone became mad and took his bow out from
his quiver and began to hit the giant. The giant then turned around
and blew his breath upon Dragging-the-Stone and blew him a long
way off. Coyote came and continued to fight the giant until the
giant became scared and went away. Then Dragging-the-Stone felt
very proud that he had conquered the giant. The people talked about
him as they went home. Not only the giant became scared, but the
chief and the braves were all also scared. When Dragging-the-Stone
reached the village the old Coyote woman said: "Old man, that man
Dragging-the-Stone has sense. He walks home and leaves my horse
at some grassy place where he can pick grass." When Dragging-the-
Stone arrived at the lodge the old woman asked where the horse was,
and he said: "I killed him. He tried to act with me as he did with you
and I shot him with my bow and arrows."

The people all became afraid of Dragging-the-Stone. The chief
gathered all his men. They were going to have a big feast and eat
roast ribs. They invited Dragging-the-Stone. The people said: "We
want Dragging-the-Stone to be our chief." When the people were all
together, Dragging-the-Stone came in and they gave him a prominent
seat. Then the chief spoke and said: "Dragging-the-Stone, I have prepared a lot of meat, for we are to have a feast." Then Dragging-the-
Stone said: "I do not eat ribs. I eat something else. If the chief

wants me to eat he must get what I like." The people were told to find out what Dragging-the-Stone ate. Dragging-the-Stone told them that it was a little piece of dried buffalo meat and a piece of buffalo tallow. He told them that when they cooked this piece of tallow to build an arbor over the fire and spread tallow over the framework. While they were cooking, Dragging-the-Stone stood up and thought to himself: "Now what am I going to do to get away from these people? I fear they will kill me." He went where these people were looking after the tallow which was spread on the framework over the fire. He told the people to sit down and he himself would do the cooking, as he was very fond of cooking. Every little while he would turn the tallow over. He noticed that the grease was running out and as it dripped into the fire it began to burn. When Dragging-the-Stone thought it was time to get away from these people, he took the tallow and swung it around the circle so that everyone in the circle received a burn. Everyone bowed down and closed his eyes to keep from being burned, and he kept swinging the tallow around until they were all burned; then he threw the fat away and ran. The people then ran after him. They caught him as he got on top of the sand bar and killed him.

Whenever people see coyotes lying on sand bars they say: "That coyote tried to fool the people, but he was found out and killed."

124. COYOTE-MAN AND HIS TRICKS.[1]

Old Coyote-Man had many tricks. He had hair upon his breast and a little upon his back. He carried a quiver made from raccoon hides. One day Coyote-Man was going along trying to find game, but he could not find any. He was going through the timber, when he came to some squirrels playing in the trees. He stood at the bottom of the tree and said: "Grandchildren, you are having such a good time, while your grandfather down here is starving. Help your poor old grandfather and give him something to eat." The Squirrels said: "You are too mean. We can not give you anything to eat." Coyote-Man kept on begging until the male Squirrel came down and said: "Now, my grand-father, you are tricky. Be careful how you cut me. You shall have something to eat if you will do just what I tell you." Then the Squirrel placed one of its hind legs against the tree and the other upon the ground. Then he told Coyote-Man to take his knife and to cut off one of his testes. As soon as Coyote-Man cut him, down came a lot of pecans, so that there

---

[1] Told by Cheyenne-Chief, Skidi. The story is told to the children so that they may be on the lookout for tricky men and those who are always bothering children.

was a big pile on the ground. Then the Squirrel ran up the tree and said: "Now, grandfather, you may eat those nuts." Coyote-Man then said: "Grandchildren, these taste very good. Grandchildren, take pity on your grandfather and teach him how to do that trick." Then the Squirrel said: "Go; you can do that three or four times a day, but not more than three or four times."

Coyote-Man ran to his home, called his wife, told her to cut him, and down poured pecans. The children gathered around and ate, and after they had eaten all of them up, he said: "Did you all have enough?" They said: "No." Then he told his wife to cut him again, and again they had pecans to eat. Four times he was cut and then he tried the fifth time. When the woman brought her knife down upon him, instead of pecans, blood flowed out and he became scared and ran to the Squirrels. He came to the Squirrels and said: "My grandchildren, I must have made a mistake. The blood is flowing from me." The Squirrels said: "That is wrong. We knew that you would not do as we told you. We will stop the blood and heal the wound, but the power is all taken from you."

He went along the banks of a creek and he found some Beavers. He commenced to beg of them for something to eat. One of the Beavers told him to go and get some bark from a cottonwood tree. When he brought the bark the Beaver told Coyote-Man to rub his hands upon the bark, so that they would become soft. Then the Beavers told him to take his knife and cut his scrotum, which he did. As soon as Coyote-Man cut himself oil came out and the Beaver poured the oil over the powdered bark. The Beaver told Coyote-Man to stir the bark up, and when Coyote-Man did that the mixture turned into pemmican. Coyote-Man ate the pemmican and then he began to beg of the Beaver to teach him to do the same thing. The Beavers taught him and told him that he could do that four times a day and no more.

Old Coyote-Man went home. He told his wife to get her knife and catch hold of his scrotum and cut it. He placed some pounded bark under him which he had gathered on his way. When she cut him the oil came out, and he poured it over the bark and made pemmican. The children ate of it, but they did not seem to get enough, so he tried it for four times. The children did not have enough, and he tried it the fifth time. When the woman cut him there came out blood instead of oil. He ran to the Beavers and told them that he had made a mistake and he wanted them to heal him. The Beavers healed him up, but they took the power from him.

Coyote-Man went along and wandered over the country. One fine day he got into a thick timber. As he went along he saw a Bear coming.

The Bear stopped and looked at him and said: "Grandfather, where are you going?" Coyote-Man said: "I am going to a village west of here." Coyote-Man asked the Bear where he was going, and the Bear said that he was going to his den. As soon as the Bear had gone, Coyote-Man ran through the timber and made a big circle. He came to a little creek. He put some mud upon his head and upon his body. Then he took white clay and put it upon his lips, so that when the clay dried it looked as if his lips were chapped.

After a while he met the Bear. Coyote-Man stopped the Bear and said: "My grandchild, you should take pity on your grandfather. You have many things to eat, while I have none. You see how your grandfather's mouth is chapped. You should give a little grease to your grandfather to grease his lips. See how his lips are chapped." The Bear said: "I know that you are tricky. I can not do that for you." Coyote-Man begged so hard that at last the Bear gave in. Then the Bear said: "Cut me on the loin and take a little tallow to grease your lips." The Bear lay down and Coyote-Man took his knife and commenced to cut the Bear. When Coyote-Man began to cut, the Bear grunted, for the cut was paining him. Then Coyote-Man would say: "Grandchild, I have just begun to cut it." Coyote-Man had already made a deep cut. Then he took one of his spiked arrows and put it into the wound and rammed it in hard. As he drove it in he said: "I thought I could fool you, Bear, and I now kill you." Coyote-Man killed the Bear. He went through a timber and found a big pile of dried limbs. He returned, skinned the Bear, and cut up the meat. Then he took the meat to where the pile of dried limbs was, carrying a little at a time. He made a big fire and began to roast some of the meat. He did not want to eat any of the meat until every piece of it was roasted. When the meat was roasted he took a thigh bone and placed it upon some leaves. He cut a big piece to eat.

Right above him he heard the squeaking of a tree. He dropped his meat and looked up and said: "Stop that noise up there. If you speak again I will come up there and kill you." He cut another piece off and just about that time the tree squeaked again and he threw down the meat. Then the squeaking continued. Coyote-Man jumped up, ran up the tree, and he saw where the two trees were rubbing, and this was what caused the noise. He placed his hands there and said: "Now squeak again and see if I don't catch you and kill you." The trees moved and caught his hand. There he sat in the tree with his hand caught. Then he would say: "My grandchild, let go of my hand now. I want to go down and eat and you can squeak all you desire." He looked and he saw a big drove of Coyotes at a distance. He began to yell and say: "Coyotes, you must not come this way, for I have a lot of cooked meat here and I do not want you to come near me." The Coyotes stopped and said: "Listen; that man is calling us. He says he has a lot of meat cooked near where he is." The Coyotes ran to where he was. They got to the meat, began to eat it, and finally they ate it all up. They then went away. Just as they went away the trees opened and Coyote-Man got loose. He went down and began to scold himself for allowing the other Coyotes to eat up his meat. He had to lick the grease which had dropped from the meat, for that was all that was left.

Coyote-Man went on through another timber, when he met a strange man. The man had on a buzzard cap, a buffalo robe, an eagle wing in his left and a gourd rattle in his right hand. Upon his back was his medicine-bag. When Coyote-Man met this man he said: "Grandchild, where are you going?" The strange man said: "I am going to a village west of here. I am doctoring the chief's son, who was wounded in battle. To-day I doctor him for the last time. I am to bathe him and then I receive my pay in presents." Coyote-Man said: "What do you do when you approach the village?" The man said: "When I approach the village I stop and sit down for a little while. Then I get up and sing:

> With a medicine-case on his back.
> With a medicine-case on his back.
> With a medicine-case on his back.
> With a medicine-case on his back.
> With a medicine-case on his back.
> With a medicine-case on his back."

As he sang he danced the way he did when he was near the village. Then the man said: "When I am through dancing I walk closer to the village and then I sing again." Coyote-Man said: "Sing it again." The man began to sing and dance. Coyote-Man began to dance with him. He kept on asking the man to sing and dance until he learned both the dance and the song. Then he asked him what he did when he went in to doctor the wounded man. The man told all that he did, and also told how he was to let all the people go out of the lodge and he was to bathe the sick man and then he was to receive his pay. When Coyote-Man thought he knew all the songs he took a club, hit the man on the head, and killed him. Then he removed his clothing and put them on himself. He went on to the village. As he went out from the timber he stopped and began to sing the song he had learned from the medicine-man. After he had sung and danced four times he went on. When he was near the village he stopped and sang and danced, just as the medicine-man had told him.

After he was through dancing he sat down upon the ground. After a while the men came out for him, placed a robe upon the ground, and placed Coyote-Man on the robe. Then these men carried Coyote-Man to the lodge. When Coyote-Man was placed in the lodge he took his bundle, put it in the lodge, and said: "You people can now go out from the lodge and stay at a distance, for I am to wash this young man and put medicine upon him." The people went out and stood some distance away. Coyote-Man took a kettle, placed it upon the fire, and went and got a piece of iron. This he placed in the fire. Then he told the wounded man to sit near the fire and he would wash his wound. The man began to feel of the wound and it was almost healed. Coyote-Man took the red-hot iron from the fire, rammed it into the side of the young man, and said: "This is the way I doctor you. I will kill you and that will be the end of you." He killed him, took out his knife, and cut him up. He cut the meat into small slices and put it in a kettle.

After he had eaten he saw a little Snake crawling up towards him, and the Coyote-Man said: "My grandson, I will give you something to eat." Coyote-Man cut a strip of meat and shoved it down into the throat of the Snake, so that it was nearly choked and could not speak. The Snake crawled out of the lodge and went to where the people were. It was windy, so that when the Snake tried to speak the people could not hear it. The Snake came close to one person and spoke to him. The Snake spoke very low, for it could hardly speak on account of the meat which was down in its throat. The person then said: "People, this Snake says something." They all stopped and listened and the Snake spoke again in a whisper and said: "That man killed the boy in the lodge some time ago, and has eaten him up."

The people then ran to the lodge and there they found the bones of the boy and some of the meat still boiling, but the man was gone. They hunted for him through the timber, but they could not find him. His medicine-bag and other things were left in the lodge.

Coyote-Man, after he left the lodge, went through the timber, and after a while he went out and began to climb a hill. As he reached the top of the hill he saw several Buzzards sitting upon the hill. Then he began to talk to the Buzzards and they listened to him. Coyote-Man asked the Buzzards to carry him up into the sky, so that he could look down as they did and see what the earth was like. Two Buzzards went away, while two remained behind. The two who remained behind told Coyote-Man to put his arms around their necks and they would take him up. When the Buzzards flew the Coyote-Man would say: "Grandchildren, wait, wait; I can not stand this. You might drop me."

Several times they flew with him, but each time Coyote-Man begged them to go back to the ground. At last the other two Buzzards told Coyote-Man that he must close his eyes. Coyote-Man closed his eyes and the Buzzards flew up. After they were away up high then they told the Coyote-Man to look. Coyote-Man looked down and he could see game upon the ground. Then he said: "My grandchildren, if I had power to fly high I could see where the game is and then go down and kill it. I would then have plenty to eat." The Buzzards kept flying with him. The other two who had left first were in the lead. After a while the two leading Buzzards circled around. Then the Buzzards told him to close his eyes. When the Buzzards swung around they came to a certain place and there the two Buzzards separated, one going one way and the other another way.

Coyote-Man was dropped into a hollow log, for the Buzzards wanted to kill him. The two who had gone on ahead of the other two found the hollow log. When they found it they brought the other two, who were flying with Coyote-Man. Coyote-Man remained in this hollow log for several days. There were holes in the sides of the hollow log. Coyote-Man began to make them a little larger, so that he could look through them. One day he heard a great noise, as if there were many people traveling. He made a big hole. He looked and saw many people traveling. They were making their camp near the log. After the women had put up their tipis they went into the timber to gather dry limbs. When Coyote-Man saw the women coming he took his quiver, cut the raccoon tails from his quiver, and stuck them into the holes of the log. When the women came and saw the raccoon tails they thought that they had found a hollow log where the raccoons stayed. When the women came to the tree they saw the tails sticking out. They caught hold of the tails and pulled them. Coyote-Man pulled inside. Then the women said: "Here are some raccoons. Let us cut the tree down and get them out." They cut the tree down, and as it fell over Coyote-Man stood up and said: "What do you women mean by cutting down my house? This is my house." He was very angry with the women, but at the same time he was thankful that they had cut down the tree.

Coyote-Man left the place and traveled on. He came to a place where there were two women gathering wood. He went by them and came to a baby tied to a baby-board standing against a tree. Coyote-Man pulled out the baby, cut off its head, and put the head in the cradle again. When the women came they took up their baby, and when they slung it upon their backs the head fell out. The two women then knew that the Coyote-Man had been there. Coyote-Man went on and came to another village.

About this time the people went out to hunt for Coyote-Man. They found him, made a big fire, and placed him upon it. After a while a noise was heard something like a gun-shot. They saw something pop from the fire. The thing flew over into the timber, and as it fell it gave one big warwhoop. The people say that instead of Coyote-Man burning up he jumped over into the timber and turned into a hairy man. He was never to associate with the people any more.

125. COYOTE TAKES THE PIPE-STICKS TO THE BEAVERS.[1]

Coyote lived in a lodge with his wife and many children. The children became hungry and so Coyote made up his mind that he would go off and hunt something for them to eat. He went towards the creek and there he found many Beavers along the banks of the stream. Coyote sat down and tried to think what would be the best way to kill some of the Beavers. He made up his mind to make pipe-sticks, and so he went back to his lodge, sat down, and made the pipe-sticks. Then he went back to where the Beavers were and asked permission that he be allowed to enter their lodge. The Beavers gave their consent. Coyote went in with the pipe-sticks and sang this song to the Beavers:

> The Beaver who swims with a stick
> Is my child, my son.
> This club hanging to my belt
> I shall use upon him.

The Beavers were satisfied. Then Coyote told them that where he lived away up on the hill was the main party of the pipe-stick people; that the Beavers would have to come and meet the party; that the Beavers were now children of Coyote's people, and that they were the Beavers' fathers. The Beavers agreed, although they had heard Coyote say in the singing something about his war club, which was in his belt.

That made them suspicious, but the majority of them thought that there was no danger, and so they agreed to go and meet Coyote upon the hill. Coyote, knowing the distance from the hill to the creek, thought if the Beavers went upon the land near the hill he could kill many of them with his club. When the Beavers came towards the hill Coyote looked down and saw that most of them were near the foot of the hill. Then he ran down with his club. As he lifted his club he shouted: "You foolish Beavers, you have no fathers to meet. It is I who am starving and I now kill you so that my children may eat you." Coyote began to kill

[1] Told by White-Horse, Pitahauirat. The story is told to the people so that they might be careful in receiving the Pipe-stick ceremony from unknown people.

the Beavers, and some of them ran away into the water. Coyote then went up and brought his children and they took the Beavers up to their lodge. There they skinned them and had plenty to eat. After they had eaten all their meat they tried to play the same trick on the Beavers again, but the Beavers would not listen to Coyote any more.

126. COYOTE AND THE ROLLING STONE.[1]

Coyote was going along, and as he had not had anything to eat for some time he was very hungry. In the evening he went to a high hill and sat down. Early the next morning he started again. He came to a big round stone. He took out his knife and said: "Grandfather, this knife I give to you as a present. I want you to help me to get something to eat."

Coyote went over a hill, and there in the bottom was a village of people. He went into the village and he could see meat hanging on poles everywhere in the camp. He went into one of the tipis and the people in the tipi roasted a piece of meat for him. Just as he was about to taste of the meat he thought of his knife and said: "Why did I give my knife to that stone? I should have kept it and then I should have been able to cut the meat without having to pull it with my hands." He asked to be excused and went out. He went to where the stone was. He said: "Grandfather, I will have to take back this knife, for I have found a village of people with plenty of meat." He went over the hills and into the bottom, but there was no village there. Coyote went back and returned the knife to the stone. He went back over the hills and there saw the village and he entered one of the tipis. They placed before him some meat. He began to chew the meat. He thought of his knife. He went back to the stone, and as he took the knife the stone said: "Why do you take the knife away from me? I am now going to kill you." Then the stone ran after the Coyote. Coyote ran and came to a den of Bears. He told the Bears that a person was running after him and he asked them to help him. The Bears said that they were not afraid of anything. They asked what the thing was, and he said it was the stone. The Bears said: "Keep on running. We can not do anything with the stone." The stone was close to Coyote when he came up to another den of Mountain-Lions. They also told Coyote to pass on, as they could not do anything for him. After a while Coyote came to a Buffalo standing all alone, but when the Buffalo found out that it was the stone running after Coyote he told him to pass on.

[1] Told by Leading-Sun, Kitkehahki. The story is told to the children so that when they give presents to stones, trees, or any other thing they must never take them away again; that if they took away the presents something would happen to them and cause their death.

At last Coyote came to a place where the Bull-Bats stayed. Coyote said: "Grandchildren, there is a person running after me." The Bull-Bats then said: "Enter our lodge and remain there." When the stone came rolling up it said: "Where is that person who came here?" The Bull-Bats did not reply and the stone became angry. Then the Bull-Bats said: "He is here and we are going to protect him." The Bull-Bats flew up and then down, and they expelled flatus on the stone. Every time they did this a piece broke off from the stone. The largest Bull-Bat came down and expelled flatus right on the center and broke the stone into pieces. Then the Coyote was told to come out and go on his way.

Coyote started off, and when he got over the hills he turned around and yelled at the Bull-Bats and said: "All you big-nosed, funny things, how you did behave to that stone." The Bull-Bats heard it and did not pay any attention, but he kept on making fun of them. Then the Bull-Bats flew up in a group, and came down, and with their wings they got the stones together again and started it to rolling, and said: "Go and kill that fellow." The stone then ran after Coyote and Coyote tried to get away, but he could not. At last he gave out. He jumped over a steep bank and the stone was right behind him. As Coyote struck the bottom, the stone fell on him and killed him. This is why we used to find dead coyotes in the hills and valleys.

127. COYOTE AND THE ROLLING SKULL.[1]

Coyote was going along, and he became very hungry. He came to a wide prairie covered with tall buffalo-grass. He stopped and sang:

> What a fine place this is;
> I wish I could run the buffalo around;
> Thus I might get something to eat.

Close by where Coyote was singing a voice spoke and said: "Stop singing and dancing around my place." Then the skull began to sing:

> Here my skull rests,
> Here my skull rests,
> Surrounded by a path.
> Here my skull rests.

[1] Told by White-Sun, Kitkehahki. This story was originally told by his grandfather, one of the leading medicine-men of the Kitkehahki. It is told to teach the children that when they find skulls upon the prairie they must not call them names nor kick them around. The children are taught by the story that skulls have supernatural power.

Here my skull rests,
But there you stand, Coyote,
Dying of starvation.
Here my skull rests.

Here my skull rests,
But there you stand, Coyote,
Awaiting the odor of meat borne by the wind
Here my skull rests.

Coyote looked up and said: "And who are you that I should be afraid of you?" Just then a skull rolled up, and when Coyote saw the skull he ran. He ran from one place to another, but the skull pursued him. At last he ran to a village of people and just as he ran into the village and called to them the skull devoured him. The people who ran out from their village were also devoured by the skull. Four girls escaped and started to run, but the skull pursued them. When the skull was about to catch one of the girls, she threw her pack strings upon the ground, and many bunches of cactus sprang up over the land. The girls ran on, and the skull tried to get over the cactus, but could not until it had tried many times. When it did get over it ran and killed the woman who had thrown the pack strings. The second woman threw her pack strings upon the ground and there was a big stream of water and a steep bank. The skull could not cross the stream of water, but somehow it managed to jump upon logs which were floating down and so crossed the stream. Then it took after the woman and killed her.

When the skull was about to overtake the other two women, one of them threw her pack strings upon the ground and there was a steep bank. But somehow the skull managed to climb up and took after the woman and killed her. Then the fourth girl, the youngest, ran and cried for help. A Bull-Bat flew by her and told her to go down into the hollow; that there she would see a man; that he alone could help her. The girl went down into the ravine and there she saw a little lodge and a small boy, as she thought, sitting outside of the lodge. She told him that a skull was coming after her. He told her to go into his lodge, and he would stay where he was. The skull came and asked the little fellow if a girl had gone on by. He paid no attention to the skull, and the skull became angry and was about to devour him, when he opened his mouth and blew with his breath a little blue bead. The blue bead struck the skull upon the forehead, killing it. The little fellow told the girl to go on her way; that the skull was killed and would never molest the people any more. The little fellow was Milk-Weed and the girl was called Rolling Skull.

128. COYOTE TURNS INTO A BUFFALO.[1]

Coyote, starving, met a Buffalo bull grazing. Coyote watched the Buffalo eat grass and said: "Grandfather, how you eat!" The Buffalo did not notice Coyote. After a while Coyote began to run around in front of the Buffalo bull. The Buffalo bull stopped eating, looked at Coyote, and said: "My grandson, why do you run around and bother me?" Coyote said: "Grandfather, you have grass to eat all over this country, and here I am starving because I can find nothing to eat." The Buffalo said: "My grandson, what you say is true, but I know you and I can not help you. You are tricky. I might do something for you, but you would do something which was wrong and you would be killed." But Coyote said: "No, my grandfather. I do not think that if you take pity on me I shall do anything wrong." The Buffalo then looked up and said: "If you are in earnest and want to be like me, go and hunt a buffalo wallow." The Coyote went and found a buffalo wallow, then he came back and told the Buffalo bull that he had found a buffalo wallow. They went along together and the Buffalo bull ran towards Coyote, and when the Buffalo bull made a motion to hook, Coyote jumped to one side and the Buffalo went by. Then the Buffalo said: "I see that what I said is true. You are not in earnest. You jump to one side. I can not do anything for you." Three times the Buffalo ran towards Coyote and every time Coyote jumped aside. The Buffalo became angry and was going away, but Coyote begged hard for him to take pity on him once more. Coyote made up his mind that he would rather be killed than starve to death, and so he stood in the buffalo wallow. The Buffalo ran towards him and tried to hook him, but when his horns touched Coyote he turned into a Buffalo, and there the two Buffalo fought with locked horns, pushing one another about. Then the Buffalo said: "My grandchild, there you are. Now you can eat all of this good grass that you see over this land. Stay with me for several days, and learn our powers. Graze upon high hills so that you can see a long distance, and when you see people coming always run. In the night follow the ravines, and when you have come to a bunch of grass and weeds sit down in the center of the weeds. In the morning go again upon the high hills and graze."

Coyote-Buffalo remained with the Buffalo. After a while the Buffalo told Coyote-Buffalo to go on and do as he had told him. He told him that whenever he sat down to always have his nose towards the wind, so

[1] Told by White-Horse, Pitahauirat. The story is told to the children so that they might learn, that whatever power they should receive from animals they must keep it to themselves and not try to give it to some one else; that if they did their power would go from them and they would be as poor as ever.

that if any people should come he could smell them for a long distance and could run from them. While Coyote-Buffalo was grazing he saw a Coyote sitting near him, and Coyote-Buffalo said: "My grandchild, what do you want?" Coyote said that he was starving and would like to be like the Buffalo, so that he could get plenty of grass to eat. Coyote-Buffalo said: "That is easy. I was a Coyote, but I was turned into a Buffalo. You find a buffalo wallow and I will take pity upon you and make you like a Buffalo. You must be brave, and then you shall be like me." The Coyote found a buffalo wallow and they went to it. Coyote-Buffalo put the Coyote into the buffalo wallow and told him to stand there. Then Coyote-Buffalo ran toward the Coyote, thinking that he would have the power to turn the Coyote into a Buffalo. He ran, and when he tried to hook the Coyote, the Coyote turned around and tried to bite him. As Coyote-Buffalo struck the Coyote he turned into a Coyote again and there were two Coyotes with their mouths locked together. When he got loose, Coyote who had been a Buffalo began to call the other Coyote names, and said: "You have done me a great wrong. I am now a Coyote again." The other Coyote ran away.

Coyote who had been a Buffalo went back to the Buffalo and said: "Grandfather, I am sorry. When I was running I fell down and I turned into a Coyote again. Take pity upon me and I will be more careful after this." The Buffalo told Coyote to find another buffalo wallow. Coyote found it and stood in the buffalo wallow, and the Buffalo ran, and as his horns struck Coyote he again turned into a Buffalo. He said: "Now, do not try to turn Coyotes into Buffalo, but stay with me."

After they were together for several days, Coyote-Buffalo said: "I will travel towards the west;" and the Buffalo said: "Good! On your way you will meet twenty Buffalo running fast. There will be nineteen Buffalo cows and one bull. When the bull sees you and stops he will say: 'Join us; let us go where the people are, so that we may receive smoke.' Do not listen to him. You must not go with him. You must stay away from him." Coyote said: "Grandfather, I will do as you say." Coyote-Buffalo went west. For several days he traveled, and one evening he heard Buffalo coming, running fast. He jumped up and stood in the pathway. The Buffalo cows passed, but when the bull came up he said: "My brother, let us go where the people are, so that we may receive smoke." Coyote-Buffalo said: "Good! I will go with you." They began to run. Towards evening they overtook the Buffalo cows and they went on together. In the evening the Buffalo sat down to rest. Then the Buffalo bull said: "It is not far to go where we are going, and there we shall receive smoke." Coyote-Buffalo said: "Let us, then, start again and get there as soon as we can." The Buffalo arose, and they ran for some time in the night. When they came to ravines they squatted down and Coyote-Buffalo said: "My brother, let us now smoke." The Buffalo bull said: "Why, do you not know what I mean when I say that we are going for smoke?" Coyote-Buffalo did not know, but he said: "Oh, I had forgotten. We are not to get smoke yet." In the morning they started again. Every time they stopped Coyote-Buffalo would say: "Let us now smoke." The Buffalo would say: "Why, do you not know what I mean when I say that we are going for smoke?" Coyote would say: "I had forgotten. I remember now what it is." Then the Buffalo started on again and at last they came close to the village. They squatted down in the ravine and sat there.

Early in the morning scouts were sent out from the people and they found the Buffalo sitting in the ravine. The scouts went and told the people that there was a herd of Buffalo close to the village. The old men cried through the village and told the men to surround the Buffalo. The men went out, surrounded the Buffalo, and they killed all the Buffalo. The men said that the Buffalo were holy and that their meat was to be taken to the lodge of the priest. Several men ran after one Buffalo that could run faster than the others. They ran this Buffalo over some hills, and just as one man got near the Buffalo, the Buffalo came to a place where there was a high precipice. The Buffalo fell as the man was about to shoot, and as he fell the Buffalo turned into a Coyote and ran away. The men were surprised when they saw the Buffalo turn into a Coyote. They went home and told about it. The old people said that this Coyote must have been turned into a Buffalo by some other Buffalo. Coyote ran back to where the Buffalo bull was grazing and said: "My grandfather, I joined those people who went to get smoke from the people. The people ran after me and I stumbled over some bad places. I fell down and turned into a Coyote. Take pity upon me and let me turn into a Buffalo again." Buffalo bull said: "Find me a buffalo wallow." Coyote found a buffalo wallow and they went to it. Coyote stood in the wallow and the Buffalo bull ran towards him and hooked him and threw him up into the air. Before he struck the ground he hooked him again and again, until he killed him. Ever since that time the Coyotes have been willing to be Coyotes, and the Buffalo have always disliked Coyotes.

129. COYOTE FAMILY RUN AFTER THE BUFFALO.[1]

There was a Coyote lodge upon the banks of a stream of water somewhere in the northern country. Coyote-Man went off on a hunt. While he was gone a bunch of Buffalo came past their lodge. The children all turned out and began to run after the Buffalo. The mother of the children came running and told them to run on after the Buffalo; that they might as well run after Buffalo as to stay there and starve. The Coyotes, with their mother, ran after the Buffalo. They began to run after the Buffalo in the morning and in the afternoon they were somewhere in the southern country. The youngest of the Coyotes began to give out. As the young Coyote fell behind he began to sing:

I only wish he knew,
That father knew of our running the Buffalo,
These running Buffalo, these running Buffalo.
These running Buffalo, these running Buffalo,

Then again, father is pleased
When his spirits are right;
And when he runs his best
His ears seem to be laughing.
These running Buffalo, these running Buffalo.

Then again, father is pleased
When his spirits are right;
And when he runs his best
His mouth laughs to the root of his ears.
These running Buffalo, these running Buffalo.

Just as the little Coyote was about to fall down and die his father overtook him and passed him. The young Coyote stopped and began to sing again: "My father will now catch up with the Buffalo and will kill one or two of them." One of the young Buffalo gave out and the Coyotes surrounded it and killed it. When they had eaten the Buffalo, the old Coyote said: "Old woman, you and I must go back to our lodge in the north. What shall we do with these children?" Young Coyote said: "Let us all scatter here and each one go wherever he chooses. In this way the country will be filled with Coyotes." They all decided to scatter out and they did so. That is why the Coyotes were found everywhere in the country.

[1] Told by Thief, Kitkehahki. The story is told to the young people to teach them that when they grow up they would go upon long hunts for buffalo. The story teaches the children that the Coyotes, by running after the buffalo, scattered out over the earth.

130. COYOTE STEALS TURTLE'S BUFFALO.[1]

Turtle was going along a sand bar, when he saw a herd of Buffalo on the other side. He cried: "Grandfather, carry me across." The Buffalo looked around at one another and said: "Poor Turtle wants you to carry him across." One said: "I will go and bring him over." The Buffalo went over and Turtle saw that the Buffalo was lean, and he said: "Grandfather, I did not mean you." Then another came and it also was lean, and Turtle refused to go with him. The Buffalo kept coming, until one came that was fat. Then Turtle said: "Now, grandfather, you are the right one to carry me across the river." The Buffalo told Turtle to sit upon his shaggy head, but Turtle said: "No; you will shake your head and drop me into the water." Then the Buffalo said: "Suppose you sit upon my back;" but Turtle said: "No." Then the Buffalo said: "Where would you like to sit?" Turtle said: "Let me sit under your tail, in your anus." The Buffalo said: "All right." Turtle sat there and the Buffalo waded the river. As the Buffalo went into the river Turtle went inside and began to chew on the entrails of the Buffalo. When the Buffalo reached the other shore Turtle jumped out and said: "Your intestines are all cut up." Buffalo began to stagger and fell to the ground and died, when Turtle began to sing:

> Flint knife, I am hunting you,
> I want to skin and cut up meat.
> Flint knife, I am hunting you,
> I want to cut and scrape my arrows.

Coyote heard Turtle singing about wanting a knife to cut meat, but Turtle denied it and said: "I am singing about wanting a knife to make arrows." Coyote's ears lay back on his head, and he was very good to Turtle and talked so kindly to him that Turtle finally admitted that he wanted a knife to cut meat with. He told Coyote about the Buffalo and they both went to the Buffalo. Then Coyote began to talk to Turtle. He said: "My grandson, let us jump over the Buffalo, and whoever jumps over the Buffalo shall own it. The loser must help the winner to cut up the Buffalo. Then we will divide the meat." Turtle agreed, because Coyote had been so kind and talked so nicely to him. Coyote smiled to himself and then offered to jump first. He jumped clear over the Buffalo. Turtle ran and tried to jump, but failed. Then Coyote claimed the Buffalo. Coyote cut up the meat and said: "My grandson,

[1] Told by Thief, Kitkehahki. The story is told to the children to teach them that when they kill game they should not be fooled by those who might misrepresent things to them.

you may take the blood and other things that are left here. I am going after my children, and when I come back we will divide the meat."

Coyote then went off after his children. While Turtle sat there watching the meat he thought to himself: "I know Coyote; he is a cheat. He will bring his children, take all the meat, and give me none." He saw two Bald-Eagles flying overhead. Turtle cried to them and said: "My grandfathers, I have some meat here. Take it up on a high tree, for Coyote is coming to take it away from me." The Bald-Eagles took the meat and flew up to a high cottonwood tree and placed it in an eagle's nest. Turtle told the Eagles to take him up there. The Eagles took Turtle up and placed him in the nest. Then Turtle made a fire and began to cook some meat. In the meantime Coyote and his children went to the place and found nothing but blood upon the ground. The children began to lick up the blood, but Coyote was very angry. He went up and down the stream, and after a while he saw the reflection of the fire in the water. He said: "There is Turtle in the water cooking the meat. I will get the meat away from him and kill him. You stay here and watch, and when you see the charred coal come up and float on the water, you may know that I have scattered his fire." Coyote dived, and his head caught between two logs under the water. The children stood upon the bank watching for the charred coals to come up. After a while they saw some things coming up. They said: "See; our father is scattering the fire of Turtle." It was Coyote's excrement, and when Turtle saw that Coyote was dead, he spoke to the children and said: "How would you like to have some meat?" They looked, and up there in the tree they saw Turtle with all the meat. Coyote's children cried and ran away.

131. COYOTE AND BEAR.[1]

Coyote was going along through the timber, when all at once a Bear jumped from the bushes and faced him. Coyote was scared nearly to death, and he said to himself: "What shall I do?" He took his bow in his hand, and beating upon it with his arrow he sang this song:

> I can still the rivers which flow and they stop.
> What shall I do with this rough-handed fellow standing before me?
> I can kill him with my bow and arrows.

At that time, it being hot weather, the waters had gone down and the bed of the river had become dry. Bear saw that the creek was nearly

---

[1] Told by White-Eagle, Skidi. This story is told to the children to teach them that they must not make war on people who have greater powers than they themselves possess.

dry and he said to himself: "This must be a wonderful man who can make the rivers and streams run dry in this way." Then he listened again and heard another song. Old Coyote sang:

> I overturned even the timber
> That extended over yonder,
> Standing yonder, with my wonderful bow.

Bear looked around and saw great big trees down, with the roots turned up. A few days before there had been a cyclone, which had blown down the trees and turned up the roots, and Bear looked at the trees that were down, and said: "Why, this is a wonderful man if he can do all this." Then Coyote sang again:

> Even the hills yonder I killed,
> Yes, even the hills yonder.
> Then this rough-chapped, flat-footed one
> I could easily kill
> With my wonderful bow.

Bear looked over the prairies and saw that there were no hills and mountains, and he believed Coyote. The people had burned the grass from the prairies so that they looked level all over. Then Coyote sang:

> I killed even the waters that
> Flowed through the land
> With my wonderful bow.

They had bright sunlight when they first met, but Coyote had seen that a fog was rising. Bear said: "This is a wonderful man, for he can make the sun disappear." Bear became afraid of Coyote and said: "Well, grandson, let us travel together." Coyote said: "All right." In the evening they made a fire, and when they had made the fire, Coyote told Bear to cook the meat on hot coals. Bear cooked the meat, and when it was done he took it off, but had one eye on Coyote all the time. When he made a motion to reach out for something he noticed Coyote jump. Bear took the piece of meat and reached out to hand the meat over to Coyote and Coyote jumped. Bear said: "Oh, yes! you have been fooling me with your big talk," and he jumped towards Coyote and Coyote ran for his life, but Bear caught him and killed him.

132. COYOTE AND BEAR.[1]

Coyote was going along and he came to thick timber. After going far into the woods he came to a cedar grove. He had a bow made of willows, so that if he pulled on it it would break easily. The bow was dirty and

[1] Told by White-Eagle, Skidi. The story is told to the children to teach them to listen attentively to the stories of other people, but not always to believe them.

greasy. As he went along he said: "I wish some wild animals would come out; I would shoot them with my bow and arrows." While thus saying, Bear came out from among the cedars, and said: "Nawa, what is that you have? Let me see." Coyote handed his bow to Bear, who pulled the string and broke the bow. Coyote then sang this song:

Father Sun, this one standing here
Has broken your bow.

Bear became frightened, for Coyote had said, "The Sun is my god." "What shall I do?" he thought. "Grandpa, do not sing any more. I will make you one," said Bear. He went into the timber and cut an ash and brought a bow already made to Coyote, for Bear had made it with his power. Coyote sang again about the Sun, and said: "It is not the right kind of wood." Bear went into the timber and brought a bow of another kind of wood, but Coyote sang again and said: "It is not the right kind of wood." Bear went and brought a plum-tree bow, which was very fine. Coyote said: "This is something like it. Now go and hide, so the Sun will not see you." Bear sneaked off. When he had gone, Coyote ran as fast as he could in another direction. The bow was a fine one. Coyote thought: "I was lucky to get away from Bear, and then to get a fine bow from him." He ran out of the timber and went on to the prairie, where he said: "I shall stay on the prairie hereafter, for Bear will kill me if he sees me again." So Coyote made his home on the prairie.

133. COYOTE SHOWS TURKEY THE SCALP-OFFERING CEREMONY.[1]

Coyote was going along all alone, when suddenly he saw Turkey. He said: "Hello! grandson, where are you going? May I go with you?" Turkey said: "Grandfather, I came all alone." Coyote said: "I want to teach you how to make fires to offer sacrifices; for before long I shall be dead, and I want to teach you these things, so that you will know them and your grandfathers will not say that I did not teach you about making the fires for making offerings to the gods in the heavens." Turkey said: "All right; I will do as you tell me." Coyote said: "Well, then, come; let us go and make a fire, and we will stand on the different corners of the fireplace, just as in the heavens the different gods stand." Coyote made Turkey believe that he knew all about the ceremony, but he was only planning to kill Turkey and take him home and eat him. Coyote made the fireplace. They both stood on the northeast of the

[1] Told by White-Eagle, Skidi. The story is told to the children so that when they grow up they shall have a desire to take scalps and make scalp sacrifices to the gods in the heavens.

fireplace, Coyote in front of Turkey, and both facing the fire, so that he could keep his eye on Turkey and finally hit him on the head with his stick.   Each stood with the left foot forward, while they grasped a stick with both hands, the left hand being in front of the right.   First they pointed the forward ends of their sticks obliquely upward, then obliquely downward; they then made one or two up-and-down motions of the body, raising the heels from the ground, the body being bent forward; all in imitation of the old priests they had seen making fire for the sacrifices of scalps, and all accompanied by the following song:

> Listen!   Attention!
> Who will eat, who will eat up
> That neck hanging there?

They went to the northwest side of the fireplace, and they went through the same performance as that of the northeast side, keeping time in their dancing to the following song:

> Listen!   Attention!
> Who will eat, who will eat up
> That which sits inside the breast?

They repeated the dance on the southwest side of the fireplace in a similar manner, while Coyote sang this song:

> Listen!   Attention!
> Who will eat, who will eat up
> That end of the backbone which carries the tail?

While Coyote was getting ready to kill him, Turkey began to suspect something and ran away to the timber on the south side of the open field where they were dancing.   When Coyote opened his eyes Turkey was gone.   He called himself names, and said: "What a fine neck he had; what a fat Turkey!   If I had only killed him instead of fooling my time away.   Now I have nothing for my children to eat, for I have let him slip away."   Then Coyote hallooed to Turkey and said: "Let's complete the ceremony; you must not be scared; my songs did not mean anything."   But Turkey never came back.

134. COYOTE AND THE DANCING TURKEYS.[1]

A bunch of Turkeys were dancing, when Coyote came up to them. "Grandchildren, you are not singing a good song; I can teach you a good song," said he.   "Very well," all the Turkeys said; "sing us a good song." Coyote sang:

[1] Told by White-Eagle, Skidi.   The story is told to the children so that they might imitate the dancing of the turkeys and should dance this dance when playing in the night.

Gizzard! Gizzard!
Lift your necks high, then low,
Waving your tails to and fro.
Tut! Tut! (Sound of turkey when jumping.)

As he sang the song the Turkeys stretched their necks and placed them on the ground, but they watched Coyote, for as he danced among them he would open his mouth as if to bite their necks. The Turkeys would say: "His mouth is open! Look out!" But Coyote sang louder. They danced and danced, and all at once Coyote jumped and bit the necks of the two biggest Turkeys and killed them. The others ran away. "Ah!" said Coyote, "I am quite a cheat; my children will have plenty to eat."

Coyote took the two Turkeys home and said: "Children, pick the feathers off and cut the meat off and put it in the pot and cook it. I am going to ask some of the chiefs to eat with me, but I will save some meat for you." He went off, and after he came back he sent his children and wife away. He went into their tipi and sat down. Once in a while he would swing the skin that hung over the entrance and say: "Nawa, take this seat." The children could hear some one else say: "Nawa, thanks;" and they thought that there were many people. After a while Coyote made a speech and said: "I have two Turkeys boiling and I invite you to help me eat them." He said "Nawa" a number of times; so the little ones thought that there were many people in the tipi. Old Coyote took the kettle off and commenced to dish out the meat. He went from one plate to another and ate all of the meat by himself. One of the children went in and saw his father eating by himself, and went back and told his mother. They all came out and made a rush into the tipi, and old Coyote ran away and the children had only bones to eat and they were left to hunt food for themselves.

135. COYOTE AND THE TURKEYS ROLL DOWN THE HILL.[1]

Coyote was going along and he saw many Turkeys sliding down a hill. "What shall I do?" he said to himself. "I will go back and get a sack and show these Turkeys something new." He got his sack and went back to where the Turkeys were. "Now, my grandchildren, I have something new. Watch me go into this sack. When I am inside tie it fast. Now roll me down the hill." As he rolled down the hill he laughed and laughed, and said: "It is very fine to roll down hill." At the foot of the hill the Turkeys untied the sack and Coyote walked up the hill with them.

[1] Told by Fox, Skidi. The story is to teach the children that when they grow up and hunt for game and kill it they should always be sure to keep watch over it and preserve it.

"Now you little ones get into this sack.   I will roll you down the hill and you will see how fine it is to roll down hill."   The young Turkeys went into the sack.   Coyote tied the sack and rolled them down hill.   The young Turkeys laughed, so the older ones thought they would try it. Coyote untied the sack and the Turkeys came out.   Then Coyote went to the top of the hill and invited the older Turkeys to get into the sack and roll down the hill.   They all went in, about sixty in number.   As he started the sack down the hill he told the young Turkeys to stay on the hill, for they would soon come up.   When the sack reached the foot of the hill Coyote swung it on his back and said: "I am a cheat."   He carried the Turkeys home to his children.   "Now, children, I have something fine in this sack.   I will go and bring your mother home.   Do not untie this sack."   He was gone but a little while when the youngest one went to the sack and untied it.   The Turkeys were very anxious to get out and made a big cackling noise, scratched the young Coyotes, and made their escape.   The young ones cried and cried.   When the old Coyote came home he found the sack empty and scolded and whipped the little Coyotes.   The little Coyotes went off crying and singing this song about their father:

> Thus father likes,
> When he is scared,
> To lay back his ears.
> Ha-o-o, haho,
> Ha-o-o, haho.

> Thus father likes,
> When he is scared,
> To open wide his mouth.
> Ha-o-o, haho.
> Ha-o-o, haho.

> He draws his knees up to his chin,
> He defecates in every direction,
> He almost loses his privates.
> Ha-o-o, haho,
> Ha-o-o, haho.

136. COYOTE AND PRAIRIE-CHICKEN.[1]

Coyote was going along looking for something to eat, when he met Prairie-Chicken.   He greeted Prairie-Chicken and said: "Prairie-Chicken, suppose we try to frighten one another and see who will get scared first." Prairie-Chicken said that he would, not suspecting that Coyote was

[1] Told by White-Sun, Kitkehahki.   This story is told to teach the children always to be on the look-out lest they be frightened by prairie chickens flying up in front of them.

planning to get a chance to kill and eat him. They selected a place where there was tall grass. Coyote hid some place in the grass and when Prairie-Chicken came along he jumped at him and tried to scare him, but Prairie-Chicken only laughed when he saw Coyote. Then Prairie-Chicken said: "Now it is my time to try to frighten you." Prairie-Chicken slipped off to a place close to a steep bank and hid there. Coyote walked all through the grass, expecting Prairie-Chicken to jump out some place. Prairie-Chicken did not appear and Coyote had forgotten all about him and started on his way, when suddenly Prairie-Chicken flew up in Coyote's face. Coyote gave a great leap, for he was frightened. He jumped over the steep bank and fell to the bottom of the canyon, where he died from his wounds.

When we see Coyotes at the bottom of steep banks and in canyons we know that some one has frightened them and that they have jumped over and so met their death through fear.

137. COYOTE AND PRAIRIE-CHICKEN.[1]

Coyote was going along and he saw Prairie-Chicken sitting on a limb. Coyote tried to get Prairie-Chicken to come down from the tree to dance with him, but Prairie-Chicken would not come. Then Coyote began to sing:

> Prairie-Chicken yonder, sitting on a limb,
> Somebody is going to bewitch you.

Then Prairie-Chicken sang:

> Who now is going to bewitch me,
> And with what shall I be poisoned?

Coyote, answering, said:

> The poison-ivy berries will poison you;
> Your mouth will get sore, you will grow large.

Coyote sang again and said:

> Prairie-Chicken yonder, sitting on a limb,
> Somebody is going to bewitch you.

Then Prairie-Chicken asked in a song:

> Who now is going to bewitch me,
> And with what shall I be poisoned?

[1] Told by Young-Bull, a little Skidi boy, eight years of age, who also sang the song in the graphophone. His mother, Woman-Newly-Made-Chief, was the daughter of Scabby-Bull, a great medicine-man among the Skidi, and who had many stories to tell about the different animals. She in turn tells the stories to her son. The story is told to the children to teach them that stones, poison-ivy, berries, etc., are poisonous for people but not for prairie chickens.

Coyote sang and said:

> The cedar berries will poison you,
> You will have a pain in your stomach.

Prairie-Chicken did not pay any attention to Coyote. Then Coyote sang again:

> Prairie-Chicken yonder, sitting on a limb,
> Somebody is going to bewitch you.

Prairie-Chicken sang:

> Who now is going to bewitch me,
> And with what shall I be poisoned?

Coyote sang and said:

> Gravel will poison you,
> With gravel you will be bewitched.

Prairie-Chicken sang:

> All of the things you mention
> I am fond of; I like to eat them.

Then Prairie-Chicken flew up and away and Coyote went his way among the hills.

138. COYOTE TRIES TO MARRY RABBIT.[1]

Coyote was going along and he met a female Rabbit. He tried to marry her, but she would not have him, and she ran away from him. Then the female Rabbit went to another Coyote and tried to marry him. The Coyote began to sing:

> Rabbit-Woman, standing here,
> Rabbit-Woman, standing here,
> Wants to marry my son,
> But one fault I find with you;
> Your nose, like the earth,
> In many places is cracked.

The Rabbit then said: "Your people and my people shall always be apart and never mix up." Then they went off.

[1] Told by Yellow-Calf, Skidi, keeper of the Big-Black-Meteoric-Star bundle. The story is told to teach the children that the rabbit-people and the coyote-people are two different sorts of animals.

139. COYOTE AND THE SALT.[1]

A long time ago the people did not have any salt. The people had heard of Coyote wandering over the land; that at one time he turned into a man, made a big fire upon a high hill, and began to roast some meat. Several of the people went up to where Coyote-Man was and he gave them pieces of roasted meat with salt on it. When the people ate the salted meat it tasted so good that when they went home they told their children to recite:

> Coyote standing yonder,
> Yonder on the hill by the fire,
> Give me some salt.
> I am going to eat soup from a wooden bowl.

The children said this many times to the Coyote-Man, and the Coyote-Man finally promised the people to lead them to a place where they could get salt. In those times the people did not have any horses, so the men and women carried south their tipis and belongings upon their backs. Coyote-Man led them. They found the salt in the south. The people dug the salt in lumps and carried the lumps home with them. Coyote-Man disappeared and was never seen again, but after that, when the children saw Coyotes upon high hills, they recited this little ritual to remind the Coyotes that they were the ones who found the salt for the people.

140. COYOTE AND THE ROSEBUDS.[2]

The Coyote people went on a buffalo hunt, and as there were no buffalo in sight they sent scouts out over the country every day to look for buffalo. One day they sent out several, and one of them went off by himself. He went up on a high hill and saw that there were rosebuds from one end of the valley to the other. He sat on the hill for a long time until he thought of a scheme. Then he went home and sang this song:

> Pah-o-o-o! I come bringing news,
> But I must have compensation.

The people listened and said: "He brings us news of buffalo. Listen to him." As he came near to the village he sang again:

---

[1] Told by Woman-Newly-Made-Chief, Skidi. The story is told to teach the people how they got their salt.

[2] Told by Thief, Kitkehahki. The story is told to the young people so that when they grow up they should never fool the people about the buffalo; that they should learn that when they saw buffalo they must go to the village and notify the priests so that the people might prepare to kill the buffalo. They are also taught in the story that they are not to turn out to be false prophets.

> You people who are camped here,
> Attention! I now say something wonderful:
> The buffalo, the buffalo,
> The buffalo have arrived.

The people gathered around and he kept on singing until some gave him presents of buffalo robes. Others gave him other presents. Then he changed his song, and sang:

> These things which you have given me,
> I do not want them.

He continued to sing until the people said: "Ask him what he wants." They asked him and he sang:

> I want the chief's daughter,
> I want the chief's daughter.

They went and begged the chief to let him have the girl, for they were hungry and they wanted Coyote to tell them where the buffalo were. They brought the girl to Coyote. Then both Coyote and the girl went into the tipi. As Coyote and the girl lay down, he sang;

> You may push my back,
> You may push my back.

Then he sang again and said:

> You have pushed me enough.
> You have pushed me enough.

After he had remained for a while with the girl he went out. A crowd had gathered to hear where the buffalo were. Coyote sang:

> As I climbed the hill yonder
> And sat on the top,
> I looked far over the country.

Then he continued to sing:

> Let the people make an opening,
> For I am hot, for I am hot.

The people made an opening. He sat on his haunches and continued to sing:

> As I sat upon the hill
> I looked down the valley;
> There, from one end to the other,
> The valley was filled
> With, with, with—rosebuds!

As he said "rosebuds," he made a leap, for the people had expected to hear him say buffalo. They closed around him, caught him, and killed him, and he was no more.

141. COYOTE AND THE ARTICHOKE.[1]

Coyote was going along a road alone, when he saw an Artichoke lying on the ground. As he passed by the Artichoke said: "Bite me." Coyote turned around and said: "I will bite you if you say anything more." Coyote started on, and the Artichoke said: "Bite me." Coyote turned around and said: "I will bite you if you say anything more." Coyote started on again, and Artichoke called: "Bite me." Coyote turned around and ate up the Artichoke. All at once he began to expel flatus. Coyote said: "Wah!" He went on and expelled flatus many times, and each time harder than before. Every time he would say: "Wonder! Wonder! Wonder!" He kept on expelling flatus, until he expelled it so hard that it made one of his legs jump up. He kept on until he began to defecate, and he stopped in a hollow, and he defecated until his own excrement washed him away.

142. COYOTE, THE PLUM TREES, AND THE GRAPE VINES.[2]

When the Coyote people were placed upon the earth, each male had a membrum which he carried around his waist. Whenever the women were swimming the men would sit upon the banks and let their membrums crawl into the water. The women would feel of them and would run out from the water, thinking that snakes were coming. The leader of these people had a membrum longer than that of any of the others. He was going along a prairie, when he heard a queer noise in the ground. He stopped and said: "Stop making that noise. I will run my membrum into you and kill you." The noise continued. He took down his membrum, stuck it into the hole, and as he pushed it into the ground something began to chew on it. When he got away from the hole he found that his membrum was only four or five inches long. It had been chewed to pieces. He began to dig and he found pieces of it in a pile. He took a handful and threw it to one side of where he was and said: "Let the plum trees grow from these, and let the trees bear plums." Then he took another handful and threw them in another direction and said: "Let the grape vines come up and bear grapes." Then he began to throw other handfuls in different directions for other berries and nuts to grow. After he had mentioned everything, the insect under the ground

[1] Told by White-Sun, Kitkehahki. This story is told to teach the people that they should not eat too many artichokes; that if they did they would expel flatus.

[2] Told by Thief, Kitkehahki. This story is told to the children to make them believe that all fruit came from the genitals of the first man placed on earth, so that the children should not eat too much fruit, but would give it to the older people.

said: "Go your way. All of your people will have a short membrum. It was never intended that you should have a long one. Now go." Coyote went on, and he found that all the others were in a condition similar to his. If that little insect had not performed the operation, all the male people would have had a membrum which would reach around their waists. In scattering the pieces he gave us plums and other berries over the land.

143. THE SKUNKS AND THE BEAVERS.[1]

There was a prairie, and upon this prairie were two lodges. In one lodge lived the Skunks. In the other lodge lived the Beavers. The Skunks became very hungry and they sent their people out to find something to eat, but they could not find anything. The old Skunk said: "Brothers, I have a plan whereby we can obtain something to eat." All the Skunks said: "What is it?" Then the old Skunk said: "Let our old woman go to the lodge of the Beavers and ask the Beavers to send one of their doctors to treat our young one." The Skunks agreed to do this. The little Skunk lay down and pretended to be sick; then the old woman was sent to the lodge of the Beavers. First the Skunk woman entered the lodge of the Beavers and sang, and in this song she said :

> I came for you, medicine-man of the Beavers;
> I left a young Skunk behind very sick,
> She is rolling upon the ground with pain.

All the Beavers said that it was too bad and that they would send White-Beaver, who knew all kinds of diseases. Said they: "Go and tell your people that White-Beaver will come to doctor the young Skunk." The old woman Skunk went back to the lodge of the Skunks, and as she entered the lodge she said: "Now lie down and be very sick." Then the other Skunks came and pretended to help hold the young Skunk, who was rolling about on the ground. After a while White-Beaver came into the lodge and went near the young Skunk. Then White-Beaver said: "The young Skunk is suffering with pain. Where is the pain?" Then the oldest Skunk said: "The pain comes from the Skunk's rectum." White-Beaver then pressed his hand upon the Skunk's rectum, and said: "It is true. The young Skunk's rectum is in bad shape. It is swollen." Then White-Beaver said: "I will suck it with my mouth. I will draw out the pain from the rectum." As the Beaver placed his mouth upon the rectum of the Skunk, the young Skunk made a discharge, so that the Beaver rolled

[1] Told by Little-Chief, Pitahauirat. The story is told to teach the children that the beaver family is a medicine family, but that the skunks have greater power than the beavers.

over upon the ground. As he did so the older Skunks got up and killed the Beaver with clubs. Then the young Skunk became well. The older Skunks then skinned the Beaver and cooked the meat and ate it. They were careful not to throw the bones out of the lodge, but to place the skin and all the bones and the entrails together, and then they took them and dumped them into the river.

The next day they sent the old woman again to the lodge of the Beavers. When the woman entered, she sang again, telling the Beavers that the young Skunk was very sick; that they wanted a doctor to come and allay her pain. The older Beavers said: "What is the matter? The Beaver who went to doctor that child is the best one we had." The woman then said: "He failed to cure her and felt so ashamed that he has gone to another place to make his home." Then the Beavers said: "We will send the next best man." The old woman Skunk went to their lodge and said: "Another one is coming." Then the young Skunk was put upon the ground and she began to cry with pain again. She stretched out her legs and the other Skunks held her down. The Beaver came in and they led him to the young Skunk. The Beaver touched the earth, then began to feel the young Skunk all over the body. When he got his hand upon the rectum of the Skunk, he said: "It is true. The young Skunk is with pain in the rectum. I will cure her by placing my mouth upon the rectum." Then the Beaver reached down his head, and as he was about to put his mouth upon the Skunk's rectum the Skunk made a discharge and blinded the Beaver, when the older Skunks took up sticks and killed the Beaver. The Skunks skinned him, cooked the meat, and saved all of the bones. The bones they placed in the skin and threw them into the water. The Skunks were getting fat. They sent for another doctor the next day, and he also came and was killed in the same way as the other two. The Skunks saved the bones and put them into the skin and threw them into the water. The next day they went for another doctor. The Beavers wanted to know where the other doctors were, but the woman Skunk said: "They were ashamed of themselves, for they did not cure our Skunk, and so they have gone to make their home in another place." Another one came and was killed in the same manner as the others. The meat was cooked and eaten; the bones were saved and all placed in the skin and thrown into the creek.

They kept on going for the Beavers until they had killed all but one, the one little one. Then the woman Skunk said: "There is but one little Beaver there and we will let it alone." They said: "Very well." The young Beaver became lonely and it came out of the lodge and went towards the creek. It sat upon the bank and cried. A diving bird came and said: "Young Beaver, what are you crying about." It said: "The Skunks invited our medicine-men to doctor their young one, and the doctors never returned." The bird said: "Come with me." The bird placed the young Beaver near the water, and said: "Jump into the water here." The young Beaver jumped into the water and came to the lodge of the other Beavers that had been killed. Then one of the Beavers came out and said to the bird: "We thank you for bringing our young one here. Tell the Skunks that they shall never be our friends; that we are their enemies, though we are glad that they placed us in the water. Here we shall make our home for all time."

Ever since, the Beavers have lived in the water, and when the people in olden times killed the Beavers they were careful not to lose any of the Beavers' bones. They would throw the bones all into the water, believing that the bones would again turn into Beavers.

144. HOW WILD-CAT KILLED THE BEAR.[1]

In the thick timber lived Wild-Cat with her young ones. One day she went off hunting. While she was gone a Bear came to her den and ate all her young ones. When the Wild-Cat came back her young ones were gone. She cried and followed the Bear's trail. As she went along she sang. After a while the Bear heard the Cat singing, and he went to meet her. When the Cat saw the Bear she called him names. The Bear became angry, but before he knew it the Wild-Cat had jumped on him; and as she was small she clung to his belly, and clawed it until she cut it open. She took out her young ones and carried them back home; then she went back to the place where she left the Bear and there she found Coyote. Coyote said: "My sister, I watched over the Bear while you were gone, so that nobody else would come to eat him up. Take what meat you want and leave the rest for me." The Cat then said: "My brother, you may have the Bear. I am glad I killed him, for he ate up my young ones, but I do not want the meat." Coyote took the Bear off to his young ones and gave them the meat, and told them that he had killed the Bear. He said: "I am a great warrior; I not only can fight in battles, but I can fight animals and kill them." Just then an old Bear came, and Coyote told the young ones to run, for he had to fight the Bear. When he saw that the young Coyotes were gone, he turned and ran in another direction. Coyote kept on running until he ran himself to death.

[1] Told by White-Eagle, Skidi. The story is told to the children to teach them that although the bear is a fierce animal, a little animal like the wild-cat could kill it if it slew its young.

145. HOW RABBIT LOST HIS TAIL.[1]

Rabbit was going along the creek, jumping here and there, and he saw the limb of a willow. He tried to jump over the limb, and as he jumped over, his tail caught on the end of the limb and he pulled so hard to get loose that he pulled his tail off. He left his tail on the limb and went on crying, and at the same time singing:

> Did I lose my tail in the timber?
> Did I lose my tail in the timber?
> My tail, Rabbit's tail?

Turtle moved out near to Rabbit. He spoke and said: "You say you lost your tail?" Rabbit said: "Yes." "Why don't you look behind you and see if your tail is not hanging on to the willows?" "Very well," said Rabbit, "I will go and hunt for my tail." "But," said Turtle, "since you have lost your tail upon the willows, the willows will have white fur at the ends in the fall, so that the people will always know that you lost your tail upon the willow limbs." Rabbit went back and there his tail was upon the willow. He jumped up and took the tail from the limb, and carried it to the Turtle, who replaced his tail. Rabbit thanked Turtle and went on his way, singing:

> Now I have my tail,
> Now I have my tail,
> Now I have my tail.
> Turtle crawling on the ground,
> Now I have my tail,
> Helped me to find it.

This is why we have white burrs upon the willows.

146. THE WHITE AND BLACK RATS.[2]

A black and a white were the first two Rats that were put upon the earth. The White Rat was going upstream to the west, while the black one was going towards the east. The Black Rat was saying: "I am hunting for food. I am hunting for food." The White Rat was also crying: "I am hunting for food. I am hunting for food." Upon the limb where they met, sat Magpie. He said: "Stop crying and listen to me." The two Rats stopped crying, and Magpie sang to the Black Rat:

[1] Told by Woman-Yellow-Corn, one of the oldest women among the Skidi, and a member of the medicine-society. The story is told to teach people how the rabbit lost its tail.
[2] Told by Woman-Yellow-Corn, Skidi. The story is told to the children to teach them that the white rats were given earth-nuts, while the black rats were given artichokes, and that these two animals gave these two things to the people for food.

Now there must be rat trails in the forest,
Now there must be rat trails in the forest,
Made by Black Rats, made by Black Rats.
The artichoke vines will climb
Upon the red willows, and there
If you dig you will find artichokes,
From this time you will find artichokes
With eyes like an ash tree.

Then Magpie sang to the White Rat:

Hunting ground beans, hunting ground beans;
That is hunting something, hunting something,
Among the willows you will find earth-nuts,
Earth-nuts by the willows under the ground.
You shall go there to the willows;
There you will find soft, crumbling soil.
Hereafter, White Rat,
You shall live on earth-nuts.

Each of the Rats went his way, singing: "The errand bird of the god in the north, who is known as 'Ready-to-Give,' has given us artichokes to eat."

Ever since that time the White Rat has been known as the ground-bean Rat and the Black Rat as the artichoke Rat.

147. TURTLE'S WAR PARTY.[1]

Turtle started on the war-path. On the way he met Mosquito. Mosquito asked Turtle where he was going and Turtle said: "We have a root sticking into us and we are mad. I am on the war-path." Mosquito then asked that he be allowed to join, and the Turtle said: "All right." After a while Cricket met the war party and asked that he be allowed to join, and they consented. The three warriors traveled on until they came to a lodge. They entered the lodge and tried to kill the people who were inside, but they were discovered. They caught Turtle, Cricket went into a hole, and Mosquito lighted on a place in the fire. They were going to put Turtle into the fire, but he said that he was not afraid of the fire and that he wished they would put him in, for he would scatter the fire all over the room. At last the people said: "Let us throw him into the water." Turtle cried and said: "I am afraid of the water." The people said: "He is afraid of the water; let us throw him into the water." They threw him into the water, and when he struck the water he raised his head, poked his tongue out to the people, and said: "The water is my home; I

[1] Told by Thief, Kitkehahki. This story is told to the children to teach them that they should not join a war party which had weak men in it, but that they should join a strong party, and theirs would be successful.

fooled you." The other members of the war party were not found. The people knew that they were still in the lodge, but they could not find them. Finally, Mosquito went out of the lodge and flew into a swampy country, where he got his legs stuck in the mud. Ever since the time of the Turtle's war party, crickets have lived in people's lodges, and mosquitoes have lived near swampy places.

148. THE ANIMALS' WAR PARTY.[1]

Many of the people once gathered together and went on the war-path. They had heard of three men who lived at a certain place who were very hard to kill. Many people had tried to kill them, but none had ever been successful, and the ground about their camp was covered with skulls of those who had tried and failed. Among the many people who went out on the war-path were three little warriors, Rabbit, Turtle, and Spider-Woman. When they were near the lodge of the three men who were hard to kill, the three little warriors boasted that they were going to kill them. They told all the men to get their bows and arrows ready; that they were about to make an attack. Rabbit charged, riding a mule, and singing this song:

> I make the charge on the first man,
> Look out!   Look out!
> Thus they are frightened away.

Then Turtle came with a spear and something on his back, and he also sang a song. The spear that Turtle had was of grass, and the thing that he had upon his back was a shield. Spider-Woman came out and said: "Kill the other two, but I want to catch the youngest of the three men." The men saw them coming, and the youngest of the three said: "Let us make a fire, for the enemy are coming. Let us cook for the enemy." The three men went out with fire in front of them, and as they came to the chief of the men on the enemy's side, the fire touched him and all of his warriors and killed them. Those whom the fire did not kill were hit upon the head with a war club and killed. At last they killed Rabbit and Turtle. The youngest of the three took Spider-Woman and had all the fun killing her. Thus the three men, who were Hawks, destroyed the great warriors who had come to kill them.

[1] Told by Thief, Kitkehahki.   This story is told to show how the rabbit, turtle, and spider-woman made a charge against the warriors who were the hawks.   The hawks were known among the Indians as warriors and they killed the rabbit, turtle, and spider-woman.   The story is to show that the warriors should always imitate the hawks instead of the rabbit, turtle, or spider-woman.

ABSTRACTS

ABSTRACTS.

1. ORIGIN OF THE CHAUI.

Tirawa creates heavens and earth and a woman. At Moon's suggestion man is sent to earth as her mate. The pair are directed as to use of terms "father" and "mother," and are instructed to build earth-lodge according to certain plan, and are told of symbolism of lodge. They are further instructed as to fireplace, altar, and sacred bundle. They are also given bow and arrow, hoe, and colored grains of corn. They are instructed how to make earthenware vessels and how to cook. Woman enters lodge first on its completion and sacrifices corn; man later sacrifices fat of animal. They eat corn meal mush and have increase. They are given dances, one of which is briefly described and is used in calling buffalo.

2. THE FOUR GODS IN THE WEST.

First, man and his wife occupy earth-lodge facing west. After they have increased they all move west. They stop and gamble. After game, man remains behind and meets strange woman covered with hair. In morning her tracks appear as animal tracks. Later, woman comes and passes near man, who runs after her, while she turns into buffalo. She leads him to her lodge. Four men sit in west, representing the four gods. In lodge are parfleches of meat. The man returns toward his home in dazed condition, is awakened by bluebird, and finding buffalo robe on his shoulders, knows that his vision is true. His people kill buffalo and sacrifice heart and tongue to four gods in the west, as directed.

3. THE SMALL-ANTS' BUNDLE AND THE BUFFALO.

Before time of corn and buffalo, people wandered about living upon roots, etc. Going north they find small game. They are led still farther north by boy who has been directed by Moon. Thus led, they arrive at their new home and build grass-lodges. Famine is imminent. The young man fasts upon hill; is directed by Moon, whose reflection he sees in water, to continue fasting; drinks of spring as commanded and encounters old woman. Second time he encounters still older woman; third time, middle-aged woman. Next time he is called to enter into cave, from which the spring issued, and old woman directs his attention to young girl, who changes herself into woman of various ages, thus representing the phases of moon which she now declares herself to be. They go outside and woman gives boy ring and javelin game for men, and basket or dice game for women. Young man returns home. They play with buffalo game sticks, while women play with dice. Young man returns to cave, sees many earth-lodges, which are really ant-hills, which she tells boy will serve as models for people's lodges. She gives him bowl of corn for the people of his village, and also some meat. With this he feeds his people, for the food is magical. He returns to old woman's lodge; is told that she proposes sending buffalo, and gives instuctions as to what is to be done with hide, skull, meat, etc. She gives boy sacred bundle, to be known as Small-Ants' bundle. Boy returns to

473

his village, where the people are clamoring for food. Chief is invited to his lodge; is told how they may obtain buffalo. Ceremonies are performed. Buffalo come, first one being sacred and treated in accordance with Moon's instructions. After people have been fed, they construct earth-lodges. Buffalo in meantime having entirely left their cave, young man places feathered stick in ground four times. He returns to cave, where men give him seeds, which he gives to his people. On returning to cave he finds that spring has become dry and cave has disappeared. The people become dissatisfied and divide up into different bands, which disperse.

4. THE FOUR GODS OF THE NORTH.

Tirawa instructs man facing north to point toward the north, his two thumbs being placed together. Upon them are imprints of two faces. On repeating this performance two additional faces appear, which represent the four gods of the north, who sent Kingfisher upon earth, who divided land from water, and being touched by the man becomes woman. Man holds ceremony in honor of four gods and transmits ceremony to his descendants.

5. LONG-TONGUE, THE ROLLING HEAD.

Four girls gathering wood make snow snakes, which they glide over ice. They are attracted toward north by strange odor. In their search for source of odor, three give up; fourth continues to cedar-covered hill, where she finds rock-lodge. Being invited, she enters lodge with young man, who claims that lodge is place of origin of scent. Inside, girl finds that lodge has no opening except small smoke hole. Young man lays down on buffalo robe and becomes old man. In lodge is sacred bundle and five rattles. In morning man, now young again, speaks, stone door moves, and he leaves lodge. Boy speaks to girl, telling her occupant of lodge is Long-Tongue, a fierce rolling skull. She is instructed how to make her escape. Her informant is Raven. As Long-Tongue enters lodge he becomes old man. Following day girl asks permission to leave lodge. Outside she picks handful of berries and is soon left alone by Long-Tongue. Again Raven addresses her. On Long-Tongue's return she louses him, throwing away ticks and cracking berries to represent killing them. Having removed last tick, Long-Tongue dies. She gathers up ticks, carries them to entrance, stone door moves, she leaves and throws ticks away and returns to lodge. Soon Long-Tongue becomes alive and again leaves lodge. At girl's request Long-Tongue brings in buffalo, which girl skins and takes care of meat. Next she makes tallow. Raven removes from sacred bundle arrow planes and flint knife. Girl makes three tallow balls. She digs hole in ground and fills it with tallow, and covers earth in center of lodge with tallow, smearing some also on side of walls and on bundle. Girl gets on Raven's back, carrying bundle of objects. They leave lodge, and when Raven grows tired he places girl on ground and flies overhead, directing her. They go toward east. Long-Tongue on return-ing finds lodge empty, but before starting on pursuit begins to eat tallow which girl had placed in lodge, thus losing much time. He returns after girl, and his pursuit is checked as she drops on ground arrow planes, which multiply and Long-Tongue attempts to gather them up. Again he begins pursuit, but stops as she strikes him with tallow ball, fragments of which he gathers and eats. She throws second and third tallow balls, checking his pursuit. She then stops him with her flint arrow-point, which multiplies. Next she stops him with arrow, which turns into dogwood timber, where Long-Tongue stops to cut arrow shaft. Next she drops sinew, which becomes buffalo, thus detaining Long-Tongue, who stops to gather sinew. Again he stops to gather turkeys, caused by the girl dropping turkey feathers. Next she drops flint knife, which makes great gulch in earth, which checks Long-Tongue's pursuit. Girl sees in front of her mound, outside which man is making bow. Girl explains her flight; is invited into mound by man, where she finds herself in lodge and sits down under sacred bundle. Long-Tongue now overtakes her and calls to owner of lodge to release her, but is struck on head by club and his skull split in two; but pieces immediately come together again. Next, man strikes him with flint axe. One piece of skull flies to west into sky and becomes moon; other piece flies up into east and becomes sun. Thus human images are found upon sun and moon. Woman lives with man and her younger brother. Later, other brothers return and they decide that girl should remain with them as their sister. They open bundle and she asks for ear of corn in it, which they finally give her, as she claims to be daughter of Evening-Star. She plants corn, which increases. In autumn she gives birth to child, whose father is North-Star, which visited her as redbird. Instructed by old man, woman now goes to her husband in north. The six brothers go to east and begin traveling toward west. In time they are to be joined by woman and her child and North-Star, at which time world will come to an end. These seven brothers were great warriors and were Hawks.

6. HOW EVENING-STAR'S DAUGHTER WAS OVERCOME.

In east is village near river. The heavenly beings come down to earth and aided by their animals they build earth-lodge, over which Evening-Star's daughter is to rule. She sends her four gods to watch over her daughter, who is guardian of bundle. Evening-Star, wife of Morning-Star, kept Morning-Star's medicine objects in bundle, among which is war club. In lodge stands heavenly gods according to their places in heavens. Evening-Star, desiring that women should be superior to men, sends her daughter to kill off all young men. People of eastern village often try to visit western village, especially to marry daughter of Evening-Star, but are always killed. Poor boy fasting is visited by red-painted strange being who wears leggings with scalps and feathers. He is given war club and is instructed how to win maiden. Boy returns home and asks old man to lead him to western village. They start west and are met by young girl. She strikes ground with war club and canyon appears in front of couple. Boy drops moccasin which bears the symbol of Morning-Star into canyon, as he had been instructed. Canyon closes; moccasin is returned. They continue and girl causes wide river in front of them, which is made to disappear by boy in same manner. Thick timber is thus also overcome. Animals appear from girl's lodge that are overcome. Boy is told that before he can marry girl he must get baby-board. In his search for board he receives help from Morning-Star and goes to animals' lodge, where he is told of beavers' lodge, where baby-boards are made, but where fire kept by Turtle is so hot as to prevent anyone from obtaining board. Coyote offers to get cradle, but is driven out by sparks. Hawk makes similar attempt. Magpie steals one, but fire follows, and it passes board to Diving Duck, who enters stream of water and fire disappears trying to follow duck. Boy takes board to girl's tipi, where it is received by one of priests and placed on west side of lodge. Boy is then told to get tying string for cradle. Again he is assisted and returns with otter string. Next, he is directed to get mat for baby-board. He is assisted by Morning-Star, who gives him arrow with which he shoots buffalo. Next he gets wild-cat's hide with hawk's assistance. First night boy attempts to enter girl's tipi he encounters serpent, which he destroys with Morning-Star moccasin. Next night on attempting to enter he encounters two bears, which he kills with moccasin. Next night he kills panthers; and next two nights he kills wild-cats and coyotes. Coyotes are willing to help and are not killed. Following night he is refused and cries till Morning-Star again takes pity on him and gives him flint stone, and directs as to what he shall do. That night boy rids girl's vagina of teeth by means of flint stone. She becomes human being and his wife. He is addressed by Morning-Star and is instructed concerning bundles, one of which is that of girl, and other, which he is to make, represents Morning-Star, the two together being Morning-Star bundles. Morning-Star, having thus aided boy by giving him instructions of various sorts, asks in return maiden in sacrifice, saying that during ceremony of sacrifice all obstacles met with in his overcoming girl should be reproduced. He is further instructed as to use of baby-board, which is to bear Morning-Star symbol. Gods now return to their places in heavens, and animals present in lodge return to timber.

7. THE DAUGHTER OF THE EVENING-STAR AND HER SACRED BUNDLE.

In sole earth-lodge beyond grass-lodge village in the west dwells beautiful girl, in attempting to marry whom many young men lose their lives. Success in attempt to marry her means sacred bundle from Tirawa, and other blessings. Rich boy decides to marry her, goes north, and fasts. On fourth day red-painted man stands by him. This man, the Sun, gives him bow and arrow, and tells him that girl is daughter of Evening-Star. Returning to his own village he starts out, accompanied by old man, to west. They encounter and overcome difficulties—deep canyon, stream of water, thick timber, two bears, and two mountain-lions. In meantime girl has been forced back toward her own lodge, and as boy strikes ground with his bow remaining animals become quiet, even great serpent. Girl, in defense of her action, accuses boy of desiring to know secrets of Tirawa. Entering lodge they find sacred bundle and four priests, representing winds, clouds, lightnings, and thunders. Boy is sent for baby-board and other accessories of cradle. In this task he is aided by mysterious being, presumably Morning-Star. The four old men now give bundle to girl, and send them forth as man and wife, men and animals in lodge returning into heavens and timber. Boy and girl return to his people and teach them to build earth-lodges, and explain symbolism of earth-lodge.

8. CONTEST BETWEEN THE MORNING-STAR AND THE MOON.

Mysterious Man, living by himself in lodge on hill overlooking valley, always returns successful from his hunt. Famine prevails in village. They desire to appeal to Mysterious Man on hill, but are afraid, on account of snakes. Spider-Woman is willing to challenge him. Chief invites the young man to be his son-in-law. He declines, for he says it is his duty to feed snakes; that he should consult with them. Again he is successful and scatters meat to feed snakes. When young man consults snakes, they express their willingness, providing young man can release them from power of witch. Next he releases buffalo from cave and people kill them. He releases buffalo again on two following days. Witch attempts to prevent him from releasing buffalo another time, and waves her robe, which has on it picture of Morning-Star. The boy shoots at this, and instead appears new moon symbol, thus revealing her true identity. Boy shoots again and quarter moon appears; again, three-quarter moon appears; fourth time full moon appears. As he shoots at it again it turns into spider, which he kills with his bow and arrow. Placing spider on his bow he shoots it into heavens, where spider remains as Moon. Young man again releases buffalo, which scatter over land; also deer, antelope, etc. He feeds snakes and returns to heavens as Morning-Star, leaving substitute in his place, who goes to village and marries. People now increase, because Spider-Woman has disappeared.

9. ORIGIN OF THE BASKET DICE GAME.

At beginning, gods make mud images of girl and boy. They come to life, and bow and arrows are given them. To determine duration of life, and whether it should be night or day, animals pass by, and as they kill spotted one, day and night intervene. Man hears dancing. Accompanied by his wife, he approaches lodge and they are invited by woman, the Moon, to enter. Within, they see four old men and many girls, daughters of Moon. Young man learns dances and receives seeds, and they are taught dice game. Woman dancing in west is Evening-Star, standing before four old men. In lodge are four other dancers, daughters of Big-Black-Meteoric Star. The two learn many things, especially symbolism of basket game, basket representing Moon, mother of all stars, who also helps Big-Black-Meteoric-Star to cure people.

10. THE ORIGIN OF A NEW BAND.

In village in north poor boy is invited to play with son of medicine-man and son of chief. He finally accepts and urges them to learn ceremonies, etc., from their fathers. When they have gained this knowledge the three set out on war-path, meet man, whom they kill, and take possession of his wives, and thus found new band, compelling their offspring and their wives to adopt their language. After a while they set out toward their former home. The poor boy goes to hill and cries. He is importuned by chief's son and medicine-man's son to desist. After repeated attempts to urge poor boy to go on, he explains as reason of his desire to remain behind his wish that, inasmuch as boys knew ceremonies of their fathers, they should found permanent band with its own place of habitation. This they do.

11. HOW THE PEOPLE GOT THE CROW LANCE.

Leader of war party announces necessity of sacrifice of raccoon. Raccoon is taken and sacrificed by fire. Some, protesting against this form of sacrifice and fearing bad luck, return home; others continue on war-path. Man who made sacrifice while out as scout is seen by remaining warriors to be attacked and overcome by warriors, who are Crows and Coyotes. Recognizing evil omen, they also return home. Man who had been killed that night is restored to life, and sees people dancing who are painted black and carry black lance. In morning he desires to follow some deer, and then some antelopes, but is restrained by Crows. Next day he kills fawn, on which he makes his meal. That night he hears strange noises from mound, but is restrained from going to place by Crows. He is restrained fourth time. But fifth time Crows disappear in tree under which man had been lying, and just then hill appears into which man is invited, where he finds himself in cave in which Crows dance and make him member of the Crow Lance society. He is taught songs and ritual. Man had been scared simply by Coyotes and Crows. Coyotes wanted to eat him up, but Crows preferred to give him their ceremonies.

12. THE ORIGIN OF THE PIPE-STICK CEREMONY.

A man in dream sees monster of immense size with head of many colors surmounted by white eagle feather. He decides to visit place where he had vision of monster. On river bank he sees water spouting. Monster lifts its head up and down from water four times, drawing its breath and drawing man toward water. On opening his eyes he finds monster and animals of all kinds. Monster proclaims that it controls all water beings. He is taught mysteries of animals and their ways of doctoring. Man on his way home collects willows with which to make image of monster in his lodge, and kills some buffalo, one of which he is to use in making effigy. Lacking further information as to how to construct effigy, he is visited in vision by monster and is told how to capture eagle in order to obtain feather for head. He is told to go to eagle's nest. The eagles are unable to help him and he meets wild-cat, representing sky and stars, which teaches him how to cheat people. Evening-Star then addresses him and gives him corn. Next, woodpecker helps him with stick upon which to tie corn, explaining that when bundle is complete it shall be efficacious in bringing rain. Ducks offer to assist, and next Owls, and next the four gods in heavens. Different animals also visit him in his visions and give him songs. He also receives a song from Sun as it comes up. He is also taught how he may decorate child to represent Tirawa during ceremony, red line of paint around face indicating that Sun has touched child. Child is to be placed on nest of oriole, thus showing that its path should be hard but safe, for oriole's nest is high in tree and can not be blown away by storms nor can snakes get at it. He is further instructed that child is to be permitted to return home and that paint on its face is to be allowed to wear off.

13. THE GIRL WHO MARRIED A STAR.

One of two girls sleeping in summer arbor wishes that she might marry star. Awakening, she finds herself in strange country, wife of star. She is warned not to dig turnips, but does so after birth of boy. While digging she sees earth below and people walking around. She saves sinew of animals killed by her husband and makes rope by which she descends with boy, but rope does not quite reach earth. Her husband discovers her absence, drops stone downward, which kills her. Boy remains near his mother for several days. During thunder shower boy follows dry path until he comes to tipi occupied by old woman and her grandson. The two boys grow up together. They are warned not to go to certain dangerous places, disobey, and destroy certain monsters—bears, monster, mountain-lion, and other wicked animals. Afterwards boys return to their country, where Star-Boy becomes great man. He disappears and is supposed to have returned to heaven.

14. THE GRAIN-OF-CORN BUNDLE.

Man of prairie hears woman crying, and going to place finds no one there. He dreams that night of seeing woman, who speaks to him. The next night he goes where he had been told to meet woman, who is beautiful. She is grain of corn, having her origin in Evening-Star. She tells man to carry her with him, keeping her in his quiver. Man goes on war-path and his guardian informs him of enemy. According to instructions, he makes sacred bundle, which contains corn. While off to gambling ground one day his mother opens bundle and converses with corn. On his return, corn tells him of fact. She also helps him on war-path, but asks him to refrain from marrying for two years and to plant her as seed corn. At proper time man marries and his descendants are many. He leaves instructions obtained from Corn-Woman concerning ceremonies, especially those respecting planting of corn.

15. THE METEORITE PEOPLE.

Wonderful being, Pahokatawa, is killed and cut up by enemy, and animals devour his flesh, but heavenly gods agree to restore him and signify their desire to earthly gods, who go and restore meat and bones, but can not find man's brains. Afterwards, he visits earth from time to time as meteorite, often warning them of enemy, and telling people that they must not be afraid of meteors or shooting stars. Afterwards, men walking over prairie dig out bright-colored stone in shape of turnip. They regard it as meteor sent by Pahokatawa. Offerings are made to it, and it is believed to be part of Morning-Star. It is believed that as long as stone is present, diseases could not enter camp.

16. BUFFALO WIFE AND CORN WIFE.

Young man in village does not associate with other boys, but daily climbs hill, where he remains by himself, paying special care to his personal adornment. On his return in evening, he is an eagle. Once while on hill he hears singing coming from Buffalo women in east and calling some one in west. Each woman has pair of moccasins, and while he is thinking which one to accept, one places one on one foot and other one on other foot, and he decides to marry them both. With his wives he returns and, with his mother, they all live together. Buffalo-Wife gives birth to boy and Corn-Wife to girl. The children quarrel over spoon and ear of corn. Mothers become angry and Buffalo-Wife leaves with her child. Corn-Wife and her child disappear under ground. Man assumes shape of eagle and flies toward east until he comes to his Buffalo-Wife and son, now a calf. At night she turns into woman and selects her tipi. Eagle-Man becomes man, enters the tipi, but is repulsed by his wife, though his little boy plays with him. In morning, wife and child turn into buffalo, and leave. He follows them as before, on across stream of water. They cross high mountains and finally enter woman's village, where man is asked to pick out his wife from other cows and his son from other calves. Before entering her lodge he calms fierce bear, whereby rock entrance to her lodge opens. Passing through, entrance falls, but he is unhurt, as he turns into breath feather. He is able to distinguish his wife, being instructed by his son to look for mark he has placed on her tail. Husband is invited into sweat-lodge, where he finds bulls which attempt to prevent him from going out. When steam heat becomes oppressive he turns into badger and thus is able to get his nose from under lodge and so can stand heat. Then husband is sent to tree with eagle nest in it, where storm rages, with lightning. On his addressing eagles storm ceases. He returns with wood. He is challenged to run race with old buffalo cow, race to be to the four ends of earth. Should he win, people are to live upon buffalo; otherwise, buffalo are to feed upon human beings. He turns himself into Magpie and they start. The old woman cow, pointing with her cane in direction, is at once there. Thus she gains on Eagle-Man, but at his request Badgers dig holes into which she falls. Thus he begins to gain. He wins, and buffalo are released from cave. Certain spotted buffalo are driven back, together with buffalo with two heads. White buffalo, however, escapes. Then old woman tries to make love to Eagle-Man and warns him not to drink water from ragged woman. He does so, thus exciting people, who accuse him of drinking chief's water, as ragged woman was chief's wife. Chief becomes angry and digs up earth. Although his body is nothing but bones, he is chief of buffalo. Eagle-Man attempts to shoot him, and is told by Mocking-Bird that vulnerable part of chief is hole in his chest. Thus Eagle-Man kills buffalo chief. Thereafter buffalo scatter and Eagle-Man returns to his people.

17. THE POOR BOY WHO MARRIED THE CHIEF'S DAUGHTER.

Poor, dirty boy is always left behind in moving camp and lives upon pieces of sinew and refuse meat. Poor people are good to him, but well-to-do mistreat him. He visits chief's tipi, but is ordered out by his daughter, although chief asks him to be seated and orders his daughter to cook for poor boy. She refuses, but offers to cook if he will provide water. Thereafter, boy often visits the chief's tipi, though abused by chief's daughter. Finally she beats him with stick and he goes upon hill and mourns. People break camp and leave behind fine horse, now badly crippled. Boy goes to pony and travels with it, and pony now rapidly regains its strength. Boy grows stronger. On journey, pony speaks to boy, telling him he had purposely lamed himself so as to be with him. He tells him to go to chief's tipi, sit at entrance, and obey chief's daughter, for from now on she will begin to love him. Presently the girl so desires boy that she goes out to find him. He offers to run away with her, asking her to get sewing implements. They make home in timber. Absence of boy and girl is noticed. Boy revisits village during attack by enemy, of which he is warned by his horse, and he succeeds in driving off enemy. Four times he assists in victory, and people give victory dance. Boy's wife enters village gaily attired, and chief rejoices to learn that his daughter married poor boy.

18. THE CANNIBAL WITCH AND THE DOY WHO CONQUERED THE BUFFALO.

Witch-Woman lives in prairie by herself with her Poor Boy and four powerful dogs. Boy has black bow with two strings and four black arrows. He is great hunter. From time to time he is urged by witch to kill human beings for her food. Boy always escapes capture because of magic flight of his arrow. Buffalo knowing woman's habits, become angry, hold council, and send two young buffalo to get boy to kill him, thus stopping witch's supply of meat. Boy in meantime, sitting on hill, has vision, goes to his grandmother and tells her that he is about to make journey. She asks for four additional bodies, which he succeeds in securing. As he is leaving he instructs witch as to care of dogs, one of them to be kept tied all the time. He travels many days without food and encounters two buffalo, one of which he shoots. As he is about to eat one of kidneys, Buffalo speaks to him, directing him to put back piece of meat he has in his hand and to look away. Turning back, he sees woman wearing new buffalo robe. She restores life to fallen Buffalo. They follow boy to hollow, where they turn into women to secure from him details of secret of his ability to kill human beings and elude pursuit. Women start to return to their country as Buffalo, and boy follows. At night Buffalo become women again and obtain further details of his secret. He even relates how he may be killed. They approach Buffalo village, where he sees Buffalo playing with game sticks. He is warned by old Buffalo that Buffalo wish to kill him. Old Buffalo is chief, who lives in west and promises to help boy. Boy follows him, and he instructs him that he is to dive four times in pond in front of tipi of Buffalo who has white spot on his forehead and who is especially desirous of killing boy. He does so, and White Spot refuses to take his usual bath. Boy is challenged to smoke contest with White Spot, but is directed by Buffalo chief as to secret of victory. In contest they are to see who can cause smoke to ascend the higher. Boy wins, as smoke from his pipe ascends on one side of the tree and comes down on other. Next, drinking contest is proposed, the object being to drain pond. Again boy is assisted, and during contest uses horns given him by Buffalo chief, which enable him to be victorious. On following day runners are to race, but the Buffalo on boy's side win, as he lashes them with his bow string. Boy now strings his bow and kills several Buffalo, but White Spot's friends attack him and he disappears. Then White Spot appeals to Buffalo women as to how to take boy, who tell him that he keeps ahead by magic of his bow, which is black snake. They finally draw near him and he hides in bunch of grass, from which he is blown by bull. Boy disappears and hides in pond, which Buffalo drink dry. As Buffalo blows his breath on mud hole in center, boy jumps on dry land and then disappears. He goes to timber and climbs high tree. Boy urinates in his robe, drops of which fall upon bulls, who think it is rain because boy has been killed, for they see no clouds. Presently bulls discover boy and they select five bulls to butt down tree, first trying to lift it up by the roots. As tree begins to totter, boy yells. His call is heard by his dogs at home, and his grandmother releases chief dog, who starts after boy, followed by others. Dogs drive away Buffalo, tree falls, and boy is unhurt. Boy tells his grandmother to cut up meat and that thereafter she should not eat human flesh. They return home and boy tells his grandmother to go north with bag of seeds, and to plant seeds, and to depend on them for her food. He releases his dog and puts on his costume. Old woman goes north. Boy goes south; is thereafter known as great warrior, and goes to land of the sun. Buffalo in council decide that they have been fairly beaten and that henceforth people should smoke, offering Buffalo whiffs of smoke; that they were beaten in the water contest and henceforth people should make spoons from their horns; that in race they were beaten and that henceforth people should be superior to them in running; and that they should seek grass when hungry and water when thirsty, so that people might find them easily; but that when people have multiplied they should use buffalo robes for children to lie upon and urinate upon, as boy had urinated upon buffalo. White Spot is killed, as are buffalo girls, and they go to north, where they now stand as minor gods and send buffalo to the people.

19. THE WARRIOR AND THE BLACK LIGHTNING ARROW.

Young man on war-path travels west to mountainous country and suffers hunger. Leader, being blamed for their misfortune, ascends hill to pray. While he is absent warriors are successful. On fourth night, man praying, facing west, is enveloped in storm, accompanied by lightning and thunder, during which he falls into trance. On awakening in morning he finds on his breast small black arrow with flint point and stone shaft. He rejoins other warriors, explains his experience, offers smoke to gods and to his arrow, promising that if he neglects arrow it may return, and he fastens arrow on necklace over his breast. They resume their journey, and next night leader in vision is visited by protector of warriors, who tells him where they may find enemy's camp. They advance, capture ponies, and escape; leader returning home offers on way horse hair to his protector. Again they set out on war-path. Encountering buffalo, he starts to kill one, but leaves his wonderful arrow and friends behind. As he aims at buffalo dark cloud comes. He runs back, obtains his arrow, and his friends attempt to help him retain it. It thunders and lightens, and blows like flapping of wings. Nevertheless, arrow makes its escape, and returns to clouds, and becomes part of lightning. The disconsolate warrior mourns; is visited by same mysterious being, who reminds him of condition under which arrow was given. He tells him he will be great warrior, but never chief. Hereafter he only goes on war party when success has been predicted for him in vision.

20. SPOTTED-HORSE, A BRAVE AND A CHIEF.

Man in dream sees mysterious being with painted buffalo robe, lariat, and bundle, and is told to stand on hill for four days, whereupon he will receive power. Obeying his instructions, he finds sun glass and blue stone, which he makes into pipe, the stem of which he does not perforate. Next he finds wild-cat, which he skins to become part of sacred bundle which he has been directed to make. Having assembled the parts of his bundle, he lights his pipe with glass, and smoke passes through stem, though it is not perforated. He is importuned by his friends to take pity on them and allow them to join him on war-path. He consents, saying that his protector is the Sun. In journeying he always passes on east side of his companions. He becomes warrior and is successful in taking ponies. He becomes chief. The bundle and accompanying rites are transmitted to young man, who changes his name with each fresh success on war-path. As Spotted-Horse-Chief he leads party against Sioux, success being attributed to rite he performs in connection with bundle.

21. THE BOY WHO WAS GIVEN POWER TO CALL THE BUFFALO.

Early in winter people travel west on buffalo hunt until they pause exhausted. A certain boy decides to look for buffalo. With moccasins filled with pemmican he starts out. Cold and discouraged he sees artichoke, which he eats, feels better, and a voice, the Wind, tells him that he has been protected since long before birth. As yet he sees no one, but hears noise like feather striking dry buffalo robe. He sees more artichokes, which he gathers, and now he sees a man wearing hawk's head dress, which he gives to boy. In return he asks that boy bring him offerings of red paint, blue beads, eagle feathers, and tobacco. Boy returns home with his artichokes, secures offerings, makes his offerings as directed, and his parents hunt artichokes, but find ground beans. Next, boy kills bear and then discovers buffalo, and becomes efficient in calling buffalo.

22. THE SON OF WIND, READY-TO-GIVE.

People preparing to break camp discover that young girl is pregnant. She, though innocent, is driven from camp with her father and sister and grandmother. Being left behind, they make grass-lodge, and girl soon gives birth to boy, at which time there is strong wind in north. Child grows rapidly, and while in timber is addressed by his father and given bird to take home. In similar manner he receives rabbit, and so day by day larger game, until he is given buffalo. On next visit boy's father appears and leads him into timber; is directed to dig in soft sand, where he finds rat's hole, beneath which are many rats and ground beans, which he takes to his grandmother On next visit he is led to discover artichokes, and next he is presented with leggings, moccasins, robe, quiver, etc. Boy returns home and tells his mother he has seen his father, who is Wind, Ready-to-Give, and that he has promised to return to them in the spring and teach them agriculture. Boy thereafter kills meat with assistance of his father, who enters lodge to visit his wife. He tells her he is angry because people made her an outcast; that her son shall eventually be chief and call buffalo. After making provision for them for winter, he returns to north. They have great success in capturing buffalo during winter. In spring boy meets his father. They return to woman and plant seeds, white corn being given to wife, yellow corn to mother, red corn to sister, and black corn to grandmother. Father then directs boy to make sacred bundle, telling him that he should place in it fire sticks, white corn, hawk skin, and sweet grass; but when he kills a buffalo he should place tobacco in its nostrils, at roots of its ears, and on top of its head, as offering. Thus the gods would know that their spirit is to dwell in buffalo skull, which is to be placed on high hill until it is clean, when it is to be taken inside his lodge and is to become part of altar. During ceremony skull is to be placed north of fireplace, to remind the people that they are to make separate offering to Ready-to-Give. In the fall Ready-to-Give, having provided for his family, returns to north, warning his family that they must shun his wife's uncles, because they were instrumental in bringing their disgrace. One of those of former village decides to return to old village to open cache hole, for his children are starving. The boy discovers man coming and he is taken into their lodge and fed. Man asks who they are, and they tell him, and he asks to see boy. Boy tells him to ask all people to return. He directs his mother to give man meat, with which he sets out. People return to old village and chief asks boy to marry his daughter, but first he gets tipi, in which he hangs his bundle, calls buffalo four times, and leads successful war party.

23. THE MAN WHO CALLED THE BUFFALO.

Boy is born with mysterious power, which he recognizes when he is old enough to use bow and arrow. He follows party hunting buffalo and discovers artichokes where tipi poles had dragged. While digging, man appears wearing black leggings with scalps and eagle feathers, buffalo robe, and eagle-skin cap. He tells boy that he has been his protector and that he is North Wind; gives him ground beans, which when put in pot multiply magically. In similar manner he receives artichokes, Indian potatoes, and buffalo meat, and on successive visits he receives still larger pieces of meat, with which his mother feeds those who are famishing. Others are invited. Boy's power increases and he is able to produce buffalo meat by reaching under buffalo robe. People recognize boy's power and chief sends for boy's father, who says that only his son has mysterious power. Boy visits North Wind and tells him to call buffalo. Boy confers with chief and asks that grass-lodge be put on west side of village. Two women enter and make moccasins. People are given to boy, who, under his direction, imitate buffalo bulls, cows, and calves, and, starting from south, pass by way of east and north about his lodge four times. Boy puts on pair of moccasins, starts toward entrance of lodge; moccasins are worn out. Women make many pairs, which he wears out during four days and four nights, fasting in meantime. Fifth day he sends two men to summit. They report four buffalo. Under boy's direction three are killed, and they are made holy. Their heads are placed toward east, so that they may be restored to life. The ribs are taken to boy's lodge, and he and chief eat. Two scouts are again sent out and report six buffalo, four only being killed. They are made holy and taken to sacred bundle tipi. Next day eight buffalo are seen, five being killed. Next day ten are seen, six being killed. That night all are ordered to keep quiet. The dogs are not allowed to bark. In night the boy yells on high hill toward the four directions. Wind begins to blow and it snows. As day breaks buffalo are seen in every direction, and upon hill is a circle of buffalo about feathered stick which boy had used in calling buffalo. Boy presents buffalo to chiefs; tells them he has fasted, but must eat grass before he may be permitted to eat. Grass is found in south with difficulty, on account of snow. When he has eaten grass he eats meat, and tells chiefs that he is not to be chief; that people were made by Tirawa, and he returns people which had been given him by chiefs. Many buffalo are killed, and as spring approaches they return to their village and plant their crops; but their crops fail, and by spring famine threatens again, the seed corn even being eaten. Chiefs in council send for boy, who tells them to call him Running-Howling-Wolf. He tells them to clean out the cache holes, to address their skin receptacles saying what kind of grain they desire, and to throw sacks into holes and cover holes up. Holes remained covered four days, and on fifth are opened and sacks are found filled with corn. Thus people are saved and boy returns to North Wind.

24. THE WONDERFUL BOY.

In village are many games, especially ring and javelin game. One boy gambles away at this game all his belongings, even his robe, his sister's robe and her trinkets. Boy lies with his sister with half robe over them. His angry father tells him to continue gambling until all the family belongings have been lost and then never to return. Boy remains sorrowing all day in lodge, and at night starts west with moccasins, arrows, leggings, and robe, part of which girl begs from her uncle. Traveling west he comes to village, visits chief tipi, and inquires if other people live farther west. Receiving an affirmative answer, he starts west, and in similar fashion visits several villages, until he comes to people who are naked and who have neither bows nor arrows, but have clubs, which they use in hunting rabbits, upon which they live. They try to detain him, but he continues onward until he encounters people without mouths, who obtain nourishment by inhaling smoke of roasting meat. They talk by signs. They feed boy and he continues on his way westward. He encounters dwarfs who kill game with slings. They challenge him to shoot hide. His bow and arrow prove superior and they wonder at his skill, and at their request he teaches them use of bow and arrow. They tell him that there are no people to west. He travels westward and at night is addressed by North Wind, who tells him of coming events. The following day he travels swiftly, seeing high peak in distance covered with eagle feathers, top of which consists of eagles. Gathering feathers, he continues to steep bank, where he spends night. He continues, and sees water and, beyond, thick fog. He is now at the horizon and is told by North Wind that under bank toward south sits buffalo, who controls big water. He is directed to throw black eagle feathers to buffalo and to ask for permission to go beyond horizon, and he rises and gives buffalo tobacco and feathers. He obtains buffalo's permission to continue. Buffalo sits down in the water, and boy, directed by North Wind, removes his clothing, wades in, and wind carries him over to opposite side. Still directed by wind, boy goes on and enters on north side the westernmost lodge, home of the four gods. North of lodge he sees pumpkin field, and on south bean field, and west of lodge corn field. Entering, he is given seat near entrance, and one of gods tells him that they know that North Wind has brought him, that he is great gambler and has lost his possessions. They tell him to look on south side of lodge, where sits South Wind, who brings bad luck. He sees ugly man with rough skin of white color and unkempt hair. He, they say, it is who brings bad luck. They tell him he is in home of Tirawa, but can not see him. They teach him ceremonies and prepare squash, beans, melons, and corn for him, priests singing in meantime. Next he is given buffalo meat. They tell him to return to his people and feed them. They give him buffalo robe, in which he wraps his seeds and food for his people, and he starts eastward. North Wind comes and covers boy and they again approach horizon, pass through water, meet buffalo, who is satisfied when he sees buffalo robe, telling boy that now he possesses buffalo's power. Buffalo is offered feathers, and boy and Wind go to eagle mound, where he gathers many feathers, which he makes into bundle. He returns home without visiting villages encountered on his way westward, being directed to prepare offerings for North Wind of blue beads, eagle feathers, red paint, sweet grass, and tobacco. As he draws near village odor of human beings overcomes him. He remains with Wind all night. Following day people see buffalo footprints. He approaches nearer village, but can not enter on account of odor. Fourth night he enters his father's lodge; directs his sister to have his father bring offerings, which he takes to North Wind. He returns, asks his father not to stop to embrace him, but to warn the people in village that he has returned. He feeds people on magic meat, which he brings from under his robe. This he does four nights, and morning of fifth day he directs people to send scouts, who shall give signal from top of hill that they see buffalo, which are now plentiful. People kill buffalo four times and perform ceremonies. In spring seeds are planted and following spring still more, and so people obtain seeds through the young gambler.

25. THE BOY WHO PREFERRED WOMAN TO POWER.

Coming Sun in a dream is told to stand on hill four days. Obeying, at end of his fast he is directed to look in certain direction and sees man in ravine going toward spring, whom he is directed to head off. He fails. He again is directed to look into valley and sees warriors driving ponies, but fails to head them off, as before. Next he fails to head off crowd of warriors who carry scalps on poles. Mysterious Being makes himself known, saying that he is North Wind; that he has all kinds of birds, animals, grass, and trees, and gives him bag of medicine, telling him that he tried to make warrior of him, that he tried to give him ponies, and tried to help him scalp the enemy; that as he had failed he would make of him a medicine-man; that whenever he should join a war party it would be successful, but that he could never be leading warrior. Also gives him eagle feather, which, if fastened to pole and used in certain way, will bring buffalo. He becomes great man, accompanies many war parties, and becomes prophet. He is assisted by his protector and is given war medicines, such as buzzard feathers, which, when worn on their heads, would cause great cloud of dust to rise and obscure warriors when they stood in circle. He calls buffalo. One night woman enters his tipi, and while he is with her young man removes feather from pole, and so he fails in calling buffalo; and thus Coming Sun loses his power, because he preferred woman to power, and becomes blind and dies.

26. THE BUFFALO GAMING-STICKS.

Ring and javelin buffalo game is given to people, and they play, singing songs. Morning after first game they see tracks on gaming field. One young man who went into field lies with woman. She gives birth to buffalo calf. Later, party hunting sees snowbird. It flies in front of them, leading them on, for they can not kill it. One by one they all cease to follow bird, except young man who had associated with woman. On summit of ridge he is able to see countless buffalo approaching. In the field is woman and her child, as cow and calf—his wife and child. Calf is always crying for its father and overhears bulls declare they will kill him. Calf tells his father how he may recognize him when bulls make him undergo certain tests. Calves are arranged in row and father is asked to recognize his son. He does so as calf winks at him. Next he distinguishes wife, for calf has placed burr on her tail. Man is permitted by bulls to return home, where he tells his people that in four days buffalo will come and they will have plenty to eat.

27. THE BOY WHO CALLED THE BUFFALO AND WENT TO NORTH WIND.

Famine prevails, and chief orders people to go west to find buffalo. They travel westward, having no success until timbered country is reached, where they are told to make their permanent village. They erect grass-lodges. Famine increases and winter is approaching. Chief sends them far into country to hunt buffalo. They prepare to leave. Coyote Boy asks his mother to make moccasins, that he may go with them. He follows them. They go west. Third night it snows, and following day Coyote Boy gives out and falls behind. Hunters press on. Clouds come from west. It snows and artichoke drops in front of Coyote Boy. He eats, and while he is eating some one addresses him. He tells him he is the author of his life and is Snow Storm. Boy sees man with buffalo robe covered with snow, and fox-skin cap with feather attached to it, which, blown by wind, strikes his robe. According to instructions boy gathers artichokes and starts home, being given power to travel fast. He gives food to his mother, which proves magical. He collects presents for his protector, who now gives him his cap and tells him he should be known as Whipping Feather and have power to travel fast and drive buffalo. Boy accompanies his parents and they find ground beans. Next he returns home with deer and then notifies people that buffalo have arrived. Boy marries and eventually goes to North Wind.

28. THE MAN WHO MARRIED A BUFFALO.

On buffalo hunt shy boy who dislikes girls has intercourse with cow. Next spring this cow has calf, which repeatedly asks for its father. With its mother they go east to find its father. They change into human beings and enter father's lodge. They tell his sister that they want to see him. He does not recognize her and does not at first acknowledge that he is father of child. She explains, and he takes them into his lodge and presents them as his wife and child. He shuns woman, but makes much of boy. Within four days she becomes exactly like other people and warns people to be on their guard against her son lest he strike their children, when his hands would be like buffalo's hoofs; also that he should not be permitted to fall lest he become buffalo. The child often takes water to his father while gambling. One day his father, losing, becomes angry and refuses to drink. His wife knows of it, leaves lodge, takes her son, and they start away. Man gets his moccasins and follows, his wife refusing to return with him. His child, pitying his father feeds him with pemmican, which falls to ground as his father strikes him on forehead, at his request. Calf brings water from ground for his father to drink, by pawing earth. On fourth day they arrive at buffalo village, where cow and calf disappear. On next day calf appears and tells his father that he is to be asked to identify his father-in-law in line of twenty buffalo. This he is able to do by tail marks on rump. On following day he identifies his mother-in-law by means of two cockle burrs on her forehead. Next day he identifies his wife by cockle burr on her tail. On following day he identifies his child as it winks at him and by cockle burr over his right eye. Buffalo now agree to allow him to remain with them, and they by magic turn him into buffalo bull. Accompanied by his wife and son and twenty buffalo they go to village of people in order that father might obtain eagle feathers, etc., as presents. This he does. He tells his people to go to certain place following morning and there find buffalo; to kill them and make them holy. Man takes three additional bunches of buffalo to his people and thereafter buffalo scatter. Once it was found out that man himself had been killed, because when his hide was removed it was discovered to be covered with feathers.

29. HOW THE WITCH-WOMAN WAS KILLED.

East of village lives Witch-Woman. Sometimes she doctors people, and other times bewitches and kills them. In village boy is born whose father is White Moccasins, a wonderful man. Child is favorite with all women, who carry him about on their backs, passing him from one to another. Witch desires child and asks Clam Shell to change places with her while she travels with people. On following morning witch obtains child and goes off with it, telling Clam Shell to follow people, so suspicion would not be cast on her. Witch carries child far to east. People mourn for child and keep abandoning their lodges until only that of White Moccasin is left. Witch stops at big water, makes grass-lodge and garden, where she remains with boy for many years, boy providing game and calling old woman his mother. He has wonderful power and is warned by Witch not to go far to east. While out playing, Crow tells him that his real parents live to west. Following day boy is enticed to west by Red Hawk, who has scalp hanging from his claw and carries war club. Boy follows till he is tired out and then lies down to sleep, Hawk dropping the scalp and club. While asleep insect tells him of his father. In morning voices cry out from every direction—tipi poles, fireplaces, grass, etc.—that he is son of White Moccasin. Finally Clam Shell tells of what had passed between her and Witch, and claims to have brought boy back through her desire, aided by the gods. At her request, boy takes Clam Shell to water and follows trail to west and comes to abandoned village site, where voices again tell him who he is. For many days he travels, always hearing singing. He enters village and is taken into chief's tipi. His father claims him and boy tells how he gained knowledge of his father. Chief asks that boy be his son-in-law. He refuses, for it is not yet time for him to marry. Led by boy they travel south and find many buffalo. They return to their old home, where boy leads war party, which is successful, and they return with scalps and ponies. He leads successful war party four times and makes four buffalo holy and takes them into lodge of priests. Then he leads party eastward until he comes to Witch's lodge, when he turns into Hawk, others turning into Owls. Hawk kills her and she becomes witch again and laughs at him, whereupon he becomes young man with war club and kills her, and he and his companions bury her. They return home. He goes to river with young boy friend and Clam Shell gives him magic power. After buffalo hunt, in which he makes four buffalo holy, he marries daughter of chief and becomes great medicine-man. His protector was Sun, and he was thereafter known as White Sun.

30. PURSUIT BY A RATTLING SKULL—THE PLEIADES.

While on buffalo hunt people camp near stream of water. Girl off gathering wood loses her way, is captured and taken to earth-lodge by Skull, who tells her that it is her duty to keep it clean; that her food is to be its scales; otherwise, she would die. Girl is missed, searched for, and given up. Skull makes several short journeys; gaining confidence in girl, he makes longer journey, and girl goes to high hill and cries. She is addressed by mysterious man, to whom she tells her trouble, and he promises to help her and gives her arrow, bladder, and cactus. She fills bladder, and water starts running toward north. Skull discovers her absence and pursues her. She sings, and mountain-lion appears and says that he has no power against that of Skull. Girl drops cactus, which magically multiplies and checks Skull's pursuit. She sings, and Bear answers her, but he is powerless. She drops bladder; wide river forms. Skull floats down river on log. Girl sings to buffalo, but he also is powerless. As Skull is about to overtake her she drops arrow and thorn trees appear. Skull blows its breath and fire burns pathway. Girl now finds lodge of brothers and sings. Three young boys come out, each with quiver and war club. They invite girl into lodge. As Skull approaches, youngest breaks it into pieces. Girl breaks Skull into smaller pieces, puts them upon fire, and burns them. Girl, with boy's aid, prepares field and plants corn, beans, and squash which she brought with her, and warns boys not to visit field until she gives them permission. In fall they gather corn and cure it and cache it. In winter older brothers return. At first they decide to send girl away, but as she has brought corn they allow her to live with them, asking youngest what relationship she shall bear, which he decides shall be that of sister. Girl discovers that brothers disappear each night, returning in morning. They are stars. Finally they decide to take her with them and she becomes seventh of the Pleiades.

31. THE POOR BOY AND THE MUD PONIES.

When dogs served as burden bearers instead of horses poor boy lives in village, to whom only chief shows friendship, for which chief is laughed at. Boy has vivid dream of two ponies, and thereafter often makes little mud ponies, and carries them in his robe and hides them outside village. He treats them as real, giving them drink and food. While sleeping in chief's lodge he again dreams of ponies and he hears Tirawa singing. In morning he goes to hill and repeats song, and some one visits him and tells him that Tirawa has given him dance, that he shall be chief, and that his ponies will live. Obtaining lariat he goes to his mud ponies, which are now living animals. He leads them to village where people revere them, as they are first ever seen. Boy marries chief's daughter, goes to war on one of his ponies, and returns victorious. He founds chief's society.

32. THE ORIGIN OF THE BUFFALO BUNDLE.

Buffalo decide to go to the people. White Spot, the leader, takes his white cow and calf and starts. Calf carries bundle and decides distance of each day's journey. They visit people and give them buffalo, which are made holy. They also capture bundle. On return white calf gives birth and leaves offspring behind. Little calf follows, claiming White Frost as its mother. Mother would not claim it and little calf says that her milk will turn black and that there would be no more white buffalo. Little calf returns to village of people and becomes a boy and grows up to be wonderful, assuming charge of the buffalo bundle. He explains use of fat in offerings, use of pipe and meat fork, and that in smoking during bundle ceremonies they should use the enemy's arrows as pipe tampers, thus making them offerings to Tirawa; for should they use their fingers in tamping, they would be offering themselves.

33. THE LAST OF THE WHITE BUFFALO.

[Similar to preceding tale. The little white calf, being disowned, turns brown.]
While on a hunt Buffalo people find a white Buffalo bull and cow. The robes are used in sacred bundles and no white Buffalo are seen thereafter.

34. THE WIFE WHO RETURNED FROM SPIRIT LAND.

Young man is continually on war-path, which he prefers to women. He finally falls in love, but must capture more ponies before he can get married. Hearing drumming and singing of warriors, he joins them and goes south toward Comanches. The girl pines for the young man, becomes sick, dies, and is buried on hill on platform which is covered with little mound. Young man rejoins his people victorious. Hearing of girl's death, he goes to her grave and mourns for many days, but finally returns to village for something to eat. He enters lodge, from which smoke issues, and sees girl, who has been buried, surrounded with all her belongings. He remains there during night, but at her request does not approach her. Thus he visits her on following nights, approaching more closely each night.   She warns him that she is ghost and may disappear, but by perseverance he might retain her.   One night spirits of children and musicians enter lodge, where fire is always burning.   He is unable to see them, but when they say they have smoke, he answers, "It is well." Thus spirits enter lodge on succeeding nights.   Each night he is able to see more plainly.   Finally leader addresses him, saying that they have taken pity on him, and warning him to guard his wife carefully.   These spirits are girl's relatives.   Girl is able to relate events in real world, and tells him that people are now returning to their village; that her four uncles are about to put offerings of fat on her grave. Each day she continues to tell what has happened.   There approaches final trial on his part to wrest her from spirit land.   As her uncles approach the grave with fat offering, he is to hold her, for her spirit each time will struggle to free itself, for spirits dislike to be troubled with human beings.   There are four trials.   He fails in first three.   Fourth time he is successful, aided by uncles, who try to hold her to earth.   At that time she flies up into air, young man trying to hold her by her hair.   After she has eaten corn and beans she announces that she will remain with them and that uncles are to remain four nights in their tipi.   After four days have passed, the people, who have been on a hunt, return to village and are informed of what has taken place.   They live with her mother for some time, but mother, becoming suspicious, goes to grave, where she digs and finds bones of her daughter. Returning, she announces her discovery, and her daughter admits that her bones are on hill, but that she is truly the spirit of her daughter.   They live happily for many years, young man being successful on war-path and woman giving birth to boy.   She may not cook nor make clothing.   Boy grows, but is not allowed to touch ground, being continually packed on some one else's back.   Husband, though his wife at first protests, takes second wife, and they live happily for many years.   Trouble finally comes, because he prefers pair of his ghost-wife's moccasins to those of his other wife. He becomes angry because his wife reproaches him for having called her ghost-wife and strikes her.   As he strikes her repeatedly she disappears.   In her place sits a whirlwind, which rises up in lodge and goes out of opening at top.   At night he goes to grave and cries, begging his wife to return.   Child is placed in bed, but in morning is dead and is buried in its mother's grave.   For four days man mourns, when his wife's spirit reappears and recounts that she has left because he struck her and she will never return, and that never again shall spirits return from spirit land.   She becomes whirlwind again and disappears.   Man dies of broken heart beside his wife's grave, but is buried in another place.

35. HOW THE WORLD IS TO COME TO AN END.

Race of giants are first race, and they are destroyed by flood, whereupon Tirawa places buffalo bull in northwest to prevent second recurrence.   Each year bull sheds a hair.   With shedding of its last hair will ensue another flood and final destruction of human beings.   Tirawa devises other ways also of destroying people. That fire might burn people, at which time, so Morning-Star said, Moon would turn red; should it turn black it would presage death of great chief; should Sun lose its brightness it would also foretell destruction of people; that North Star might eventually move, which would also be sign of world's end.   Morning-Star also tells people that pathway (Milky Way) leading from North to South Star is road of death, and that South Star occasionally moves up towards north to see if North

Star is still standing in its place, in which case it moves back toward south; that, according to Morning-Star, during first great council of stars, when position of each was to be determined, an old and a young person became sick; they were placed upon a stretcher and carried by certain stars, preceded by chief medicine-man, and the group goes around North Star; that there will come time when South Star will capture people who were carrying stretcher; that South Star, god of death, would then take possession of earth; that meteors would fly through sky and all rivers would rise, and that animals, otter, beaver, etc., would drift downstream carry-ing out people like human beings. Clam Shell would carry out some like babies, and some would be in shape of birds. Some of signs have come to pass. Moon has turned black several times, but time for end of world is not yet come. Time will be determined by North and South Stars. At that time people will turn into stars and go to south, all stars first falling from heavens and mingling with people. One time men preparing for war party see that Moon has turned black. Some, recognizing the evil omen, wish to postpone party; others decide to go on. They are surrounded and many warriors and chiefs are killed, only one escaping.

36. THE TALKING MEMBRUM VIRILE.

Young man while hunting, after urinating strikes his membrum and asks it if it sees buffalo. Finally it answers, "Yes," and continues to say that it sees buffalo, and does not stop until addressed by his mother-in-law. He is so ashamed that he leaves and is never heard of.

37. THE HERMAPHRODITE.

Young man, caring nothing for women, is visited by young girl. He bathes in spring. In dream he sees Spider-Woman, spirit of spring, and she tells him that he will be like woman. He becomes sick, and medicine-men declare that he is becoming woman, being bewitched by Spider-Woman. Only moss from spring can cure him, but none is to be found, for Spider-Woman caused it to disap-pear. He is so ashamed he commits suicide rather than be hermaphrodite.

38. THE SCALPED MEN.

Leader of war party carries sacred bundle on his back, but never makes smoke offering. Others complain. Scouts report small village, which they attack and find many enemies. They are surrounded and all scalped. After enemy leave they come together, and leader as spokesman declares that being scalped they would be ashamed to return to their people. They agree to live among hills. After several years, man while on hunt encounters these scalped people singing as scabs drop from their heads. He shoots at them and they run to their cave and disappear in cave, and he reports to his people fate of lost war party.

39. HANDSOME-BOY AND AFTER-BIRTH BOY.

Poor boy likes chief's daughter and is invited by her to her lodge. Boy does not go, fearing chief. Girl visits his lodge, but he refuses to lie with her. She pro-poses that they elope and they make preparations. At night, after she has driven horses to water, she meets him and they travel south to heavily timbered river valley, where they build grass-house and live alone.   She gives birth to boy and man buries after-birth by elm tree.   Child grows rapidly.   Father goes off to hunt.   Woman places sleeping child on bed.   She hears voices, and strange beings with long spines at their joints, and with two eyes, one in front and one behind, enter lodge.   She is asked to feed them, but is warned that she must not call them names, which she does as they are leaving, whereupon they return, kill her, and take her away.   They do not see boy.   Father returns, and follows trail of strangers until it is lost in timber, but sees grass-lodge and hears voices, so that he knows cannibals are about to eat his wife.   He and his child live together.   While father is off hunting strange boy appears.   Boys play together.   Stranger disappears as father approaches. Boy tells his father of strange boy and he lays plans to capture him, recognizing that it is his own son born from after-birth.   First he hides, but is recognized by strange boy by his odor.   Older boy finally captures him by tying his hair with strings, and strange boy surrenders.   The three live together many years and boys grow up and hunt with bow and arrows.   They are warned by their father against dangerous places.   They go to river and get in bull-boat which, when half way across river, pitches, whereupon boys fly up as geese, older boy being afraid and requiring urging. Next they go to steep bank covered with snakes, which are unable to bite them, for one of boy's feet and legs are covered with flint stones, while other has soles like horned toad and his legs are covered with turtle shells   They kill four largest rattle-snakes, skins of which they take home and put at entrance of lodge, to scare their father.   Next they go to foot of hill and clouds assemble and it thunders and lightens.   They go to top of high tree, where they find red-painted being, or Thunder, which they throw down out of tree.   Next they find Lightning, then Loud-Thunder, then Wonderful-Lightning.   They take them home to their lodge.   Father protests that they should not molest these heavenly beings, but boy protests that they should not live in tree, and causes one of them to fly to west to sound thunder first in spring.   With him is sent one of lightnings.   Other thunder and lightning are sent to south, from which point they are to travel to earth and occasionally kill people. Father is provoked because they have overcome these heavenly gods and warns them not to go to certain place.   They go into timber where trees are dead and leaves are yellow, and find grass-lodge of sharp-elbowed people who killed their mother. They are welcomed and kettle is placed on fire.   At proper time boys step upon kettle, overturn it, causing steam.   Cannibals scald and fight each other, while the lodge burns up.   Younger brother takes leader and tells him that he and his people shall become locust trees.   Father, learning of their feat, becomes alarmed and decides to run away, fearing for his life.   He provides food and water for boys, and leaves.   Boys, who had become charred leaves and were thus enabled to escape from burning grass-lodge, return home.   They go to Wood Rats' nest under elm tree, where the younger brother says that he received his power, and that Wood Rats are his grandmothers and fed him, and there it is he says that real lightning warned him of beings who pretended to be lightnings, and these were those which boys despoiled of their power.   Woman feeds boys, and they leave, hunting their father, asking animals they encounter if they have seen him.   They also ask insects and bugs.   Finally they return to lodge and Mouse directs them to wooden mortar, which, because it helped boys' father to escape, is again to be used and not to be burned in future.   In morning they find their father's trail, and with it they enter the underground world and follow trail until they come to village of people.   They pass through additional villages until they come to village of bad people. They shake their heads, which makes sound like rattles, and they cause death of all people in village, one starting in on west side and other on east. People die whether they look at them or not. Passing on, they encounter their father's tracks by stream of water. On opposite side they encounter strange being, who challenges them. Younger brother is victorious and conquers Lizard through his ability to cause his feet to turn into flint stone. They finally enter village which contains their father. Again they kill people, including their father, whose body they carry to high hill. Then they make a funeral pyre with four willow, cottonwood, box-elder, and elm poles. They ascend with him in rising smoke.

40. LONG-TOOTH-BOY.

A man and his wife travel east to country of small ponds where they live by themselves for many years. Woman gives birth to child and dies, after-birth being thrown by father into water. He feeds child with animals' milk. In his absence strange boy comes and plays with his son. He has long teeth and is called Long-Tooth-Boy. Older son tells his father of strange boy and he plans to capture him by strategy, first turning into parfleche; but Long-Tooth-Boy recognizes him and jumps into pond. Man mourns and is addressed by buffalo, who tells him to kill him, remove his bladder, fill it with air, and tie it to head of Long-Tooth-Boy. This is done, and so Long-Tooth-Boy is captured in water. Boys are warned against visiting dangerous places. They disobey, visit steep bank, where they encounter water monster, which has swallowed their father. Leaving their bows and arrows on bank they fill their pockets with stones, slide down beaver path, and as they touch water they turn into foam. Foam floats down river and into mouth of monster. Then they become human beings, but do not find their father. They make their way out and Long-Tooth-Boy breaks his bow and arrows and plays with them inside monster's mouth. With flint stones he makes spark which he throws inside monster, and bow and arrows are burned. Suddenly monster bursts and is thrown upon ground. With sinew strings they drag home its skin, which they had blown off. They give it to their father for tobacco pouch. They go to river, attempt to cross on fallen log, but old woman on opposite side causes log to stand on end and grow up like tree. She spits upon it; it grows cold and sleets. Around tree are many human skulls. Old woman leaves, thinking they will soon perish. Long-Tongue-Boy gnaws steps on tree whereby they descend. They plan the old woman's death. Long-Tooth-Boy becomes raccoon, which older brother kills, and at old woman's request takes it into her lodge. Inside lodge he places meat in pot, and on top, head resting upon paws, being careful not to cut intestines. Big fire is kindled under pot and soon raccoon sticks out its tongue, which is signal for older brother to leave lodge. Old woman, owing to heat in lodge, has removed her garments; pot now boils over and splashes on woman, who falls toward fire and is killed. Elder brother then takes meat and places it on skin, wraps it up, and throws it into pond. Thus Long-Tooth-Boy is restored to life. Witch hears of Long-Tooth-Boy's deeds and decides on his death. Warriors join her and they travel east. She turns into yellow bird and alights on opening of lodge. Long-Tooth-Boy directs his father to kill it. He shoots twice, but misses it, whereupon bird flies down, takes man by hair, and disappears with him into sky. Each of brothers shoots his arrows up into sky, following their father. They alight and see yellow feathers on ground. They advance and find warriors dancing. Long-Tooth-Boy disguises himself, enters witch's village, and takes buffalo hide, asking in which tipi old woman is hid. He sees his father sitting by witch, who recognizes him. He returns to his brother. The two go to gopher hill and throw up handful of earth, causing dust storm, in midst of which they enter tipi where their father is confined. There everyone has covered his head, and boys escape. In the night they re-enter lodge, find witch asleep, cut off her head, and take their father with them. The three bounce up and down in air old woman's head, screaming. Returning home, Long-Tooth-Boy is about to scalp old woman, but begs that her head may be placed on pole outside of lodge where she is to remain and serve as sentinel.

41. LONG-TOOTH-BOY.

A man and his wife travel south and erect grass-lodge by creek. Woman is confined: after-birth is thrown into water. Shortly woman dies and boy is nourished by milk of animals. While absent, boy is visited by his brother born from after-birth. In attempting to capture after-birth boy man hides, but is detected by his odor. Next, he is covered up in hole, which he leaves and returns with two bladders blown up and containing rattles, one of which he directs his son to tie to the hair of his younger brother. Father now crawls from his hiding place and boy is captured in water. They live together, but younger brother grows long teeth like those of beaver, with which he injures his father, whereupon with stone he files them down. Father warns them against visiting dangerous places. One day they go to Long-Tooth-Boy's lodge, which was under water. Within lodge is sage floor, and bows and arrows which he has taken from his brother. He gives his brother one of two finely braided antelope hide strings, to one end of which is flint. They go to steep bank and are addressed by voice which tells them that it has devoured their father. Water monster is slain, as in preceding tale, except that fire is kindled inside monster, heat causing bladder to burst. Skin is taken home. Next, they visit snake's den. They escape being bitten by standing upon flint stone, which increases its height. Snakes eject venom at boy, which he diverts by waving his flint stone. He shoots snake with his arrow, which flashes like lightning, causing snake to burst with noise like thunder. Other snakes escape to their holes. Boys take skin home. They go to high hill, where they see boys sliding from its top on buffalo-rib sleds. They rub themselves with their magic stone. Boys kick the two brothers, but do not injure them. At bottom are many human skeletons. At next attempt the boys kick brothers on back over kidneys. The leader of the boys is spotted calf. They take its skin home. They go south to cedar timber, meet red painted man with bear-claw necklace and carrying war club. Before he strikes boy he is killed with arrow. Approaching, they find not man, but cinnamon bear, whereupon they tell bear to disperse, and take skin home. Next, they go to river, where old woman throws log across water, which when they start to cross stands up and grows into tree, and weather turns very cold. Long-Tooth-Boy blows his breath on his brother and he turns into snowbird. He also becomes bird and they fly to earth. They go to old woman's lodge and in contest dance on side of precipice. She challenges elder boy to jump and he is killed at bottom. Long-Tooth-Boy dances with old woman. He jumps and lands safely, old woman following. As she flies through air he blows his breath and her body falls on one side and her skin on other. He kicks his brother's feet, saying, "Awake," and they take old woman's skin home with them. They return to river, on bank of which are many skeletons. Near by is fire. Near fire is man groaning. He asks boys to warm their feet and step upon his back to relieve his suffering. With his magic flint Long-Tooth-Boy turns his legs into stone, stamps upon man, and kills him, and they find that being is catfish, which has caused death of many people by asking them to doctor it by stepping upon spines on its back, which kills them. Go east to den of mountain-lions, largest of which is struck upon head with arrow, and boys ride it home. Other lions are caused to disperse. Soon after sky is filled with dust, caused by buffalo scattering over country, for they are angry because Long-Tooth-Boy killed spotted calf. To escape danger Long-Tooth-Boy takes his father and brother to open place and they make circle of smooth stones. In morning stones have grown high, forming corral with single entrance. They make dogwood arrows. Buffalo come from west and north. They try to butt down stones and fail, some even smashing their skulls. Buffalo scatter. Few are killed. Long-Tooth-Boy directs his father to go east and bring his people. He is gone several days. By his return stones of the corral have become normal size. Long-Tooth-Boy addresses people, telling them he has overcome all bad animals. He teaches them, gives them buffalo, tells them he is about to leave, that his power comes from clouds, that they may obtain power from him where they see lightning strike, where they will find a flint stone. He directs that his brother's skull shall be placed in stone circle. He smokes with his brother and in night disappears. In his place is large-sized flint. This is placed in sacred bundle.

42. BURNT-BELLY AND HIS DREAMS.

Apart from village live man and his sister. He is often visited by poor Burnt-Belly, who is always begging food. He addresses him as brother-in-law and tells his sister that Burnt-Belly is her future husband. Thus he made fun at his expense. Burnt-Belly goes to stream of water, where he has vision, in which he is addressed by finely costumed man, who tells him that he is to become great warrior. He tells him that young man's power comes from Sun, that this power is in his shield, and that Burnt-Belly is to ask for his shield. They follow war party and Burnt-Belly is told that he will be spoken to again. He does as directed. Joins war party in spite of protest, and takes scalp, which he gives to leader. Again he has dream on bank of river, where he is asked to fast for four days. Then he is told to dive into water four times and stand on bank. He does so and finds himself beautifully costumed. On his way back he meets sister and excites her admiration. As she returns from river with water he asks for drink. She hesitates, and follows young man to her brother's lodge, where they spend night together. Brother-in-law is pleased that his sister is married. Shortly afterward boy repulses attack of enemy and soon leads successful war party. People wonder who he is and he tells them.

43. THE BOY WHO WORE A WOODPECKER CAP.

On one side of stream is village. On west are many ponds with islands, on which lives strange boy who wears cap of woodpecker scalps. He has otter quiver and black bow. He wears leggings from which hang owls' heads, which hoot at night. Strange woman braves dangers of water animals and swims over to boy's island. She addresses him as grandchild and tells him it is time for him to return to his people. She gives him magic arrow, by which he can get across water. This is not woman, but moon, and travels as swan. She watches over people. In night boy goes to village on his arrow. He enters lodge and girl takes his bow and arrow and other belongings and hangs them up. Her bow, a snake, and the birds permit her. People in lodge say that they are poor and can not feed him. He goes out and returns with pecans, etc., and sends for chief and tells him to surround timber. They do so and find nests of ground-beans and many animals. These were found there because boy had made mud images in night. He returns to his island and shortly revisits village. He produces more game and is called wonderful. Third time they find buffalo in timber and he returns to his island home. Bear-Man has been growing jealous of this boy and digs hole into which boy falls as he shoots himself across lake. He is robbed of his clothing and left in hole. Birds on clothing peck Bear-Man and snake arrows and bow bite him, but he goes through village, enters chief's lodge, and gains favor of all chief's daughters but youngest. He fails to produce game as boy had done. Boy remains in hole five days and is discovered by old woman's grandchild. They rescue boy and feed him, begging corn for him. He calls his rescuer "uncle," and gets him to bring material for bow and arrows. They go into timber and find rat, which they shoot for their supper. Next, they find porcupine, raccoon, quails, prairie chickens, turkeys, fawn, deer, elk, and finally buffalo. Every day boy kills game and they have plenty to eat. With the skins old woman builds fine tipi. People are surprised at prosperous condition of old woman and her two boys and some suspect that man in chief's lodge is impostor. Youngest daughter of chief makes her home with old woman and boy tells her of his treatment by Bear-Man, whereupon she returns home, takes boy's clothing, quiver, etc., and restores them to him, snakes and birds expressing their joy. People begin to attack impostor. He turns into bear, but is chased out of village by firebrands. Boy brings game for people for last time and gives them seeds to plant and teaches them agriculture. He teaches them ceremonies, and disappears.

44. THE SHOOTING OF THE SQUIRREL'S NOSE.

Chief's tipi stands on north side of village by itself, near stream of water. Near by is ravine with forked cottonwood. East of village is little grass-house where poor woman and her child live. People urinate against their tipi, and maltreat them. She is called grandmother because she is poor. Chief's children amuse themselves by shooting at squirrel which has made its home in cottonwood tree. No one could kill it. Eldest daughter has father announce that whoever could kill squirrel might marry her. This is difficult, because only nose of squirrel is visible. Boys all make bows and arrows, including Burnt-Belly, son of poor woman. He has power of bringing buffalo by using ring and javelin game in their lodge. They fill many parfleches with meat. Although he is laughed at, he enters contest for chief's eldest daughter. He shoots squirrel, but prize is claimed by man with bear claws. Nevertheless he obtains several hairs of squirrel. Impostor takes squirrel to chief's lodge and marries two eldest daughters, youngest refusing him. Squirrel skin in chief's lodge fails to emit light, as had been expected. Impostor promises people buffalo, and failing, says it is because youngest daughter does not marry him. She runs off to old woman's lodge. Asked why she did not marry man, youngest daughter says she does not believe in him. Girl is given food and sent home. Boy's grandmother visits chief to ask for girl in marriage. Chief leaves decision with his daughter. She favors proposal, boy is brought, and they are married. Young couple are mistreated by older sisters. On fourth day Burnt-Belly enters lodge as eagle. As he turns into human form he wears fine eagle feather garments. Two eldest sisters now try to claim him as their husband. He rejects them and tells chief to warn people to get ready for buffalo hunt. He leads people into timber. They find much small game. Next, they find buffalo. Boy is given a new tipi, where he lives with his grandmother and his wife.

45. ORIGIN OF THE CLAM SHELL.

Man captures diving duck, which he takes home and releases at his wife's request. Later, wife gives birth to girl called Young Duck. Child has ways of duck. Child makes small hole in tipi, fills it with water, and sits on it, imitating duck. She requires her mother to wash her face from that water. She grows rapidly, and becomes beautiful, with very long hair. In vision she is told to get stick with crook at end, and carrying-straps. She often goes to timber with girls for firewood, and by means of her magic crook she can draw down dry limbs from trees. She becomes leader of girls in getting firewood. Young men court her with games and flutes. She finally recognizes Hawk and gives him permission to visit her. He begs of animals that he may become human being, whereupon he marries girl. She still continues her old habit. Old woman becomes jealous of girl, follows her to timber, and kills her, sticking fire-hardened stick into her ear. Old woman blows in girl's mouth, takes off her skin down to her waist, substitutes her own skin, throws girl into stream, and returns as young girl. She tries to act like young duck, and for a while is not detected. Soon her skin begins to rot. Medicine-men are sent for. They fail. Finally, Crow doctor comes, and at once recognizes old woman, while Hawk goes to river and hears voice of his wife singing. Old woman is thrown into water and her child is killed. Husband turns into hawk, flying up and down creek for four days. Then he sees smoke issuing from tipi in valley. Entering, he finds woman and four girls and his wife, who at first refuses to see him. Upper part of her body now resembles that of old woman, her skin being wrinkled and her ears hanging down. She asks her husband to fly up in air with her, then to drop her. Next day he takes her to high hill and turns into hawk, places her upon his back, flies upward, and lets girl fall. He discovers that she is Clam Shell, outside rough like witch's skin, inside with smooth and delicate surface like that of young girl.

46. THE POOR BOY WHO TURNED INTO AN EAGLE.

When no people lived on earth, at direction of Morning-Star, Moon sends down woman and Morning-Star, his younger brother. Boy calls woman "niece." They are placed near stream of water and food is given them. In spring clearance is made and woman plants corn, tying up remaining seeds and warning her uncle not to touch them. While she is at work boy eats up seeds. Enraged, she whips him, and he sings, turning gradually into eagle, whereupon he flies up and off in spite of her protests. She follows him to lodge of beavers. They agree to help her, digging hole which they cover with limbs, placing woman inside, and overhead animals simulate death to attract Eagle. Finally, Eagle comes, but is not fooled. Badgers are helpless. Woman goes on and elks try to help her to catch her brother in same manner; likewise buffalo. They tell her that they all know this Eagle; that he is Morning-Star, chief of the heavenly gods, who desires only human flesh. They agree to help to capture him. So many buffalo die, making great odor. They take girl and cut her open, place her on arbor, and then Magpie comes, and also Crow and Coyote, to feed. Finally, Eagle alights upon the arbor; says that he is willing to eat of human being, at which other animals begin to eat. As the Eagle is looking for girl's heart she grabs his legs and he becomes boy again, and he says that henceforth when people live on earth an enemy shall be sacrificed to Morning-Star, but not until many have been made holy. The two disappear in dark clouds, she returning to Moon, boy to east, where he stands behind his brother.

47. THE POOR BOY WHO LOST HIS POWER.

Burnt-Belly and his mother live in deserted village. They are very poor. He soils his robe; she strikes him and he turns into Eagle, in spite of her protests. It continually hovers near her, finally becoming boy again after her repeated solicitations. She makes bows and arrows for him each morning, then buffalo, and he kills game and finally buffalo. People return to village. They move into timber where they continue to have plenty of meat. Chief, fearing boy's power, invites him to call buffalo. Boy disappears as eagle several days. Returning, he directs successful buffalo hunt. Boy and his mother are invited to live in village. Boy declares that impossible, and at his suggestion chief moves his village near boy's lodge, and chief offers him his daughter; but boy refuses, as proper time has not arrived. Girl visits boy's tipi and lies with him, whereupon boy loses his power, whereas if he had not done this and had called buffalo four times he would have been permitted to marry and retain his power.

48. THE FLINT MAN.

Man travels to far prairie country, and finds man of flint emitting sparks of fire, who has power to transform himself into any creature and to see great distances. He renders himself invisible by asking man to smoke, smoke getting in his eyes. Flint man bestows upon him power to turn to stone; also to bring rain during drought, by lifting piece of flint upward to heaven and placing it on ground and sprinkling water upon it, whereupon clouds will form and it will rain. With pieces of flint he will also be able to cure sick. Flint man thereupon turns into blue flint and diminishes in size until he is little stone, bearing on one side picture of moon and stars and on other of sun. Man takes it home and places it on his altar. He invites his friends, who bring offerings to stone. He hears of monster by big lake. He visits monster and sees human bones lying about. He kills the monster, which is catfish, by trampling upon his back. He escapes death, for his feet have turned into flint and spines on monster's back do not enter his feet. People visit monster and take its fat for medicines. Next, he slays seven spotted calves, who are always challenging strangers to slide down hill with them on buffalo-rib sled. Next, he visits gluttonous buffalo bull in west. Bull tries to gore him, but he is turned into flint. Bull breaks off its horn and man kills it with his arrow. He becomes frightened as he realizes that he has killed chief of buffalo. People are all frightened. They surround village with stones, which grow, making a high corral about village. People see cloud of dust reaching to sky, made by buffalo, which attack village, but are unsuccessful, whereupon they scatter over earth. Following day stones of corral are reduced to their natural size. Flint man loses his magic stone, which angers gods, who send rainstorm, lightning strikes him, and he is placed in heavens.

49. THE TURKEY RITUAL.

Village crier announces approach of enemy. All turn out and meet many warriors, who are turkeys, sages of land from which they have come, and they tell people where they are going, in order that people may hunt them for food.

50. THE BOY WHO TURNED INTO A PRAIRIE DOG.

A village lies between hill and creek, across which is Prairie Dog town. Bright Eyes, good-looking little boy in love with girl, repeatedly waits for her at spring. She tells him she does not love him. Grieving, boy sets out alone to east and crosses river and enters Prairie Dog town, where he marries young Prairie Dog and lives with them. His mother grieves for him and tracks him by his tears and footprints. She remains there several days mourning. In vision is addressed by beautiful young girl and told that her son is happy; that he has forgotten about his people, except his mother. She is directed to bring to hole certain black arrow from boy's quiver. She does so, and as Prairie Dog leaves hole he jumps at arrow and becomes her son again. Boy returns home, followed by his Prairie Dog wife, who is pregnant. She rolls herself in dust and becomes woman. They live together happily and have many children. He becomes great man, but is warned by his Prairie Dog wife that he shall never associate with girl through grief for whom he had left his village. This girl meets him, talks with him, says she is sorry she acted as she did, and they lie together. On returning home he finds wife and child, who do not heed his instructions, but cross stream and turn into Prairie Dogs. From that time on boy has bad luck and dies broken-hearted.

51. THE GAMBLER AND THE GAMING-STICKS.

Two wonderful brothers live in village, from which many young men have gone to another village, whence they never returned, for in that village lives Gambler and Spider-Woman, his wife. Older brother visits Gambler's village; is met by Gambler's errand man, who invites him into village and provides for his comfort. He is warned by people of village against Gambler. He is invited to eat with Gambler. As he eats of human eyes he loses his power. They play on following day, he uniformly loses, and finally his life, the witch woman cutting off his head, which she hangs up in lodge. Younger brother sends birds to look for his brother. Raven informs him of what has happened and boy starts for Gambler's village. Here he is welcomed and treated as had been his brother. Instead of eating of human eyes in Gambler's tipi, he carries bowl of food to tipi where he is to spend night. He remains there five days and Gambler attempts to feed him on human brains and human ears. On fourth night boy goes to buffalo wallow where there are many buffalo skeletons. He cries by side of bull's skull, which offers to help him. Active young bull offers to help him, bellows, he is surrounded by spirits of buffalo, and in their midst is black javelin. Another bull in similar manner becomes white javelin. This one is to be played with by Gambler, for being young this bull had never associated with cow and hence could not overtake ring in game. Cow in similar performance turns into ring. Buffalo promise their help; tell boy to place ring on black stick and hang it in his tipi that night, and give him instructions as to game. Following morning he plays with Gambler, witch woman being present with her quirt with which she proposes to kill boy after his life has been won. For a while boy loses. Finally he stakes his life. When boy aims at Gambler's javelin and breaks it, Gambler asks that game be postponed, but boy declares he will win or lose all, and asks Gambler to get another set; but Gambler has none and boy says he has set in his lodge, and Gambler sends his errand man, Coyote, after them. Coyote is scared by spirits of buffalo within lodge. Again he is sent and is so scared that he defecates. Blackbird is sent and returns with javelins. Gambler chooses white javelin. Before beginning final game they bet, in addition to their lives, all their friends, winner having the privilege of killing loser and his party. Gambler's white javelin enters ring, but ring leaves it and takes its place on black javelin. Next, boy makes a successful throw. So they play on, boy being successful and winning everything back. Gambler tries to stop game by pretending that he has broken leg, but taunted by boy he continues. With last successful throw of boy javelins turn into buffalo and run away. Gambler, his family and friends are all put to death.

52. YOUNG HAWK HUNTS FOR HIS MOTHER.

Hawk, great warrior, lives with his wife and child. While absent one day his wife disappears. Her son hunts for her in under-world. He travels through different villages. Father, returning, starts after little boy. All three find each other and turn successively, as they are struck by father, into Hawks, killing snake, which had stolen woman.

53. THE DOG-BOY WHO MARRIED THE CHIEF'S DAUGHTER.

White Moccasin's wife gives birth to dog, which he throws into creek. Dog is rescued by Clam Shell, who says that it is witch who has thrown him into water, and tells him to follow trail of his people. Looking around, he finds that he is now boy. Looking around again he discovers quiver. He goes to his village, where he announces that he is White Moccasin's child; is taken to chief's lodge, where he remains. On buffalo hunt he is leading spirit, and returning marries chief's daughter. They have many children. One day he goes south, sees deer, looks again and deer has become girl, who warns that his father is trying to kill him, but that she will protect him. Boy returns, invites men to his lodge, including his father, and challenges him to contest. His father has no power over him, but boy waves his hand and his father begins to butt his head against everything he encounters. White Moccasin's friends try to kill boy with clubs, and he yells, and his enemies, including his father, fall down.

54. SUN-RAY WHO MISTREATED HIS WIFE.

Man and his wife live alone. He is good hunter, bringing home much game, but treats his wife meanly and she tries to leave him, though is always unsuccessful, finding herself at each attempt inside rattle hanging at his belt. She tells people of her husband's cruelty, and lives with them. Her husband returning home from hunt goes to village, points his rattle toward it, his wife does not appear, and he goes to other villages doing the same until his wife appears in his rattle, and he takes her to their home. Again he goes on hunt, and woman goes to creek and cries. Beavers take her into their lodge. Husband again recovers her by his rattle, and warns her that she can not escape from him, and in his anger throws hot coals at her. She becomes a mole, digs down under mortar, escapes from lodge, passes out on ground, and goes to distant village, leaving no trail, for she has covered her feet with grass. He enters village as sun ray, discovers her, and she returns to his rattle. He becomes man and people abuse him, saying that he belongs in heavens and has no right to mistreat an earthly woman. He throws rattle on ground and woman wakes up. He pulls string of his rattle, she enters, and he takes her home and releases her. He now repents and returns, placing her in his rattle and takes her home. He becomes Sun-Ray and goes back to sun.

55. HAWK SLAYS THE FIRE-KEEPER.

In beginning, Fire-Keeper has his home with people in west, but he does not like them. On west of their village is deep river, across which live two Hawk brothers. They have magic log by which they cross river. Older crosses and gets wife, daughter of priest. Fire-Keeper, priest's brother, decides to kill young man, because he was not consulted regarding marriage. After a while woman gives birth to boy. Husband crosses river and visits his brother during fog. As he leaves log he is seized by mysterious being. Being strips him of his clothing and burns it and he loses his eyes. His captor leads him for many days till they arrive at his home, where he is made slave. Child cries for his father. Mother goes to lodge of her brother-in-law across river. Brother takes child, but it cries louder. She takes her child and hunts her husband. At river's bank she discovers fragments of his clothing, and she follows his tracks toward west until she comes to big fire inside tipi. Then she discovers her uncle, painted red, and her husband, who is made to stir fire. Woman begs in vain for her husband. Her blind husband comes out of lodge and his child stops crying. She enters and secures her husband's half-burned war club and they travel east many days. At his request she leads him up on rocky hill with steep sides, places him at edge with his feet hanging down, and pushes him over at his earnest request before sunrise. She starts toward foot of precipice and encounters her husband in his normal condition, fully costumed. He starts forward to revenge himself on her uncle, and she goes to her brother-in-law and they go to her people, who are awaiting her husband. At night they see fire flying through sky and they know that he has killed Fire-Keeper. He did this by turning into Hawk, striking Fire-Keeper on head. Then turning into human being, he threw fire through sky in different directions, announcing that warriors should receive help from stars' light. On his return home he is thanked by animals and by birds, who call him Warrior-Bird. Brothers tell girl's father that when they die their skulls should be kept in sacred bundles, to use as protectors while on war-path; that priests (owls) should remain at home as guardians of people.

56. THE SINGING HAWK.

In grass-lodge, representing first lodge on earth, priests hold their ceremonies and women bring offerings of food.   Once Coyote people, including all animals, go on buffalo hunt.   Hawk acts as scout.   He travels nearly around world.   As he returns home he finds buffalo.   Thus people sing songs he sang, recounting their travels, that they may find buffalo near at home.

57. THE BOY WHO MARRIED A BUFFALO.

Daughter of Buffalo chief visits boy and his sister.   Boy has one red and one black arrow.   He shoots cow with arrow, which penetrates only beneath skin, and boy follows, hoping to regain his arrow.   At night tipi appears, in which he sleeps. In morning tipi has become Buffalo, which he follows throughout day.   Boy is angry.   At night he again enters magic tipi; finds woman covered with robe.   He again follows.   Third night woman tells him of her love for him and feeds him, and they pass night as man and wife.   In morning she is Buffalo.   They travel on and encounter old bull, to which boy offers tobacco, and they enter Buffalo's village, where he is received kindly by some, hostilely by others.   Girl's uncle, White-Spot Buffalo, jumps at boy, but boy shoots him with arrow.   Next, he kills girl's father, who also has white spot on his forehead.   All buffalo become angry and try to kill him, but each time he turns into breath feather.   They ask for sacrifice of smoke, and he takes certain buffalo to his village, which are killed and their meat made holy.   Their spirits return to Buffalo village with news.   Boy travels with Buffalo as feather.   He becomes Buffalo, as is proved by people killing buffalo whose hide was covered with feathers.

58. BUFFALO WIFE AND THE DISPERSION OF THE BUFFALO.

A young boy dislikes women.   Being blackbird he escapes them.   West is village of Buffalo, and young man learns that in that village is girl who dislikes men. He decides to marry her.   She also hears of him.   Each decides to visit the other, and they meet on high hill between villages.   They compare notes and each returns home.   Girl by river bank sings of her lover.   Coyote hears her and schemes how to get her.   Coyote pricks his horse with cockle burrs and rides to girl, but boy has arrived first and takes girl to his tipi, where she is fed and they go to girl's father, who is glad, and sends for Buffalo and they are given smoke.   Buffalo chief decides to send eight of Buffalo to people to be killed.   Their meat is made holy, and Buffalo chief is pleased and sends more of his people.   Each day a larger number is sent, and finally Buffalo scatter for benefit of people.   As Buffalo wife wore an elk dress, so must woman in ceremonies when her husband makes Buffalo holy.   Thus also they wear eagle feather on their heads, imitating her.   She finally makes her husband angry and he flies away as blackbird and thereafter lives among buffalo.

59. THE POOR BOY WHO WANTED TO BE MARRIED.

Poor boy living with his grandmother wanders from village, and while asleep is addressed by buffalo chief's son, who says that his home is beyond mountains, where buffalo live in great cave.   Boy is asked to return on following day.   Returning, he is led to place of buffalo, while from side of hill comes little calf.   He is warned to so place himself as not to see manner of calf's exit. He is instructed to shoot calf, which he takes home. From this time on he brings larger buffalo home each day. Grandmother jerks meat and stores it in parfleches. Girl visits lodge and is fed. Boy again encounters his benefactor, who gives him full costume. He asks his grandmother to go to chief's lodge and ask for his girl in marriage. Chief promises his answer next day. In meantime youngest daughter of chief again visits them and tells of her love for boy. She carries meat home, which she gives to her parents in night. On old woman's return next day chief consents to his daughter's marriage. He enters chief's tipi, and being finely arrayed other daughters, who formerly despised him, now wish to marry him. He takes youngest daughter back to his grandmother's lodge, where they have feast, inviting chief. People are starving and boy calls buffalo four times, and buffalo become numerous. Boy remains faithful to his young wife. They have many children.

60. THE BUFFALO AND RED-SPIDER-WOMAN'S DAUGHTER.

Red-Spider-Woman, living in center of earth, controls corn, beans, etc., and has many daughters. Buffalo live in north, their chief having son named Curly-Eyes. Buffalo in council decide to send four of their number to south to look for better land, Curly-Eyes being one of party. On their journey they meet Red-Spider-Woman and her daughters, Curly-Eyes falling in love with one of them. Reporting fact to his father, he is told it will be necessary to buy her in order that he may bring her home. Then delegations are sent offering old woman, first, valley full of buffalo, then two valleys full, then half land full, and finally land full. Still old woman refuses, whereupon buffalo decide to move to her country. They travel south many years. Curly-Eyes and other buffalo see girl. Old woman's fields are trampled. She stands on prairie and begins to disappear in ground. They kill her. Buffalo chief announces that her body shall remain in ground as medicinal root, from which is derived squash medicine. Hereafter buffalo cover earth.

61. THE SINGING BUFFALO CALF.

Buffalo calf traveling with party dreams that they are to be surrounded, killed, and consecrated. Dream comes true. Buffalo are satisfied as long as they are consecrated.

62. THE BUFFALO AND THE DEER.

Buffalo and deer dispute concerning relative merits of their meat for the purpose of consecration. Deer becomes angry, and, running amongst the people who are on hunt, is shot and consecrated. Consequently, deer are always first consecrated when upon hunt.

63. THE UNFAITHFUL BUNDLE-KEEPER.

Famine prevails. Buffalo are far in west. They have council and decide that chief's daughter should lead them to people. She puts bundle on her back and divides them into four herds, first herd being sent to south of village and is killed. Second herd fares same on north side, and still third. Fourth herd approaches village from west, she remaining behind with bundle. During slaughter of this herd she gives birth to calf in ravine and joins those who escape slaughter, who now return home.   Calf is taught by Wind name of its father and mother, and starts home singing of its parentage.   People are surprised, for they thought girl maiden.   When chief is assured that girl is mother of calf, she is commanded to cease carrying sacred bundle.   Henceforth, witch woman shall not carry bundle, and women of high birth, though unmarried, occasionally have children.

64. THE HUNGRY COYOTE.

Coyote is famishing, hears tramp of buffalo and sees calf.   He questions calf, who sings to him, in meantime passing on by and thus escaping with its life, while Coyote dies of hunger.

65. THE GATHERING OF THE PRIESTS.

In village of Coyotes they are about to open sacred bundle and women are told to bring firewood, but they are on hunt, except one girl.   She grinds corn and makes mush, which she takes to priests' lodge.   Priests are very grateful and sing her praises.   Buffalo hunters are unsuccessful, but, because of mush, priests keep bundle open, singing all night.   In morning hunters are successful.

66. THE MAN WHO SANG TO COYOTE.

In winter time people tell Coyote stories.   It is winter time, and in every lodge they are telling Coyote tales.   Young man goes on hunt, encounters Coyote, and starts to shoot him, but stops for fear of bad luck.   Thereafter he is lucky while on hunt, for sparing Coyote's life.

67. HOW THE CANNIBAL SPIDER-WOMAN WAS OVERCOME.

Wonderful boy wearing his robe wrong side out sets out to find Spider-Woman's village, who kills people in tree-climbing contest.   He is met by boy of her village, who takes him into his lodge and his mother warns him of Spider-Woman.   He is invited to Spider-Woman's lodge by Eyes-Wide-Open, her errand man.   He is offered human brains, but refuses to eat.   In morning boy asks to be left alone in lodge.   He smears his body with white clay, spotting it with black, and ties feathers in his scalp-lock.   He goes to contest and wagers his life against that of Spider-Woman and her children.   Spider-Woman climbs tree, which falls, but she is not hurt.   Boy prepares to climb, sings a song, and Eyes-Wide-Open asks to join his side, to which Spider-Woman assents.   He throws robe aside, climbs tree, which falls, and he is unhurt.   People run to Spider-Woman and kill her and her people, who are thrown into ravines over country.   Eyes-Wide-Open is also killed.   Boy declares there shall be no more cannibalism and causes tree to fall.   He tells woman in whose lodge he has stayed over night that she and her child thereafter shall live about old trees, and they become mice, while he and his people shall live in tops of trees, and he becomes speckled woodpecker.   Thus it is that woodpeckers live in tops and mice among roots of hollow trees.

68. THE WITCH-WOMAN WHO STOLE THE WONDERFUL BUFFALO ROBE.

In village lives Witch-Woman who kills many people and is great thief. She also has power to turn people into animals. People try to kill her, and pound her with sticks, cut her with knives, but in vain. They appeal to priest, and he sings songs which foretell of the death of old woman. In spring stranger visits them wearing robe painted with stars, clouds, lightning, sun, moon, swallows, and flies. He is challenged by deer who belongs to old woman to race. Boy is victorious. Boy one day is gambling. False alarm of enemy is given. In confusion woman steals his robe. She taunts him and tells him he will never find it again. She is wearing it as skirt. Boy sings four times. Old woman recognizes his power, gives up robe, and she is taken up to heavens in rainstorm, and is thrown back into mud ravine and begins to urinate, and henceforth is spring. Boy says that thereafter she would either be spider or black-tailed deer, that his work is done, that he represents North Wind. And he becomes speckled snowbird and flies to north.

69. HOW THE CANNIBAL WITCH-WOMAN WAS OVERCOME.

Boy goes to village, where he is invited by Eyes-Wide-Open, Coyote, to eat with Witch-Woman. He refuses to eat and she challenges him to contest. On morrow they dive into river, both remaining under water until afternoon. Old woman is victorious, boy is killed, and woman places his head with her other trophies. Dead boy's twin brother sets out to find him; arrives at village. On night before contest he goes to river bank and cries. Beaver comes and takes boy into Beavers' lodge, and in council they decide to help him. They feed him with meat of young beaver's leg, which has been boiled, bone of which is thrown into water. Young Beaver who thus lost his leg dives into water and returns with his leg intact. Beaver chief gives boy blue mud, with which he paints himself. On following day contest takes place. As boy dives he enters Beavers' lodge, where again Beaver's leg is cut off. While meat is cooking boy sleeps, while Beaver watches bank to see if old woman has appeared. By night old woman thinks she must be victorious and appears on bank. Watcher informs Beavers, who awaken boy, who eats, and Beaver's leg is restored and boy appears above water victorious. Witch people are killed and trampled into ground, water being forced from old woman, and she becomes spring near river.

70. THE GIRL WHO CALLED THE BUFFALO.

Coyote and his wife, Spider-Woman, are famishing. Each day he cuts small piece from her dress which he eats. He goes far into country, but finds no game. In evening he smells roasting meat and follows odor for four days. He finds tipi; is invited in; young girl is sitting on west. On floor of tipi is placed sweet grass. Coyote tells her of his condition. She asks him to await her brothers' return. There is rushing noise in sky and Bald Eagle enters. He is followed by White Eagle, black and other eagles. Each calls Coyote grandfather, but he can not see them. Next, comes Hawk, then Crow, then Magpie. Eagles take girl on south side of tipi and swing her from two lariats which hang from sky. She flies away toward west. As she returns buffalo follow her. Eagles take girl into tipi, while Crow flies among buffalo, saying, "Caw! Caw!" thus killing two buffalo. Coyote is told to

help himself to meat.   He remains several days, becoming fat.   He starts home
with load of meat, which his wife prepares, and they invite leading men of village to
feast.   Coyote again goes to girl's home, and is again given meat, which he takes
home.   As he returns for meat third time he is accompanied by another Coyote,
who has begged permission to follow him.   As brothers are absent and Coyotes are
hungry, they ask girl if they may swing her and not await her brothers' return.
They swing her.   She nearly disappears from sight.   So many buffalo come that
Coyotes are scared and run into tipi.   Buffalo return to west and Coyotes go home.
Coyote again goes after meat, but sister has disappeared and brothers are hunting
her.   Crow suspects Coyote and tells him that he must help them to find her.   Again
birds are sent out and told not to return without having found girl.   All return except
Blackbird, who reports next day that girl was with buffalo.   On following day
Eagle, Hawk, Crow, and Blackbird are selected to go after girl.   They find buffalo
playing ring and javelin game, girl being ring.   This enrages Blackbird, who reports
what he has seen.   Coyote asks them to besmear him with pine pitch, except his
feet.   Coyote leads rescuing party, composed of Badger, Rabbit, Fox, Prairie
Chicken, Crow, Blackbird, Magpie, Hawk, and Eagle, Blackbird acting as guide.
Having gone distance, Badger digs hole for Fox, another one for Rabbit, and farther
on one for Coyote.   Coyote approaches gaming ground.   Buffalo are about to hook
him, but one calls attention to his pitiable condition, so he is unmolested.   As ring
rolls close to Coyote he gapes and tells ring to come closer.   Next, ring rolls straight
to Coyote, who passes it to Rabbit, who runs on and enters his hole, where he passes
it to Fox.   Thus ring is passed to Prairie Chicken and to other birds, buffalo following.   Last to receive ring is Eagle, who flies up with it into heavens, whereupon
buffalo decide to scatter over land and allow themselves to be killed.   Girl is restored to her people, whom she tells that each year maiden must be sacrificed, or
otherwise buffalo would not offer themselves to people.

71. WOOD-RAT-WOMAN WHO WISHED TO BE MARRIED.

Young Eagle chief visits village where he falls in love with young girl, who easily
surpasses other girls in bringing wood from timber, on account of her magic crook
and pack straps.   Going home he tells his father of girl, and his father moves his
village near village of girl.   Their marriage takes place.   She continues to bring
home from timber neat loads of dry cottonwood sticks.   She meets old woman, who
gives her roots which cause her to sleep.   Old woman blows her skin off from her
waist up and throws girl into water, while old woman thereafter takes girl's place.
She soon emits bad odor.   Otter is sent for to doctor her, and, failing, Beaver is
sent for, and then Buzzard, who recognizes old woman as Wood-Rat and orders
them to burn her.   Young man mourns by creek four days and recovers his wife.

72. THE WITCH-WOMAN WHO WISHED TO BE MARRIED.

Young man marries beautiful young girl by name of White Duck.   Old woman
becomes jealous of girl and kills her by thrusting dogwood stick into her ear, which
she does while girl is in timber after wood.   She then clothes herself in girl's skin,
throws girl into water, and returns and takes girl's place in tipi.   She becomes sick,
medicine-men are sent for, Raven recognizes her and orders her burned up.   Young
man mourns his wife and flies into sky as Hawk.

73. THE BASKET GAME, OR THE WOMAN IN THE MOON.

Spider-Woman and her people control seeds. When people visit her for seeds they are challenged and killed. In contest they jump up, storms are called, and they are frozen. Two young men decide to put end to Spider-Woman. They come to her corn-field with its grass-lodge and many skulls. They are warned by daughter against old woman, especially not to eat of food which she will offer them, for it will be human flesh. They are welcomed to old woman's lodge, are offered food, of which they eat, first having eaten some medicine. Boys leave lodge and emetic takes effect. Again they take medicine and eat of bowl of human eyes, and again they go out and allow emetic to take effect. Following morning they are fed squash, which is human ears. They vomit it up. They prepare to play game, covering their bodies with white clay, and from their eyes extend little black streaks. They begin to dance up and down by steep bank, which old woman pushes her victims over. As they dance old woman sings of snowstorm and other storms, but boys turn into snowbirds. She sings of air and they become larks. She then acknowledges defeat and offers her daughter to boys. They express wish to continue game; and they sing about storms, etc. Old woman survives until they sing of grasshoppers, which fly around and under her and take her up to Moon, hanging from which often a piece of her dress may be seen. Grasshoppers continue their flight to Sun, where they may be seen in summer time.

74. THE GIRL, SPIDER-WOMAN, AND THE BALL GAME.

Lame man and his niece live alone. He disappears each day, often remaining away late, which angers girl, and she tells him not to go so far away. Once while he is gone being takes girl to far country in wind. There she meets Spider-Woman, who tells her that she must play game of double ball. Girl cries and is taken to lodge of Wood-Rat. Errand man appears that evening and invites girl to feast with Spider-Woman. Girl goes to Spider-Woman's lodge, who whispers to herself that she will place girl's head among her skulls. Girl refuses to eat human eyes, and in night she asks birds to tell her uncle that she needs his help. Girl asks for four days' time and goes to hill and cries. In meantime uncle returns, misses girl, takes double ball game from bundle, places himself on them, strikes his ankle with stick, making motion as if throwing balls into air, and balls carry him. Thus he goes south looking for his niece, then west, then north. Not finding her, he returns home and a little bird offers to lead him to his niece, and flies toward east. Uncle finds niece and he gives her double ball with which to play, and blows his breath on string so that it will not break. When time for game comes, uncle tells her to strike him several times upon his ankle with stick. Game begins. As they progress, string holding balls breaks, and Spider-Woman suggests that they stop, but girl insists that they should use her set. She begins to beat her uncle's feet and presently twin balls appear. Thereafter she is uniformly successful, finally winning Spider-Woman and her people. Old Woman is killed and burned, and jumps from fire into grass as spider. Girl whips her uncle's feet, placing balls near them, and thus they enter his feet again, and he says that so it is that they rid themselves of Spider-Woman, and that hereafter people may have rheumatism and require bent sticks for support.

75. THE BOY WHO KILLED THE CANNIBAL WITCH.

Young man wandered about country, finding many human skulls. He finds lodge about which are playing three ugly girls and one beautiful girl. Three ugly girls enter lodge and youngest warns him against her mother, who is cannibal. In morning young man is asked into lodge, is offered food repeatedly, but it has no effect upon him. Old woman challenges him to dance, but he becomes snowbird and then lark, whereupon he carries old woman up to moon. Then he returns, dismisses three oldest girls and takes youngest girl to his village as his wife. She prepares garden and plants different kinds of seeds. In meantime he goes to west and brings buffalo, which power he has obtained from larks.

76. THE WITCH-WOMAN AND HER HOME.

Hunter goes east to grass-lodge, which he is invited to enter by Witch-Woman. He partakes of food, dies, and his head is hung up in her lodge. After four days his wife sends her son to look for his father. She challenges boy to dance, but first she suspends about his neck his father's head, which is held in place by cord passing from ear to ear. Witch-Woman is about to kill boy, rescuers appear, and she is burned. She bursts open and croaking tree frog springs upon tree.

77. THE MEDICINE-CHILD AND THE BEAVER MEDICINE.

Young boy acts peculiarly, playing always by himself, imitating the ways of a doctor, in which he often has great success. Powerful medicine-man of neighboring tribe hears of boy's ways, is jealous, and decides to visit him. He offers him tobacco from skunk-skin pouch. They smoke together. Again he, with his wife, visits boy and his mother, and continues relating to boy stories of his medicine. Several visits thereafter are made, and he and his wife bring presents and ask boy to relate stories of his medicine. Whereupon boy tells him he has no power whatever, that he has never been initiated into any mysterious lodge, and if he has cured people it has been without his knowledge of the origin of his curative power. Old man is enraged and on fourth night again offers boy smoke. Boy faints. He is awakened by old man, who, with his wife, goes home. Thereafter boy feels peculiar in his stomach. He shows increasing signs of pregnancy, and sets out to die in strange country. He travels south, then west, going to dangerous places and tempting wild animals to slay him. On hill he hears noises, which he follows to large new tipi. Is repeatedly warned not to approach, but in spite of protest enters. He expresses his willingness to die. Little people sit around lodge, one queerly-dressed man being on south side, who wears white streaks of paint on his face, and over him hang lariats and downy feathers. They decide that raccoon and muskrat and two errand men should decide whether or not they would offer him help. They express their willingness, but other animals' lodges must be consulted, and the peculiar man on south is instructed to take boy to next animals' lodge. Boy closes his eyes and strange being flies up with him on his back. Within second animals' lodge he finds that man who carried him is Hawk. Hawk explains their errand; animals express their willingness to help him, but lack power. Errand men of this lodge are Buzzard and Magpie. Magpie visits other animals' lodges, and finally Pahuk, chief of animals' lodges. They instruct Magpie to invite animals to report at Pahuk, and Buzzard is instructed to bring boy thither. As Magpie makes rounds of lodges they select delegates to go to Pahuk. Buzzards take boy, one carrying him at time and being relieved by others, two flying beneath one carrying boy. As boy enters lodge at Pahuk he becomes conscious and sees four little men at west whom he had seen at first animals' lodge, and who are Ground Hogs. Beavers, chief medicine-men, instruct Otters to cure the boy, but they are unable. Next, Bears are asked, and other animals in lodge. All are unable, until priests, Ground Hogs, are asked. Boy is placed on south side of lodge. Chief Ground Hog then sticks his nose in bowl of water, moves his jaws, and vomits up bone. Other Ground Hogs do same, continuing until they have exhausted their power. Bears then take up work, youngest cutting open boy's belly with his claw and removing flesh therefrom, which he throws to little animals, upon which, all medicine-men in lodge rush upon boy, exerting their several powers. They work over boy until the wound is healed, and he again becomes conscious. Boy is instructed to leave lodge during daytime and to return during nights. For several days he subsists upon seeds, berries, and small game, which he kills with bow and arrow which he has made. During night he is instructed in animals' mysteries. Finally, he is told to return to his village, where his parents have come to regard him as dead. His parents are asked to prepare food for him and call in his friends and relatives. When they come, boy collects from them presents, which he takes to Pahuk. Throwing two parfleches of presents into water he follows them and finds himself in animals' lodge. They are thankful for presents, but as there are not enough for all animals present, he returns for more, after which he is given power to slay enemies. Boy is permitted to kill smallest Ground Hog, which has power to kill enemies, removing skin, but keeping skull in the skin. He is taught feats of sleight-of-hand. News spread rapidly that mysterious boy has returned as great medicine-man, and old medicine-man of neighboring village decides to visit him with his wife, and they renew their story-telling contests. Next, boy visits old man in his village. Boy smokes old man's pipe, but does not swallow smoke. Old man smokes boy's pipe and becomes sleepy. Chief of village attempts to bribe boy to kill medicine-man, but boy refuses. After he and old medicine-man have smoked again, boy goes to creek, breaks hole in ice, dips nose of his Ground Hog in water, water stirs, and animal appears with piece of liver in its mouth. Blood appears on ice and about are pieces of entrails. Old medicine man is killed by boy, his wife removing his robe in morning and finding him dead, with pit of his stomach sunken in. All are glad of his death. Boy now enters medicine-men's lodge and dances with them and performs sleight-of-hand. Visiting Potawatami admire boy and invite Pawnee to bring him to their village. Pawnee go and are well received. After they have had their performance boy asks his friends to guard him during the night, as Potawatami are trying to bewitch him, and toward morning he hears someone groaning near entrance, He follows this man home and finds that it is Potawatami-medicine man. Pawnee start for home, boy saying that he has been bewitched, and they hurry him to stream at his request, into which they must plunge, whereupon thing within him which bewitches him will attempt to escape; that as it appears at his mouth they must grab it and throw it away; otherwise, he will die. Thus young man is rescued, and while they remain camping near river they are informed of death of Potawatami medicine-man who tried to overcome boy.

They return home and next year young man gives medicine ceremony and does many wonderful performances and becomes leading medicine-man, commanding cottonwood tree to grow from cottonwood stick.   Following year young man again has his performance, this time making beaver-lodge and making use of powers of beavers in which he thrusts sticks through cheeks of his friends, swallows willow poles, commands dead loon to fly about lake, etc.   He lives to old age and transmits his beaver medicine to his son.

78. THE ORIGIN OF THE LOON MEDICINE CEREMONY.

Poor boy is befriended by chief, with whom he is invited to live, where he looks after chief's ponies.   Chief's son and poor boy are great friends.   Chief's son is in love with daughter of another chief of village.   He is continually with her, but decides not to mary her.   To secure excuse for not marrying her he gets poor boy to lie with her.   He tells girl should she refuse he will never marry her.   The girl objects and refuses.   He attempts this second time, getting poor boy to dress in his clothing and to meet girl outside village in night; whereupon he discloses his identity and tells her of deception, that he himself would marry her.   He returns, obtains his belongings, while she obtains hers, and they journey south, killing game as they go. Her relatives ask chief's son her whereabouts.   Careful examination of young men in village reveals absence of poor boy, and it is known he has left with chief's daughter.   Poor boy and girl travel south to Pahuk, where they make grass-lodge and live. As she is getting water in pond she sees Loon, and later finds nest with two young birds.   She tries in vain to capture them.   She sleeps late one morning and they hear Loons talking, asking why their mother has not come.   She goes to pond and they allow themselves to be captured.   Thereafter, Loons pass each night with couple, returning to ponds during day.   Loons tell them that they will have no children; but that they will give them their power.   One day man follows Loons to water, which they enter, making great noise, sparks flying upward.   Loons and other water birds swim about in pond and downy feathers form in shape of earth mound, and man is taught mysteries of water fowl.   At Loons' suggestion man goes on hunt and returns with many ponies.   Loons are anxious that they should all return to their village, and they start out, woman carrying Loons.   They enter village and people are frightened, thinking they are enemy, for they had been gone four years.   Man gives several ponies to chief's son and tells him he has been to Pahuk, and chief's son invites him and Loons to eat with them.   War party is formed and ponies are brought home.   Chief's son then leads war party and poor boy assists him, and they take one of Loons with them, which guides and protects them.   They return with scalps and ponies.   They again go on war party and young man of village attempts to visit young's man wife, but Loon which has remained with her makes noise in protest and is mistreated.   On that night woman's husband on war-path knows that something is wrong and they set out for home.   Arriving, he finds Loon is ill, and it tells man that his wife has been unfaithful during his absence, and that man who has been with her has mistreated him.   Loon dies.   Young man takes his skin, and shortly after skin of other Loon, which also dies.   Then he drives his wife from his lodge, telling her never to return.   Thereafter, Loons are used on altar of medicine-man.   He finally dies of broken heart, but leaves his medicines to chief's son.

79. THE LIGHTNING'S MEDICINE CEREMONY.

Girl is born with birthmark on her forehead. She has mysterious ways; seems always to be counting stars; on which account she is allowed unusual freedom. She becomes beautiful young woman, and takes good care of her bed and pillows. One clear day she prophesies rain. All are surprised. During rainstorm girl lies near fireplace covered up. Lightning flashes, smoke fills lodge, and all are stunned. When they recover, father goes to his daughter, sees smoke coming from her head through round hole, hole extending through the pillow beneath her head and on into ground, from which smoke is pouring. Father digs into ground and comes to an object of many colors shaped like woman. People bathe in cedar-nut tea, in which has been placed scent of skunk, and bathe themselves in smoke from cedar leaves, and their face is smeared with mud from where lightning struck. All pray to stone, especially father. Lodge is swept and people bathe. Storm has disappeared. Following day father calls council. Smoke is offered to stone, which now seems heavy, though small. Girl is buried on hill. Father does not mourn, for he believes that gods in heavens took his daughter. In dream he sees her, and birthmark on her forehead especially as bright star, but on back of her head are eleven eagle feathers arranged like crescent moon. She tells her father that she is now living with moon, and says that lightning did not kill her, but stone which fell from heaven. She tells her father to make his bed on north side of stone, which he shall keep in lodge, and that stone will speak to him. Father at first can not see, for light of girl has dazzled him. Then he sees, although it is night. He reports to his wife what he has seen in his vision. He makes his bed by stone, and in vision man stands at head of his bed and tells him that he has loved his daughter; that he has killed her and he has lost his place in heavens and will remain with him; that he should make him up into a bundle, wrapping him in soft downy feathers; that he is medicine-man and will teach him his power. Following day father paints himself and goes to high hill in west and fasts. In dream he is again visited by this man, who tells him to cease fasting. Several nights after it rains, and spirit of stone tells him he should go to certain animal-lodge. He again fasts on hill during rainstorm, and is told to go to Swimming Mound animal-lodge; that he is to carry stone with him and remain on Swimming Mound until it thunders; that he will see Lightning strike place it has before struck many times. He is to go there and he will find hole, which he is to enter, leaving stone at entrance. Farther in he will find himself in large lodge, where he will hear animals playing on notched stick; that animals will go to entrance, see stone, and ask man to remove it; that he is to tell animals that he will remove stone if they will give him their power. Early in morning he arises, prays to stone, informs his friends of his vision, and they set out and journey to Swimming Mound. Though there is no sign of storm, as soon as he places stone on hill storm arises. He hears noise of rubbing of notched stick, and of people drumming, On second night he again hears strange noises, and whistling like wind, and he sees many elk. He faints, and is given power from elks, who fear stone and ask him to remove it, saying that it draws lightning and will kill them. Next, eagles visit him, and on account of their fear of stone give him power. Next night noises are heard and people sing like geese. Fire comes up from river and he sees all kinds of animals swimming. He pays no attention to them, and following day sun comes up and many colors are visible in every direction, like countless rainbows. At night he begins to be afraid. Green light shines from stone and he prays that his fear may leave him.   He continues mourning and again hears noises which seem to come from timber.   Fear is again taken from him as he sees green color of stone.   Man appears before him, stone shining brightly.   Man wears bear robe, with two great tusks, and bear claws about his ankles.   He breathes colored dust, which stone dispels.   Being tells man that he is afraid of stone, that lightning will kill his child. He turns into bear and walks off.   Following day clouds tremble in heavens as if crazy.   By evening dark cloud comes from west.   Lightning comes in his direction. He hears crying of animals.   Lightning flashes and rain pours down.   Noise passes, sounding like hailstorm.   Lightning now repeatedly strikes certain spot on river's bank.   He is stunned by lightning, and swoons, and stone man addresses him, telling him that animals have never been friendly with man before; that they are now to give him power.   He asks to be carried to place where lightning struck.   Man takes up stone and goes to hole where lightning has struck, prays to stone, and enters animals' lodge.   Mink passes in and goes to entrance and reports to other animals.   They send messenger to him to ask him to remove stone, telling man that he is fire maker, and is willing henceforth to live among people.   Animals confer and finally tell him that they will give him their power.   Animals walk around fire while he enters lodge.   In front of him he sees pieces of ice, which animals tell him they have taken from his stomach.   He is to swallow them again and animals would give him power to blow objects into people's stomachs.   As he takes his seat in circle in lodge he sees scalped man and tells tale of his power, and other animals give him their medicine.   Thereupon, man brings stone into lodge.   Animals blow their breath upon it, Skunk being last, saying that he also has power to make rainbows, and he gives man power to cure people with lightning.   Animals then tell man that he has formed stone medicine-lodge; that one altar shall contain mysterious stone, that second altar shall be Beavers', and that they will teach him power of sleight-of-hand and many songs.   He is guided out of lodge and sees clearly in night and enters his home with stone, skin, etc., which have been given him.   In morning he makes offering of smoke to sun, asking it to confirm all that has happened.   He disappears every day, returning every day with roots and herbs, one day in crazed condition, being under influence of some animal.   He is watched and appears as deer, as coyote, and as eagle.   Thus he was guided in his search for medicines.   Then they return to their own village.   Each night on way he sings his songs and tells his friends of his experiences, and he takes presents to animals.   In fall timbers are gathered for medicine-lodge, and, after successful buffalo hunt in winter, lodge is erected.   Man invites his tribesmen and explains to them all that has happened. They make altars in medicine-lodge, using skins of birds and animals.   Four ash limbs are obtained, which are decorated and notched on one side.   Cottonwood saplings are placed about altar, and also willows.   As they visit timber for these trees, medicine-man occasionally grunts and throws others down.   As they arise, some vomit corn-cobs, others pieces of root.   They bathe, cut trees, and return to lodge.   On way back medicine-man grunts and all fall to their knees.   Thus he finds out animal power of each man, for when wounded he would imitate animal from which he obtained his power.   Booths for different medicine-men are made inside lodge, and each man takes his medicines into his booth.   On following day medicine-men go to far-away timber and return with cedar tree.   This is selected for bear medicine-man.   In night they perform, and man makes lightning appear.   Each man throws up his animal's power and their power is seen sitting on ground.   After dance all sit down, then each man picks up his power and swallows it.   For many nights they perform. Distinguished warrior asks permission to join in final sleight-of-hand performances. Permission being given, he disappears for three days while he makes preparations. He goes into enemy's country wearing his war paints, and returns with many ponies. Returning, as he goes through village he sees poor boy, whom he takes into his lodge and asks him to help him. In afternoon they go to high hill, into which they dig and obtain clay, with which boy makes four mud ponies, and places them in path of sun ray in lodge to dry. In night two go to medicine-lodge with clay ponies. He sings and mud ponies walk around. At end of performance they leave lodge, the boy carrying ponies, which he throws into water. Thereafter, this warrior is known never to capture pony, for his power was taken from him because he has thrown mud ponies into creek. In summer people go hunting, and medicine-man takes his stone medicine with him. They are attacked by enemy. One of their number goes to near-by Potawatami village and asks their people for assistance. They send twenty warriors, who attack enemy, for they are giants, and enemy are overthrown. Thereupon, Pawnee cut out hearts of enemy, which they place in their medicine-bags, and smear their faces with blood. Owner of stone medicine is not killed, but bundle is lost.

80. EARLY MIGRATIONS AND THE STONE-MAN MEDICINE-LODGE.

Man and wife have two sons and many daughters. Each of sons takes wife. Thereupon, father makes lodge on each side of his own for each of his sons. Thus were formed three Pawnee villages—that of father being Pitahauirat; one on right, Chaui; one on left, Kitkehahki. The three original lodges faced west. Older son is told by his father that he should obtain power from animals and have roots and herbs, while younger son is told that he should learn power of stones and obtain their strength. Kitkehahki go south, and Chaui west, while Pitahauirat stay in east. Pitahauriat were favored by Tirawa, and Chaui were watched by heavenly gods, and Kitkehahki people understood power of stones. Especially did they talk with certain stone god who made them famous. Among Chaui young man disappears and returns famous, and is known as Animal Boy. Among Pitahauirat is man known as Cheat Coyote, or Crow Feathers, who is great thief. Crow Feathers becomes jealous of Animal Boy's costume, and meeting him in timber challenges him to turn into some animal. Boy becomes eagle, and is commanded by Crow Feathers to remain eagle and Crow Feathers returns to village clad in Animal Boy's costume. East of village poor man and his wife live in poor grass-lodge. As she is gathering grass bird drops down in front of her. She looks and finds boy baby. They care for child, which grows rapidly. In few days he asks for bow and arrow, which are given him. Next, he asks for spider-web ring. As woman rolls it for him he shoots at it and there appears dead buffalo. Thus for many succeeding days he brings buffalo. His power is not recognized, for he continues ragged and dirty. No one yet knows he is Animal Boy who disappeared, and who was taken into animals' lodge and given great power. Kitkehahki man in west is addressed by Stone-Man and given power to ward off arrows. On his return to his people he behaves insolently and they try in vain to kill him. They are hungry, for red fox has carried away game, and chief announces that whoever will kill it may marry his eldest daughter. Animal Boy goes to timber, and, with others, prepares trap. Fox is caught in Animal Boy's trap and Animal Boy grabs at its tail as it swings in the air from pole, but can not pull it down, and only gets hair from its tail. Crow Feathers comes along, claims fox, strikes down Animal Boy, and marries chief's daughter. Boy returns home, and hair which he has becomes whole hide of fox. People visit Crow Feathers' tipi to see fox. Hairs fall from it and are blue in color, not red. Buffalo do not approach village, but boy continues to obtain buffalo by his magic ring. One day Animal Boy sends his grandmother to chief's lodge with roll of pemmican. She is to sit at entrance and drop it, and, on leaving, chief is to ask what it is, and she is to tell him it is piece of fat with which she greases her boy's eyes. She does as she is told and is followed home by chief's youngest daughter, who sees true red fox and many parfleches with buffalo meat. Then boy tells old woman of visit of chief's young daughter, and sends his grandmother with parfleche of meat and red fox to chief's lodge. She goes to chief and tells him what her boy has said. Chief invites his friends and they are astonished at fox, for it makes his lodge very red. Chief announces that Animal Boy shall marry his daughter. Boy is sent for, enters his father-in-law's lodge, and shortly after they leave and go to pond, where boy bathes, appearing fine looking, wearing woodpecker cap and star-painted robe. They make their home with Crow Feathers and his wife. In night Crow Feathers sees stars on boy's robe sparkle like fire. Crow Feathers' wife is angry at herself at having been deceived. Following day boy goes to timber and returns with woodpecker on his head that flops its wings and whistles. That night Crow Feathers tries to imitate him, throwing coals of fire upon his own robe, which burns up. In morning he sets out with woodpecker tied on his head. It pecks at him and he bleeds. Soon Animal Boy tells chief to announce arrival of buffalo. They find buffalo and all have chance in slaughter. Crow Feathers finds one buffalo which he finally kills, but it is lean and thin. He takes meat home. Animal Boy pulls hair from some buffalo and hairs become hearts. He pulls beards of others, and hairs become tongues. From tail of fat cow he pulls hair, which becomes whole buffalo, and he is first to get home. His wife makes drying frame. Late at night Crow Feathers enters with his lean meat, which he removes from his pony's back. He is more enraged than ever at Animal Boy and tries to kill him, but animals kill Crow Feathers, and he is found dead in bed. All now recognize Animal Boy's wonderful power except Stone-Man, who encounters boy's wife on her way to spring, and demands that she let him drink. Girl tells her husband what Stone-Man has done. Boy takes his bow and arrow and goes among hills, where he finds Stone-Man. He shoots at him with arrow, but arrow flies back. Stone-Man, fearing boy, goes west with his wife and travels to hilly, stony country and he lies down near hot spring. He drives buffalo west by his magic power. He and his wife make earth-lodge. On altar he places stone. He captures many buffalo, meat of which his wife jerks. They have many buffalo robes. His wife gives birth to girl and dies, and Stone-Man lives with his daughter. Animal Boy loses his wife and leaves people, who are dissatisfied, for there are no buffalo. Chief asks young men to go in pairs through country looking for buffalo. Some in west find earth-lodge, which they enter and find Stone-Man and his daughter, who questions them about Animal Boy. Being told that Animal Boy has lost his wife and disappeared, he is pleased and gives them food. During night they hear strange noises in lodge. In morning each man is given parfleche of meat, being told to return to his people. They return, relate their adventures, and thus Kitkehahki move west to Stone-Man's country. Stone-Man sees handsome young man in their number and selects him for his son-in-law. That night he tells his son-in-law what he expects of him. During night they lie still, for Stone-Man can hear every movement and orders them to be quiet. Ascertaining that boy has no magic power, he challenges him to play ring and javelin game. They play inside lodge and Stone-Man throws boy into spring of boiling water, in which he disappears. Few days after other young men are invited to lodge, and he selects son-in-law, and discovering he has no power he also is destroyed. Many young men are similarly destroyed. Each time he selects a son-in-law he promises buffalo to people. Animal Boy in his wanderings is informed by animals of current events, and is told to return to his people. He arrives as they are entering lodge of Stone-Man and accompanies them and is selected as Stone-Man's son-in-law, but first asks permission to be accompanied by his two errand men. Permission is granted and he at once sends to chief to inform him that buffalo will appear at daybreak. In night Stone-Man's daughter tells her husband that she recognizes him and hopes that he will kill her father. Following day in hunt Animal Boy brings in meat, which angers Stone-Man, and he tells boy that he has not yet married his daughter, but must first bring him some plums, which must be fresh. Although it is winter time boy goes south, summons aid of different bears, who take him to plum bush, growl, boy shakes bush, and obtains plums. He returns with only perfect fruit to his father-in-law, who refuses to eat them. Then he tells his son-in-law to get good material for bow and arrows. Boy goes to southwest and mountain-lion furnishes him with bow, wood being imitation ash and sinew from his own tail, in imitation of buffalo sinew. Then boy prays to rushes, spreads his robe under them, shakes rushes, pulls up four stems, puts them in his robe, throws robe upon the ground four times, and arrows appear, one red, one white, one yellow, and one black. He goes to rocks and stones, cries, and is told to put arrows in his robe with flint stones, and to throw robe upon ground four times. He does so and arrows are flint-tipped. He gives bow and arrows to his wife, who gives them to her father, who complains that they are not good, and asks that they be tipped with hawk feathers, and that he be furnished gray wolf-skin quiver. Following day boy cries; hawks answer and drop their finest feathers. He prays again and wolves appear, and chief offers four of their number. Boy spreads his robe over them, shakes them, and there appear four wolf hides. These are given to father. He now begins to be satisfied, fills one quiver with bow and arrows, and asks that he be given three other bows and sets of arrows for other quivers. The boy appears with them and by magic transforms hides into quivers, and Stone-Man expresses satisfaction. He tells him that on following day he will play ring and javelin game with him as final test of fitness to be his son-in-law. That night boy leaves lodge and receives power from beaver. They play game a while and Stone-Man pushes boy toward spring, but he falls across hole with speed of otter and not into it. Several times he is pushed and escapes every time. He then turns into otter and Stone-Man declares himself beaten. In night he confesses that he had intended to turn people into stone, and he asks for young buffalo. In night boy goes east and cries. Man with dirty face and long hair, in robe, stands by him, saying he is leader of buffalo, and he offers to take boy to stone from which Stone-Man obtains his power. They go to hill where they find large stone, from which boy is directed to break many small pieces. He works all night and thus power is withdrawn from Stone-Man. They return to buffalo herd, which stands up and surrounds boy, and young buffalo of great power and flint horns offers himself for contest. In forenoon they reach Stone-Man's lodge. Stone-Man admits to himself boy's great power and declares he will never obtain his daughter. Buffalo runs to north side of lodge, panting as if winded.

Stone-Man takes one of his quivers, goes out and shoots buffalo, but point of arrow stops in buffalo's hair.   Stone-Man shoots at it many times, emptying his first quiver, and so he continues, exhausting one quiver after another, until he begins on arrows of fourth, which are four that were colored and that are only rushes.   He shoots his last arrow and runs past buffalo, who gets up and hooks Stone-Man, piece of stone falling from him, whistling through air.   Buffalo continues knocking pieces from him, and young man's two errand men batter him to pieces, while girl throws pieces into boiling spring, from which steam issues, filling lodge and ascending from top.   Boy and girl leave lodge, returning in morning, when they find that it has turned into earth-lodge of solid stone.   Thus there are geysers in west. Young man takes his wife home, starts an animal-lodge, and performs many miracles, in which his wife takes part, even flint-pointed arrows dropping from her body. Lodge which he founded is known as Stone-Medicine lodge, for on altar is piece of stone which girl has saved, which is part of her father.   Once Sioux attack village and keeper of stone drops it into river.   It is never found, but ceremony is transmitted by boy and his wife to their children.

81. THE FOSSIL GIANT MEDICINE-LODGE.

Man from hunting party near Swimming Mound enters timber and falls asleep on high hill.   He is addressed by giant, who tells him that many of giant people were drowned in that place, and that their bones are thereabouts, and that upon south side of hill he will find one of his thigh bones; that he is to take it and it will give him great power.   On waking, man sees no one, but goes and finds bone.   Carved on it is man and woman, skull, bow and arrows, and many stars.   On head is carved sun and moon.   He takes it home and makes it into bundle.   Again he dreams of this giant, and it tells him how to hold ceremony, and in his dream he hears songs which he is to sing in ceremony.   Years after, he holds ceremony, and those associating with him in ceremony are known as Medicine-Stone people.   This man becomes great medicine-man, and in doctoring uses dust from bone.   In great smallpox epidemic those who touch bone are immune.   Ceremony no longer exists.

82. THE SQUASH MEDICINE.

Before ordinary people is race of giants so large that they could carry buffalo. They have no fear of wild animals or heavenly gods.   They revile sun, call thunder names, turning their backs to it, and Tirawa decides to destroy them, and he sends rain, but though it does not rain very hard buffalo in west move and water breaks through and covers earth.   Giants are washed away and left on steep banks and other high places, on which they sink into soft earth, being covered with lightnings and clouds.   Thus power should remain in them, useful in after-ages for medicines, while bones should have healing power.   When ordinary people come to be on earth Big-Black-Meteoric-Star visits man, telling him to dig in certain place, where he would find great root, which contains power; that this root sprung from giant. Star also explains how giants had been destroyed, and instructs man exact ways of obtaining root, preparing it, etc.   Man realizes root star has spoken of is one people are afraid of, because it has odor such as human beings emit from their axillæ.   In spite of fear for this root, man is discovered one day digging one out.   He sings songs which he has been taught.   People lose their fear and join him, and he tells of his vision. After uncovering it he smokes to star and to root, addressing it as "father" and "mother." As he prays to it water oozes from root, whereby he knows that it commands to be removed, for if it had burst he would know that it was angry and was turning its odor upon the people. Men sit in circle west of root, place their hands on it, and thank it. Women come with hoes, one standing in each direction. Men smoke to Mother Earth, saying that they are about to dig into her to remove root; that root is one of her children, and thanking her for having received root and for having preserved it for them. Women sing. Woman in west represents birth; one in east, power of young life; in north, chief or warrior, and in south, land of the dead. They dig, exposing root, and it is seen that it is in form of human being. Root is removed and laid on west side. Hole is filled up. All sit down. Man fills his pipe, smokes to star in east, to Tirawa above four whiffs, to four gods of east, again to Mother Earth, four whiffs to head of root, one whiff each to right arm, right hand, left foot, and left hand, and one whiff to stomach. Drawing his hand over pipestem he then addresses root as "father," saying that gods taught him how to remove it; that earth was willing for it to be removed, and that root itself signified its assent by shedding water; that they are to place it in their medicine bundle and feel that its spirit is with them. Root is then carried to man's tipi, which has been swept and new mats placed on ground. It is placed west of fireplace and people sing songs. Again man smokes as before, and root is cut up, being supplicated that it may not be angry. Man then asks each medicine-man from what part of root he desires piece. He himself retains central part, and tells medicine-men to guard carefully part which they have received. In night he sees woman clothed in black, with soft downy feathers. In her left hand she has clam shell, and in her right, powdered root. She sings song, dropping some of root into clam shell. Thus she teaches man how to use root in doctoring. He learns that he has been addressed by root herself. He becomes a great medicine-man.

83. ORIGIN OF THE GEESE MEDICINE.

Young man who often goes with war parties is in love and often visits spring to see girl, but she flees from him. He therefore tries to associate with other girls in order to provoke her jealousy, and thinks that thus he may win her, but all girls refuse to associate with him, and he decides to stay with an ugly young man who is favorite with girls. He goes to his tipi and stays with him many nights, asking him why it is that girls seem so fond of him. Ugly young man tells him he got his power from antelope, and he, being requested, takes him to river that he may obtain this power. At river's bank he ties lariat around his waist and suspends him from bank, tying other end of lariat to tree. He is then left for four days, seeing fire and water each night. On fourth night he faints and finds himself in animals' lodge. They speak to him and tell him they know why he has come; that elk is in charge of lodge, but that his companion should have entered lodge with him. They tell him what he must do in order to obtain power. On fifth night he finds himself again on bank. Ugly young man then takes him to fire, where they eat. They return home, and ugly young man takes down his sacred bundle, removing flute red painted, which is of root and strings of elk hide, which he gives to young man. Tells him how to use it, warning him not to court married women or young girls. Handsome young man thereupon makes his home with ugly young man and he paints himself and goes

with his flute out around village.   He does this for four nights, whereupon girl he
especially loves appears and follows him to his lodge, where she remains all the next
day.   Girl's relatives hunt her, and young man and girl set out to journey toward
east, until they come to swamp, where girl sees two goslings.   These she rears as
pets, making moccasins for them in winter and feeding them corn and dried meat.
Husband goes off and returns with ponies, being watched in meantime by one of
geese.   Eventually they return to their village, where they make their lodge at edge.
They invite people, who see geese at entrance.   They are astonished, because geese
act like human beings.   Girl's father is now proud of his son-in-law.   They live
together, keeping homely young man with them.   One of geese dies, while other flies
away, first telling them that they are to have two children, one of which will die
young, and other will live to be great.   Years after, girl gives birth to boy, and then
another.   One grows up to be young man and dies; other becomes great warrior.
Chief offers to make him chief, but he declines, remaining great medicine-man, and
founding Geese medicine-lodge.   His father and mother die of old age and he
becomes leading medicine-man, also dying of old age after being father of many
children.

84. THE WONDERFUL BOY WHO KILLED HIS FATHER.

Sleight-of-hand performances are continued for many months in medicine-
lodge.   Stranger comes and shows great skill.   Leading Medicine-Man relates at
home of stranger's skill, and his son asks his mother to help him enter lodge.   She
protests, for boy is too young as yet and has received no instructions from his father.
Boy leads his mother to creek, where she is told to bathe.   While in water boy turns
into swan.   On way home they take two squashes.   His mother makes booth for
him in medicine-lodge.   Therein squashes are rid of their seeds and boy fills them
with swan down.   Seeds are buried west of village.   In night during perfomance boy
asks assistance of medicine-men.   Two young men assist him, they are given knives,
and cut two squashes in two, which now appear whole again.   His mother brings in
bowl of water, boy sings, and squirts water upon squashes, thereby forming pool
under them, whereupon squashes sing like swans.   They become swans and follow
him.   He puts his hand on their necks and they are again squashes.   All rejoice over
power of young man.   Young man's father worries over great power boy has shown
and hurries ceremony to end.   People prepare for buffalo hunt, cacheing their food.
On hunt young man is told to stay by his father, especially should he run after
buffalo cow.   Man follows cow far away from crowd, leaves boy to skin cow, claiming his preference to look for enemy, and shoots his son, who, when he recognizes
that it is his father who has shot him, dies.   Returning home at night with meat,
he pretends to know nothing about his son's whereabouts, and mourns his death.
On night of return to their village young man quietly enters his lodge, awakens his
mother, tells her to keep quiet, and goes to his uncle's lodge.   News spreads that
young man has returned.   His father sends for him, offering him his medicines, etc.,
and enlisting his wife's aid, but boy refuses to return.   When mother visits boy he
tells her what has happened to him; that after his death he found himself in Swimming Mound, where his swans had taken him.   They plan to kill man.   Boy takes
from his bundle a bone of a sunfish, and blows his breath upon it.   Thus bone
flies into man and kills him.   Boy grows up to be great medicine-man.

85. THE MEDICINE-MAN WHO KILLED HIS SON.

Boy is told that it is now time that he should join his father's medicine-lodge. He goes to lodge and prays to his father to receive him. Father refuses. Thereupon, he takes presents of many kinds, but his father is firm. Then mother takes her bundle and arrows, and she and her son, with downy feathers, robe, and some earth, enter lodge; but father does not recognize boy. In afternoon they enter lodge, singing about diving ducks. That night medicine-men perform sleight-of-hand. In morning they are asked to go to creek, where she and her boy are to perform. She jumps in with two gourds in her hand, holding them under water. On bringing them up gourds are soft down. Releasing them, they float downstream. Waving hands, they come upstream to her. Immersing them, they become gourds again. Boy is given gourds, jumps into water, releases them, and they come up as ducks and swim about in water, and then turn into gourds. Boy's father has remained in lodge, stung with jealousy and envy. All go on buffalo hunt, and medicine-man takes his son with him. When two are far from crowd, he accuses his son of attempting to outdo him in sleight-of-hand; shoots him in side with arrow, and throws him into river. He pretends ignorance, and joins his wife in mourning boy's death. Boy floats downstream to animals' lodge, where animals carry his body, beaver on one side and otter on other and led by mink, to Pahuk. He is taken in. Arrow is extracted and beaver and otter restore him to life. They send him home for tobacco, feathers, beads, and sweet grass. These he obtains through his mother, who goes through village collecting them from sacred bundles. Boy takes presents to animals' lodge and returns home, but does not associate with his father. Boy one night tells his mother what his father has done; among other things, that his father on throwing him into creek had told animals he gave them his boy to eat, but that animals had taken pity on him. He tells his mother that, if she thinks his father should die, she should take little water dog which she had to the creek, dip it into water, and if it came up with piece of liver in its mouth, she would know that animals at Pahuk had eaten up his father's intestines. This she does, and boy thereafter becomes leader of medicine-lodge.

86. THE CHIEF'S SON WHO RECEIVED THE ANIMAL POWER.

Man leads to Pahuk, far away, universally liked son of chief. There they sit down on bank. Man ties rope around boy and suspends him over bank, telling him to pick up eagle and woodpecker feathers which are scattered about. The boy does so and asks man to pull him up, but man has disappeared. He cries for help, and realizes that he is pregnant. Animals carry boy into their lodge and decide to help him. They act upon him, first Buffalo, then Elk, jumping over him. Then Bear cuts boy open, takes out bones of child, throws them away, and heals wound. Snake gives him bone from sunfish with which to strike his enemies. Buffalo gives him whistle upon which to blow when in trouble. Bear gives him dust to be used as paint upon sick people. Each of animals teaches him some power. Eagle teaches him how to fly and Duck to swim and dive. Boy is hungry, and animals send Crow to west, Beaver to north, Otter to east, and Fox to south, for food. After he has eaten, Beaver tells him it is time to go home, and Owl, Buffalo, and two Crows accompany him to his village. They leave boy just outside village. In night boy enters village, and following day presents are made to him. He then sends for his deceiver, takes him to creek, touches water, and he is dragged under and is never seen thereafter.

87. THE THUNDER-BIRD CEREMONY.

Two hermaphrodites digging artichokes see strange man. One of them slips around behind him and kills him with hoe. They return home and relate their adventure. People go to see dead man. His face is painted and his head is bloody, as though he has been scalped. That night they dance scalp dance. Shortly after, grandfather takes his young grandson, leads him to dead man, and boy counts coup on him. They remove downy feathers from man's head and cut off scalp-lock, which is fastened on pole and placed in front of their lodge. Boy sees this man in dream, who tells him that he is Thunder-Bird, and boy now sees a great bird like a crane talking to him. Bird again becomes man and tells him that he will give him power. Next day he throws away scalp, but keeps feather and always carries it with him. Once while on buffalo hunt boy sees the man in vision, and is told to visit him. He does so, leaving his feather as directed on tree. By pond he sees man turning into crane and into man again. He takes boy into cleared place with altar in west, where stands bird. In south of place is Bird-That-Never-Moves. Man then teaches boy ceremony and many sleight-of-hand performances during several days. He returns to his village, encountering his father crying on hill. They go farther and find his mother mourning. Boy asks that neither of his parents touch him. During hunt boy directs that they should kill many buffalo and prepare them for ceremony. Boy enters medicine-men's lodge with his bundle. He is painted with blue clay. His friends make many offerings to him. He is given seat in south. His performances are wonderful, for he is not yet medicine-man. He turns downy feather into Thunder-Bird; makes skull, which he places in east; makes Thunder-Bird to disappear, along with sun crane in south. At boy's request his friends prepare for him medicine-lodge and he gives ceremony which is called elk dance, because large crane in west of lodge has feathers on its head like deer antlers.

88. PROUD BOY AND THE ANIMAL MEDICINE.

Three bands of Pawnee unite in great medicine-lodge. Procession is formed to obtain tree to be used in lodge. In crowd is poor boy who afterwards is known as Proud Boy. He falls in love with daughter of leading man, but she pays no attention to him. Scouts are sent ahead and return with news that enemy is near tree which has been selected. Old warrior is sent to kill him. Girl is selected to cut tree. On return to village with tree is race, which is won by girl, prize being that she may live with priest until end of season. Ceremony is held and tribes return to their village. Following year ceremony repeated, and Proud Boy watches for girl, who appears beautifully costumed. Boy asks his father for clothing, but receives only waistband. Again they go after tree and race back to village, which girl wins again. There is a dispute over race, and they decide to repeat it, but girl's father asks that it be postponed until next day. Her father paints buffalo calf robe for her to wear. In race she wears her black moccasins and skirt and calf robe. They race, but girl outstrips the best runners, and Proud Boy's determination to marry girl is greater than before, because he knows that she possesses wonderful power. For winning race girl receives red ointment and lives with priest, sitting under bundle all time. She does not like this, but priest warns her that she must sit still or wind would hear her and not send buffalo. If she should play, buffalo would leave and gods in west would think that people only wanted dry heat in summer. So she lives with priest. They go on buffalo hunt and she carries bundle. Hunt is successful and girl is given heart and tongue of buffalo. Before they near the village on their return scouts who have been sent ahead return and report that their crops during their absence have not been molested. Crops are now gathered and bundle is opened and they have ceremony, during which girl is relieved of her ointment and gods take their eyes off from her, and she now becomes like other girls. Food is offered to girl first, and after ceremony she is handed to her grandfather and taken home. Girl is now known as Yellow-Corn. Boy tries to marry her, pleading that his father is great warrior and has many ponies and scalps, but girl's father refuses, because boy has never been on war-path and taken scalps. Boy becomes sad and wanders over country. He no longer plays with boys, nor listens to old men. Next year boy learns that Yellow-Corn has married greatest warrior in her village. He becomes more despondent than ever. People go hunting to country where animals abound, and Proud Boy goes to water dogs, where he remains, people mourning him as dead and returning home. Going through timber he sees girl, but on embracing her he finds it is deer. He mourns and tells animals to kill him. In evening he awakes from sleep and finds himself surrounded by birds, who tell him they have taken pity on him. They give him root to eat, and in night owls and water dogs come to him. In morning buffalo gives him robe bearing picture of sun, from which buffalo got his power, telling boy, should he be killed, to throw robe over himself and birds would wake him from sleep. Boy again sleeps and finds himself in animals' lodge. Four bears give him power to conquer enemy. They also give him medicines and tell him to use their picture on his lodge. Mountain-Lion, Buffalo, Eagle, Owls, and all other birds address him, telling him to put their picture also upon his tipi. Buffalo tells him that first buffalo he shall kill will be himself. That he is to take its scalp and place it upon pole at head of his bed. Proud Boy now sets out to find his people, and arrives after several days at dusk. Next day he appears, gaily costumed, with his face painted, and in his hand he carries eagle fan. He rides to playground on his pony, which is variously painted. He boasts of what he will do in overcoming enemy, and he now receives name of Proud Boy. People kill many buffalo and return to their village, where they have ceremonies of thanksgiving. Following winter they do not have to go on hunt, for buffalo appear near village. Proud Boy then obtains buffalo scalp as he has been directed. In spring big ceremony is again held by three tribes. Proud Boy's tipi is erected, and on little mound to west is erected cedar tree. As other tribes appear Proud Boy, mounted on his painted pony, tells that he is going to see woman who has refused him. Several bands appear, but girl is not among them. She finally comes with her mother, whom Proud Boy asks for her daughter. She consents, and Proud Boy takes Yellow-Corn to his tipi and asks his mother to bring them food, and they eat. He tells her of his love for her and she acknowledges hers for him, and tells him that she is married and that it would be better that she return to her mother's tipi, for her husband, who is a great warrior, will soon return home. Proud Boy says that he is not afraid of her husband, and girl finally consents to remain with him. Girl's mother misses her and after hunting her finds her with Proud Boy, but Proud Boy refuses to give girl up, although she begs girl to return on following day. Many ceremonies are held, but Proud Boy and girl remain alone in their tipi. Now warriors return victorious, bringing many scalps. Yellow-Corn's husband is told of his wife's desertion. He goes to his tipi, apparently not caring, but his brothers reproach him, telling him he has been great warrior, has made many sacrifices, and they taunt him because he leaves his wife with Proud Boy. He finally gives in and decides to accompany them to kill Proud Boy. Proud Boy, hearing of their intention, tells his father to have no fear, but to cover them side by side with his robe and to leave them. In night he eats of root which has been given him and gives some to Yellow-Corn. She expresses her willingness to die with him. Early in morning Proud Boy holds buffalo scalp to rising sun and he paints Yellow-Corn and again gives her some root. They seat themselves in front of buffalo scalp. Girl's husband and his friends come and shoot them and kill them and ride over them on their horses. Father and mother take bodies, place them on bed, and cover them with painted robe, as directed, and tipi is closed. People wonder why parents do not mourn. At noon dust rises straight up from tipi and there are noises inside, such as made by mountain-lion, buffalo, birds, etc. Again dust is seen and noises are heard, and for two additional times. Then Proud Boy comes out of his tipi in afternoon and asks his mother to prepare food for them. Boy tells his father that he shall not use his weapons against his enemies, but that they shall die. Next morning boy takes from beneath bed water dog, which he points towards his enemies. At noon Yellow-Corn's first husband is found dead, and thereafter each day one of his friends who helped him to attack Proud Boy dies. They offer to make Proud Boy chief. He declines, becomes medicine-man, healing sick and teaching his power. People began thereafter to paint their tipis in imitation of his.

89. THE BEAR MEDICINE-MAN.

Little boy alone in timber tries to shoot Magpie. It runs from him and entices him on day after day until boy comes to thick timber. In vision man stands before him, painted black, with feather head-dress, telling boy that bird which he has followed is medicine-men's errand man and that he is bird; that boy is to return to his people and to return to him several years later. Magpie then leads boy back to his village. Among Skidi is medicine-man who is jealous of all other medicine-men. He has great power, visiting graves to obtain human ears, etc., which he uses in killing people. He hears of little Chaui boy who has followed Magpie and invites him to his tipi, where he is given pipe to smoke and bowl of mush, which is really human flesh. Boy now returns to timber again, being led by Magpie, who takes him to animals' lodge, for boy is now in dangerous condition. He finds himself lying on fireplace, which is in shape of turtle. In his vision he finds himself in another place, surrounded by rushes. He sees man covered with mud emitting fire from his eyes and mouth. This being tells him that he is turtle and that he has carried boy; that he is fireplace of animals' lodge. He teaches him how in medicine-men's lodge he may shoot at turtle fireplace, whereupon it will move about lodge, and boy again finds Magpie in timber and in his vision he sees fire coming from water. He becomes unconscious and finds himself in lodge with animals sitting in groups. Magpie explains to medicine-men that boy has been fed by Skidi medicine-man with poisonous food, which has formed into clay ball in his stomach, which is increasing in size; that he, Magpie, has never before asked favor of animals, but that he now asks that they take pity on this boy. Animals shout approval, and healing doctor,

Beaver, begins trying to heal boy. They work over him with their mouths, grunting, but are not able to accomplish anything. Other animals try and fail, and boy is taken to another animals' lodge. For several days he follows Magpie, now suffering under increasing weight in his stomach. He lies down to sleep and again sees fire coming from water, and he finds himself in animals' lodge. Magpie tells medicine-men that he has taken boy to Pahuk; that they could not do anything for him; whereupon medicine-men say that if at Pahuk nothing could be done, they can do nothing. Boy is then taken to Spring Mound, where neither catfish, mink, raccoon, otter, nor beavers are able to help him. They return to Pahuk. Clay ball is now much larger and boy is weaker than ever and very thin. He faints at entrance and animals take boy in. They decide to appeal to chief who controls all animal medicine-lodges. Magpie flies after him, taking presents. Dust comes in at entrance, which, settling down, appears as bear, who so stands that it may look at sun. Bear is addressed by animals, and they explain that they wish him to cure boy. Bear offers to use his power if he may eat piece of boy's liver. Permission being granted, bear works over boy, cuts him open, takes out large stone, eats piece of boy's liver, screams and jumps over him, blows his breath upon boy's mouth, wound closes, and boy is healed, but seems as if dead. Bear commands other animals to restore him to life. They fail, whereupon bear blows his breath in his nostrils and boy regains consciousness. He is now told that he has power to cut people open and eat their liver, power never before given to human beings. Boy is sent home, where he does many wonderful feats. News of his fame reaches Skidi medicine-man, who again invites boy to his lodge. They talk of their medicines, and boy opens his hand, disclosing bear claw. He closes it and medicine-man drops dead, whereupon Skidi thank him for ridding them of an evil doctor. Boy becomes great, and in his medicine performances produces live bear. He also belongs to deer society, and in quarrel reveals his power to cause fireplace to move, and deer people yield to boy. He receives name Smoking-With-the-Bear, for he always smokes to rising sun and to bears. His secrets are lost with death of Medicine Sun, last of bear family.

90. THE BEAR MEDICINE.

On buffalo hunt chief's boy keeps with him in his lodge poor boy, son of poor parents. Boy is ashamed because his father has no success in killing buffalo. Father tells boy about mysterious animals in cedar-covered country to west, and boy decides to go and be slain by animals. He throws away his blanket and goes west into mountains, finds trail like human pathway, which he follows until he comes to hole, which he enters and finds it to be home of bears. He plays with cubs for a while, and mother warns him that her husband has wonderful power, given by sun, and is most dangerous bear in country, and she points to great pile of bones of animals which her husband has eaten; also to clothing belonging to captured people. Boy tells her that he is not afraid to die. On approach of her husband, mother bear tells boy to embrace one of cubs. Thus boy is found by old bear, who, entering, exclaims that he smells human being. He orders boy to let go cub. Boy refuses and cub asks his father to take pity on boy. Father quiets down, exhaling colored dust. He tells boy he is leader of bears; that arrows of man will not pierce his side, and that he is son of sun. He decides to teach boy his power. He then turns his family and himself into human beings, and they sing bear songs.   He shoots boy in side with arrow, but boy is unharmed.   He blows colored dust on boy, shoots arrow through him, and they restore him to life.   He then transforms his wife and child into bears, and they roll him over and he becomes bear again.   They turn boy into bear, then into human being, and he is told of movement of his people, that they are about to return home, and that he should go with them, but not to forget bears, for he is one of them.   Bear takes him to cedar tree, from which he takes down bear claw and hangs it about boy's neck.   He tells boy that he has power to blow colored dusts, which will heal sick.   He warns him that he must be careful among his own people, for he possesses canine teeth like bear; that he shall live to old age and that when bear dies he shall die.   He directs boy to go to animals' lodge, where he will learn to be medicine-man.   Boy returns home.   People return to their village and are attacked by enemy, who are driven away, one man being injured.   He is doctored by different medicine-men, but they fail to cure him.   Boy visits him, blows different dusts upon wound, and heals him.   Boy's fame as medicine-man goes through village.   In his doctoring he sings bear songs, and all know that he has visited bears.   He has his lodge swept and asks that all leave.   He takes down his bear claw and four colored feathers.   He goes to ponies which he has received as his fee for doctoring wounded man, passes his hands over bear claw and feathers, thus thanking bears for first gift he has ever received.   Then he sings song calling spirits of bears to him, and he smokes to them.   He sends for chief's son, who begs poor boy to teach him his power.   Boy is unable, for chief's son is to be chief, and may not be medicine-man.   He may not have bear spirit, for thus he might kill people, which chiefs should not do.   He offers his friend his choice of robes he has received as presents; also pony.   He makes his home with poor boy.   Enemies attack village, and boy wearing his bear claw and feathers and painting his face red, with black streaks down each eye, attacks enemy and kills many, and village rejoices in boy's honor.   He becomes leader of bear dance.   In winter they go on buffalo hunt, at which time chief's boy kills buffalo cow, which they make holy.   In spring boys go toward northwest until they come to animals' lodge.   Poor boy cuts meat in small pieces and gives it to chief's boy, and lowers him by lariat over steep bank, where he fastens meat to stick in bank.   He asks chief's boy if he is willing to be suspended over bank until animals receive him.   As he says "Yes" he prepares two short dogwood sticks, sharpened at one end, while chief's boy sits with his back to sun, that sun may tell bears that poor boy is sending substitute.   He places two dogwood skewers into skin of boy's back and lowers him over bank to where parfleche is hanging.   He notices that night that chief's boy feeds birds as they come to him.   On fifth morning poor boy awakens from his bed on bank and chief's son is standing by him, fully clad in ceremonial garments and bearing bundle.   They start home, and following day go to chief's lodge, where all are glad to see them.   Chief's son tells his father of having been received in lodge, where he was taught power of medicine-men.   He collects presents for animals, delivers them, and returns next day.   In fall the two boys enter medicine-lodge, and perform many wonderful feats.   The two become most powerful medicine-men, and chief's boy becomes chief.   As they grow old first one to receive power grunts.   He takes up his robe, embraces his friends, and leaves lodge and people hear scream of bears.   Boy disappears, for it is his time to die, as bear is now dead.   Chief's son continues bear dance, marries, and has many children, and passes on to them mysterious power which he had learned in animals' lodge.

91. THE BEAR MEDICINE AND CEREMONY.

Man kills bear while his wife is with child. Girl is born, possessing spirit of bears. When her finger nails are trimmed she nearly dies. She grows to womanhood, has three children, first two dying in infancy, Third child, boy, when about ten years old, is taken with party on hunt. Boy returns sick. Medicine-men fail to cure him, he dies and is buried, and his mother mourns at his grave for several days. She returns from hunt, having cut her hair and gashed her arms and legs. A hunting party returns, reporting that grave of boy has been robbed. She goes to grave, finding her son's body exposed. She mourns by grave four days, when she goes to drooping cedar tree under which she crawls, fearing animals. In night she hears bear growling. Bear speaks to her, saying that they have taken pity on her. She is asked to follow bear, sliding down steep bank and entering bears's den, which is like lodge. There she meets his wife and six cubs. She is asked to run after cubs, and is told that she may have children equal to number of cubs that she can catch. After much difficulty she is able to catch two cubs. She is told that she may take them home. Bear blows colored breath upon her face, telling her that thus she may restore wounded men. Next, bear's wife hugs woman, coughs up piece of cherry, which woman eats; also piece of hackberry and piece of bullberry, and these she told woman are to be used in doctoring. Bear gives her paint and red feather, while his wife gives her yellow paint and a yellow feather, saying that she is to use them, too, in doctoring. She is instructed to make tipi of buffalo hides, and on it to paint yellow circle, black band and red band, picture of cedar tree, and owls, who guard bears' den. She is also told to kill two cubs when she gets them home and to make sleeping bags of their hides for her children; that spirit of cubs will return to bears. She starts home with bears, one of which strays away. Other bear she carries into village, although bear does not like odor of human beings. In night in vision she sees woman bear, who tells her not to be afraid to kill cub. She kills cub, tans skin, which she paints yellow, placing yellow feather on its head. She hangs skin up on pole so that sun may strike it. Thus spirit of bear is present with woman. Whenever she is touched she grunts like bear. When woman's husband returns he recognizes her power. Enemy attack village; she gives red paint and feathers to her husband. Enemy's arrows do not affect him. He fights bravely. After battle, wounded man is brought to them. As he grunts like bear, they send for woman. Tipi is prepared, she and her husband put on their paints, she sings bear song, grunts like bear, and in morning she inhales power from sun and her husband smokes to it. They go to wounded man's lodge. She blows different colored breaths upon wound, which becomes fresh, and blood flows. She becomes savage like bear, and cedar leaves are burned. Four days later she and her husband again doctor wounded man in similar fashion. Fourth time wounded man begins to get well. Man she has cured sees woman often in his dreams as cinnamon bear, and he decides to become poor through offerings he proposes to make to her. She learns of his thought, goes to him and tells him that he is not to worry about recompensing her. He is made member of bear society and she feeds him from her mouth with cherries. He makes her many presents, at which time she opens her bundle, placing her bear hide on west of fireplace with paints and feathers by it. She then passes her hand through mouths of ponies which have been given her for healing wounded man, mixing saliva of ponies with tobacco and offering it to different gods and to the bears. Then woman tells her husband of songs she has learned and of her visit to bears' lodge.   Several years afterward she gives birth to son, who is never sick; later, to girl, and thereafter to many children. They all die, except first two.   Husband kills many buffalo, they make tipi, and she originates bear dance.   She warns her husband that arrows will be powerless against him unless they strike him on hands.   One time camp is attacked, woman's husband fights bravely, but is wounded in many places.   His wife, learning of fact, asks for menstruating woman.   His niece comes forward, is taken to wounded man, but they are too late, for he is dead.   For many months she mourns her husband. She teaches her boy bear mysteries.   She is visited by a Chaui, who, being sincere in spirit, is taught bear dance.   He remains with her several years, caring for her children.   She often performs in medicine-lodges.   She lives to old age and her son becomes one of four leaders of bear ceremony.

92. THE BUFFALO POWER AND THE WILD HORSE DANCE.

Famous and powerful chief has many wives.   Youngest of wives gives birth to son, who is great favorite with his father.   Boy is taught to believe that he will succeed his father.   Boy is encouraged by his father to join war parties.   He joins many, but they are unsuccessful, and warriors decide that it is on account of chief's son that they always meet with mishap.   Thereafter, he is not allowed to join warriors, and is called Poor Boy.   The boy's father and mother are ashamed of him and grow angry at him.   He becomes despondent and decides to leave home, taking with him pair of moccasins filled with corn and another with pemmican. Taking his quiver, robe, and lariat, he starts west, eating few kernels of corn each day. His food soon becomes exhausted and he grows weak.   He goes up on high hill to die.   From hill he sees big lake, around which people seem to be standing.   He goes to lake and drinks, and tells lake that this seems to be good place to die.   He removes his clothing, makes it into bundle, and throws it into lake, offering it to spirit of lake. In vision two clouds of dust approach from west.   First is made by two horses, who circle lake and return; next, by two buffalo, who also return.   Again he sees dust and horses and buffalo are together.   They pass over him, trampling him.   Big drove of buffalo next appears and tramples him further, and boy seemingly is killed.   Some one touches him, he stands up, and finds himself in lodge beneath lake. On north side are men imitating horses; on south side are men imitating buffalo. Leader of buffalo tells him that they have sent for him, that they have taken pity on him.   They are to make a medicine-man of him and teach him buffalo and wild horse dances.   They tell boy that he should first report to his parents, who now mourn for him, and return to animals' lodge with usual presents.   They then turn into horses and buffalo and again trample upon him, and he finds himself by lake, and by his side stands black horse, which carries him home.   On way boy is told to eat grass as horse does.   Each day horse circles about boy to refresh his strength. Horse takes him to his father's village.   He returns to horse presently, having obtained presents from his parents, and is again taken to animals' lodge.   Horses give him spear, shield, and black lariat.   Buffalo give him wool and paint.   He returns home.   At once he takes poor boy, who has befriended him, and alone they go on war path and capture many ponies.   Again they go on war-path, and boy becomes famous as warrior.   Village is attacked by enemy, and boy paints his horse and himself and takes his shield, robe, and spear, which he waves at enemy while they shoot at him. Having frightened enemy he orders his side to attack. He at once becomes famous and is offered chief's daughter in marriage, and he becomes chief of tribe. In marrying chief's daughter he provokes jealousy of young man of tribe, who goes to girl's brother and bears false witness about his sister's husband. Husband has told his brother-in-law that he must not ride black or dun horse while hunting. Chief's son disobeys, rides dun horse to buffalo hunt, buffalo kill him and horse. Chief's son-in-law realizes by his magic power what has happened and informs his father-in-law. They send for boy. He is placed on east side of village. Chief's son-in-law then asks that all keep quiet and closely guard their horses. Horses then begin to neigh and rumbling noise is heard, and just as sun rises in east black and dun horses run over boy, trampling him. Husband then tells his wife to go to east of village and arouse her brother; to tell him he has been sleeping too long. She does so and restores him to their father. Some doubted this man's ability to restore his brother-in-law, and to prove his power when they are on war-path he throws his lariat over his shoulder, storm comes from heavens and covers enemy and they are scattered, and party captures enemy's horses. At another time his village is attacked and he throws his spear among enemy and it makes great noise as it falls, and deep ravine opens up between them and village. All now know that man is powerful, but jealous man continues to cause chief's son to make trouble for him, and again girl's brother mounts his dun horse in attack against enemy. Husband tells his wife that her brother has now caused his death, for when black and dun horses fight together in same battle he must die. He then turns over to her his belongings, telling her to keep them for her children. He mounts his black horse, goes in among enemy, and is killed, together with horse. His brother-in-law on dun horse is also killed, along with horse. Woman gives her husband's lariat and other wonderful belongings to one of her sons, who becomes medicine-man and continues wild horse dance.

93. THE ORIGIN OF THE BUFFALO CEREMONY.

Men play ring and javelin game. Howling Fox never plays, but watches them. One day he hears rumbling noise pass toward east beneath playgrounds. In evening noise passes to west. In night he is told to remain on playground next day. In morning he bathes, and after breakfast takes his pipe and tobacco to grounds, where he sits in his usual place at northeast corner. After game he remains, and woman addresses him, coming from west. He recognizes her as buffalo. She tells him that she has six sons and one daughter. Daughter is missing and she has searched all over country for her. She tells Howling Fox she will give him great power if he will find her daughter; that she is ring which is used by one of gamblers. She tells him to collect rings and bring them to her and she will recognize her daughter. On following day he visits different lodges, begging that they lend him their gaming rings. He takes rings to his own lodge, which he has had swept, and places them west of fireplace and makes smoke offering to heavens and to each of rings, praying to them for mercy. He hides rings under his pillow. In evening, after men have ceased playing, he takes rings to grounds and places them on north side. He hears rumbling sound from beneath ground; as it draws nigh he hears rattling of hoofs. Buffalo draws near and turns into woman. She examines rings and detects her daughter, whom she says she will take with her, leaving it to buffalo to decide whether she shall remain ring or become buffalo. She promises to watch over him and gives him paint which he may spread across his mouth in order that he may heal sick. She now becomes buffalo, and, as requested, he ties ring between her horns to her hair, and she disappears. He thanks gods in heavens that he has been permitted to see wonderful buffalo. In morning he returns two rings and begs man whose ring he has not returned not to question him, for he shall be compensated. In fall village goes to southwest to hunt buffalo. They meet with no success. Howling Fox meets buffalo woman, who tells him she is there to help him; that he is to tell people to go to northwest. Fearing chief, he makes him offering of food and suggests that they discontinue traveling southwest and go northwest. Next morning they set out in that direction and travel slowly, for people are weak. They travel for several days. One night Howling Fox again meets buffalo woman. She tells him to make earth-lodge, its entrance to face west; that she shall return in four days and shall want offerings of feathers, etc. He again offers meat to chief and tells him that he desires earth-lodge, which is built. Fourth night Howling Fox meets buffalo woman and gives her presents. He goes with her to buffalo wallow, where she becomes buffalo. He follows her until they come to bulls, where he ties presents on their horns. She becomes woman again and tells him that in few days they shall have buffalo, and gives him power to call buffalo, for buffalo rejoice that she has found her daughter. She covers him with her robe and blows her breath, causing great wind. When wind dies down he finds that he is at home. In morning he tells chief that they shall soon have buffalo. When lodge is finished Howling Fox again meets woman, who tells him that she has brought bulls for people. She enters Howling Fox's lodge; instructs him how to arrange it. On following day people are warned to keep away from lodge. Howling Fox makes great fire and in evening scatters ashes over floor and out to entrance. In night woman returns with buffalo bull, who sits down in west of lodge. Smoke is offered him, and woman says that her father is satisfied. Bull leaves and another enters to receive smoke, and so on during night buffalo enter lodge to receive smoke. Woman gives Howling Fox buffalo meat, and when chief is invited in morning he is feasted and is surprised to see hoofprints on ashes. Warriors are sent for and they eat. Then spies are sent over hills to look for buffalo. They come back, reporting that they have seen none. They are sent out again and report having seen several bulls in ravine. They return with news, receive smoke in lodge, and crier summons people to make attack, announcing that ribs, tongues, and hearts are to be brought to Howling Fox's lodge. They gather about his lodge, where he instructs them that they are not to break open skulls with stones in order to obtain brains, and that one cow they must not kill, for she is messenger. Leader of surround is chosen. Many bulls are killed, cow being permitted to escape. As bulls are skinned, eagle feathers and native tobacco are found on their heads, and they know that Howling Fox has been instrumental in bringing them. Howling Fox is given many presents and ponies. People kill buffalo four times and they return to their permanent village, Howling Fox alone staying behind. He is visited by buffalo woman during nights and is taught buffalo dance and ceremony, which on his return to the people he institutes. He wears gaming ring from cow on his left arm and is owner of ring. He gives presents of buffalo robe and pony to man and teaches him ceremony. Shortly after, Howling Fox dies, because, as was said, he gave all his knowledge to another man.

94. THE BUFFALO MEDICINE DANCE.

People are on buffalo hunt and are attacked by bull, who enters sacred tipi and tears it to pieces. Man is sent for who understands spirits of buffalo. In afternoon dark clouds gather, rainstorm follows, and woman is blown away. After storm, people are addressed by buffalo, who tells them that their sacred belongings shall be restored. Buffalo disappears. Again buffalo appears and invites some of buffalo medicine-men to go with him to buffalo country. They travel until they come to steep bank, where they enter buffalo lodge, passing on way through deep water. In lodge they find bear and buffalo, who perform feats of sleight-of-hand. During performance animals arise, snort, and downy feathers fall from their mouths. One buffalo blows upon reed whistle and swallows it, throwing up feathers. He tells medicine-men that he gives them ceremony, that they shall have buffalo skull to which they shall make offerings, for spirit of buffalo will reside in skull, and that skull will inform them through dreams as to what they shall do in ceremony. People return to village and perform ceremony.

95. THE WOMAN AND BUFFALO DANCE.

Unmarried woman gives birth to child, and because people are angry at her they leave her behind when they go on hunt, Child cries, she tries in vain to stop it, starts west, and on hill finds buffalo bull, who blows smoke from his mouth and gives woman root with which to doctor child. He rolls on ground and robe appears, in which she is told to wrap child. Bull blows and calls three other bulls. They blow their breath upon child. Buffalo cow comes. Child is placed by cow and sleeps. When it awakes it is well. Buffalo tell woman that root will drive away wild beasts and that she is to bathe child. She starts off, passes snake, and it dies on account of root. Man comes to her lodge and offers to be her husband. He learns of her power and they return west to thank buffalo, and he is taught buffalo dance. He finds rattle where buffalo rolls upon ground, which bears picture of buffalo skull. He is to use it in doctoring. Buffalo rolls again and makes whistle, from each end of which hangs moon-shaped shell. In doctoring, man is to blow whistle, whereupon he will see bull's shadow. If shadow does not appear, patient is to die. When boy grows up he becomes great medicine-man and is taught buffalo dance.

96. THE BUFFALO MEDICINE DANCE.

Boy meets old buffalo on hill who tells him that he is getting old. Buffalo takes pity on boy while boy feeds him. He hands boy little ball from his stomach, which, when he smells it, will enable him to see buffalo. He gives him whistle and some roots which he is to use in doctoring. In buffalo dance he is to chew piece of ball, eat of root, and paint his face with mud from buffalo wallow and eat piece of it, whereupon he will have buffalo spirit and people will give him many presents. He gives him power to heal wounds, but not sickness. Boy returns and tells his father of his adventure; they return to buffalo, which is now dead. Then, as he has been directed by buffalo, he cuts off its tail and piece of scalp. In next medicine-lodge, boy dances buffalo dance, using robe, which changes its color.

97. THE BUFFALO GAME MEDICINE.

Man whose medicines are herbs sleeps in open, sees in sky stars which appear as sticks and rings of javelin game.   In his sleep man appears to him and tells him to make gaming sets up as he has seen, that he is to play game on west side of village, for there is home of buffalo.   He is not to play in east, for it is home of diseases, nor in south, for it is home of dead, nor in north, for from that direction enemies come. He is to make ash bow and dogwood arrows.   With them he is to kill two buffalo bulls, using their hides for wrapping for two javelins.   In selecting wood for his javelins he is to darken his enemy's visage by cutting on north side, he is to fight disease by cutting on east side, he is to ward off death by cutting on south side, and then to cut tree down on west side.   Thus the leaves of tree will be preserved.   He is to smoke to heavens to remind them that they gave him game.   Wood for second javelin is to be obtained in same way.   Sticks are to be length of his body and they are to represent men.   He is to obtain two other sticks shorter than first two, and they are to represent one-horned buffalo in west.   Sticks are to be spliced in pairs. He is to kill buffalo cow, placing her head toward east, so that buffalo will follow him, and remove skin from about vulva with which he is to make ring.   He then takes gaming sticks, representing at one end ears and single horn.   Two cross sticks are tied on to represent legs; front stick representing sun, and hind one, moon, for they were first to play game in heavens, moon winning and giving sticks to men.   After sticks are prepared one is charred black to represent darkness, night, or north; other is left white to represent light, day, or south.   Next, he prepares ring, to which he ties white bead, representing star which gave him game.   They start to play game, ring being carried by his granddaughter, for ring represents granddaughter of men. At gaming ground they smoke to star, to earth, and to ring and javelin.   In playing, they are to count one hundred and twenty, or number of fingers and toes on six individuals, value of count being determined by relation of ring to different parts of javelin.   Losing side is to furnish fire in which to boil meat for offering.   At end of game pieces of heart and tongue are offered to sun, moon, and stars, and game and player is rubbed with fat.   In night he is again visited and told to make ring from buffalo calf, on which he is to put blue bead to represent Tirawa, and that ring will represent earth.   In doctoring, should sick person have played with sticks, he is to go to gaming ground and take dust from center of ring where it has stopped and let sick person smell of it and then rub it over his body.   Other men make gaming sets in imitation of this one.   Owner with black javelin in medicine-lodge uses it as pipe-stem, although javelin is not perforated.

98. LOST WARRIOR AND THE SINGING BUFFALO MEDICINE.

Warriors are taken by enemy.   One hides, and in returning home loses his way. He cries to spirits.   On hill he hears buffalo cow singing in east.   Cow teaches man many mysteries, and gives him power to travel without fatigue and to capture ponies.   He sings song which he learns from buffalo at sunrise.   Thereafter, he is always successful while on war-path.

99. THE BUFFALO MEDICINE WAR SHIELD.

Man on hill is envious, seeing that boy is talking with girls, for girls have refused to talk with him. He cries on second hill farther away from village, and then wanders off and remains all winter. He returns in spring and does not enter village, for he has no home. He sets out after herd of buffalo, seeing among them woman. He asks her to marry him. He goes with her to buffalo village and woman's uncle tells him that he wants presents of scalp and blue beads. Boy returns to his village, enters chief's tipi, obtains presents, and offers them to buffalo. They are thankful and give boy shield, which he is to wear upon his left shoulder. Boy returns with his wife to his village. It is attacked by enemy. He uses his shield in battle and kills many. He shows greater bravery in second and third attacks upon village. On fourth attack in his excitement he wears his shield on his right shoulder. He is wounded and taken home to die. In night buffalo bull makes water in front of his tipi. In morning boy rubs some of mud over his face and returns and lies down, whereupon many buffalo roll about in his tipi. Great dust appears. Boy rolls in dust again and becomes man with buffalo robe on his shoulder. He is known thereafter as wonderful man. Buffalo warn him never to put buffalo horn or hoof in fire. Long time after, careless person, not knowing of restriction, throws spoon into fire in his tipi and man dies.

100. THE MAN WHO MARRIED A DEER.

Young man on hunt goes to Pahuk, where he associates with woman who turns into deer. Angry because he has been deceived, he shoots at deer several times, but can not kill it. He follows deer to swamp, where it becomes woman. They lie together, and both become deer and wander over country, and woman gives birth to two fawns. In meantime she teaches him deer power. He is now able to transform himself into deer or back into man at his will. She takes him to his people and he enters medicine-lodge and asks permission to perform. When they give it he returns to his wife, and she and two fawns turn into human beings. They enter village, but odor of people is offensive. Man and his wife and child enter medicine-lodge. They borrow pair of deer antlers, sing, man places antlers on his head and he becomes deer. Next, he puts fawn skin over his boy and boy turns into fawn. Then he turns fawn into boy. At end of performance medicine-men acknowledge his great power and make him their leader. They live with people many years. Woman tells her husband that she must now leave him. She becomes black-tailed deer and runs off. Man is unhappy. His children grow up and both marry, his boy possessing great power. When man sees that his children are happy, he goes into timber and never returns.

101. THE DEER DANCE.

Man wanders away from village to mountains, and on hill in dream sees black-painted man standing by him wearing buffalo robe. He tells him he is errand man of deer society, and that he is to take him to their lodge. Man looks around and sees no one, but in sky sees Raven, who has been speaking to him. Raven directs him to top of mountains, where he hears great noise. At entrance of lodge man addresses him and tells him it is he who has spoken to him in vision, and that he had become raven, and as man seems afraid to go to animals' lodge he has caused many ravens to make noise like human beings.   They enter lodge, where man finds many animals, elks being leaders.   They sing, and all have turned into people, each after his kind.   They dance and sing, and eat red beans, some of which they give to man, who becomes very ill.   He believes himself dead and visits heavens and sees Tirawa sitting in earth-lodge holding bow in his left hand and sage in his right.   Tirawa puts wild sage on ground, moves it, and red beans appear.   Tirawa tells him he is to return to his people and teach them this dance.   At daylight people turn into animals and birds and leave lodge,   They return each night for four nights, and man returns to his people.   On his way home he makes songs commemorating his introduction to lodge, and he institutes deer dance.

102. THE WOLF WARRIOR.

Man is separated from war party, goes on hill and hears old wolf singing toward heavens.   Wolf addresses man and gives him root which he is to powder and mix with clay and snuff it while on war-path, whereupon root will relieve his fatigue.   Man is instructed to make wolf robe.   He asks wolf for long life and tells wolf that he will always smoke to him.   Wolf asks man to spend night with him, for it is to be his last.   As sun appears in morning wolf dies, crying with his last breath to sun, whereupon man, as directed, cuts around wolf's nose and strip down his back, which he is to wear on his scalp-lock, thus keeping with him spirit of wolf, which will enable him to live to old age.   After taking skin from wolf, man returns home, where he has been regarded as lost.   He is often absent from village.   He disguises himself and accompanies victorious war party, but claims no credit.   In fall he again joins war party.   Each day, though he remains behind, he scouts in advance of others, telling them at night what he has seen.   They fail to find Comanche and start toward Osage country.   He scouts again and reports having seen Cheyenne and Arapaho.   He captures many ponies, which he gives to leader.   When ponies are divided he takes one, while each of warriors receives pony, even those who have gone on war-path for first time.   They burn grass as signal of their victorious approach, and paint their faces with charred grass.   Wolf Man becomes famous as warrior, and thereafter is leading scout.   Famous leader rides war party into Mexico.   Wolf Man and companion are leading scouts.   They seem never to tire.   They discuss their power, Wolf Man explaining how he received his from wolf, while other man gives him root which he uses as relief from fatigue.   This be obtained from horse in dream.   These two travel incredible distances each day.   They return home successful and they become close friends.   Wolf Man dies of old age, his last moment coming as ray of sunlight rests on him, and thus he dies as wolf has died.

103. THE COYOTE AND WOLF MEDICINE.

Man meets Coyote, who offers him his pipe.   After he has smoked, Coyote takes him to his people, where he meets wolves and coyotes.   There Coyote introduces man as his brother.   Coyotes roll in dust and give him root which will cure hydrophobia.   They give him other medicines for urinary troubles.   Next, wolves roll in dust and give man whistle, blowing of which will cure sickness.   Another Coyote gives him bone with which to kill people.   Coyote gives him bone for war club.   Another Coyote gives him piece of his skull, which he is to place on his forehead to prevent people from bewitching him.   He returns home, blowing on his whistle on way as directed.   Animals hear him.   He becomes medicine-man.

104. THE SCALPED-MAN MEDICINE.

Party meeting success returns again to enemy's country, but fare badly. Man is wounded in flight. He is necessarily abandoned, his friends giving him food and drink. In night woman addresses him, telling him that she has only done it to scare him. He misses some of his meat. Several nights he hears strange voices and misses portion of his food each time. When last piece is gone, he asks mysterious being to kill him. Scalped-Man appears and takes him to his home in big cave, on floor of which is spread wild sage. By fireplace is buffalo skull with offerings about it, and many parfleches of meat, and buffalo robes. Each day Scalped-Man leaves cave, but wounded man discovers no exit. As Scalped-Man returns, wounded man hears voices and then laughter of Scalped-Man. He thinks he hears his parents calling him, but is warned by Scalped-Man not to try to escape. Scalped-Man teaches him ventriloquism and sleight-of-hand performances, and heals his wound, and gives him eagle feather which he is to wear in his hair to represent Scalped-Man. Feather, and paint which he gives him for his body, will enable him to run fast like wind, and when fleeing from his enemy he is also to spit on his hands and wet soles of his feet. Wild sage in his hands will turn into arrows. In dismissing him Scalped-Man warns him never to tell of his abode in cave, or he will take away his power. Man returns to place where warriors had left him. There he is found by his friends, and he asks them for certain presents, which he takes to Scalped-Man and then returns home. In medicine-lodge he exhibits his power and becomes medicine-man. Village is attacked, one of enemy having power to divert arrows from his body. Medicine-man leaves his lodge by Scalped-Man's power, approaches enemy from behind and they turn on him, but he wards off their arrows. Man among enemy, who shows same power, rushes upon him, and he strikes him with club which Scalped-Man has given him. Enemy are now easily overcome. He becomes great warrior, and finally commits suicide, grieving for his friend Scalped-Man, who disappears.

105. HOW THE PAWNEE GOT THE EAGLE DANCE.

People move their village and man disappears. Two years after when on hunt lost man returns to them, wearing buffalo robe covered with feathers and head-dress of feathers. He does not associate with other men. He disappears again for short while and returns with feathers, which he makes into bundle. He is looked upon as wonderful. Really he has no power, but often visits feather-covered hill where he stands and prays. He ponders as to how he may obtain secret of hill. He goes to gaming grounds, takes his nephew on his back to feathered hill, cries, and drops boy down hole into eagles' den, saying to animals that he offers his nephew for them to devour. He cries several days thereafter, but receives no power. Boy's parents do not know what has become of him. Eagles receive boy, but are angry at man who has made such sacrifice, for they were about to give him power. As he has become impatient they decide to punish him. On east side of den are two old featherless Eagles, parents of all Eagles. They decide to keep child and teach him their power. All Eagles approve. They fly around boy and scatter feathers. Again they fly around him and he is covered with soft down. They do this several times, placing him on south side, and he is now young Eagle, and not yet able to fly. He lives with young Eagles and eats meat which is brought each afternoon by old Eagles.

At night they take bones out of cave and drop them over country. He is taught to fly, but is not yet permitted to return to his own country. He then begins to bring in young animals, which he offers to old Eagles. When he brings in deer they know that he is strong and that it is time for him to return to his people. They ask boy to lead them to his uncle's home, where they enter his village on south side where men are playing stick game. Sitting watching game is boy's uncle. He recognizes him, and two Eagles circle about him and take him up into sky and drop him and he falls into Eagles' den. He is placed in front of old Eagles and they spit upon him for several days and his bones are scattered one by one over earth. People in their fright remove their village, and site becomes known as Place-Where-the-Eagles-Carried-Off-a-Man. Boy remains with Eagles several years, and old Eagle offers him his skin, by means of which he may keep his spirit and tells boy that he should grow old like old Eagle. He gives him claw which he is to wear when fighting enemy, and paint to wear upon his body and bone from wing for whistle. They promise to watch over him in sickness. He is told to get eagle-wing fan, by means of which they will breathe and revive spirits of sick. He is to kill young fawn and make rattle to use in his doctoring, which he is to shake and odor will arouse animal spirits. Ten Eagles fly with boy to his home. They alight on mound in village, fly around him, and he becomes boy and enters his village, finding his parents still mourning for him. He gives his mother his bundle to be placed on altar in west. News then rapidly spreads through village of boy's return, and manner of his uncle's death and reason therefor. War party sets out. Four days thereafter boy becomes eagle, and hurries after them, becoming boy again just before he overtakes them. In attacking, boy is first. He takes two scalps, which he gives to leader, retaining small piece of each. In night boy becomes eagle and returns to his village, outstripping war party. On relating next day of success of war party he is not believed, for his power of flight is not known. In few days warriors return and it is now known that boy has told truth. He becomes great warrior and decides to enter medicine-lodge, in which he causes his eagle skin to turn into live eagle. Next, he becomes chief and dies in old age and transmits his power.

106. THE DOG MEDICINE.

Boy resting on hill is spoken to by dog, who tells him he has taken pity on him and will help him to marry certain girl who has refused him. Boy goes south and sings song which Dog has taught him, and girl comes to him and they are married. They go to Dog, who tells boy that he is to call him brother. Dog gives him buffalo robe, eagle fan, bone whistle, and rattle. Whistle he is to use in his ceremony and whenever he wants Dog. Dog gives him medicines and Dog dance, and tells him he should capture pony he is to give him when he is upon war-path. He will know it by star upon its forehead. Pony is to be Dog himself. Dog has power to blow smoke from its mouth. Boy originates war party; they go south, capture ponies, one of which has star on its forehead. In medicine dance boy appears with feathers on his head. When he dances he seems to be surrounded by sparks of fire. In doctoring sick man he sings songs and spits up small dog hide with picture of moon upon it. Patient is put to sleep upon this and becomes well. He institutes Young Dog dance.

107. BURNT BELLY AND THE DOG.

Old woman lives in grass-lodge with her grandson. They are poor and boy begs food. Boy finds Dog, which he feeds, and Dog brings them meat. In dream Dog tells boy to go on war-path and that he will protect him. He and his Dog go to enemy's country. Dog aids boy in capturing horse. Chief's son now takes interest in poor boy and he is asked to treat Dog kindly. On hunt poor boy kills several buffalo with arrows given him by chief's son. Chief's son has no success and poor boy gives him buffalo. Dog again visits boy in dream, telling him to go on war-path. Accompanied by chief's son he sets out and captures many ponies. Dog now tells him it is time to kill enemy and gives him owl feathers, bone whistle, and red paint, for sun is his father, and he tells boy that sun is protecting him and that father of Dogs sits near Tirawa. They go to enemy's village and return home with scalps. He returns with scalps four times and is now recognized as warrior. He marries. He goes on war party, for Dog has told him he will watch over his wife. Nearing village Dog meets him wagging his tail. Thus he knows that his wife has been faithful. He goes on war-path many times. Once man visits his wife and kicks Dog. As husband returns Dog does not meet him and he realizes that something is wrong. He hunts up Dog and they go to high hill. His friends visit him, offering him pipe. He refuses even chief's son. Boy and Dog sit on hill until they finally turn into red sandstone.

108. THE EAGLE AND THE SUN-DANCE.

Poor young man goes on hill, cries, and he hears drumming on fourth night plainly. Visiting river where drumming is heard, he hears whistling. Looking overhead, he sees Eagle, who speaks to him. Eagle flies around boy, then off to timber. He returns, and boy follows him until he finds birds sitting in circle, two swans in center drumming, and birds are all whistling. Eagle tells him they are to give him their dance. He is to dance four days, during which time he must fast. Swans tell him that they are leaders of dance and that their spirits will follow him home; that he will dream of dance and in dream will be instructed. He is to give dance when buffalo bones are seen on high hills. Owls circle about him and teach him songs. Thereafter, he institutes Sun-Dance.

109. THE SKELETON MAN AND THE SUN-DANCE.

Man and his wife on hunt make grass-lodge. Each day he returns with meat, which they cook outside. Something approaches from timber one day. They enter their lodge and skeleton follows them, rattling as it drops to ground. Woman is afraid to touch bones, but man gathers them in robe and voice whispers to him, telling him that he is Knee-Prints-Upon-the-River-Banks. Woman being frightend is sent home next day and skeleton smokes with man. In one whiff he finishes pipe. He tells man he controls all animals and birds and teaches him Sun-Dance.

110. THE WOMAN WHO IS BEWITCHED BY A FOX.

Young girl strays off by herself while women are gathering wood. She finds hollow tree blown over by wind. Within it she discovers child with small face, long hair, thin arms, and long finger nails. Child reaches out its arms to her. Girl is frightened. She looks again and child motions to her, and she sees that its face is painted yellow and its forehead black. She calls women, who look into log, but child has disappeared. Girl screams like Fox, and Fox runs from them, and girl acts like Fox. At home medicine-man is sent for, who doctors girl, placing her over smoke, which she inhales. She vomits, throwing up white clay and Fox hair. Man sucks upon her body, drawing out hairs. She becomes well. Many years after she has a pain in her wrist, sore forms, and white clay appears. She is then fully recovered. She lives to old age and has many children.

111. GHOST-MAN WHO BECAME A WHIRLWIND.

Man lives in graveyard. People see whirlwinds about him and he is considered ghost. He cures sick man by throwing dust into air, which envelops man as whirlwind. He also cures people who become sick on dreaming of dead people. Once he himself becomes whirlwind while doctoring and falls down as skeleton.

112. THE MAN WHO WENT TO SPIRIT LAND.

Poor boy rejected by girl goes on war-path, captures fleet pony, and so is able to kill buffalo. Next, he counts coup, women dance in his honor, and girl marries him. In few days she dies and he mourns by her grave. In night he is told to leave grave, as his wife is dead. He persists, however, in mourning, and mysterious boy tells him finally that he will take him to his wife. Young man travels south for many days, being accompanied by strange boy, although he can not see him. He imagines himself surrounded by ghosts, but is told not to give up. He sees bright tipi; he is warned not to enter, but goes in and finds old woman on south side. She asks him what he seeks, and he tells her, and she lets him continue on his journey, telling him that way to spirit land is dark; that he must cross black stream of water on log; should he fail to cross log he will die; and she gives him four clay balls, and tells him how to use them. He continues, crosses black water, and enters village. It is now light. On south men and women stand in circle, his wife among them. As she passes him he strikes her with clay ball. He does this fourth time, whereupon she addresses him. He begs her to return with him, and she hesitates long before she decides. They set out upon their return, and find old woman's tipi. She gives them something to eat and keeps them for some time, teaching him elk dance and giving him whistle and red beans, eating of which will enable him to commune with spirits. She gives him four more balls, which when thrown will turn to buffalo. They start on their journey. When he has thrown last ball and killed last buffalo mysterious being who accompanies him leaves him, telling him that he is Wind. Young man and his wife journey on to his village. They live happily for some time, but women become fond of him on account of elk dance which he has instituted. He does not remain true to his wife and she dies second time. He mourns at her grave and Wind tells him that having disobeyed his wife he can not regain her. He teaches his ceremony to his friends and wanders off to die.

113. THE SPIRIT WIFE AND THE WHISTLE DANCE.

Man recently married leaves his wife and goes on war-path. Upon returning, he finds that people have gone on hunt. He follows them and her father tells him that she is dead. He goes to her grave and mourns. A boy asks him if he really loves his wife and places his hands upon him, and man finds himself in different country. At night he sees bright tipi, which he enters, finding old woman. Floor of tipi is covered with sage, and upon it many fox skins, eagle feathers, etc. She gives him four mud balls. He continues his journey, crossing log, which shakes at first, but becomes quiet, and man declares his readiness to die. He enters village in spirit land and by means of balls attracts attention of his wife, who follows him. They set out for home, he receives balls from old woman which become buffalo, and she gives him elk dance and rattle, telling him that warriors who have died on plains make their home in rattle. She also gives him whistle. They continue traveling through space. Finally they all land and husband is instructed to have his wife sleep each night in bed of cactus, which by morning has caused her nerves to assume normal condition. Arriving home, wife remains apart from people for several days, on account of their odor. In night boy is told that it is Breath or Wind who has assisted him, and that he is to obey his wife. He goes on war-path, carrying his rattle. Near enemy he removes handle, particles of dust fly out from rattle and become armed warriors. They attack village, killing many and capturing ponies. He holds rattle up and warriors enter, becoming dust. He becomes famous warrior, always traveling alone. Women desire to marry him. He takes second wife. His first wife tells him that he must remember her and must be kind to her. Once in visiting his second wife he becomes angry and speaks in slighting terms of his first wife. When he returns to his first wife he finds her bones upon bed. They are placed in grave, where he mourns, but no spirit addresses him. He institutes whistle dance, teaches people how to bewitch, and teaches power of bewitching by throwing red beans into air.

114. HANDSOME-BOY.

Boy is carefully guarded and well clothed by his parents and is called Handsome-Boy. He hears warriors talking. and in night he wonders why his father does not send him on war-path. In night girl visits him, but he repels her and she scornfully tells him that as he has achieved no reputation as warrior he should not act in that manner. When she leaves he ponders over what she has told him, arises, captures two of his ponies, and sets out, traveling many days. He has no fire utensils and eats raw flesh. In dream, man with bear-claw necklace and scalped-fringed leggings speaks to him, telling him to go to high hill. From hill he sees people coming up from water who look like eagles. He puts his hand to ground, arises, and finds flint knife. He goes to water and sees buffalo. He kills one and skins it with his flint knife. He is again addressed in night and is told to go to another hill. Arriving at hill he sees sparks passing from one weed to another, which he at first believes to be fire-flies. He takes stick from center of hill, and then another, and uses them with his flint in making fire, using sand also. Thus he makes fire and thereafter cooks his food. He enters prairie-dog town and in dream is again addressed by mysterious being. In morning he kills buffalo and jerks meat, and remains there several days. One night he hears people dancing and singing that Handsome-Boy has killed an enemy. Mysterious being speaks to him and tells him that he is to fight enemy. He hears singing and dancing as before. He goes in; he sees people dancing, and they are prairie dogs, which run into their holes. He throws tobacco in hole to show his gratitude for them singing and asks them to help him. He mounts one of his ponies, rides on high hill at sunrise, and sees man. He returns to his camp, paints himself and his pony, and meets man and takes his scalp, which he puts on long pole. In night he again hears dancing and next day he again offers prairie dogs tobacco. He is warned by mysterious being that in three days he is to have hard fight, but that he must not be afraid, and on third day he meets lone enemy, scalps him, removes his war bonnet, is surrounded by other enemies, kills several, and takes their scalps. He is again addressed by mysterious being, who tells him to go north. He takes his two ponies, releasing one he had captured, to big mountain, on top of which he sees fresh earth and hole. In hole he sees footprints of child. Removing his clothing, he enters hole, which enlarges. Desiring to see end, he runs and hears whistling. He meets dwarf, which allows him to pass. Passage-way grows lighter and he sees his two ponies and village, at edge of which he is addressed by man as "Nephew," who stands him on his feet, and sage is burned with hot coals on four sides of him, and he is given small sage ball to eat and told to swallow saliva. After four days his uncle tells him that it is time to leave, that they have watched over him, and dead people pass through passage; that it is good for young man to die in battle, and warriors find the passage easy and are gladly received; that people who die on sick beds have hard journey; that people who commit suicide never journey through that passage—should they enter, dwarf drives them back. Again he is bathed in sage smoke and is told to return to his people. He runs through passage, encountering dwarf, who asks him to stop, and boy now sees mysterious being who has before addressed him many times, and he tells him he is Wind and he will be with him on war-path and give him courage. Wind gives him paint, whistle, and downy feather, and tells him that should enemy shoot feather he will die. Boy runs through passage-way and starts north. Each night Wind visits him, telling him to decorate his leggings with pieces of scalps. He also tells boy that his parents have adopted child, for they believed him dead; that he must not be angry at them. Outside his own village he meets boy and accompanies him home. He is invited to Crazy Dog dance. There Handsome-Boy sees his father and mother. Next day his mother sends invitation for supposed stranger to her lodge to eat. His parents do not recognize him and he grieves because he is asked not to sit on bed. He goes to dog dance, sits on south side, and takes part, but enemy appear and all go out to defend village. Handsome-Boy enters fight with boy who has befriended him. The two kill enemies and count coup, and they take many scalps. Handsome-Boy returns to his new home and is received with honor, for with him their son has counted coup. Women dance scalp dance and Handsome-Boy hears same shouting as he heard in prairie-dog town. He gives away many presents. Next day as he approaches lodge where Crazy Dog dance is to be held, he finds pony tied to spear, thus indicating that pony is to become property of whosoever will take scalp. During dance, Handsome-Boy's friend recounts his deeds, whereupon Handsome-Boy relates his adventures. All rejoice, and father and mother ask Handsome-Boy to return to his old home, but he refuses. After dance he divides his ponies between two lodges. Enemy is attacked and Handsome-Boy takes up spear which has been thrust in ground, and with it kills four. Tying four scalps to spear, he takes it to lodge of those who mourn and is given pony, which he presents to his adopted father. He now marries, and they have boy, but his wife is mean. He is chosen leader of hunt. Mysterious being directs him to herd of buffalo. His wife asks him what he should do if she were unfaithful, and tells him that she is sought by other men. He must not strike her, however, for thus he has been instructed by spirits. His wife thereupon taunts him, whereupon he goes off to mourn. Beautiful girl appears and asks him to be her husband. They return to village as man and wife and enter lodge which girl's father has prepared for her, and he smokes with his father-in-law. Feast follows. They remain together four days and nights. Handsome-Boy's child cries for its father. It is not known what has become of him. Mother discovers her husband with his new wife by following direction indicated by child. She takes child to its grandmother, telling her that she must take it to its father. When father sees child it stops crying. Child's mother enters tipi, calls him names, and as he does not reply she draws knife and is about to strike him, but Handsome-Boy 's second wife prevents her, and men rush into tipi and kill her. People rejoice because of her death, for they know she has been mean to Handsome-Boy, and no one is punished. Handsome-Boy grieves and chiefs try to console him, offering to make him chief. He can not accept, for he has been struck by woman. He has leggings prepared with scalp-locks and necklace of scalps. In night he tells his relatives of his visit to spirit land, directing them how to live and how to die in battle. Next day he disappears.

115. THE WEEPING CEDAR TREE.

War party hunts enemy. In mountainous country they hear woman crying. They are selected to hunt her. They are led away by crying and find cedar tree. One, believing this to be bad omen, returns home. Other warriors continue and all are killed.

116. BIG TURTLE.

Warrior borrows friend's bundle and leads on war-path. On journey they meet big Turtle. Two young men climb upon its back to ride Turtle. They become fast. Others mount Turtle's back and also become fast. One member is told to return home and relate fate of party to their friends. Turtle goes to big water and disappears with warriors. One directed to return home remains, and in dream sees other men in lodge under water. He returns home with his tale. Afterwards he goes to place, is taken into water where in animals' lodge he is taught many mysteries by Turtle, their leader. People are jealous of power which boy shows in medicine dance, which he has been taught. They go to water and dip it out with buckets and find skeletons of men, but no trace of Turtle. Animals are displeased and take away boy's power.

117. COYOTE AND THE SCALPED-WOMAN.

Coyote meets Scalped-Woman on hill and makes fun of her head, which he likens to mush pot boiling over. She runs after him and he changes into old man with whiskers. He stands by tobacco patch. She asks him about Coyote. He knows nothing and she goes off. He again overtakes her as Coyote and turns into warrior, and she asks him if he has seen Coyote. He again becomes Coyote and calls her names; she starts after him and he crawls into hole, and she follows him and gets fast. He has connection with her; she marries him and he deserts her.

118. HOW A WITCH-WOMAN WAS KILLED BY A COYOTE.

Coyote meets Spider-Woman on island. Desiring to gain her friendship, he moves his membrum back and forth through foliage. She laughs until she dies.

119. COYOTE MARRIES HIS DAUGHTER.

Coyote while with his family on hunt feigns illness, is buried, first telling his wife that she is to marry their daughter to man making arrows.   Next day mother and daughter see man making arrows.   Coyote follows them and enters lodge, pretending to be blind in one eye.   He accompanies hunting party, gets hearts and tongues, which he sends to his wife, saying that he, chief, presents them.   While they are cooking, he enters and asks for his daughter in marriage.   In his happiness he forgets himself, opens both eyes, and is recognized by his wife. who kills him with club.

120. COYOTE AND HIS TWO WIVES MEET WONDERFUL-BEING.

Coyote and his two wives go south.   They meet Wonderful Being.   Women being afraid are told by Coyote to put pebbles in their robes so that they will rattle. They dance while Wonderful-Being comes up, and sing song about having killed wonderful man.   He becomes afraid and runs away, whereupon Coyote and his wives run home, his older wife dying on way with fright.

121. COYOTE TRIES TO FOOL RAIN GODS.

Coyote almost perishes from thirst and offers his heart and tongue to gods in west if they will send rain.   Clouds form and it rains.   Coyote drinks.   He continues drinking and withdraws his promise.   It continues raining, and Coyote runs and is killed in hailstorm.

122. COYOTE AND THE PRIESTS.

Coyote, Fox, Rabbit, and Spider-Woman act as scouts on buffalo hunt.   They report to priests' lodge having seen many buffalo.   After slaughter they carry much food to priests' lodge, and their daughters carry wood to priests' lodge.

123. COYOTE WHO CALLED HIMSELF DRAGGING-THE-STONE.

Coyote decides to leave his village and visit another Coyote village.   As he approaches they are gambling.   He announces himself as Dragging-the-Stone, and being dressed like warrior they are afraid of him.   He is invited to chief's lodge, but refuses.   He is next invited to feast with giant, and refuses.   He also refuses to feast with bravest warrior in village.   All are afraid of him.   He camps with poor couple in village.   Chief calls for scouts to look for buffalo.   They return and all set out for hunt.   Coyote is invited, paints himself, and rides old woman's horse, which he kills because its penis is on its back.   He walks on and man gives him buffalo. He begins to skin it and giant comes, ordering him and his friends to leave buffalo, as it his.   Coyote is second time ordered to leave buffalo.   They quarrel and Coyote strikes giant with his bow.   Giant with his breath blows Coyote away, but Coyote returns to fight and giant runs off scared.   His reputation increases throughout village.   All are afraid of him.   In feast Coyote is given prominent place and is offered ribs, which he declines.   Being asked about his favorite piece, he says he prefers small piece of jerked meat and some tallow, and asks that they build little arbor over fireplace.   As he is fond of cooking, he asks them to sit down and he spreads the tallow on rack and it begins to drift into fire.   Then Coyote swings tallow about, thus burning people and causing them to cover their heads, whereupon he starts to run, but they overtake him on sandbar and kill him.

124. COYOTE-MAN AND HIS TRICKS.

Coyote passing through timber finds squirrels playing in trees and tells them he is starving and asks them to feed him. They accuse him of knavery, but he begs, and male squirrel descends and tells Coyote to remove one of his testes, whereupon pecans appear. Coyote returns home, has his wife operate on him, and they obtain pecans. She does this four times, but fifth time blood appears, for she has done it once too often; whereupon he returns to squirrels, who heal his wound, but tell him he has lost power. He continues traveling and meets Beaver, and begs food. Beaver instructs him to get cottonwood bark and macerate it between his hands. Then Beaver cuts Coyote's scrotum, oil appears, which is mixed with bark, and pemmican is formed. Coyote is taught trick, but is warned he must not do it oftener than four times a day. He goes home, disobeys their injunction, and returns to Beaver to heal him. He meets Bear, who tells him that he is going to his den. Coyote runs on ahead, daubs his head with mud, and puts white clay on his lips to make them appear chapped. He again meets Bear and begs for food, especially for grease for his lips. Bear finally consents to allow Coyote to cut him in loin. He cuts deeply and thrusts in his arrow, killing bear. He finds pile of dry limbs, to which he carries bear meat and roasts all of it before eating any. Overhead he hears squeaking noise, made by two limbs rubbing, and orders them to stop. Enraged because they do not, he climbs tree and puts his hand between them and is caught. Coyotes appear, eat up his meat, and run away. The tree releases him and he continues in quest of food. He meets medicine-man, asks him how he doctors sick, and obtains medicine-man's song and dance; whereupon he kills medicine-man, dresses himself in his costume, enters village, dancing on way, pretending to doctor sick boy, but kills him with red-hot iron. He cuts boy up in small pieces and puts him in kettle. Snake appears and Coyote gags it with piece of meat. Snake goes to people and with difficulty tells them that Coyote killed sick boy. People run to village, but Coyote has disappeared. He runs through timber and sees Buzzards on hill. He asks them to carry him up into sky. They do so and he discerns game far below. Presently two Buzzards carrying him separate and Coyote falls to earth, alighting in hollow log, where he remains for several days. He enlarges holes in log. People camp near him and he cuts tails from his raccoon-hide quiver and sticks them through holes, and woman gathering wood calls her companions and they cut tree down for raccoons. He feigns anger at them. He travels on and meets two women gathering wood, and near by baby-board. He takes out baby, cuts off its head, and replaces head in cradle. Women discover deed and they recognize it as work of Coyote. All are now angry at him, and they capture him and throw him on fire, but he jumps out with popping noise and becomes little hairy man.

125. COYOTE TAKES THE PIPE-STICKS TO THE BEAVER.

Coyote's wife and child are hungry. He encounters beavers, makes pipe sticks, which he carries to beavers' lodge. Thus beavers become his children. On invitation they meet Coyote on hill far from creek, where pipe stick dance is to be held. He kills many with his club. He tries in vain thereafter to repeat trick on beavers.

126. COYOTE AND THE ROLLING STONE.

Coyote looking for food gives his knife to big, round stone, asking it to help him find food.   He enters lodge in village and sees meat and regrets his foolishness in having given away his knife.   He returns to stone, takes his knife with him, returns toward village, but village has disappeared.   He gives his knife again to stone.   He returns and discovers village second time.   He goes back to stone and takes his knife.   Stone starts after him.   He asks help of bears, but they claim they are powerless; likewise, mountain-lions and buffalo.   Bull bats offer protection and he enters their lodge.   They expel flatus on stone as it approaches, breaking it in pieces.   Coyote starts on his way again, but makes fun of bull bats, whereupon they fly about stone fragments, reassemble them, and stone again pursues Coyote and kills him.

127. COYOTE AND THE ROLLING SKULL.

Coyote sings about hunting buffalo on prairie.   Buffalo skull taunts him. Coyote replies insultingly to Skull, and it pursues him into village and devours him and all people except four girls.   They flee and Skull takes after them.   As it approaches closely, one girl throws her packstring on ground and cactus appears. Coyote overtakes her and kills her.   Next, Skull's flight is retarded by second woman's packstring, which forms steep bank and creek.   He crosses on floating logs, overtakes girl, and kills her.   Third woman with her packstring makes ravine, but Skull gets over and kills her   Youngest cries for help.   Bull bats direct her to hollow.   There she finds small lodge and small boy.   He tells her to enter his lodge. Skull appears and demands girl, and boy blows blue bead from his mouth, which strikes Skull, breaking it in two.   Boy is Milkweed.

128. COYOTE TURNS INTO A BUFFALO.

Starving Coyote meets buffalo bull eating grass, envies him his ease in obtaining food, and desires to learn to imitate buffalo.   After repeatedly fleeing for his life, he allows buffalo to charge upon him in buffalo wallow, and he becomes buffalo and remains with them.   He is told to sit while resting with his nose toward wind, to detect odor of approaching enemy.   Coyote begs Coyote-Buffalo to make him also buffalo.   He attempts to do so, but becomes himself coyote.   He returns to buffalo, asking them to transform him again into buffalo.   They do so.   Coyote travels west and is warned that he will meet nineteen cows and bull, and that he is to refuse invitation from bull to travel to land of human beings.   Coyote meets bull and accepts his invitation.   They travel on many days, Coyote each night proposing that they smoke, but bull tells him it is not yet time.   Hunters surround buffalo and kill all except one, which runs very fast.   As they are about to shoot it, it falls over precipice and becomes Coyote again.   Coyote returns to buffalo and asks them to make him buffalo once more.   They pretend to repeat performance, placing him in buffalo wallow, where he is gored to death.

129. COYOTE FAMILY RUN AFTER THE BUFFALO.

While Coyote is on hunt his wife and child run after buffalo.   Coyote overtakes them and kills buffalo, whereupon they decide not to travel longer as one family, but to scatter out over country.

130. COYOTE STEALS TURTLE'S BUFFALO.

Turtle begs Buffalo to carry him across river. Entering Buffalo's anus, he gnaws at his intestines and kills him. Then Turtle sings of his desire for knife. Coyote hears him and offers knife, whereupon Coyote proposes that they have test of skill in jumping over buffalo, winner to receive buffalo and loser to help him cut it up, meat being divided. Coyote wins, Turtle cuts up Buffalo, while Coyote goes after his family. Turtle recognizes Coyote's deception, cries to two eagles flying overhead and asks them to take him and meat up to their nest in cottonwood tree. There Turtle makes fire and cooks meat. Coyote returns with his children. He presently discovers reflection of fire in water. Thinking it is Turtle, he dives in, his head is caught between two logs, and his excrement floats to top, which Turtle sees and asks Coyote's children how they would like to have some meat. They cry and run away.

131. COYOTE AND BEAR.

Coyote is nearly scared to death upon meeting Bear. He sings of his power to stop rivers. Bear believes him wonderful, for being summer time rivers are dry. Coyote sings about turning trees to hills, and Bear believes him wonderful. They travel together and Bear cooks meat. Bear reaches for something, scares Coyote, and Bear recognizes that he has been deceived by Coyote's big talk. He kills Coyote.

132. COYOTE AND BEAR.

Coyote makes imitation bow and meets Bear, who breaks Coyote's bow. Coyote then addresses sun, accusing Bear of having broken his bow. Bear is alarmed at his sacrilegious act and makes Coyote another bow; whereupon Coyote tells him to hide, that sun may not see him. Coyote congratulates himself on his escape and decides to make his home on prairie.

133. COYOTE SHOWS TURKEY THE SCALP-OFFERING CEREMONY.

Coyote meets Turkey and offers to teach him how to make fire for offerings. Fireplace is made and both face it. While Coyote sings they go through movements of offering scalp to fire. Turkey becomes suspicious and escapes while Coyote's eyes are closed. Coyote reproaches himself for permitting Turkey to get away.

134. COYOTE AND THE DANCING TURKEYS.

Coyote comes upon some dancing Turkeys and offers to teach them better dance. He bites off heads of two. Others run away. He takes two Turkeys home and asks children to cook meat while he goes to invite chief. He returns alone and sends his wife and children outside and pretends to be entertaining guests, eating all meat himself. One of children discovers deception, tells mother, but Coyote escapes and children have only bones for their meals.

135. COYOTE AND THE TURKEYS ROLL DOWN THE HILL.

Coyote sees Turkeys sliding down hill and gets his sack and tells them he has new method. He gets into sack and rolls down hill, laughing on way and declaring it fine fun. Then he persuades Turkeys to roll down, first young ones. Next, he gets large number of older Turkeys in sack, telling young ones to remain on hill. When sack reaches bottom, he takes it up and carries it home, warning his children not to untie it while he goes after their mother. Youngest child unties sack and Turkeys escape, and children make fun of their father in song.

136. COYOTE AND PRAIRIE CHICKEN.

Coyote meets Prairie Chicken and they have contest, seeing which can frighten other. Coyote hides in tall grass and jumps at Prairie Chicken. Prairie Chicken laughs. Then Prairie Chicken hides near steep bank. Coyote wanders about, forgetting Prairie Chicken. Nearing bank, Prairie Chicken flies up, and Coyote in his fright leaps over bank and is killed.

137. COYOTE AND PRAIRIE CHICKEN.

Coyote meets Prairie Chicken sitting on limb and invites him to come down and dance with him. Prairie Chicken refuses and Coyote threatens it with various poisons. Prairie Chicken replies that he is fond of things Coyote mentions, and flies away.

138. COYOTE TRIES TO MARRY RABBIT.

Coyote tries to marry Rabbit; she refuses. Then Rabbit tries to marry Coyote, but Coyote finds fault with Rabbit because it has cracked nose, and says that Rabbits and Coyotes will never intermarry.

139. COYOTE AND THE SALT.

People have no salt and they go to place where Coyote roasts his meat, where they beg salt of him. He gives it to them. Coyote disappears, and thereafter when children see coyotes on hill they sing song to remind them that coyotes gave them salt.

140. COYOTE AND THE ROSEBUDS.

Coyote hunting for buffalo climbs hill and sees valley full of rosebuds. He goes to village and tells people that he brings great news. As reward he must have chief's daughter. After he has lain with her he announces that he has seen (asking the people to step back because he is very warm)—rosebuds, and leaps for his life, as he knows that the people will be angry at him for having deceived them. They kill him.

141. COYOTE AND THE ARTICHOKE.

Coyote going along road is challenged by Artichoke to bite it. He does so and devours Artichoke. He soon begins to expel flatus, which, increasing, lifts him from ground. He is finally washed away by his own excrement.

142. COYOTE, THE PLUM TREES, AND THE GRAPE VINES.

At first Coyotes have membrum long enough to go around their waist. They would conceal themselves on banks, sending them into water to fool women, who would flee, thinking them snakes. Chief Coyote one day hears noise in ground, unwinds his membrum, and sticks it into hole. It is gnawed into pieces. He digs, recovers pieces, and throws handful in one direction, commanding that plum trees shall grow. He orders another handful thrown in another direction, which shall produce grape vines. Another handful produces berry bushes, and again from another handful rise nut trees. Whereupon insect in ground tells him that thereafter Coyotes shall no longer have long membrums.

143. THE SKUNKS AND THE BEAVERS.

Skunks become hungry and plan to secure food by strategy. They send old woman to Beavers' lodge, asking them to send medicine-man to doctor young Skunk. Beavers send White Beaver, who enters Skunks' lodge. In attempting to draw pain from pretending sick Skunk with his mouth, he is told that pain is in rectum, whereupon he receives discharge, rolls over, and is killed by older Skunks. Thus they obtain food. Next day they resort to same plan, sending old woman to Beavers for medicine-man. She tells them that man who was sent day before was so ashamed of his incompetence that he wandered off. They send another medicine-man, who is killed in same manner. Thus one after another of Beavers is killed by Skunks, until there is only one left. This Beaver becoming lonely, goes to creek and cries. Diving bird takes him into water, where he finds lodge of Beavers which have been killed. Since then Beavers live in water and are at enmity with Skunks. People are careful to throw beaver bones into water that they may again become beavers.

144. HOW WILD-CAT KILLED THE BEAR.

Wild-Cat goes hunting, and Bear comes to her den and eats all her young ones. Wild-Cat follows Bear's trail and calls Bear names. They fight, and Wild-Cat claws Bear's stomach open, removes her young ones, and carries them home. Returning to dead bear, she finds Coyote, who claims that he is guarding her prey for her. Wild-Cat is grateful and presents Coyote with whole bear, who takes it home to his family, telling them that he killed bear. Old bear now passes by and Coyote tells young ones to escape while he fights him. He then runs away himself until he kills himself with fright.

145. HOW RABBIT LOST HIS TAIL.

Rabbit loses his tail jumping over willow limb and sings about his loss. Turtle tells him to hunt for his tail among willows where he will find it, but that henceforth willow will bear white fur in recognition of event. Rabbit recovers his tail, gives it to Turtle, and Turtle restores it.

146. THE WHITE AND BLACK RATS.

Two rats hunting for food are addressed by Magpie, who tells Black Rat where he will find artichokes, and White Rat where he will find ground nuts. Since then, rats have used these for food.

147. TURTLE'S WAR PARTY.

Turtle is joined on war-path by Mosquito and Cricket. They capture Turtle, but Cricket escapes in hole and Mosquito alights near fire. They are about to throw Turtle into fire, but he warns them that he will scatter fire about lodge. When they propose throwing him into water he protests that he is afraid of water, whereupon they throw him in, and he tells them that he has fooled them.

148. THE ANIMALS' WAR PARTY.

Rabbit, Turtle, and Spider-Woman on war-path hear of three men who are hard to kill; that ground about their camp is covered with skulls. They boast of their power. They are killed by enemy, who carry firebrands. Those not killed by fire are killed by war clubs. The enemy are foxes.

CPSIA information can be obtained at www.ICGtesting.com
Printed in the USA
LVOW12s0933180913

352925LV00001B/9/A